AF836457

Methods of Terrorism Financing

Internationales und Europäisches Strafverfahrensrecht

Herausgegeben von Hans-Heiner Kühne und Robert Esser

Band 21

PETER LANG

Fabian Maximilian Johannes Teichmann

Methods of Terrorism Financing

Criminal procedural obstacles to the prevention of crime in Germany, Liechtenstein, Austria and Switzerland

PETER LANG

Bibliographic Information published by the Deutsche Nationalbibliothek
The Deutsche Nationalbibliothek lists this publication in the Deutsche Nationalbibliografie; detailed bibliographic data is available online at http://dnb.d-nb.de.

ISSN 1611-275X
ISBN 978-3-631-86432-6 (Print)
E-ISBN 978-3-631-86495-1 (E-PDF)
E-ISBN 978-3-631-86496-8 (EPUB)
DOI 10.3726/b18903

© Peter Lang GmbH
Internationaler Verlag der Wissenschaften
Berlin 2021
All rights reserved.

Peter Lang – Berlin · Bern · Bruxelles · New York ·
Oxford · Warszawa · Wien

All parts of this publication are protected by copyright. Any utilisation outside the strict limits of the copyright law, without the permission of the publisher, is forbidden and liable to prosecution. This applies in particular to reproductions, translations, microfilming, and storage and processing in electronic retrieval systems.

This publication has been peer reviewed.

www.peterlang.com

Abstract

While the measures and organizations for combating terrorism financing have already been adequately studied, little concrete information is known about terrorist financiers' procedures. This study addresses this research gap and illustrates which criminal procedural obstacles significantly impede the fight against terrorism financing and other crime. In addition, suggestions for legislative reform are developed to enable more effective crime fighting and prevention.

Foreword

I would like to express my special thanks to Prof. Dr. Dr. h.c. mult. Hans-Heiner Kühne, who first learned of this research project during our joint stay at the National Academy of Legal Sciences of Ukraine in 2017 and who, as a mentor, has since then continuously encouraged, supported and provided me with valuable advice. It is thanks to him that the present work may now appear in his series on European and international criminal procedure law. I would also like to thank Professor Dr Robert Esser for his willingness to review the work in his capacity as co-editor and all those who participated in the empirical study. The present work is dedicated to my grandparents, Elisabeth and Maximilian Zeiller, who made my education possible.

Table of contents

I. Bibliography

Abadie, A., and Gardeazabal, J. (2008). 'Terrorism and the World Economy', *European Economic Review*, 52 (1), 1–27.

Abrahamsen, R., and Williams, M. C. (2009). 'Security Beyond the State: Global Security Assemblages in International Politics', *International Political Sociology*, 3 (1), 1–17.

Abrahms, M. (2012). 'The Political Effectiveness of Terrorism Revisited', *Comparative Political Studies*, 45 (3), 366–393.

Abuza, Z. (2002). 'Tentacles of Terror: Al Qaeda's Southeast Asian Network', *Contemporary Southeast Asia*, 24 (3), 427–465.

---- (2003). 'Funding Terrorism in Southeast Asia: The Financial Network of Al Qaeda and Jemaah Islamiya', *Contemporary Southeast Asia*, 25 (2), 169–199.

Acharya, A. (2009). 'Small Amounts for Big Bangs? Rethinking Responses to "Low Cost" Terrorism', *Journal of Money Laundering Control*, 12 (3), 285–298.

Alford, D. E. (1993). 'Anti-Money Laundering Regulations: A Burden on Financial Institutions', *North Carolina Journal of International Law and Commercial Regulation*, 19 (3), 437–468.

Allen, W. (2003). 'The War Against Terrorist Financing', *Journal of Money Laundering Control*, 6 (4), 306–310.

Alonso, R., and Reinares, F. (2005). 'Terrorism, Human Rights and Law Enforcement in Spain', *Terrorism and Political Violence*, 17 (1–2), 265–278.

Andenaes, J. (1952). 'General Prevention. Illusion or Reality?' *The Journal of Criminal Law, Criminology, and Police Science*, 43 (2), 176–198.

---- (1971). 'The Moral or Educative Influence of Criminal Law', *Journal of Social Issues*, 27 (2), 17–31.

---- (1975). 'General Prevention Revisited: Research and Policy Implications', *The Journal of Criminal Law and Criminology (1973-)*, 66 (3), 338–365.

Arin, K. P., Ciferri, D., and Spagnolo, N. (2008). 'The Price of Terror: The Effects of Terrorism on Stock Market Returns and Volatility', *Economics Letters*, 101 (3), 164–167.

Aufhauser, D. D. (2003). 'Terrorist Financing: Foxes Run to Ground', *Journal of Money Laundering Control*, 6 (4), 301–305.

Aydinli, E. (2006). 'From Finances to Transnational Mobility: Searching for the Global Jihadists' Achilles Heel', *Terrorism and Political Violence*, 18 (2), 301–313.

Bachner-Foregger, H. (2018). *Strafprozessordnung – StPO 1975* (24th edn). Vienna: Manz.

Badey, T. J. (1998). 'Defining International Terrorism: A Pragmatic Approach', *Terrorism and Political Violence*, 10 (1), 90–107.

Balasubramaniyan, V. (2015). 'Understanding the Costing Decisions Behind Terror Attacks – An Analytical Study', *Journal of Money Laundering Control*, 18 (4), 475–487.

Baldus, M. (2016). 'Art. 10'. In V. Epping, and C. Hillgruber (eds), *Beck'scher Online-Kommentar Grundgesetz* (29th edn). Munich: Beck Verlag.

Baldwin Jr, F. N. (2004). 'The Rule of Law, Human Rights and Proportionality as Components of the War Against Terrorism: Is the US Judiciary in Self-Imposed Exile?' *Journal of Money Laundering Control*, 7 (3), 218–253.

–––– (2005). 'The Financing of Terror in the Age of the Internet: Wilful Blindness, Greed or a Political Statement?' *Journal of Money Laundering Control*, 8 (2), 157–158.

Balkin, J. M. (2008). 'The Constitution in the National Surveillance State', *Minnesota Law Review*, 93, 1–25.

Balkin, J. M., and Levinson, S. (2006). 'The Processes of Constitutional Change: From Partisan Entrenchment to the National Surveillance State', *Fordham Law Review*, 75, 489–536.

Bandyopadhyay, S., Sandler, T., and Younas, J. (2014). 'Foreign Direct Investment, Aid, and Terrorism', *Oxford Economic Papers*, 66 (1), 25–50.

Bantekas, I. (2003). 'The International Law of Terrorist Financing', *The American Journal of International Law*, 97 (2), 315–333.

Barkin, A. A. (2003). 'Corporate America – Making a Killing: An Analysis of Why It Is Appropriate to Hold American Corporations Who Fund Terrorist Organizations Liable for Aiding and Abetting Terrorism', *California Western Law Review*, 40, 169–193.

Baron, B. F. (2004). 'Deterring Donors: Anti-Terrorist Financing Rules and American Philanthropy', *International Journal of Not-for-Profit Law*, 6 (2), 1–32.

Barrett, R. (2009). 'Time to Reexamine Regulation Designed to Counter the Financing of Terrorism', *Case Western Reserve Journal of International Law*, 41, 7–18.

–––– (2011). 'Preventing the Financing of Terrorism', *Case Western Reserve Journal of International Law*, 44, 719–736.

Barry Johnston, R., and Carrington, I. (2006). 'Protecting the Financial System from Abuse: Challenges to Banks in Implementing AML/CFT Standards', *Journal of Money Laundering Control*, 9 (1), 48–61.

Barry Johnston, R., and Nedelescu, O. M. (2006). 'The Impact of Terrorism on Financial Markets', *Journal of Financial Crime*, 13 (1), 7–25.

Basile, M. (2004). 'Going to the Source: Why Al Qaeda's Financial Network is Likely to Withstand the Current War on Terrorist Financing ', *Studies in Conflict & Terrorism*, 27 (3), 169–185.

Basse, D. M. (2017). 'Art. 1 ff.'. In: P. V. Kunz, T. Jutzi, and S. Schären (eds), *Geldwäschereigesetz (GwG)*, pp. 1–44. Bern: Stämpfli.

Baum, B., and Palm, F. (1994). 'On the Constitutional Problem of "Grand Eavesdropping"', *Juristenzeitung*, 49 (9), 447–454.

Baum, G. R., and Schantz, P. (2008). 'The Amendment of the BKA Act: A Legal Policy and Constitutional Critique', *Journal of Legal Policy*, 41 (5), 137–140.

Beekarry, N. (2011). 'International Anti-Money Laundering and Combating the Financing of Terrorism Regulatory Strategy: A Critical Analysis of Compliance Determinants in International Law', *Northwestern Journal of International Law & Business*, 31, 137–194.

Begorre-Bret, C. (2005). 'The Definition of Terrorism and the Challenge of Relativism', *Cardozo Law Review*, 27, 1987–2004.

Bell, R. E. (2004). 'The Confiscation, Forfeiture and Disruption of Terrorist Finances', *Journal of Money Laundering Control*, 7 (2), 105–125.

Benthall, J. (2007). 'The Overreaction Against Islamic Charities', *Isim Review*, 20, 6–7.

Bernsmann, K., and Jansen, K. (1998). 'Secret Investigative Methods and Their Control', *StV*, 4, 217–231.

Betti, S. (2006). 'The Duty to Bring Terrorists to Justice and Discretionary Prosecution', *Journal of International Criminal Justice*, 4, 1104–1116.

Beukelmann, S. (2017). 'Online-Durchsuchung und Quellen-TKÜ', *NJW Spezial*, 14, 440.

Biersteker, T. J., and Eckert, S. E. (eds) (2007). *Countering the Financing of Terrorism*. Abingdon: Routledge.

Bizer, J. (2007). 'Gegen die Online-Durchsuchung', *Datenschutz und Datensicherheit - DuD*, 31 (9), 640.

Blackett, A. (1998). 'Globalization and Its Ambiguities: Implications for Law School Curricular Reform', *Columbia Journal of Transnational Law*, 37, 57–80.

Blomberg, S. B., Hess, G. D., and Orphanides, A. (2004). 'The Macroeconomic Consequences of Terrorism', *Journal of Monetary Economics*, 51 (5), 1007–1032.

Bock, M. (1991). 'Ideas and Chimeras in Criminal Law. Legal Sociological Comments on the Dogmatics of Positive General Prevention', *Journal of the Whole Science of Criminal Law*, 103 (3), 636–656.

Bogner, A., Littig, B., and Menz, W. (2014). *Interviews With Experts: A Practice-Oriented Introduction*. Wiesbaden: Springer-Verlag.

Böhme, R., Christin, N., Edelman, B., and Moore, T. (2015). 'Bitcoin: Economics, Technology, and Governance', *The Journal of Economic Perspectives*, 29 (2), 213–238.

Böckenförde, T. (2008). 'Auf dem Weg zur elektronischen Privatsphäre: Zugleich Besprechung von BVerfG, Urteil v. 27. 2. 2008 – "Online-Durchsuchung"', *Juristenzeitung*, 63 (19), 925–939.

Bossong, R. (2012). 'Peer Reviews in the Fight Against Terrorism: A Hidden Dimension of European Security Governance', *Cooperation and Conflict*, 47 (4), 519–538.

Boudreaux, P. (1989). 'Booth v. Maryland and the Individual Vengeance Rationale for Criminal Punishment', *The Journal of Criminal Law and Criminology (1973)*, 80 (1), 177–196.

Bowen, G. A. (2005). 'Preparing a Qualitative Research-Based Dissertation: Lessons Learned', *The Qualitative Report*, 10 (2), 208–222.

Bowers, C. B. (2008). 'Hawala, Money Laundering, and Terrorism Finance: Micro-Lending as an End to Illicit Remittance', *Denver Journal of International Law and Policy*, 37, 379–419.

Brantingham, P. J., and Faust, F. L. (1976). 'A Conceptual Model of Crime Prevention', *NPPA Journal*, 22 (3), 284–296.

Brodeur, J. P. (1992). 'Undercover Policing in Canada: Wanting What Is Wrong', *Crime, Law and Social Change*, 18 (1), 105–136.

Brooks, R. C., Riley Jr, R. A., and Thomas, J. (2005). 'Detecting and Preventing the Financing of Terrorist Activities: A Role for Government Accountants', *The Journal of Government Financial Management*, 54 (1), 12–18.

Brounen, D., and Derwall, J. (2010). 'The Impact of Terrorist Attacks on International Stock Markets', *European Financial Management*, 16 (4), 585–598.

Brown, D. K. (2002). 'The Warren Court, Criminal Procedure Reform, and Retributive Punishment', *Washington and Lee Law Review*, 59, 1411–1428.

Brown, J. R., Cummins, J. D., Lewis, C. M., and Wei, R. (2004). 'An Empirical Analysis of the Economic Impact of Federal Terrorism Reinsurance', *Journal of Monetary Economics*, 51 (5), 861–898.

Brunnhofer, M., and Leimgruber, D. (2017). 'Art. 5'. In: P. V. Kunz, T. Jutzi, and S. Schären (eds), *Geldwäschereigesetz (GwG)*, pp. 280–286. Bern: Stämpfli.

Bruns, A. (2019). '§§ 100a–11a'. In: R. Hannich (ed.), *Karlsruher Kommentar zur Strafprozessordnung (StPO)* (8th edn), pp. 444–640. Munich: Beck Verlag.

Brunst, P. W. (2011). 'Staatlicher Zugang zur Identität, *Datenschutz und Datensicherheit - DuD*, 35 (9), 618–623.

Buckler, K. (2008). 'The Quantitative/Qualitative Divide Revisited: A Study of Published Research, Doctoral Program Curricula, and Journal Editor Perceptions', *Journal of Criminal Justice Education*, 19 (3), 383–403.

Bures, O. (2010). 'EU's Fight Against Terrorist Finances: Internal Shortcomings and Unsuitable External Models', *Terrorism and Political Violence*, 22 (3), 418–437.

---- (2013). 'Public-Private Partnerships in the Fight Against Terrorism?' *Crime, Law and Social Change*, 60 (4), 429–455.

Campbell, L. M. (1999). 'Defending Against Terrorism: A Legal Analysis of the Decision to Strike Sudan and Afghanistan', *Tulane Law Review*, 74, 1067–1096.

Carter, T. S., Carter, S. S., and Claridge, N. E. (2008). 'Impact of Anti-Terrorism Legislation on Charities in Canada: The Need for Balance', *International Journal of Civil Society Law*, 6, 42–77.

Cassani, U. (2003). 'Le train de mesures contre le financement du terrorisme: une loi nécessaire?' *RSDA Revue Suisse de Droit des Affaires et du Marché Financier*, 75 (6), 293–313.

Cassella, S. D. (2004). 'Terrorism and the Financial Sector: Are the Right Prosecutorial Tools Being Used?' *Journal of Money Laundering Control*, 7 (3), 281–285.

Cassese, A. (2001). 'Terrorism Is Also Disrupting Some Crucial Legal Categories of International Law', *European Journal of International Law*, 12 (5), 993–1001.

Chen, A. H., and Siems, T. F. (2004). 'The Effects of Terrorism on Global Capital Markets', *European Journal of Political Economy*, 20 (2), 349–366.

Chesney, M., Reshetar, G., and Karaman, M. (2011). 'The Impact of Terrorism on Financial Markets: An Empirical Study', *Journal of Banking & Finance*, 35 (2), 253–267.

Christen, M., Küng, M., and Lange, M. (2018). 'Die Finanzierung von Kriegsmaterialproduzenten als politischer Streitpunkt', *Sicherheit und Recht*, 3, 208–215.

Chodosh, H. E. (1998). 'Comparing Comparisons: In Search of Methodology', *Iowa Law Review*, 84, 1025–1132.

Choi, S. W. (2010). 'Fighting Terrorism Through the Rule of Law?' *Journal of Conflict Resolution*, 54 (6), 940–966.

Choudhry, S. (1998). 'Globalization in Search of Justification: Toward a Theory of Comparative Constitutional Interpretation', *Indiana Law Journal*, 74, 819–892.

Chukwuemerie, A. I. (2006). 'International Legal War on the Financing of Terrorism: A Comparison of Nigerian, UK, US and Canadian Laws', *Journal of Money Laundering Control*, 9 (1), 71–88.

Clunan, A. L. (2006). 'The Fight Against Terrorist Financing ', *Political Science Quarterly*, 121 (4), 569–596.

Coninx, A. (2016). 'Legal Philosophical Foundations of Punishment and Recent Developments in the Law of Measures', *Law*, 16, 157–179.

Cooper, H. H. (2001). 'Terrorism: The Problem of Definition Revisited', *American Behavioral Scientist*, 44 (6), 881–893.

Corlett, J. A. (2006). 'Forgiveness, Apology, and Retributive Punishment', *American Philosophical Quarterly*, 43 (1), 25–42.

Cox Jr, L. A. T. (2008). 'Some Limitations of "Risk = Threat × Vulnerability × Consequence" for Risk Analysis of Terrorist Attacks', *Risk Analysis*, 28 (6), 1749–1761.

Creswell, J. W. (2012). *Qualitative Inquiry and Research Design: Choosing Among Five Approaches*. Thousand Oaks: Sage Publications.

---- (2013). *Research Design: Qualitative, Quantitative, and Mixed Methods Approaches*. Thousand Oaks: Sage Publications.

Creswell, J. W., and Miller, D. L. (2000). 'Determining Validity in Qualitative Inquiry', *Theory Into Practice*, 39 (3), 124–130.

Crimm, N. J. (2003). 'High Alert: The Government's War on the Financing of Terrorism and Its Implications for Donors, Domestic Charitable Organizations, and Global Philanthropy', *William & Mary Law Review*, 45, 1341–1350.

---- (2004). 'Post-September 11 Fortified Anti-Terrorism Measures Compel Heightened Due Diligence', *Pace Law Review*, 25, 203–218.

---- (2008). 'The Moral Hazard of Anti-Terrorism Financing Measures: A Potential to Compromise Civil Societies and National Interests', *Wake Forest Law Review*, 43, 577–626.

Croissant, A., and Barlow, D. (2007). 'Following the Money Trail: Terrorist Financing and Government Responses in Southeast Asia 1', *Studies in Conflict & Terrorism*, 30 (2), 131–156.

Crouch, M., and McKenzie, H. (2006). 'The Logic of Small Samples in Interview-Based Qualitative Research', *Social Science Information*, 45 (4), 483–499.

Curran, V. G. (1998a). 'Cultural Immersion, Difference and Categories in US Comparative Law', *The American Journal of Comparative Law*, 46 (1), 43–92.

---- (1998b). 'Dealing in Difference: Comparative Law's Potential for Broadening Legal Perspectives', *The American Journal of Comparative Law*, 46 (4), 657–668.

Curti, H. (1999). 'Punishment and General Prevention: An Empirical Evidence for the Federal Republic of Germany', *Journal of Legal Policy*, 32 (6), 234–237.

Daly, K. (2000). 'Revisiting the Relationship Between Retributive and Restorative Justice'. In H. Strang, and J. Braithwaite (eds), *Restorative Justice: Philosophy to Practice*, pp. 33–54. Farnham: Ashgate.

Dalyan, S. (2008). 'Combating the Financing of Terrorism: Rethinking Strategies for Success', *Defence Against Terrorism Review*, 1 (1), 137–153.

Danziger, Y. (2012). 'Changes in Methods of Freezing Funds of Terrorist Organisations Since 9/11: A Comparative Analysis', *Journal of Money Laundering Control*, 15 (2), 210–236.

Davis, K. E. (2003). 'Legislating Against the Financing of Terrorism: Pitfalls and Prospects', *Journal of Financial Crime*, 10 (3), 269–274.

Day, J. P. (1978). 'Retributive Punishment', *Mind*, 87 (348), 498–516.

DeFord, W. (2005). 'The Dilemma of Expressive Punishment', *University of Colorado Law Review*, 76, 843–860.

De Goede, M. (2003). 'Hawala Discourses and the War on Terrorist Finance', *Environment and Planning D: Society and Space*, 21 (5), 513–532.

De Koker, L. (2006). 'Money Laundering Control and Suppression of Financing of Terrorism: Some Thoughts on the Impact of Customer Due Diligence Measures on Financial Exclusion', *Journal of Financial Crime*, 13 (1), 26–50.

Den Boer, M., and Monar, J. (2002). 'Keynote Article: 11 September and the Challenge of Global Terrorism to the EU as a Security Actor', *JCMS: Journal of Common Market Studies*, 40 (s1), 11–28.

Denkowski, C. (2008). 'The Inclusion of Digital surveillance in Federal and State Police Law – A Legal Policy Sketch on the Expected Federal Constitutional Court Decision', *New Criminal Policy*, 20 (1), 5–8.

Derungs, C., and Gmünder, E. (2017). 'Art. 22a AMLA'. In P. V. Kunz, T. Jutzi, and S. Schären (eds), *Geldwäschereigesetz (GwG)*, pp. 574–584. Bern: Stämpfli.

Dishman, C. (2005). 'The Leaderless Nexus: When Crime and Terror Converge', *Studies in Conflict & Terrorism*, 28 (3), 237–252.

Dix, G. E. (1974). 'Undercover Investigations and Police Rulemaking', *Texas Law Review*, 53, 203–294.

Dobrauz-Saldapenna, G., and Derungs, C. (2017). 'Art. 3 AMLA'. In P. V. Kunz, T. Jutzi, and S. Schären (eds), *Geldwäschereigesetz (GwG)*, pp. 170–196. Bern: Stämpfli.

Donatsch, A. (2017). 'Advances in Law Enforcement', *SJZ*, 113, 285–292.

Donatsch, A., Thommen, M., and Wohlers, W. (2017). *Strafrecht IV – Delikte gegen die Allgemeinheit* (5th edn). Zurich: Schulthess.

Döbeli, T. (2015). 'Blockieren – Beschlagnahmen – Einfrieren', *AJP*, 9, 1237–1248.

Dölling, D., Entorf, H., Hermann, D., Häring, A., Rupp, T., and Woll, A. (2006). 'Zur generalpräventiven Abschreckungswirkung des Strafrechts – Befunde einer Metaanalyse', *Soziale Probleme*, 17 (2), 193–209.

Dölling, D., and Hermann, D. (2012). 'Zur generalpräventiven Abschreckungswirkkung des Strafrechts bei jungen Menschen'. In Detusche Vereinigung für Jugendgerichte und Jugendgerichtshilfen e.V. (ed.), *Achtung (für) Jugend! Praxis und Perspektiven des Jugendkriminalrechts- Dokumentation des 28. Deutschen Jugendgerichtstages vom 11. bis 14. September 2010 in Münster* (1st edn), pp. 427–439. Mönchengladbach: Forum Verlag Godesberg GmbH.

Duttge, G. (1996). 'Strafprozessualer Einsatz von V-Personen und Vorbehalt des Gesetzes', *JZ*, 51 (11), 556–565.

Dragu, T., and Polborn, M. (2014). 'The Rule of Law in the Fight Against Terrorism', *American Journal of Political Science*, 58 (2), 511–525.

Drakos, K. (2004). 'Terrorism-Induced Structural Shifts in Financial Risk: Airline Stocks in the Aftermath of the September 11th Terror Attacks', *European Journal of Political Economy*, 20 (2), 435–446.

Dreher, A., and Gassebner, M. (2008). 'Does Political Proximity to the US Cause Terror?' *Economics Letters*, 99 (1), 27–29.

Dreher, A., Gassebner, M., and Siemers, L. H. (2010). 'Does Terrorism Threaten Human Rights? Evidence from Panel Data', *The Journal of Law and Economics*, 53 (1), 65–93.

Dumitriu, E. (2004). 'The EU's Definition of Terrorism: The Council Framework Decision on Combating Terrorism', *German Law Journal*, 5, 585–602.

Eggimann, P. (2013). 'Neuer Regulierungsschub im Datenschutzrecht?' *Sic!*, 2, 112–116.

Eldor, R., and Melnick, R. (2004). 'Financial Markets and Terrorism', *European Journal of Political Economy*, 20 (2), 367–386.

Elo, S., and Kyngäs, H. (2008). 'The Qualitative Content Analysis Process', *Journal of Advanced Nursing*, 62 (1), 107–115.

Elu, J. U., and Price, G. N. (2012). 'Remittances and the Financing of Terrorism in Sub-Saharan Africa: 1974–2006', *Peace Economics, Peace Science and Public Policy*, 18 (1), 1–40.

Enders, W., and Sandler, T. (1996). 'Terrorism and Foreign Direct Investment in Spain and Greece', *Kyklos*, 49 (3), 331–352.

Enders, W., Sachsida, A., and Sandler, T. (2006). 'The Impact of Transnational Terrorism on US Foreign Direct Investment', *Political Research Quarterly*, 59 (4), 517–531.

Engel, M. E. (2004). 'Donating Blood Money: Fundraising for International Terrorism by United States Charities and the Government's Efforts to Constrict the Flow', *Cardozo Journal of International & Comparative Law*, 12, 251–296.

Eschelbach, R. (2000). 'Rechtsfragen zum Einsatz von V-Leuten', *StV*, 7, 390–399.

---- (2020). '§§ 110a–110c'. In H. Satzger, and W. Schluckebier (eds), *Strafprozessordnung mit GVG und EMRK* (4th edn). Cologne: Carl Heymanns Verlag.

Eugster L., and Katzenstein, A. (2014). 'Art. 196–457 StPO', In M. A. Niggli, M. Heer, and H. Wiprächtiger (eds). *Schweizerische Strafprozessordnung/ Jugendstrafprozessordnung (StPO, JStPO)* (2nd edn). Basel: Helbing Lichtenhahn.

Ewald, W. (1995a). 'Comparative Jurisprudence (I): What Was It Like to Try a Rat?' *University of Pennsylvania Law Review*, 143 (6), 1889–2149.

---- (1995b). 'Comparative Jurisprudence (II): The Logic of Legal Transplants', *The American Journal of Comparative Law*, 43 (4), 489–510.

Fabrizy, E. (2014). *Strafprozessordnung – StPO und wichtige Nebengesetze* (12th edn). Vienna: Manz.

Favarel-Garrigues, G., Godefroy, T., and Lascoumes, P. (2011). 'Reluctant Partners? Banks in the Fight Against Money Laundering and Terrorism Financing in France', *Security Dialogue*, 42 (2), 179–196.

Fereday, J., and Muir-Cochrane, E. (2006). 'Demonstrating Rigor Using Thematic Analysis: A Hybrid Approach of Inductive and Deductive Coding and Theme Development', *International Journal of Qualitative Methods*, 5 (1), 80–92.

Ferrara, N., and Salmina, E. (2016). *Die Weissgeldstrategie wird zum Strafrecht. Der neue Art. 305bis StGB: Die Steuergeldwäscherei und ihre Auswirkungen auf die internationale Rechtshilfe*. Bern: Stämpfli.

Fezer, G. (1995). 'Zum Einsatz Verdeckter Ermittler', *JZ*, 50 (19), 970–972.

Fink, N. (2016). 'Art. 13'. In V. Epping, and C. Hillgruber (eds), *Beck'scher Online-Kommentar Grundgesetz* (29th edn). Munich: Beck Verlag.

Fiolka, G. (2018). 'Terrorismusfinanzierung'. In M. A. Niggli, and H. Wiprächtiger (eds), *Basler Kommentar zum Strafrecht I* (4th ed.). Basel: Helbing & Lichtenhahn.

Fischer, T. (2020). *§ 89c StGB. Kommentar Strafgesetzbuch mit Nebengesetzen* (67th edn). Munich: C. H. Beck Verlag.

Fiss, O. (2006). 'The War Against Terrorism and the Rule of Law', *Oxford Journal of Legal Studies*, 26 (2), 235–256.

FitzGerald, V. (2004). 'Global Financial Information, Compliance Incentives and Terrorist Funding', *European Journal of Political Economy*, 20 (2), 387–401.

Fitzpatrick, J. (2003). 'Speaking Law to Power: The War Against Terrorism and Human Rights', *European Journal of International Law*, 14 (2), 241–264.

Flanigan, S. T. (2006). 'Charity as Resistance: Connections Between Charity, Contentious Politics, and Terror', *Studies in Conflict & Terrorism*, 29 (7), 641–655.

Fletcher, G. P. (1998). 'Comparative Law as a Subversive Discipline', *The American Journal of Comparative Law*, 46 (4), 683–700.

---- (1999). 'The Place of Victims in the Theory of Retribution', *Buffalo Criminal Law Review*, 3 (1), 51–63.

Foot, R. (2007). 'The United Nations, Counter Terrorism and Human Rights: Institutional Adaptation and Embedded Ideas', *Human Rights Quarterly*, 29 (2), 489–514.

Forman, M. M. (2006). 'Combating Terrorist Financing and Other Financial Crimes Through Private Sector Partnerships', *Journal of Money Laundering Control*, 9 (1), 112–118.

Forster, M. (2003). 'The Criminal Liability of Supporting (Especially Financing) Terrorism Al-Qaïda, ETA, Brigate Rosse – Swiss Anti-Terrorism Criminal Law Under Scrutiny', *Swiss Journal of Criminal Law – ZStrR*, 121, 423–447.

---- (2005). 'Zur Abgrenzung zwischen Terroristen und militanten "politischen" Widerstandskämpfern im internationalen Strafrecht – Am Beispiel des serbisch-kosovo-albanischen Bürgerkrieges', *Zeitschrift des Bernischen Juristenvereins – ZBJV*, 141, 213–238.

---- (2006). 'Terrorist Mass Murder of Civilians as a "Legitimate Struggle for Freedom" (in the Sense of Art. 260quinquies § 3 StGB) by Virtue of "Prohibition of Analogy?"' *Swiss Journal of Criminal Law – ZStrR*, 124, 331–338.

---- (2015). 'Strafrecht / Marksteine der Bundesgerichtspraxis zur strafprozessualen Überwachung des digitalen Fernmeldeverkehrs'. In L. Gschwend, P. Hettich, M. Müller-Chen, B. Schindler, and I. Wildhaber (eds.), *Recht im digitalen Zeitalter. Festgabe Schweizerischer Juristentag 2015 in St. Gallen* (1st ed), pp. 613–635. Zürich/St. Gallene: Dike Verlag.

---- (2018). 'Art. 24–27 StGB'. In M. A. Niggli, and H. Wiprächtiger (eds), *Basler Kommentar zum Strafrecht I* (4th ed.). (4th edn). Basel: Helbing & Lichtenhahn.

Frankenberg, G. (1985). 'Critical Comparisons: Re-Thinking Comparative Law', *Harvard International Law Journal*, 26, 411–456.

Freedman, M. G. (2010). 'Prosecuting Terrorism: The Material Support Statute and Muslim Charities', *Hastings Constitutional Law* Quarterly, 38, 1113–1154.

Freeman, M. (2011). 'The Sources of Terrorism financing: Theory and Typology', *Studies in Conflict & Terrorism*, 34 (6), 461–475.

Frey, B. S., Luechinger, S., and Stutzer, A. (2007). 'Calculating Tragedy: Assessing the Costs of Terrorism', *Journal of Economic Surveys*, 21 (1), 1–24.

Froschauer, U., and Lueger, M. (2003). *The Qualitative Interview: On the Practice of Interpretative Analysis of Social Systems*. Vienna: WUV.

Ganor, B. (2002). 'Defining Terrorism: Is One Man's Terrorist Another Man's Freedom Fighter?' *Police Practice and Research*, 3 (4), 287–304.

---- (2008). 'Terrorist Organization Typologies and the Probability of a Boomerang Effect', *Studies in Conflict & Terrorism*, 31 (4), 269–283.

Gardella, A. (2003). 'The Fight Against the Financing of Terrorism Between Judicial and Regulatory Cooperation', *Studies in International Financial, Economic, and Technology Law*, 6, 109.

Gardner, K. L. (2007). 'Fighting Terrorism the FATF Way', *Global Governance: A Review of Multilateralism and International Organizations*, 13 (3), 325–345.

Garrick, B. J., Hall, J. E., Kilger, M., McDonald, J. C., O'Toole, T., Probst, P. S., and Zebroski, E. L. (2004). 'Confronting the Risks of Terrorism: Making the Right Decisions', *Reliability Engineering & System Safety*, 86 (2), 129–176.

Gearty, C. (2005). '11 September 2001, Counter-Terrorism, and the Human Rights Act', *Journal of Law and Society*, 32 (1), 18–33.

Gerber, D. J. (2000). 'Globalization and Legal Knowledge: Implications for Comparative Law', *Tulane Law Review*, 75, 949–976.

Gercke, B. (2017). 'Gesetzliche Regelung des Einsatzes von V-Leuten im Rahmen der Strafverfolgung? *StV*, 37 (9), 615–629.

---- (2019). '§§ 94–111q StPO'. In B. Gercke, K. P. Julius, D. Temming, and M. A. Zöller (eds), *Strafprozessordnung* (6th edn). Heidelberg: C. F. Müller Verlag.

Gibbs, J. P. (1989). 'Conceptualization of Terrorism', *American Sociological Review*, 54 (3), 329–340.

Gilmore, W. C. (2004). *Dirty Money: The Evolution of International Measures to Counter Money Laundering and the Financing of Terrorism* (Vol. 599). Strasbourg: Council of Europe.

Girodo, M. (1991). 'Drug Corruption in Undercover Agents: Measuring the Risk', *Behavioral Sciences & the Law*, 9 (3), 361–370.

Glaeser, E. L., and Shapiro, J. M. (2002). 'Cities and Warfare: The Impact of Terrorism on Urban Form', *Journal of Urban Economics*, 51 (2), 205–224.

Gläser, J., and Laudel, G. (2010). *Experteninterviews und qualitative Inhaltsanalyse: als Instrumente rekonstruierender Untersuchungen*. Wiesbaden: VS Verlag für Sozialwissenschaften.

Godenzi, G. (2012). 'Strafbare Beweisverwertung?' *AJP*, 9, 1243–1254.

Goldby, M. (2010). 'The Impact of Schedule 7 of the Counter-Terrorism Act 2008 on Banks and Their Customers', *Journal of Money Laundering Control*, 13 (4), 351–371.

Gordon, R. K. (2010). 'Losing the War Against Dirty Money: Rethinking Global Standards on Preventing Money Laundering and Terrorism Financing', *Duke Journal of Comparative & International Law*, 21, 503–565.

Graf, J. P. (2017). *Beck'scher Online-Kommentar StPO* (27th edn). Munich: Beck Verlag.

---- (2018). *Strafprozessordnung mit Gerichtsverfassungsgesetz und Nebengesetzen* (3rd edn). Munich: C. H. Beck Verlag.

Graneheim, U. H., and Lundman, B. (2004). 'Qualitative Content Analysis in Nursing Research: Concepts, Procedures and Measures to Achieve Trustworthiness', *Nurse Education Today*, 24 (2), 105–112.

Gross, E. (2001). 'Legal Aspects of Tackling Terrorism: The Balance Between the Right of a Democracy to Defend Itself and the Protection of Human Rights', *UCLA Journal of International Law & Foreign Affairs*, 6, 89–167.

Guillaume, G. (2004). 'Terrorism and International Law', *International & Comparative Law Quarterly*, 53 (3), 537–548.

Gul, T. G., Hussain, A. H., Bangash, S. B., and Khattak, S. W. K. (2010). 'Impact of Terrorism on Financial Markets of Pakistan (2006–2008)', *European Journal of Social Sciences*, 18 (1), 98–108.

Günther, R. (2016). '§§ 110a–110c'. In H. Schneider (ed.), *Münchner Kommentar zur StPO* (1st edn.), pp. 1381–. Munich: Beck Verlag.

Gurulé, J. (2010). *Unfunding Terror: The Legal Response to the Financing of Global Terrorism*. Cheltenham: Edward Elgar Publishing.

Gurung, J., Wijaya, M., and Rao, A. (2010). 'AMLCTF Compliance and SMEs in Australia: A Case Study of the Prepaid Card Industry', *Journal of Money Laundering Control*, 13 (3), 184–201.

Halberstam, M. (2002). 'The Evolution of the United Nations Position on Terrorism: From Exempting National Liberation Movements to Criminalizing Terrorism Wherever and by Whomever Committed', *Columbia Journal of Transnational Law*, 41, 573–584.

Hamilton, H., and Smykla, J. O. (1994). 'Guidelines for Police Undercover Work: New Questions About Accreditation and the Emphasis of Procedure Over Authorization', *Justice Quarterly*, 11 (1), 135–151.

Hamin, Z. (2017). 'Recent Changes to the AML/CFT Law in Malaysia', *Journal of Money Laundering Control*, 20 (1), 5–14.

Hansjakob, T. (2005). 'Erste Erfahrungen mit dem SPTA aus anwaltlicher Sicht'. *Anwaltsrevue*, 2, 54–67.

---- (2008). 'Zwangsmassnahmen in der neuen Eidg. StPO', *Schweizerische Zeitschrift für Strafrecht - ZStrR*, 1, 90–120.

---- (2016). 'Das neue SPTA', *Schweizerische Zeitschrift für Strafrecht - ZStrR*, 134, 429–444.

Hardouin, P. (2009). 'Banks Governance and Public-Private Partnership in Preventing and Confronting Organized Crime, Corruption and Terrorism Financing', *Journal of Financial Crime*, 16 (3), 199–209.

Hardouin, P., and Weichhardt, R. (2006). 'Terrorist Fund Raising Through Criminal Activities', *Journal of Money Laundering Control*, 9 (3), 303–308.

Hasler, A. (2016). 'Gesetzgebung', *Forumpoenale*, 3, 182–183.

Hassemer, W. (1992). 'Warum man den «Grossen Lauschangriff» nicht führen sollte', *Deutsche Richterzeitung*, 357–358.

Häusermann D. (2017). 'Autonome Systeme im Rechtskleid der Kapitalgesellschaft', *AJP*, 2, 204–219.

Healy, M., and Perry, C. (2000). 'Comprehensive Criteria to Judge Validity and Reliability of Qualitative Research Within the Realism Paradigm', *Qualitative Market Research: An International Journal*, 3 (3), 118–126.

Hegmann, S. (2017). *Beck'scher Online-Kommentar StPO* (27th edn). Munich: Beck Verlag.

Heintschel-Heinegg, B. (2018). '§ 89c StGB'. In B. Heintschel-Heinegg (ed.) *Kommentar Strafgesetzbuch* (3rd edn). Munich: C. H. Beck Verlag.

Heng, Y. K., and McDonagh, K. (2008). 'The Other War on Terror Revealed: Global Governmentality and the Financial Action Task Force's Campaign Against Terrorist Financing', *Review of International Studies*, 34 (3), 553–573.

Henrichson, C., and Delaney, R. (2012). 'The Price of Prisons: What Incarceration Costs Taxpayers', *Federal Sentencing Reporter*, 25, 68–80.

Herzfeld, M. (2003). 'Restricting the Flow of Funds From US Charities to International Terrorist Organizations – A Proposal', *The Tax Lawyer*, 56 (4), 875–901.

Hett, W. (2008). 'Digital Currencies and the Financing of Terrorism', *Richmond Journal of Law & Technology*, 15, 1–43.

Hetzer, W. (2008). 'Deutsche Umsetzung neuer europäischer Vorgaben zur Bekämpfung der Geldwäsche und der Terrorismusfinanzierung, *EuZW*, 19 (18), 560–565.

Hilf, M. (2017). 'Art. 37'. In P. V. Kunz, T. Jutzi, and S. Schären (eds), *Geldwäschereigesetz (GwG)*, pp. 774–787. Bern: Stämpfli.

Hilger, H. (1992). 'Neues Strafverfahrensrecht durch das OrgKG, *NStZ*, 12 (11), 523–526.

Hill, J. (1989). 'Comparative Law, Law Reform and Legal Theory', *Oxford Journal of Legal Studies*, 9, 101–115.

Hillgruber, C. (2016). 'Art. 1'. In V. Epping, and C. Hillgruber (eds), *Beck'scher Online-Kommentar Grundgesetz* (29th edn). Munich: Beck Verlag.

Hinnen, T. M. (2004). 'The Cyber-Front in the War on Terrorism: Curbing Terrorist Use of the Internet', *The Columbia Science and Technology Law Review*, 5 (5), 1–42.

Hirsch, C. (2001). 'Policing Undercover Agents in the United Kingdom: Whether the Regulation of Investigatory Powers Acts Complies With Regional Human Rights Obligations', *Fordham International Law Journal*, 25, 1282–1334.

Hofmann, M. (2005). 'The Online Search – State "Hacking" or Permissible Investigative Measure', *Neue Zeitschrift für Strafrecht*, 25, 121–176.

Hoffman, M. B., and Goldsmith, T. H. (2003). 'The Biological Roots of Punishment', *Ohio State Journal of Criminal Law*, 1, 627–641.

Hoffmann-Riem, W. (2008). 'Der grundrechtliche Schutz der Vertraulichkeit und Integrität eigengenutzter informationstechnischer Systeme, *Juristenzeitung*, 63 (21), 1009–1022.

Holder, W. E. (2003). 'The International Monetary Fund's Involvement in Combating Money Laundering and the Financing of Terrorism', *Journal of Money Laundering Control*, 6 (4), 383–387.

Hömig, D. (2009). 'Die aktuelle Entscheidung «Neues» Grundrecht, neue Fragen?', *JURA – Juristische Ausbildung*, 31 (3), 207–213.

Hornung, G. (2007). 'Ermächtigungsgrundlage für die «Online-Durchsuchung»?' *Datenschutz und Datensicherheit – DuD*, 31 (8), 575–580.

---- (2008). 'Ein neues Grundrecht, *Computer und Recht*, 24 (5), 299–306.

Howard, M. (2002). 'What's in a Name? How to Fight Terrorism', *Foreign Affairs*, 81, 8–13.

Hroub, K. (2006). 'Hamas: Politics, Charity, and Terrorism in the Service of Jihad', *Journal of Palestine Studies*, 35 (4), 73–75.

Hsieh, H. F., and Shannon, S. E. (2005). 'Three Approaches to Qualitative Content Analysis', *Qualitative Health Research*, 15 (9), 1277–1288.

Hudson, B. A. (1994). 'Beyond Proportionate Punishment: Difficult Cases and the 1991 Criminal Justice Act', *Crime, Law and Social Change*, 22 (1), 59–78.

Hunt, J. (2011). 'The New Frontier of Money Laundering: How Terrorist Organizations Use Cyberlaundering to Fund Their Activities, and How Governments Are Trying to Stop Them', *Information & Communications Technology Law*, 20 (2), 133–152.

Hughes, J. (2007). 'The Chechnya Conflict: Freedom Fighters or Terrorists?' *Demokratizatsiya*, 15 (3), 293–311.

Hutchinson, S., and O'Malley, P. (2007). 'A Crime-Terror Nexus? Thinking on Some of the Links Between Terrorism and Criminality', *Studies in Conflict Terrorism*, 30 (12), 1095–1107.

Irwin, A. S., and Milad, G. (2016). 'The Use of Crypto-Currencies in Funding Violent Jihad', *Journal of Money Laundering Control*, 19 (4), 407–425.

Irwin, A. S., Slay, J., Raymond Choo, K. K., and Liu, L. (2012). 'Are the Financial Transactions Conducted Inside Virtual Environments Truly Anonymous? An Experimental Research From an Australian Perspective', *Journal of Money Laundering Control*, 16 (1), 6–40.

Jacobson, M. (2010). 'Terrorist Financing and the Internet', *Studies in Conflict & Terrorism*, 33 (4), 353–363.

Jaggi, E. (2015). 'Die Revision des SPTA', *Schweizerische Zeitschrift für Strafrecht – ZStrR*, 133, 276–294.

Jahn, M., and Kudlich, H. (2007). 'Die strafprozessuale Zulässigkeit der Online-Durchsuchung', *Juristische Rundschau*, 2, 57–61.

Jamwal, N. S. (2002). 'Hawala – The Invisible Financing System of Terrorism', *Strategic Analysis*, 26 (2), 181–198.

Jean-Richard-dit-Bressel, M. (2014). 'Art. 269, 272, 275–278 StGB'. In M. A. Niggli, M. Heer, and H. Wiprächtiger (eds), *Basler Kommentar zur schweizerischen Strafprozessordnung* (2nd edn). Basel: Helbing Lichtenhahn.

Joh, E. E. (2009). 'Breaking the Law to Enforce It: Undercover Police Participation in Crime', *Stanford Law Review*, 62, 155–198.

Johnson, J. (2003). '11th September, 2001: Will It Make a Difference to the Global Anti-Money Laundering Movement?' *Journal of Money Laundering Control*, 6 (1), 9–16.

---- (2008a). 'Is the Global Financial System AML/CFT Prepared?' *Journal of Financial Crime*, 15 (1), 7–21.

---- (2008b). 'Third Round FATF Mutual Evaluations Indicate Declining Compliance', *Journal of Money Laundering Control*, 11 (1), 47–66.

Jositsch, D. (2005). 'Terrorismus oder Freiheitskampf? – Heikle Abgrenzungsfragen bei der Anwendung von Art. 260quinquies', *ZStrR*, 123, 458–470.

Jositsch, D., and von Rotz, M. (2016). 'Das Finanzmarktstrafrecht der Schweiz – Status quo unter Einbezug der neusten Gesetzesänderungen, des internationalen Einflusses sowie der anstehenden Neuerungen', *SZW*, 16, 592–608.

Jutzi, T. (2017). 'Art. 7a ff. GwG'. In P. V. Kunz, T. Jutzi, and S. Schären (eds), *Geldwäschereigesetz (GwG)*, pp. 310–319. Bern: Stämpfli.

Kahn-Freund, O. (1974). 'On Uses and Misuses of Comparative Law', *The Modern Law Review*, 37 (1), 1–27.

Kalin, W., and Kunzli, J. (2000). 'Article 1F (b): Freedom Fighters, Terrorists, and the Notion of Serious Non-Political Crimes', *International Journal of Refugee Law*, 12, 46–78.

Kaufmann, A. F., Meltzer, M. I., and Schmid, G. P. (1997). 'The Economic Impact of a Bioterrorist Attack: Are Prevention and Postattack Intervention Programs Justifiable?' *Emerging Infectious Diseases*, 3 (2), 83–94.

Keene, S. (2007). 'Hawala and Related Informal Value Transfer Systems – An Assessment in the Context of Organized Crime and Terrorist Finance: Is There Cause for Concern?' *Security Journal*, 20 (3), 185–196.

Kemper, M. (2007). 'Requirements and Content of Digital surveillance in the Prosecution of Criminal Offences', *Journal of Legal Policy*, 40 (4), 105–109.

Kennedy, D. (1997). 'New Approaches to Comparative Law: Comparativism and International Governance', *Utah Law Review*, 545–637.

Kennedy, R. (1999). 'Is One Person's Terrorist Another's Freedom Fighter? Western and Islamic Approaches to "Just War" Compared', *Terrorism and Political Violence*, 11 (1), 1–21.

Kerr, O. S. (2008). 'Updating the Foreign Intelligence Surveillance Act', *The University of Chicago Law Review*, 75 (1), 225–243.

Kersten, A. (2002). 'Financing of Terrorism – A Predicate Offence to Money Laundering?' In M. Pieht (ed.), *Financing Terrorism*, pp. 49–56. Dordrecht: Springer Netherlands.

Kessler, M. A., and Waygood-Weiner, A. (2017). 'Art. 10a GwG'. In P. V. Kunz, T. Jutzi, and S. Schären (eds), *Geldwäschereigesetz (GwG)*, pp. 441–460. Bern: Stämpfli.

Kindhäuser, U. (2017). '§ 89c StGB'. In U. Kindhäuser (ed), *Strafgesetzbuch, Lehr- und Praxiskommentar* (7th edn), pp. 536–538. Baden-Baden: Nomos-Verlag.

Killias, M., Kuhn, A., Dongois, N., and Aebi, M. (2009). *Grundriss des Allgemeinen Teils des schweizerischen Strafgesetzbuches*. Bern: Stämpfli.

Klabbers, J. (2003). 'Rebel With a Cause? Terrorists and Humanitarian Law', *European Journal of International Law*, 14 (2), 299–312.

Knodel, T. (2014). Art. 285a StPO. In M. A. Niggli, M. Heer, and H. Wiprächtiger (eds). *Schweizerische Strafprozessordnung/Jugendstrafprozessordnung (StPO, JStPO)* (2nd edn). Basel: Helbing Lichtenhahn.

Koh, W. T. (2007). 'Terrorism and Its Impact on Economic Growth and Technological Innovation', *Technological Forecasting and Social Change*, 74 (2), 129–138.

Kracauer, S. (1952). 'The Challenge of Qualitative Content Analysis', *Public Opinion Quarterly*, 16 (4) 631–642.

Kramer, B. (2019). *Grundlagen des Strafverfahrensrechts – Ermittlung und Verfahren* (8th edn). Stuttgart: Kohlhammer Verlag.

Krey, V., and Heinrich, M. (2019). *Deutsches Strafverfahrensrecht* (2nd edn). Stuttgart: Kohlhammer Verlag.

Krüger, R. (1993). 'Undercover Investigations in Criminal Proceedings and the Inviolability of the Home', *Journal of Legal Policy*, 26 (4), 124–127.

Kugelmann, D. (2014). *BKA-Gesetz* (1st edn). Munich: Beck Verlag.

Kunreuther, H., Michel-Kerjan, E., and Porter, B. (2003). *Assessing, Managing, and Financing Extreme Events: Dealing With Terrorism*. National Bureau of Economic Research Working Paper No. 10179.

Kutty, F. (2001). 'Canada Calling: Canadian Muslims Concerned About New Charity Law', *The Washington Report on Middle East Affairs*, 20 (4), 25–35.

Kühl, K. (2018). '§ 89c StGB'. In K. Lackner, and K. Kühl (eds), *Strafgesetzbuch (StGB) Kommentar* (29th edn), pp. 699–734. Munich: C. H. Beck Verlag.

Kühne, H. (2015). *Strafprozessrecht – Eine systematische Darstellung des deutschen und europäischen Strafverfahrensrechts* (9th edn). Heidelberg: C. F. Müller Verlag.

Lagodny, O. (1996). 'Verdeckte Ermittler und V-Leute im Spiegl von § 136 a StPO als «angewandtem Verfassungsrecht»', *StV*, 3, 167–172.

Latimer, P. (2005). 'Bank Secrecy in Australia: Terrorism Legislation as the New Exception to the Tournier Rule', *Journal of Money Laundering Control*, 8 (1), 56–65.

Legrand, P. (1995). 'Comparative Legal Studies and Commitment to Theory', *The Modern Law Review*, 58 (2), 262–273.

Léonard, S., and Kaunert, C. (2012). 'Combating the Financing of Terrorism Together? The Influence of the United Nations on the European Union's Financial Sanctions Regime'. In O. Costa, and K. Jørgensen (eds), *The Influence of International Institutions on the EU*, pp. 111–134. London: Palgrave Macmillan.

Leuzinger, A. (2014). 'Verdeckte Einvernahme – nach Mr. Big und allgemein, *Forumpoenale*, 3, 165–167.

Levi, M., Halliday, T., and Reuter, P. (2014). *Global Surveillance of Dirty Money: Assessing Assessments of Regimes to Control Money-Laundering and Combat the Financing of Terrorism.* Final Report to International Monetary Fund.

Levitt, M. (2003). 'Stemming the Flow of Terrorist Financing: Practical and Conceptual Challenges', *Fletcher Forum of World Affairs*, 27, 59–70.

Levitt, M. A. (2002). 'The Political Economy of Middle East Terrorism', *Middle East Review of International Affairs*, 6 (4), 49–65.

Li, Q., and Schaub, D. (2004). 'Economic Globalization and Transnational Terrorism: A Pooled Time-Series Analysis', *Journal of Conflict Resolution*, 48 (2), 230–258.

Liebi, M., and Lionel, C. (2017). 'Art. 4'. In P. V. Kunz, T. Jutzi, and S. Schären (eds), *Geldwäschereigesetz (GwG)*, pp. 197–279 Bern: Stämpfli.

Linn, C. J. (2005). 'How Terrorists Exploit Gaps in US Anti-Money Laundering Laws to Secrete Plunder', *Journal of Money Laundering Control*, 8 (3), 200–214.

Lobel, J. (1999). 'The Use of Force to Respond to Terrorist Attacks: The Bombing of Sudan and Afghanistan', *Yale Journal of International Law*, 24 (2), 537–557.

Looney, R. (2003). 'Hawala: The Terrorist's Informal Financial Mechanism', *Middle East Policy*, 10 (1), 164–167.

López-Rivera, O., and Headley, B. (1989). 'Who Is the Terrorist? The Making of a Puerto Rican Freedom Fighter', *Social Justice*, 16 (4), 162–174.

Lowe, P. (2006). 'Counterfeiting: Links to Organised Crime and Terrorist Funding', *Journal of Financial Crime*, 13 (2), 255–257.

Luban, D. (2002). 'The War on Terrorism and the End of Human Rights', *Philosophy & Public Policy Quarterly*, 22 (3), 9–14.

Luchsinger, R. (2017). 'Art. 9 ff.'. In P. V. Kunz, T. Jutzi, and S. Schären, (eds), *Geldwäschereigesetz (GwG)*, pp. 349–418. Bern: Stämpfli.

Lundy, J. R. (1968). 'Police Undercover Agents: New Threat to First Amendment Freedoms', *The George Washington Law Review*, 37, 634–668.

Lutz, D. S. (2002). 'Was ist Terrorismus? Definitionen, Wandel, Perspektiven, *Sicherheit und Frieden (S+F) / Security and Peace*, 20 (1), 2–8.

Lutz, P. (2016). 'Fresh Up: GwG für Rechtsanwälte und Notare', *Anwaltsrevue*, 16, 487–493.

Lutz, P., and Kern, M. (2017). 'Geldwäscherei und das qualifizierte Steuervergehen von Art. 305bis Ziff. 1bis StGB', *SJZ*, 113, 97–106.

Maclin, T. (2007). 'The Bush Administration's Terrorist Surveillance Program and the Fourth Amendment's Warrant Requirement: Lessons from Justice Powell and the Keith Case', *UC Davis Law Review*, 41, 1259–1325.

MacMull, J. G. (2004). 'Removing the Charitable Veil: An Examination of US Policy to Combat Terrorist Funding Charities Post 9/11', *New England Journal of International and Comparative Law*, 10, 121–136.

Makarenko, T. (2004). 'The Crime–Terror Continuum: Tracing the Interplay Between Transnational Organised Crime and Terrorism', *Global Crime*, 6 (1), 129–145.

Malkawi, B. H., and Malkawi, H. O. (2007). 'Anti-Terrorist Finance Provisions in Jordan: Important Step but Insufficient', *Journal of Money Laundering Control*, 10 (2), 180–188.

Markesinis, B. (1990). 'Comparative Law – A Subject in Search of an Audience', *The Modern Law Review*, 53 (1), 1–21.

Marron, D. (2008). 'Money Talks, Money Walks: The War on Terrorist Financing in the West', *Policing*, 2 (4), 441–451.

Marshall, M. N. (1996). 'Sampling for Qualitative Research', *Family Practice*, 13 (6), 522–526.

Marx, G. (1977). 'Undercover Cops: Creative Policing or Constitutional Threat?' *The Civil Liberties Review*, 4, 34–44.

Marx, G. T. (1980). 'The New Police Undercover Work', *Urban Life*, 8 (4), 399–446.

---- (1982). 'Who Really Gets Stung? Some Issues Raised by the New Police Undercover Work', *NPPA Journal*, 28 (2), 165–193.

---- (1987). 'The Interweaving of Public and Private Police in Undercover Work', *Private Policing*, 23, 172–193.

Masciandaro, D., and Portolano, A. (2003). 'It Takes Two to Tango: International Financial Regulation and Offshore Centres', *Journal of Money Laundering Control*, 6 (4), 311–330.

Masciandaro, D. (2004). 'Migration and Illegal Finance', *Journal of Money Laundering Control*, 7 (3), 264–271.

Mattei, U. (1994). 'Efficiency in Legal Transplants: An Essay in Comparative Law and Economics', *International Review of Law and Economics*, 14 (1), 3–19.

Mayer, J. (1999). 'Verdeckte Ermittlungen: Zulässigkeit und rechtliche Grundlagen des Einsatzes nicht offen operierender Polizeibeamter, *Kriminalistik* 49–57.

Mayring, P. (2010). *Qualitative Content Analysis: Principles and Techniques*. Weinheim: Beltz.

Mays, N., and Pope, C. (2000). 'Assessing Quality in Qualitative Research', *BMJ: British Medical Journal*, 320 (7226), 50–60.

McCloskey, H. J. (1967). 'Utilitarian and Retributive Punishment', *The Journal of Philosophy*, 64 (3), 91–110.

McCulloch, J., and Carlton, B. (2005). 'Preempting Justice: Suppression of Financing of Terrorism and the War on Terror', *Current Issues in Criminal Justice*, 17, 397–412.

McCulloch, J., and Pickering, S. (2005). 'Suppressing the Financing of Terrorism Proliferating State Crime, Eroding Censure and Extending Neo-Colonialism', *British Journal of Criminology*, 45 (4), 470–486.

---- (2009). 'Pre-Crime and Counter-Terrorism Imagining Future Crime in the "War on Terror"', *British Journal of Criminology*, 49 (5), 628–645.

McCulloch, J., Pickering, S., McQueen, R., and Tham, J. C. (2004). 'Suppressing the Financing of Terrorism', *Current Issues in Criminal Justice*, 16, 71–78.

Merlonghi, G. (2010). 'Fighting Financial Crime in the Age of Electronic Money: Opportunities and Limitations', *Journal of Money Laundering Control*, 13 (3), 202–214.

Middlebrook, S., and Hughes, S. (2013). 'Virtual Uncertainty: Developments in the Law of Electronic Payments and Financial Services', *The Business Lawyer*, 69 (1), 263–273.

Miller, G. I. (1987). 'Observations on Police Undercover Work', *Criminology*, 25 (1), 27–46.

Mitsilegas, V., and Gilmore, B. (2007). 'The EU Legislative Framework Against Money Laundering and Terrorist Finance: A Critical Analysis in the Light of Evolving Global Standards', *International and Comparative Law Quarterly*, 56 (01), 119–140.

Molo G., and Drzalic, J. (2019). 'Can Cryptocurrencies Be Compliant?' *AJP*, 28, 50–57.

Moreillon, L., and Lubishtani, K. (2018). 'Selected Aspects of the Criminalisation of Terrorism. A Study of Swiss, German, French and English Comparative Law (1/2)', *Swiss Criminal Review – SPR*, 4, 499–521.

Morse, J. M., Barrett, M., Mayan, M., Olson, K., and Spiers, J. (2002). 'Verification Strategies for Establishing Reliability and Validity in Qualitative Research', *International Journal of Qualitative Methods*, 1 (2), 13–22.

Müller, T. (2017). 'Art. 7 AMLA'. In P. V. Kunz, T. Jutzi, and S. Schären (eds), *Money Laundering Act (AMLA)*. Bern: Stämpfli.

Myers, M. D. (1997). 'Qualitative Research in Information Systems', *Management Information Systems Quarterly*, 21 (2), 241–242.

Nakajima, C. (2006). 'Intensified Efforts to Fight Money Laundering and Terrorist Financing – More Changes for the UK Financial Services Industry?' *Journal of Money Laundering Control*, 9 (3), 1–6.

Navias, M. S. (2002). 'Finance Warfare as a Response to International Terrorism', *The Political Quarterly*, 73 (s1), 57–79.

Nitsch, V., and Schumacher, D. (2004). 'Terrorism and International Trade: An Empirical Investigation', *European Journal of Political Economy*, 20 (2), 423–433.

Norgren, C. (2004). 'The Control of Risks Associated with Crime, Terror and Subversion', *Journal of Money Laundering Control*, 7 (3), 201–206.

Norman, T. L. (2010). *Risk Analysis and Security Countermeasure Selection*. New York: CRC Press.

Orlova, A. V., and Moore, J. W. (2004). 'Umbrellas or Building Blocks: Defining International Terrorism and Transnational Organized Crime in International Law', *Houston Journal of International Law*, 27, 267–310.

Othman, R., and Ameer, R. (2014). 'Institutionalization of Risk Management Framework in Islamic NGOs for Suppressing Terrorism Financing: Exploratory Research', *Journal of Money Laundering Control*, 17 (1), 96–109.

Paeffgen, H. (2017). '§ 89c StGB'. In U. Kindhäuser, U. Neumann, and H. U. Paeffgen (eds), *Strafgesetzbuch* (5th edn), pp. 536–538. Baden-Baden: Nomos-Verlag.

Parnell, G. S., Smith, C. M., and Moxley, F. I. (2010). 'Intelligent Adversary Risk Analysis: A Bioterrorism Risk Management Model', *Risk Analysis*, 30 (1), 32–48.

Passas, N. (2003). 'Hawala and Other Informal Value Transfer Systems: How to Regulate Them?' *Risk Management*, 5, 49–59.

---- (2005a). 'Indicators of Hawala Operations and Criminal Abuse', *Journal of Money Laundering Control*, 8 (2), 168–172.

---- (2005b). 'Law Enforcement Challenges in Hawala-Related Investigations', *Journal of Financial Crime*, 12 (2), 112–119.

---- (2006a). 'Demystifying Hawala: A Look Into Its Social Organization and Mechanics', *Journal of Scandinavian Studies in Criminology and Crime Prevention*, 7 (S1), 46–62.

---- (2006b). 'Setting Global CFT Standards: A Critique and Suggestions', *Journal of Money Laundering Control*, 9 (3), 281–292.

Paté-Cornell, E., and Guikema, S. (2002). 'Probabilistic Modeling of Terrorist Threats: A Systems Analysis Approach to Setting Priorities Among Countermeasures', *Military Operations Research*, 7 (4), 5–23.

Pathak, R. (2003). 'The Obstacles to Regulating the Hawala: A Cultural Norm or a Terrorist Hotbed', *Fordham International Law Journal*, 27, 2007–2061.

Peers, S. (2003). 'EU Responses to Terrorism', *International and Comparative Law Quarterly*, 52 (01), 227–243.

Perri, F. S., and Brody, R. G. (2011). 'The Dark Triad: Organized Crime, Terror and Fraud', *Journal of Money Laundering Control*, 14 (1), 44–59.

Perry, N. J. (2003). 'The Numerous Federal Legal Definitions of Terrorism: The Problem of Too Many Grails', *Journal of Legislation*, 30, 249–274.

Petri, T. B. (2008). 'The Federal Constitutional Court's Ruling on "Digital surveillance"', *Datenschutz und Datensicherheit – DuD*, 32 (7), 443–448.

Petzsche, A. (2013). *Strafrecht und Terrorismusbekämpfung*. Bern: Stämpfli Verlag.

Pfeiffer, M. (2005). *Strafprozessordnung* (5th edn). Munich: Beck Verlag.

Pfitzmann, A. (2008). 'Contra Online-Durchsuchungen', *Informatik-Spektrum*, 31 (1), 65–69.

Piers, M. J. (2004). 'Malevolent Destruction of a Muslim Charity: A Commentary on the Prosecution of Benevolence International Foundation', *Pace Law Review*, 25, 339–354.

Pieth, M. (2002). 'Financing of Terrorism: Following the Money'. In M. Pieth (ed.), *Financing Terrorism*, pp. 115–126. Dordrecht: Springer Netherlands.

---- (2006). 'Criminalizing the Financing of Terrorism', *Journal of International Criminal Justice*, 4 (5), 1074–1086.

Ping, H. E. (2008). 'The Measures on Combating Money Laundering and Terrorism Financing in the PRC: From the Perspective of Financial Action Task Force', *Journal of Money Laundering Control*, 11 (4), 320–330.

Pizam, A., and Smith, G. (2000). 'Tourism and Terrorism: A Quantitative analysis of Major Terrorist Acts and Their Impact on Tourism Destinations', *Tourism Economics*, 6 (2), 123–138.

Plöchl, F. (2018). '§ 278d StGB'. In F. Höpfel, and E. Ratz (eds), *Wiener Kommentar zum Strafgesetzbuch* (2nd edn). Vienna: Manz.

Pohl, H. (2007). 'On the Technology of Surreptitious Digital surveillance', *Datenschutz und Datensicherheit – DuD*, 31 (9), 684–688.

Polenz, S. (2018). 'Verfassungsrechtliche Grundlagen des Datenschutzes. In J. Taenger, and J. Pohle (eds), *Computerrechts-Handbuch* (34th edn). Munich: Beck Verlag.

Pollinger, Z. A. (2008). 'Counterfeit Goods and Their Potential Financing of International Terrorism', *The Michigan Journal of Business*, 1 (1), 85–102.

Pope, C., Ziebland, S., and Mays, N. (2000). 'Analysing Qualitative Data', *British Medical Journal*, 320 (7227), 114–116.

Posner, R. A. (2008). 'Privacy, Surveillance, and Law', *The University of Chicago Law Review*, 75 (1), 245–260.

Prabha, K. (2000). 'Defining Terrorism', *Strategic Analysis*, 24 (1), 125–135.

Raghavan, S. V., and Balasubramaniyan, V. (2012). 'Financial Facilitators: An Important Component of Terror Networks', *Journal of Money Laundering Control*, 15 (3), 294–303.

Raphaeli, N. (2003). 'Financing of Terrorism: Sources, Methods, and Channels', *Terrorism and Political Violence*, 15 (4), 59–82.

Razavy, M. (2005). 'Hawala: An Underground Haven for Terrorists or Social Phenomenon?' *Crime, Law and Social Change*, 44 (3), 277–299.

Reimann, M. (2002). 'The Progress and Failure of Comparative Law in the Second Half of the Twentieth Century', *The American Journal of Comparative Law*, 50 (4), 671–700.

Reindl-Krauskopf, S. (2011). *Code of Criminal Procedure* (21st edn). Vienna: Manz.

Reitz, J. C. (1998). 'How to Do Comparative Law', *The American Journal of Comparative Law*, 46 (4), 617–636.

Rice, D. (2013). 'The Past and Future of Bitcoins in Worldwide Commerce', *Business Law Today*, 1–4.

Ridley, N. (2008). 'Organized Crime, Money Laundering, and Terrorism', *Policing*, 2 (1), 28–35.

Riklin, F. (2014). *StPO Kommentar – Schweizerische Strafprozessordnung mit JStPO, StBOG und weiteren Erlassen*. Zurich: Schulthess.

Riles, A. (1999). 'Wigmore's Treasure Box: Comparative Law in the Era of Information', *Harvard International Law Journal*, 40, 221–284.

Rios Insua, D., Rios, J., and Banks, D. (2009). 'Adversarial Risk Analysis', *Journal of the American Statistical Association*, 104 (486), 841–854.

Roach, K. (2011). 'The Air India Report and the Regulation of Charities and Terrorism Financing', *University of Toronto Law Journal*, 61 (1), 45–57.

Roberge, I. (2007). 'Misguided Policies in the War on Terror? The Case for Disentangling Terrorist Financing from Money Laundering', *Politics*, 27 (3), 196–203.

Roberts, A. (2000). 'Crime Creation? Some Questions of Fairness and Efficacy in Covert Operations', *The Police Journal*, 73 (3), 263–276.

Rodin, D. (2004). 'Terrorism Without Intention', *Ethics*, 114 (4), 752–771.

Rogall, K. (1987). 'Strafprozessuale Grundlagen und legislative Probleme des Einsatzes Verdeckter Ermittler im Strafverfahren', *JZ*, 42 (18), 847–853.

Rolfe, G. (2006). 'Validity, Trustworthiness and Rigour: Quality and the Idea of Qualitative Research', *Journal of Advanced Nursing*, 53 (3), 304–310.

Rosand, E. (2003). 'Security Council Resolution 1373, the Counter-Terrorism Committee, and the Fight Against Terrorism', *The American Journal of International Law*, 97 (2), 333–341.

Rosenthal, G. (2005). *Interpretative Social Research, an Introduction.* Munich: Juventa.

Ross, J. E. (2007). 'The Place of Covert Surveillance in Democratic Societies: A Comparative Study of the United States and Germany', *The American Journal of Comparative Law*, 55 (3), 493–579.

---- (2008). 'Undercover Policing and the Shifting Terms of Scholarly Debate: The United States and Europe in Counterpoint', *Annual Review of Law and Social Science*, 4, 239–273.

Roth, M. P., and Sever, M. (2007). 'The Kurdish Workers Party (PKK) as Criminal Syndicate: Funding Terrorism Through Organized Crime, a Case Study', *Studies in Conflict & Terrorism*, 30 (10), 901–920.

Roy, S. (2007). 'Hamas: Politics, Charity and Terrorism in the Service of Jihad', *Middle East Policy*, 14 (2), 162–167.

Ruby, C. L. (2002). 'The Definition of Terrorism', *Analyses of Social Issues and Public Policy*, 2 (1), 9–14.

Ruebner, R. (2002). 'Democracy, Judicial Review and the Rule of Law in the Age of Terrorism: The Experience of Israel – A Comparative Perspective', *Georgia Journal of International and Comparative Law*, 31, 493–546.

Ruff, K. A. (2005). 'Scared to Donate: An Examination of the Effects of Designating Muslim Charities as Terrorist Organizations on the First Amendment Rights of Muslim Donors', *N.Y.U. Journal of Legislation & Public Policy*, 9, 447–502.

Rux, J. (2007). 'Ausforschung privater Rechner durch die Polizei- und Sicherheitsbehörden – Rechtsfragen der «Online-Durchsuchung»"', *JuristenZeitung*, 62 (6), 285–295.

Sacco, R. (1991). 'Legal Formants: A Dynamic Approach to Comparative Law (Installment I of II)', *The American Journal of Comparative Law*, 39 (1), 1–34.

Sadat, L. N. (2004). 'Terrorism and the Rule of Law', *Washington University Global Studies Law Review*, 3, 135–154.

Irwin, S.M.A., Choo, K. K. R., and Liu, L. (2011). 'An Analysis of Money Laundering and Terrorism Financing Typologies', *Journal of Money Laundering Control*, 15 (1), 85–111.

Sandelowski, M. (1994). 'Focus on Qualitative Methods. The Use of Quotes in Qualitative Research', *Research in Nursing & Health*, 17 (6), 479–482.

Sanderson, T. M. (2004). 'Transnational Terror and Organized Crime: Blurring the Lines', *SAIS Review of International Affairs*, 24 (1), 49–61.

Saul, B. (2005a). 'Attempts to Define "Terrorism" in International Law', *Netherlands International Law Review*, 52 (1), 57–84.

---- (2005b). 'Definition of "Terrorism" in the UN Security Council: 1985–2004', *Chinese Journal of International Law*, 4 (1), 141–166.

Schaeffer, E. C. (2008). 'Remittances and Reputations in Hawala Money-Transfer Systems: Self-Enforcing Exchange on an International Scale', *Journal of Private Enterprise*, 24 (1), 95–117.

Schäfer, J. (2017). '§ 89c StGB'. In K. Miebach (ed.), *Münchener Kommentar zum Strafgesetzbuch* (3rd edn), pp. 157–164. Munich: C. H. Beck Verlag.

Schantz, P. (2007). 'Verfassungsrechtliche Probleme von «Online-Durchsuchungen»', *Kritische Vierteljahresschrift für Gesetzgebung und Rechtswissenschaft (KritV)*, 90 (3), 310–330.

Schären, S. (2017). 'Art. 2'. In P. V. Kunz, T. Jutzi, and S. Schären (eds), *Geldwäschereigesetz (GwG)*, pp. 45–124. Bern: Stämpfli.

Scharf, M. P. (2000). 'Defining Terrorism as the Peace Time Equivalent of War Crimes: A Case of Too Much Convergence Between International Humanitarian Law and International Criminal Law', *ILSA Journal of International & Comparative Law*, 7, 391–398.

---- (2004). 'Defining Terrorism as the Peacetime Equivalent of War Crimes: Problems and Prospects', *Case Western Reserve Journal of International Law*, 36, 359–374.

Schenke, W. R. (2019). '§ 49 BKA Law'. In W. R. Schenke, K. Graulich, and J. Ruthig (eds). *Sicherheitsrecht des Bundes* (2nd edn), pp. 341–343. Munich: C. H. Beck Verlag.

Scheuerman, W. E. (2006). 'Survey Article: Emergency Powers and the Rule of Law After 9/11', *Journal of Political Philosophy*, 14 (1), 61–84.

Schinkelshoek, M. (2015). 'Scope of Application of Art. 9 § 1 lit. b Anti-Money Laundering Act (AMLA)', *AJP*, 15, 481–486.

Schmid, A. P. (1996). 'The Links Between Transnational Organized Crime and Terrorist Crimes', *Transnational Organized Crime*, 2 (4), 40–82.

---- (2004a). 'Frameworks for Conceptualising Terrorism', *Terrorism and Political Violence*, 16 (2), 197–221.

---- (2004b). 'Terrorism – The Definitional Problem', *Case Western Reserve Journal of International Law*, 36, 375–420.

Schmid, N., and Jositsch, D. (2017). *Swiss Code of Criminal Procedure – Practical Commentary* (3rd revised edn). Zurich: Dike.

Schneider, F. (2010). 'Turnover of Organized Crime and Money Laundering: Some Preliminary Empirical Findings', *Public Choice*, 144 (3–4), 473–486.

Schott, P. A. (2006). *Reference Guide to Anti-Money Laundering and Combating the Financing of Terrorism*. Washington, D.C.: World Bank Publications.

Schubarth, M., and Vest, H. (2013). *Commentary on Swiss Criminal Law*. Bern: Stämpfli.

Schwaighofer, K. (2010). '§ 278d StGB'. In C. Bertel, and K. Schwaighofer (eds), *Österreichisches Strafrecht, Besonderer Teil II (§ 169 bis 321 StGB)* (9th edn) p. 217, Vienna: Österreich GmbH Verlag.

Scott, D. (1995). 'Money Laundering and International Efforts to Fight It', *Public Policy for the Private Sector*, 48, 1–6.

Seifert, J. (1992). 'From Eavesdropping to "Grand Eavesdropping". May There Be Total Surveillance of the Home?' *Critical Justice*, 25 (3), 355–363.

Senechal dela Roche, R. (2004). 'Toward a Scientific Theory of Terrorism', *Sociological Theory*, 22 (1), 1–4.

Shahin, W. (2013). 'Compliance With International Regulation on AML/CFT: The Case of Banks in Lebanon', *Journal of Money Laundering Control*, 16 (2), 109–118.

Shapiro, J. N., and Siegel, D. A. (2007). 'Underfunding in Terrorist Organizations', *International Studies Quarterly*, 51 (2), 405–429.

Sharp, F. C., and Otto, M. C. (1910). 'A Study of the Popular Attitude Towards Retributive Punishment', *The International Journal of Ethics*, 20 (3), 341–357.

Shelley, L. I., and Picarelli, J. T. (2002). 'Methods Not Motives: Implications of the Convergence of International Organized Crime and Terrorism', *Police Practice and Research*, 3 (4), 305–318.

---- (2005). 'Methods and Motives: Exploring Links Between Transnational Organized Crime and International Terrorism', *Trends in Organized Crime*, 9 (2), 52–67.

Shehu, A. Y. (2010). 'Promoting Financial Sector Stability Through an Effective AML/CFT Regime', *Journal of Money Laundering Control*, 13 (2), 139–154.

Shelley, L. I., and Melzer, S. A. (2008). 'The Nexus of Organized Crime and Terrorism: Two Case Studies in Cigarette Smuggling', *International Journal of Comparative and Applied Criminal Justice*, 32 (1), 43–63.

Simser, J. (2011). 'Terrorism Financing and the Threat to Financial Institutions', *Journal of Money Laundering Control*, 14 (4), 334–345.

Singelnstein, T., and Derin, B. (2017). 'The Law to Make Criminal Proceedings More Effective and Practical', *NJW*, 70 (37), 2646–2652.

Sinha, G. (2013). 'AML-CTF: A Forced Marriage Post 9/11 and Its Effect on Financial Institutions', *Journal of Money Laundering Control*, 16 (2), 142–158.

Slaughter, A. M. (1999). 'Judicial Globalization', *Virginia Journal of International Law*, 40, 1103–1124.

Spalek, B., and O'Rawe, M. (2014). 'Researching Counterterrorism: A Critical Perspective From the Field in the Light of Allegations and Findings of Covert Activities by Undercover Police Officers', *Critical Studies on Terrorism*, 7 (1), 150–164.

Sproat, P. A. (2010). 'Counter-Terrorist Finance in the UK: A Quantitative and Qualitative Commentary Based on Open-Source Materials', *Journal of Money Laundering Control*, 13 (4), 315–335.

Stergiou, D., and Stergiou, D. (2016). 'ISIS Political Economy: Financing a Terror State', *Journal of Money Laundering Control*, 19 (2), 189–207.

Sternberg-Lieben, D. (2019). '§ 89c StGB'. In A. Schönke, and H. Schröder (eds), *Strafgesetzbuch Kommentar* (30th edn), pp. 1333–1334. Munich: C. H. Beck Verlag.

Stessens, G. (2001). 'The FATF "Black List" of Non-Cooperative Countries or Territories', *Leiden Journal of International Law*, 14 (01), 199–207.

Stotter, H.J. (2008). '§ 278d StGB'. In H.J. Stotter (ed.), *Das liechtensteinische Strafgesetzbuch* (2nd edn), pp. 708–716. Vaduz: Ex Jure Verlagsanstalt.

---- (2012). *The Liechtenstein Code of Criminal Procedure (StPO)* (1st edn). Triesen: Ritter.

Stratenwerth, G. (2011). *Schweizerisches Recht – Allgemeiner Teil*. Bern: Stämpfli.

Stratenwerth, G., and Wohlers, W. (2013). *Schweizerisches Strafgesetzbuch – Handkommentar*. Bern: Stämpfli.

Stromseth, J. E. (2003). 'The Security Council's Counter-Terrorism Role: Continuity and Innovation', In J.E. Stromseth, *Proceedings of the ASIL Annual Meeting*, 97, pp. 41–45. Cambridge: Cambridge University Press.

Szasz, P. C. (2002). 'The Security Council Starts Legislating', *The American Journal of International Law*, 96 (4), 901–905.

Teichmann, F. (2017a). 'Die Bekämpfung der Terrorismusfinanzierung – Ein aussichtsloser Weg?' *ius.full*, 3, 95–100.

---- (2017b). 'Geldwäscherei in der Immobilienbranche, *Kriminalistik*, 3, 194–198.

---- (2017c). 'Twelve Methods of Money Laundering', *Journal of Money Laundering Control*, 20 (2), 130–137.

---- (2016a). *Umgehungsmöglichkeiten der Geldwäschereipräventionsmassnah men*. Zurich: Schulthess Verlag.

---- (2016b). 'Wie sinnvoll ist die Abschaffung des Bargelds zur Bekämpfung der Geldwäscherei und der Terrorismusfinanzierung' *ius.full*, 6, 154–161.

---- (2016c). 'Geldwäscherei in der Schweiz, *ZRFC – Risk, Fraud & Compliance*, 4, 163–166.

---- (2016d). 'Geldwäscherei im Schmuckhandel, *ius.full*, 5, 120–127.

Tewksbury, R. (2009). 'Qualitative Versus Quantitative Methods: Understanding Why Qualitative Methods Are Superior for Criminology and Criminal Justice', *Journal of Theoretical and Philosophical Criminology*, 1 (1), 38–58.

Tewksbury, R., Dabney, D. A., and Copes, H. (2010). 'The Prominence of Qualitative Research in Criminology and Criminal Justice Scholarship', *Journal of Criminal Justice Education*, 21 (4), 391–411.

Thelesklaf, D. (2009). 'Art. 9 ff. GwG'. In D. Thelesklaf, R. Wyss, D. Zollinger, and M. van Thiel (eds), *GWG Kommentar*. Bern: Orell Füssli.

Thistle, C. (2008). 'A First Amendment Breach: The National Security Agency's Electronic Surveillance Program', *Seton Hall Law Review*, 38, 1197–1232.

Thomas, E., and Magilvy, J. K. (2011). 'Qualitative Rigor or Research Validity in Qualitative Research', *Journal for Specialists in Pediatric Nursing*, 16 (2), 151–155.

Thony, J. F., and Png, C. A. (2007). 'FATF Special Recommendations and UN Resolutions on the Financing of Terrorism: A Review of the Status of Implementation and Legal Challenges Faced by Countries', *Journal of Financial Crime*, 14 (2), 150–169.

Tierney, M. (2017). 'Well Funded and Dangerous: Assessing the Islamic State's Financing Operations', *Journal of Money Laundering Control*, 20 (2), 1–20.

Tilly, C. (2004). 'Terror, Terrorism, Terrorists', *Sociological Theory*, 22 (1), 5–13.

Tofangsaz, H. (2012). 'A New Approach to the Criminalization of Terrorist Financing and Its Compatibility With Sharia Law', *Journal of Money Laundering Control*, 15 (4), 396–406.

---- (2015a). 'Rethinking Terrorist Financing; Where Does All This Lead?' *Journal of Money Laundering Control*, 18 (1), 112–130.

---- (2015b). 'Terrorism or Not Terrorism? Whose Money Are We Looking For?' *Journal of Financial Crime*, 22 (3), 378–390.

Travalio, G. M. (2000). 'Terrorism, International Law, and the Use of Military Force', *Wisconsin International Law Review*, 18, 145–192.

Trechsel, S., and Pieth, M. (2018). *Schweizerisches Strafgesetzbuch – Praxiskommentar* (3rd edn). Zurich: Dike.

Truby, J. (2016). 'Qatar's Progress Towards Preventing Terror Finance Through the Abuse of Charitable Status and the Financial Sector', *Journal of Money Laundering Control*, 19 (4), 500–516.

Tupman, W. A. (2009). 'Ten Myths About Terrorist Financing ', *Journal of Money Laundering Control*, 12 (2), 189–205.

Twining, W. (1999). 'Globalization and Comparative Law', *Maastricht Journal of European & Comparative Law*, 6, 217–243.

Vaismoradi, M., Turunen, H., and Bondas, T. (2013). 'Content Analysis and Thematic Analysis: Implications for Conducting a Qualitative Descriptive Study', *Nursing & Health Sciences*, 15 (3), 398–405.

van den Haag, E. (1986). 'Punishment: Desert and Crime Control', *Michigan Law Review*, 85 (5), 1250–1260.

van Hoecke, M., and Warrington, M. (1998). 'Legal Cultures, Legal Paradigms and Legal Doctrine: Towards a New Model for Comparative Law', *International and Comparative Law Quarterly*, 47 (3), 495–536.

van Munster, R. (2004). 'The War on Terrorism: When the Exception Becomes the Rule', *International Journal for the Semiotics of Law*, 17 (2), 141–153.

Veng Mei Leong, A. (2005). 'Definitional Analysis: The War on Terror and Organised Crime', *Journal of Money Laundering Control*, 8 (1), 19–36.

Verdugo-Yepes, C. (2008). 'Enhancing International Cooperation in the Fight Against the Financing of Terrorism', *Journal of Global Change and Governance*, 1 (3), 1–27.

Vest, H., and Schuhbarth, M. (2007). *Offences Against the Public Peace (Art. 258–263 StGB)* (1st edn). Bern: Stämpfli.

Viles, T. (2008). 'Hawala, Hysteria and Hegemony', *Journal of Money Laundering Control*, 11 (1), 25–33.

Viritha, B., Mariappan, V., and Haq, I. U. (2015). 'Suspicious Transaction Reporting: An Indian Experience', *Journal of Money Laundering Control*, 18 (1), 2–16.

Vlcek, W. (2006). 'Acts to Combat the Financing of Terrorism: Common Foreign and Security Policy at the European Court of Justice', *European Foreign Affairs Review*, 11, 491–507.

---- (2008). 'Development vs. Terrorism: Money Transfers and EU Financial Regulations in the UK', *The British Journal of Politics and International Relations*, 10 (2), 286–302.

von Heintschel-Heinegg, W. (2016). *Beck'scher Online-Kommentar StGB* (33rd edn). Munich: Beck Verlag.

von Hirsch, A. (1991). 'Proportionality in the Philosophy of Punishment: From "Why Punish?" to "How Much?"', *Israel Law Review*, 25 (3–4), 549–580.

---- (1992). 'Proportionality in the Philosophy of Punishment', *Crime and Justice*, 16, 55–98.

von Ins, P., and Wyder, P. (2018). 'Art. 179bis'. In M. A. Niggli, M. Heer, and H. Wiprächtiger (eds), *Basler Kommentar zum Strafrecht II* (4th edn). Basel: Helbing Lichtenhahn.

von Winterfeldt, D., and O'Sullivan, T. M. (2006). 'Should We Protect Commercial Airplanes Against Surface-to-Air Missile Attacks by Terrorists?' *Decision Analysis*, 3 (2), 63–75.

Wachtel, J. (1992). 'From Morals to Practice: Dilemmas of Control in Undercover Policing', *Crime, Law and Social Change*, 18 (1–2), 137–158.

Warbrick, C. (2004). 'The European Response to Terrorism in an Age of Human Rights', *European Journal of International Law*, 15 (5), 989–1018.

Ward, C. A. (2003). 'Building Capacity to Combat International Terrorism: The Role of the United Nations Security Council', *Journal of Conflict and Security Law*, 8 (2), 289–305.

Waszak, J. D. (2004). 'The Obstacles to Suppressing Radical Islamic Terrorist Financing', *Case Western Reserve Journal of International Law*, 36, 673–710.

Watson, A. (1978). 'Comparative Law and Legal Change', *The Cambridge Law Journal*, 37 (02), 313–336.

---- (1995). 'From Legal Transplants to Legal Formants', *American Journal of Comparative Law*, 43, 469–476.

Webster, D. W., Bulzacchelli, M. T., Zeoli, A. M., and Vernick, J. S. (2006). 'Effects of Undercover Police Stings of Gun Dealers on the Supply of New Guns to Criminals', *Injury Prevention*, 12 (4), 225–230.

Wedgwood, R. (1999). 'Responding to Terrorism: The Strikes Against Bin Laden', *Yale Journal of International Law*, 24, 559–576.

Weder, U. (2018). StGB Kommentar. In: A. Donatsch, S. Heimgartner, B. Isenring, and U. Weder (eds), *StGB Kommentar*. Bern: Orell Füssli.

Weil, S. (1992). 'Undercover Investigations in Criminal Proceedings and the Inviolability of the Home', *Journal of Legal Policy*, 25 (7), 243–247.

Weiner, B., Graham, S., and Reyna, C. (1997). 'An Attributional Examination of Retributive Versus Utilitarian Philosophies of Punishment', *Social Justice Research*, 10 (4), 431–452.

Weintraub, S. (2002). 'Disrupting the Financing of Terrorism', *Washington Quarterly*, 25 (1), 53–60.

Weissenberger, P. (2018). 'Art. 143bis'. In M. A. Niggli, M. Heer, and H. Wiprächtiger (eds), *Basler Kommentar zum Strafrecht II* (4th edn). Basel: Helbing Lichtenhahn

Wheatley, J. (2005). 'Ancient Banking, Modern Crimes: How Hawala Secretly Transfers the Finances of Criminals and Thwarts Existing Laws', *University of Pennsylvania Journal of International Economic Law*, 26, 347–378.

Whittemore, R., Chase, S. K., and Mandle, C. L. (2001). 'Validity in Qualitative Research', *Qualitative Health Research*, 11 (4), 522–537.

Winer, J. M. (2008). 'Countering Terrorist Finance: A Work, Mostly in Progress', *The ANNALS of the American Academy of Political and Social Science*, 618 (1), 112–132.

Winer, J. M., and Roule, T. J. (2002). 'Fighting Terrorist Finance', *Survival*, 44 (3), 87–104.

Wong, K. (2006). 'The NSA Terrorist Surveillance Program', *Harvard Journal on Legislation*, 43, 517–534.

Wyss, R. (2009). 'Art. 1 ff.'. In D. Thelesklaf, R. Wyss, D. Zollinger, and M. van Thiel (eds), *GwG Kommentar*. Bern: Orell Füssli.

Yoo, J. (2006). 'The Terrorist Surveillance Program and the Constitution', *George Mason Law Review*, 14, 565–600.

Zagaris, B. (2004). 'The Merging of the Anti-Money Laundering and Counter-Terrorism Financial Enforcement Regimes After September 11, 2001', *Berkeley Journal of International Law*, 22, 123–158.

---- (2007). 'Problems Applying Traditional Anti-Money Laundering Procedures to Non-Financial Transactions, "Parallel Banking Systems" and Islamic Financial Systems', *Journal of Money Laundering Control*, 10 (2), 157–169.

Zeidan, S. (2003). 'Desperately Seeking Definition: The International Community's Quest for Identifying the Specter of Terrorism', *Cornell International Law Journal*, 36, 491–496.

Zerbes, I. (2011). *Wiener Kommentar StPO*. Vienna: Manz.

Ziercke, J. (2008). 'Pro Online-Durchsuchung', *Informatik-Spektrum*, 31 (1), 62–64.

Zöller, A. M. (2018). '§ 89c StGB'. In J. Wolter (ed.), *SK-StGB, §§80–173. vol. III* (9th edn). Cologne: Carl Heymanns Verlag.

Zöller, M. (2009). *Terrorismusstrafrecht – Ein Handbuch*. Heidelberg: C. F. Müller Verlag.

II. Internet sources

Federal Council (2007). 'Draft for the Federal Act on Measures to Safeguard Internal Security', <http://www.news-service.admin.ch/NSBSubscriber/message/attachments/8731.pdf>, accessed 1 May 2017.

Der Bundesrat (2011). 'Bericht und Vorentwurf über die Revision des Bundesgesetzes vom 6. Oktober 2000 betreffend die Überwachung des Post- und Fernmeldeverkehrs (SPTA)', <https://www.admin.ch/ch/d/gg/pc/documents/1719/Bericht_V_Ueberwachung_des_Post-_und_Fernmeldeverkehrs.pdf>, accessed 1 May 2017.

FINMA (2006). 'Bekämpfung der Terrorismusfinanzierung, <https://www.finma.ch/FinmaArchiv/bpv/d/themen/00711/index.html?lang=de>, accessed 6 April 2017.

FINMA (2017). 'Finanzsanktionen im Zusammenhang mit Terrorismus und Terrorismusfinanzierung', <https://www.finma.ch/de/dokumentation/internationale-sanktionen-und-terrorismusbekaempfung/finanzsanktionen-gegen-terrorismus/#Order=4>, accessed 6 April 2017.

Hansjakob, T. (2011). 'Einsatz von GovWare – zulässig oder nicht? Zum Einsatz von Computerprogrammen bei der Überwachung der Internet-Telefonie, <http://www.hansjakob.ch/thomas/jusletter_einsatz_govware.pdf>, accessed 2 May 2017.

Nationalrat (2016). 'Bundesgesetz, mit dem die Strafprozessordnung 1975 und das Staatsanwaltschaftsgesetz geändert werden, <https://www.parlament.gv.at/PAKT/VHG/XXV/ME/ME_00192/fname_521691.pdf>, accessed 1 May 2017.

Time (2015). 'Spreading Fear Is Frighteningly Cheap', <http://www.zeit.de/wirtschaft/2015-11/terrorismus-finanzierung-islamischer-staat-fatf-peter-neumann>, accessed 6 April 2017.

III. List of abbreviations and acronyms

(*no.*)	Subsection	
Art.	Article	
AML	Anti-money laundering	
AMLA	Swiss Anti-Money Laundering Act	
AT-StGB	Austrian Criminal Code	*(Strafgesetzbuch)*
AT-StPO	Austrian Code of Criminal Procedure	*(Strafprozessordnung)*
B-VG	Austrian Federal Constitutional Law	*(Bundes-Verfassungsgesetz)*
BGE	Swiss Federal Court ruling	(*Bundesgerichtsentscheid*)
BKA Law	Law on the Bundeskriminalamt and the Cooperation between Federal and State Authorities in Criminal Police Matters	
BV	Swiss Federal Consitution	*(Bundesverfassung)*
BVerfG	German Federal Constitutional Court	*(Bundesverfasssungs-gericht)*
BVR	German Federal Constitutional Court ruling	
BWIS	Swiss Federal Act on Measures to Safeguard	*(Bundesgesetz über die* Internal Security *Massnahmen zur Wahrung der inneren Sicherheit)*
CFT	Counter the financing of terrorism	
CH-StGB	Swiss Criminal Code	

CH-StPO	Swiss Code of Criminal Procedure	
DE-StGB	German Criminal Code	
DE-StPO	German Code of Criminal Procedure	
E.	Consideration (in Federal Court rulings)	*(BGE Erwägung)*
ECHR	European Convention on Human Rights	
EmbA	Swiss Federal Act on the Implementation of International Sanctions (Embargo Act)	
FATF	Financial Action Task Force	
FINMA	Swiss Financial Market Supervisory Authority	*(Finanzmarktaufsicht)*
FIU	Financial Intelligence Unit	
FL-StGB	Liechtenstein Criminal Code	
FL-StPO	Liechtenstein Code of Criminal Procedure	
GG	Basic Law for der Federal Republic of Germany	*(Grundgesetz)*
IntelSA	Swiss Federal Act on the Intelligence Service (Intelligence Service Act)	
KYC	Know your customer	
lit.	Letter	
LV	Liechtenstein Constitution	*(Verfassung des Fürstentums Liechtenstein)*
MROS	Swiss Money Laundering Reporting Office	
no.	number	

OECD	Organisation for Economic Co-operation and Development	
PKK	Kurdistan's Workers' Party	
SPTA	Federal Act on the Surveillance of Postal and Telecommunications Traffic	
SPG	Due Diligence Act	*(Sorgfaltspflichtgesetz)*
StGG	Austrian Basic State Law	*(Staatsgrundgesetz)*
StGH	Liechtenstein Constitutional Court	*(Staatsgerichtshof)*
ÜBFT	International Convention for the Suppression of the Financing of Terrorism	*(Internationales Übereinkommen zur Bekämpfung der Finanzierung des Terrorismus)*
WMA	Swiss Federal Act on War Material (War Material Act)	

1. Introduction

This book examines the barriers and hurdles in the fight against and prevention of crime in the criminal procedure context viewed through the lens of combating the financing of terrorism in Germany, Liechtenstein, Austria and Switzerland. Counter-terrorism continues to be a central issue as the self-proclaimed 'Islamic State' (IS) keeps the world on tenterhooks. Terrorist attacks in Europe and battles over territory in Syria dominate media coverage. Despite the general census being that terrorism must be fought, there is disagreement about which is the correct approach to take.

One approach to tackling counter-terrorism is to dry up terrorist funding streams. The underlying logic of this approach is that many forms of terrorism come at a cost, and terrorists are likely to be limited in their options to carry out terrorist acts if they lack adequate funding. This is logical in that terrorists rely on weapons and explosives, among other things, to carry out their attacks. However, this argument must also be contextualized within the recent attacks that took place in Nice, Berlin and Stockholm. In those three cases, stolen lorries were used as the means of committing the crimes, which means that these attacks were executed at a relatively low cost. It should be noted that financing acts of terrorism is surprisingly inexpensive, with the average attack costing only US$ 10,000.[1]

Although not every terrorist attack is associated with high costs, and it is certainly possible to injure or even kill many people at a fairly low cost (and consequently gain free publicity via the media), it is reasonable to assume that larger terrorist organizations, such as IS or Al-Qaeda, require considerable financial resources in order to maintain their networks. Consider, for example, the payments that must be made to fighters in Syria who are defending IS territory. Funding is necessary to create safeholds and offer training opportunities for terrorists from all over the world. It is therefore in the interest of the international community to combat terrorism financing by weakening terrorist organizations and restricting their ability to fund and carry out major terrorist attacks.

This book uses the definition of terrorism financing found in Art. 260^{quinquies} CH-StGB, which is explained in more detail in Section 2.1, to explore questions surrounding how to define and combat terrorism financing; the existing

1 Time, 2015: pp. 1 ff.

mechanisms of terrorism financing are discussed in Section 2.2. An in-depth analysis of the available literature on the subject of terrorism financing highlights the strengths and weaknesses of the existing measures in place to combat it. In particular, the current research on terrorism financing focuses on examining statistical data on terrorists' sources of income and wealth transfer, but it must be assumed that there is an extraordinarily high number of unreported cases that do not feature in the statistics. However, thus far, there has been no investigation into how an intelligent terrorist financier would go about creating and subsequently transferring specific assets with the lowest possible risk of detection for the purposes of funding terrorism.

The aim of this study is to anticipate the actions of intelligent perpetrators and to develop proposals for legislative measures to combat terrorism financing more effectively. Therefore, the perspective of intelligent perpetrators is taken and methods for generating revenue sources and transferring assets are developed. These methods serve as the basis for an analysis of the weaknesses in the fight against terrorism from the perspective of criminal procedure.

Above all, weak points in the fight against terrorism financing in Germany, Liechtenstein, Austria and Switzerland will be analysed in terms of criminal procedure law. In particular, this book will show how intelligent terrorist financiers operate and what difficulties arise for investigators in terms of criminal procedure law. To this end, selected instruments used by investigators will be examined in the light of their practical relevance and analysed on a comparative legal basis. Finally, suggestions for legislative improvement will be developed.

First, to carry out a preliminary study, fifteen informal interviews with illicit financial service providers will be conducted in order to exploratively investigate which sources of income terrorists use and how they might transfer their funds. Building on the results of the preliminary study, fifteen semi-structured expert interviews with investigators are analysed in the context of a summary qualitative content analysis according to Mayring.[2] This process will examine how intelligent terrorist financiers must proceed in concrete terms in order to generate and transfer assets for terrorism financing with as little risk as possible.

Subsequently, how selected instruments of criminal procedure could help investigators in Switzerland to more effectively combat the methods of terrorism financing described in the discussion of the empirical results will be presented. In doing so, the current legal situation in Switzerland will be taken as a starting point and then supplemented by taking comparative legal cues from Germany,

2 Mayring (2010).

Liechtenstein and Austria in order to examine the question in greater detail. Ultimately, the aim is to provide suggestions for legislative reform in Switzerland to enable even more effective combating and prevention of crime in Germany, Liechtenstein, Austria and Switzerland.

One suggestion is that investigators should be permitted to engage in digital surveillance. Skilful offenders do not communicate openly with other individuals about their plans. Therefore, digital surveillance is often the only means available with which to identify so-called lone wolves and prove that they have violated Art. 260^{quinquies} CH-StGB. In many cases, this can only be achieved by penetrating and searching data processing systems without being noticed.

Another suggestion is that the powers of undercover investigators should be extended so that they may avoid detection. As a rule, undercover investigators are relatively easy for offenders to identify because, with few exceptions, undercover investigators are not permitted to commit criminal offences.

2. The state of research and research gaps

This chapter presents the state of research on terrorism financing, any gaps in the research and the methodological approach underlying this study. The aim of this chapter is not to compile an encyclopaedia of literature on the topic of terrorism financing, rather, it is to lay the theoretical groundwork for the empirical study that will follow. This requires that the reader be given an overview of the current state of research in order to explain why an investigation of the research questions is meaningful and necessary.

As the first step, the term 'terrorism financing' is defined for the purposes of this work. Subsequently, terrorists' sources of income and how they transfer assets for the purpose of terrorism financing will be presented. Furthermore, existing measures for the purpose of combating terrorism financing are considered. Finally, a research gap is identified.

2.1 Definition of terrorism financing

To be able to combat terrorism financing, the phenomenon must first of all be defined.[3] Unlike other crimes, terrorism and terrorism financing are not easy to define.[4] Despite intensive efforts by the international community, it has not yet succeeded in agreeing on a uniform definition of terrorism financing.[5] The absence of a uniform definition of terrorism financing is due in part to the fact that it is difficult to develop a uniform definition of terrorism and the international community cannot reach a consensus on this matter.[6] For example, a distinction must be made between freedom fighters and terrorists, and the United States alone already utilizes several different definitions of terrorism.[7] Moreover,

---

3 Veng Mei Long, 2005: p. 19.

4 Tofangsaz, 2015: p. 386; Cooper, 2001: p. 881 f.; Ruby, 2002: p. 9 f.; Tilly, 2004: p. 5 f.; Lutz, 2002: p. 2 f.; Saul, 2005a: p. 57 f.; Saul, 2005b: p. 141; Senechal dela Roche, 2004: pp. 1 f.; Begorre-Bret, 2005: pp. 1987 f.; Scharf, 2000: p. 391; Gibbs, 1989: pp. 329 f.; Schmid, 2004a: pp. 40 f.; Schmid, 2004b: pp. 375 f.; Rodin, 2004: pp. 752 f.

5 Dalyan, 2008: p. 138; Cassese, 2001: p. 993; Zeidan, 2003: p. 491 f.; Dumitriu, 2005: p. 237 f.

6 Guillaume, 2004: p. 544; Badey, 1998: p. 90 f.; Prabha, 2000: p. 125.

7 Scharf, 2004: p. 359; Ganor, 2002: p. 287; Howard, 2002: p. 8 f.; Kennedy, 2009: p. 1 f.; Hughes, 2007: p. 293; Klabbers, 2003: p. 299 f.; Lopez-Rivera & Headley, 1989: p. 162; Kalin & Kunzli, 2000: p. 46 f.; Orlova & Moore, 2004: p. 310; Perry, 2003: p. 249 f.

the term is misused by various groups around the world to justify even more radical approaches.[8] This in turn raises questions regarding law enforcement. Finally, it is unclear whether the offence of financing terrorism has been committed when the perpetrator has financed a group that may not be clearly defined as a terrorist group.

Switzerland has defined terrorism financing in Art. $260^{\text{quinquies}}$ CH-StGB. Other laws, such as the Federal Act on Combating Money Laundering and Terrorism financing, refer to this definition. This definition therefore also serves as the basis for the present work. With Art. $260^{\text{quinquies}}$ CH-StGB, the Convention for the Suppression of the Financing of Terrorism, which was adopted in New York on 9 December 1999, was finally implemented in Switzerland. Article $260^{\text{quinquies}}$ CH-StGB reads as follows:

Financing of terrorism

1. Any person who collects or makes available assets with the intention of financing a crime of violence intended to intimidate the population or to coerce a State or an international organisation into doing or failing to do something is liable to a custodial sentence not exceeding five years or to a monetary penalty.
2. If the perpetrator merely accepts the possibility of terrorism financing, he is not liable to prosecution under this provision.
3. The act is not considered to be the financing of a terrorist offence if it is directed towards the establishment or restoration of democratic conditions and the rule of law or the exercise or safeguarding of human rights.
4. (1) shall not apply if the financing is intended to support acts that are not inconsistent with the rules of international law applicable in armed conflicts.[9]

Article $260^{\text{quinquies}}$ CH-StGB is dealt with in detail in the following chapter (2.1.1). Consequently, no further discussion is provided here.

In Germany, terrorism financing has been defined in § 89c DE-StGB as follows:

(1) Whoever collects, receives or makes available property with the knowledge or intention that it will be used by another person to commit
   1. murder (§ 211), manslaughter (§ 212), genocide (§ 6 of the International Criminal Code), a crime against humanity (§ 7 of the International Criminal Code), a war crime (§§ 8, 9, 10, 11 or 12 of the International Criminal Code),

8 Forster, 2005: p. 215.

9 Art. $260^{\text{quinquies}}$ CH-StGB.

a bodily injury under section 224 or a bodily injury causing serious bodily or mental harm to another person, in particular of the kind referred to in § 226,
2. an extortionate kidnapping (§ 239a) or a hostage-taking (§ 239b),
3. offences under §§ 303b, 305, 305a or offences dangerous to public health in the cases of §§ 306 to 306c or 307 (1) to (3), section 308 (1) to (4), § 309 (1) to (5), §§ 313, 314 or 315 (1), (3) or (4), § 316b (1) or (3) or § 316c (1) to (3) or § 317 (1),
4. offences against the environment in the cases of § 330a (1) to (3),
5. offences under section 19 (1) to (3), § 20 (1) or (2), § 20a (1) to (3), § 19 (2) No. 2 or (3) No. 2, § 20 (1) or (2) or § 20a (1) to (3), in each case also in conjunction with section 21, or under § 22a (1) to (3) of the War Weapons Control Act,
6. offences under § 51 (1) to (3) of the Weapons Act,
7. an offence under § 328 (1) or (2) or § 310 (1) or (2),
8. an offence under § 89a (2a)

is punishable by imprisonment for a term of six months to ten years. Sentence 1 shall apply in the cases of numbers 1 to 7 only if the offence specified therein is intended to intimidate the population in a substantial manner, to coerce an authority or an international organisation unlawfully by force or by threat of force, or to eliminate or substantially impair the fundamental political, constitutional, economic or social structures of a state or an international organisation, and by the manner of its commission or its effects is likely to cause substantial damage to a state or an international organisation.

(2) Any person who collects, receives or makes available assets under the condition of subsection (1) sentence 2 with a view to committing one of the offences referred to in subsection (1) sentence 1 himself shall also be punished.
(3) Subsections (1) and (2) also apply if the offence is committed abroad. If it is committed outside the Member States of the European Union, this shall apply only if it is committed by a German or a foreigner with a livelihood in Germany or if the financed offence is to be committed in Germany or by or against a German.
(4) In the cases of § 3 sentence 2, the prosecution shall require the authorisation of the Federal Ministry of Justice and Consumer Protection. If the offence is committed in another Member State of the European Union, the prosecution shall require the authorisation of the Federal Ministry of Justice and Consumer Protection if the offence is neither committed by a German nor the financed offence is to be committed in Germany nor by or against a German.
(5) If the assets involved in an offence under subsection (1) or (2) are of minor value, the sentence shall be imprisonment for a term of three months to five years.
(6) The court shall mitigate the penalty (§ 49 (1)) or may refrain from imposing a penalty if the culpability of the offender is slight.
(7) The court may, at its discretion, mitigate the penalty (§ 49 (2)) or refrain from punishing the offender in accordance with this provision if the offender voluntarily abandons further preparation of the offence and averts or substantially reduces a danger caused and recognised by him that others will further prepare this offence or carry it out, or if he voluntarily prevents the completion of this offence. If,

> without any action on the part of the offender, the designated danger is averted or substantially lessened or the completion of the act is prevented, his voluntary and sincere efforts to achieve this goal shall suffice.[10]

In § 89c DE-StGB, Germany has created a uniform and independent offence with a minimum term of imprisonment that is modelled on Switzerland's Art. 260^{quinquies} CH-StGB.[11] The similarities particularly relate to the gathering and making available of assets, although they do not narrow them down in terms of value. From a subjective point of view, there is considerable similarity with regard to the dolus directus of the first and second degree, which can be found in Art. 260^{quinquies} (2) of the Swiss Criminal Code and in Art. 2 (1) of the UN Convention for the Suppression of the Financing of Terrorism.[12] In contrast to the Swiss Criminal Code, the German Criminal Code does not distinguish between whether assets were received once or more often.[13]

In order to meet international requirements, § 89c (1) nos 1 to 8 DE-StGB refer to numerous criminal offences that protect both individual legal interests and community legal interests. Pursuant to § 1, sentence 2, a regulation applies to cases of sub-section 1, nos 1 to 7, which corresponds to that of § 129a (2) DE-StGB. This ensures that § 89c DE-StGB can only be applied to circumstances that apply to terrorism. In the literature, § 89c DE-StGB is often criticized for its definiteness and proportionality, which are constitutionally mandated.[14] Section 89c DE-StGB distinguishes between whether the terrorist act is to be committed by a third party or the financier, but there are no further differences in content between § 89c (1) (commission of the act by a third party) and (2) (commission of the act by the financier).[15] Furthermore, the act to be financed must – either in terms of the manner of its commission or its effects – be capable of causing substantial damage to the state or an international organization in order to be considered terrorism.[16]

Section 89c (1) DE-StGB regulates the collection and receipt of assets and the making available of the same for the purposes of terrorism financing.[17] It should be noted that at least two persons should be involved and outwardly

---

10 § 89c DE-StGB.
11 Fischer, 2020: § 89c DE-StGB point 2.
12 Zöller, 2018: § 89c DE-StGB point 3.
13 Fischer, 2020: § 89c DE-StGB point 4.
14 Schäfer, 2017: § 89c DE-StGB point 1.
15 Sternberg-Lieben, 2019: § 89c DE-StGB point 2.
16 Fischer, 2020: § 89c DE-StGB point 6.
17 Schäfer, 2017: § 89c DE-StGB point 9.

visible conduct is required. This ensures that only the collection, but not the gathering, of assets meets the requirements of the offence. With regard to the collection of assets, the focus must particularly be on the regularity and consistency of the receipt of or demand for assets.[18] In particular, the receipt of assets is to be understood as conduct that includes the acceptance of but not the solicitation of assets.[19] With regard to receiving assets, it should be noted that a certain degree of decision-making autonomy over the assets can be assumed. Making assets available, on the other hand, is understood to mean the handing over of assets.[20] This also includes the indirect transfer of assets to third parties. This can take place, for example, via bank transfer or by handing over the assets to third parties.[21] This is to be distinguished from everyday inflows of assets, such as salary payments, which are not deemed offences.[22]

Assets are thus considered to include money and all other objects of monetary value and instrumentalities.[23] These can be movable or immovable. Rights are also eligible to be considered for this purpose.[24] The latter are likely to be of particular interest with regard to the development of cryptocurrencies and other blockchain technologies, such as tokens. It is now also possible to securitize rights and use blockchain technology for this purpose. The definitions of terrorism financing are largely identical in Germany, Liechtenstein, Austria and Switzerland. Section 89 (1) DE-StGB regulates the financing of third-party acts. It should be emphasized that this does not only refer to serious acts of violence endangering the state but to any type of terrorist offence.[25] In § 89c (2) DE-StGB, the same acts as in sub-section 1 are made punishable offences. In particular, preparatory acts, which were previously unpunishable, are now punishable. This excludes everyday transactions that are based on a legal obligation. Everyday inflows of assets are not covered by § 89c DE-StGB.[26]

From a subjective point of view, conditional intent suffices for the action to be considered terrorism financing.[27] The perpetrator's intent must also be for the

18 Paeffgen, 2017: § 89c DE-StGB point 7; Schäfer, 2017: § 89c DE-StGB point 8.
19 Schäfer, 2017: § 89c DE-StGB point 10.
20 Paeffgen, 2017: § 89c DE-StGB point 8; Paeffgen, 2017: § 89c DE-StGB point 7.
21 Kühl, 2018: § 89c DE-StGB point 2.
22 Schäfer, 2017: § 89c DE-StGB point 11.
23 Fischer, 2020: § 89c DE-StGB point 2.
24 Schäfer, 2017: § 89c DE-StGB point 12.
25 Paeffgen, 2017: § 89c DE-StGB point 9.
26 Schäfer, 2017: § 89c DE-StGB point 13; Paeffgen, 2017: § 89c DE-StGB point 13; Kindhäuser, 2018: § 89c DE-StGB point 2.
27 Schäfer, 2017: § 89c DE-StGB point 14.

assets to be used for a terrorist act.[28] However, a distinction must be made here between acts committed by others and the perpetrator's own acts. In the case of acts committed by others, within the scope of § 89c (1), either a dolus directus of the second degree (i.e. certain knowledge that other persons intend to commit a criminal act within the meaning of § 89c (1) sentence 1 DE-StGB and that the assets concerned are to be used for this purpose) or acting with a corresponding intention is required. If it is a perpetrator's own act, as per § 89c (2) DE-StGB, a dolus directus of the first degree (i.e. real intent) is required. A catalogue of offences is applied, which is based on § 129a DE-StGB. The offences are listed in § 89c (1) sentence 1, nos 1 to 8 DE-StGB.[29] It is not necessary to repeat the catalogue of offences here, as the text of the law is also printed. It is worth mentioning, however, that § 89c (1) sentence 2 DE-StGB requires that the offences listed in subsection 1, sentence 1, nos 1 to 7 DE-StGB have a special purpose and suitability.[30]

Section 89c (3) DE-StGB regulates the provision's applicability to offences committed abroad. In particular, a distinction is made between offences committed within and outside the European Union. The latter are subject to restrictive conditions. The provision is reminiscent of § 89a (3) DE-StGB.[31] Certain foreign offences are placed under an enabling provision. This provision is reminiscent of § 89a (4) DE-StGB.[32] Similar to § 89a DE-StGB, the unlawfulness is judged according to general principles. It is considered unlawful if the elements of the offence are met; in particular, if no grounds for justification are apparent.[33]

In the former § 89a (4) DE-StGB, materiality of the property contribution was a prerequisite, with which the legislator has deliberately dispensed.[34] Instead, § 5 provides for a minimum sentence in an aggravated case and § 6 for a mandatory reduction and a potential waiver of punishment. It has been argued in the literature that this technique is a violation of the principle of proportionality. It has been suggested that it increases the possibilities for preventive police measures.[35] It should be noted that in the case of minor culpability, the court is required to mitigate the sentence under § 49 (1) DE-StGB. Alternatively, it may

28 Sternberg-Lieben, 2019: § 89c DE-StGB point 9.
29 Schäfer, 2017: § 89c DE-StGB point 15; Schäfer, 2017: § 89c DE-StGB point 16.
30 Schäfer, 2017: § 89c DE-StGB point 17.
31 Schäfer, 2017: § 89c DE-StGB point 18.
32 Schäfer, 2017: § 89c DE-StGB point 19.
33 Schäfer, 2017: § 89c DE-StGB point 20.
34 Kindhäuser, 2018: § 89c DE-StGB point 6.
35 Paeffgen, 2017: § 89c DE-StGB point 10.

also refrain from imposing the penalty. The low value of the assets no longer results in impunity, as before, but leads to a reduction of the sentence by half.[36] From the author's point of view, it is problematic that the value of the assets has not been limited. Thus, very low-value assets (e.g. a few euros for a few rounds of ammunition) also fall within the scope of § 89c DE-StGB.[37] In theory, a limit of €50.00 could be set as the minimum in Germany. Abroad, one could take into consideration the typical circumstances where the offence took place. The latter, however, would likely be difficult for German judges to assess.[38]

Section 89c DE-StGB was designed as an abstract endangerment offence, with perpetration and participation being governed by the general principles. Attempts to finance terrorism on the other hand, are not punishable.[39] Offences falling within the scope of § 89c DE-StGB are regarded as predicate offences punishable in addition to the offence and, within the framework of the concurrence of laws, take second place to offences committed at any stage and in any form of participation.[40]

In Austria, terrorism financing is regulated in § 278d AT-StGB:

(1) A person who provides or collects property with the intent that it be used, even if only in part, to execute
1. air piracy (§ 185) or deliberately endangering the safety of aviation (§ 186),
2. an extortionate kidnapping (§ 102) or a threat thereof,
3. an attack on the life, limb or freedom of a person protected under international law, or a violent attack on a dwelling, official room or means of transport of such a person, which is likely to endanger the life, limb or freedom of that person, or a threat thereof,
4. an intentional endangerment by nuclear energy or ionising radiation (§ 171), a threat thereof, an unauthorised handling of nuclear material or radioactive substances (§ 177b), any other criminal act for the purpose of obtaining nuclear material or radioactive substances or a threat to commit theft or robbery of nuclear material or radioactive substances in order to compel another to act, acquiesce or refrain from acting,
5. a significant attack on the life or limb of another at an airport serving international civil aviation, destruction of or significant damage to such an airport or to aircraft thereon, or disruption of the services of the airport, provided that the act

36 Von Heintschel-Heinegg, 2016: § 89c DE-StGB point 15; Sternberg-Lieben, 2019: § 89c DE-StGB point 14.
37 Zöller, 2018: § 89c DE-StGB point 12.
38 Zöller, 2018: § 89c DE-StGB point 21.
39 Zöller, 2018: § 89c DE-StGB point 5.
40 Paeffgen, 2017: § 89c DE-StGB point 17.

is committed with the use of a weapon or other device and is likely to jeopardise security at the airport,

6. an offence committed in a manner described in §§ 185 or 186 against a ship or fixed platform, against a person on board a ship or fixed platform, against the cargo of a ship or a navigational facility,
7. transporting an explosive device or other lethal device to a public place, governmental or public facility, public transportation system, or utility, or using such means with the intent to cause death or serious bodily injury to another or extensive destruction of the place, facility, or system, if the destruction is likely to cause substantial economic harm,
8. an offence intended to cause death or serious bodily harm to a civilian or other person not taking an active part in hostilities in an armed conflict, where that offence, by its nature or circumstances, is intended to intimidate a section of the population or to coerce a government or an international organisation to do or abstain from doing something,
9. any other offence under § 278c (1), any offence under §§ 278e, 278 f or 278g or the recruitment of another to commit a terrorist offence under section 278c (1) nos 1 to 9 or 10,

shall be punishable by a term of imprisonment of between one and ten years.

(1a) Likewise to be punished is anyone who provides or collects assets for
1. another person whom he knows to be committing acts under subsection (1), or
2. a member of a terrorist group which he knows is directed to commit acts referred to in paragraph 1,

(2) The offender shall not be punished under subsection (1) or subsection (1a) if the offence is punishable by a more severe penalty under any other provision.[41]

Section 278d of the Austrian Criminal Code is also to be regarded as a type of preparatory offence.[42] It was created as a catch-all offence and serves to implement the UN Convention on the Financing of Terrorism BGBI. III 2002/102 and UN Security Council Resolution 1373 (2001).[43] In particular, it is intended to ensure that the financing of terrorism is already punishable.[44] The offence is the intentional provision or collection of assets to be used for the execution of one or more of the catalogue offences mentioned in §§ 1 to 8.[45]

Similar to Germany, Switzerland and Liechtenstein, all types of assets in Austria are considered assets. These can be tangible, intangible, movable or

41 § 278d AT-StGB.
42 Plöchl, 2017: § 278d AT-StGB point 1.
43 Fabrizy, 2018: § 278d AT-StPO point 1.
44 Plöchl, 2017: § 278d AT-StGB point 1.
45 Plöchl, 2017: § 278d AT-StGB point 2.

immovable. The type of acquisition does not play a significant role here. In particular, the transfer of rights is also conceivably an asset. Similar to Germany's § 89c–e DE-StGB, § 278d (1) AT-StGB does not provide for a materiality limit. In the literature, however, the opinion has been expressed that a one-time, minor payment does not necessarily have to constitute an offence.[46] The list of catalogue offences in § 278d AT-StGB is partly explicit and partly implicit,[47] but the individual catalogue offences are not listed here in light of the fact that the text of the law is also printed.

It is a criminal offence to provide as well as to collect assets if they are to be used for the execution of one of the catalogue offences mentioned in § 278d AT-StGB, and paragraph 1 explicitly refers to the intent to use as being required.[48] Paragraph 1a refers to knowledge being necessary. Both forms of commission are taxative and thus legally equivalent. This is referred to as an alternative mixed offence. Under the provision of assets, the granting of the de facto power of disposal is ultimately required.[49] Collecting assets is to be understood as any activity aimed at the transfer or accumulation of assets.[50]

Section 278d (1) of the Austrian Criminal Code is designed as an intentional offence, whereby dolus eventualis within the meaning of § 5 (1) is sufficient.[51] This must, however, refer to all elements of the offence. What is required is, among other things, an offence-specific extended (contingent) intent with regard to the use of the assets for the execution of one of the catalogue offences mentioned in nos 1–8. In this context, the term 'intent to use' is also used. The decisive factor is that this intent must already be present at the time the assets are collected or made available. This constitutes the wrong. An actual execution of the catalogue offences, on the other hand, is not required.[52] Section 278d (1a) AT-StGB also refers to a crime of intent. However, since no intent to use the assets is required here, the financing of individual terrorists (e.g. by paying for their living expenses) is already a constituent element of the offence.[53]

---

46 Plöchl, 2017: § 278d AT-StGB point3; Plöchl, 2017: § 278d AT-StGB point 4.

47 Plöchl, 2017: § 278d AT-StGB point 5.

48 Plöchl, 2017: § 278d AT-StGB point 18; Bertel & Schwaighofer, 2010: § 278d AT-StGB point 1.

49 Plöchl, 2017: § 278d AT-StGB point 18; Plöchl, 2017: § 278d AT-StGB point 19.

50 Plöchl, 2017: § 278d AT-StGB point 20.

51 Fabrizy, 2018: § 278d.

52 Plöchl, 2017: § 278d AT-StGB point 21.

53 Plöchl, 2017: § 278d AT-StGB point 21/1.

Section 278d AT-StGB is designed as a so-called independent preparatory offence, and both the attempt and the withdrawal, in the sense of § 16 AT-StGB, are possible – it is an 'offence of success'. The offence of providing assets is deemed to have been completed once the assets have actually been handed over to third parties, or at least once a de facto power of disposal over them has been granted to another.[54] With regard to the collection of assets, the offence is deemed to have been completed as soon as the offender receives the corresponding assets. However, criminal acts of attempt are also conceivable. These include, among others, appeals for donations.[55] Section 278d AT-StGB is designed as a general offence. Thus, the general principles for participation apply.[56] Contributory offences are only considered to have been attempted and are thus not punishable (§ 15 (2) AT-StGB) unless the funds collected or provided are used for a catalogue offence mentioned in § 278d (1) AT-StGB.[57] Section 278d AT-StGB provides for a prison sentence of one to ten years, and exemptions from punishment have been abolished by BGB i I. 2013/134.[58]

If the means provided are actually used for the execution of a terrorist offence, the offender is considered to be a regular contributory offender in the sense of § 12 of the Austrian Criminal Code (third case). In this case, § 278d AT-StGB takes a back seat to the more severely punished offence due to the subsidiarity clause anchored in § 278d (2) AT-StGB.[59] If the withdrawal from an attempt to commit a catalogue offence listed in § 278d (1), nos 1 to 8 AT-StGB takes place and consequently remains unpunished, § 278d AT-StGB and the associated punishments apply.[60] Since the international guidelines do not provide grounds for the annulment of a sentence on the basis of active remorse, this was also not adopted in § 278d of the Austrian Penal Code.[61]

Liechtenstein's § 278d FL-StGB is almost identical to Austria's § 278d AT-StGB:

---

54 Plöchl, 2017: § 278d AT-StGB point 23.
55 Plöchl, 2017: § 278d AT-StGB point 24.
56 Plöchl, 2017: § 278d AT-StGB point 25.
57 Bertel & Schwaighofer, 2010: § 278d AT-StGB point 1.
58 Plöchl, 2017: § 278d AT-StGB point 26.
59 Plöchl, 2017: § 278d AT-StGB point 27.
60 Plöchl, 2017: § 278d AT-StGB point 28.
61 Plöchl, 2017: § 278d AT-StGB point 29.

(1) Whoever provides or collects property with the intent that it will be used, even if only in part
   1. for the execution of
      (a) air piracy (§ 185) or deliberate endangerment of the safety of aviation (§ 186),
      (b) an extortionate kidnapping (§ 102) or a threat thereof,
      (c) an attack on the life, limb or freedom of a person protected under international law, or a violent attack on or threat of an attack on the home, official residence or means of transport of such a person, which is likely to endanger the life, limb or freedom of that person,
      (d) an intentional endangerment by nuclear energy or ionising radiation (§ 171), a threat thereof, a criminal act to obtain nuclear material or radioactive substances or a threat to commit theft or robbery of nuclear material or radioactive substances in order to coerce another to perform, acquiesce in or refrain from any act,
      (c) a significant attack on the life or limb of another person at an airport serving international civil aviation, destruction of or significant damage to such an airport or to aircraft thereon, or disruption of the services of the airport, provided that the act is committed with the use of a weapon or other device and is likely to jeopardise security at the airport,
      (f) an offence committed in a manner described in §§ 185 or 186 against a ship or fixed platform, a person on board a ship or fixed platform, the cargo of a ship or a navigational facility,
      (g) the transport of an explosive device or other lethal device to a public place, a government or public facility, a public transportation system, or a utility system, or the use of such means with the intent to cause death or serious bodily injury to another or extensive destruction of the place, facility, or system, if the destruction is likely to cause particularly great economic harm,
      (h) an act intended to cause death or serious injury to a civilian or to any other person not taking an active part in the hostilities in an armed conflict, when that act, by its nature or circumstances, is intended to intimidate a section of the population or to coerce a government or an international organisation to do or abstain from doing something; or
   2. by a person or an association (§ 278b (3)) who commits an act referred to in no 1 or participates in such an association as a member (§ 278b (2)) shall be punished with imprisonment for a term of one to ten years.

(2) The offender shall not be punished under subsection (1) if the offence is punishable by a more severe penalty under any other provision.[62]

Consequently, the provision or collection of assets intended to finance one of the catalogue offences listed in § 278d (1) FL-StGB is punishable in Liechtenstein. Assets of all kinds are eligible for this purpose. Similar to Austria, Germany and

62 § 278d FL-StGB.

Switzerland, tangible, intangible, movable and immovable objects are considered assets for the financing of terrorism within the scope of § 278d FL-StGB.[63]

On the subjective side, conditional intent within the scope of § 5 (1) FL-StGB is sufficient. It is thus required that the offender at least considers it possible that the assets provided or collected will be used to commit one of the catalogue offences listed in § 278d (1) FL-StGB. Since the text of the law is also printed, listing of the individual catalogue offences of § 278d (1) FL-StGB is dispensed with here. With regard to further explanations of § 278d FL-StGB, reference is made to § 278d of the Austrian Criminal Code, which uses almost the same wording.

Despite their utility, four different definitions of terrorism financing cannot serve as the basis for an empirical study. It is therefore necessary to select one of the four definitions mentioned above. Since this definition should also be known to the interview partners in each case, the version that is easiest to understand should be selected. While the definitions used in Germany, Liechtenstein and Austria are all detailed and list individual offences that are to be included in the offence, the Swiss definition is the simplest. It is therefore particularly well suited for the purposes of the present study, especially because Art. 260^{quinquies} CH-StGB served as the basis for § 89c DE-StGB. In the following, Art. 260^{quinquies} CH-StGB and secondary Swiss criminal law will be discussed in more detail, and selected aspects of criminal law will be dealt with through the lens of Art. 260^{quinquies} CH-StGB.

2.1.1 Selected aspects of criminal law

Although the focus of this paper is not on the definition of terrorism financing under criminal law, and thus existing definitions can be used for the empirical investigation, the author will point out some selected weaknesses of the existing regulations. The aim of these remarks is not to create an alternative to the current commentaries; rather, a few selected aspects will be considered.

In particular, contingent intent and negligence will be addressed below. This is relevant from a practical point of view because skilful terrorist financiers can always claim that they only had charitable intentions. Those who can plausibly demonstrate this may get off scot-free. Consequently, the offence described under Art. 260^{quinquies} CH-StGB is a rather blunt sword in the fight against the financing of terrorism.

63 Stutter, 2006: 711.

In such cases, making a distinction from other criminal offences may provide a remedy. In particular, it can be argued that the financier of terrorism could be prosecuted for aiding and abetting more serious offences for which, under certain circumstances, contingent intent is also sufficient. In this case, the above-mentioned problem of the exclusion of contingent intent and negligence can be at least partially compensated for. At the same time, however, the level of punishment under Art. $260^{\text{quinquies}}$ CH-StGB should not go unmentioned. Sanctioning the financing of terrorism with a custodial sentence of up to five years or a fine does not have a particularly deterrent effect. However, the question arises as to whether terrorist financiers can be deterred at all by custodial sentences. After all, at least some terrorists are prepared to die to achieve their goals.

Finally, secondary criminal law, in particular the Federal Act on Combating Money Laundering and Terrorism financing (Anti-Money Laundering Act, AMLA), is also briefly considered. This law also sanctions negligent acts. However, only traders and financial service providers are subject to the AMLA.

2.1.1.1 Art. $260^{\text{quinquies}}$ CH-StGB

For the purposes of this study, the definition of terrorism set out in Art. $260^{\text{quinquies}}$ CH-StGB will be used. It reads as follows:

> Whoever, with intent to finance a crime of violence intended to intimidate the population or to coerce a State or an international organization to do or refrain from doing something, collects or makes available assets, shall be punished by imprisonment for a term not exceeding five years or a fine.[64]

In contrast to the German definition found in § 89c DE-StGB, Swiss Art. $260^{\text{quinquies}}$ CH-StGB refrains from offering a detailed enumeration of all possible terrorist activities.[65]

It is worth noting, however, that according to Art. $260^{\text{quinquies}}$ (2) CH-StGB, recognizing the possibility of funds being used for terrorism financing is not punishable under this provision: 'If the offender merely accepts the possibility of terrorism financing, he is not liable to prosecution under this provision'.[66]

Furthermore, acts aimed at the establishment or restoration of democracy and the rule of law or at the protection of human rights are excluded from the offence of financing terrorism. This potentially opens the door to abusive

---

64 Art. $260^{\text{quinquies}}$ (1) CH-StGB.

65 von Heintschel-Heinegg, 2016; § 89c DE-StGB point 1 f.

66 Art. $260^{\text{quinquies}}$ (2) CH-StGB.

behaviour: 'The act shall not be deemed to be financing of a terrorist offence if it is directed towards the establishment or restoration of democratic conditions and the rule of law or the exercise or preservation of human rights'.[67]

In addition, Art. 260^{quinquies} (1) CH-StGB states that conflicts in conformity with international law are excluded from the prohibition of terrorism financing: 'Paragraph 1 shall not apply where the financing is intended to support acts not inconsistent with the rules of international law applicable in armed conflicts'.[68]

Despite the weaknesses mentioned, the definition of terrorism financing used in Art. 260^{quinquies} CH-StGB covers all the essential elements of the offence. The AMLA of 10 October 1997 further specifies the measures to combat terrorism financing. In addition, it should be emphasized that terrorism financing should be distinguished from so-called 'finance warfare'.[69] However, these further definitions or delimitations are not decisive for the purposes of this study because the criminal law definition is primarily decisive for the implications of the work of criminal procedure law.

This study is primarily concerned with cases of application of Art. 260^{quinquies} CH-StGB and their implications in terms of criminal law. Consequently, the focus of the work is not on a dogmatic discussion of Art. 260^{quinquies} CH-StGB. Nevertheless, it is essential to present the subjective and objective elements of the offence in summary form in order to highlight which conduct constitutes the offence.

2.1.1.2 The facts of the case

The objective elements of the offence in Art. 260^{quinquies} (1) CH-StGB include the collection or making available of assets.[70] The object of the offence is therefore all types of assets.[71] However, it is not necessary for these assets to have actually facilitated a terrorist act.[72] The term 'assets' was taken from Art. 305bis CH-StGB regarding money laundering. Thus, it is ultimately based on Art. 70 CH-StGB which addresses confiscation.[73] In particular, the norm is intended to help close

---

67 Art. 260^{quinquies} (3) CH-StGB.

68 Art. 260^{quinquies} (4) CH-StGB.

69 Navias, 2002: p. 5.

70 Stratenwerth & Wohlers, 2013: p. 508.

71 Trechsel & Pieth, 2018: p. 1316.

72 Vest & Schuhbarth, 2007: p. 98.

73 Fiolka, 2018: Art. 260^{quinquies} CH-StGB point 15.

criminal liability gaps that arise when the requirements of Art. 260ter or 260bis CH-StGB are not met.[74] It is a catch-all provision.[75] To date, Art. 260^quinquies CH-StGB is the only provision in Switzerland's penal code that sanctions the financing of terrorism.[76]

According to Art. 1 (1) of the International Convention for the Suppression of the Financing of Terrorism (ÜBFT), financial resources refers to:

> assets of every kind, tangible or intangible, movable or immovable, however acquired, and legal documents or instruments of any kind, including electronic or digital, evidencing title to or interest in such assets, including, but not limited to, bank credits, travelers checks, cashier's checks, money orders, stocks, securities, bonds, drafts, and letters of credit.[77]

Thus, all assets are eligible to be used for terrorism financing.[78] In particular, both legal and illegal sources of income are considered.[79] This represents a significant divergence from Art. 305bis CH-StGB's definition of money laundering, which is limited to assets derived from a crime.[80]

Both the collection and the making available of assets are covered by the offence.[81] In a narrow sense, collecting includes the willingness to accept assets in an unspecified amount, whereas making assets available grants a third party the power to dispose of them.[82]

According to the wording used in subsection (2), the subjective elements of the offence in Art. 260^quinquies CH-StGB require intent.[83] What is meant here is direct intent of the first degree.[84] In particular, contingent intent is to be excluded in order to ensure that the minimum requirements of the principle of certainty are not undercut by the advancement of criminal liability.[85] This is intended to ensure that the financing of freedom fighters does not fall within the scope of Art. 260^quinquies CH-StGB.[86]

---

74 Stratenwerth & Wohlers, 2013: p. 508.
75 Christen et al., 2018: p. 211.
76 Moreillon & Lubishtani, 2018: p. 512.
77 Art. 1 (1) ÜBFT.
78 Fiolka, 2018: Art. 260^quinquies CH-StGB point 15.
79 Stratenwerth & Wohlers, 2013: p. 508.
80 Vest & Schuhbarth, 2007: p. 99.
81 Trechsel & Pieth, 2018: p. 1317.
82 Fiolka, 2018: Art. 260^quinquies CH-StGB point 18 f.
83 Stratenwerth & Wohlers, 2013: p. 508.
84 Trechsel & Pieth, 2018: p. 1317.
85 Fiolka, 2018: Art. 260^quinquies CH-StGB point 20.
86 Stratenwerth & Wohlers, 2013: p. 509.

In addition, the concept of violent crime must be defined on the basis of Art. 2, no 1 lit. b of the International Convention for the Suppression of the Financing of Terrorism. Violent crime is also referred to in Article 260ter CH-StGB and describes acts that are punishable by a custodial sentence of more than three years and that involve making a physical impact on people or property. Legitimate acts (i.e. justified violent crimes) are distinguished from this.[87]

Furthermore, the concept of civilian intimidation must be considered, which is as vague a term as 'intimidation',[88] since the entire population does not necessarily need to be intimidated. What matters most is whether the intended act is capable of significantly shaking the civilian population's sense of security. For civilian intimidation, proving contingent intent is sufficient.[89]

With regard to the concept of coercion, recourse can be had in the definition found in Art. 181 CH-StGB. Only a state or an international organization can be considered a victim of coercion.[90] However, with regard to violent crime, there is a special feature that the means of coercion is always illegal. Consequently, whether the aim of the coercion was legal or illegal is irrelevant.[91]

Finally, it should be emphasized that criminal liability is excluded in the case of legitimate violent crimes.[92] This provision exists due to the lack of uniformity in the definition of terrorism mentioned at the outset.[93] In particular, the context of the restoration of democratic conditions and the rule of law, as well as the exercise and preservation of human rights, must be taken into account.[94] The standards of the European Convention on Human Rights (ECHR) as well as other relevant conventions under international law apply.[95] Furthermore, criminal liability is excluded in the case of offences that are in conformity with international law.[96]

Last but not least, there are still numerous loopholes in the law that encourage terrorism financing and should not be discounted. For example, cash payments in excess of CHF 100,000 are still relatively easy to make.[97]

---

87 Fiolka, 2018: Art. $260^{\text{quinquies}}$ CH-StGB point 25.
88 Vest & Schuhbarth, 2007: p. 100.
89 Fiolka, 2018: Art. $260^{\text{quinquies}}$ CH-StGB point 31 f.
90 Trechsel & Pieth, 2018: p. 1317.
91 Fiolka, 2018: Art. $260^{\text{quinquies}}$ CH-StGB point 35 f.
92 Stratenwerth & Wohlers, 2013: p. 509.
93 Fiolka, 2018: Art. $260^{\text{quinquies}}$ CH-StGB point 42 f.
94 Trechsel & Pieth, 2018: p. 1318.
95 Fiolka, 2018: Art. $260^{\text{quinquies}}$ CH-StGB point 52 f.
96 Trechsel & Pieth, 2018: p. 1318.
97 Jositsch & von Rotz, 2016: p. 592.

2.1.1.3 Contingent intent and negligence

Article 260quinquies CH-StGB requires intentional action, and this should be emphasized.[98] The perpetrator must therefore have been aware of what they were doing.[99] As explained above, Art. 260quinquies CH-StGB provides that perpetrators who merely accept the possibility of terrorism financing are not liable to prosecution under this provision.[100] This poses a problem for the prosecuting authorities in that it requires the perpetrators to prove intent. A clever perpetrator will always claim to have acted without knowledge and will plead that under no circumstances would they have intentionally supported terrorists.

In addition, according to Art. 260quinquies (2) CH-StGB, conditional intent is not sufficient when using the funds.[101] The collection, forwarding or making available of financial resources is not punishable if the perpetrator (even negligently) does not realize that these funds are flowing in whole or in part into terrorist channels.[102] In the case of donations, it is difficult to ascertain whether the financier knew that the donated funds were supporting a terrorist organization in Syria, for example, or whether the financier may actually have been acting in good faith and fully intended to donate to an aid organization for underage refugees.

Art. 260quinquies (2) CH-StGB explicitly excludes the possibility of contingent intent. This means that intent, i.e. certain knowledge or success, is required. The ratio legis underlying the exclusion of contingent intent is plausibly comprehensible. Accordingly, Art. 260quinquies CH-StGB represents an advanced shift of criminal liability.[103] Consequently, particularly high subjective requirements must be imposed in order not to violate the requirement of certainty. Thus, the commission of terrorist attacks must constitute the goal of the financier of terrorism.[104]

In particular, the perpetrator must have certain knowledge that the person or group they are supporting is comprised of one or more terrorists who are planning and carrying out violent crimes.[105] However, the violent crime being financed does not necessarily have to be a terrorist attack. Rather, the aim of this

---

98 Stratenwerth & Wohlers, 2013: p. 509.
99 Killias et al., 2009: p. 29.
100 Art. 260quinquies CH-StGB.
101 Stratenwerth & Wohlers, 2009: p. 499.
102 Donatsch et al., 2017: p. 216.
103 Trechsel & Vest, 2013: p. 1317.
104 Cassani, 2003: p. 297; Forster, 2003: p. 444.
105 Weder, 2018: p. 480.

violent crime must be either to intimidate the population – at least in part – or to compel a state or an international organization to do or refrain from doing something. According to the current legal situation, the act must be suitable to financially support the execution of a violent crime.[106]

The legislature has explicitly excluded contingent intent in Art. 260quinquies CH-StGB in order to prevent charitably motivated donations from constituting the offence of terrorism financing.[107] This raises significant questions from a practical perspective. For example, the question arises as to how donations to an organization that both finances terrorism and operates schools and hospitals should be dealt with. Nor is it clear how deliberately funding terrorism could pose a greater threat than simply accepting it. Ultimately, in both cases, attacks are financed and human lives are endangered.[108]

The requirement of direct intent is positive in that it would not make sense to punish a donor acting in good faith. At the same time, however, the question arises as to whether a minimum of caution should not also be expected of donors. It could thus also be argued that anyone who does not reasonably assume that the assets they have provided are not intended to be used for terrorist activities is liable to prosecution. The indeterminacy is thus due to the formula of contingent intent.[109]

The parliamentary debate expressed concern that anyone who could not rule out the misuse of their funds for terrorist purposes would already be liable to prosecution.[110] However, this concern is unfounded as long as the persons concerned have documented that there were no indications of terrorism financing being involved and that they had made all reasonable enquiries to ensure that their funds would not be misused for terrorism purposes.

In this context, the question arises as to what measures can be reasonably taken in order to rule out accidentally supporting terrorism financing. In principle, the proportionality of the measures must be taken into account here. The specific expense could be determined by taking into account the amount of the transaction, any suspicious facts and knowledge of the persons involved. Thus, a donation of CHF 1 million to a charity active in Syria would certainly be subject to a higher standard of due diligence than a payment of CHF 500 to a charitable

106 Donatsch et al., 2017: p. 217.
107 Weder, 2018: p. 481.
108 Fiolka, 2018: Art. 260quinquies CH-StGB point 21.
109 Jositsch, 2005: p. 462.
110 Fiolka, 2018: Art. 260quinquies CH-StGB point 21.

institution based in Switzerland. Although even in the case of the latter it can never be completely ruled out that the funds could benefit the financing of terrorism, the donor does not have to assume this unless there are indications to the contrary.

It is also unclear how to deal with direct second-degree intent (i.e. simple intent). The dispatch on Art. 260^{quinquies} CH-StGB states that this provision should only be applicable if the financing of terrorism can be regarded as the actual objective of the perpetrator.[111] The intent would therefore have to relate to the financing of a specific terrorist act.[112] However, this raises the question as to whether this must be the ultimate goal of the perpetrator. This would probably have to be negated.[113]

Finally, the distinction between direct intent in the second degree and contingent intent can be made based on the fact that in the case of contingent intent, the offender merely accepts a risk, but in the case of direct intent in the second degree, an unavoidable secondary consequence of the act must be assumed (e.g. the financing of the terrorist's livelihood).[114]

This raises the question of how to deal with a situation wherein someone finances the livelihood of a terrorist. This is particularly problematic if the terrorist is already determined to commit an attack and uses the benefits received to prepare for it.[115] Conceivable support payments would include money to pay for accommodation and food so that the perpetrator could concentrate on preparing for the attack. However, this would be almost impossible to prove. A financier can always claim to have merely supported a fugitive without knowing about the terrorist activities being planned.

In this context, it should be emphasized that intentional acts pursuant to Art. 260^{quinquies} CH-StGB are also to be assumed if the perpetrator knows that the group they are supporting is planning and carrying out violent crimes.[116] However, the dispatch assumes that Art. 260^{quinquies} CH-StGB should only be applied if the financing of terrorist acts is the actual goal of the perpetrator.[117]

111 Message, 2002: p. 5442.

112 Schubarth & Vest, 2013: Art. 260^{quinquies} CH-StGB point 14.

113 Message, 2002: p. 5442.

114 Fiolka, 2018: Art. 260^{quinquies} CH-StGB point 22; Schubarth & Vest, 2013: Art. 260^{quinquies} CH-StGB point 16.

115 Fiolka, 2018: Art. 260^{quinquies} CH-StGB point 22.

116 Stratenwerth & Wohlers, 2013: p. 509; Forster, 2003: p. 444.

117 Message, 2002: p. 5442.

At this point, it should also be borne in mind that contingent intent and conscious negligence do not differ on the knowledge side.[118] Negligence within the meaning of Art. 12 (3) CH-StGB presupposes that the offender either does not consider the consequences of their conduct due to imprudence contrary to their duty or at least does not take them into account. Imprudence is in particular contrary to duty if the offender does not exercise the degree of caution that is reasonable in the circumstances and according to their personal circumstances.[119]

The direct intent of the first or second degree required by Art. 260^{quinquies} (2) CH-StGB refers only to the intention to finance terrorism. Contingent intent is sufficient for the objective of violent crime. However, this sets the bar high enough for a successful prosecution. In the vast majority of cases, it is unlikely that the authorities will succeed in proving the perpetrator's intent with regard to the intention to finance. This applies all the more as soon as the perpetrator is represented by a lawyer.

Finally, however, the question arises as to what extent the perpetrator can succeed in proving intent in the first or second degree. A skilful perpetrator will always plead that they acted in good faith. Supposed charitable donations or support payments to relatives serve as a possible justification. In these cases, it is up to the relevant prosecuting authorities to prove the perpetrator's intent.

The problem of proving direct intent can be partially solved – at least in cases where a specific terrorist attack was actually financed. In particular, the financier can be prosecuted for aiding and abetting the principal offence, provided that they at least acted with possible intent.[120] An aider and abettor is anyone who intentionally assists in the commission of a crime. The nature of the aiding and abetting is irrelevant. In particular, any subordinate contribution that significantly facilitates the principal offence is covered.[121]

However, the question arises as to what extent it is possible to establish a causal link between the terrorist act and the financial support. In particular, this empirical study shows how skilful perpetrators can make it almost impossible to trace their transactions. The fact that law enforcement authorities must prove that the financier acted intentionally further complicates gathering evidence.

---

118 Niggli & Maeder, 2013: Art. 12 CH-StGB point 58.

119 Art. 12 (3) CH-StGB.

120 Donatsch et al., 2017: p. 218.

121 Killias et al., 2009: p. 94.

2.1.1.4 *Exculpation according to Art. 260^{quinquies} (3) and (4) CH-StGB*

In addition to the problem of the requirement of direct intent, a further challenge arises from a subjective point of view in the application of Art. 260^{quinquies} CH-StGB. In particular, it requires that the perpetrator intends to finance an act of violence that has the effect of intimidating the population or coercing a state or an international organization.[122] However, Art. 260^{quinquies} (3) CH-StGB provides grounds for exculpation. In particular, the act is not considered to be terrorism financing 'if it is directed towards the establishment or restoration of democratic conditions and the rule of law or the exercise or preservation of human rights'.[123] This exclusion of criminal liability for allegedly legitimate crimes of violence was not provided for in the original version of Art. 260^{quinquies} CH-StGB.[124] It was only added as a result of the preliminary consultative parliamentary commission of the Council of States.[125]

Accordingly, support for freedom fighters should not fall within the scope of Art. 260^{quinquies} CH-StGB.[126] Thus, the financing of the (re-)establishment of democratic conditions or the rule of law should not be punishable.[127] Those who financially support parties in a civil war that respect the international humanitarian law of war or freedom fighters who take action against oppression and occupation are therefore not liable to prosecution, provided that they choose appropriate means of violent resistance to achieve their objectives.[128]

The background to this addition can be explained by the inconsistent definition of terrorism mentioned above.[129] In the absence of a clear definition of terrorism, it is ultimately debatable whether a violent criminal should be considered a terrorist or a freedom fighter.[130] Consequently, the Swiss Parliament was concerned that Art. 260^{quinquies} CH-StGB would mean that those who fight for human rights or support this fight financially would have to reckon with criminal prosecution.[131] However, this exclusion of criminal liability for legitimate violent crimes has been met with criticism in the doctrine. Ultimately,

---

122 Thelesklaf, 2009: Art. 260^{quinquies} CH-StGB point 12.
123 Art. 260^{quinquies} (3) CH-StGB.
124 Fiolka, 2018: Art. 260^{quinquies} CH-StGB point 42.
125 Forster, 2003: p. 445.
126 Stratenwerth & Wohlers, 2013: p. 509.
127 Trechsel & Pieth, 2018: p. 1318.
128 BGE 131 II 235, E. 3.3.
129 Forster, 2003: p. 445.
130 Fiolka, 2018: Art. 260^{quinquies} CH-StGB point 42.
131 Message, 2002: p. 5440.

all terrorists pursue political goals. Therefore, if terrorism is seen merely as a matter of perspective, it will hardly be possible to apply Art. $260^{quinquies}$ CH-StGB in practice.[132]

One of the problems is that the distinction between legitimate freedom fighters, parties in a civil war and suspected terrorists is extraordinarily difficult.[133] Ultimately, a not inconsiderable margin of discretion arises here. This can only be closed to a limited extent, even within the framework of objective considerations. If a perpetrator invokes this as grounds for justification, what they understood the democratic and constitutional conditions to be at the time of the offence and how their act of financing was intended to contribute to the establishment or restoration of these conditions must be investigated and ultimately also proven. However, it is unclear how this can be objectively understood. In fact, an intelligent perpetrator can always claim that at the time of the crime, they were only aiming at the establishment of democratic and constitutional conditions,[134] and it would be difficult or even impossible to prove them wrong.

With regard to determining guilt, the assessment of the circumstances must not be based on political considerations but on the perpetrator's ideas.[135]

A clever perpetrator may claim that their intention was merely to establish democratic conditions and the rule of law. Consider for example a perpetrator who has already been proven to have intentionally transferred assets to an association in Syria. Despite clear evidence pointing to the funding of terrorism, this perpetrator could plead that they simply wanted to support a group working towards the restoration of democratic conditions and the rule of law and that they had only inadvertently donated to the IS.

The problem is that in almost all cases, the perpetrator will find ways to justify their actions. After all, it cannot be assumed that a perpetrator who wishes to finance terrorism will resort to such means because they are very satisfied with the conditions where the terrorist activities will take place. Rather, in almost all cases, a problematic situation will present itself through different perspectives and offer a correspondingly large scope for debate. As a rule, it is only possible to judge ex post whether certain activities were successful or not.[136]

---

132 Jositsch, 2005: p. 464; Fiolka, 2018: Art. $260^{quinquies}$ CH-StGB point 43.
133 BGE 130 II 337, E. 6.
134 Thelesklaf, 2009: Art. $260^{quinquies}$ CH-StGB point 14.
135 Thelesklaf, 2009: Art. $260^{quinquies}$ CH-StGB point 14.
136 Jositsch, 2005: p. 463 f.

Furthermore, it must not be forgotten that terrorist activities are usually directed against random victims. These persons are often subjected to great suffering. Under certain circumstances, there is a danger to life and limb.[137] A question therefore arises as to whether, from the point of view of the rule of law, it is acceptable for some people to experience great suffering if a greater goal is being pursued, such as the establishment of democratic conditions and the rule of law.

Moreover, terrorist attacks usually intimidate or unsettle the civilian population.[138] It is unclear whether terrorist attacks can ever be carried out in the best interests of civilians. Proponents argue with the great benefit of possible changes. The author takes an extremely sceptical view of this and argues that terrorist attacks cannot, under any circumstances, be a suitable way of bringing about change, and thus their funding can never be justified.

Ultimately, the existing rule forces criminal courts to make a distinction between legitimate violent crimes and acts of terrorism.[139] Therefore, financing the assassination of a head of state can thus, at the discretion of the criminal judge, be qualified either as an act of terrorism or as freedom fighting, with the latter of the two leading to impunity under Art. $260^{quinquies}$ CH-StGB.[140]

If a perpetrator uses certain means to fight dictatorial regimes or regimes that systematically violate human rights, it is necessary to differentiate between these acts and acts of terrorism. In the case of serious violent crimes, for example, the murder of a head of state mentioned above, the political character of the assassination would in principle tend to be negated. However, exceptions are conceivable – consider a civil war context. In this case, tyrannicide can, under certain circumstances, represent the only practicable means of achieving certain goals.[141]

It goes without saying that hopefully it would not occur to any jurist gifted with reason to qualify the terrorist attacks carried out by the IS as indicative of a legitimate fight for freedom. However, there is ultimately no guarantee of this.[142] It should also be remembered that so-called 'legitimate crimes of violence' could also be justified without Art. $260^{quinquies}$ CH-StGB. Finally, there are extra-legal grounds for justification in Switzerland.[143] For example, a proportionate

137 Fiolka, 2018: Art. $260^{quinquies}$ CH-StGB point 43.
138 Fiolka, 2018: Art. $260^{quinquies}$ CH-StGB point 43.
139 Cassani, 2003: p. 301.
140 Schubarth & Vest, 2013: Art. $260^{quinquies}$ CH-StGB point 24.
141 BGE 131 II 235, E. 3.3; BGE 130 II 337, E. 3.3; BGE 128 II 355, E. 4.2; BGE 109 Ib 64, E. 6a.
142 Forster, 2006: p. 332.
143 Forster, 2005: p. 217; Fiolka, 2018: Art. $260^{quinquies}$ CH-StGB point 44.

resistance to illegal acts can qualify as self-defence, as a state of necessity or as safeguarding legitimate interests and thus be justified.[144] Consequently, even in the absence of Art. $260^{quinquies}$ (3) CH-StGB, it would not be mandatory to designate such perpetrators as terrorists and their benefactors as terrorist financiers.[145]

Furthermore, the International Convention for the Suppression of the Financing of Terrorism (ÜBFT) does not provide for any exceptions within the meaning of Art. $260^{quinquies}$ (3) CH-StGB. Consequently, Art. $260^{quinquies}$ CH-StGB is an insufficient and inadequate implementation of the ÜBFT. This problem can be solved, at least in part, by an exceptionally restrictive interpretation of Art. $260^{quinquies}$ CH-StGB. In particular, the proportionality of the offences and the objectives must be considered.[146]

In addition, a question arises as to which criteria can be used to assess democratic conditions and the rule of law. It seems obvious to base the assessment on Swiss constitutional law,[147] but can these standards then be applied in other countries as well? Finally, cultural and historical differences must be taken into account. It would be downright presumptuous to apply Swiss standards in North Africa, but at the same time, criminal courts can hardly be expected to follow their own standards and procedures for each country to be judged. This potentially raises a significant problem in practice.

The task delegated by the legislature to the criminal courts of defining what constitutes a 'politically legitimate' use of force and what is considered 'terrorism' must be described as extremely delicate, to say the least.[148] Finally, differentiating terrorists from other criminals and defining resistance fighters are among the most difficult tasks faced by criminal law, which requires particularly careful clarifications in this regard, and clarifications of possible civil war backgrounds are especially necessary.[149]

Furthermore, what is meant by the 'establishment or restoration' of democratic conditions or the rule of law must also be clarified. This expression suggests that no democratic or constitutional conditions existed at the time that an alleged terrorist act was financed.[150] Answering this question is moot when it

144 Fiolka, 2018: Art. $260^{quinquies}$ CH-StGB point 26.
145 Forster, 2005: p. 217; Fiolka, 2018: Art. $260^{quinquies}$ CH-StGB point 44.
146 Cassani, 2003: p. 302; Forster, 2003: p. 445; Forster, 2006: p. 336; Fiolka, 2018: Art. $260^{quinquies}$ CH-StGB point 45; Jositsch, 2005: p. 466 f.
147 Fiolka, 2018: Art. $260^{quinquies}$ CH-StGB point 49.
148 BGE 130 II 337, E. 3.3.
149 BGE 130 II 337, E. 6; BGE 133 IV 58, E. 5.
150 Fiolka, 2018: Art. $260^{quinquies}$ CH-StGB point 50.

comes to assessing acts of terrorism in Switzerland or Germany, since there is no doubt about the rule of law and democratic conditions in these countries; however, the Swiss Federal Supreme Court (BG) has explicitly emphasized that in the case of supporters of resistance organizations, serious terrorist crimes cannot be inferred without further investigation.[151]

It should also be emphasized that the cumulative enumeration of democratic and constitutional conditions in Art. $260^{\text{quinquies}}$ (3) CH-StGB indicates that exculpation is only applicable if both constitutional and democratic – and not only democratic – conditions are to be established. This is of particular importance because otherwise acts of terrorism in states governed by the rule of law that are non-democratic would fall within the scope of application of Art. $260^{\text{quinquies}}$ (3) CH-StGB.[152] In such cases, specific indications of the terrorist nature of the act would have to be taken into account.[153]

In addition, how the Federal Supreme Court views criminal organizations under Art. 260ter CH-StGB also provides valuable guidance. According to this, organizations that 'struggle for political power in their home country or wage a struggle for freedom against dictatorial regimes' using appropriate but non-criminal means are not considered criminal.[154]

Moreover, the exercise or preservation of human rights must also be addressed. This means that human rights must first be defined. The standards of the ECHR and the Swiss constitution should be applied here. However, it should not be forgotten that acts of terrorism also frequently violate human rights. This raises the question of whether an act of terrorism can be legitimized by the exercise of human rights.[155] In the author's view, the legitimization of acts of terrorism must be denied on principle. Otherwise, one would have to assume that the lives of a few random victims are worth less than the human rights of the rest of the population. This can hardly be reconciled with rule of law principles. In particular, serious violent crimes committed against civilians, which serve as the systematic intimidation of a population or the coercion of states and international organizations, are always characterized by their terrorist nature.[156] However, the Federal

151 BG 130 II 337, E. 7.1.

152 Fiolka, 2018: Art. $260^{\text{quinquies}}$ CH-StGB point 51.

153 BG 131 II 235, E. 3.5.

154 BG 131 II 235, E. 2.12; BG 130 II 337, E. 3.4; BG 128 II 355, E. 4.3; BG 125 II 569, E. 5c.

155 Fiolka, 2018: Art. $260^{\text{quinquies}}$ CH-StGB point 52.

156 BGE 131 II 235, E. 3.5.

Supreme Court provides for exceptions if the offence 'would constitute the only available means to achieve a central humanitarian objective'.[157]

Furthermore, remember that the above-mentioned protection of human rights founded in the Swiss constitution and in the ECHR cannot be applicable to all regions of the world. Western Europe has an exceptionally high standard of human rights. Consequently, the Swiss standard for human rights cannot be applied unconditionally to other states. An exceptionally restrictive interpretation of Art. $260^{quinquies}$ (3) CH-StGB is therefore unavoidable.[158]

Hence, the 'Brigate Rosse', ETA and Al-Qaeda are terrorist criminal organizations according to Art. 260ter, no 1 CH-StGB.[159] In conclusion, it can be stated that the deletion of Art. $260^{quinquies}$ (3) CH-StGB without replacement would be desirable and sensible. This is particularly true in view of the significant potential for abuse of this as grounds for exculpation.

The situation is different in the case of Art. $260^{quinquies}$ (4) CH-StGB, which regulates the exclusion of criminal liability in the case of violent crimes that conform to international law. Accordingly, Art. $260^{quinquies}$ (1) CH-StGB 'does not apply if the financing is intended to support acts that are not in conflict with the rules of international law applicable in armed conflicts'.[160] This brings Art. $260^{quinquies}$ CH-StGB in line with international law. In particular, art. $260^{quinquies}$ is intended to ensure that acts of violence permitted by international law do not fall within the scope of Art. $260^{quinquies}$ CH-StGB.

However, Art. $260^{quinquies}$ (4) CH-StGB does not constitute a significant obstacle to criminal prosecution, since international law can be taken as the basis. For example, the financing of measures initiated by UN resolutions is legal.[161] These resolutions are unambiguous and do not give the criminal court an excessively wide margin of discretion. Moreover, under normal circumstances, ordinary terrorist financiers are unlikely to succeed in invoking such UN resolutions or other instruments of international law as grounds for justification of their actions. Subsidiarily, conformity with the international humanitarian law of war could also be relied upon here.

In summary, Art. $260^{quinquies}$ (4) CH-StGB is significantly less problematic than Art. $260^{quinquies}$ (3) CH-StGB. However, the latter creates high hurdles to

---

157 BGE 130 II 337, E. 3.3; BGE 128 II 355, E. 4.2; BGE 109 Ib, 64, E. 6a.

158 Fiolka, 2018: Art. $260^{quinquies}$ CH-StGB point 53.

159 BGE 131 II 235, E. 2.12; BGE 128 II 355; E. 2.2; BGE 125 II 569, E. 5c.

160 Art. $260^{quinquies}$ (4) CH-StGB.

161 Fiolka, 2018: Art. $260^{quinquies}$ CH-StGB point 55.

overcome which can also be problematic, particularly in cases of international criminal judicial assistance. Finally, the dual criminality required does not apply if there are grounds for exculpation under Swiss criminal law.

2.1.3 Delimitation

A question also arises as to how to deal with cases which do not merely feature the financing of terrorism but in which the perpetrator, through their financial contribution, has deliberately enabled another serious criminal offence, such as intimidation of the civilian population within the scope of Art. 258 CH-StGB. It should be noted that Art. $260^{\text{quinquies}}$ CH-StGB is subsidiary to the (attempted) perpetration of and participation in principal terrorist acts.[162] This at least partially solves the problem of proving intent as discussed above. If the subjective elements of Art. $260^{\text{quinquies}}$ CH-StGB are not fulfilled or cannot be proven, but the terrorism financing was successful and a concrete act of terrorism was actually financed, then the financier can be prosecuted for aiding and abetting the principal offence, provided they acted with at least probable intent.[163]

Consider Arts 221–230 CH-StGB (i.e. felonies and misdemeanours dangerous to the public), homicide in the sense of Arts 111–117 CH-StGB and bodily injury in the sense of Arts 122–126 CH-StGB, as well as endangering life and health in the sense of Art. 129 CH-StGB. Subsidiary consideration should also be given to Arts 230bis–236 CH-StGB, namely crimes and offences against public health, and Arts 237–239 CH-StGB, referring to crimes and offences against public transport. All these offences are exemplary, the fulfilment of which could be made possible by Art. $260^{\text{quinquies}}$ CH-StGB.

Consider, for example, the financing of an act punishable under Art. 223 CH-StGB, namely causing an explosion, or murder within the meaning of Art. 112 CH-StGB. The attacks in London in Spring 2017 showed that perpetrators may only need access to a vehicle and some commercially available knives in order to kill people indiscriminately. Anyone who finances such acts could possibly be considered an accomplice, indirect perpetrator or secondary perpetrator. In addition, aiding and abetting these acts should also be illuminated.

The vast majority of legal doctrine supports considering the aiding and abetting of a violent crime if the financing contributed to the implementation thereof.[164] An aider and abettor intends to promote the principal offence and

162 Trechsel & Pieth, 2018: p. 1319.

163 Donatsch et al., 2017: p. 218.

164 Stratenwerth & Wohlers, 2013: p. 509.

accepts that their assistance will at least facilitate the offence. In this respect, the person acts intentionally.[165] However, contingent intent is sufficient.[166] Nevertheless, the aider and abettor accepts that the principal offender will act intentionally.[167]

The accomplice's contribution to the crime must also be subsidiary, meaning that the violent crime must not depend substantially on the actions of the accomplice. Thus, the accomplice must not appear as the main perpetrator.[168] Otherwise, it would be a case of complicity. The accomplice therefore has no animus auctoris.[169] In particular, contributing to the fulfilment of the offence of aiding and abetting must merely promote the offence but not constitute a conditio sine qua non within the meaning offered by the theory of equivalence.[170] However, the aider and abettor's assistance must actually contribute to the main offence and increase its practical chances of success. In this context, the term 'promotion causality' is also used.[171]

An accomplice intentionally assists the principal offender.[172] Causality of assistance means that the principal offender must derive a concrete practical benefit from the accessory's contribution to the offence.[173] This means that the contribution to the offence must be made by the time the principal offence has been completed.[174] However, the principal offender does not necessarily have to know about this benefit, and nor does the principal offender necessarily have to derive any benefit from the accessory's contribution.[175]

Particularly relevant in the case of terrorism financing appears to be the question of the extent to which supposedly harmless everyday transactions or services typical of the person's profession (e.g. in money transfer services) can qualify as aiding and abetting if they serve to further a criminal offence.[176] The

---

165 Forster, 2018: Art. 25 CH-StGB point 3.

166 BGE 121 IV 109, E. 3a; Fiolka, 2018: Art. 260^{quinquies} CH-StGB point 67; Cassani, 2003: p. 303.

167 BGE 117 IV 186, E. 3.

168 BGE 120 IV 265, E. 2c.

169 Forster, 2018: Art. 25 CH-StGB point 3.

170 BGE 121 IV 109, E. 3a.

171 BGE 129 IV 124, E. 3.2; Forster, 2018: Art. 25 CH-StGB point 8.

172 BG 1B_467/2016.

173 Forster, 2018: Art. 25 CH-StGB point 10.

174 BGE 98 IV 83, E. 2c.

175 Forster, 2018: Art. 25 CH-StGB point 12; BGE 121 IV 109, E. 3a.

176 Forster, 2018: Art. 25 CH-StGB point 30.

Federal Supreme Court has not yet answered this question conclusively.[177] The most sensible approach would appear to be to rely on the knowledge and intent of the perpetrator.[178] This is particularly true in view of the practice of the Federal Supreme Court, which lends great weight to the knowledge of the participant in a criminal offence.[179] This means that, in order to establish aiding and abetting, the criminal use must be both obvious and recognizable.[180]

Attempted aiding and abetting is not punishable.[181] This explains, among other things, the scope of application of Art. 260quinquies CH-StGB. Ultimately, Art. 260quinquies CH-StGB is a catch-all offence that is applicable, among other things, if the principal offence was not successful or if no connection can be proven between the perpetrator's act of financing and a concrete act of terrorism.

It should also be noted that Art. 260quinquies CH-StGB is also subsidiary to the attempt of the principal offence.[182] This is plausible insofar as it is obvious that a perpetrator who has attempted to kill several people should be punished primarily for the attempted homicide. However, if the terrorist financier's contribution to the offence goes beyond aiding and abetting, they may qualify as an accomplice. CH-StGB does not contain a definition of perpetration. In principle, a perpetrator is someone who objectively controls both the 'whether' and the 'how' of the possible execution of the offence and thus has the power to commit the offence and has the corresponding will. A participant, on the other hand, is someone who does not control 'whether' and 'how' but makes it dependent on the will of a third party; thus they do not have the power to commit the offence but nevertheless cause or encourage it to be committed.[183]

In the context of co-perpetration, the offence-specific characteristics are to be examined on the objective side, with imputation taking place in the case of the act of commission if the decisive characteristic was not itself realized. According to the established case law of the Federal Supreme Court, a co-perpetrator is considered someone

> who intentionally and in a decisive manner cooperates with other perpetrators in the resolution, planning or execution of an offence, so that he stands as the main participant; in this regard, it depends on whether the contribution to the offence is so essential

177 BGE 120 IV 265, E. 2c.
178 Forster, 2018: Art. 25 CH-StGB point 32.
179 BGE 121 IV 109, E. 3.
180 Forster, 2018: Art. 25 CH-StGB point 38.
181 BGE 130 IV 131, E. 2.4.
182 Fiolka, 2018: Art. 260quinquies CH-StGB point 67; Trechsel & Pieth, 2018: p. 1319.
183 Forster, 2018; Art. 24 CH-StGB point 7.

> for the execution of the offence according to the circumstances of the specific case and the plan of the offence that it stands or falls with him.[184]

Thus, the contribution of the co-perpetrator must be essential to the commission of the offence. Nevertheless, the accomplice does not have to have been directly involved in the main offence. Moreover, the accomplice does not have to have been in charge of the offence in order to be prosecuted. Co-perpetration of the decision-making, planning or co-ordination may be sufficient grounds for prosecution.[185]

From a subjective point of view, co-perpetration requires intent within the meaning provided by Art. 12, § 2 CH-StGB and a joint intention to commit the offence (i.e. an intention to commit the offence or animus auctoris). The joint decision can also be implied. In addition, contingent intent is sufficient.[186]

Furthermore, it is not necessary for the accomplice to be involved from the outset. They may join in at a later point in time, but no later than the completion of the offence. In these cases, one speaks of successive complicity. For example, psychological or intellectual influence could also suffice. An accomplice having a passive role during the planning phase and the actual execution of the offence is also conceivable.[187] What is required, however, is at least a motivating act.[188]

There is disagreement as to whether there is real competition between Art. 260^{quinquies} CH-StGB and Art. 260ter CH-StGB. Some of the doctrine affirms this.[189] The majority, however, argues that Art. 260ter CH-StGB takes precedence over Art. 260^{quinquies} CH-StGB, as the latter is merely conceived as a catch-all offence for the former.[190]

It must also be emphasized that the grounds for exclusion set out in Art. 260^{quinquies}, paras 2–4 CH-StGB do not apply to Art. 260ter CH-StGB and therefore have no effect. If an offender intentionally finances persons who ex post turn out to be members of a terrorist organization, the financier is liable to prosecution under Art. 260ter CH-StGB if it can be proven that they at least knowingly accepted the involvement of the persons they supported in the terrorist organization.[191]

---

184 BGE 133 IV 76, E. 2.7; BGE 130 IV 58, E. 9.2.1.

185 BGE 133 IV 76, E. 2.7; BGE 130 IV 58, E. 9.2.1; Forster, 2018: Art. 24 CH-StGB point 8.

186 BGE 126 IV 84, E. 2c.

187 Forster, 2018: Art. 24 CH-StGB point 12; BGE 128 IV 11, E. 2a.

188 Forster, 2018: Art. 24 CH-StGB point 14; BGE 127 IV 122, E. 2b.

189 Stratenwerth & Wohlers, 2013: p. 509.

190 Fiolka, 2018: Art. 260^{quinquies} CH-StGB point 69; Forster, 2003: p. 446 f.; Cassani, 2003: p. 304.

191 Fiolka, 2018: Art. 260^{quinquies}, CH-StGB point 69.

In practice, this means that in the event of successful terrorism financing, proof of contingent intent could suffice. This explains why Art. 260^{quinquies} CH-StGB is often regarded as a catch-all offence. However, it should also be borne in mind that a skilful offender could avoid the fulfilment of further offences, and thus only Art. 260^{quinquies} CH-StGB would be applicable. This would mean that the low penalty of a maximum of five years' imprisonment would apply.

Furthermore, it should be noted that there is genuine competition between Art. 260^{quinquies} CH-StGB and Art. 305bis CH-StGB.[192] The latter applies if incriminated assets are used to finance terrorism. This can already be assumed to be the case when terrorists' livelihoods are funded using assets derived from crimes.[193] However, this competition must be put into perspective from a practical point of view. Intelligent terrorist financiers are likely able to avoid using incriminated assets. After all, they would not want to risk facing the scrutiny of investigators due to the origins of the assets even before they are able to be used (i.e. before they are used to finance terrorism).

If the terrorist financier is preparing acts that are solely intended to finance terrorism, Art. 260^{quinquies} CH-StGB takes precedence. Otherwise, it is subsidiary to the punishable preparatory acts within the meaning of Art. 260bis CH-StGB, which take precedence if the perpetrator is also involved in other crimes.[194] This particularly applies to organizational arrangements for the preparation of other offences.[195]

Finally, it should be mentioned that Art. 260^{quinquies} CH-StGB can coincide with various other laws such as the Embargo Act (EmbA) or the War Material Act (WMA). According to Art. 11 EmbA, only the law that provides for the most severe penalty is applicable. This applies in particular to conflicts between the EmbA and the WMA.[196] However, this rule should also apply by analogy to any conflicts between Art. 260^{quinquies} CH-StGB and the EmbA. Consequently, Art. 260^{quinquies} CH-StGB is superseded by Art. 9, (2) EmbA (for a serious case), but at the same time, it takes precedence over Art. 9 (1) EmbA.[197] Accordingly, there is no real competition.[198]

---

192 Trechsel & Pieth, 2018: p. 1319.

193 Fiolka, 2018: Art. 260^{quinquies}, CH-StGB point 70; Cassani, 2003: p. 305; Trechsel & Vest, 2013: p. 1198.

194 Trechsel & Pieth, 2018: p. 1319.

195 Engler, 2013: Art. 260bis CDE-StGB point 5.

196 Trechsel & Pieth, 2018: p. 1319.

197 Art. 9 EmbA.

198 Fiolka, 2018: Art. 260^{quinquies} CH-StGB point 71.

A question also arises as to how competing offences between Art. 260quinquies CH-StGB and the WMA are to be considered. This applies in particular to the financing elements of Art. 33 (1), lit. f WMA and the promotion elements of Art. 34 (1), lit. c WMA and Art. 35 (1), lit. c WMA.[199] In these cases, the WMA offences take precedence over Art. 260quinquies CH-StGB because the WMA offences are also punishable in the case of negligence. Thus, Art. 260quinquies CH-StGB is to be regarded as subsidiary to the WMA.[200]

2.1.4 The level of penalties

Furthermore, it must be questioned whether the penalty provided for in Art. 260quinquies CH-StGB is appropriate. A violation of Art. 260quinquies CH-StGB is punishable by imprisonment of up to five years or a fine.[201] However, it is unclear whether terrorist financiers would be deterred by a higher penalty. After all, these perpetrators may be people who are prepared to die to achieve their goal or even die during the commission of their crime, like suicide bombers. It is therefore questionable whether a higher threat of punishment would be a suitable means of dissuading these perpetrators from committing their crime in the first place.

At the same time, a question arises as to whether it makes sense to punish a perpetrator who may not be prepared to die – but who nevertheless finances terrorism – with a prison sentence of a maximum of five years. Such a perpetrator might consciously accept this risk but might be deterred by a higher penalty. A higher penalty is possible in any case where the perpetrator has successfully financed an attack. Opponents of an increase in the possible punishment as part of a reform of Art. 260quinquies CH-StGB could thus argue that the higher punishment is given in cases involving a concrete threat to life and limb anyway. Even in cases where there is an attempt to commit a more serious offence, Art. 260quinquies CH-StGB plays only a minor role.

Nevertheless, the question arises as to how to deal with cases in which the financing of terrorism can be proven but the causal link to a specific attack cannot be established. This becomes a problem when the perpetrator has financed a terrorist organization such as the IS or Al-Qaeda.

As a rule, long prison sentences represent a considerable burden for the offender and the general public.[202] Thus, and also with regard to the costs

199 Art. 33 f. WMA.

200 Fiolka, 2018: Art. 260quinquies, CH-StGB point 72.

201 Art. 260quinquies CH-StGB.

202 Henrichson & Delaney, 2012: p. 68 f.

associated with a custodial sentence for the general public, a question arises as to whether this is proportionate and desirable.[203] While the necessity of custodial sentences is debatable, there seems to be consensus that a custodial sentence is proportionate, given the significant threat to life and limb associated with the financing of terrorism and the need to prevent the perpetrator from continuing to finance terrorism. In this context, the custodial sentence has both retributive and preventive purposes.

The retributive measure represents the response to the act of terrorism financing that has already been committed and relates to the culpable commission of the offence.[204] At the same time, however, it is also intended to prevent further offences of the same kind from being committed, which is why the penalty always also has preventive features. In this context, a conceptual distinction must be made between the specific offender (i.e. special prevention) and the general public (i.e. general prevention).[205]

General prevention is understood to be the deterrence of the general public through the sanctioning of criminal offences.[206] It should be noted that the punishment should not only have a deterrent effect but must also ensure that the offence is sanctioned as well.[207] If it is clear to citizens that prosecution is virtually impossible, since it is almost impossible to prove that the offender acted intentionally – and even in the event of a conviction, an exceptionally lenient sentence can be expected – it can be assumed that the deterrent effect is limited.

Retributive theories of punishment are often referred to in the literature as 'absolute' because they supposedly lack social utility.[208] In this context, they are often equated with the punitive element of revenge. However, this makes little sense, as revenge does not entail social utility.[209] Rather, the focus should be on deed-proportional retribution, that is, a callous and rational instrument.[210]

Consequently, the punishment should be proportional to the crime.[211] A distinction is made between ordinal and cardinal proportionality.[212] Cardinal

---

203 Coninx, 2016: p. 157.

204 McCloskey, 1967: p. 91; Corlett, 2006: p. 26; Brown, 2002: p. 1411 f.; Sharp & Otto, 1910: p. 341 f.; Fletcher, 1999: p. 51 f.; Day, 1978: p. 498 f.

205 Coninx, 2016: p. 158.

206 Andenaes, 1952: p. 176; Andenaes, 1971: p. 18; Andenaes, 1975: p. 339.

207 Donatsch, 2017: p. 292.

208 Weiner et al., 1997: p. 431.

209 Boudreaux, 1989: p. 177 f.

210 Coninx, 2016: p. 157 f.

211 Hudson, 1994: p. 59 f.; Hoffman & Goldsmith, 2003: p. 638.

212 Van den Haag, 1986: p. 1254; von Hirsch, 1991: p. 549 f.

proportionality provides that both the most severe and the most lenient punishment should be defined. Ordinal proportionality also provides for proportionality to be graded in relation to the individual offences. With regard to terrorism financing, it is therefore necessary to take into account how other offences are punished.[213]

The question also arises as to whether offenders may be punished solely for the purposes of retribution or whether preventive measures may also be pursued on a secondary basis.[214] Preventive punishments can sometimes also be justified in the fight against terrorism financing. After all, the security of the general public is at stake. However, a strict differentiation between retributive and preventive penalties in the context of terrorism financing is almost superfluous. A retributive punishment, proportionate to the gravity of the crime, will always have a preventive effect as well.[215]

Expressive theories of punishment are also based on the idea that punishment is a social necessity because it contributes to social understanding.[216] These theories advocate reappraisal between the actors involved. Crime prevention does not play a primary role.[217]

Negative general prevention attempts to deter citizens as a whole from committing a crime.[218] This is usually achieved by means of deterrent punishments, whereby a differentiation can be made between the threat of punishment and the imposition of punishment.[219] Since cases of terrorism financing are likely to be of potential interest to the media and the wider public, it can be assumed that both the threat of punishment and the imposition of punishment play a role.

The deterrence theory assumes that citizens are aware of the penalty and act according to the threat of punishment.[220] This is an intuitive assumption that is difficult to test empirically. For example, the probability of being caught could also play a certain role. In addition, with negative general prevention there is often the risk that the punishment could be unjust and too far-reaching.[221]

---

213 von Hirsch, 1992: p. 57; Brantingham & Faust, 1976: p. 549 f.; Coninx, 2016: p. 160.
214 Coninx, 2016: p. 161.
215 Daly, 2000: p. 33 f.
216 DeFord, 2005: p. 843 f.
217 Coninx, 2016: p. 161.
218 Dölling et al., 2006: p. 193.
219 Coninx, 2016: p. 163.
220 Dölling & Hermann, 2012: p. 427 f.
221 Coninx, 2016: p. 164.

For this reason, positive general prevention is frequently resorted to, particularly in Germany.[222] The assumption here is that punishing the individual leads to the general public being informed about the legal norms and the sanctions associated with their violation and that trust in the penal norms grows as a result.[223] Consequently, communication should also take place with citizens who behave in a law-abiding manner.[224] The concept of positive general prevention seems particularly suitable for combating terrorism financing. Finally, it is important to inform the population about the offence of terrorism financing. This is particularly important in order to ensure that offences committed through negligence are avoided.

However, it should be noted at the same time that the existing provision of Art. 260^{quinquies} CH-StGB does not do justice to the explanations outlined above. A custodial sentence of a maximum of five years for the financing of terrorism does not appear to be particularly effective, either retributively or preventively. After all, as a rule, human lives are endangered by the financing of terrorism. However, as long as no concrete connection with a specific act or organization can be proven, no other offences apart from Art. 260^{quinquies} CH-StGB may be fulfilled. This means that the perpetrator would face a maximum prison sentence of five years. This is not particularly dissuasive, either for the offender himself or for the general public. A combination of positive and negative general prevention seems appropriate here. However, this presupposes a higher level of punishment and the punishment of acts committed negligently or possibly with intent.

2.1.5 The Anti-Money Laundering Act

Finally, it is also worth briefly examining regulations outside of the Swiss Criminal Code. In this context, the AMLA stands out. This is a special law that applies exclusively to financial intermediaries and persons who trade commercially in goods and accept cash in the process. A distinction must be made between financial intermediaries in the narrower and broader sense.[225] Financial intermediaries in the narrower sense (such as bankers) are supervised by the Swiss Financial Market Supervisory Authority (FINMA) or the Gaming Commission. Financial intermediaries in the broader sense (such as rating agencies or realtors) are not

222 Curti, 1999: p. 234 f.
223 Bock, 1991: p. 636 f.
224 Coninx, 2016: p. 164.
225 Basse, 2017; Art. 1 AMLA point 45; Art. 2 (1) AMLA.

prudentially supervised by FINMA, but from a functional perspective, they also provide financial intermediation services.[226]

Financial intermediaries are obliged to report suspicions of a terrorism connection.[227] Lawyers and notaries, on the other hand, are only obliged to report their suspicions if they have not come into contact with the assets in the course of their profession-specific activities (i.e. through the provision of accessory services).[228]

The reference in Art. 1 AMLA to Art. 260^quinquies CH-StGB makes it clear that the AMLA draws on the definition of the financing of terrorism enshrined in the Swiss Criminal Code.[229] This illustrates how closely linked Art. 260^quinquies CH-StGB and the AMLA are.[230] Moreover, the majority of cases of terrorism financing are already covered by supporting a criminal organization within the scope of Art. 260ter no. 1 (2) CH-StGB, which takes precedence over Art. 260^quinquies CH-StGB.[231]

It is interesting to note that numerous services that could be relevant to terrorism financing do not fall within the scope of the AMLA. For example, the activities of governing bodies in all operating companies do not fall within the scope of application of the AMLA.[232] Another example is the transport of valuables. In principle, these are suitable for transferring terrorists' assets. However, if the transporter does not offer any additional financial services, the AMLA is not applicable.[233]

Article 3 et seq. AMLA also set out the obligations of financial service providers. According to the Federal Supreme Court, financial intermediaries have a guarantor position.[234] This entails duties to act.[235] In particular, the contracting party must be identified by presenting an evidential document, among other things, which has to be checked for authenticity.[236] At least the standard of a general plausibility check and the consideration of generally accessible

226 Schären, 2017; Art. 2 AMLA point 2.
227 Jositsch & von Rotz, 2016: p. 600.
228 Lutz, 2016: p. 487.
229 Wyss, 2009: Art. 1 AMLA point 4a.
230 Basse, 2017: Art. 1 AMLA point 50.
231 Basse, 2017: Art. 1 AMLA point 57.
232 Lutz, 2016: p. 487.
233 Wyss, 2009: Art. 2 AMLA point 16.
234 BGE 136 IV 188, E. 6.2.
235 Lutz & Kern, 2017: p. 99.
236 Art. 3 AMLA.

information apply. Under certain circumstances, it may be useful to examine the identification document under UV light. In the past, identification by means of a digital certificate was not permitted.[237] However, since the release of FINMA Circular 2016/7, a variety of digital identification options have been made available, such as by means of video – provided that an equivalent implementation of due diligence is guaranteed.[238]

In addition, the beneficial owner must be identified.[239] In practice, this is usually done by signing a corresponding form. It is true that financial intermediaries must observe due diligence rules and identify the beneficial owner,[240] and a person controlling a legal entity is generally considered to be the beneficial owner;[241] however, financial service providers and traders may generally assume that the contracting party is the beneficial owner. Only if there are indications to the contrary must further clarifications be made.[242] This illustrates how easy it would be in most cases to use people operating in the background. If they behave inconspicuously and declare in writing that they are themselves the beneficial owners, no further clarification is required in many cases.

Only if in the course of the business relationship doubts arise as to the identity of the contracting party or its economic justification must renewed clarifications take place.[243] The standard for doubt is set relatively low. The legislator expects the financial service provider to document the identity and the beneficial ownership continuously and correctly. As soon as there are indications that the information is incorrect, a new determination must be made.[244] In particular, there is an in-depth duty to clarify identities with regard to foreign 'politically exposed' persons and persons closely associated with them.[245]

Furthermore, there are additional obligations to clarify the nature and purpose of the business relationship desired by the contracting party in the sense of a risk analysis.[246] If transactions appear unusual or if there are indications of terrorism financing, the financial intermediary must clarify their purpose and

237 Wyss, 2009; Art. 3 AMLA point 8 f.
238 Dobrauz-Saldapenna & Derungs, 2017; Art. 3 AMLA point 46.
239 Art. 4 AMLA.
240 BG 1B_86/2016, E. 6.2.
241 Liebi & Lionel, 2017; Art. 4, § 38.
242 Wyss, 2009: Art. 4 AMLA point 3 f.
243 Art. 5 AMLA; Brunnhofer & Leimgruber, 2017: Art. 5 AMLA point 3.
244 Wyss, 2009: Art. 5 AMLA point 4 f.
245 BG 1B_86/2016, E. 6.2.
246 Basse, 2017: Art. 6 AMLA point 1.

the economic background.[247] Transactions may be considered unusual if their legality is not readily apparent.[248]

There are also various documentation obligations.[249] These go beyond the information collected as a result of Arts 3–6 AMLA and serve to verify compliance with the AMLA obligations.[250] In particular, evidence is required that allows for a reliable judgment of compliance with the provisions of the AMLA. Thus, not only business transactions but also reports made and training and organizational measures must be documented.[251] These documents must be kept in such a way that competent third parties can form an opinion.[252] This safekeeping duty applies to all necessary documents.[253]

However, the documentation requirements are at least eased for assets of low value.[254] If the business relationship only involves assets of low value, and there are no grounds for suspicion of money laundering or terrorism financing, compliance with the due diligence requirements set out in Arts 3–7 AMLA can be waived.[255] The threshold for low-value assets benefits financial intermediaries by preventing excessive costs from arising. This also applies to new business areas such as micropayments via the Internet.[256] However, this poses a considerable risk in terms of terrorism financing through smurfing.[257] Finally, it is only possible to determine whether there are indications of terrorism financing within the clarification framework.

Article 7a AMLA poses a challenge in the fight against terrorism financing. On the one hand, it could be used by terrorists to engage in so-called smurfing (i.e. deliberately undermining the thresholds for more detailed investigations and thus preventing the transaction from being reported to the reporting office for money laundering). On the other hand, it enables financial intermediaries to carry out smaller transactions without incurring excessive costs. If micropayments were to be combined with more in-depth compliance obligations, this could lead to

247 Art. 6 AMLA.
248 BGE 143 II 162, E. 4.2.2.
249 Art. 7 AMLA.
250 Müller, 2017: Art. 7 AMLA point 1.
251 Wyss, 2009: Art. 7 AMLA point 3.
252 BG 1B_86/2016, E. 6.2.
253 BG 1B_249/2015, E. 7.1.3.
254 Jutzi, 2017; Art. 7a AMLA point 2.
255 Art. 7a AMLA.
256 Wyss, 2009; Art. 7a AMLA point 1.
257 Jutzi, 2017; Art. 7a AMLA point 9.

excessively high fees and cause a shift of these transactions to non-regulated channels, such as hawala banking.

Financial service providers' organizational measures must also be considered. Pursuant to Art. 8 AMLA, financial intermediaries must take the measures necessary in their field to prevent money laundering and terrorism financing. This includes, among other things, appropriate staff training and viable controls.[258] These measures must be documented and, in the case of complex suspicious cases, handed over to the competent authorities.[259]

However, Art. 8 AMLA goes beyond the implementation of Arts 3–7 AMLA by stipulating an independent duty of due diligence for financial intermediaries. This conclusion is reached in particular in the context of a systematic interpretation, as Art. 8 AMLA is listed under the heading 'Due diligence obligations'.[260] Therefore, banks must have adequate compliance departments and delegate the review of complex matters to external consultants.[261]

The next step is how a financial intermediary must proceed if they know or has a reasonable suspicion that the assets involved in the business relationship are serving to finance terrorism within the meaning of Art. 260^{quinquies} (1) CH-StGB. According to Art. 9 (1), lit. a no. 4 AMLA, in such cases, a report must be made immediately to the Money Laundering Reporting Office.[262] This is not a duty of due diligence but a measure which the financial intermediary is obliged to undertake.[263] The duty to report also applies if negotiations to enter into a business relationship have been broken off on suspicion of money laundering or terrorism financing.[264]

The report shall be made in writing by means of a form.[265] In any case, the financial intermediary, the contractual partners, the beneficial owner, any other persons involved and the findings of the background investigation must be reported. In addition, copies of the account opening forms, identification documents and account statements must also be enclosed. However, it is only possible to enclose the account documents if the account has already been

258 Jutzi, 2017; Art. 8 AMLA point 5; Art. 8 AMLA.
259 BG 1B_249/2015, E. 7.1.5 f.
260 Wyss, 2009; Art. 8 AMLA point 2.
261 BG 1B_86/2016, E. 6.5.
262 Art. 9 AMLA.
263 Thelesklaf, 2009: Art. 9 AMLA point 3 f.
264 Schinkelshoek, 2015: p. 481 f.
265 Luchsinger, 2017: Art. 9 AMLA point 90.

opened. Under certain circumstances, reporting after a preliminary meeting would also be possible and useful.[266]

In the past, the financial intermediary had to freeze the assets entrusted to them immediately after making the report. The freeze had to be maintained until a ruling was received from the prosecution authority but for no longer than five working days from the time of the report.[267] The purpose of the asset freeze was to prevent the perpetrators from withdrawing the assets.[268] However, only entrusted assets were affected. Cash transactions were not covered. Moreover, an asset freeze only took place after a suspicious activity report was filed.[269] Since 1 January 2016, in the case of reports pursuant to Art. 9 (1) lit. a AMLA, the financial intermediary is only required to freeze the assets if they are forwarded to the prosecution authorities.[270] For reports under Art. 9 (1) lit. c AMLA, on the other hand, the freezing of assets must be carried out immediately after a suspicious activity report is made. This applies in particular to cases in which, on the basis of investigations carried out in accordance with Art. 6 (2) AMLA, there is reason to believe that the data held by FINMA, the Swiss Federal Gaming Board or a self-regulatory organization, for example, in accordance with Art. 22a AMLA, could be affected.[271] Pursuant to Art. 22a AMLA, data received by FINMA or the Federal Gaming Board from another state and relating to persons who have been placed on a list pursuant to UN Security Council Resolution 1373 (2001) on account of terrorist activities or providing support for such activities are forwarded to financial service providers.[272]

Co-operation between banks and authorities with regard to asset freezing works well in practice.[273] The AMLA does not provide for a sanction in the event of a breach of the asset freeze. However, this weakness is compensated for by the Swiss Criminal Code, since failure to freeze assets may constitute money laundering within the scope of Art. 305bis CH-StGB or even the financing of terrorism within the scope of Art. 260^{quinquies} CH-StGB. It would also be conceivable for the state to claim compensation on the basis of Art. 59 CH-StGB.[274]

266 Thelesklaf, 2009: Art. 9 AMLA point 3 f.
267 Art. 10 AMLA.
268 BG 6B_907/2009, E. 9.4.2.
269 Thelesklaf, 2009: Art. 10 AMLA point 2 f.
270 Art. 9a AMLA in conjunction with. Art. 10 (1) AMLA.
271 Art. 9 (1), lit. c AMLA.
272 Derungs & Gmünder, 2017: Art. 22a AMLA point 1 ff.
273 Döbeli, 2015: p. 1241.
274 Thelesklaf, 2009: Art. 10 AMLA point 9.

Furthermore, Art. 10a AMLA provides for an information freeze. In its original form, this provided that neither the persons concerned nor third parties could receive information from the financial intermediary during the asset freeze.[275] Since 1 January 2016, this information freeze has applied for an indefinite period, but the measure must be ordered secretly.[276] The Federal Supreme Court had left open the question of the legal basis for this ban on disclosure,[277] and since 1 January 2016, there has been an explicit legal basis in Art. 10a AMLA. However, there is still no constitutional basis for long-lasting information blocks.[278]

This is problematic insofar as the asset freeze conflicts with the ban on information since surely the financial intermediary cannot be expected to lie to their client. At the same time, however, the question arises as to how to react if the client, who is unaware of the asset freeze, wishes to dispose of their assets.[279] Thus, the law in fact requires the financial intermediary to lie to their client. This becomes particularly problematic when the financial intermediary also acts as their client's lawyer. After all, a lawyer owes their client a duty of care. The idea that a lawyer could be obliged to deliberately lie to their client hardly seems compatible with their professional duties under the Advocacy Act.

In these cases, the asset freeze is unlikely to be concealed from the client in reality. Nevertheless, the information freeze takes precedence over the asset freeze so that the client is not warned of it. In any case, the financial intermediary must contact the Money Laundering Reporting Office (MROS) before carrying out the transaction, and the latter may inform the prosecution authorities. The prosecution authorities have the necessary procedural powers to resolve the dilemma between the information and asset freezes.[280]

In order to protect the financial intermediary from a penalty or liability as a result of the report, Art. 11 AMLA contains a penalty and exclusion of liability for reports made in good faith.[281] Liability would only be conceivable in the event of careless clarification or a denunciatory report.[282]

275 Art. 10a AMLA.
276 Döbeli, 2015: p. 1238.
277 BGE 131 I 425, E. 2 f.
278 Kessler & Waygood-Weiner, 2017: Art. 10a AMLA point 36.
279 Thelesklaf, 2009: Art. 10a AMLA point 1.
280 Thelesklaf, 2009: Art. 10a AMLA point 1.
281 Art. 11 AMLA.
282 Thelesklaf, 2009: Art. 11 AMLA point 2.

It should also be mentioned at this point that the asset freeze could be misused as a means of political pressure. It is therefore essential that it is always critically scrutinized. Under no circumstances should it be used to put clients under pressure.[283] At the same time, it must be ensured that financial intermediaries do not have to fear facing consequences under criminal or civil law if they have fulfilled their reporting obligations in good faith and implemented an asset freeze.[284]

Supervision, administrative assistance and the processing of personal data will only be dealt with summarily in this study, as they are only of secondary importance for the assessment of possible practices undertaken by terrorist financiers. In any case, the exchange of information between authorities enshrined in Art. 29 AMLA should be emphasized in a positive light since it permits authorities to share information.[285]

Under Article 29a AMLA, the criminal justice authorities are also obliged to use their own initiative to report to MROS all pending proceedings, judgments and discontinuation orders that are related to the scope of application of the AMLA.[286] Pursuant to Art. 32 AMLA, co-operation with foreign financial intelligence units is also possible.[287]

Anyone who intentionally violates the reporting obligation is punished by a fine of up to CHF 500,000 pursuant to Art. 37 (1) AMLA. Interestingly, Art. 37 (2) AMLA also makes a negligent breach of the reporting obligation punishable. However, the fine in this case is only CHF 150,000 and is thus significantly lower.[288] This also applies if a report is made late. Nevertheless, it is noteworthy that the AMLA sanctions both intentional and negligent acts and thus goes well beyond Art. 260^{quinquies} CH-StGB.[289]

A negligent breach of the reporting obligation is punishable if the financial intermediary has not reported a reportable fact that has a recognizable criminal background. In practice, recognizability plays a decisive role. Contingent intent, on the other hand, exists if the financial intermediary knowingly accepts that an offence has been committed but fails to make further inquiries and reports.[290]

283 Döbeli, 2015: p. 1237 f.
284 Luchsinger, 2017: Art. 11 AMLA point 6.
285 Art. 29 AMLA; Thelesklaf, 2009: Art. 29 AMLA point 1.
286 Art. 29a AMLA.
287 Art. 32 AMLA.
288 Art. 37 AMLA.
289 Hilf, 2017: Art. 37 AMLA point 32.
290 Thelesklaf, 2009: Art. 37 AMLA point 6 f.

In summary, therefore, it can be said that the AMLA places a considerable burden of responsibility on financial service providers to combat terrorism financing.[291] However, the sensibility of the measures that have been discussed in this section can be debated. This criticism is not directed against the financial intermediaries themselves but against the legislative measures to which they are subject and which, while appearing helpful in theory, actually offer very few practical benefits.

Ultimately, the reporting procedures and clarifications outlined above are only helpful if financial intermediaries are able to identify suspicious circumstances. However, this is unlikely to be the case with regard to terrorism financing. While money laundering is much easier to detect because the assets originate from a crime, terrorism financing may lie in the future. This means that the financial service provider would need to be able to anticipate the client's criminal conduct in order to make a timely report. This is unlikely to be possible.

While it could be argued that a financial service provider can report suspicious transactions and impose an asset freeze before execution, such reporting is unlikely to provide much insight, as the individuals concerned can always claim to have intended a legitimate transfer. It may be difficult to prove otherwise.

The effectiveness of the investigations carried out by financial service providers should also not be overestimated. These enquiries become obsolete as soon as straw men are used. They present their genuine identity documents and confirm that they are the beneficial owners. In addition, they explain the origins of the assets in a plausible manner.

The AMLA should also be criticized for only applying to financial intermediaries and traders since other industries, such as the transportation of valuables, are also used for terrorism financing. However, the purely physical transport and storage of assets does not qualify as financial intermediation within the scope of Art. 2 (3) AMLA. Thus, it would make sense to extend the scope of application of the AMLA.[292]

Further complicating matters is that the AMLA is not consistently applied to financial intermediaries. Hawala bankers and providers of illegal financial services are good examples. These operate underground and are not subject to any form of supervision. Consequently, they neither clarify the economic justification nor the identity of their business partners.

291 Döbeli, 2015: p. 1237 f.

292 Art. 2 (2) lit a no 1 AMLA.

The distribution of the burden of proof under the AMLA is problematic. In principle, it is the state's responsibility to prove the facts of the case against the accused. The accused may not be required to incriminate themselves. As outlined above, the AMLA obliges financial intermediaries to take appropriate measures to prevent money laundering and terrorism financing and to report suspicious circumstances.[293] In addition, supporting documents must be prepared in such a way that knowledgeable third parties can form an opinion.[294] However, this becomes problematic once these reports are used against the financial intermediary itself and handed over to the public prosecutor's office.[295]

Under certain circumstances, the financial intermediary may have had to provide information that is self-incriminating. However, according to the principle of nemo tenetur se ipsum accusare, no one has to self-incriminate in criminal proceedings.[296] Consequently, accused persons are not obliged to testify.[297] According to the established practice of the Federal Supreme Court, the accused may also not be forced to testify by means of pressure or have their silence used against them as an indication of culpable conduct.[298]

Via a detour, namely the MROS or FINMA, there is thus an obligation for the bank and its employees in certain constellations to incriminate themselves, which is inadmissible under criminal procedure and constitutional law.[299] Finally, the financial intermediary must provide the information. In certain circumstances, however, this would result in self-incrimination. However, the prohibition of the obligation to incriminate oneself is partially undermined here, since Art. 9 AMLA is an administrative law instrument. From the author's point of view, later use of the information obtained on this basis in a criminal trial is out of the question, at least in the case of natural persons. In the case of legal persons, on the other hand, this seems to be permissible.[300] This is particularly the case if there is an obligation under administrative law to produce and retain the relevant documents and to make them available to the authorities upon request.[301]

293 BG 1B_85/2016, E. 4 f.
294 Art. 7 AMLA.
295 Donatsch, 2017: p. 290.
296 Article 6 (1) ECHR.
297 BGE 138 IV 47.
298 BGE 131 IV 36, E. 3.1; BGE 130 I 126, E. 2.1.
299 Donatsch, 2017: p. 290.
300 BGE 142 IV 207, E. 8.3.3.
301 BGE 140 II 384, E. 3.3.4.

The Federal Supreme Court rejects the above argumentation and counters that companies are not human beings and are not therefore granted full human rights. This argumentation would be justifiable if the Federal Supreme Court did not at the same time invoke in connection with Art. 102 CH-StGB the claim that a company can act intentionally (i.e. with knowledge and will). In this respect, a question arises as to whether a pluralism of methods applies.[302]

Finally, the author would like to comment on the protection of legal financial service providers who invest large amounts in their compliance measures every year. The Federal Supreme Court has noted that compliance requirements have increased in recent years, both nationally and internationally.[303] If a bank employee fails to meet their compliance obligations and does not report a money laundering incident to MROS, then both the employee and the bank are punished under the current law.[304] This is particularly true with regard to corporate criminal liability within the scope of Art. 102 CH-StGB.[305] At this point, it becomes clear what problems are associated with the 'outsourcing of criminal prosecution tasks' to private companies.[306] At the same time, however, it is important to bear in mind that Art. 102 CH-StGB has thus far primarily been a problem in theory. From a practical point of view, it can be pointed out that only a fraction of the reports to MROS result in convictions for money laundering within the scope of Art. 305bis CH-StGB or for financing terrorism within the scope of Art. 260^{quinquies} CH-StGB.

The author recommends rethinking the duties of financial service providers and questioning the more than unclear effectiveness of these compliance efforts.[307] Within the framework of this empirical study, it will be shown how easily intelligent perpetrators can circumvent even supposedly sophisticated compliance systems. Therefore, in the field of combating terrorism financing, it is primarily the state that is called upon to act. After all, the fight against terrorism financing has not so far had the desired effect, and a 'de-cluttering' of (financial market) criminal law could possibly provide a remedy.[308] However, it is also fair to point out at this juncture that existing international standards cannot be ignored. Switzerland must adapt to international regulations.

---

302 Donatsch, 2017: p. 290 f.
303 BGE 143 II 162, E. 4.4.3.
304 Donatsch, 2017: p. 291.
305 BG 6B_124/2016, E. 4.
306 Donatsch, 2017: p. 291.
307 Alford, 1993: p. 437 f.
308 Jositsch & von Rotz, 2016: p. 608.

2.1.6 Conclusions

Article 260^{quinquies} CH-StGB can be described as a 'blunt sword' in the fight against international terrorism. First of all, it should be pointed out that the exclusion of contingent intent regulated in Art. 260^{quinquies} (2) CH-StGB makes it virtually impossible to prosecute intelligent perpetrators. As will be shown in the discussion of the empirical results, even without such obstacles on the side of the subjective elements of the offence, it is hardly possible to identify clever terrorist financiers and prove their misdeeds. However, the exclusion of negligence and contingent intent further complicates prosecution.

Now, it could be argued that the restrictions of Art. 260^{quinquies} (2) CH-StGB on the offender's intent should not play too great a role in practice, since in the case of an offence of success, other offences for which contingent intent is sufficient are fulfilled anyway. Although this is conceivable in principle, the requirements for proving causality should not be underestimated. This particularly applies to lone offenders who do not necessarily fall within the scope of Art. 260ter CH-StGB. Finally, in these cases, one would have to provide concrete proof of the causal connection between the financing and the promotion of a particular terrorist act. This too is unlikely to succeed in many cases.

The ratio legis for meeting the high requirements of Art. 260^{quinquies} CH-StGB on the subjective side is understandable – the legislature wanted to prevent legitimate donors from having to fear criminal prosecution for supporting aid organizations. This is a legitimate concern. At the same time, however, it must not be forgotten that completely excluding donors from fulfilling compliance obligations ultimately creates 'fool's freedom' for legitimate donors and terrorist financiers. The latter will always claim to be among the former and to have had no intention whatsoever to fund terrorism. Tolerating this ultimately grants impunity to terrorist financiers. This is unacceptable for reasons of general prevention.

In this context, exculpation under Art. 260^{quinquies} (3) and (4) CH-StGB poses a further problem. Terrorist financiers could claim that they had only the intention of promoting the (re)establishment of the rule of law and democracy. Under these circumstances, it is likely to be difficult to prove that the perpetrator intentionally financed terrorism.

The penalty set out in Article 260^{quinquies} CH-StGB is also rather low. A maximum sentence of five years' imprisonment seems rather low in view of the scope of possible offences and their negative effects. It could be argued that in the case of successfully executed offences, other elements of the offence are fulfilled anyway and thus a higher sentence can be imposed.

However, the purpose of an article in the Swiss Criminal Code cannot be that one must trust that other elements of the offence are fulfilled and thereby solve the problems associated with requirements that are too high on the subjective side and a sentence that is too low. Since the requirements on the subjective side are so high, a higher sentence would be justifiable. Finally, the same would only apply if it were proven that the offender had deliberately financed terrorism.

The AMLA should be viewed positively insofar as it compensates to a certain extent for the problem of intent and imposes higher requirements – at least on persons falling within the scope of the AMLA. At the same time, evasion of the Swiss Criminal Code and a reliance on the AMLA cannot represent the sense and purpose of a norm found in the Swiss Criminal Code.

In summary, it can be stated that adjustments to Art. 260^{quinquies} CH-StGB are necessary in order to make it an effective instrument in the fight against terrorism financing. At the same time, however, no undue expectations should be placed on this article. The following conditions (indicated in bold lettering) could be added to Art. 260^{quinquies} CH-StGB:

Financing of terrorism

1 Any person who collects or makes available assets with the intention of financing a crime of violence intended to intimidate the population or to coerce a State or an international organisation into doing or failing to do something is liable to a custodial sentence not exceeding **ten** years or to a monetary penalty.
2 If the perpetrator merely accepts the possibility of terrorism financing, the penalty is a custodial sentence not exceeding **five** years or a monetary penalty.
3 The act is not considered to be the financing of a terrorist offence if it is aimed at the establishment or restoration of democratic conditions and the rule of law or the exercise of or respect for human rights **and has been authorised by the competent authority.**
4 (1) shall not apply where the financing is intended to support acts which are not contrary to the rules of international law applicable in armed conflicts.

This article would undoubtedly make Art. 260^{quinquies} CH-StGB a more effective instrument in the fight against terrorism financing. In particular, the adjustments highlighted above would at least partially solve the problem of the exclusion of contingent intent.

Differentiating between direct intent and contingent intent or negligence seems appropriate with regard to the level of punishment. This would also make it possible to prosecute offenders who have not demonstrably acted with intent. At the same time, the different levels of penalty would take account of the offender's intent or negligence.

The grounds for exculpation do not constitute an obstacle in the revised form of Art. $260^{\text{quinquies}}$ CH-StGB insofar as § 3 provides for authorization by the competent authorities. It would be conceivable here, for example, to declare MROS competent. The idea behind the authorization procedure is that very few terrorist financiers will disclose the actions they have planned to the authorities.

In view of the potentially far-reaching consequences of the offence, it would appear appropriate to adjust the level of punishment. In particular, for reasons of general and specific prevention, a higher penalty should encourage offenders to refrain from financing terrorism. In addition, it must be ensured that negligent acts are also sanctioned. At the same time, a retributive penalty also appears justified in cases of terrorism financing.

The present proposals for the amendment of Art. $260^{\text{quinquies}}$ CH-StGB do not claim to be ideal but serve as food for thought. Ultimately, Art. $260^{\text{quinquies}}$ CH-StGB has numerous weaknesses that could be at least partially compensated for by the proposed amendments outlined above. At the same time, it must be pointed out that terrorism financing could not be eliminated through the implementation of the aforementioned amendments but only combated somewhat more effectively.

However, since the focus of this study is not on criminal law, but on the concrete procedures of terrorist financiers and their associated implications in terms of criminal procedure, we will refrain from going into more detail on criminal law. Nevertheless, it was necessary to highlight the above-mentioned weaknesses of criminal law in order to provide a suitable basis for a discussion of the empirical results. In particular, the empirical study will show that even in the event of an adaptation of Art. $260^{\text{quinquies}}$ CH-StGB, it is likely to remain difficult to prove that intelligent perpetrators are financing terrorism. This is also in view of the fact that criminal prosecution is and remains a national matter, ultimately, although perpetrators are increasingly acting across borders.

For this reason, the procedures of the perpetrators have been highlighted to suggest ways to relieve the burden on financial service providers. Finally, the compliance measures provided for by law only make sense if they can actually be used to combat the financing of terrorism. However, this is not the case. It is therefore appropriate to critically question the sense and purpose of these measures.

2.2 Literature

While the fight against money laundering has been in investigators' sights since the mid-1980s, that against terrorism financing was only intensified after the events of 11 September 2001 (9/11). The measures taken before 9/11 were not sufficient, which was ultimately reflected in the terrorist attacks that took place.[309] Since the 9/11 attacks, countries around the world have reaffirmed their support for the 'financial war' against terrorism and have taken legislative action to prosecute terrorists and terrorist financiers for their acts.[310] In addition to the military responses to 9/11, many countries focused on measures to combat the financing of terrorism due to the fact that countries with political ties to the USA in particular had to fear terrorist attacks taking place in their own territories.[311] These tasks are global and cannot be handled by a single nation.[312]

There are a variety of possible measures available to combat terrorism, ranging from the calculation of probabilities[313] to protective measures for civil aviation[314] and conventional warfare.[315] Restricting the mobility of terrorists is also often presented as an effective tool.[316] However, combating the financing of terrorism seems to be one of the most sensible and effective approaches to take in this regard.

The logic underlying this approach is plausibly understandable. Terrorism costs money, and terrorists need money to be able to carry out terrorist attacks.[317] The 9/11 terrorist attacks would hardly have been possible without access to the necessary financial resources, and that is why Al-Qaeda has long been the focus of the fight against terrorism financing.[318] After all, Al-Qaeda is often regarded as the prime example of a modern terrorist group.[319]

---

309 Davis, 2003: p. 269 f.; Pieth, 2002: p. 115 f.; Weintraub, 2002: p. 53.

310 Betti, 2006: p. 1104.

311 Dreher & Gassebner, 2008: p. 29.

312 Barrett, 2009: p. 9; Norgen, 2004: p. 201.

313 Pate-Cornell & Guikema, 2002: p. 5 f.; Cox, 2008: p. 1749; Norman, 2010: p. 978; Garrick et al., 2004: p. 129 f.; Parnell et al., 2010: p. 32 f.; Rios et al., 2009: p. 841 f.

314 Von Winterfeldt & O'Sullivan, 2006: p. 63.

315 Lobel, 1999: p. 537 f.; Wedgwood, 1999: p. 559 f.; Campbell, 1999: p. 1067; Travalio, 2000: p. 192 f.

316 Aydinly, 2006: p. 301 f.

317 Freeman, 2011: p. 461.

318 Gurule, 2010: p. 21 f.; Crimm, 2003: p. 1345; Gurule, 2010: p. 52 f.

319 Zöller, 2009: p. 97.

However, it should not be forgotten that the costs of terrorist attacks are not always high. While the 9/11 attacks cost an estimated US$500,000, the costs of everyday attacks, such as those regularly carried out by suicide bombers, are far lower.[320] Finally, the acquisition of small arms and raw materials for bombs sometimes requires only very small amounts of financing.[321] Nevertheless, it is reasonable to assume that even partial success in combating terrorism financing could make it more difficult for terrorists to operate.[322] Thus, it can be reasonably assumed that terrorist attacks can be prevented by combating terrorism financing.[323]

Terrorist groups not only require financial resources to fund their attacks, but they also generally have a significant organizational infrastructure that they have to maintain, which is associated with high costs (e.g. the financing of mercenaries).[324] Terrorist organizations also need to continuously recruit new members to join their forces, which involves advertising costs.[325] The costs of these efforts depend predominantly on the size of the organization and the scope of the respective campaign.[326] Moreover, terrorists operate internationally – consider, for example, the global presence of Al-Qaeda or the IS. The costs of maintaining their organizational infrastructure are usually higher than those of their actual operations (i.e. the terrorist attacks), and weakening this infrastructure can significantly contribute to the fight against terrorism.[327] Funding problems have significantly weakened terrorist organizations in the past.[328]

Moreover, it is often argued that the costs of combating terrorism financing are disproportionate to its benefits. Apart from the fact that this argument obviously does not place too great a value on human life, it is also wrong from an economic point of view. The secondary costs of terrorist attacks are significant,[329] and Al-Qaeda's costs of the 9/11 attacks alone exceeded the US$500 billion estimated by Osama Bin Laden, if one considers the US' retaliation in Iraq and

320 Pieth, 2006: p. 1076.
321 Danziger, 2012: p. 227.
322 Weintraub, 2002: p. 59.
323 Dalyan, 2008: p. 138.
324 Simser, 2011: p. 334 f.; Ganor, 2008: p. 287 f.; Freeman, 2011: p. 462.
325 Jamwal, 2002: p. 181.
326 Bell, 2004: p. 105.
327 Gurule, 2010: p. 73 f.; Gardner, 2007: p. 326.
328 Shapiro & Siegel, 2007: p. 405 f.
329 Frey et al., 2007: p. 1 f.

Afghanistan which has put significant economic strain on these countries and terrorist organizations located there.[330]

Moreover, one should not ignore the possible negative effects of a terrorist attack on a country's economy.[331] The uncertainty associated with terrorist attacks leads to, among other things, a decline in investment. While the benefit to terrorists in the form of political concessions by governments is usually small or non-existent, damage is done nonetheless. This is especially true for financial markets, as in the case of airline stocks after 9/11.[332] However, in the recent past, the markets seem to have recovered quite quickly.[333] In certain circumstances, it has been possible to observe a hardening effect of a terrorist attacks, significantly reducing uncertainty as market participants gain experience in dealing with such scenarios. However, declining consumption has also been observed as consumer behaviour is influenced by terrorism.[334]

Another benefit of the fight against terrorism financing is knowledge gains. In the course of investigating terrorists' financing channels, one often comes across networks of persons who support terrorist groups. Records of the terrorists themselves may lead to conclusions about the use of funds. This can provide insights into the organizational structures of these groups. The terrorists' asset transfers also leave traces that can be analysed years later.[335]

In some circumstances, it can even be helpful to observe known financing channels over a longer period of time in order to gain insights into those behind them.[336] This analysis should not be limited to a few countries, such as Afghanistan, Iraq and Syria, as the region of Southeast Asia also plays an important role. Ultimately, terrorism financing is a global problem.[337]

---

330 Barrett, 2009: p. 8.

331 Brown et al., 2004: p. 861 f.; Kaufmann et al., 1997: p. 83 f.; Gläser & Shapiro, 2002: p. 205; Pizam & Smith, 2000: p. 123 f.; Nitsch & Schumacher, 2004: p. 423; Blomberg et al., 2004: p. 1007 f.; Koh, 2007: p. 129.

332 Abadie & Gardeazabal, 2008: p. 2; Enders & Sandler, 1996: p. 331; Enders et al., 2006: p- 517 ff.; Abrahms, 2012: p. 366 f.; Chesney et al., 2011: p. 253 f.; Eldor & Melnick, 2004: p. 368 f.; Gul et al., 2010: p. 98 f.; Brounen & Derwall, 2010: p. 585 f.; Drakos, 2004: p. 436.

333 Chen & Siems, 2004: p. 350.

334 Arin et al., 2008: p. 164 f.

335 Simser, 2011: p. 336.

336 Simser, 2011: p. 335.

337 Abuza, 2002: p. 428.

At this point, the fight against terrorism financing is obviously worthwhile, especially in light of the fact that states around the world have succeeded in transferring a large part of these costs to private companies — first and foremost, financial service providers. However, this poses a problem because it ultimately means that a public task, namely the fight against terrorism financing, has been placed to a significant extent in private hands.

The legislative measures taken after 9/11 focused in many cases on combating money laundering.[338] This approach was based, among other things, on the assumption that money laundering would also be used for the purposes of terrorism financing.[339] However, this premise is not necessarily based in fact because intelligent perpetrators do not use incriminated assets in order to finance terrorism.

Therefore, differentiating between money laundering and terrorism financing is not only useful but necessary. After all, money launderers and terrorists pursue different goals and use means of different origins. The greatest similarity between terrorism financing and money laundering in these cases is that both offences involve money.[340] Moreover, in both cases, the international financial system is abused for criminal purposes.[341] However, in the case of terrorism financing, no integration of the assets into the economic cycle is necessary.[342] Thus, the literature even speaks of a forced marriage of the fight against money laundering and terrorism financing.[343] This is reflected, among other things, in the fact that legislative measures are often aimed at combating money laundering and terrorism financing.[344]

Money launderers divide their activities into three stages, namely placement, layering and integration. Placement initially involves the mere placement of the incriminated assets. In the context of layering, the aim is to conceal the origin of the incriminated assets. In the context of integration, complete integration into the legal economic cycle should ultimately take place.[345]

While money laundering assets are in principle incriminated and must originate from a predicate offence, legal assets can also be used for terrorism financing. Furthermore, the purpose of money laundering is to integrate incriminated

338 Kersten, 2002: p. 49.
339 Johnson, 2003: p. 10.
340 Roberge, 2007: p. 196 f.
341 Zöller, 2009: p. 612.
342 Tofangsaz, 2015: p. 112 f.
343 Sinha, 2013: p. 142.
344 Hetzer, 2008: p. 561.
345 Zöller, 2009: p. 607.

assets into the legal financial and economic cycle. In contrast, the primary objective of terrorism financing is to be able to use assets for terrorism purposes. Thus, the primary objective is to channel non-incriminated assets to terrorist groups. In simple terms, one could say that terrorism financing involves the use of legal assets for illegal purposes. Money laundering, on the other hand, involves the introduction of incriminated assets into the legal economy. The two phenomena are thus mirror images of each other.[346]

In addition, private companies in particular, especially financial service providers, have been made responsible for preventing terrorism financing.[347] However, they do not always pay attention to sufficient controls and the assumption of responsibility.[348] After all, clever perpetrators could set up a bank and thus avoid having to answer annoying queries from compliance departments. It should also be borne in mind that many measures could merely lead to terrorism financing being shifted to other areas.[349]

An important approach in the fight against terrorism financing is the focus on preventive measures. Ideally, the perpetrators' behaviour can be anticipated and the crime prevented.[350] This is particularly true in view of the fact that terrorists often behave rationally and know the limits of their budgets. Within these limits, utility maximization often takes place. Rational behaviour can be anticipated.[351]

There are numerous microeconomic and macroeconomic approaches to measuring the volume of terrorism financing.[352] However, these approaches will not be discussed here. On the one hand, this is due to the fact that a high number of unreported cases must be assumed and making valid estimates appears to be almost impossible. It is not possible to estimate the volume of terrorism financing even in partial areas, such as that of charitable organizations,[353] and there are no reliable figures from international organizations on which to draw – only vague estimates from journalists and researchers.[354]

On the other hand, estimates of the volume of terrorism financing are not necessary to answer this study's research questions. Finally, it is sufficient to assume

346 Zöller, 2009: p. 612.
347 Barrett, 2011: p. 720.
348 Passas, 2006a: p. 281 f.
349 Gurung et al., 2010: p. 184.
350 McCulloch & Pickering, 2009: p. 628.
351 Li & Schaub, 2004: p. 232.
352 Samantha Maitland Irwin et al., 2011: p. 88.
353 MacMull, 2004: p. 122.
354 Stergiou, 2016: p. 189 f.

that terrorism financing continues to play a significant role for terrorists. The aim of this study is to anticipate the modus operandi of intelligent perpetrators and to strengthen the criminal procedural capabilities of investigators. It must be borne in mind that even low-cost attacks can be very damaging and impactful.[355]

In summary, despite the low costs associated with certain attacks, combating terrorism financing remains important overall.[356] While combating terrorism financing cannot prevent all terrorist attacks from occurring, it can weaken terrorist organizations and help investigative authorities gain valuable intelligence. This is particularly true with regard to the perpetrators' organizational structures.

Basically, there are two starting points for combating terrorism financing. On the one hand, the sources of income must be identified and eliminated. On the other hand, terrorists must be prevented from transferring assets. In doing so, not only must the traditional methods used by terrorist financiers be taken into account but also innovative methods.[357] Ultimately, however, it must also be borne in mind that counter-terrorism is only possible at the international level.[358]

2.2.1 Sources of revenue

Terrorist financiers benefit from a variety of different revenue streams, and they have both legal and illegal sources of income.[359] In addition, donations play a significant role in funding their activities.[360] Skilled terrorist financiers rely on legally acquired assets.[361] Terrorist financiers' revenues can also be categorized according to five criteria, namely quantity, legitimacy, reliability, control and simplicity.[362] Three main categories of funding sources can be identified in the literature: donations, support from states and assets from the commission of general criminal offences. Furthermore, proceeds from legal transactions also appear to play a certain role.[363]

There are states that support terrorist groups for political or religious reasons.[364] State support was once a major source of income for terrorists; however, this has

355 Balasubramaniyan, 2015: p. 482.
356 Acharya, 2009: p. 295.
357 Marrcon, 2008: p. 441; Baldwin, 2005: p. 150
358 Forster, 2003: p. 425.
359 Dalyan, 2008: p. 139.
360 Raphaeli, 2003: p. 59; Croissant & Barlow, 2007: p. 151.
361 Simser, 2011: p. 335.
362 Freeman, 2011: p. 463.
363 Zöller, 2009: p. 613.
364 Zöller, 2009: p. 614.

changed fundamentally since the end of the Cold War.[365] As a result of the pressure exerted by the international community, this support has declined considerably over the past thirty years.

At least since the attacks of 9/11, state support for terrorists has played only a very small role, if any at all. The decline in state support has forced terrorists to adapt their strategies.[366] As a result, terrorists now focus primarily on non-state sources of revenue, such as by gaining financial support through donations from their supporters.[367] In particular, donations from private individuals can play a significant role.[368] These are often gathered in the context of holding cultural events, collecting membership fees for associations or through collection campaigns.[369] Zakat, which is a form of alms in Islam intended to ensure a balance between the poor and the rich, should be considered here.[370] Islam defines who should receive zakat. Among other things, zakat balances the disparity between the wealthy and less wealthy social classes, which serves to maintain social harmony.[371] It is important in this context to remember that the financing of terrorism is prohibited under Sharia law.[372]

Muslim banks often take zakat into account in their transactions. This is especially true for banks that operate under the Sharia legal system. These are not allowed to grant interest. The zakat is forwarded as a donation to charitable organizations. These transactions often take place outside the ordinary books of account and are therefore difficult to trace. This is further complicated by the fact that the relevant banks often destroy the transaction receipts for the zakat.[373] Consequently, charities are often used to channel funds to terrorist groups by functioning primarily as fronts and cover addresses that help to collect, manage and forward funds for terrorist purposes.[374]

However, in order to avoid penalizing honourable and legitimate organizations, a distinction should be made between people who donate intentionally

365 Makarenko, 2004: p. 130.
366 Winer, 2008: p. 114; Hatchinson & O'Malley, 2007: p. 1095.
367 Dalyan, 2008: p. 139; Tierney, 2017: p. 15; Flanigan, 2006: p. 641 f.; Engel, 2004: p. 251 f.; Roy, 2007: p. 162 f.; Hroub, 2006: p. 73.
368 Bierstecker et al., 2007: p. 40 f.
369 Dalyan, 2008: p. 140.
370 Raphaeli, 2003: p. 61 f.
371 Crimm, 2008: p. 580; Zöller, 2009: p. 613.
372 Tofangsaz, 2012: p. 396 f.
373 Zöller, 2009: p. 614.
374 Zöller, 2009: p. 614.

to terrorists and those who actually want to support a charitable cause.[375] It is possible that donations can be misappropriated. Therefore, it is important that both donors and the governing bodies of charitable organizations exercise the necessary caution.[376] Due diligence must ultimately be performed by the donor as well.[377] Finally, the donor may be able to discern whether a charitable organization is pursuing legal or illegal purposes by relying on Internet sites and information from official bodies, for example, for clues, as fraudulent charities certainly exist.[378] Press reports can also be informative.

Furthermore, it must be noted that the black sheep among the charitable organizations are ultimately responsible for honest donors and honourable charitable organizations without terrorist connections being unfairly penalized. Due to the reputational risks associated with donations and the possibility of criminal prosecution, donors have become increasingly cautious.[379] Honourable donors who do not wish to fund terrorism under any circumstances may decide not to donate. This means that honest charities will be disadvantaged by the behaviour of a few bad apples.[380]

However, terrorist organizations are also developing independent fundraising structures that depend less on wealthy individuals and are aimed more at training forces to collect donations abroad. As a result, small donations are collected from unsuspecting donors in many places. For example, a suitably official purpose for gathering funds would be under the guise of supporting Syrian refugees.[381] Subsequently, the money from these unsuspecting donors is transferred to Syria and used to finance IS fighters.

However, there are also donors who are undeterred by the risk. For example, recruits of terrorist organizations, who serve as foreign terrorist fighters, often donate. These individuals travel from abroad to war zones and provide financial support to the troops they join. The exact amounts they contribute are not known, but the literature assumes an average value of US$2,500 per foreign terrorist fighter.[382]

---

375 Abuza, 2003: p. 171; Levitt, 2002: p. 54; Freedman, 2010: p. 1113 f.; Kutty, 2001: p. 25 f.; Carter et al., 2008: p. 42; Roach, 2011: p. 45; Benthall, 2007: p. 6.

376 Crimm, 2003: p. 1342.

377 Crimm, 2004: p. 203 f.

378 Raphaeli, 2003: p. 62 f.

379 Barrett, 2011: p. 723.

380 Othman & Ameer, 2014: p. 96 f.; Piers, 2004: p. 339 f.

381 Basile, 2004: p. 169.

382 Simser, 2011: p. 335.

Furthermore, terrorists seem to make use of legal sources of income as well. Investments in securities and real estate, as well as the sale of publications, play an important role in generating funds.[383] Reports mention investments in the wood and paper industry, hospital facilities, fishing fleets and honey trading.[384] Al-Qaeda's investments in Al-Barakaat's financial and telecommunications empire are mentioned here as an example. Another example of a legal source of income is the Kurdistan Workers' Party (PKK)'s investments in media companies in Europe.[385] The aforementioned problem that incriminated assets also offer starting points for criminal prosecution for money laundering has not escaped the attention of terrorists. They are thus increasingly trying to shift their sources of income to legitimate businesses and companies.[386]

Terrorists have numerous illegal sources of income.[387] In this area, there seems to be a current trend towards regional revenues. On the one hand, terrorists 'tax' the activities of other criminals, such as drug farmers, and they also commit crimes themselves. In doing so, terrorist financiers appear to draw on a wide range of criminal activities.[388] These include smuggling, fraud, theft, drug trafficking, kidnapping, robbery, extortion and money laundering.[389] This brings to mind South American paramilitaries and courier groups, as well as Islamist groups in the Balkans, who have in the past often resorted to narcotics crime to finance themselves. Other groups, such as ETA in the Basque Country, have resorted to kidnapping and then demanding ransom.[390] Al-Qaeda, for example, has kidnapped foreigners in West Africa and extorted ransoms. Boko Haram has stolen cars and robbed banks and jewellery stores.[391] However, fraud appears to be a particularly central source of income for terrorists. In addition, counterfeiting goods also appears to play some role and is becoming increasingly important for terrorists.[392] However, drug trafficking appears to be the most important illicit source of income. In this respect, fundraising by terrorist groups also provides an entry point for prosecution based on money laundering.[393]

---

383 Dalyan, 2008: p. 140.
384 Zöller, 2009: p. 616.
385 Winer & Roule, 2002: p. 89; Roth & Sever, 2007: p. 913.
386 Zöller, 2009: p. 615.
387 Zöller, 2009: p. 614; Simser, 2011: p. 335.
388 Makarenko, 2004: p. 130; Linn, 2005: p. 209.
389 Dalyan, 2008: p. 140.
390 Zöller, 2009: p. 615.
391 Barrett, 2011: p. 723.
392 Perri & Brody, 2011: p. 44 f.; Pollinger, 2008: p. 86; Lowe, 2006: p. 257.
393 Bantekas, 2003: p. 318; Zöller, 2009: p. 615.

Terrorists appear to have close links with organized crime.[394] This link has existed since the end of the Cold War. However, it can be assumed that this link has grown in recent years due to the increasing globalization of crime as well as simplified communication.[395] Terrorists and members of organized crime often prefer the same methods to raise and transfer funds.[396] It should be noted that the organizational and operational structures of terrorist groups and organized crime share certain similarities. For example, investigative authorities force both to decentralize their structures to a certain extent.[397] However, criminals and terrorists often pursue different goals.[398]

Furthermore, there are numerous sources of income that straddle the boundary between legal and illegal. This applies, for example, to so-called hawala shops (i.e. parallel banking systems). The proceeds of these hawala activities are partly used for terrorism financing. Whether hawala activities are legal or illegal ultimately depends on national legislation and how it deals with financial service providers.[399]

Furthermore, terrorist organizations are increasingly assuming state roles in order to finance themselves. This is not only true of IS – Al-Shabaab has, for example, levied taxes on local businesses, demanded customs duties for crossing roads, engaged in trade and maintained a port.[400]

Nor should the role of the Internet in terrorism financing be underestimated. The Internet is of paramount importance to international terrorists. Terrorist groups often have websites, which range from offering an Internet presence in different languages to hosting chat rooms.[401] Consequently, the Internet serves to facilitate international terrorist groups' ability to organize attacks on the one hand and on the other hand to disseminate propaganda and share expertise and ideological convictions. It is thus, in the broadest sense, a PR tool that is used for both advertising and strategic purposes. The boundaries between actual terrorist-motivated criminals and their supporters are blurred.

The Internet can also be seen as a springboard to real, physical terrorism.[402] The Internet can therefore also be used to plan a crime. In this context, the

394 Ridley, 2008: p. 29 f.; Makarenko, 2004: p. 130.
395 Verdugo-Yepes, 2008: p. 3.
396 Shelley & Picarelli, 2005: p. 53
397 Sanderson, 2004: p. 49; Dishman, 2005: p. 237.
398 Shelley & Picarelli, 2002: p. 305 f.; Schmid, 1996: p. 40 f.; Shelley & Melzer, 2008: p. 43 f.
399 Abuza, 2003: p. 171.
400 Barrett, 2011: p. 724.
401 Zöller, 2009: p. 347.
402 Zöller, 2009: p. 357.

Internet plays an important role as a means of communication. Conceivable instruments here include emails, discussion forums, chats and newsgroups, as well as so-called messenger services. There, information can be exchanged decentrally and in real time.[403] Furthermore, the Internet can also be used as a source of information.[404] In addition, the Internet is suitable for the dissemination of terrorism-related content. Along with extensive self-presentation, the recruitment of new members and the collection of funds are also possible over the Internet.[405]

Fundraising is of particular importance for the present work. In this context, appeals for donations are often published on websites. These usually include account information so that any supporters can transfer the desired amounts. There are even Internet shops where missives, propaganda videos or even posters can be purchased and paid for by credit card. In some cases, appeals for donations have even been published on YouTube. Arabic-language videos in particular are posted online.[406] Often, the proceeds collected on the Internet do not go directly to terrorist organizations but first are funnelled to supposed aid or charitable organizations offering financial support for widows and orphans of suicide bombers, for example. Funds are also collected to provide food or school supplies for terrorist trainees. Supporters can even choose whether they would rather invest in military operations or in social causes.[407]

2.2.2 Capital transfer

In addition to significant and continuous sources of income, terrorists need the ability to transfer assets across borders.[408] The numerous money laundering methods available, ranging from real estate to jewellery trading, suggest that terrorist financiers can also resort to many different methods of transferring assets.[409] Nevertheless, the fight against terrorism financing is not hopeless because the financial sector has an important role to play.[410] This is primarily because

403 Zöller, 2009: p. 358.
404 Zöller, 2009: p. 362.
405 Zöller, 2009: p. 373 f.
406 Zöller, 2009: p. 376.
407 Zöller, 2009: p. 377.
408 Fitzgerald, 2004: p. 387 f.
409 Teichmann, 2017c: pp. 130 ff; Teichmann, 2017b: pp. 194 ff; Teichmann, 2016a: pp. 8 ff; Teichmann, 2016b: pp. 154 ff; Teichmann, 2016c: pp. 163 ff; Teichmann, 2016d: pp. 120 ff.
410 Teichmann, 2017a: pp. 95 ff.; Gurule, 2010: p. 151 f.

terrorists have resorted to the banking system in the past to transfer assets. Basically, a distinction must be made between central financial service providers, other financial service providers and non-financial service providers.[411] Central financial service providers are banks. Other financial service providers include asset managers, which are subject to self-regulatory organizations. Non-financial service providers include all institutions that cannot be assigned to either of the former two categories. It should be noted that financial service providers could be involved in the transfer of assets for the purposes of terrorism financing as perpetrators, accomplices or victims.[412]

Financial service providers are fundamentally interested in combating terrorism financing in order to avoid reputational risks and a possible loss of trust.[413] Multinational companies cannot afford the risks associated with violating rules on combating terrorism financing.[414] In addition, financial service providers are suitable for supporting the investigative work of the authorities because they collect data. Banks, for example, know from precisely where their customers have drawn money.[415] Suspicious transactions, such as on the Turkish border with Syria, can provide clues for further investigation.

As a general rule, it should be noted that terrorist financiers may be more likely to operate in retail banking than in private banking because terrorists do not need large assets to fund their attacks.[416] Thus, it is not sufficient to limit the compliance measures of financial service providers to clients with significant assets.

Due to the increasing surveillance of the formal banking system, terrorists are now resorting to other forms of wealth transfer. Among other things, hawala banking plays a decisive role here.[417] A basic distinction is made between national and international hawala banking. It should be noted that hawala banking is often combined with transactions processed through the official banking system. This ultimately further complicates the traceability of transactions. In some circumstances, hawala services also include small loans.[418]

---

411 Dalyan, 2008: p. 140; Schott, 2006: p. 24 f.

412 Barry Johnston & Nedelescu, 2006: p. 7.

413 Beekarry, 2011: p. 152.

414 Zagaris, 2004: p. 153.

415 Barrett, 2011: p. 730.

416 Pieth, 2006: p. 1077.

417 Dalyan, 2008: p. 140.

418 Jamwal, 2002: p. 182; De Goede, 2003: p. 517; Bowers, 2008: p. 379 f.

Hawala structures vary widely and do not have a uniform appearance. They are often found where official banking systems are rather weak.[419] They range from small offices in Southeast Asia to backrooms in Europe.[420] These offices are often based on the reputation of individual hawala bankers.[421] However, these banks usually do not have a banking license and are therefore not subject to any controls.[422] Thus, they are well suited to facilitate criminal activities.[423]

Nevertheless, it should be noted that in most cases, traces of transactions are left behind, as certain transactions are usually documented in hawala banking as well. For example, hawala bankers can be identified by means of so-called settlement transactions, which are conducted between two hawala bankers in different locations to settle their accounts.[424] Due to their fragmented structures, however, they are difficult to infiltrate in any other way, which is why procedures adapted to local conditions appear necessary.[425]

Hawala systems do offer social benefits, and hawala banking is the not only way for terrorist financiers to transfer assets.[426] Despite the lack of infrastructure in countries such as Afghanistan and Somalia, which do not have developed banking systems, hawala banking ought to be regulated nonetheless.[427] At the same time, a question also arises as to how effective the regulation of hawala banking would be.[428]

So-called cash couriers (i.e. the personal transfer of assets) also appear to be gaining importance in terrorism financing.[429] These have been used by Chechens, for example.[430] However, there are also known cases of deliveries to Yemen of foreign currency.[431]

In addition, the money transfer service providers frequently used by migrants must be taken into account. The use of these providers often varies due to local

419 Zagaris, 2007: p. 157 f.
420 Looney, 2003: p. 165.
421 Schaeffer, 2008: p. 95 f.
422 Schneider, 2010: p. 477.
423 Passas, 2005a: p. 112; Wheatley, 2002: p. 347 f.
424 Passas, 2006b: p. 46; Passas, 2005b: p. 172.
425 Pathak, 2003: p. 2061.
426 Viles, 2008: p. 25 f.
427 Passas, 2003: p. 58; Razavy, 2005: p. 277 f.
428 Keene, 2007: p. 185.
429 Dalyan, 2008: p. 140.
430 Ridley, 2008: p. 29 f.
431 Cassella, 2004: p. 285.

cultural circumstances, but it presents a challenge when it comes to combating terrorism financing.[432] Migrants often wish to transfer legitimate assets to their home countries.[433]

Furthermore, the role of the Internet in transferring assets intended for terrorism financing should not be neglected; consider, for example, electronic payment transactions.[434] Ultimately, it is possible for terrorists to launder their assets via the Internet and thus disguise the origins of the funds.[435] Sending funds via the Internet is cheap, anonymous, secure and not tied to any particular location. These are ultimately ideal conditions for terrorist financiers to operate within.[436]

Electronic currencies also pose a challenge in this context. While electronic currencies have been around since the early 2000s, FarmVille Credits and Linden Dollars have been of little use in real life, unlike Bitcoin, which was invented in 2008.[437] Bitcoin, by contrast, appears to be used by terrorist financiers to raise funds.[438] Bitcoin and other electronic payment methods represent a novelty and a significant challenge in the area of terrorism financing.[439] They were not developed by legislators and their legal advisers but by computer scientists. Their transactions are irreversible. Honest behaviour and use at an early stage of development or proliferation are rewarded. Concentration of power is prevented by mechanisms in the algorithm. It is correspondingly difficult to regulate Bitcoin.[440] This is all the more true in light of the fact that in many cases, no value is placed on establishing the identity of the beneficial owner.[441]

In addition, the use of shell corporations for terrorism financing has been considered in the literature, highlighting that corporations could be set up to channel assets. Once these corporations are no longer needed, they can be liquidated. This approach makes particular sense if legal entities can be established with little effort, at a low cost and possibly even without disclosing the beneficial owner.[442] This particularly applies in connection with so-called tax havens.[443]

---

432 Vlcek, 2008: p. 296.
433 Masciandro, 2004: p. 296 f.
434 Jacobson, 2010: p. 358.
435 Hunt, 2011: p. 145.
436 Hinnen, 2004: p. 1.
437 Rice, 2013: p. 1 f.
438 Irwin & Milad, 2016: p. 407.
439 Merlonghi, 2010: p. 202.
440 Böhme et al., 2015: p. 213 f.; Middlebrock & Hughes, 2013: p. 273.
441 Irwin et al., 2012: p. 6 f.
442 Häusermann, 2017: p. 207.
443 Weintraub, 2002: p. 55.

In summary, terrorist financiers have a variety of different methods with which to transfer assets at their disposal. The literature does highlight which approaches might play a role; however, how intelligent perpetrators would have to proceed in order to finance terrorism with as little risk as possible is not demonstrated. Therefore, while the existing explanations can provide an initial indication of the approaches taken by terrorist financiers, they do not provide in-depth insight. Consequently, a research gap has been identified that this study aims to fill. First, however, we will look at counter-terrorism financing organizations in order to show what organizational measures have been taken to date.

2.2.3. Organizations combating the financing of terrorism

In light of increasing globalization, it is not enough to combat terrorism financing at the national level.[444] Ultimately, more intensive international co-operation is necessary to be able to combat terrorism financing more effectively. It cannot be assumed that one state alone could meet this challenge. This can be observed in the freezing of assets at the international level. Consequently, intensive international co-operation is necessary to effectively combat terrorism financing.[445]

The increasing internationalization of the fight against terrorism financing is also due in part to novel methods of wealth transfer. Hawala banking and Bitcoin transactions enable perpetrators to transfer large assets between countries within minutes. In this context, a question arises as to whether cryptocurrencies can ever be compliant with anti-money laundering and terrorism financing provisions. It is obvious that individual countries, whose jurisdiction ends at the national border, can only meet this challenge to a limited extent. In many cases, international co-operation is inevitable. At the same time, international co-operation also helps to improve and further develop national methods that countries can employ to combat terrorism financing.[446]

The Organisation for Economic Co-operation and Development (OECD)'s Financial Action Task Force (FATF) probably plays the most important role in ensuring there is international co-operation in the fight against terrorism financing.[447] Since its foundation in 1989, the FATF has been trying to set new standards in the area of combating terrorism financing.[448] Following the 9/11

444 Beekarry, 2011: p. 149; Gardella, 2003: p. 121
445 McCulloch & Pickering, 2005: p. 486; Gurule, 2010: p. 233 f.
446 Molo & Drzalic, 2019: p. 56.
447 Gilmore, 2004: p. 89 f.
448 Levi et al., 2014: p. 10.

terrorist attacks, the FATF immediately began to seek new ways to combat terrorism financing more effectively.[449]

In particular, the FATF's peer review process plays an important role and has contributed to a continuous strengthening of regulations and their implementation.[450] This is partly because the FATF has succeeded in creating a global network of governmental and non-governmental bodies. Among other things, the FATF helps to continuously develop compliance measures to address the evolution of criminal behaviour. The FATF standards are more a code of conduct than legislative measures.[451] However, they have been widely accepted and implemented around the world.[452] Recently, for example, the Malaysian government has made significant adjustments to combat terrorism financing more effectively. Measures in Lebanon have been similarly successful. Nevertheless, implementing FATF standards remains a challenge for smaller countries with limited resources, like India, which still has a long way to go.[453]

The United Nations also plays a leading role in the fight against terrorism financing at the international level.[454] The UN Security Council Resolutions, the UN List of Names and the Bush Lists are among the most important steps taken in the fight against terrorism financing. The UN Security Council has both built on its existing measures and introduced significant innovations in the aftermath of the 9/11 attacks in 2001.[455]

UN Resolution 1373 is particularly innovative as it obliges states to take certain steps, such as freezing assets of suspected terrorists. Unlike its predecessor, Resolution 1267, the list of suspects is not directed against a specific regime, such as the Taliban or Al-Qaeda, but against terrorists in general. Resolution 1373 is thus innovative because it goes much further than previous resolutions. Resolution 1269 also prohibits all forms of terrorism; however, it does not contain any control mechanisms.[456]

---

449 Pieth, 2006: p. 1074.

450 Beekarry, 2011: p. 143; Bossong, 2012: p. 519 f.; Scott, 1995: p. 1 f.; Stessens, 2001: p. 199 f.

451 Heng & McDonagh, 2008: p. 572.

452 Levi et al., 2014: p. 10; Beekarry, 2011: p. 161; Barrett, 2011: p. 727.

453 Hamin, 2017: p. 6 f.; Shahin, 2013: p. 109 f.; Sheyu, 2010: p. 139 f.; Viritha et al., 2015: p. 2 f.

454 Vlcek, 2006: p. 493.

455 Stromseth, 2003: p. 41.

456 Halberstam, 2002: p. 584; Ward, 2003: p. 290.

It is important to note that these are ultimately only guidelines, and each state can develop and apply its own lists of suspected terrorists or terrorist financiers. The USA also makes its findings available to other states. The terrorist lists published by the UN Security Council are also shared with financial intermediaries. The UN Counter Terrorism Committee also plays a central role in planning further measures.[457]

The International Monetary Fund (IMF) also plays a role in the fight against terrorism financing. Among other things, the IMF monitors the activities of the FATF.[458] Furthermore, the World Bank is also involved.[459] For example, the World Bank and the IMF co-operate in developing measures to support the FATF.[460]

In addition, there are numerous regional organizations combating the financing of terrorism. The following organizations are listed as examples. To avoid confusion, the English-language designation is used in each case:

- Caribbean Financial Action Task Force
- Eurasian Group
- Eastern and Southern Africa Anti-Money Laundering Group
- Intergovernmental Action Group Against Money Laundering
- Asia/Pacific Group on Money Laundering
- Financial Action Task Force of Latin America (GAFILAT)
- Middle East and North Africa Financial Action Task Force (MENAFATF)
- Select Committee of Experts on the Evaluation of Anti-Money Laundering Measures (MONEYVAL)

All of these groups address regional specificities, but it should ultimately be noted that the global standards are set by the FATF.[461] In addition, regional organizations often rely on technocratic support.[462]

Naturally, the European Union has also taken action. Immediately after the 9/11 attacks, the EU expressed its solidarity with the USA in an exceptionally emotionally worded declaration, the so-called 'Joint Declaration on Terrorist Attacks in the US'. Further steps taken by the EU were significantly influenced by the United Nations. For example, EU position 2001/154/CFSP,[463] aiming to freeze

457 FINMA, 2006: p. 1 f.; FINMA, 2017: p. 1 f.; Rosand, 2003: p. 341.
458 Holder, 2003: p. 385; Levi et al., 2014: p. 10.
459 Weintraub, 2002: p. 57.
460 Dalyan, 2008: p. 145.
461 Johnson, 2008a: p. 10.
462 Aufhauser, 2003: p. 303.
463 Den Boer & Monar, 2002: p. 12.

the assets of Bin Laden and his close associates, is based on UN Security Council Resolution 1333.[464]

Finally, it should also be mentioned that the co-ordination of measures to combat terrorism financing often already fails at the national level. For example, the fight against terrorism financing often entails a relaxation of banking secrecy.[465] This also raises the question of what interest a country like the Cayman Islands has in relaxing banking secrecy in order to combat terrorism financing.[466]

Offshore centres often do not have the resources required to successfully implement restrictive compliance rules.[467] However, the fight against terrorism financing could also provide an opportunity to encourage offshore centres in particular to co-operate more profoundly with the rest of the world and correct their past mistakes.[468]

The fight against terrorism financing is a complex matter. It cannot be assumed that a single approach will lead to success. Rather, a combination of different approaches is necessary. Long-term measures are needed that will continue despite changes in personnel.[469] In addition, international co-operation must be strengthened.[470] In particular, the legislative measures to combat terrorism financing should be designed in an internationally uniform manner.[471] The scope for interpreting rules must also be as restrictive as possible in order to ensure legal certainty for financial service providers.[472] The next section will focus on measures to combat terrorism financing.

2.2.4 Measures to combat the financing of terrorism

One of the greatest challenges for investigators is the use of Islamic banks by terrorist groups. First, these Islamic banks are often not within the immediate reach of investigative authorities. They are usually subject to foreign financial supervision and often have no points of contact in the countries where the investigating authorities are based. At the same time, these banks often use the so-called zakat system to generate funds for terrorist groups. They also readily provide so-called

464 Leonard & Kaunert, 2012: p. 117.
465 Clunan, 2006: p. 569; Latimer, 2005: p. 62 f.
466 Waszak, 2004: p. 709.
467 Masciandaro & Portolano, 2003: p. 211.
468 Allen, 2003: p. 309.
469 Hardouin & Weichhardt, 2006: p. 303; Bures, 2010: p. 432.
470 Levitt, 2003: p. 68.
471 Chuckwuemerie, 2006: p. 71 f.
472 Nakajima, 2006: p. 6.

'forwarder accounts' to facilitate the injection of funds. These bank accounts are usually held by what looks to be at first glance unsuspicious organizations, such as charities. In addition, so-called 'operational accounts' are kept, which are managed by particularly trustworthy members of the terrorist group.[473]

Investigations are complicated by the fact that offshore banks help to transfer terrorists' assets. Investigating authorities often do not have direct access to these offshore banks. Furthermore, many offshore banks are considered very secretive. On the one hand, they invoke banking secrecy to advance their business model. On the other hand, they are probably also partly motivated by the desire to avoid having to disclose illegal transactions.[474]

One challenge for investigators that at first glance seems banal (but which in practice also cannot be ignored) is the different spellings of terrorist groups or their supposed charities. Especially in translations, there can easily be more than twenty different spellings used for the same person or organization. This makes database-driven matching much more difficult.[475]

Another significant challenge for investigators is the transfer of assets outside the banking system. Hawala banking is one such example. Here, assets are moved through informal global networks. Hawala bankers conduct only a fraction of their transactions through the formal banking system. Typically, a phone call from one hawala banker to another hawala banker is sufficient to initiate a disbursement to a specific person in another country. Hawala bankers keep records among themselves. However, these records are usually rudimentary in nature and very difficult or completely impossible for investigators to trace. Transactions through the official banking system are carried out only to clear any 'spikes'. However, settlement can also take place in other ways, such as through the transfer of precious stones.[476]

In addition, the smuggling of cash also poses a challenge for investigators. These transactions are mostly untraceable. Messengers are used to transport cash or other assets (gold, diamonds, etc.) across borders.[477] Another challenge is that investigators often do not have the necessary expertise to combat tourism financing. This is due in part to the fact that both the fight against terrorism and the fight against financial crime are two extraordinarily complex matters to

473 Zöller, 2009: p. 616.
474 Zöller, 2009: 616.
475 Zöller, 2009: p. 617.
476 Zöller, 2009: p. 617 f.
477 Zöller, 2009: p. 618.

tackle. In order to be able to effectively combat terrorism financing, specialist knowledge is required with regard to both terrorist and financial structures.[478]

Finally, it should not be forgotten that relatively few financial resources are required to carry out terrorist attacks. While it is true that terrorist organizations require considerable resources to maintain their organizational structure, transfers and other transactions made to and in other countries in order to finance attacks are relatively difficult to identify in international payment transactions.[479] Nevertheless, investigations into these transactions are useful in the fight against terrorism financing. In particular, such investigations provide pertinent information regarding the structures of terrorist groups. Valuable information can be obtained on the basis of payment flows.[480]

There are various measures to combat terrorism financing. In principle, a division into five groups is useful:

- Freezing of assets intended for terrorism financing;
- Implementation and enforcement of regulatory measures to prevent the misuse of the international financial system for the financing of terrorism;
- Implementation of international standards to combat terrorism financing;
- Criminal proceedings against terrorist financiers and their helpers;
- Civil actions by victims of terrorist attacks.[481]

Nevertheless, improving national legislative measures and promoting international co-operation should not be neglected.[482] One problem, however, is that financial service providers may be combating terrorism financing primarily to avoid facing reputational risks and penalties rather than to actually prevent terrorist activities.[483] Finally, a lack of integrity and the breaching of rules by banks are severely sanctioned by the relevant authorities.[484] This leads to reputational risks.[485]

There are criteria that allow banks to identify terrorist financiers at an early stage; some signs are P.O. box addresses or frequently changing addresses, as well as the opening of accounts with cash in amounts ranging from US$3,000 to

478 Zöller, 2009: p. 619.
479 Zöller, 2009: p. 618 f.
480 Zöller, 2009: p. 620.
481 Gurule, 2010: p. 6.
482 Ping, 2008: p. 321.
483 Barrett, 2011: p. 730.
484 Barry Johnston & Carrington, 2006: p. 48.
485 Hardouin, 2009: p. 202.

US$5,000 by supposed students.[486] Asset freezing is considered an important tool in the fight against terrorism financing.[487] However, it should be borne in mind that frozen assets have often had to be unfrozen in the past.[488]

Ultimately, in the fight against terrorism financing, a balance must always be struck between the principles of the rule of law and extending the reach of investigators. At the same time, it should also be borne in mind that the task of combating terrorism financing cannot be entrusted entirely to private companies. This is ultimately a sovereign task of the state.[489]

Consequently, there are considerable doubts as to the effectiveness of the existing measures to combat terrorism financing.[490] The assumption that financial service providers might be able to proactively identify secret preparations for suicide attacks is rather unrealistic. The nineteen terrorists who carried out the 9/11 attacks had opened bank accounts beforehand, but their transactions were in no way illegal or suspicious.[491] Ultimately, the assets transferred by terrorists comprise only a very small fraction of the total amount circulating in the international financial system.[492]

Finally, it should not be forgotten that smaller transactions for the purposes of terrorism financing can get lost in the multitude of everyday transfers. While transaction analyses do take into account anomalies and lead to reviews by compliance officers, it is not reasonable to assume that every transaction will be reviewed in detail. Skilled perpetrators are likely to succeed in plausibly justifying their transfers.

Moreover, it should also be recalled at this point that partnerships between the public administration and private companies primarily promote efficiency but not necessarily security.[493] The privatization of tasks is not unusual in the context of the fight against terrorism; consider, for example, the tasks that were transferred to the American security company Blackwater whose 'contractors' had been sent to Iraq to fight terrorism.[494] However, conflicts of interest inevitably arise.

---

486 Brooks et al., 2005: p. 15.
487 Gurule, 2010: p. 194 f.
488 Tupman, 2009: p. 190 f.
489 Barrett, 2011: p. 730.
490 Levi et al., 2014: p. 9.
491 Pieth, 2006: p. 1077; Barrett, 2011: p. 721.
492 Weintraub, 2002: p. 57.
493 Burres, 2013: p. 451.
494 Abrahamsen & Williams, 2009: p. 1 f.

Banks and the state usually have diverging interests. Banks often intend to maximize their profits. The state, on the other hand, must ensure public safety, among many other things. The latter, however, is ultimately only an indirect interest of banks. The state has created incentives and control mechanisms to mitigate the principal–agent problem that exists at this point. Banks are monitored by the financial supervisory authority (control) and face draconian penalties if they violate the rules (disincentives).

It should also be borne in mind that the banks' compliance measures could exclude individuals from the international financial system.[495] Finally, identifying beneficial owners is time-consuming and expensive. As a result, compliance investigations are likely to turn into a loss-making business for financial service providers in many cases. This is all especially true in regions with economically weak clients, such as large parts of Africa.

Another problem is the transfer of information from public authorities to private companies.[496] Authorities tend to keep information about terrorist activities secret. Exchanging information is important, however, because otherwise banks do not know who is the focus of the authorities' investigators and who might make suspicious transactions.[497] At the same time, this usually secret information must not be leaked to unauthorized third parties. Often, an unofficial exchange of information is also maintained.[498]

The problem of information exchange could be solved by limiting the tasks of financial service providers, for example. Instead of assigning the verification of suspicious transactions to the financial service providers, this task could be assigned to financial intelligence units, and the bank's duty could be limited to the transmission of suspicious data.[499]

However, the fight against terrorism financing cannot be limited to financial service providers. Digital currencies are increasingly posing a challenge for investigators. The situation is similar with parallel banking systems.[500] Cash couriers should not be neglected, either.[501]

495 De Koker, 2006: p. 27 f.
496 Barrett, 2011: p. 729; Kunreuther et al., 2003: p. 6.
497 Forman, 2006: p. 112 f.
498 Favarel et al., 2011: p. 191.
499 Gordon, 2010: p. 565.
500 Hett, 2008: p. 2; Gardella, 2003: p. 134 f.
501 Barrett, 2011: p. 720.

It is also important to continuously monitor the non-profit sector.[502] Ultimately, charities need to be more regulated. This may also lead to legitimate charities receiving fewer donations. Nevertheless, it is important to ensure that donations do not flow to terrorist organizations. This is especially true with regard to the tax deductibility of donations.[503]

It is important that charities are monitored at the international level. Qatar, for example, has already made progress in this regard, but the system there still has significant weaknesses.[504] It is up to the international community to put pressure on countries with weaker compliance measures while offering support, particularly in view of the fact that, as a rule, a few weak links in the compliance chain are enough to make the system very vulnerable.

This also raises a question regarding whether legislative measures should be taken to stop the spread of new currencies that could be suitable for terrorism financing.[505] It is important that the regulatory measures taken to combat terrorism financing are continuously adapted. Developments such as new currencies must also be taken into account.[506]

Furthermore, it is important to hold accountable any natural or legal person who directly or indirectly finances terrorism. This also applies to companies that place advertisements on networks associated with terrorists.[507]

There is also a question surrounding how international efforts can be unified and actually applied, although legislative sovereignty rests with the individual states.[508] However, if the efforts are not unified, the costs will be high and the benefits could be low, as possibilities for circumvention will remain.[509] The persistence of circumvention possibilities and inconsistent procedures has led to significant delays in the past.[510] It is therefore important that the measures to combat terrorism financing are actually implemented and that opportunities for circumvention are eliminated.[511] Finally, it is in the interest of all states to combat terrorism financing in order to protect their own interests.[512]

---

502 Mitsilegas & Gilmore, 2007: p. 131; Baron, 2004: p. 1 f.
503 Ruff, 2005: p. 447; Herzfeld, 2003: p. 875 f.
504 Truby, 2016: p. 500 f.
505 Mitsilegas & Gilmore, 2007: p. 131.
506 Gardella, 2003: p. 134.
507 Barkin, 2003: p. 193.
508 Dalyan, 2008: p. 145; Szasz, 2002: p. 53.
509 Johnson, 2008b: p. 62.
510 Thony & Png, 2007: p. 164.
511 Malkawi & Malkawi, 2007: p. 180 f.
512 Elu & Price, 2012: p. 32.

However, no exaggerated expectations should be placed on the fight against terrorism financing. Ultimately, this is not a panacea but an instrument that should be combined with other approaches, such as classic surveillance measures.[513]

In the fight against terrorism, criminal law must be supplemented with criminal procedure measures. In particular, possibilities for clandestine criminal procedural measures must be created, and there is even talk of developing special criminal procedural law for the purposes of combating terrorism.[514]

That the rule of law must be respected in the context of the fight against terrorism financing should also be pointed out.[515] This is particularly salient because special powers are often granted to the authorities in view of the risk of a terrorist attack. A question arises as to what the measures to combat terrorism financing mean for democracy and human rights.[516] In the past, the presumption of innocence in particular ceased to be given its due consideration.[517] However, the impact of the measures taken on banks and their clients must not be neglected. Here, there may be significant restrictions on possible business relationships.[518]

2.3 Research gap, research questions and research objective

A significant research gap was discovered when carrying out the literature review. Specifically, it was found that measures to combat terrorism financing have been outlined in detail and there are also numerous articles on the organizations entrusted with combating terrorism financing. However, the literature on terrorists' sources of income and the possibilities for the transfer of assets by terrorist financiers is rather sparse.

Above all, the literature has not yet sufficiently investigated how perpetrators must proceed in order to finance terrorism with as little risk as possible to

---

513 Sproat, 2010: p. 331.

514 Petzsche, 2013: p. 229.

515 Baldwin, 2004: p. 245; Sadat, 2004: p. 154 f.; Choi, 2010: p. 940 f.; Fiss, 2006: p. 235; Scheuermann, 2006: p. 61 f.; van Munster, 2004: p. 141 f.; Ruebner, 2002: p. 493 f.; Dragu & Polborn, 2014: p. 511 f.

516 Peers, 2003: p. 235; McCulloch et al., 2004: p. 74; Fitzpatrick, 2003: p. 241 f.; Alonso & Reinares, 2005: p. 265 f.; Luban, 2002: p. 9 f.; Gearty, 2005: p. 18 f.; Dreher et al., 2010: p. 65 f.; Warbrick, 2004: p. 989 f.; Foot, 2007: p. 489 f.; Gross, 2001: p. 89 f.

517 McCulloch & Carlton, 2005: p. 398.

518 Goldby, 2010: p. 364.

themselves and what the implications are for criminal procedure law in Germany, Liechtenstein, Austria and Switzerland. This work aims to close this gap.

Consequently, this book is concerned with investigating the following research questions:

- What sources of revenue can terrorists use?
- How do terrorists transfer assets?
- What tools are available to investigators in Germany, Liechtenstein, Austria and Switzerland to combat terrorism financing?
  - What difficulties arise for investigators in Germany, Liechtenstein, Austria and Switzerland in connection with digital surveillance?
  - What difficulties arise for investigators in Germany, Liechtenstein, Austria and Switzerland in connection with undercover agents?
- How can the tools used by investigators in Germany, Liechtenstein, Austria and Switzerland be improved upon?

The objective of this research is to anticipate the modus operandi of intelligent terrorist financiers and to develop suggestions for the Swiss legislature in order to promote a more effective fight against terrorism financing. In doing so, the concrete approaches taken by perpetrators will be illuminated, along with the difficulties that exist for investigators in terms of criminal procedure and how these could be eliminated.

3. Empirical investigation

3.1 Research methodology

The methodological approach is divided into several steps. This takes into account the fact that it is difficult to anticipate the concrete modus operandi of terrorist financiers. Thus, as part of a preliminary study, interviews were conducted with providers of illegal financial services (i.e. those facilitating the acts of alleged terrorist financiers). Subsequently, as part of the main study, the results of the preliminary study were examined in more detail in semi-structured expert interviews. This provided the basis for a comparative legal study. The main focus of the preliminary and main studies was to empirically investigate the sources of income and transfer possibilities available to terrorist financiers and the resulting difficulties these pose for investigators. Based on these empirical results, a functional comparative law analysis was then conducted to determine the extent to which changes in the law would make it possible to combat terrorism financing more effectively.

This three-stage model makes sense and is necessary insofar as it would not be expedient to limit oneself to a functional comparison of laws. Finally, solutions-oriented proposals for changes in the law can only be made if there has been an in-depth analysis of the problem and why the previous solutions have failed. At the same time, however, it is not very useful to merely point out how intelligent terrorist financiers operate. After the procedures have been explained, possible solutions leading to a more effective fight against terrorism financing will be proposed.

In the following, each of the three stages of the analytical model on which this study is based is analysed in depth. In particular, how the author approached the research and the research methods that were applied will be demonstrated while acknowledging that this is not intended to serve as a textbook on the methodological approach and therefore the explanations will be limited to the essentials.

3.1.1 Preliminary study

Terrorist financiers and their helpers (i.e. providers of illegal financial services) are ideally suited to reporting on their concrete procedures themselves, as they can draw on their personal breadth of experience to offer examples. However, these individuals fear facing criminal consequences for owning up to their activities and are therefore generally unwilling to share their extensive knowledge with researchers. This is especially true with regard to possibly being tape recorded, although this would allow for a more detailed evaluation to take place.

It is therefore natural to conduct informal interviews with such individuals. In this preliminary study, fifteen informal interviews were conducted with providers of illicit financial services to explore (a) the sources of income that terrorists use and (b) how they transfer their funds.

Table 1: Interview partners

Interview partners	Industry	Country	Interview language
Interviewee 1	Justice	Russia	Russian
Interviewee 2	Financial services	Italy	Italian
Interviewee 3	Consulting	Russia	Russian
Interviewee 4	Justice	Russia	Russian
Interviewee 5	Financial services	Switzerland	German
Interviewee 6	Diamond trade	Italy	Italian
Interviewee 7	Consulting	Kazakhstan	Russian
Interviewee 8	Consulting	Dubai	English
Interviewee 9	Financial services	Liechtenstein	German
Interviewee 10	Consulting	Germany	German
Interviewee 11	Justice	Ukraine	Russian
Interviewee 12	Financial services	Austria	German
Interviewee 13	Consulting	Russia	Russian
Interviewee 14	Consulting	Russia	Russian
Interviewee 15	Consulting	Monaco	Italian

The interview partners (see Table 1) were selected on the basis of their professional expertise and personal experience. The author deliberately chose interview partners from various countries outside the field of investigation of this study, which focuses on Germany, Liechtenstein, Austria and Switzerland, since terrorism financing is generally a transnational crime. However, only interview partners who involved at least one of the countries examined in this study in their approach were selected because how perpetrators proceed elsewhere, such as in South America and Asia, is of only limited relevance to the fight against terrorism financing in Germany, Liechtenstein, Austria and Switzerland. How terrorist financiers and their auxiliaries from Kazakhstan, Russia or Dubai use the countries examined in this study as they carry out their activities is certainly relevant to this research, and thus it was highly appropriate to conduct interviews with these individuals.

For confidentiality reasons, it is not possible to provide more detailed information about the interview partners, as the author has committed to maintaining their anonymity and wishes to continue this scientific work going forward. The conversations were conducted openly (i.e. without an interview guide) and took place in informal settings. The answers were recorded using memory protocols. This approach is not optimal in terms of the research methodology, as memory protocols are obviously incomplete and may be biased in terms of the content recalled. Thus, they are not comparable to detailed transcriptions of tape recordings and offer far fewer possibilities for sound analysis. At the same time, for the reasons explained above, they represent the only possibility for collecting data in the closest environments of terrorist financiers that can subsequently be verified in expert interviews with investigators, advisors and compliance experts.

The informal expert interviews were conducted with persons who could be assumed to have experience with or knowledge of illegal financial services. The subject of the interviews, however, was not on any specific offences – the interviews merely focused on hypotheses about possible modus operandi of intelligent perpetrators. The author did not learn of any specific crimes during the interviews. Nevertheless, the interview partners were assured anonymity. Prior to the interviews, the interview partners were informed about the purposes of the research and asked not to talk about specific crimes or reveal any personal details. This prevented the author from otherwise being mistaken for an undercover investigator. Moreover, if the author had become aware of criminal offences (e.g. those representing a concrete danger to life and limb) in the course of his research, it would have been essential from his point of view to inform the competent authorities. Since the conversations held were exclusively for research purposes and did not take place in the context of an investigation, no specific criminal offences were discussed at any time.

3.1.2 Main study

Qualitative research methods also appear to be particularly suitable for the main study due to its exploratory nature.[519] Since this is a new field that has not yet been investigated in depth, no prior hypothesis generation was possible. The findings of the preliminary study, while valuable and helpful in planning the main study, were ultimately not detailed enough to be used as a basis for hypothesis formation. Recording the interviews held during the preliminary study was not possible for the reasons explained above, and thus the analysis may be of limited

519 Creswell, 2013: p. 183 f.; Crouch & McKenzie, 2006: p. 483 f.; Bowen, 2005: p. 208 f.

use to readers. Due to the exploratory nature of this study and the lack of a basis for solid hypothesis development to take place, carrying out a quantitative main study seemed rather unlikely.[520]

In order to examine the results of the preliminary study in more detail and to compensate for the research's methodological weaknesses, a total of fifteen exploratory expert interviews were conducted that could be recorded. A theory- and rule-driven approach was chosen in order to build on existing theoretical knowledge and to allow the expert community to reconstruct how the author arrived at the results.[521] The goal of these exploratory expert interviews was to provide initial access to a new field and to concretize and structure in a meaningful way certain processes for solving a scientific problem.[522] A quantitative investigation would have been unsuitable for the purposes of this study due to its lack of openness and the exploratory approach necessary in casu.[523]

The findings of the main study can serve as a basis for the formation of new hypotheses.[524] The objective was to develop a sound theoretical understanding of terrorism financing that could serve as a basis for more effective crime prevention.[525] The principle of openness was taken into account, and, above all, great importance was attached to remaining open to new information both during the interviews and in the course of the subsequent analysis.[526]

The interview partners were selected for their particular expertise in the field of terrorism financing.[527] Who was deemed a suitable expert was ultimately determined by the specific research interest of the present study and the social representativeness of the expert.[528] In order to gain in-depth insight, it was necessary to interview carefully selected experts. Laypersons are generally not familiar with the compliance mechanisms of financial service providers or the procedures of terrorist financiers and would therefore only have been able to provide limited information on these topics.[529]

---

520 Tewksbury, 2009: p. 901 f.; Tewksbury et al., 2010: p. 391 f.; Buckler, 2008: p. 383 f.
521 Gläser & Laudel, 2010: p. 31.
522 Froschauer & Lueger, 2003: p. 17.
523 Kracauer, 1952: p. 631; Myers, 1997: p. 241 f.
524 Bogner et al., 2015: p. 23.
525 Froschauer & Lueger, 2003: p. 19.
526 Gläser & Laudel, 2010: p. 30.
527 Creswell, 2013: p. 189 f.
528 Bogner et al., 2015: p. 11.
529 Gläser & Laudel, 2010: p. 117.

In particular, it was necessary to interview experts who, based on their practical and experiential knowledge in the area of terrorism financing, had the ability to meaningfully structure the field of action and address specific problem areas.[530] It was therefore important to select experts who could go beyond the findings of the existing literature and draw on existing, systematized empirical knowledge about the concrete approaches taken by terrorist financiers.[531]

It was therefore of fundamental importance to check in advance which experts were familiar with the topic of terrorism financing. Finally, the interview partners needed to possess the necessary information and knowledge to contribute to this research.[532] This was achieved through a literature review and Internet searches.[533]

The selection of the interview partners also took into account which of them were accessible.[534] Some experts could also be recruited from the author's personal network that was formed by carrying out scientific research in this field in the past. This made it considerably easier to get past gatekeepers such as administrative assistants.[535] In all cases, contact was made in writing and those contacted were provided with information about the aims of the research.[536] A brief explanation of why the participant being recruited had been selected as being particularly suitable for the present study was also included.[537]

Being able to gather a sufficient amount of data is important to ensure the reliability of the study results.[538] Statistical methods are of very limited use in primarily qualitative studies, which is why – in addition to practical reasons – theoretical saturation was the primary consideration when selecting the number of suitable interview partners.[539] Interviews were conducted until statements began to be repeated. In particular, the following fifteen people were interviewed (see Table 2):

530 Bogner et al., 2014: p. 13.
531 Froschauer & Lueger, 2003: p. 53.
532 Gläser & Laudel, 2010: p. 117.
533 Bogner et al., 2014: p. 35.
534 Froschauer & Lueger, 2003: p. 64.
535 Bogner et al., 2014: p. 37.
536 Gläser & Laudel, 2010: p. 162.
537 Froschauer & Lueger, 2003: p. 66.
538 Creswell, 2012: p. 52.
539 Gläser & Laudel, 2010: p. 100; Marshall, 1996: p. 522 f.; Rosenthal, 2005: p. 85 f.

Table 2: Interview partners

Interview partners	Industry	Country	Interview language
Interviewee 1	Money transfer services	Germany	German
Interviewee 2	Consulting	Switzerland	German
Interviewee 3	Banking	Germany	German
Interviewee 4	Antiques trade	Germany	German
Interviewee 5	Prosecutor's office	Switzerland	German
Interviewee 6	Financial market authority	Austria	German
Interviewee 7	Consulting	Switzerland	German
Interviewee 8	Banking	Germany	German
Interviewee 9	Investigative agency	Germany	German
Interviewee 10	Investigative agency	Austria	German
Interviewee 11	Financial market authority	Switzerland	German
Interviewee 12	Banking	Germany	German
Interviewee 13	Financial intelligence unit	Liechtenstein	German
Interviewee 14	Consulting	Switzerland	German
Interviewee 15	Ministry of Finance	Austria	German

As Table 2 shows, experts working for financial service providers, consulting firms and investigative and supervisory authorities were interviewed to allow different perspectives to be taken into account. As some of the interviewees work in very exposed positions, all statements are presented anonymously.[540] Finally, it was important to ensure that the interview partners would not be harmed by the publication of the results.[541] Therefore, it was imperative to take an ethical approach to describing the results.[542]

Furthermore, it was important to collect the correct data and to query it throughout the interviews.[543] During the interviews, primarily procedural and interpretive knowledge was requested because technical knowledge (i.e. data and facts) could be obtained from other sources, and data and facts on the volume of terrorism financing have only limited value since the actual extent of terrorism financing is likely to be difficult to assess.[544] It can be assumed that the number

540 Bogner et al., 2014: p. 89.
541 Gläser & Laudel, 2010: p. 50.
542 Creswell, 2012: p. 56.
543 Creswell, 2013: p. 189.
544 Bogner et al., 2014: p. 18.

of unreported cases is high, which is why the investigators' case numbers do not play a major role in this study. This study assumes that illegal financial services providers who are dedicated to facilitating terrorism financing are both intelligent and educated.[545] Ultimately, the aim of this study is to anticipate the methods used by intelligent perpetrators financing terrorism because these have not yet attracted much scholarly attention.

Interview partners' statements are often influenced by the context of the interview[546] and depend on perceptions of the interviewer's professional competence and a normative evaluation thereof.[547] It is the job of the interviewer to guide the conversation and encourage the reproduction of knowledge without distorting the results.[548] In this study, the interviewer established himself as a co-expert in order to promote the exchange of knowledge and information on an equal footing.[549]

Several topics had to be covered in the course of the interviews, which is why it was obvious to develop a guideline.[550] In order to ensure that the semi-structured expert interviews were conducted properly, the guide presented in Appendix 2 was developed. This served to ensure optimal preparation and implementation.[551] By choosing a semi-structured interview guide, the questions were defined ex ante, but the interviewee was given sufficient freedom to answer them as they wished.[552] This was particularly necessary because this study was exploratory and the interviewer could therefore not know ex ante which areas might be particularly relevant from the experts' points of view.

The interviews conducted can be roughly divided into three phases, namely the interview initiation, the narrative and inquiry phase and the interview conclusion. While the establishment of a relationship of trust was the main focus of the initial phase of the interview, and the narrative and inquiry phase formed the main part of the interview, any gaps were closed in the conclusion of the interview. This division ensured an optimal flow of the interview and the most comprehensive data collection possible.[553]

545 Raghavan & Balasubramaniyan, 2012: p. 294 f.
546 Gläser & Laudel, 2010: p. 111 f.
547 Bogner et al., 2014: p. 51.
548 Gläser & Laudel, 2010: p. 112.
549 Bogner et al., 2014: p. 52.
550 Gläser & Laudel, 2010: p. 111.
551 Bogner et al., 2014: p. 27.
552 Gläser & Laudel, 2010: p. 41.
553 Froschauer & Lueger, 2003: p. 69 f.

Since this is not a quantitative study, the questions in the individual interviews were adapted to suit the context. However, this did not impair comparability.[554] Particularly relevant topics were also revisited in the final phase of the interview.[555]

The questions were also partly adapted to apply to the respective interview partner based on the principle of openness.[556] For example, it made more sense to look at certain aspects of money transfer service providers in more detail by asking questions of a compliance officer working for a money transfer service provider than it would have to have asked other interview partners the same questions. Furthermore, the order of the questions was also adjusted depending on how the interview progressed by ensuring that it flowed as naturally as possible.[557] Ultimately, the order in which the topics were discussed was irrelevant.

The expert interviews were audio-recorded with the explicit consent of the interview partners and subsequently transcribed in full.[558] This was to avoid the loss of information associated with memory transcripts. The material for analysis is thus available in the form of a written text. Refining the statements was generally avoided here in order to ensure that the interview partners' statements were as authentic as possible. Ultimately, any refinement would have involved a certain degree of discretion, which would have potentially distorted the results.[559]

Recording conversations can make interview partners feel insecure, making them sometimes reticent to reveal all of their knowledge.[560] After the end of the official interview and the associated switching off of the recording device, the interview partners were then given the opportunity to add further statements in an informal conversation. The knowledge gained in these informal conversations was recorded in post-interview memos. In addition, the interview context was also documented.[561] This was to ensure that the findings were as comprehensive as possible.

In the next step, the information collected in the interviews had to be evaluated.[562] It was important not to falsify the interview partners' statements. This depended significantly on the skills of the author.[563] Information was

554 Bogner et al., 2014: p. 28.
555 Froschauer & Lueger, 2003: p. 73.
556 Gläser & Laudel, 2010: p. 150.
557 Bogner et al., 2014: p. 29.
558 Creswell, 2013: p. 193 f.; Gläser & Laudel, 2010: p. 157.
559 Mayring, 2010: p. 53; Bogner et al., 2014: p. 40 f.
560 Creswell, 2013: p. 193.
561 Bogner et al., 2014: p. 59; Bogner et al., 2014: p. 61; Froschauer & Lueger, 2003: p. 74.
562 Bogner et al., 2014: p. 72.
563 Creswell, 2013: p. 194 f.; Pope et al., 2000: p. 114 f.

systematically extracted from the texts. Furthermore, information that was not relevant for the purposes of this study had to be removed. The content of the interviews was therefore analysed in a systematic, rule- and theory-based manner.[564] The analysis of the interviews was based on qualitative content analysis according to Mayring (2010).[565] This analysis offers the possibility to systematically process large amounts of text.[566] Categories are at the heart of qualitative content analysis, and it is important to define the exact procedure ex ante.[567]

In qualitative content analyses, a graduated procedure is applied.[568] First, the units of analysis are determined. Then, the content-bearing elements of the text are paraphrased. Then, the level of abstraction is determined, and the paraphrases are generalized at this level. The next step is an initial reduction phase in which meaningless paraphrases are deleted. In the following reduction phase, the statements are clustered at the desired level of reduction. Furthermore, a category system is formed, which is checked in the last step on the basis of the source material.[569]

This procedure was facilitated by using the analysis software MAXQDA.[570] First, relevant original statements were selected as units of analysis.[571] Subsequently, these statements were paraphrased in a two-stage process. In the first stage of paraphrasing, gross errors were removed. In the second stage of paraphrasing, unnecessary information was deleted and the sentence was rephrased. In the subsequent generalization stage, the statement was reduced to its core content. The following examples are intended to illustrate the procedure:[572]

564 Gläser & Laudel, 2010: p. 206; Creswell, 2013: p. 194 f.; Graneheim & Lundman, 2003: pp. 105 ff.

565 Mayring, 2010: p. 13 f.

566 Froschauer & Lueger, 2003: p. 111.

567 Mayring, 2010: p. 49; Hsieh & Shannon, 2005: p. 1286.

568 Froschauer & Lueger, 2003: p. 99.

569 Mayring, 2010: p. 68.

570 Froschauer & Lueger, 2003: p. 92.

571 Elo & Kyngäs, 2008: p. 110.

572 Please note that the statements were originally made in German and translated for the purpose of the demonstration.

Example 1:

Original statement:

I think that's another area where perhaps there's a weakness in counter-terrorism financing, that the regulators or investigators are actually too slow. (Interviewee 8)

Paraphrasing 1:

I think a weakness of terrorism financing is that regulators or investigators are too slow.

Paraphrasing 2:

One weakness of counter-terrorism financing is that regulators or investigators are too slow.

Generalization:

Investigative agencies are too slow.

Example 2:

Original statement:

And the/just these splinter groups, these attackers from Paris and Brussels, probably now also in Istanbul, that's not costly, a few thousand euros that they need to buy their resources, so to speak, to pay rent, to buy food. The weapons are also not terribly expensive. You can do it for a few thousand euros. (Interviewee 14)

Paraphrasing 1:

These splinter groups, these attackers of Paris and Brussels, probably also in Istanbul, that's not costly, a few thousand euros that they need to buy resources, so to carry rent, to buy food. The weapons are not insanely expensive either. You're in for a few thousand euros there.

Paraphrasing 2:

The splinter groups in Paris, Brussels and Istanbul only need a few thousand euros to buy food and pay the rent. Weapons are not particularly expensive either. A few thousand euros is enough.

Generalization:

Strikes are not costly.

<u>*Example 3:*</u>

Original statement:

First of all, yes, one has a primary goal. The IS, the Islamic State, wants to finance itself. It's not exactly thinking, 'what happens if there's an investigation somewhere?' (Interviewee 9)

Paraphrasing 1:

One has a primary goal. The Islamic State wants to fund itself. IS doesn't think about what happens if there's an investigation going on somewhere.

Paraphrasing 2:

The Islamic State's primary goal is to fund itself. This does not take into account any possible investigation.

Generalization:

Investigative procedures do not deter offenders.

The next step was the reduction and the development of the category system. The category system developed in this thesis is not explicitly based on the literature review presented in Chapter 2.2 but was developed inductively on the basis of the interviews.[573] Namely, themes frequently mentioned by the interview partners were first marked in the text. Each relevant statement made by the interview partners was assigned to one of the following categories. Statements that were more general in nature and applicable to multiple revenue streams or transfer opportunities were grouped into the 'general statements' category.[574] Thereafter, both revenue sources and transfer opportunities were considered in greater depth. Finally, instruments for combating terrorism financing were discussed:

<u>General statements</u>

- Capital transfer
- Revenue sources
- Perpetrator
- Investigative authorities
- Necessary measures

573 Mayring, 2010: p. 83; Fereday & Muir-Cochrane, 2006: p. 80 f.

574 Vaismoradi et al., 2013: p. 404.

Revenue sources

- Legal
  - Real estate
  - Stock exchange transactions
  - Trade
- Illegal
  - 'Taxes'
  - White-collar crime
  - Organized crime
  - Petty crime
- Challenges for investigators

Transfer options

- Banking system
  - General suitability
  - Concrete procedure
  - Detection risks
- Parallel banking systems
  - General suitability
  - Concrete procedure
  - Detection risks
- Personal transfer
  - General suitability
  - Concrete procedure
  - Detection risks
- Cryptocurrencies
  - General suitability
  - Concrete procedure
  - Detection risks
- Money transfer systems
  - General suitability
  - Concrete procedure
  - Detection risks

Counter-terrorism instruments

- Undercover investigators
- Digital surveillance

- Administrative and judicial assistance
- Trade secrets

General statements on terrorism financing are considered first in order to provide a basis for the further findings and to explain the logic underlying the formation of further categories. For example, the statements on perpetrators help explain why trivial ways of looking at things were out of the question. Subsequently, how terrorists finance themselves and how they transfer their assets is presented. Last but not least, the suggestions for improvement in order to more effectively fight terrorism (as mentioned by the interview partners) are highlighted to create a basis for the comparative law study.

Section 4 reproduces numerous quotations from the interviews, making it clear from which statements the results were obtained.[575] In addition, quotations help to present further information and thus make the results appear more vivid.[576]

Finally, the quality of the present study must be assessed.[577] In order to be able to assess the quality of the empirical investigation, it is helpful to be able to judge whether and to what extent a thorough treatment of the research question was successful by means of a consideration of the course of the investigation.[578] In doing so, it should be taken into account that no absolutely accurate and exclusively valid interpretation of the findings was possible. Nevertheless, the results of the study show considerable objectivity, reliability and validity.[579] This was particularly checked within the framework of a reflective analysis by the author as well as through triangulation.[580]

The next step is to interpret the results of the main study.[581] Based on the interpretation of the results, a functional comparative law study will analyse the extent to which adjustments to the Code of Criminal Procedure could combat terrorism financing more effectively. In doing so, both the sources of income and the transfer possibilities of terrorist financiers will be taken into account, and the approaches for improvement proposed by the experts will be analysed in detail.

---

575 Please note that these statements were translated from German into English.

576 Gläser & Laudel, 2010: p. 274; Sandelowski, 1994: p. 479 f.

577 Creswell, 2013: p. 201.

578 Bogner et al., 2014: p. 93; Thomas & Magilvy, 2011: p. 151 f.

579 Froschauer & Lueger, 2003: p. 103; Mayring, 2010: p. 51; Morse et al., 2002: p. 13 f.; Healy & Perry, 2000: p. 118 f.; Mays & Pope, 2000: p. 50 f.; Whittemore et al., 2001: p. 522 f.; Rolfe, 2006: p. 304 f.

580 Creswell & Miller, 2000: p. 127.

581 Gläser & Laudel, 2010: p. 268.

3.1.3 Criminal procedural issues

The aim of this book is to make recommendations for legislative measures in Switzerland based on the results of the empirical study through an explicit comparison with other countries.[582] Such a comparison forms the basis for possible reforms. This should lead to a strong theoretical and practical standing.[583] The aim is to apply as broad an approach as possible, in that not only is a strict comparison of rules carried out but the applicability of these rules in practice can also be taken into account.[584]

Unlike those found in other approaches, such as comparative law studies for anthropological purposes, the focus of this book is on developing solutions to a practical problem identified in the main study.[585] Excessive theorizing is therefore refrained from to preserve the practical relevance of the book – particularly the focus on solving specific problems.[586]

In principle, considering the examples provided by other legal systems is helpful in developing proposals for legislative measures. The overlaps between different legal systems as a result of globalization can lead to significant progress.[587] Both established principles and innovative approaches can be taken into account.[588] This is particularly the case with regard to social change and associated societal changes.[589] At the same time, it should also be taken into account that many countries have societal commonalities and could thus apply the same or similar rules in certain circumstances.[590] Examining other legal systems can therefore help to develop new approaches; however, a single standard approach to comparative law analysis does not exist.[591]

First of all, the research question must be defined.[592] In casu, the aim is to examine how the legal systems in Germany, Liechtenstein, Austria and

582 Reitz, 1998: p. 618.
583 Chodosch, 1998: p. 1027; Hill, 1989: p. 102; Ewald, 1995a: p. 2139.
584 Van Hoecke & Warrington, 1998: p. 495 f.
585 Sacco, 1991: p. 1 f.
586 Markesinis, 1990: p. 1 f.
587 Riles, 1999: p. 222; Choudry, 1998: p. 819 f.; Slaughter, 1999: p. 1103 f.; Gerber, 2000: p. 949 f.; Twining, 1999: p. 217 f.; Blackett, 1998: p. 57 f.
588 Fletcher, 1998: p. 684.
589 Kahn-Freund, 1974: p. 4.
590 Watson, 1978: p. 315; Ewald, 1995b: p. 489 f.; Mattei, 1994: p. 4.
591 Reimann, 2002: p. 673.
592 Zweigert & Kötz, 1996: p. 33

Switzerland deal with the challenges of combating terrorism financing. The comparison could take place on philosophical, dogmatic, historical and sociological levels.[593] Ultimately, cultural differences could also influence the results of the comparative law analysis.[594] All these approaches could lead to new perspectives.[595] In the present case, however, the focus is on the investigation of criminal procedural hurdles, which were identified in the main study.

In order to do justice to the practical relevance of the present work, the author analyses selected aspects of criminal procedure law in Germany, Liechtenstein, Austria and Switzerland based on the results of the main study. The legal situation in Switzerland is taken as a starting point and considered in detail. Based on the approaches developed for Switzerland, the legal situations in the other three countries are also examined and suggestions for improving or supplementing the existing regulations are discussed.

The author believes that this approach is most likely to generate a practical result. A purely summary and comparative presentation of the regulations in different countries would be more suitable for an encyclopaedia than for making the case that legal reform in necessary. Thus, the comparative law study presented in this work does not claim to be exhaustive. Rather, the aim is to discuss selected aspects that are particularly relevant in practice and to develop proposals for legislative measures to be taken.

3.2 Empirical results

The empirical results are presented below. In particular, the results of the preliminary study are first discussed in summary form. A detailed qualitative content analysis was not possible for the reasons mentioned above, namely the difficulty in gaining access to the interview partners, the inability to obtain consent to record and the resulting lack of interview transcripts. Therefore, the author's memory transcripts are summarized. However, this is not a major limitation of the present study, as the preliminary study was only intended to serve as a starting point for the main study.

Subsequently, the author will present the results of the main study. Since a large number of statements are involved and a formulated summary would either

593 Frankenberg, 1985: p. 428.

594 Curran, 1998a: p. 44; Kennedy, 1997: p. 636; Watson, 1995: p. 470; Legrand, 1992: p. 262.

595 Curran, 1998b: p. 657.

go beyond the reasonable scope of the present work or would be associated with a significant and not inconsiderable selection of the statements by the author, the findings are presented in tabular form for the sake of brevity.

Nonetheless, all essential statements are provided. Repetitive statements have been excluded from the main text but have been included in Appendix 1. The findings already presented in tabular form have not been expanded on as this would not have added any additional knowledge, increased the author's scientific output or ultimately benefited the reader.

However, the results of the main study have been summarized in an executive summary to facilitate the reading thereof and highlight its key findings. Although this is ultimately an additional table, on the one hand it proves useful for the reader, but on the other hand it also shows that the author is able to select as well as highlight key statements and thus underlines the value of the scientific achievement. For a discussion of the findings tabulated in this section, please refer to section 4.

3.2.1 Preliminary study

The preliminary study has shown that terrorist financiers use both legal and illegal sources of income. In the case of the latter, white-collar crime and organized crime seem to be particularly prominent. However, petty crime also appears to play some role. The main features of the methods mentioned by the interview partners are presented below. It should be borne in mind that, in principle, any activity that generates an income is suitable for financing terrorism.

Nevertheless, it makes sense to show which activities are actually used by terrorist financiers and how they are carried out. Only in this way can weaknesses in the fight against terrorism financing ultimately be identified and subsequently remedied. The aim of the preliminary study was to outline the basic procedures of terrorist financiers in order to identify and narrow down the subject of the main study. The author therefore expressly points out that the methods described below will be explained in more detail as part of the evaluation of the results of the main study.

In order to provide the reader with an initial overview and to facilitate the comparison of the results of the preliminary and main studies, the findings of the preliminary study have been summarized in the following two tables (Tables 3 and 4):

Table 3: Revenue sources

Illegal sources of income	Legal sources of income
- Sales tax fraud - Trade in CO_2 emission allowances - Trade in raw materials - Trafficking in narcotics - Trafficking in organs - Human trafficking - Pimping - Protection racket - Extortionate kidnapping - Online fraud - Insurance fraud	- Real estate - Stock exchange transactions

Table 4: Capital transfer

Transfer methods
- Transfers to Turkey - Hawala transfer (parallel banking systems) - Personal transfer - Electronic currencies (cryptocurrencies)

VAT fraud, which is often referred to as carousel fraud, continues to be very popular among professional terrorist financiers. In its basic form, Company A is founded in Country of Origin X, which exports goods or services to Company B in Country Y. This export is exempt from value-added tax within the European Union. Company B in Country Y sells these goods to Company C in Country Y, incurring VAT, which is not usually paid immediately. Company C in turn sells the goods to Company A in Country X. This export is VAT exempt, which is why Company C has the VAT refunded by the tax authorities. Ideally, the refund to Company C occurs before Company B has paid its sales tax liability. Company B then disappears from the market before the VAT can be enforced by the relevant tax authority.

In the past, goods that were easy to transport, such as computer chips or mobile phones, were preferred for VAT fraud. However, due to legislative measures, such as the reverse charge procedure, as well as increased attention by the tax authorities with regard to import and export transactions involving certain goods, terrorist financiers have switched to other industries. In particular, trade in branded clothing, which also has a high commodity value and is easy to transport, is playing an increasingly important role. Trade in textiles is also an industry that is frequently characterized by transnational transactions, even in the context of legal transactions.

Appointing young people who want to go on jihad as the managing directors of the legal entities through which carousel fraud is being carried out is also a means of evading detection. On the one hand, this has advantages in that these individuals are provided with an unsuspicious environment which they can use to argue that they are in no way interested in leaving for Syria. On the other hand, those involved in the carousel fraud are no longer tangible for the investigating authorities, which protects those who are behind it. Moreover, these people do not usually insist on profit sharing.

A special form of carousel fraud is *trading in CO2 emission certificates*. However, this form of terrorism financing is becoming increasingly less important. The approach is analogous to the basic form of carousel fraud described above; however, instead of mobile phones, computer chips or textiles, CO_2 emission certificates are traded. Since these do not have to be physically exported, they can be channelled through companies in several countries within a very short time, which massively limits their traceability. However, this type of fraud has been known about for years and is actively being combated by the reverse charge procedure. Nevertheless, this method of terrorism financing will probably continue to be used in practice.

Furthermore, *commodity trading* is used for terrorism financing, particularly when terrorist groups have succeeded in capturing oil refineries and are using them to extract and process oil. However, this form of terrorism financing has also been on the decline in recent years, as experience has shown that oil platforms captured by terrorists become targets for air strikes and the export of crude oil is difficult due to logistical problems. Furthermore, potential buyers are coming under political pressure.

Terrorist financiers are also increasingly involved in organized crime. In this context, *trafficking in narcotics* plays an important role. A distinction can be made between two possible approaches, both of which are often employed by the same perpetrator(s). On the one hand, areas controlled by terrorists in certain countries are suitable for the cultivation of narcotics that are then exported to Europe. Smuggling routes are used for this purpose. For example, airplanes, trucks and ships that deliver relief supplies and usually return unloaded are instead used to transport narcotics.

Once the goods have been exported to Europe, they are sold in small quantities to the end consumer by terrorist financiers' auxiliaries in large cities. Ideally, the entire price paid by the end consumer remains in the hands of the terrorist financiers. In particular, refugees from Arab countries are currently being specifically recruited to sell narcotics in Europe. These individuals are particularly suitable candidates from the perspective of terrorist financiers due to their religion, their supposed loyalty to their compatriots, their difficult economic situation and their lack of access to alternative gainful employment. They are also given guarantees that their families will be taken care of if they are caught and sentenced to prison.

In addition to trafficking in narcotics, *trafficking in organs* also plays a role in terrorism financing. In this context, people resident in Europe who are in need of a donor organ are offered help via personal networks. Subsequently, potential donors are sought in areas controlled by terrorist groups. The same are either persuaded monetarily or forcibly induced to donate. Organ harvesting usually takes place in Turkey or the Balkans. The donors are brought to the country of organ removal via the usual refugee routes. Subsequently, the organs can either be transplanted in the country of removal or exported to another country.

Human trafficking, especially in labour and refugees, also plays a significant role. Refugees from terrorist-controlled areas are smuggled into Europe and exploited there as workers who are paid extremely low wages. In this way, the terrorist financiers earn money from the flight itself and also from the work. However, this is offset by the terrorists' essential interest in maintaining the population of the areas they control, since customs duties and taxes can be collected there.

Pimping also seems to play a certain role in terrorism financing. As a line of business, this is currently being developed. Although prostitution itself contradicts the religious convictions of the terrorist financiers, this source of income also seems to be desired for the financing of certain terrorist activities. Primarily, refugees are recruited to offer protection to prostitutes in exchange for a portion of the prostitute's income. If the protection offered is not accepted, violence is usually used to force acceptance.

In addition, terrorist financiers are dedicated to *extorting protection money*. For this purpose, too, refugees are specifically recruited to offer their protection to business people and demand monetary compensation. If the protection is not taken up, there are first 'friendly' reminders and then massive intimidation to force acceptance. Refugees are particularly suitable perpetrators because they often have little to lose and thus accept very low profit margins. In the process, terrorist financiers specifically target easily manipulated, poorly integrated refugees who are ideally easy to radicalize.

Another line of business in which terrorist financiers engage is *extortionate kidnapping*. On the one hand, people are kidnapped in terrorist-controlled areas and released again in exchange for very high ransoms. At the same time, however, people are also kidnapped in Europe and released for relatively small ransoms in order to prevent the law enforcement authorities from becoming involved. However, kidnappings in terrorist-controlled areas appear to be the more significant source of revenue.

Petty crime also contributes to terrorism financing. Young refugees are specifically recruited to commit property crimes in Europe. The *theft of sneakers* in a Berlin department store which are subsequently sold on the black market is ultimately suitable for financing terrorism. Refugees who are not integrated and do not have legal sources of income are usually easy to recruit for such activities. Ideally, they become radicalized and act without profit sharing for the purposes of financing terrorism. Alternatively, small profit shares are paid.

Furthermore, *fraud in the context of online auctions* also seems to play a certain role in terrorism financing. Several approaches are possible here. On the one hand, non-existent goods can be auctioned off. Subsequently, the buyer is asked to transfer the money not via an auction platform's escrow system but directly – preferably via money transfer systems. However, the goods are never delivered. Alternatively, the accounts of existing users are hacked and false account details are provided to buyers of goods in the name of the genuine seller. In both cases, money is transferred to the terrorist financiers.

Terrorist financiers also appear to use *insurance fraud* for their own purposes. This usually involves deliberately causing damage in order to obtain cash payouts from insurers. Preference is given to faking damage to vehicles and the theft of luxury goods. Consistent care is taken not to cause excessive damage in order to avoid attracting increased attention from insurers.

A special form of insurance fraud is the *establishment of car rental companies*. These car rental companies lease vehicles from well-known manufacturers and insure them. Subsequently, these vehicles are rented out to front men and taken abroad. Once the vehicles are abroad, the alleged theft is reported to the relevant authorities and the insurance company.

Finally, it should be mentioned that legal transactions are also capable of financing terrorism. This represents by far the greatest hurdle for investigators to overcome and is accordingly frequently used by terrorist financiers. For example, legal *real estate transactions* are carried out. The proceeds are officially taxed and then a portion is used for terrorism financing. However, since the underlying source of income for terrorism financing is not incriminated, the fight against terrorism financing only succeeds if the intended use of the funds can be proven.

Stock exchange transactions appear to be similarly popular among terrorist financiers. Analogous to the real estate transactions mentioned above, a detection problem arises here as well because stock exchange transactions are not illegal per se. Provided that the terrorist financier does not make any direct transfers to terrorist organizations, this method of financing terrorism can rarely be proven.

This raises the question of how do terrorist financiers transfer their money? In principle, a distinction should be made between legal and illegal sources of income and between cash and electronic assets. Legal assets pose the least challenge to terrorist financiers. After all, they can legally transfer officially taxed income from real estate and stock exchange transactions abroad. This can be plausibly justified by spreading assets abroad to diversify risk. For example, a *transfer to Turkey* is conceivable. There, the money is withdrawn in cash and handed over to a terrorist near the border with Syria. As a rule, even if detected, this crime is unlikely to be proven.

The transfer of illegal funds is more complicated. If cash is involved, a *hawala transfer* is an option. In this case, sums of money are settled among Muslims. Hawala transactions exist all over the world and are usually subject to no or extremely few identification requirements. The cash is handed over in a hawala shop in Munich, for example, and within a few minutes, a terrorist can collect it in a hawala shop in Turkey. The hawala system is based primarily on trust and personal networks. Customers thus benefit from the fact that hawala bankers do not actually have to transfer the money but create a two-way settlement system. In this example, the money is not actually transferred from Munich to Turkey. Rather, both hawala bankers simply make a note in their accounts that the transaction has taken place. As soon as another customer wants to transfer money from Turkey to Munich, the transaction is settled. Any surpluses can be adjusted periodically – once a year, for example.

Alternatively, the *personal transfer of cash* is also an option. The route known as the 'Balkan route' in the context of the refugee crisis can obviously be used to facilitate this. As long as it is possible to travel in one direction, it should also be possible to travel in the other. Terrorist financiers can therefore either travel themselves via the Balkan route to Turkey and then to Syria or send a messenger.

If the terrorist financiers have incriminated assets in *electronic currencies*, it makes sense to process the transfer in these electronic currencies. Bitcoin, among others, is used for this purpose. However, according to the interviewees, this method is rarely used. Personal transfers and transfers via banks or hawala transactions are obviously preferred.

In summary, terrorist financiers and their auxiliaries have access to a wide range of possible sources of income and methods for transferring assets. However, since the informal expert interviews were not recorded and thus not transcribed, it was necessary to conduct a main study with formal expert interviews. This was particularly necessary in order to gain more in-depth insights into the concrete practices of terrorist financiers which could serve as a basis for making recommendations for legislative measures.

3.2.2 Main study

The results of the expert interviews, which were transcribed and evaluated within the framework of a qualitative content analysis according to Mayring[596], are presented below. In order to enable the clearest possible presentation, the results were first summarized in a table in the form of an executive summary. The category system serves as the basis for this. The executive summary is intended to provide the reader with a brief initial overview.

In order to ensure the greatest possible transparency of the results, the author has supported each of the statements made in the summary presentation with a citation. These citations can be found in Appendix 3. In addition, Appendix 1 contains a table with all the relevant statements made by the interviewees, which enables the reader to see how extensively the individual experts have commented. In principle, the citations could have been summarized in a continuous text. However, this would have made it more difficult to read.

First, general statements by the interview partners on sources of income, the transfer of assets, offender characteristics, strengths and weaknesses of the investigating authorities and necessary measures are commented on. Subsequently, legal and illegal sources of income are presented.

In the next step, five methods of wealth transfer are explained. Namely, bank transfers, parallel banking systems, money transfer systems, cryptocurrencies and physical transfers are examined in more detail.

Finally, the instruments of counter-terrorism, in particular the exchange of information between private individuals and the authorities, undercover investigators, digital surveillance and administrative and legal assistance, as well as the handling of professional secrets, are discussed.

The following section is limited to a summary presentation of the statements of the interview partners, and a discussion of the empirical results is presented in Chapter 4 (see Tables 5–8).

---

596 Mayring (2010).

3.2.3 Executive summary

Table 5: General statements

Asset Transfer	Revenue sources	Perpetrator	Investigative authorities	Necessary measures
- Advancing technology and trend towards mobile payment services - Non-regulated industries - Any type of asset transfers suitable for terrorism financing - Transfer of funds both domestically and abroad - Normal bank accounts mostly inconspicuous - Transaction analyses helpful to a limited extent, since the use of funds lies in the future. - IS has learned from Al-Qaeda	- Funds often not incriminated - Administrative loopholes - Even small amounts are sufficient for attacks - Terrorist groups are self-financing - Mixing of legal and illegal sources of income - Terrorism can also be financed by means of crime, e.g. guns - Income in own domain	- Intelligent - Well trained - Have access to technical literature - Have plausible explanations for behaviour - Learning from money laundering methods - Trained to avoid leaving traces - Only small-time offenders get caught - Trend away from large organizations towards individual perpetrators - Single perpetrator difficult to identify - Organizations behave like states - Previously only asset preservation; today, targeted development of new sources of income - Already weakened by counter-terrorism measures	- Slow - Need counter-terrorism financing for tax tracing - Focus on combating money laundering - Are not familiar with the modus operandi of terrorist financiers - International co-ordination required - Existing measures aimed at combating large organizations - Knowledge based on evaluation of 9/11 and analysis of Al-Qaeda - Watchlists - Offender profiles	- Promote exchanges between investigative authorities and private parties and between Financial Intelligence Units (FIUs) and intelligence services - Deterrent penalties - Analysis and measures derived from it - Use financing flows to draw conclusions about the environment - Drying up of financial flows - Consider a combination of several factors - Increased counter-terrorism assistance to countries neighbouring crisis areas - Safeguarding of funds - No overreaction

Table 6: Revenue sources

Legal sources of income	Illegal sources of income
- Borrow from banks - Taking out loans from private individuals (contact via Internet platforms) - Management of a construction company - Trading activities - Salary - State support	- Compulsory levies (taxes) - Looting - Protection fees - Expropriation - Petroleum trade - Trade in cultural goods - Sales tax fraud via company constructs - Fraud - Counterfeit products - Fraudulently obtaining student loans - Drug trafficking - Insurance fraud - Kidnappings - Human trafficking - Misuse of telephony systems - Blackmail - Theft

Table 7: Capital transfer

	General suitability	Concrete procedure	Detection risks
Banking system	- More extensive controls than in other industries - Perpetrators often difficult to distinguish from other customers - Banks see only a fraction of the process - Mixing the fight against terrorism financing with measures to combat money laundering - Even high-risk countries such as Turkey are not considered suspect per se - Crisis countries such as Syria do not have appropriate infrastructure	- Marshal - Ensure legal source of funds - Avoid high-risk countries - Disclose alleged business partners - Ensure plausible, comprehensible explanations for transactions - Use online banks - Use specialized financial service providers for specific regions - Choose banks with branches abroad and use lower audits within group structures - Use Turkish banks with branches in Germany - Create invoices, orders and financing documents	- Transaction analyses - Known typologies for the detection of foreign terrorist fighters - No anonymous transactions possible - Checking the background of customers and payments - Persons with Arabic names suspected - Beneficial owners of the beneficiary are often not known - Routine analysis of the press - Traceability of the documentation significantly reduces the risk of detection

Table 7: Continued

	General suitability	Concrete procedure	Detection risks
	- Quick transfers - Smaller amounts do not attract attention	- Provide documentation to the bank upon first request - Use well-prepared documents with stamp - Provide documents in foreign languages - Establish a company in Turkey	- Transfer of larger amounts increases risk of detection - Criminal purpose cannot usually be established - Suspicious transactions get lost among legitimate transactions - Cash withdrawal in border area with Syria highly suspicious
		- Consultancy and investment as justification for capital requirements - Establish a limited liability company with business relations in Turkey - Funeral homes - Use companies with cash payment - Using cultural associations and foundations as cover - Referrals to reputable Non-Governmental Organizations (NGOs) - Create legal structures for lobbying and advertising - Use refugees as a cover - Procure website and trade register entry - Seek judgments by default - Use referrals to sick family members - Carpet purchase or wallet loss as reasons for cash withdrawals in Istanbul - Use being a tourist from Qatar to explain remittances from abroad to Germany - Cash withdrawals and subsequent distribution of funds - Take advantage of the lack of co-operation between the authorities in Dubai and China - Cash withdrawals	- Difficult to differentiate between terrorism financing and legitimate cash withdrawals

(*continued on next page*)

Table 7: Continued

	General suitability	Concrete procedure	Detection risks
		- Use notarial certification - Using biases to create low-risk profiles - Make frequent transfers to increase plausibility - Involve experts - Distribute assets - Avoid prepaid cards - Use tour operator - Use company structure in transportation	
Parallel banking systems	- No supervision - Concealment of the beneficial owner - Difficult access - Serious - Cost-effective - Infrastructure available in conflict areas - Combination with bank transfer possible - Especially suitable for ransom payments	- Cash transactions based on trust and middlemen - Contact by members of certain ethnic groups - Aid agencies as a cover - Combination with trade and use of fictitious invoices - Avoid general invoices for services - Use difficult-to-determine values for machines in calculations - Procure documents - Clearing (settlement of peaks) via banks - Physical transport of cash - Involve countries without advanced banking systems - Impossibility of transfer from crisis area via bank as possible justification	- Clearing via banks - Lack of supervision - No AML or know your customer (KYC) standards - No identification of the beneficial owner possible
Cryptocurrencies	- Parallel currency exchangeable into common currencies - No regulation or supervision - Alternative to classic bank transfers - Lack of transparency - Anonymity - Low storage risk; easy to hide - Not a common currency in retail - Popular on the darknet	- Create and provide computing capacity - Create an e-wallet - Constantly changing, inexpensive notebooks - Use publicly accessible WIFI networks - Acquisition of Bitcoin with cash or tangible assets - Find Bitcoin exchange or exchange partner - Investment of assets in Bitcoin - Payment of extortion money in Bitcoin - Using Bitcoin to pay for weapons on the darknet	- Authorities not up to date - Electronic traces - Assignment of Bitcoin to the beneficial owner is difficult

Table 7: Continued

	General suitability	Concrete procedure	Detection risks
Money transfer systems	- Quick - Cheap - Difficult to attribute to a specific person - Infrastructure on the recipient side may be limited	- Sending money to Turkey, e.g. to family members - Use digital natives - Marshal - Allow different people to act under the same name - If necessary, use public documents to provide plausible evidence of the purpose of the payment - Avoid cities bordering Syria	- Proximity to Syria increases risk of detection - Transactional analysis - Consider real-time criteria - Consider ex post analyses - Avoid known profiles (male, between 18 and 30 years old) - Facebook search - Avoid networks between people - Do not exceed certain sums - Consider motion profiles - Verification standards for mobile phone shops rather low
Personal transfer	- Refugee routes ideal for money transfer - Cash transport of funds for purchases	- Use refugee routes - Use trade routes (land routes) - Involve experienced smugglers and traffickers - Use prepaid cards - Use border between Turkey and Syria	- Travel to Syria is suspicious - Preparation of the trip to Syria attracts attention

Table 8: Counter-terrorism instruments

Exchange of information between private parties and public authorities	**Undercover investigators**	**Digital surveillance**	**Administrative and judicial assistance**	**Trade secrets**
- Exchange of lists of dangerous persons between authorities and financial service providers - Exchange of typologies between public authorities and financial service providers - Lack of control over information exchanged	- Investigations without classical intelligence are difficult - Targeted use necessary - Insider knowledge required - Without undercover investigators, there is hardly any chance of success - Undercover investigators with a migration background ideal but difficult to recruit - V-men are easier to recruit - Cost and personnel intensive - Weak legal basis - Decentralized organization of the IS as an obstacle - Ideal for sleeper cells in Europe, e.g. Belgium - Lone wolf not available	- Effective and efficient - Data protection hurdles - Individual elements as circumstantial evidence - Vulnerable to abuse	- Obsolete system of mutual assistance - Money often faster than administrative assistance - Immediate action required - Linking data and targeted use of large data volumes - Forwarding of information to selected countries - Promote informal co-operation between financial intelligence units	- Professional secrets as a concealment tool - Align standards on notarization with those of financial service providers - Use information only for counter-terrorism purposes - Transparent person as an ideal case

3.2.4 Documentary citations

In Appendix 3, each of the statements mentioned in the executive summary is presented with a citation, the corresponding generalization according to Mayring (2013) and the respective interviewee. This is to ensure that the reader can easily understand how the individual elements of the executive summary came about – the findings of the executive summary are based entirely on the statements of the interviewees and have not been distorted.

In order to guarantee the authenticity of the data, the citations were transcribed verbatim and not refined. This means that passages emphasized by the interview partners are shown in capital letters. In addition, all filler words such as 'um' and grammatical errors were also included. This is to ensure that the reader can view unaltered original statements and their generalization. The interpretation of the original statements is reserved for the next chapter (Chapter 4), which is dedicated to the discussion of the empirical results. It should be noted that for the purpose of this interpretation, the quotes were translated into English. However, the data in the appendix was not translated to maintain transparency and the integrity of the data.

The presentation of the empirical results in tabular form should enable the reader to gain a quick overview of the findings of this study. Alternatively, the results could also have presented as graphs. However, this would have had the disadvantage of lacking clarity. Due to the size of the tabular presentation, this has been included as Appendix 3.

The formal expert interviews were extremely productive. In particular, it was possible not only to confirm the findings of the preliminary study but to deepen them and to substantiate them with quotations. The category system allows the statements to be presented clearly. The empirical results and individual methods of terrorism financing are discussed in the following chapter (Chapter 4). In particular, the methods used by the perpetrators and the resulting challenges for law enforcement agencies will be examined.

4. Discussion of the empirical results

This discussion of the empirical results will explain how intelligent terrorist financiers behave and what challenges their actions pose for the investigating authorities entrusted with combating terrorism. In doing so, basic statements on transfers of assets, sources of income, possible perpetrator profiles, the challenges faced by the investigating authorities and necessary measures to be taken are addressed. Where useful and necessary, these individual areas of interest have already been listed in separate tables in the previous chapter (Chapter 3) and will also be discussed separately in the present chapter. However, in order to avoid a logical break and to explain why these areas in particular are again highlighted separately, it makes sense to first discuss the fundamental findings and lay the foundation for the subsequent discussion. Therefore, this chapter begins with a general overview of the most significant problem areas and their associated challenges. Subsequently, core areas are discussed in greater depth.

The interview partners' statements form the basis of the following discussion; in many cases, the considerations are supported by a quotation. These quotations are refined and partly abridged statements from the interview partners that can be found in their original form in Appendix 3. The refinement and shortening of the statements serves to facilitate readability. However, as the quotes in Appendix 3 are presented in their original form, the transparency of the work is not significantly affected by this approach. Nevertheless, where reasonable and possible, excessive smoothing has been avoided in order to preserve the authenticity of the statements. Although the presentation of the statements leads to a repetition of content, it allows the reader to understand the basis for the discussion without tedious reference to other chapters or the Appendix. In addition, not all of the issues raised in the discussion are supported by original quotations. The presentation is merely exemplary in nature and intended to help the reader better understand the views of the interviewees.

Since the current state of research on the concrete modus operandi of terrorist financiers is not very informative, it is not possible in many places to confront the statements of the interview partners with relevant references from the literature. The author has deliberately limited himself to quoting only relevant sources.

In addition, it is expressly pointed out that the following explanations are intended to illustrate the procedures of an intelligent perpetrator. Finally, methods of terrorism financing must be anticipated in order to prevent them.

Only if investigators and legislators are aware of the possible modus operandi of intelligent perpetrators can they respond to them in the best possible way. This research intends to help investigators and lawmakers identify the modus operandi of intelligent perpetrators at an early stage in order to be able to combat them more effectively. It is not intended to serve as a guide to terrorism financing.

4.1 General statements

4.1.1 Capital transfer

In principle, it should be noted that any type of asset transfer is suitable for terrorism financing. Although normal bank accounts are usually inconspicuous because the use of funds lies in the future and transaction analyses are thus of only limited use, progressive mechanization and a trend towards non-regulated industries and mobile payment services can be observed. The transfer of funds can take place both domestically and abroad, which makes analysis even more difficult. In addition, new terrorist groups such as IS have learned lessons from Al-Qaeda.

The fact that any type of asset transfer can be used for terrorism financing complicates the work of investigators immensely:

> I'll give you an example, but this is such a favourite topic with me here that I could rant about it for hours, that certain areas are incredibly harshly regulated and some areas, however, where it's obvious from my perspective that nothing is happening there by choice. (Interviewee 8)

Contrary to popular belief, it is not sufficient to focus on financial service providers. Funds intended for terrorism financing can also be transported in cash or in kind, for example. Thus, less heavily regulated industries must also be in the sights of the investigation.

In addition, there is the advancing mechanization and the trend towards mobile payment services: 'For me, the progressive mechanization of it all is also, I don't want to say a risk, but also a fact that has made the job harder' (Interviewee 8). It is possible to transfer amounts between people in different jurisdictions within seconds. These are often very small amounts that are sent by migrants to people in their countries of origin, such as by providing legitimate financial support to family members back home. It is reasonable to assume that the majority of these transactions are legal. However, it cannot be denied that these forms of money transfer are vulnerable to abuse. After all, the money is transferred within seconds, and, despite sophisticated transaction analyses that identify any accumulation of risk, it cannot be assumed that every transaction is adequately checked.

Nevertheless, financial service providers in general and banks in particular appear to play some role in terrorism financing. This is particularly obvious because the accounts of terrorist financiers are difficult to distinguish from those of other account holders. Unlike money launderers, terrorist financiers often have no difficulty in proving the source of their funds. Often, the assets intended for terrorism financing originate from the properly taxed transactions of legitimate merchants. Since possible crimes are thus exclusively in the future, it is in many cases almost impossible to anticipate them and to seize the funds. After all, no criminal offence has yet been committed.

The fact that the criminal conduct in many cases lies in the future and not in the past also explains why transaction analyses are of only limited use. It is true that suspicious sources of funds come to light. However, the use of funds can only be controlled to a limited extent. Further complicating matters is the fact that the IS has apparently learned from (and continues to learn from) the example set by Al-Qaeda – but the investigative authorities' tactics are also evolving. Nevertheless, it would be erroneous to assume that terrorist groups do not carry out situation analyses. Based on past experience, it can be assumed that their methods of asset transfer are constantly improving.

It should also be borne in mind that both the financing of terrorist activities at home and abroad must be prevented. This gives rise to various scenarios. For example, businessmen in Switzerland could try to support the IS in Syria. On the other hand, the IS could also try to finance attacks in Central Europe and transfer assets to Germany for this purpose. It is also entirely conceivable that terrorist groups could transfer assets within Europe. This results in a multitude of possible scenarios that must be considered in the context of a comprehensive analysis.

4.1.2 Sources of revenue

One of the biggest challenges relating to combating terrorism financing is that, unlike money launderers, terrorists do not necessarily have to deal with incriminated assets. In fact, the funds are often not incriminated. In other cases, there is a mixture of legal and illegal sources of income. Moreover, even relatively small amounts are sufficient for attacks, which under certain circumstances can also be supported by means of crime, such as the supply of firearms.

Moreover, skilled terrorists are capable of funding themselves: 'So just as a terrorist organization, I would look at: Can I finance myself? Then of course I'm much more independent and can tap into land and sources where I know there are always victims we can choose from' (Interviewee 14). It can therefore be assumed that terrorists could be financially independent and have their own sources of income.

As a general principle, it must be borne in mind that intelligent terrorist financiers do not work with incriminated assets. Probably the lowest-risk form of terrorism financing involves the use of legally acquired funds. This ultimately ensures that investigative proceedings are made considerably more difficult. Finally, by using assets derived from a crime, the terrorist financier would be exposed to the risk of being prosecuted for money laundering within the scope of Art. 305bis CH-StGB:

> When it comes to money laundering, we're practically paranoid already, looking: Where could something bigger come in? In the case of terrorism financing, we already have funds that have been declared clean, that have already been audited – so that's practically the difference, a really exciting topic, in my opinion – that they don't arouse any suspicion at first. (Interviewee 8)

The exclusive use of non-incriminated assets eliminates this risk. Since in many cases terrorism financing is still in the future and has not yet taken place, seizure of the assets is ruled out in many cases.

Alternatively, perpetrators could combine legal and illegal sources of income to make it more difficult to trace the origin and use of funds. Funds that do not officially exist are usually not missed. If, contrary to expectations, they do turn up, the official source of income is used to justify their origin. For example, a retailer with both official and unofficial sources of revenue may keep them in the same cash box. Since the retailer conceals the amounts intended for terrorism financing from tax authorities, initially no one notices that funds are being diverted for terrorist purposes.

It must also be borne in mind that even small amounts are sufficient to finance attacks:

> These splinter groups, these attackers from Paris and Brussels, probably now also in Istanbul, that is not expensive, a few thousand euros that they need to buy their resources, so to speak, to pay rent, to buy food. The weapons are also not terribly expensive. You can do it for a few thousand euros. (Interviewee 14)

A suicide bomber can easily acquire firearms and explosives in considerable quantities and kill countless innocent people with a budget of less than

US$10,000.[597] This means that analyses must not be limited to supposedly large organizations and amounts.

Moreover, it should not go unmentioned that terrorism financing is ultimately also possible through criminal means. For example, instead of money terrorist financers can provide guns, explosives or components for bombs for terrorist organizations. This approach to terrorism financing appears to be less common at first glance, but should nevertheless not be underestimated under any circumstances.

The possible income sources for terrorists are wide-ranging and both official and unofficial. In particular, it must be assumed that terrorist groups can also finance themselves through income generated in their own areas of control. This is problematic in that these territories often lack rule-of-law mechanisms to combat terrorism financing and perpetrators can operate there in a legal vacuum without regulation.

4.1.3 Perpetrators

The perpetrators of terrorism financing are presumably intelligent and well-educated and have access to specialist literature. They have also learned how to move funds without being detected from money laundering methods. Consequently, they have plausible explanations for their behaviour. Since many perpetrators are trained to avoid leaving traces of their activities, only small-time offenders are usually caught.

The trend is shifting away from large organizations as terrorist financiers and moving towards individual perpetrators who are usually more difficult to identify. Terrorist organizations themselves sometimes behave like states. Whereas in the past, their focus was often only on preserving their existing assets, today, they are concerned with the targeted development of new sources of income. However, it should also be noted that many existing terrorist organizations have already been significantly weakened by counter-terrorism measures.

The financing of terrorism is ultimately a feasible but rather complex task. Consequently, according to the experts interviewed, the perpetrators are usually intelligent. The following considerations should therefore not only be aimed at anticipating the behaviour of fanatical perpetrators but in particular at analysing rational approaches to terrorist financiers. In many cases, the perpetrators are well trained and specifically look for weak points:

---

597 Time, 2015: p. 1 f.

> I mean, one should not be under the illusion that – especially in the case of terrorism – it is all just – in inverted commas – some fanatics who want to blow up skyscrapers and then drag some people down with them. They exist too, but there are probably also highly intelligent people in the background who, with a comparable education, are really looking for the weak points. (Interviewee 8)

Thus, not only are uneducated individuals, small-time criminals and vulnerable migrants involved in financing terrorism, but so too are lawyers, business economists and professionals. This must be kept in mind by financial intermediaries when assessing the plausibility of the stories and documents presented by the perpetrators.

Moreover, it is important to recognize that the literature on terrorism financing summarized within the scope of the literature review is not only available to academics and investigators but also, as a rule, to offenders: 'Gee, what does the expert recommend? (laughs) I mean, what's the best way to launder money? (takes breath) There's so much available on the Internet now' (Interviewee 1). It can therefore be assumed that intelligent and educated perpetrators inform themselves in advance. The methods they choose are likely to be correspondingly sophisticated. This is particularly true because many of the methods used by money launderers can also be used in the area of terrorism financing. Ultimately, it cannot be conclusively clarified what proportion of perpetrators are intelligent, well-trained and expertly informed, but it can be assumed that there are both amateurish offenders and highly professional ones.

However, in order to devise preventive measures and further develop criminal procedural options for combating terrorism financing more effectively, it is primarily professional perpetrators who are of interest, as the worst-case scenario should be assumed as a matter of principle. If legislators give investigators the ability to act effectively and efficiently against intelligent perpetrators, it stands to reason that it should also be possible to put a stop to less skilful terrorist financiers. It is therefore helpful to use clever perpetrators as a yardstick against which to measure the rest.

At the same time, one should not place unrealistic expectations on the insights this study is able to provide. The following discussion of the approaches taken by intelligent terrorist financiers can undoubtedly help to better anticipate the behaviour of perpetrators and respond accordingly. However, it is important to acknowledge that certain approaches that require few resources can be difficult to anticipate.

4.1.4 Investigating authorities

Investigative authorities are relatively slow when it comes to investigating cases of terrorism financing (e.g. due to bureaucratic obstacles or lack of relevant information) and continue to focus on combating money laundering. As a result, they are sometimes unfamiliar with the modus operandi of terrorist financiers. In addition, they are accused of using the fight against terrorism financing for launching investigations into tax matters. Furthermore, the existing counter the financing of terrorism (CFT) measures are geared towards combating large organizations, as the knowledge underlying the investigations is based on the evaluation of 9/11 and an analysis of Al-Qaeda. However, in addition to perpetrator profiles, there are also terrorist watchlists which, with the appropriate international co-ordination, can certainly lead to promising results.

One of the biggest weaknesses of investigative agencies is that they are slower in following the traces of the offenders than offenders are in successfully conducting their crime: 'I think that's another area where perhaps there's a weakness in counter-terrorism financing, that the regulators or investigators are actually too slow' (Interviewee 8). This slowness is frequently due to the fact that investigating officers, unlike offenders, must abide by laws and regulations. In addition, there are often conflicts of jurisdiction, for example between the German state criminal investigation offices and the German Office for the Protection of the Constitution, which potentially slows down processes even further. A personnel shortage is also undeniable.

Moreover, the existing resources of the investigating authorities are often used for money laundering proceedings and only secondarily for combating terrorism financing: 'When it comes to reviewing transactions, uh, ultimately the mindset, but also on anti-money laundering (AML), uh, on money laundering, on patterns of money laundering, uh, but terrorism financing just doesn't exist in minds yet' (Interviewee 7). On the one hand, this is due to the fact that money laundering is more widespread and larger in volume than terrorism financing. On the other hand, however, the money laundering problem has also been known about for some time, which is why investigators are often more familiar with it.

One concern is that investigating authorities may not be sufficiently familiar with the modus operandi of terrorist financiers: 'The patterns of terrorism financing, I think, are not even known by most people. And that's why it's just difficult to identify them as well' (Interviewee 7). This assumption is not true for specialized units in most cases, as financial intelligence units usually have expert knowledge. Therefore, it can be assumed that the interview partners' statements refer to other investigators, such as fraud units. To what extent an investigator who uncovers an insurance fraud in a large German city thinks about the possible use of the incriminated assets resulting from this crime to finance terrorism is unknown. The difficulty here lies in particular in the fact that in the case of terrorism financing, the use of the funds lies in the future and is therefore in many cases not immediately obvious. Unless the investigator recognizes the actual purpose of the insurance fraud before them, namely terrorism financing, this case is unlikely to be referred to specialist investigators. The same is probably true for the theft of sneakers that are subsequently sold. Raising awareness is therefore needed among the vast majority of investigators to ensure that terrorism financing is detected and can subsequently be combated.

Furthermore, it was expressed during the expert interviews that investigations to combat terrorism financing may be misused for tax investigation purposes. This is plausible insofar as it can reasonably be assumed that private sector actors, such as banks, are more co-operative in the context of combating terrorism financing than in the case of enquiries into the tax honesty of their clients due to the associated reputational risks. It is true that aiding and abetting a lack of tax honesty is not necessarily received positively by the public. However, the potential reputational damage from fiscal crimes is disproportionate to the reputational consequences associated with financing terrorist activities. It is therefore important not to misuse the instruments available for combating terrorism financing for tax investigations so as not to jeopardize the willingness of private-sector actors to co-operate.[598]

Another of the investigative authorities' weaknesses is the level of international co-operation required in the fight against terrorism financing: 'The second difficulty that I would think of with this is that it simply requires a very high level of co-ordination between authorities nationally and also internationally. Because there are very different authorities involved in the fight throughout' (Interviewee 10). Terrorism financing is not usually a national problem; rather, it is an international problem because the perpetrators move across borders. On the one hand, their movements serve to thwart investigators; on the other hand, cross-border activity is often simply a necessity. For example, in order to finance terrorism, sometimes income is generated in one country and needed in another to finance an attack. Increased international co-ordination is therefore essential to identify the source and movement of these funds. However, at the level of financial intelligence units, where the exchange of information is paramount, communication is undoubtedly easier than in criminal proceedings, which as

598 Ferrara & Salmina, 2016: p. 88.

a rule involve greater formal hurdles and in practice are often associated with lengthy requests for administrative and judicial assistance. In addition, certain countries that are used by terrorists no longer have the necessary infrastructure to participate in international co-operation (e.g. Syria).

Furthermore, many of the investigators' approaches are geared towards combating large organizations:

> The whole thing has been originally aligned on the premise that terrorism financing is actually financing terrorist organizations as a large organization or as a large network and especially as a unified network and therefore something that is tangible and can be financed on a large scale; I think that was basically the ulterior motive. (Interviewee 6)

At first glance, this quote may make sense, as large organizations are potentially planning large attacks. However, it can be assumed that the intelligent and well-trained perpetrators mentioned above have also analysed the situation and may increasingly resort to relying on smaller structures. It is therefore important that investigating authorities keep an eye on both large and small organizations.

In addition, it is important to bear in mind that the knowledge of the investigating authorities is largely based on the evaluation of the terrorist attacks that took place on 9/11 and the findings derived from their investigations of Al-Qaeda. However, continuously developing knowledge is of prime importance since one cannot and must not assume that perpetrators are working with outdated information.

Many measures to combat terrorism financing are also based on terrorist watchlists. Although these are an important tool for gaining initial insights, their utility should not be overestimated. After all, such lists are almost always incomplete. In addition, there is often confusion in terms of which persons in particular are being targeted due to common names and other factors. It is therefore of central importance to give lists of persons the appropriate weight.

Offender profiles also play an increasingly important role for investigating authorities. These are made available, often in a reduced form, to private sector players such as banks in order to identify certain individuals at an early stage. However, a dilemma regularly arises here. On the one hand, it makes sense for intelligence services and police authorities to share these profiles in the most detail possible in order to enable potential perpetrators to be identified at an early stage. At the same time, however, it is likely that sharing detailed intelligence with a wide range of private sector actors may lead to a degree of indiscretion. If every bank compliance officer has access to this information, it is only a matter of time before these insights reach the perpetrators themselves. Once it becomes known on the perpetrator side which actors are considered suspicious, targeted circumvention of these profiles may occur.

4.1.5 Measures required

To engage in a more effective fight against terrorism financing, exchanges are needed between investigative authorities and private individuals, as well as between financial intelligence units and intelligence services. Detailed analyses, measures derived from them and deterrent penalties are also needed. In particular, it should be borne in mind that the drying up of financial flows and the seizure of funds represent only one segment of the many measures that can be taken. At the same time, understanding the financing flows also allows conclusions to be drawn about the terrorists' environment. In this context, increased support for the countries neighbouring crisis regions in particular can also make a valuable contribution to the fight against terrorism financing. Nonetheless, despite the seriousness and threatening nature of terrorism financing, we must refrain from overreacting.

Exchanges between investigative authorities and private sector actors must undoubtedly be encouraged. This applies in particular to co-operation between investigative authorities and banks. Without the help of the former, the latter are often only able to create helpful perpetrator profiles to a limited extent in order to identify potential terrorist financiers at an early stage. At the same time, banks' Suspicious Activity Reports are essential for investigators.

Engaging in an efficient, uncomplicated exchange of information without bureaucratic hurdles to overcome is often crucial to the success of investigations. The most comprehensive approach possible is important here, as terrorist financiers are no longer just individuals but a multitude of individuals: 'So, and that already looks different from what we had ten years ago, where we always typically tried to find this financial supporter, this sheikh, who supports Al-Qaeda, we are already more broadly positioned today' (Interviewee 13). It is therefore crucial that public authorities are as broadly based as possible.

However, co-operation between financial intelligence units and intelligence services also needs to be strengthened.

> I think generally we have, well we have an important role of intelligence on the one hand and we have an important role of financial investigators on the other and the two haven't even sat down in the same room yet, yeah? (Interviewee 13)

If information from one authority is not passed on to other authorities, this can prevent conclusions from being drawn by combining data from different sources. Furthermore, it is also essential to deal responsibly with information that for the most part is classified. One possible solution is to make information accessible only to certain individuals within an authority in order to prevent secrets from being leaked and the source of the betrayal from being traced.

In addition, deterrent penalties are necessary to increase prevention in general. However, this raises the question of the extent to which terrorist financiers can be influenced by such penalties. An intelligent and educated offender will take the threat of punishment into account when committing a crime, but an extremist who is prepared to carry out a suicide attack in the name of religion is unlikely to be deterred by the threat of imprisonment for a violation of Art. 260^{quinquies} CH-StGB. However, it can be assumed that not every financier of terrorism is sufficiently radicalized to completely disregard the consequences of their actions. Thus, deterrent penalties do have a certain potential to contribute to a more effective fight against terrorism financing.

An analysis of financing flows also allows for conclusions to be drawn about the environment of possible attackers. Understanding how previous attacks were financed and who was involved is fundamentally important to making it possible to track down extended terrorist cells and prevent further attacks from occurring.

In order to ensure that the analysis of funding flows does not stop at national borders, it is essential to support crisis areas and their neighbouring countries in the fight against terrorism: 'What we can do is make sure that the money doesn't keep flowing, but the IS, is just already, because it's going out mainly through smuggling, it's actually up to the neighbouring countries' (Interviewee 13). This is ultimately the only way to ensure that terrorist financiers cannot hide behind certain national borders. The types of support range from training programmes to data and information exchanges to joint analyses.

It is also important that the funds intended for the financing of terrorism can be seized and recovered in a timely manner, although this is an ongoing a challenge – particularly in circumstances requiring international co-operation. However, the confiscated funds must not be misused in other ways or end up financing terrorism in a roundabout way.

Finally, it should also be mentioned that an overreaction to the threat of terrorism financing is unlikely to be helpful. It is simply not possible or reasonable for banks to implement measures to screen every customer and every transaction in detail, nor is it an economically justifiable use of their resources. Skilled perpetrators will continue to succeed in financing terrorism in the future, no matter what. However, the probability of identifying these perpetrators in a timely manner can be significantly increased. This research aims to help make this a reality.

4.2 Sources of revenue

The following presentation of potential sources of income for terrorist financiers is exemplary and aims to expand on the statements made in Section 4.1.2. In particular, specific examples provided by the interviewees will be used to illustrate how skilful terrorist financiers might proceed in financing terrorism. This should help to illustrate the extensive range of options available to terrorists and how difficult it would be to eliminate all of their sources of income. The primary objective of Section 4.2 is thus to demonstrate that perpetrators have access to a variety of ways of financing terrorism.

In order to analyse the examples offered by the interviewees, they will be critically assessed. How perpetrators might proceed in carrying out their activities will also be outlined. While not all forms of legal and illegal sources of terrorist income can be presented in detail within the scope of this work, simply listing the possible sources of income would also be too superficial of an approach to take. The author therefore devotes at least one paragraph to each method to present the most important elements of the approaches and the associated risks, as well as the required resources. This analysis does not claim to be exhaustive and merely serves the purpose of providing plausibility as to how a terrorist financier might proceed. Nevertheless, these examples can help investigators to anticipate a terrorist's behaviour.

In the present case, differentiating between legal and illegal sources of income is almost inevitable. The interview partners were responsible for selecting the methods discussed, and it is explicitly pointed out that other methods would also be possible. However, it is not necessary to present all potential sources of income in order to prove that terrorism can be financed relatively easily and to emphasize that the focus of the fight against terrorism financing should be in the area of asset transfers if one does not want to place all sources of income under the shadow of suspicion. Nonetheless, outlining the breadth of possible methods can help raise awareness among investigators in different areas and thus create built-in hurdles for terrorist financiers.

4.2.1 Legal sources of revenue

The range of legal sources of income for terrorist financiers is broad, and those presented below are merely examples offered by the interviewees. The legal sources of income mentioned by the experts are considered particularly suitable for terrorism financing, but this in no way excludes other sources of income. The methods emphasized by the experts are very widespread and, in many cases, obvious, as they can be realized with relatively little effort and in the vast majority of cases do not require much technical expertise. There are myriad ways to generate legal income, and the procedures described below merely serve the purpose of illustrating how perpetrators might proceed.

Acquiring loans from banks and from private individuals seems to be a popular means of gaining financing. Running a construction company or a trading company would also be a suitable front. In addition, persons can also spend their salary payments and state support payments on terrorism financing.

Loans from banks are particularly suitable for offenders who wish to finance a one-time offence. This applies in particular to perpetrators who wish to carry out the act themselves and who may reasonably expect die in the course of executing it. In these cases, the perpetrator does not plan to ever repay the loan.

If the perpetrator does not plan to carry out the act themself or die in the execution thereof, then loans from private individuals are appropriate. To source private loans, specialized Internet platforms are sometimes used:

> That is, you say, I have such and such a credit need here, such and such a price I'm willing to pay, and the platform actually just makes the contact between the credit seekers and other people who say, okay, I'll give money for it. (Interviewee 8)

Private individuals generally have fewer options for taking action against defaulting debtors. This is particularly true in view of the fact that the average private individual who grants a private loan generally does not maintain their own debt collection department and has limited familiarity with debt collection procedures. Therefore, if the perpetrator does not carry out the attack to be financed themself, they have less to fear in terms of civil proceedings in the aftermath of the attack. They may even be able to repay the loan to avoid attracting attention.

Provided that the perpetrator does not require a substantial amount of money, their regular income may be sufficient to finance a terrorist attack, particularly since US$10,000 is sufficient to finance an attack in many cases.[599] For example, the attacks that took place on 22 March 2017 in London only required a rental car and a knife, neither of which was expensive.

The same seems to be true for the generation of funds through state support, for example, in the form of social benefits: 'So, that can be legitimate sources of income, that can be a salary, that can be unemployment benefits, government benefits, that can be anything' (Interviewee 6). This form of financing attracts particular attention from the public since it means that taxpayers' money is

599 Time, 2015: p. 1 f.

ultimately being used to fund acts of terrorism. Many perpetrators have the opportunity to apply for financial support in their respective target country (e.g. in the form of social assistance) and can then devote themselves to preparing an attack at their leisure and at the state's expense.

At the same time, the scale of an attack that can be carried out relatively inexpensively cannot begin to compare with the impact of the attacks of 9/11. Thus, if a perpetrator does need more significant amounts, they could, for example, engage in a commercial activity or run a construction company:

> They have very normal incomes. The one that Bin Laden was heir to [was] a big construction company in Saudi Arabia and [he] was a millionaire and thus, quite simply probably, financed the attacks in 9/11 by coming out of legal construction companies/ out of the profits of a construction company or a corporation he financed his/the people who did the attacks to the extent necessary. (Interviewee 9)

High-profit companies, like construction companies, appear to be particularly suitable for generating income for terrorism financing, especially if part of the company's income is not officially declared. Many clients are open to the idea of forgoing an invoice in exchange for a small discount on the invoice amount and paying at least part of the work done in cash. This usually saves the customer from paying the full VAT and the contractor from paying any income or profit tax. If the buyer does not require a receipt, the trader can refrain from recording the transaction altogether. Parallel accounting practices ultimately generate funds that can be used for terrorism financing without creating gaps in the company's official books.

The foregoing shows that terrorist financiers can draw on a variety of revenue sources. Legal sources of income, as outlined in this section, have the great advantage of not attracting attention. In the worst-case scenario, terrorist financiers would have to answer for tax offences. However, very few cases are likely to attract much suspicion in terms of contributing to terrorism financing.

The statements of the interview partners are consistent with the findings of the literature review. Consider, for example, Al-Qaeda's investments in Al-Barakaat's financial and telecommunications empire.[600] The PKK's investments in media companies in Europe also fall into this category.[601] In addition, it can be assumed that investments in securities and real estate as well as the sale of publications play an important role in generating funds.[602] However, the findings

600 Winer & Roule, 2002: p. 89.
601 Roth & Sever, 2007: p. 913.
602 Dalyan, 2008: p. 140.

of the interview partners go much further than those found in the literature, as a broader spectrum of funding sources was revealed.

The fact that the interviewees made no reference to state support as a means of financing terrorism shows that much has changed in this area since the end of the Cold War.[603] Terrorists are now more likely to focus primarily on non-state sources of revenue.[604] Moreover, although the role played by donations has been discussed extensively in the literature, it was not brought into focus by the experts in the interviews.[605]

4.2.2 Illegal sources of income

Terrorists' illegal sources of income can basically be divided into two subcategories. On the one hand, the IS in particular has sources of income in the areas it occupies, which are also referred to below as 'territory'. These sources of income include, above all, the collection of compulsory levies (i.e. taxes and customs duties) as well as protection fees. However, looting and expropriation also seem to play a significant role. Furthermore, the IS's trade in oil and cultural goods should also be mentioned in this context. It is not possible for European investigative authorities, due to their lack of jurisdiction and sovereign power, to combat the IS within its own territory. Thus, only the transfer of these funds to Europe can be prevented.

On the other hand, terrorists also generate revenues in Europe through fraud – specifically insurance and VAT fraud – counterfeiting of products, obtaining educational loans by fraudulent means, drug trafficking, the misuse of telecommunications equipment, extortion and theft. Human trafficking also lies at the interface between Europe and the territories of certain terrorist groups such as the IS.

Among the many illegal sources of revenue, compulsory levies, often referred to as taxes or customs duties, seem to play an important role, particularly in the territory of the IS: 'So that's already, I'll say, this claim, Islamic State, who see themselves as a state, who have a certain infrastructure, so that requires "some taxation"' (Interviewee 7). These taxes are levied directly in the areas concerned and are similar to Western taxation systems in terms of their basic features, although significant deviations can certainly be observed. Thus, income taxes

603 Makarenko, 2004: p. 130.
604 Dalyan, 2008: p. 139.
605 Biersteker et al., 2007: p. 40 f.

and customs duties are levied on the import or export of goods in IS-controlled territories, and tax rates vary according to religion.

Furthermore, terrorist organizations charge protection fees as a means of generating income. The modus operandi here is similar to that of organized crime in Southern or Eastern Europe. The perpetrators create dangers for their victims and then offer protection in return for payment. This practice is particularly common in areas controlled by terrorist groups. However, it is also a possible source of income in Europe.

Expropriation also appears to be a major source of new assets for terrorists. This mainly affects landowners and shopkeepers, and the latter are deprived of the goods in their shops. Since these assets are not transferred to Europe, their relevance is minor to the present work.

In addition, the IS also seems to finance itself through looting. In particular, museums and places where archaeological excavations take place are looted of their artefacts. Sculptures and individual pieces of temples are also sometimes taken and sold. Museums are therefore particularly suitable for plunder, as the goods are already catalogued and prepared, whereas theft from excavation sites is costly and requires a certain level of expertise for the post-processing of the find.

In this context, trafficking in cultural goods should be highlighted as it represents an interface between terrorism financing taking place in IS territory and in Europe. Traditional trade routes are often used to smuggle movable property acquired through looting in Syria. These trafficking routes could well be countered with the support of IS's neighbouring countries. It is also important to ensure that items derived from looting cannot be sold in Europe (e.g. through the compulsory presentation of documents of origin).

Trade in oil also plays a crucial role in financing terrorism:

> And/and I mean, not speaking from experience there, but my guess is just relatively big, what we've seen, for example, when the whole Iran Oil-for-Food Programme was going on. These are these trade routes. I mean, it's been proven by now that in the time of the 90s and 2000s, when this Oil-for-Food Programme was running, that the black market for oil was also partly running through Turkey. (Interviewee 7)

IS has significant oil reserves in its territory and, to some extent, has the infrastructure to extract and transport this oil. However, it is unclear how much oil the IS actually sells. On the one hand, this is because the infrastructure needed for oil production has suffered from the ongoing war in Syria and related airstrikes. On the other hand, international pressure on the countries neighbouring IS territory has also increased, making any transport of oil more difficult. Nevertheless, it can still be assumed that the IS generates at least part of its income from the trade in oil, although there are no reliable figures estimating its worth.

However, terrorists do not have to limit themselves to illegal sources of income in areas under their control. Among other things, sales tax fraud via company constructs comes into question here. This involves reclaiming sales taxes that were never paid as part of a carousel fraud. This method is advantageous for terrorist financiers in that the financing of terrorist attacks is rarely considered as a possible motive for the crime. The disadvantage, however, is that the investigating authorities are now aware of this method, which means that it can only be implemented in a very complex manner and by relying on people with the appropriate expertise. A question therefore arises as to whether this method could be a viable model for terrorist financiers. In view of the risks involved, the answer must be no.

In addition, fraud also appears to play some role in generating revenue streams for terrorism financing: 'So now, if you look at fraud also as white-collar crime, then yes, any form of crime that produces money to fund terrorists like this is an issue' (Interviewee 14). However, white-collar crime in many cases requires greater expertise than that which is needed for the other methods described in this chapter. In particular, due to the complexity of the offence, more extensive investigations are necessary in most cases, which, for example, target the perpetrator's web of lies. As a result, in practice, investigators are more concerned with the offender and their statements than they would be in cases pertaining to offences that are less personal and more tangible. This is disadvantageous in view of the fact that the perpetrator wants to avoid coming under suspicion of terrorism financing. Nevertheless, investigators should always consider terrorism financing as being a possible destination of fraudulent funds.

Insurance fraud might be the most likely candidate for terrorism financing because it can in many cases be carried out rather simply and does not require in-depth specialist knowledge. Hypothetically, a fictitious car accident could be agreed upon by two parties who have colluded. Unlike many other fraud scenarios, a fake car accident does not require any special expertise in order to build a complex web of lies. All that is ultimately required is to collude with a second driver and cause a fender bender at a low speed to defraud insurers. However, while this is a trivial form of revenue generation to implement, it is also ultimately a model that cannot be repeated as often as desired. At best, it is suitable for funding small to medium-sized strikes.

The situation is different with counterfeit goods. In certain circumstances, these represent ongoing and reliable sources of income: 'And I know that counterfeit products have funded some terrorist groups in the past' (Interviewee 14).

According to the interviewees, product counterfeiting is popular among terrorist financiers because counterfeiting is in many cases a criminal act that leads to significant cashflows quickly. Although amateurs in this field do not necessarily make millions, it should be possible to finance a small to medium-sized attack without much difficulty.

The fraudulent use of educational loans also plays a non-insignificant role in financing terrorism because although obtaining these loans generally requires a certificate of enrolment, the authenticity thereof is not checked consistently. Since the loans are relatively small in value, not every document presented by applicants is verified. This means that terrorist financiers can obtain cash without having to overcome major hurdles by forging a certificate of enrolment and using it to apply for a small loan for educational purposes.

Ultimately, narcotics trafficking remains an important source of income for terrorists, as certain areas that are either controlled or at least populated by terrorists are suitable for narcotics cultivation:

> Other terrorist organizations that don't have that or they're clearly involved in drug trafficking, clearly, [...] and that's still operating, and the question is can you get on top of that and in countries like Pakistan, I think that's completely impossible. (Interviewee 14)

This means that terrorist financiers can operate relatively freely and undisturbed in these areas of cultivation, which are often not governed by the principles of the rule of law. It is therefore all the more important to block the export routes for these drugs and to prevent their sale in Europe. However, in the context of proceedings for violations of the Narcotics Act, terrorism financing is rarely considered as a possible motive, and perpetrators are unlikely to raise this subject willingly during questioning. It is reasonable to expect them to cite either greed or support for needy family members as motives. It is therefore essential that investigators in such proceedings should not only analyse offences against the Narcotics Act and, in some circumstances, possible money laundering in connection with assets derived from a crime, but they should also consider other possible motives such as terrorism financing.

One source of income that has attracted relatively little attention to date is kidnapping in Europe. It is common knowledge that terrorist groups repeatedly kidnap people in their territories in order to extort ransom money:

> Yes, the classic kidnappings. So no matter where, whether that's IS or that's the case in Pakistan or that's the case in, still, Latin America is the case or that's the case in Africa, where just a Western hostage. Really, that's an investment. (Interviewee 14)

Some states are suspected of paying for the release of their kidnapped citizens; others do not allow themselves to be blackmailed. It is clear that a relatively large sum of money can be made through kidnapping in the course of a one-off act. It would therefore be logical if terrorists were to utilize kidnappings in Europe as a source of income. In order to reduce the risk of being caught while releasing victims in exchange for money, they could focus on either extorting smaller sums or receiving payment in a territory they control. It is questionable whether wealthy individuals would involve the police in a ransom demand for CHF 300,000. In many cases, it would probably be in the best interests of the relatives of the victim to comply with the kidnappers' demand not to involve the police. However, if the ransom were handed over in an IS-controlled area, larger sums would also be entirely possible.

Engaging in other forms of blackmail is also conceivable. Should important information, such as Western companies' trade or business secrets, fall into the hands of terrorists, they could attempt to blackmail the companies. This is particularly problematic for prosecutors because terrorists tend to retreat to areas under their control in order to carry out their deeds.

Another potential source of income at the interface between the Western world and IS-controlled areas is human trafficking. By extending its territory, the IS repeatedly succeeds in bringing people of other religions under its control. In certain circumstances, these people can be sold at a profit.

Furthermore, according to the interviewees, the fraudulent use of data processing systems for terrorism financing is also a problem. In particular, the manipulation of telephony systems to dial premium telephone numbers seems to be suitable for this purpose:

> There were phone numbers hacked. Unused telephone numbers, if you take a large company. They have an internal telephone system with lots of internal numbers. And if you know that no one is working on this number at the moment, that this number is not assigned internally, and you then manage to hack into such a number, then you can generate calls via this number. (Interviewee 5)

Calls made in this way to premium numbers result in the payment of high fees, some of which the perpetrators collect. This approach has the advantage that it can be implemented in electronic form and thus from abroad. However, it should be noted that a certain level of expertise in the information technology (IT) sector is generally required for this method to be used, and it is unclear to what extent terrorists have the necessary knowledge.

One final and rather banal form of terrorism financing should not go unnoticed, namely theft. This is ultimately a form of terrorism financing that in many cases can be implemented without special expertise and should be relatively inconspicuous.

In summary, terrorists have access to a variety of possible sources of revenue. It is simply not possible to eliminate each of them. Nevertheless, it is useful to raise awareness of the threat of terrorism financing among investigators in various fields in order to identify early on that terrorists are involved. However, combating terrorism financing is an extraordinarily complex matter that cannot be tackled by selective interventions like other forms of crime.

The findings of this empirical study extend far beyond those of other studies. It is true that the existing literature has also referred to regional sources of income, the taxation of the activities of other criminals and drug cultivation in particular.[606] However, the interviewees were able to provide much more detailed information on these sources of terrorism financing, and the experts succeeded in pointing out concrete procedures that had not yet been sufficiently considered in the literature reviewed.

The literature does also assume that terrorists resort to a variety of illegal sources of income to fund their activities.[607] These include smuggling, fraud, theft, drug trafficking, kidnapping, robbery, extortion and money laundering.[608] However, the range of practices identified by the interviewees in this study is much broader and represents a significant increase in empirical knowledge gained through this investigation.

Nevertheless, it should also be mentioned that within the framework of the literature review, some sources of income were identified that were not mentioned by the interview partners at all or only in different contexts, such as hawala banking. The literature review suggested that the proceeds of these hawala activities are partly used for terrorism financing, whereas 'he interview partners considered hawala banking not only a source of income but also a form of wealth transfer.[609]

4.3 Capital transfer

The previous section has shown the variety of revenue sources available to terrorist financiers. However, what is common among many of these sources of income is that sooner or later assets have to be transferred. This can take place

606 Simser, 2011: p. 335; Makarenko, 2004: p. 130.
607 Linn, 2005: p. 209.
608 Dalyan, 2008: p. 140.
609 Abuza, 2003: p. 171.

between purely financing parties and the executing terrorists on the one hand and between different countries on the other.

However, it must be explicitly pointed out that while the transfer of assets is an extremely important starting point for investigations, other approaches should also be taken into account. After all, it may be possible for perpetrators who concentrate on small-scale attacks to finance them without having to transfer assets.

In addition to banking and parallel banking systems, cryptocurrencies such as Bitcoin and so-called money transfer systems are discussed below. Furthermore, the personal transfer of assets is also discussed. Due to its particular complexity and the hurdles created by compliance departments for terrorist financiers, the analysis of the banking system is naturally somewhat more extensive than that of the other sectors and procedures.

4.3.1 Banking system

4.3.1.1 Banking system – general suitability

In principle, the banking system is characterized by more extensive controls than other sectors. Nevertheless, in many cases, terrorist financiers are difficult to distinguish from other clients – mainly because banks only see a fraction of the process and in many cases have to rely on the information provided by the client. In addition, measures to combat terrorism financing are in many cases mixed with those to prevent money laundering, thereby blurring the focus. This is extremely problematic because remittances ensure the rapid transfer of money and smaller amounts often go unnoticed. Since high-risk countries such as Turkey are not considered suspicious per se, and transfers to the border area of Syria are thus still possible, the banking system's general suitability for the transfer of assets intended for terrorism financing can certainly be assumed.

Banks generally have particularly strict control mechanisms. In contrast to many other industries, the financial sector maintains extensive compliance departments that establish control mechanisms and review individual transactions to ensure that they comply with the rules. Therefore, at first glance, banks might be considered rather unsuitable for the transfer of assets intended for terrorism financing; however, this is a fallacy:

> So again, not that the banks are all clean, please don't take it that way, but I think the likelihood that you can still represent something through the banks is significantly more difficult or less likely than if you go into other areas. (Interviewee 8)

A more detailed analysis shows that the existing control mechanisms can be circumvented relatively easily, largely due to the fact that in many cases it is difficult to distinguish terrorist financiers from other bank clients: 'And it is inconceivably difficult in my understanding to distinguish the few bad guys – and I think they are really few – from the overwhelmingly good' (Interviewee 8). This applies mainly to intelligent perpetrators who are familiar with the average profiles of dangerous persons. It can therefore be assumed that intelligent terrorist financiers do not make an appearance themselves if they meet the criteria of suspected person profiles and watchlists developed by the investigating authorities and shared with the banks. Nevertheless, these perpetrator profiles are ultimately useful since there are always perpetrators who do not have the necessary expertise to avoid detection and thus act carelessly. As a rule, however, these are likely to be less important members of terrorist groups. In principle, it can be stated that terrorist financiers are difficult to distinguish from other bank customers and banks are therefore still likely to be suitable for the transfer of assets intended for terrorism financing.

Since many banks mix up the fight against terrorism financing with the prevention of money laundering, compliance measures are often only partially effective:

> On the one hand, identifying the beneficial owner and then monitoring the transactions and matching them against lists, sanctions lists, EU lists, money laundering, checklists, et cetera. In other words, I don't think there's a lot of sensitivity about what the difference actually is exactly between terrorism financing or money laundering. (Interviewee 7)

Ultimately, terrorism financing and money laundering are two fundamentally different offences. It is true that legislators around the world have combined both offences in the same laws, such as the Swiss Federal Act on Combating Money Laundering and Terrorism financing of 10 October 1997. However, this does not change the fact that money laundering basically starts with incriminated assets (i.e. assets originating from a crime) and is usually aimed at making it more difficult to trace the origin or at thwarting confiscation, which is often achieved by integrating the assets into the legal economic cycle. In the case of terrorism financing, the starting point is often different, since the assets do not necessarily have to be incriminated. Moreover, the offence does not aim at integration into the legal economic cycle but at the opposite, namely a detachment from legal structures. Since the criminal acts of terrorist financiers lie in the future and their transactions are in many cases not based on prior unlawful acts, applying the same measures used to combat money laundering to terrorism financing is often ineffective. This is another reason why banks are still suitable for terrorism financing.

Furthermore, it is still possible to transfer funds to risky countries such as Turkey. These transactions are not automatically considered suspicious:

> Just because they are now on the border there with the crisis areas and there is a certain amount of influence throughout the country, that doesn't mean that every business activity in Turkey is illegal per se or ultimately money laundering or terrorism financing is automatically suspected. (Interviewee 7)

This means that banks enable terrorists to transfer funds cheaply and securely from Central Europe to the border with Syria. Therefore, banks are significantly better suited to terrorism financing than other mechanisms, such as physical transfers, which involve higher costs and risks.

One problem, however, is that crisis countries, such as Syria, no longer have the appropriate infrastructure to receive remittances from Central Europe. This means that terrorist financiers have to switch to sending funds to neighbouring countries instead. However, this is not a significant problem for the perpetrators (consider the banks in Turkey mentioned above) and does not limit the general suitability of banks for the transfer of assets intended for terrorism financing.

This is particularly true because terrorist financiers often transfer smaller amounts: 'But other than that, it's extremely difficult to tell because, as I said, it's often smaller amounts that don't stand out in a big way either going in or going out' (Interviewee 3). It is simply not economically viable to review every small transaction in detail. It is true that transaction analyses can be used to identify and selectively analyse certain trends and anomalies; however, it cannot be assumed that every transaction intended for terrorism financing will be uncovered by transaction analyses.

In addition, transfers usually have to be executed quickly. This means that there is usually a relatively short time frame for checking individual transactions. It is certainly possible to block transactions in order to check them more closely and, if necessary, report them to the relevant reporting offices. However, this may not be the case for the majority of transactions.

In summary, it can be said that despite certain compliance measures, banks are still suitable for the transfer of assets in the context of terrorism financing, especially for intelligent and well-trained perpetrators who inform themselves in advance about the banks' preventive measures and act accordingly. Due to the low costs and the possibility of transferring large sums relatively risk-free, banks are likely to remain an instrument of choice for terrorist financiers. It goes without saying that further differentiation between banks is necessary, as not all financial service providers are equally suited to the transfer of assets to or from certain territories. Banks with many Turkish customers who regularly make legitimate remittances to their home country are likely to tend to be more suitable for the transfer of terrorist funds to Turkey than a financial institution that has little to no business relations with Turkey. However, it is reasonable to assume that intelligent perpetrators also take this into account.

4.3.1.2 Banking system – concrete approach

Now that it has been sufficiently demonstrated that banks are in principle likely to be suitable for terrorism financing, the question arises as to how intelligent terrorist financiers actually proceed. In this subsection, the perspective of perpetrators who act as skilfully as possible will be taken. If it is possible to anticipate their behaviour, it should also be possible to identify perpetrators who act less intelligently. However, it would not be sufficient to restrict the analysis to the banal procedures of less skilled perpetrators, as it is reasonable to assume that intelligent people also finance terrorism.

First of all, it can be assumed that intelligent perpetrators use either online banks or financial service providers specializing in certain regions. Banks with branches abroad also seem to be suitable, as this means that transfers can be processed internally within the group, and thus lower standards can possibly be expected during verification. For example, Turkish banks with branches in Germany may be suitable. However, intelligent perpetrators avoid sending funds to high-risk countries such as Iraq.

Furthermore, it should be emphasized that thoughtfully acting perpetrators use straw men, i.e. persons who act on their behalf, and ensure a legal source of funds. In doing so, they deliberately manipulate preconceptions to create supposedly low-risk profiles. In addition, they promptly disclose alleged business partners as well as provide plausible, traceable explanations for their transactions and back them up with documents such as invoices and order confirmations.

In this context, documents are provided in foreign languages and stamps are usually used. Professional perpetrators may even set up their own companies in Turkey to serve as a cover for terrorism financing. Possible explanations offered for their transactions include consultations and investments. Those who regularly transfer money to Turkey not only set up companies there but also in Germany or Switzerland, for example. Ensuring that they have entries in the commercial register and informative websites are considered particularly helpful in this context. The purpose of the front company is chosen in such a way that any transactions can be made plausible. For example, funeral homes, tour operators or logistics providers are suitable for this purpose. Alternatively, cultural associations, NGOs or charitable foundations could also be used as a cover. In addition, legal structures for lobbying and advertising could be created. One can seek default judgments or have contracts notarized in order to justify payments and support any queries with documentation.

In any case, it is obvious that terrorist financiers aim to divide larger amounts of money into smaller transactions in order to attract less attention. In addition, a skilled perpetrator could make frequent transactions using the appropriate structure. Finally, perpetrators might also consult with experts before executing the transaction in order to choose the lowest-risk approach.

On the other hand, those who only want to transfer small amounts can, among other things, resort to using refugees who claim to be making transfers to sick family members back home. Alternatively, they could also fake a carpet purchase or the loss of a wallet in the centre of Istanbul, for example. If, on the other hand, they want to transfer funds not to Syria but to a Central European country, they could pretend to be Arab tourists vacationing in Munich. They could then withdraw the transferred amount in cash and distribute it to any accomplices. The use of prepaid cards, on the other hand, is generally avoided by terrorist financiers because these are already the focus of investigators.

It is reasonable to assume that perpetrators integrate online banks into their transactions. This is simply because banking relationships in this case are not based on personal contact between the customer and the bank's employees. For people who have something to hide, this can be advantageous because they can provide their information in writing and thus in a considered manner. In addition, it is more difficult to expose written lies, as the customer's voice, gestures and facial expressions cannot be included in the analysis of the validity of their statements.

Furthermore, financial service providers specializing in certain regions or cultures are also suitable for terrorism financing: 'They also have, I'll say, specialist service providers, I don't want to call it ethnic banking now, that sounds so strange, but who specialise precisely in certain ethnic groups' (Interviewee 8). For example, Turkish banks with branches in Germany are particularly suitable for transfers from Germany to Turkey because these banks process a large number of transfers from Germany to Turkey and a transaction with a Turkish connection would go relatively unnoticed.

Alternatively, terrorist financiers could of course choose German or international banks in Turkey:

> So I go to HSBC in Germany with my money, say: Here, put into my account such and such amount, and now why don't you transfer that into my account at HSBC in, I don't know, let's take Turkey or let's take Iran or wherever they have a presence. (Interviewee 8)

For terrorist financiers, this offers an advantage in that intra-group transfers are generally subject to less detailed scrutiny: 'After all, I don't check with us within the corporate structure to see if it's okay' (Interviewee 8). Finally, there is an implicit assumption that intra-group compliance is working and that the parties have already been reviewed.

Nevertheless, terrorist financiers sensibly avoid transactions with overly risky countries such as Iraq. Such transactions have the disadvantage that they are automatically subject to more detailed scrutiny, as Iraq is considered to be a high-risk country for terrorism financing. It can therefore be assumed that taking the risk of having to make declarations is primarily reserved for legitimate transactions that are actually business related and can only be carried out via Iraq. As a rule, terrorist financiers choose less suspicious countries.

The fact that Turkey is repeatedly referred to in this work should not lead to misunderstanding. The references to Turkey are based on the statements of the interview partners who repeatedly highlighted Turkey as a particularly suitable pathway for terrorism financing due to its geographical proximity to Syria on the one hand and its regulatory weaknesses on the other.

In order to endure possible investigations without the banks reporting to the competent authorities, clever terrorist financiers generally do not use incriminated assets. When using funds derived from a crime, there is ultimately a double risk of discovery – the bank could report its suspicion of both money laundering and terrorism financing to the authorities. Thus, from the perspective of terrorist financiers, it makes no sense to transfer incriminated assets through the banking system to fund terrorism. If funds originating from a crime need to be transferred, it makes more sense to use one of the other methods presented in this paper, such as the personal transfer.

Moreover, it is not necessary for terrorist financiers to act in their own name. Usually, they look for straw men to carry out the transactions in someone else's name. For this purpose, they choose individuals who will not draw suspicion and who can plausibly explain transfers to the terrorist financiers' target country without encountering any problems:

> That is common. So this is not only in the field of terrorism, but quite other, um, criminal activities, such as human trafficking, human smuggling or drug trafficking, then usually people are fronted. That's such a behaviour that is quite well known, and you find that in the scene as well. (Interviewee 1)

For example, it makes sense to use Turkish migrants with elderly parents living in Istanbul. A transfer of CHF 2,000 can usually be plausibly justified as a living allowance or as assistance in paying a medical bill.

When selecting stooges, skilful terrorist financiers take common prejudices into account. The author explicitly distances himself from these prejudices but points out that our society continues to be shaped by certain stereotypes. Intelligent perpetrators use these stereotypes to appear as unsuspicious as possible: 'An intelligent person embraces those biases and actually looks: how do I get a profile in surveillance, which is low-risk?' (Interviewee 8). Using people who might typically quickly come under suspicion as stooges is avoided. People who would not normally be considered terrorists are targeted instead, such as young mothers or senior citizens.

Should larger transfers become necessary, the justifications provided by the stooges must be stronger and more sophisticated. Here, the key to success for terrorist financiers ultimately lies in being able to provide detailed explanations for the transactions. These explanations must be plausible in order to withstand at least cursory scrutiny.

In addition, it is important for terrorist financiers to be able to promptly disclose the explanations for their transactions. They willingly provide information about their business partners: '[So] that you really know which client I'm dealing with and more importantly, who are my client's business partners' (Interviewee 8). This means that stories are constructed in advance and disclosed upon first request:

> I don't know if I would come like that in the first place. But if the question comes, I would deliver that right away and say, 'Yes, of course. We understand that you have compliance obligations, you have education obligations, and we know that. It's not the first time we've been asked. Here you go, here are the documents'. (Interviewee 14)

If the terrorist financier is initially thrown off by the bank's queries and struggles to provide an explanation, they will ultimately miss the opportunity to immediately rebut the bank's initial suspicions. This means that the bank could carry out further clarifications to ensure the validity of the transaction.

In order to rebut any initial suspicions of illicit activities, the perpetrator ideally submits supportive documents. This is done not only because documents convey a certain credibility and substantiate the stories being told but also because doing so gives the bank the opportunity to document its investigations cleanly and without great effort. Although there are probably banks that are interested in preventing the financing of terrorism, most financial service providers are primarily concerned with protecting themselves from sanctions. Therefore, a clean paper trail detailing the bank's adherence to compliance measures is in many cases more important for the bank than the actual fight against terrorism financing. After all, provided the bank can prove that it has taken all reasonable organizational measures to prevent the offence, it will ultimately not face significant sanctions. A smart terrorist financier takes into account the bank's priorities and paves the way for compliance officers by presenting credible documents that the bank can include in its files.

Terrorist financiers use invoices and payment confirmations, among other things, for this purpose. However, there is always the question of the volume of the transaction. Simple invoices are usually sufficient for the transfer of smaller amounts. For example, a Turkish person living in Germany could present fictitious medical bills from family members in Istanbul to justify their remittances to Turkey. It is quite plausible that a Turkish person would want to support their family members and therefore transfer money to Turkey to serve this purpose. A Syrian perpetrator could also pretend to want to support sick relatives back home by sending funds:

> Someone sent his brother 1,000, 2,000 euros and he had the problem here in court, or not him, but the justice system had the problem of proving that it was IS financing, when he said, 'my brother was ill, I had to pay his doctor/he had to pay a doctor's bill. That's a purely family matter, I had to pay him/he's in Syria, I don't even know what/I don't know anything about IS', he then said, 'I sent him 1,000 or 2,000 euros or dollars because he told me he needed the money. He's sick'. (Interviewee 9)

Even if it should turn out ex post that the money transferred was used to finance terrorism, it cannot be proven that the perpetrator knew this in advance at this point. They can claim to have acted only with the intention of supporting a sick relative.

Using Turkish medical bills as a front offers an additional advantage because they are written in a foreign language: 'So that starts with the fact that when in doubt, you can't speak the language, or if push comes to shove, you can't even decipher the writing' (Interviewee 8). If the originator of the transfer does not use a bank specializing in transfers to Turkey, a more detailed review of the matter is likely to fail from the start due to the compliance officers' lack of knowledge of the Turkish language. This may be particularly helpful where genuine documents are not involved. However, in the case of medical invoices, there is nothing to prevent terrorist financiers from using genuine documents as they are easy to obtain. For example, one could ask their relatives in Turkey to hand over their last ten medical bills. In so doing, it is also possible to deceive banks with Turkish-speaking compliance officers. However, the applicability of this approach is obviously limited to smaller amounts. It is simply not plausible for a Turkish person to spend six-figure euro amounts each year to pay the medical bills of their extended family members living in Turkey. Where the upper limit lies in an individual case cannot ultimately be determined without taking into account the client's income and personal assets, so no precise figures are given here.

Another way of transferring smaller amounts is to present order confirmations. These can also be obtained with relatively little effort. For example, the use of stamps can lend increased credibility to the documents. However, this is a considerable fallacy, as stamps are ultimately very easy to forge. They can usually be obtained conveniently via the Internet. Unless they are specially protected stamps, such as those of notaries and doctors, there are often no queries.

Another plausible explanation for the transfer of small amounts to Turkey is the support of family members of refugees:

> And what I can imagine is, of course, when you talk about the area of transactions to Turkey, that you have, of course, in the context of the refugee movement, that we have, of course, many people who have immigrated from the crisis areas, where there are terrorist activities, I say, to Western or near-Western countries, have now established a legal identity or a legal life there, are registered, have a business, et cetera. And there you can trace the history, where do these people come from, what kind of connections do they have, that's hard to trace. (Interviewee 7)

Refugees should have no trouble justifying their personal relationships with certain areas. It is not uncommon for families to be separated from each other while fleeing conflict zones, and the need to support family members living elsewhere is also understandable.

If no refugees are available as stooges, a terrorist financier could also physically travel to Turkey and pretend to have lost their wallet or want to buy an expensive carpet:

> So I just bring up the example of someone having a large amount of money in Istanbul and has an Arabic-sounding name but with French citizenship. Maybe it's a good family man who wants to buy a carpet, or who has had his wallet stolen and urgently needs cash to pay for his hotel. (Interviewee 13)

In these examples, the perpetrator withdraws money from their German or French account at an ATM in Istanbul and hands over the cash to a terrorist organization. In the end, these justifications are also plausibly comprehensible and the investigating authorities are unlikely to succeed in proving the opposite.

While making a cash withdrawal in Istanbul should not generally be suspicious, even making a similar transaction on the border with Syria can hardly be plausibly justified, and terrorist financiers already know this. There have been some perpetrators who, on the last leg of their journey to Syria, have withdrawn cash from ATMs in Turkey near the Syrian border which has understandably raised suspicion and led to further investigations. Making cash withdrawals in tourist cities, such as Istanbul or Antalya, on the other hand, which are visited by hundreds of thousands of innocent Central Europeans every year for holiday purposes, is not only unsuspicious but for practical reasons cannot be further verified. After all, compliance officers cannot be expected to scrutinize the transactions of every holidaymaker in Turkey. This would be simply impossible. Therefore, this offers an excellent cover for smaller amounts.

For larger amounts, it might be helpful to use genuine notarized documents. Many civil law contracts do not require public certification; however, this does not mean that notarization is impossible. For example, in order to give a loan agreement greater credibility, terrorist financiers could have it notarized by a notary in Germany or abroad:

> You have, of course, I say, because of the linguistic differences and the distance, nevertheless, not the chance to somehow put all this into reasonable doubt. Especially when you bring this example with the notarial certification, et cetera then, no. (Interviewee 7)

This ultimately facilitates the bank's compliance review since on the one hand it may rely on a public deed and on the other hand it can carry out a review with relatively little effort. Finally, the bank can contact the certifying notary and enquire whether the deed is genuine. However, a material verification of the contents of the deed is not mandatory for the notary and is often not possible.

Although there are notaries who exercise appropriate caution and take a closer look at the parties and the objectively significant contractual points before notarization, a question arises as to whether the notary has an interest in engaging in a material review of the loan agreement. Ultimately, it is not possible for a notary to do this conclusively, and considering the fees paid for the notarization, the notary is likely to limit their contribution to doing what is necessary and only correcting obviously incorrect information.

Insofar as terrorist financiers embrace the utility of the public deed or frequently require invoices and order confirmations, it is obvious that they need to directly or indirectly control the parties noted on the deeds. For this purpose, it is a good idea for them to set up legal entities that carry out transactions between themselves. Consultancy and investment companies, among others, seem to be particularly suitable for this purpose.

Consultancy firms offer an advantage in that their services can hardly be objectified. It is true that it is now difficult to freely invent services rendered and charge for them without any actual activity, as evidence of the work performed is occasionally required; however, it is not usually possible to attribute a specific value to the work performed by consultants. There is usually some discretion exercised in this regard. On the one hand, this is due to different hourly rates, but on the other hand, it is also due to the fact that the time spent is difficult to measure and the pricing is correspondingly non-transparent.

The same is true for investment companies such as venture capital and private equity firms. The value of an investment in another company is ultimately in the eye of the beholder. While there are a variety of valuation methods, they are fundamentally susceptible to manipulation. For example, although a discounted cash flow analysis allows the value of a company to be determined in a perfectly understandable analysis, ultimately the result can be easily influenced by adjusting the interest rate. This means that payments for the purchase or sale of shares can be justified.

For example, a terrorist financier could purchase shares in a medium-sized company from the party to be financed. The parties have the share purchase agreement publicly notarized. In addition, an auditor is commissioned to determine the value of the company. Subsequently, the publicly notarized share purchase agreement, the valuation report and extracts from the commercial register are submitted to the bank to enable the transaction to be executed. At this point, the bank relies on documents with increased credibility. Many banks will be satisfied with this approach.

If a more detailed review of the matter does occur, it is important for terrorist financiers to ensure that the companies involved not only exist but can be easily found on the Internet. A convincing Internet presence ultimately helps to increase the credibility of the operation and to document the review. Finally, the compliance officer in charge can save the content of the website and place it in the file. This should allow the compliance officer to approve the transaction without being negligent.

Those who do not already have companies but would still like to finance terrorism on a large scale and, above all, on a regular basis, have the option of founding corresponding companies. This is ultimately possible to do with relatively little effort in Central Europe and Turkey. The business of the front company is chosen in such a way that any transactions it undertakes can be made plausible. In contrast to consulting companies and investment companies, which help to explain one-off larger transactions, funeral companies, tour operators or logistics companies are suitable fronts for regular transactions.

The advantage of establishing such companies in Central Europe and Turkey is that although a more detailed clarification of the business and its purposes is usually made at the beginning of the business relationship with the bank, similarly detailed examinations of individual transactions are often dispensed with afterwards. In addition to justifying transfers abroad, having a good story to tell also immediately makes plausible the personal presence of terrorist financiers in certain regions:

> So a classic, I'll say, which also went through the press at the time, you open a funeral home. Sounds a bit strange at first, but if you say: Well, we just have a lot of people who want to be buried in their home country, then you definitely have someone who can plausibly explain to you why they are regularly down on the ground in the Middle East. (Interviewee 8)

If a bank enters into a business relationship with an internationally active funeral home company, the compliance department will certainly check whether the company actually carries out international funerals. However, this review usually takes place at the beginning of the business relationship. As soon as the compliance officer has confirmed the first funerals of Turks residing in Germany or Switzerland taking place in Turkey, it will hardly take the trouble to check every single transaction thereafter in a similarly conscientious manner. Any review of further transactions will focus primarily on anomalous transfers and may include a check of common transactions. Ideally, then, a skilled terrorist financier actually runs a funeral home that organizes international funerals and then allows transactions intended for terrorism financing to be buried in amongst the legitimate remittances.

Furthermore, the terrorist financier could also operate a logistics company:

> Oh, I suddenly start transferring money to Turkey or Russia or, I don't know, somewhere, that's conspicuous. But if I go there and say: So, I have an international company here, I do transport, I have a nice homepage for it, where I can also see: 'Look, he transports to the Middle East'. Because of me, he also says he specializes in, I don't know, transporting patients or something similar. Then it works out wonderfully. (Interviewee 8)

Ultimately, the plausibility of the story is always important. It is quite conceivable that an internationally active logistics company will need to make legitimate transfers abroad.

The same applies to tourism companies. Those that regularly sell Turkish holidays to clients in Germany usually have to pay hotel and resort bills in Turkey. This means that these companies make a large number of legitimate transfers from Germany to Turkey, and these could be used as a cover for terrorism financing transactions. The same applies to logistics companies that regularly transport goods between Turkey and Central Europe.

Alternatively, cultural associations, NGOs or charitable foundations can also be used as cover:

> They can be foundations, they can be cultural associations, they can be some kind of support groups that give themselves some kind of outward appearance, as I said,

> all these cultural associations that you have here, all these NGOs, some kind of non-governmental organizations that give themselves some kind of appearance as being charitable, benevolent. But behind that, in the end, there is an organization that is close to a political organization, a terrorist organization. (Interviewee 7)

However, terrorist financiers generally avoid utilizing non-profit organizations because, in principle, a transfer from a Turkish cultural association is viewed more critically than a similar transaction from a tour operator. This is simply because non-profit organizations have repeatedly come under suspicion for serving the purposes of financing terrorism. Intelligent terrorist financiers are well aware of these prejudices, even though they are of course unjustified in many cases.

Should a perpetrator still wish to use an NGO to send funds, they will make plausible the story behind the transaction:

> Of course, it always has to be in the recipient's name, if you can Google it and it's an NGO that you can trace, then that's fine with us. If it goes, let's say, to the Red Crescent, that's fine with me too. If, on the other hand, it's somewhere I really couldn't trace, then we'd be more suspicious. (Interviewee 3)

A clever perpetrator therefore ensures that their Internet presence is beyond reproach and may also organize a corresponding entry to be made in an official register.

Advertising and lobbying structures are also of limited use to terrorist financiers. While these structures can certainly be used to justify payment flows, the difficulty in tracing the actual activity and its value is an obstacle in many cases. In particular, payments to lobbyists could also trigger corruption investigations. Therefore, these structures are now avoided by skilled terrorist financiers.

A very clever method of terrorism financing, on the other hand, is the obtaining of default judgments. In this case, the paying party allows itself to be sued by the receiving party before a court in Switzerland. It is obvious that the summary procedure within the scope of Arts 248 ff. CH-StPO and ordinary proceedings in the sense of Arts 219 ff. CH-StPO would also be possible. The trick used by the terrorist financiers is that the claimant justifies their claim in great detail and with documentary evidence. For example, the failure to repay a loan within the scope of Arts 312 ff. Code of Obligations could be asserted. The defendant disputes the claim in a general way (i.e. by means of the formula 'in its entirety and in all details') but fails to substantiate even in principle why the claim is unjustified. Rather, the defendant engages in appellatory criticism which is in no case suitable for raising doubts about the plaintiff's statements.

Should the case reach the stage of a courtroom hearing, the defendant's defence is emotional but factually unsubstantiated. In each case, the plaintiff justifies their claim in detail, credibly and with reference to the applicable laws. Taking into account the maxim of negotiation and disposition, the judge ultimately has no choice but to approve the claim. Naturally, the defendant waives the right to a written statement of the reasons for the judgment in order to at least keep the court costs within reasonable limits.

Subsequently, the respondent contacts their bank and orders the transfer of the amount awarded in the court judgment to the other party. Should any queries arise from the compliance department, the respondent promptly submits a copy of the judgment obliging them to make the payment. In the absence of a statement of reasons explaining the judgment, the bank is unable to question why the claim was approved and typically assumes that the court has reviewed all the facts. However, the entire case was a farce.

Since such legal proceedings are a rather complex method of terrorism financing, it is obvious that experts should be consulted: 'I think there are people on the opposite side now who know the structures and can exploit those structures' (Interviewee 8). However, it is not necessary for the terrorist financier to inform the expert of their actual motives. It is sufficient to mandate a lawyer to assert a claim arising from a loan relationship within the meaning of Arts 312 ff. OR. The lawyer does not necessarily have to know that the true purpose is terrorism financing. The defendant, on the other hand, does not need to rely on any special expertise – they simply need to argue their case banally and unobjectively to ensure that the claim is approved.

Apart from the default action, most of the procedures previously mentioned that can be used for the purposes of financing terrorism are more suitable for smaller amounts. It therefore makes sense for terrorist financiers to split up larger amounts into smaller transactions order to attract less attention: 'Then, if you're also kind of splitting and staying below any critical thresholds, you don't stand a chance as a bank' (Interviewee 7). However, the exact amount that constitutes the threshold varies depending on each individual case.

The focus of this section is primarily on the transfer of assets from Central Europe to terrorist-controlled areas. However, the reverse is also possible. For example, a terrorist financier from Syria could pose as an Arab tourist in Munich and have funds transferred to an account in Dubai. The transferred amount is then withdrawn in cash in Munich and distributed to accomplices in Germany. The use of prepaid cards is avoided in this context because investigators have been focusing on their use since the 2016 Paris attacks. Therefore, an intelligent terrorist financier refrains from regularly making transactions with prepaid cards to avoid attracting unnecessary attention.

This section has presented a variety of ways in which assets can be transferred through the banking system for the purposes of terrorism financing. The breadth of methods outlined is based not only on the wide-ranging expertise of the interviewees but above all on the needs of terrorist financiers. In particular, a distinction must be made between small and large transactions and between one-off and regular transactions.

This section has shown that, despite all compliance efforts, using the banking system is still suitable for terrorism financing. Some of the concrete approaches taken by intelligent perpetrators have been explained to substantiate this claim. At the same time, however, it must be emphasized that only a fraction of the possible approaches can be dealt with within the scope of this work. For example, some of the various methods could be combined, thus resulting in several more possible avenues to explore – ultimately, one could devote a separate chapter to each of the majority of the methods. The purpose of this section, however, is primarily to give the reader an overview of several of the more prominent methods and to pick up on the essential points. It does not claim to be exhaustive.

The purpose of this research is not to provide guidance on terrorism financing. Rather, the aim is to identify gaps in the system so that they can be closed through appropriate measures. However, it must be borne in mind that it will not suffice to tighten or intensify banks' compliance measures. A global approach that also takes the instruments of criminal procedure into account and raises awareness among other professional groups, such as judges and notaries, is crucial to ensure that the fight against terrorism financing is successful.

4.3.1.3 Banking system – detection risks

The detection risks associated with the individual methods aforementioned should also be considered. First of all, banks' transaction analyses should be mentioned. However, known typologies of so-called foreign terrorist fighters are also increasingly being used. Persons with Arabic-sounding names, for example, are considered particularly suspicious.

Carrying out transactions anonymously is generally no longer possible, and in certain circumstances, banks do background checks on their customers' transactions. However, this poses a relatively limited risk to terrorist financiers because the beneficial owners on the receiving end often remain a mystery to the bank. Moreover, clearly traceable documentation significantly reduces the risk of detection. Consequently, a the future criminal intent behind a transaction cannot usually be established in the present. Suspicious transactions often get lost among legitimate ones. Only transfers of large amounts of money typically increase the risk of detection.

Nevertheless, it can be assumed that terrorist financiers do not act negligently, and both banks and perpetrators keep up to date with the news cycle. While it is usually difficult to differentiate between terrorism financing and legitimate cash withdrawals, thanks to the media, it should by now be common knowledge that cash withdrawals made in areas bordering Syria are considered highly suspicious.

The detection risks associated with individual methods of transferring funds should not be neglected. In particular, it is important to highlight the banks' transaction analyses. These aim to identify and possibly block anomalous transactions and are often based on the customer's profile, their previous transactions and their individual business relationships. It is true that this is a very significant risk for terrorist financiers. However, it is relatively easy to circumvent this risk by always ensuring that the transactions carried out are compatible with the profile of the customer relationship. For example, a transfer from an established tour operator who has been making transfers to Turkey for years is less suspicious than a transfer from a twenty-year-old German citizen who is transferring funds to Turkey for the first time. The latter will most likely have to answer queries from the bank. In the case of the former, on the other hand, the bank will assume that it is an ordinary transfer within the scope of the business's established purpose and, as a rule, will not carry out a separate check of the individual transaction.

In addition, banks regularly make use of the foreign terrorist fighter profiles provided to them by the authorities. These are often further developed internally by the financial service providers in co-operation with the authorities:

> Usually, that's also how it is in our house, we develop typologies, we have for example here/That I think, also one of the leading institutes that have now developed typologies, especially in the US then co-operation with the authorities, but also here in Europe, and here also specifically in Germany, for example foreign terrorist fighters, to identify their behaviour in the financial area. (Interviewee 1)

These profiles cannot be presented in this paper because they are confidential documents intended exclusively for the internal use of banks' compliance departments and may not be published. However, it can be assumed that intelligent perpetrators have gained at least rudimentary knowledge of certain search profiles either through their contact with bankers or through an analysis of the press. It should be common knowledge, for example, that young men who are not gainfully employed and are closing their savings accounts in order to go on a long trip tend to be more suspicious than middle-aged German women who withdraw no more than ten per cent of their checking account balance under the guise of wanting to buy a new handbag. The profiles of foreign terrorist fighters thus only pose a challenge for rash perpetrators and can be circumvented by the targeted use of supposedly unsuspicious straw men.

The same applies to people with Arabic surnames. These are generally considered particularly suspicious because many bank employees hold certain prejudices. Although these prejudices are unfounded in the majority of cases, they could nevertheless give rise to more detailed queries and a more thorough examination of the matter: 'That was then a striking number of people involved in these money flows, all with Arab names' (Interviewee 5). Intelligent offenders are aware of these biases and, if they have something to hide, avoid entering into banking relationships in their own name.

In addition, anonymous transactions are generally no longer possible: 'The likelihood of someone slipping in there who is completely anonymous and somehow gets in by accident, that's actually not representable or is not possible' (Interviewee 8). Financial service providers around the world are making efforts to identify beneficial owners in order to be able to trace transactions as thoroughly as possible. While this poses a certain risk for terrorist financiers, the targeted use of front men can also help here.

However, straw men may well have to endure a background check on the transaction as well: 'We really know our client and we also know the client's background' (Interviewee 8). In the vast majority of cases, it is sufficient to provide a plausible explanation. Moreover, in the case of larger transactions, anyone who can back up their explanation with suitable documentation generally does not have to fear any further investigation of the matter by the bank.

It is therefore essential for terrorist financiers to keep good records of any transactions they make: 'If someone is really that precise in their approach, really, I'll say, there's a traceability from the records, I think, frankly, you don't get that one in doubt at all' (Interviewee 8). Good documentation is usually comprehensible and plausible. The documentation should also appear credible and pass at least a cursory examination without raising suspicion. This means that skilful terrorist financiers craft background stories that make good business sense, are logical and can immediately and easily be supported with documentation upon request. This significantly reduces the risk of detection.

At this point, questions regarding the authenticity of the document might arise. It is much less risky to work with genuine documents. Even if a document were a genuine certification of false facts, this would usually not become known until a preliminary investigation at the earliest. Banks do not check many records that look genuine at first glance. However, if they do make an effort to verify the authenticity of the document, they are likely to rely in the vast majority of cases on the assurance of authenticity given by a notary.

It therefore makes sense for intelligent perpetrators to use genuine public deeds from abroad for larger transactions. Should the bank verify the transaction, the public notary will confirm the authenticity of the underlying document. The bank should normally rely on this assurance. After all, it can record that it has reviewed the transaction and even contacted the notary public. Thus, the bank has ultimately fulfilled its compliance obligations. However, this does not take into account the fact that in many cases the notary is not required to conduct a substantive review of the matter.

The risk of detection can be further reduced by ensuring that suspicious transactions are subsumed into legitimate transactions. For example, not all transactions involving Turkey can be specifically scrutinized:

> Well, especially to question, that would be like asking, all vehicles heading to the compass direction of Turkey, or maybe even going directly to Turkey, would have to be subject to a special control. So the question is, to what extent is this still practicable? Probably 99.9 per cent of remittances are completely legitimate, and in this mass of financial flows there will be one or the other euro that might be transferred to them by sympathizers to, I don't know, family members or anyone else or people who are active in the combat zone or at least commute there again and again. (Interviewee 6)

A skilled terrorist financier does not engage in a transaction that would immediately catch the eye of a compliance officer. Conducting a wire transfer to finance terrorism without raising suspicion would only be possible under special circumstances with outstanding documentation. An example of this would be a court judgment requiring the principal to pay a certain sum to the recipient. In the vast majority of cases, however, it is easier to consider which transactions do not stand out and to spread larger amounts over several smaller transfers.

Larger transfers generally increase the risk of detection because they attract attention, and a more detailed investigation of larger transfers is justified from a business perspective. A payment of CHF 500 from Switzerland to Turkey should not, as a rule, take up several hours of a compliance officer's time, as this effort would hardly be justifiable from the perspective of the bank which is striving to make a profit. On the other hand, a transfer of CHF 5,000,000 may well justify a compliance offer spending several days researching its validity. As mentioned above, such large transfers only make sense from the perspective of a terrorist financier if they can provide excellent documentation guaranteed to remove any shadow of a doubt at first glance. Otherwise, the risk of detection is significantly increased by the transfer of excessively large amounts.

From the perspective of terrorist financiers, it is also useful that the beneficial owners on the receiving end of the transaction often remain a mystery to the bank. This means that in many cases, the bank has no way of verifying the beneficial owner. It is forced to rely on the compliance of the bank on the receiving end instead, and in most cases, it is not empowered to exchange detailed information about transactions with other banks' compliance officers. This would ultimately be a violation of banking secrecy.

Another challenge in combating terrorism financing is that the offence being funded is usually going to be committed in the future. The risk of detection of acts that have not yet been carried out is therefore extremely low. Finally, in most cases, it will be difficult to prove that a perpetrator intends to finance terrorism. Once the perpetrator has carried out the act, it may already be too late. This is especially true if the perpetrator expects to die as a result of carrying out the financed attack. Only perpetrators who limit themselves to financing terrorism and do not carry out terrorist attacks themselves would still have to fear criminal prosecution.

In summary, it appears that terrorist financiers are particularly targeted by compliance officers and investigators, thereby significantly increasing the risk of detection, if they act carelessly or imprudently. However, it cannot be assumed that terrorist financiers act negligently as a matter of principle. As discussed above, the risk of detection can be minimized by acting logically. In many cases, the perpetrators are also aware of this and behave accordingly.

In particular, it can be assumed that banks follow the news:

> You can't avoid analysing the press these days. If you find out that there is someone who is not legitimate, then you should really start thinking in your bank why they might not want to have this business partner in the future. (Interviewee 8)

It can also be assumed that perpetrators regularly analyse the news as well. Thanks to the Internet, this does not even require much effort. Before planning a transaction, they can gather information via the Internet about the latest developments in the field of compliance and ensure that the parties involved are beyond reproach. The Internet can be used to check how other terrorist financiers have proceeded in their attempts to send funds by revealing who has been caught and how, and who and what are considered suspicious. This again significantly reduces the risk of detection.

For example, it is now common knowledge that cash withdrawals in the areas bordering Syria are considered highly suspicious, but cash withdrawals by terrorist financiers in other countries, such as Germany or Switzerland, are hardly distinguishable from legitimate transactions. It is reasonable to assume that terrorists therefore avoid making cash withdrawals in areas bordering Syria.

In terms of an overall assessment, the risk of terrorism financing via the banking system being detected is already low in principle. By taking a reasonably well-thought-out approach, the risk can be significantly reduced and in many cases virtually eliminated. At this point, it might be obvious to call for stricter compliance rules for banks. However, this makes little sense, as even an expansion of the existing compliance measures would not significantly increase terrorist financiers' risk of detection.

4.3.1.4 Banking system – overall assessment

The literature review showed that financial service providers are fundamentally working to combat terrorism financing in order to avoid reputational risks and maintain public trust. In addition, the penalties associated with breaches of the rules have been considered.[610] Unsurprisingly, therefore, the expert interviews highlighted the fact that banks monitor their clients' transactions and know who has drawn money and from where.[611]

However, the expert interviews also revealed that it is almost impossible to identify a clever terrorist financier who behaves like any other customer. This is primarily due to the fact that intelligent perpetrators often do not make use of incriminated assets and the sources of their funds are therefore not suspicious. This means that the only clue left to identify is the intended use of the funds. However, this lies in the future. If the client is able to tell a plausible story and, if necessary, back it up with documents, it is unlikely that a bank's transaction analyses will be successful in identifying the funds as being intended for terrorism purposes.

The author would like to explicitly point out at this point that this is not intended as a criticism of banks. Rather, it is up to legislators to realistically assess financial service providers' capabilities and to supplement them with other measures. The longstanding practice of outsourcing law enforcement tasks to private companies has not achieved the desired effect.[612]

610 Beekarry, 2011: p. 152; Zagaris, 2004: p. 153.
611 Barrett, 2011: p. 730.
612 Donatsch, 2017: p. 291.

4.3.2 Parallel banking systems

4.3.2.1 Parallel banking systems – general suitability

In addition to the regulated banking system, so-called parallel banking systems also appear to play a role in terrorism financing. Since these systems are generally not supervised by state authorities, in most cases they do not have sufficient compliance measures in place to prevent them from being used for terrorism purposes. This may make it considerably easier to conceal the identity of the beneficial owner. In addition, parallel banking systems can often be combined with transactions via regulated banks.

In particular, so-called hawala systems seem to play a decisive role in financing terrorism. Hawala systems are based on trust and networks. Hawala bankers usually have a day job and offer money transfer services on the side. The funds are not actually transferred but merely credited to another hawala banker elsewhere. This means that a hawala banker can take money from a customer in Zurich, and if this money is destined for a recipient in Syria, then the hawala banker in Zurich can inform their counterpart in Syria that they have just received a specific amount. After deducting a commission, the recipient can then collect the funds from the hawala banker in Syria. Both hawala bankers make a note in their files that a transaction has taken place and that the banker in Syria has a credit balance against the banker in Switzerland. If, in the course of a subsequent transaction, a client wishes to transfer funds from Syria to Switzerland, then the system works in reverse and the credit balance is – at least partially – settled between the hawala bankers. Any surpluses can be settled periodically (e.g. annually). Such parallel banking systems are legal in many countries.

Gaining access to these parallel banking systems is difficult; however, those who succeed in overcoming the hurdles often benefit from a reputable and cost-effective service. In particular, these parallel banking systems often have an infrastructure in place in areas of the world from which regulated banks have already withdrawn. This makes parallel banking systems particularly suitable alternatives for collecting ransom payments, among other things.

The fact that parallel banking systems generally do not have sophisticated compliance measures makes them particularly attractive for terrorism financing: 'That is of course already an area where there is no supervision and which is not transparent at all, and that of course offers quite a lot of opportunities to also move assets from A to B' (Interviewee 14). In these circumstances, terrorist financiers do not have to worry about concealing their transactions. Unusual transfers are also rarely noticed due to the lack of transaction analysis taking place. Moreover, parallel banking systems do not usually report suspicious transactions to the competent authorities because this would ultimately incriminate the providers of these services. Finally, parallel bankers do not have a licence to carry out this activity in Germany, Austria, Switzerland and Liechtenstein.

Sending funds using a combination of parallel banking systems with transactions made via regulated banks can create traceability difficulties for investigators that terrorist financiers exploit. This especially applies if the perpetrator primarily uses the regulated banking system and resorts to parallel banking systems as a supplement for the purposes of concealment. However, it should be emphasized at this point that the smuggling in and out of assets could ultimately cause a stir among regulated financial service providers.

Nevertheless, not everyone has easy access to parallel banking systems. These are often closed systems that are only available to certain groups of people: 'So you'd have to be from that ethnic group to get that primal confidence from hawala there' (Interviewee 15). Although belonging to a certain cultural group can significantly facilitate gaining access to parallel banking, personal contacts are ultimately necessary (which terrorist financiers are likely to have).

Another major advantage of parallel banking systems is that they are extremely cost-effective due, in part, to the lack of compliance measures mentioned at the outset. Furthermore, parallel bankers often do not work full-time as financial service providers but regard the provision of these services as a sideline, which is why they can accept lower margins.

Since the services provided by parallel banking systems are in many cases based on trust, and the reputation of the individual and their family is usually highly valued in the cultural circles typically involved, the providers of these services are generally considered reputable: 'People are very serious because they risk a lot if it doesn't work out' (Interviewee 11). The social reputations of service providers are considered a means of guaranteeing their professionalism and reliability.

Another advantage of parallel banking systems is that they also function in remote regions of the world: 'Of course, that was a big issue with Al-Qaeda, you know, because the main thing there was just to get money into the conflict area, and hawala was almost the only way to do that' (Interviewee 13). Parallel bankers are often found in areas from which regulated banks have long since withdrawn. This can be advantageous for terrorist financiers in that they can use them to transfer funds to IS-controlled areas of Syria, for example.

Finally, parallel banking systems can also be used for ransom payments. In particular, terrorist financiers who have kidnapped a person could demand payment of the ransom via parallel banking systems. This allows the ransom to be transferred across several countries within a relatively short period of time, making traceability considerably more difficult.

In conclusion, parallel banking systems are excellent options for terrorism financing, mainly because of the lack of regulation of these systems and the resulting anonymity they provide. Moreover, the presence of parallel banking systems in remote regions is also a key advantage in terms of terrorism financing. Finally, parallel banking systems transfer assets from Europe to terrorist-controlled areas (e.g. from supporters in Central Europe to IS fighters in Syria) that would not be possible via regular banking systems. It can therefore be assumed that parallel banking systems will fill this gap in the legal banking system.

4.3.2.2 Parallel banking systems – concrete approach

Now that it has been established that parallel banking systems are certainly suitable for financing terrorism, the concrete approach taken by intelligent perpetrators will be described below. Basically, trust-based cash transactions using middlemen (e.g. hawala bankers) are suitable for this approach and rely on members of certain ethnic groups to make contact.

For the transfer of larger sums to remote regions, aid organizations are also suitable covers. Alternatively, the use of fictitious invoices is also conceivable. For example, commercial transactions with values or services that are difficult to quantify could be used, although it may be necessary to obtain documents to substantiate these transactions, especially if clearing (i.e. settlement of peaks) is to take place via banks.

In most cases, however, the physical transportation of cash is likely to suffice. To do so, perpetrators deliberately involve countries without advanced banking systems. In these cases, the impossibility of transferring funds via a bank even serves as a justification for resorting to parallel banking systems.

First, the terrorist financier must find suitable parallel bankers. If they do not already know of any, they must look for appropriate contacts to be made through intermediaries and trusted persons:

> This hawala system for example, because it's just based on middlemen and trust, yeah, where ultimately at the end of the day, sometime a clearing takes place, but it's all cash based, and you just have your middlemen sitting somewhere, where of course, as someone who's used to a Western banking system, you have no access at all, because it's just a completely parallel banking system, right. (Interviewee 7)

In doing so, however, the perpetrator must proceed carefully so as not to attract attention, especially if they are in Central Europe. After all, parallel bankers have no particular interest in doing business with terrorist financiers since unregulated financial service providers do not want to attract the attention of the authorities. Thus, it makes sense for perpetrators to be discrete in their enquiries about ways to transfer money from Germany to Syria, perhaps claiming to need to help their friends or family members as a cover.

Those who belong to certain cultural circles are likely to have a much easier time of it in this context:

> But there are, let's say, groups of people from certain regions, and they want to transfer money to their home countries, and if you know you have a community, let's say of Asians or Filipinos, or that can also be Brazilians, and you have access to these groups, then you can ask: 'Where can I transfer money cheaply?' And they immediately say: 'Go to him!' or 'Go to that woman!' (Interviewee 14)

The perpetrator may also cite the lack of banking infrastructure in certain regions as their justification for choosing a parallel banking system:

> For some, there are also purely practical reasons why, even if the person is in Vienna and theoretically already has an account here, they still have to resort to hawala, simply because you have the difficulties in Country B, which in that case is Syria, and you can't do anything else because otherwise you won't get the money across the border. That would be one direction. Of course, in the other direction, the whole thing is more accessible, no question. (Interviewee 6)

The transfer of assets can therefore also take place from Syria to Germany.

Moreover, these weaknesses of the banking system are already known in certain regions. They can thus be chosen as a justification for certain courses of action:

> We also have to say that we know this from reports, from people who have come from the crisis areas in Syria and have sought asylum here. They often no longer have the possibility to access regular financial means, theoretically, if they have assets at home or bank balances or otherwise have credit balances in banks or other accounts, they can no longer access them. Simply because there are blocks, will be on the part of the organizations that currently occupy a certain area or it's just still the Syrian government, they are then sometimes dependent on such networks as a hawala network to fall back on. (Interviewee 6)

Ultimately, it is irrelevant whether the infrastructure is actually non-existent. What is important is that this story gives the terrorist financier the opportunity to make plausible the reason why it was necessary to resort to a parallel banking system to transfer funds.

Anyone who regularly transfers large sums of money will sooner or later hit the limits of hawala bankers' credulity by using the above approach of referring to needy family members or friends. In these cases, terrorist financiers can set up an aid organization as a cover. These aid organizations are indeed occasionally forced to resort to parallel banking systems as part of their everyday business:

> I actually know it off the record from, I'll say, aid organizations that have the problem. Imagine you're a relief organization and there's been a disaster somewhere in an area where there's just no Western bank that will accept dollars or anything. (Interviewee 7)

A skilled terrorist financier can use a supposed aid organization as a cover. This aid organization collects 'donations' for needy people in Syria, for example. Since the Syrian banking system no longer functions well in all parts of the country, these amounts are transferred to regions that are in particular need. In doing so, the terrorist financier resorts to parallel banking systems. This approach is ultimately plausible, credible and also known in the literature (e.g. in the paying of zakat).[613] While some people may donate specifically for the purposes of funding terrorism, others actually want to support a charitable cause.[614]

Alternatively, the terrorist financier could use fictitious invoices for goods or services:

> If you combine that, or that's sort of mixed with trade, or that a delivery of goods is made or not made, or an invoice is raised but not delivered and then of course you have the ability again to move assets from A to B. (Interviewee 14)

However, in each case, there is the question as to which route the money must take. Ultimately, it is not plausible for a Syrian living in Germany to pay large bills in Syria using hawala banking. In business terms, it would make much more sense to transfer the money to an account at a regulated bank in Turkey, as the counterparty in Syria risks the total loss of funds by utilizing parallel banking systems in Syria.

However, the use of fictitious invoices for services rendered or machinery purchased may be used in balancing peaks. Ultimately, a parallel banker cannot declare to their principal bank that they are engaging in parallel financial services on the side, without being subject to supervision, and now wish to balance some of this business through their regular bank account. This would most likely result in a report being made to the relevant authorities. Therefore, in such cases,

---

613 Bierstecker et al., 2007: p. 40 f.; Dalyan, 2008: p. 140; Raphaeli, 2003: p. 61 f.

614 Abuza, 2003: p. 171; Levitt, 2002: p. 54; Freedman, 2010: p. 1113 f.; Kutty, 2001: p. 25 f.; Carter et al., 2008: p. 42; Roach, 2011: p. 45.

the use of fictitious invoices or contracts is quite conceivable. This especially applies in cases of parallel bankers who provide their unofficial financial services alongside an official trading activity.

For example, a parallel banker based in Germany who has a credit balance with another member of the parallel banking system based in Syria could pretend to have delivered construction machinery to Syria: 'What is the value of a product or how can they determine if this machine really costs that much 100,000 euros or not?' (Interviewee 14). Ideally, the parallel banker actually does deliver older machinery to Syria but charges an inflated price for it. The payment is thus made to both repay the parallel banker for the actual purchase price of the machinery and to offset the surplus created through the provision of financial services.

The problem with the above-mentioned balancing of peaks by means of trading in machinery lies on the one hand in the complexity of this approach and on the other in the associated costs. Ultimately, a corresponding underlying transaction (i.e. in casu the sale of a machine) must be created and then settled in a way that covers the costs. In view of the associated transport costs, this is likely to be associated with a relatively high margin as a rule.

Alternatively, the terrorist financier could simply falsify the invoices for the construction machinery and present them to the bank. However, this runs the not inconsiderable risk of facing further scrutiny by the bank, as the bank might want to see copies of customs documents as well. This would mean the terrorist financier has to forge those documents too. Generating forgeries is problematic from the perspective of perpetrators because they are relatively easy to expose by making a simple enquiry to the competent customs authorities as to their authenticity.

Because of these challenges in clearing surpluses through banks, it stands to reason that parallel bankers are more likely to use cash to clear peaks. While this creates some transport risks and the risk of receiving counterfeit money, no data trails are left behind. Alternatively, settlement takes place via clearing within a network of parallel bankers.

Clearing among parallel bankers who are connected in a network seems to be widespread, especially in the area of hawala banking. This is understandable, as it avoids the aforementioned difficulties in the area of the transport of cash and the forgery of documents. At the same time, clearing among multiple parallel bankers also implies some data collection is taking place and ultimately some record keeping. This could, if discovered by investigators, serve as sufficient evidence to launch criminal proceedings against the parallel bankers identified.

Due to these risks, which are by no means negligible and which will be discussed in more detail in the next section, terrorist financiers who carry out transactions via parallel banking systems must be prepared to explain their actions. Probably the most valid argument for using parallel banking systems is the lack of an official banking infrastructure in certain regions.

4.3.2.3 Parallel banking systems – detection risks

As mentioned above, clearing through banks is one of the biggest risks of parallel banking systems since terrorist financiers using parallel banking systems often benefit from their lack of supervision and regulation. Parallel banking systems often do not have compliance officers, which is why the beneficial owner is not usually identified. Clearing is problematic because it often involves regulated banks: 'Especially with peak clearing, you can probably see that in certain banks, via certain methods' (Interviewee 1).

Banks have compliance departments that will question the source of unusual payments. However, the players involved cannot state that the funds constitute the settlement of surpluses of a parallel and unregulated banking system without expecting a report to be made to the relevant authorities. This means that other motivations are given for these transactions instead, which are likely to be fictitious and thus carry a detection risk.

The detection risk associated with clearing is most likely to be mitigated by the physical settlement of surpluses. Ultimately, it is not absolutely necessary to settle surpluses via the banking system – couriers can be used instead and any peaks can be settled in cash.

Since parallel banking systems are often not regulated and are in fact not supervised, using this method has fewer risks for criminals. It is effectively impossible to reliably control parallel bankers, so although money laundering laws would theoretically apply to them in certain cases, in practice they are not enforced:

> They are, if you look at it very drastically, then in Germany at least they are also subject to the Anti-Money Laundering Act, and would actually also have to, if they have suspicious cases, report them. But you won't see that. Nobody in this industry does that, because they are not supervised by a supervisory authority like the credit institutions are now. There are just the trade supervisory offices, but they do not look into such areas. (Interviewee 1)

In particular, these systems do not have compliance officers who can verify the identity of the beneficial owner. The business relationship is usually based exclusively on trust. As a result, the terrorist financier does not usually have to go to the trouble of inventing a plausible story to justify their transaction. Nor do they often have to present any form of identification and are therefore able to conceal their true identity.

However, there is a certain risk of loss in parallel banking systems. Since transactions are primarily based on trust, it is not often possible to sue for any claims. This raises questions as to what happens if the money does not reach the recipient.

It can also be assumed that the authorities are aware of parallel banking systems and have them in their sights. Ultimately, these systems are ideally suited for the transfer of illegal assets. It can therefore be assumed that authorities are attempting to gain insight into the clientele of parallel bankers through undercover investigators and high-tech monitoring options.

In conclusion, the risks associated with parallel banking systems are relatively low since perpetrators do not have to carry out the transactions themselves and can send stooges in their place, making it a very safe method from the perspective of maintaining anonymity. Only the risk of loss is a concern for them. However, parallel banking systems could soon attract public attention due to increasing awareness of their activities.

4.3.2.4 Parallel banking systems – overall assessment

As mentioned in the literature review, terrorist financiers resort to alternative means, such as hawala banking, to transfer assets.[615] Such hawala mechanisms are particularly popular beyond the limits of the regular banking system.[616] In these cases, transactions are often processed through the reputation of individual hawala bankers.[617] However, these hawala bankers are not subject to any control.[618] Thus, such parallel banking systems are exploited for the purposes of engaging in criminal activities.[619] Consequently, it is not surprising that the interviewees mentioned that hawala banking could play a crucial role in handling transfers of funds for the purposes of terrorism financing.

Although valued for its anonymity, hawala banking does leave some identifying traces behind.[620] For example, hawala bankers can be identified through

615 Dalyan, 2008: p. 140.
616 Zagaris, 2007: p. 157 f.
617 Schaeffer, 2008: p. 95 f.
618 Schneider, 2010: p. 477.
619 Passas, 2005a: p. 112; Wheatley, 2002: p. 347 f.
620 Passas, 2006b: p. 46.

so-called settlement transactions.[621] However, the procedures described by the interviewees make it clear that these risks of detection can be reduced with relatively little effort. In sum, the interview partners' statements were generally in line with the findings presented in the literature, as the latter also drew the conclusion that hawala banking can play a significant role in terrorism financing. However, the interviewees' statements offer much more detail with regard to the specific procedures employed by intelligent perpetrators. The literature has not yet presented to this extent how intelligent perpetrators of terrorism financing would have to proceed in order to transfer assets via hawala banking and evade detection. The findings based on an analysis of the existing literature and the empirical study therefore represent a significant expansion of existing knowledge by showing that parallel banking systems are very well suited for the transfer of assets intended for terrorism financing.

4.3.3 Cryptocurrencies

4.3.3.1 Cryptocurrencies – general suitability

Cryptocurrencies offer another means of transferring assets. These are ultimately unregulated parallel currencies that can be exchanged for common currencies. They therefore represent an alternative to traditional transfers and guarantee a high degree of anonymity due to their lack of transparency. They also have a low storage risk, as they are easy to hide. However, it must be kept in mind that while these currencies are popular on the darknet, they are largely unsuitable as a means of regular payment.

Cryptocurrencies are not subject to supervision. This means that they could in principle be more suitable for terrorism financing than currencies issued by governments. Finally, the transfer of cryptocurrencies is generally the responsibility of online platforms or exchanges, and making points of contact with financial service providers that could lead to investigations can be avoided: 'It should actually be possible to do it without ever having a financial institution come into contact with it' (Interviewee 7). It is not usually necessary to involve regulated financial service providers in the transfer of cryptocurrencies, which is why compliance measures can be circumvented with very little effort. This leads to low costs and low transport risks. Furthermore, cryptocurrencies are a valid alternative to remittances: 'Yeah, so why should I somehow, let's say, really badly,

621 Passas, 2005b: p. 172.

let's say, make a transfer, when I can just use an encryption system like that, artificial currency, to actually represent anything I want?' (Interviewee 8).

However, cryptocurrencies are often associated with high volatility due to their lack of regulation. This means that although one may assume low transport risks, one may certainly also assume a significant risk of loss as a result of price fluctuations. This affects the suitability of this method for the transfer of assets for the purposes of terrorism financing.

Cryptocurrencies are also usually characterized by a high degree of anonymity, making them particularly suitable for purchases on the darknet: 'But you have no idea who's behind a Bitcoin address. It's completely anonymous, encrypted, you have no idea who's behind it' (Interviewee 14). For example, weapons and explosives can be purchased on the darknet and paid for with cryptocurrencies: 'Bitcoin and Co. already have a certain popularity in criminal circles. I would be surprised if not only normal narcotics offences or other, much more serious offences are committed here, but also precisely something like terrorism financing' (Interviewee 6).

While useful for making purchases on the darknet, cryptocurrencies are rather useless in most other areas of commerce: 'Just, it's just difficult because I can't use Bitcoin to buy things at Aldi or at the gas station' (Interviewee 15). For example, it might be difficult to rent a car with or pay the rent in a cryptocurrency without causing a stir. Skilled terrorist financiers act as inconspicuously as possible and avoid engaging in unusual behaviour. The scope of use of cryptocurrencies is thus likely to be limited to the darknet and the transfer of incriminated assets. Using cryptocurrencies to integrate incriminated funds into the legal economy is considered rather unlikely.

While it is certainly possible to exchange cryptocurrencies back into government-issued currencies, in many cases this exchange must be carried out using a regular bank account. This ultimately means that the supposed greatest advantage of cryptocurrencies for criminals – namely its anonymity – is lost. While terrorist financiers could also make use of specialist bureaux de change or front men, the question is whether this would attract unnecessary attention. Ultimately, one could use a bank account in the name of a straw man from the outset and not have to resort to cryptocurrencies at all.

Cryptocurrencies are therefore primarily suitable for areas of application in which bank transfers are of limited use. This tends to apply whenever compliance measures need to be avoided and anonymity must be preserved.

4.3.3.2 *Cryptocurrencies – concrete approach*

Cryptocurrencies are a complex topic. The possible approaches to their use vary greatly, and it would go beyond the scope of this paper to explain every conceivable variant in detail. Therefore, this discussion of the interviewees' statements focuses on the approaches that are particularly suitable for terrorism financing and deliberately avoids providing basic explanations about cryptocurrencies.

Using cryptocurrencies requires computing capacity and an e-wallet (i.e. a purse for the corresponding cryptocurrency). Skilled terrorist financiers usually work with constantly changing, inexpensive notebooks and publicly accessible WLAN networks. The acquisition of cryptocurrencies is ideally done with cash or tangible assets using so-called local directories that make it possible to find exchange partners. Subsequently, cryptocurrencies can be used as an investment opportunity or as a means of payment on the darknet, such as to acquire weapons or explosives. It can also be used as a means of paying ransom demands. This method is preferred over cash due to the anonymity associated with it.

The terrorist financier must first gain access to the necessary hardware in the most discreet way possible. Using cryptocurrencies requires computing capacity which can be procured by constantly changing notebooks that are not used for other purposes, such as exchanging messages with other terrorists: 'Then you buy a cheap computer, a cheap notebook and then you're in for a few hundred francs and that's nothing. And then you change the thing again and throw that away' (Interviewee 14). Furthermore, an intelligent perpetrator purchases these notebooks using cash so that they cannot be linked to any credit card details.

In order to carry out cryptocurrency transactions with these notebooks, the terrorist financier uses only publicly accessible and constantly changing WLAN networks: 'Yeah, like I said, the public networks, it's like that. Where no cell phone number is necessary to log in. There are still people who don't protect their network and so on and so forth' (Interviewee 14). A smart perpetrator is careful never to use a personal or workplace network, focusing on using networks provided in restaurants and cafés instead. Clever perpetrators do not use these places more than once, which makes it much more difficult to identify them.

The terrorist financier behaves like any other user of cryptocurrencies in order not to attract attention. They will maintain a so-called e-wallet and the corresponding software on their devices: 'You also need an electronic wallet, an e-wallet to go with it and just the address or just the physical, electronic address' (Interviewee 14). The e-wallet is used to store the cryptocurrencies. Terrorist financiers will often have several e-wallets to distribute the risk.

In addition, an intelligent perpetrator refrains from acquiring cryptocurrency by transferring it to a trader or an exchange. Instead, a clever terrorist financier resorts to exchange offers between private individuals found through so-called local directories: 'You go to privates where you can buy cryptocurrencies and deposit the other money or assets on consideration' (Interviewee 14). It makes sense for terrorist financiers to use local directories in other cities to disguise their true identities. They then acquire cryptocurrencies either in exchange for cash in other currencies or by using tangible assets to barter.

Alternatively, the terrorist financier could use specialized bureaux de change. These are often attached to Internet cafés or similar providers. However, there is a risk that the bureau de change will require an identification document. If it does, the terrorist financier can employ a stooge who can identify themselves without any problems.

Online exchanges, on the other hand, are rather unsuitable for the purposes of terrorism financing, primarily because they are easier for authorities to monitor. From the perspective of investigators, it is obvious to place the focus of surveillance in the area of cryptocurrencies on online platforms. While it is entirely conceivable that someone might invest in cryptocurrencies because they are hoping for significant price growth and view these currencies (which are not issued by governments) as an interesting investment opportunity, there are also serious buyers and sellers on the Internet who prefer to pay with cryptocurrencies.

Why would someone resort to cryptocurrencies and not to currencies issued by governments and low-cost, easy-to-use online payment services? From the perspective of honest and reputable sellers, it hardly makes sense to limit payment options to cryptocurrencies. After all, this significantly limits the customer base, as the majority of potential buyers usually have no experience with cryptocurrencies. From the buyer's point of view, the various advantages offered by other payment options, such as the recovery of amounts already paid in the event of fraudulent actions, are lost. So, from the investigators' point of view, this raises the question of why upstanding citizens would use cryptocurrencies at all.

One possible explanation for the preference for cryptocurrencies is the lack of traceability they offer, which can be observed as part of the anonymity of the system. This makes particular sense if the parties have something to hide. For example, it stands to reason that narcotics, weapons and explosives should not be paid for with a credit card unless a person wants to be caught. In these cases, cryptocurrencies offer a suitable alternative. However, investigators know this too. Therefore, reasonable offenders assume that interfaces between cryptocurrencies and other currencies are monitored. Online platforms are ultimately particularly easy to monitor because doing so can be done electronically, remotely and therefore cost-effectively. By contrast, observing all participants in a local directory would be significantly more costly. Thus, online platforms are rather unsuitable for the acquisition of cryptocurrencies for all but the most upstanding of citizens.

However, the situation changes fundamentally as soon as cryptocurrencies are used as a means of payment. While online platforms are rather unsuitable for buying cryptocurrencies, they remain useful when it comes to spending the foreign currency that has been acquired. Criminals can use the acquired cryptocurrency to buy weapons and explosives on the darknet, but how are cryptocurrencies transferred from the buyer to the seller? In this case, a face-to-face meeting would ultimately be far too risky for both parties; therefore, it makes sense to use an online transfer of cryptocurrencies instead, as investigators are likely monitoring the darknet and will use face-to-face meetings between buyers and sellers as opportunities to make arrests.

The situation is similar with the payment of ransom in the context of kidnappings because the transfer of the ransom money has always represented the greatest risk for kidnappers. In this particular case, it may well make sense from the perspective of terrorist financiers to demand that the ransom is paid in cryptocurrencies, especially if the paying and receiving parties are located in different countries.

It is important to remember that cryptocurrencies can also be used for discrete investments:

> I sold my property and now I'm investing it in Bitcoin. I could have invested it in precious metal, invested it in shares, then the bank would still have some control over it, because it would be booked in a securities or precious metal account, but that wouldn't be the case with Bitcoins. (Interviewee 14)

The advantage of such investments is primarily their anonymity. However, such investments are usually associated with very high volatility.

4.3.3.3 Cryptocurrencies – detection risks

The detection risks associated with cryptocurrencies are relatively low, largely due to the fact that the authorities are often not up to date regarding the possibilities of innovative technologies. In addition, identifying the beneficial owners of cryptocurrency is usually difficult. However, the terrorist financier does leave electronic traces when using this method.

Leaving electronic traces is problematic insofar as it is uncertain to what extent these can be evaluated forensically in the future: 'But yes, there's always a risk of leaving traces, yes. But it's exactly the same with cash. You can't integrate large sums of cash somehow invisibly into the market. It's always going to show up somewhere' (Interviewee 14). Today, cryptocurrencies are considered largely anonymous. A perpetrator who intends to finance a terrorist attack that will lead to their own demise is very likely to benefit from this anonymity. However, it is unclear whether a perpetrator who wishes to finance an attack but not carry it out will have to reckon with considerable risks of detection in the medium to long term. Finally, it can be assumed that technologies that are considered secure today will be obsolete in a few years. The traces, on the other hand, will remain.

A few ways of dealing with the above-mentioned technological development was mentioned at the beginning in the form of the use of straw men and constantly changing both computers and public WLAN networks, although at present, 'attribution of Bitcoin or currency to a beneficial owner is extremely difficult' (Interviewee 11). Nevertheless, a certain residual risk remains with the perpetrator, as it is unclear what possibilities for tracing will arise as a result of further technical development in the future. Currently, the authorities often lag behind technologically: 'So I personally would go much more in the direction of these new technologies. That's where the authorities are really still behind' (Interviewee 14). However, it cannot be assumed that authorities will give free rein to new technologies by not even attempting to police them.

In summary, then, despite their supposed anonymity, cryptocurrencies are associated with significant risks of detection, primarily because resorting to using cryptocurrencies already raises suspicion. While not all users of cryptocurrencies are criminals, there is a widespread belief that cryptocurrencies are preferentially used for illicit transactions. After all, these currencies are usually rather unsuitable forms of payment for life's necessities, and it is ultimately difficult to plausibly justify their use.

Skilled terrorist financiers avoid undertaking this risk. They act reasonably inconspicuously so as not to attract the attention of the investigating authorities. Moreover, they always act in such a way that they can plausibly explain their behaviour. While cryptocurrencies appear at first glance to be quite suitable for terrorism financing, this analysis was able to establish that the detection risks associated with this method outweigh the risks and that parallel currencies are thus only likely to come into question for terrorists in exceptional cases.

4.3.3.4 Cryptocurrencies – overall assessment

Through the course of the literature analysis, it became clear that Bitcoin and other electronic means of payment pose a challenge in the area of terrorism financing.[622] These means of payment do not require the identification of the beneficial owner.[623] This was not a problem with early forms of cryptocurrencies, which were virtually unusable in everyday life.[624] Bitcoin, on the other hand, is suitable for transferring donations.[625] It is therefore not surprising that the interviewees also consider cryptocurrencies a suitable instrument for terrorist financiers to use. The interviewees succeeded in showing how intelligent terrorist financiers would have to proceed in concrete terms in order to transfer assets by taking as little risk as possible with the help of cryptocurrencies. Thus, it is possible to speak of a significant gain in knowledge in this case as well. Cryptocurrencies are ideally suited for the transfer of assets intended for terrorism financing.

4.3.4 Money transfer systems

4.3.4.1 Money transfer systems – general suitability

So-called money transfer systems are fast and inexpensive – they are also characterized by the difficultly of identifying beneficial owners in transactions. Although the infrastructure on the recipient side may be limited, they are extremely popular, especially among migrants with relatives abroad. As a result, terrorist financiers' use of these systems can be difficult to detect, especially since they offer a wide range of legal services. For example, it is perfectly legitimate for someone to send money to relatives abroad via one of the well-known money transfer service providers such as Western Union that can be found in all major train stations. Many migrants and refugees can be found in Germany, Liechtenstein, Austria and Switzerland who still have relatives back home that they are keen to support financially.

Money transfer systems allow their users to transfer money to another country within minutes. In many cases, this can be done without requiring an elaborate registration process. This means that terrorist financiers can operate efficiently and flexibly with the help of these service providers. Although the transaction fees are somewhat higher than they are for bank transfers or in the transfer of cryptocurrencies, money transfer systems do not usually require the

622 Merlonghi, 2010: p. 202.
623 Irwin et al., 2012: p. 6 f.
624 Rice, 2013: p. 1 f.
625 Irwin & Milad, 2016: p. 407.

same compliance measures that banks do or expensive hardware like computers for cryptocurrencies.

Since in many cases the transfer is not preceded by a registration process, the identification provided by the persons involved usually offer the only evidence that can be used in a transaction analysis: 'That's already appropriate in the sense that, again, there's no legitimized, fixed account behind it, meaning there's no permanent infrastructure that can be attributed to an individual' (Interviewee 6). The use of front men, who can be chosen either deliberately or at random, makes it significantly and permanently more difficult to attribute a transaction to a specific person. The anonymity of the terrorist financier can thus be guaranteed with relatively little effort.

The biggest weakness of this method is the possibly non-existent infrastructure on the receiving end: 'That's where remittance-wise, you might really still resort to money transfers, although again, I think by now the infrastructure is just unlikely to be there on the receiving end in a country like Syria' (Interviewee 6). For example, large parts of Syria are no longer served by money transfer systems. It may therefore be necessary to combine or replace money transfer systems with another method, such as the use of parallel banks.

4.3.4.2 Money transfer systems – concrete approach

Money transfer systems are often used to send money to family members. It is precisely this legitimate purpose that terrorist financiers use to disguise the true intent of their transactions. They also make use of digital natives or straw men. For example, skilled terrorist financiers can have different people act on their behalf and send funds. The transfer of larger amounts is usually backed up with public documents to plausibly support the purpose of the payment. In addition, sending money from towns bordering Syria is avoided.

The first thing to note is that an intelligent terrorist financier will not transfer money in their own name; instead, they will use front men for this purpose: 'Here we are with the straw man issue. It's quite common that third parties are put forward. It's like in all criminal areas, including drug trafficking and money laundering' (Interviewee 1). Both traditional straw men and digital natives are eligible for this purpose.

Digital natives have the advantage of being useful for carrying out the online services of money transfer providers: 'These are young men who grew up digital and are familiar. I mean, Bin Laden probably didn't know what e-banking was, they know what e-wallets are here, yeah?' (Interviewee 13). However, these online services are particularly vulnerable to money laundering, and their use is more likely to arouse suspicion than a supposedly naive housewife appearing in a physical shop asking to transfer a small amount of money home to her parents.

A clever terrorist financier first analyses how blameless individuals use money transfer service providers and then copies their modus operandi. Money transfer service providers are preferred by people with a migration background who want to transfer assets to their home country. Often the focus is on supporting family members. An intelligent terrorist financier seeks out people from a particular target destination and asks them to make transfers to their close relatives. The terrorist financier's contacts in the country then receive the transferred money from the straw men's relatives.

The straw men who are used also continuously change. This prevents money transfer providers from targeting the terrorist financier's known front men. As a result of the continuous changes, no trends can be identified within the framework of the transaction analyses. It is also conceivable that different people might transfer money under the same name: 'That there have also been such transfers, from different people but under the same name, that is also very well known' (Interviewee 6). As a rule, a profile is created that appears unsuspicious and can be used for all transactions. However, this leads to an accumulation of risks, which is why this approach offers limited utility.

However, when using stooges, it should be kept in mind that there may well be family members who transfer funds to terrorists for their everyday needs. So it cannot be assumed that every transaction within a family is unsuspicious:

> Yes, we see that/I mean, you see that too, we also have examples here where you just said, a father who was also in this age group, who sent money to his son, who was in Syria and also participated in the fight. That's when I said the son just wanted to buy a Coke, didn't have the money. And he lacked certain Western amenities. Because of this situation, money was transferred through us, we reported it to the police, the police informed us again afterwards that it was really so dire that the boy had certain needs there and indeed also wanted to drink Coke and needed money for that. (Interviewee 1)

Intelligent terrorist financiers not only refrain from sending unnecessary transactions simply to provide someone with Western comforts, but they also take into account that transactions between family members are by no means considered unsuspicious in every case.

In addition, intelligent perpetrators split up larger amounts to deliberately remain below the threshold values that would otherwise lead to more detailed investigations. Money transfer service providers carry out thousands of transactions every day. It is simply not reasonable to analyse each of these transactions in detail. Therefore, clever terrorist financiers try not to attract attention by sending extraordinarily high amounts.

If larger sums are transferred, they must be made plausible by using documentation. Intelligent perpetrators therefore prepare public documents that help them to explain their transactions: 'But of course, if there's an official stamp on it, an authority, an employee will believe it more than if it's some wishy-washy paper. And then they often won't follow up on it' (Interviewee 1). However, perpetrators' documentation is not limited to deeds from public authorities; they could also have something notarized by a lawyer or notary. For example, a perpetrator could present a publicly certified joint and several guarantee and state that the debtor is unfortunately insolvent and that they, as the guarantors, would like to pay off the debt.

Sending money to cities bordering Syria or even destinations within Syria, if they are still offered, should be avoided at all costs. This would ultimately lead to more detailed investigations. Sending a transfer to Istanbul or Antalya, however, is less suspicious. After all, it is plausible that a Turkish woman living in Germany would want to transfer money to family members in Turkey.

4.3.4.3 Money transfer systems – detection risks

Terrorist financiers must consider both transaction analyses and real-time criteria when using money transfer systems as a method of sending and receiving funds. Proximity to the Syrian border, for example, significantly increases the risk of detection. Ex post analyses should also be kept in mind. Furthermore, money transfer service providers usually have certain perpetrator profiles that trigger a more in-depth investigation of their activities. In addition, Facebook searches are often carried out by investigative authorities. Larger amounts also trigger further checks. Movement profiles are also created, and networks between individuals are analysed. At the same time, the standard of verification is generally rather low in the case of mobile phone shops that offer money transfer services as a supplement to their range of services.

Certain behaviours, such as traveling to and preparing to travel to Syria, increase the risk of detection: 'So if they want to travel to Syria now, for example, we see that those have a certain behaviour, how they move, where they receive money or also send money' (Interviewee 1). In addition to movement profiles, which will be discussed in more detail below, other patterns also emerge. These relate, among other things, to the amount and frequency of the amounts drawn and the counterparty of the respective transaction.

Money transfer service providers use real-time criteria to assess their clients' transactions. Since the money to be transferred can usually be withdrawn by the counterparty within a few minutes, the analysis must be carried out quickly. Randomly selected transactions are also examined in greater depth. It is therefore essential to have plausible and conclusive explanations ready, even for small amounts.

Ex post analyses are significantly more robust than meeting real-time criteria. Here, payment flows are analysed over a longer period of time and the underlying stories are looked at in more detail. Terrorist financiers cannot therefore expect to have avoided attracting suspicion simply because the transaction has been completed. It is quite possible that in individual cases, even transactions that have already been completed will still be reported to the authorities. It is therefore important that the claims made by terrorist financiers are also plausible in the long term.

Similar to banks, money transfer service providers also have perpetrator profiles to help them identify particularly suspicious persons:

> If I put it in general terms, we know that it's often young men who are between 18 and 30 years old, for example. We also see an increase in women who support this and also become active. But there we would have something, so to speak, it's often young men who have a certain history. So possibly non-Germans, but who have a German ID, but were born somewhere else and behave in a certain way. (Interviewee 1)

As a result, skilled terrorist financiers avoid using particularly suspicious-looking individuals to conduct their transactions. The profiles that are considered highly suspicious are usually created by authorities and shared with numerous financial service providers. It is therefore not impossible to find out which individuals are currently perceived as suspicious.

It is hardly surprising that money transfer service providers also use the Internet for research purposes. Compliance officers particularly rely on Facebook to find evidence of unskilled perpetrators sympathizing with extreme views:

> We also see sympathizers with certain characteristics who are then, for example, also active in a kind of press work. With press work, I am talking about Facebook or other social networks, internet platforms, where you can recognize suspicious behaviour with certain methods or can also investigate persons. (Interviewee 1)

Skilled perpetrators, on the other hand, know that compliance officers search for information on the Internet, among other places, and they use social media to back up their stories. For example, someone declaring that they urgently need to send money to Turkey to support a sick relative might post a photo of their supposed relative in hospital on Facebook and include a brief caption stating the situation. In this post, they might say that they pray for their beloved family member's speedy recovery and promise to provide financial support. Should a money transfer service provider's compliance officer search for information about the suspicious customer, they will find evidence that seemingly supports the explanation given to the service provider's employees.

Another risk that should not be overlooked is the movement profiles created by money transfer service providers since these make it possible to track the movements of terrorist financiers who regularly receive funds in their own name:

> They're sort of on their way to Syria, and they might go back after half a year. So something like that, so now for whatever reason, they come back to Germany. These are behaviours that we see. And there are also certain criteria that we have now developed, which you will certainly also find elsewhere, at other institutions, which then lead to a conspicuousness, and which is then specifically processed by employees with us, who look at this incident and research it and then consider further possibilities. (Interviewee 1)

It is obvious that a person who uses money transfer services first in Frankfurt, for example, and then in Istanbul and then again on the Turkish border with Syria would attract the attention of compliance officers. A smart perpetrator uses multiple identities instead and refrains from drawing funds at the border with Syria:

> If you then move near the Syrian border, then we know that there are also many of these people who have a certain profile and a certain type of behaviour, in terms of financial transfers, and also, if they then go to Syria, or wherever they move to, uh there you have certain characteristics that you can also then recognize via analysis. (Interviewee 1)

So the trail of an intelligent terrorist financier typically ends in Istanbul or even before it.

Networks between people are also the focus of the analyses of money transfer service providers. The aim is to identify the well-known 'spider in the web'. This is a central person who receives money transfers from various of the money transfer service provider's customers: 'You also see certain networks where transactions between certain […] people from different European countries […]. And they are then like a kind of spider in a network [that is] also recognizable' (Interviewee 1). Intelligent terrorist financiers know that creating such central persons is an unnecessary accumulation of risk. If the central person were to be exposed, all the contacts who have transferred them money would automatically come under suspicion. Therefore, intelligent perpetrators refrain from creating such spiders in the web.

Larger transfer amounts trigger controls and abort transactions: 'And you exceed a certain amount, then we don't allow the withdrawal, we send the money back, and then we respond further' (Interviewee 1). However, this is generally known and should not come as a surprise to terrorist financiers. Less well known are the actual thresholds for triggering in-depth investigations, as these are continually being adjusted. However, it should be clear to any reasonable perpetrator that a transfer of CHF 20,000 via a money transfer service provider is highly unusual and can hardly be plausibly justified due to the associated fees. A transfer of CHF 150, on the other hand, is within the usual range and arouses considerably less suspicion. This means that a clever perpetrator splits up larger amounts and transfers them in the names of different people.

For the transfer itself, clever perpetrators resort to branches of money transfer service providers that do not specialize in financial services but have another primary source of business. It is reasonable to assume, for example, that owners of mobile phone shops that offer supplementary money transfer services do not have extensive expertise in the compliance area, which makes it significantly easier for perpetrators to make the transaction plausible:

> The standard of verification and the standard of care is not what most countries would like to see, particularly when such transactions are initiated with mobile phone shops or other traders who are acting as agents for these big companies. We know that too. (Interviewee 6)

While it is reasonable to assume that in many cases any employee or representative of a money transfer service provider will have some basic knowledge of compliance, it is simply not reasonable to expect mobile phone salespeople to have a depth of knowledge that is remotely close to the knowledge possessed by those working full-time in financial services.

In summary, money transfer service providers are in principle largely well suited for terrorism financing. In particular, the use of front men and the splitting of larger amounts, as well as the avoidance of an accumulation of risks with individual persons, allows funds to be transferred over large distances within a short period of time. Provided that the terrorist financier does not make a personal appearance, the risk associated with this method is exceptionally low.

4.3.4.4 Money transfer systems – overall assessment

The literature review found that the use of money transfer systems, while varying due to cultural differences, poses a significant challenge in combating terrorism financing in almost every form.[626] This is particularly so because it is difficult to

626 Vlcek, 2008: p. 296.

distinguish between migrants who legitimately wish to transfer assets back to their home countries and terrorist financiers. The interviewees not only confirmed the findings of the literature review but added to them.[627] In doing so, they have shown how perpetrators would have to proceed in concrete terms in order to transfer assets for the purposes of terrorism financing with the help of money transfer service providers. Based on the above explanations of the concrete procedure and the compliance mechanisms that are relatively easy to circumvent, it can be assumed that despite all the efforts of the money transfer service providers to prevent it, this is a suitable method for terrorists to transfer assets. However, this observation should not be seen as a reproach against money transfer service providers but rather serve as a warning to legislators.

4.3.5 Personal transfer

4.3.5.1 Personal transfer – general suitability

The most banal method of personal transfer is probably the personal transport of assets. Refugee routes are supposedly excellent for transferring money as they could be used to pay cash for local purchases.

Since refugee routes have been little monitored, at least in the past, and it has been possible to travel from Turkey to Germany without encountering border controls, it is reasonable to assume that this route is also open from Germany to Turkey and has some significance for terrorism financing: 'I think that's probably one of the main channels, that's my personal opinion' (Interviewee 6). Terrorist financiers could use these routes to either transport cash themselves or use messengers. Once the cash arrives in Turkey or Syria, it can be used to make purchases.

As refugee routes are generally poorly monitored, they are also likely to be suitable for transporting cash: 'If you get people over there, then of course you get cash or assets over there' (Interviewee 7). After all, cash is usually easier to hide than a living person.

Once the cash arrives at its destination, purchases can be made with it without leaving any evidence behind in the form of a data trail: 'Yes, well, I think the last thing to go is cash. So they need the money […] to be able to make purchases' (Interviewee 14). Thus, it is also conceivable that this method is combined with other approaches and that only in the last step of the financing of terrorism is a personal transfer of funds used.

627 Masciandro, 2004: p. 296 f.

The personal transfer offers a great advantage in that no financial service providers are involved and compliance measures can thus be cleverly circumvented. At the same time, however, this method is associated with a considerable risk of loss and relatively high costs (including high travel costs) – it also relies on the trustworthiness of numerous confidants. Messengers who undoubtedly know what they are transporting can simply disappear with the money.

4.3.5.2 Personal transfer – concrete approach

Skilled terrorist financiers use refugee and trafficking routes. They involve experienced smugglers and traffickers in the process when necessary. For example, they use the border between Turkey and Syria to move assets. The use of prepaid cards is possible but highly risky, as investigators already focus on them.

As indicated above, the terrorist financier uses existing refugee and trafficking routes: 'You have there relatively often in mind something like in Syria, where there has been a relatively unmolested border with Turkey, where you also know that very many people and goods cross this border and relatively freely' (Interviewee 6). These routes are mostly tried and tested and not usually monitored. Due to the large number of people travelling along them, it should be possible to avoid drawing attention to the individual.

Those who do not have the necessary knowledge of suitable routes themselves call in experienced experts, such as smugglers and traffickers: 'There are logisticians, smugglers, whatever you want to call them' (Interviewee 7). If it is possible for these people to transport refugees without detection, it should also be possible for them to accompany terrorist financiers to their destination. However, the terrorist financiers do not identify themselves as such; rather, they pose as refugees or journalists.

Terrorist financiers usually carry the assets to be transferred in cash. Alternatively, one could also think about the use of prepaid cards: 'And right now, if we're talking about cash values or just prepaid cards. I mean, that's probably even easier then smuggling any people over where you need papers et cetera' (Interviewee 7). Prepaid cards reduce the risk of loss, but they are also ultimately the focus of investigators. Their use would also leave an unwanted data trail.

4.3.5.3 Personal transfer – risks of detection

The risks associated with this method are relatively low. However, it should not be forgotten that simply traveling to Syria or areas know to be controlled by terrorists is already highly suspicious activity. Even the preparation of such a trip could attract unwanted attention.

Since travel to Syria is considered suspicious, the perpetrator must adopt a suitable cover: 'But if he were to travel to Syria, we'd already have plenty of suspicions to report him' (Interviewee 3). For example, the perpetrator could pretend to be a journalist or a refugee aid worker. However, this is only possible if the cover is actually partially true and the perpetrator is already working as such. Otherwise, the cover is not sustainable.

In addition, the terrorist financier must expect to encounter customs controls. Should they attempt to transport larger amounts of cash, this could trigger customs procedures. However, it is unclear whether this would give rise to suspicions of terrorism financing.

In summary, this method can be described as low risk since it is highly unlikely that the perpetrator will come under suspicion of terrorism financing provided that they can plausibly explain the reasons for their trip to Syria and they do not encounter a customs check where the cash they are carrying is revealed.

4.3.5.4 Personal transfer – overall assessment

Personal transfers are also well known in the literature. 'Cash couriers' (i.e. those who carry out the personal transfer of assets) are allegedly gaining importance in terrorism financing.[628] The use of cash couriers by Chechens, among others, is known.[629] Furthermore, there have been similar cases in Yemen.[630] Nonetheless, the approaches highlighted by the interviewees have made it clear that this method is likely to involve very high costs. While the risk of detection is low, the cash couriers could lose the assets, be robbed or intentionally embezzle it. Thus, in summary, this approach tends to be less suitable for the transfer of assets intended for terrorism financing. The findings of the empirical study complement those of the literature review in that attention is drawn to the hurdles associated with this method. Given the merits of the other approaches outlined in this chapter, it can be assumed that physical transfers are likely to play a rather minor role.

4.4 Counter-terrorism instruments

The foregoing has shown how easy it is to generate and subsequently transfer funds for terrorism financing. Since simply any source of revenue is suitable for

628 Dalyan, 2008: p. 140.
629 Ridley, 2008: p. 29 f.
630 Cassella, 2004: p. 285.

terrorism financing, it cannot reasonably be argued that one must merely eliminate the possibilities for generating financial resources to prevent the financing of terrorism. This would be desirable but hardly enforceable.

On the other hand, it is certainly possible to sensitize investigators in all areas to terrorism financing. This can help to ensure that perpetrators who have supposedly 'only' evaded taxes or defrauded companies are targeted by terrorist investigators as well. It is therefore important to consider all criminal acts that are capable of generating funds as potentially being intended for terrorism financing. Of course, the author does not expect every investigation to be extended by an extensive procedure to clarify the potential link to terrorism financing, but it may well make sense to carry out at least cursory checks on the planned use of funds.

However, since the use of funds for terrorism financing usually lies in the future, and legal sources of income are certainly also suitable for terrorism financing, the key to success in combating terrorism financing can be found in identifying the transfer of assets. As soon as assets have to be transferred, several people are usually involved. This is where undercover investigators, for example, can come into the equation.

One of the questions asked in the expert interviews was what improvements would investigators like to see in order to be able to combat terrorism financing even more effectively. Five focal points emerged in the responses. The experts would like to see a more intensive exchange of information between private individuals and the authorities, more efficient administrative and legal assistance and more possibilities for undercover investigations and digital surveillance. In addition, it was suggested that professional secrecy should be questioned and that certain groups of persons who are subject to professional secrecy should at least be subject to compliance obligations.

The following discusses the approaches taken by investigators. Since combating terrorism financing is ultimately an interdisciplinary challenge, all proposals taken up by investigators are considered. However, this research primarily addresses criminal law and criminal procedure issues. Therefore, the focus of the comparative law analysis in the next section is on the possibilities for improvement in terms of criminal procedure.

The intention here is not to conflate factual and legal problems. Rather, the aim of this section is to highlight selected weak points from the perspective of practitioners. The dogmatic analysis is presented in the following section.

4.4.1 Exchange of information between private parties and public authorities

An important component of promoting the exchange of information between private parties and the authorities are the watchlists that are made available to financial service providers. However, the lack of control over the information exchanged remains a challenge.

Watchlists contain the names of suspicious persons:

> That would of course be interesting for financial service providers and also for banks, if one could get this list, and could then also research more specifically and also then in exchange make the information available to the authorities. And these are of course people also, who may not yet be in the stage of a terrorist, and perhaps somewhere in the preliminary stage somewhere in the broadest sense related to it, perhaps not, perhaps also innocently got into it. (Interviewee 1)

A comprehensive exchange of information on so-called dangerous persons could therefore help to identify suspicious persons more quickly and reduce the number of false suspicions. As soon as such a person tries to make a transaction, the financial service providers involved can report the incident to the authorities. These lists are undoubtedly important, but they are usually incomplete. So the fact that a person is not already on such a list does not mean that their transactions are harmless. Moreover, these lists are sometimes kept nationally and are not always the same.[631] However, the United Nations Security Council consolidated list is forwarded to financial intermediaries in Switzerland.[632]

As these lists are incomplete, so-called offender profiles are also used. These are created by the authorities and shared with financial service providers:

> We also work together with the authorities, for example, with the Federal Criminal Police Office or with the Office for the Protection of the Constitution, where you think about it and also disclose it relatively openly: How does someone behave, a sympathizer who supports IS, or how does a foreign terrorist fighter behave? (Interviewee 1)

These offender profiles, which are developed in co-operation between compliance officers from private companies and employees of public authorities, are intended to help financial service providers identify suspicious persons at an early stage and to initiate further investigations. In addition to certain suspicious characteristics, suspicious behaviour is also described.

---

631 FINMA, 2006.

632 FINMA, 2017.

However, the exchange of information outlined above entails the risk that confidential information held by the authorities may fall into the hands of terrorist financiers: 'Of course, you always have the problem, even if you give lists like that to private institutions, that then they're not really under control anymore and then they might end up in hands where they're not supposed to go' (Interviewee 1). Ultimately, this information must be shared with a large number of people. There is a risk that terrorist financiers or their contacts will become aware of the confidential information and use it to their advantage.

A data leak could lead to terrorist financiers knowing the perpetrator profiles and thus knowing which individuals are considered particularly dangerous by financial service providers. Conversely, however, these profiles can also be used to determine how a supposedly unsuspicious person should appear. Perpetrators could use this knowledge to appear accordingly unsuspicious and to undermine the compliance measures of financial service providers.

This dilemma can only be solved to a certain extent. One possible approach is that authorities' sharing of information with private individuals should be limited. For reasons of the rule of law, this is in any case unavoidable in certain cases:

> On the other hand, from the point of view of the authorities, with all the office work, with prevention, a very high degree of compartmentalization is absolutely necessary. In other words, for reasons of the rule of law, this information cannot be passed on. (Interviewee 12)

In addition, strict secrecy rules could be imposed on private companies. However, the secrecy rules already exist, and restricting access to important information would make it more difficult for financial service providers to identify perpetrators in a timely manner. This cannot be what the legislature had in mind. Ultimately, the UN Security Council lists will also be passed on to financial service providers.[633]

However, since the focus of this research is on criminal procedural issues, the exchange of information between authorities and private parties will not be discussed in detail. The author is of the opinion that this exchange is important and should be further intensified. The author does not consider it sensible to restrict the exchange of information in order to keep offender profiles secret.

---

633 FINMA, 2017.

4.4.2 Undercover agents

The use of undercover investigators is considered particularly promising in the field of combating terrorism financing, partly because investigations without 'classic intelligence' are often difficult. Insider knowledge is therefore required, and the targeted use of undercover investigators is necessary. In particular, undercover investigators with a migration background are sought. However, these people are difficult to recruit. Undercover agents (i.e. informants) are considered easier to recruit. In any case, undercover investigators are costly and personnel intensive.

Since terrorism financing mostly applies to events that will take place in the future, and it is important to anticipate terrorist attacks in order to prevent them, investigations are difficult without classical intelligence: 'I think without that kind of information you'll never get there otherwise. If you really have to go through the chain of custody with administrative assistance, you're never going to get there' (Interviewee 7). It is simply not sufficient to wait for terrorist attacks to take place and then try to trace the financing of these acts ex post by means of administrative assistance.

Assuming that terrorist financiers are, at least in part, intelligent and educated, it is natural to assume that they are adept at disguising themselves as well. Thus, insider knowledge of their operations is required. This can be obtained by undercover agents who penetrate the criminal milieu and pose as terrorists: 'Yeah, that's probably one of the most essential or the smartest forms of combat because you can really maybe target the individual cells here' (Interviewee 6). In order to penetrate the milieu, it is advantageous to already belong to certain cultural or religious groups. In this context, it is important to address the circumstances and characteristics of the individual terrorist cells.

With regard to Islamist terrorism, it could therefore be helpful to recruit undercover agents from a religious and immigrant background. However, this is difficult in practice, as these individuals usually wish to maintain a certain loyalty to their compatriots:

> It's a bigger hurdle to get colleagues who want to be undercover in the field – I haven't had any luck up to this point. They've got a bit of an, an ethnic loyalty there. Problem of ethnic loyalty even had that they say, 'nah, I don't want that. I don't like that'. So, the extraction of undercover agents, you don't imagine that's too easy. (Interviewee 9)

Recruiting suitable undercover officers with a migration background is therefore difficult and time-consuming.

Even if undercover officers can be recruited, infiltration requires time and money, which is why such operations are considered costly and personnel intensive: 'Is also very time-consuming, very costly, personnel intensive. Long-standing investigations that is' (Interviewee 5). It is therefore all the more important to optimize the legal framework and organizational procedures in order to create sufficient resources for the actual investigative work to take place.

It seems to be easier to recruit informants. They are already in place and therefore do not have to be established at a great expense to investigative agencies: 'undercover agents, well, that's more likely to happen now, that you have people from the scene directly who then work for the police. This is also quite common in right-wing extremism and left-wing extremism' (Interviewee 9). In addition, these people often already have knowledge of facts relevant to investigators. The disadvantage, however, is that the use of undercover agents can only be planned to a limited extent.

The decentralized organization of the IS makes the work of undercover investigators more difficult: 'Relatively difficult for IS itself because this organization is very cleverly structured, they don't actually have a headquarters there where you can sneak one in and then find out everything, [it's] a very decentralized organization' (Interviewee 13). However, this poses only a limited problem in the fight against terrorism financing. It is reasonable to assume that only cells that are connected to each other also transfer assets between them. Undercover investigators can start with these transfers.

Sleeper cells in particular can be identified by undercover agents: 'So I think the Belgian cell and so on, those are worthwhile targets for undercover agents' (Interviewee 13). These cells often spend a long period of time planning and financing an attack. They are usually comprised of small groups of people. Inserting an undercover investigator into these structures is difficult but certainly possible.

'Lone wolves', however, are indeed hard for even undercover agents to catch:

> The lone wolf who's there somewhere at home watching violent videos and kind of radicalizing and then renting a truck, they're not going to, there's not that many undercover agents, so if they're going to go after everybody there one or three or five and we don't have the resources there. (Interviewee 13)

However, the lack of accessibility of lone wolves is not only due to a limited number of undercover officers but also to the isolation of the perpetrator. Perpetrators who are radicalized via the Internet and do not talk to anyone about their plans are almost impossible to expose. If they finance their attacks themselves and do not need any significant means to do so, they will probably not be deterred from carrying out their deeds even by undercover agents. After all, in this case, the perpetrator is not dependent on transferring funds either. It is thus hardly possible to unmask these types of perpetrators. This helps to emphasize that undercover agents are a valuable tool, but they are not a panacea. Therefore, it is also important to use other tools, such as digital surveillance, to identify lone wolves.

Probably the greatest weakness of undercover investigations is the large bureaucratic and legal hurdles that must be overcome. Often a lot of time passes before an undercover investigator can start their work. It is therefore important to use what are already scarce resources in the most targeted way possible:

> I think you have to take the limited resources you already have with undercover officers, which is highly risky for them as well, you have to go where it makes the most sense, and that's probably in tracking down and infiltrating recognized cells that have a high probability that one of them will then actually carry out an attack. (Interviewee 13)

It should therefore be emphasized that it is important to use undercover agents in an as-focused manner as possible. At the same time, however, it is also necessary for undercover investigators to pre-emptively infiltrate various suspicious groups in order to identify possible attack plans in advance, even if these suspicions are not yet substantiated at the beginning of the investigation.

In addition, the following section examines how the conditions for authorizing an undercover investigation could be adapted to promote a more efficient fight against terrorism financing. This should enable undercover agents to undertake more successful operations. In the past, experts have repeatedly criticized the weak legal basis used for undercover investigations: 'Yes, well with us, it already starts with the legal basis that we are actually not allowed to do that or we are set such narrow limits' (Interviewee 5). It must therefore be clarified within the framework of the comparative law analysis to what extent legislative measures could contribute to a more effective use of undercover investigations for the purposes of combating terrorism financing.

4.4.3 Digital surveillance

Digital surveillance is an effective and efficient crime-fighting instrument. They are particularly useful when undercover investigators reach their limits. Even lone wolves need to obtain information, and this is usually done via the Internet. However, there are considerable data protection hurdles to overcome. It is also unclear how much circumstantial evidence might ultimately be sufficient to justify such an operation. Moreover, digital surveillance is extremely vulnerable to abuse.

Digital surveillance is particularly helpful when undercover investigations reach their limits. Lone wolves who do not talk to other people about their plans of attack cannot be reached by undercover investigators. However, these individuals may be radicalized via the Internet. In addition, they often obtain information about possible courses of action via the Internet:

> I think that the fact that such attacks happen again and again and that we know that these people have been radicalized on the Internet or through certain material on the Internet, and yet we have not found out about these people, shows all the more how difficult it simply is. These are simply areas of regulation or simply areas of life that simply affect everyday life as everyone knows it in our country. And these are then only small elements that can possibly give an indication. (Interviewee 6)

At the same time, it must be borne in mind that digital surveillance offer important indications but ultimately only individual elements of the bigger picture. Therefore, complementary offline investigations are often necessary. Nevertheless, the potential of digital surveillance should not be underestimated.

In the context of digital surveillance, investigators can hack the computers of perpetrators without the latter becoming aware of it. In this way, it is possible to monitor the activities of perpetrators while they continue to believe that they are unobserved. This approach is often more effective and less expensive than classical approaches such as surveillance.

In addition, digital surveillance is easier to document than the findings of undercover investigators. While undercover investigators take down their statements and may subsequently have to testify as witnesses, recordings on data carriers[634], provided they can be clearly attributed to the perpetrator, are much easier to exploit because they are available in digital or transcripted form.

Digital surveillance is also exceptionally fast and cost-effective since one investigator can observe the activities of several offenders simultaneously and from a distance. While whole teams have to be deployed for physical surveillance, one IT expert is usually sufficient to carry out an online search from their own office. This saves valuable time.

The speed of this method is also due to the fact that fewer formal limits often have to be observed: 'As I said, also valuable here, of course, because fast and just not stopping at any boundaries, formal boundaries' (Interviewee 13). While the presence of the person concerned is required or at least desired in the case of a physical search or seizure, digital surveillance can usually be carried out in the absence of the suspect. This means that important time can be gained from an investigative tactical point of view. This is particularly true with regard to the time pressure associated with cross-border asset transfers.

634 Mediums such as hard disks that allow data to be saved in encrypted form.

In summary, digital surveillance is an extremely promising investigative tool. Not using them would lead to a lower level of security:

> So probably the recipe in that is, yes, these opportunities have to be used, we owe that to people if they want security, or we have to be honest enough to go to people and say, 'This could be done, we're not going to do that, with that said, security is not 100 per cent'. (Interviewee 13)

One could therefore argue that it is possible and reasonable to use digital surveillance. Should one decide against the use of this instrument, one would at least have to document the reasons for this clearly.

Moreover, a question is also raised with regard to who may use such instruments in the context of the international and global fight against terrorism. The experts interviewed expressed their concerns in this regard: 'So I'll say once, if a German federal prosecutor's office does something like that, then I have no problem with it, if Russian domestic intelligence does it, then (laughter) is probably not so great' (Interviewee 13). The author has no concerns here as long as the intelligence gathered is only used to combat terrorism financing.

Indeed, there is also a significant potential for digital surveillance to be abused 'because of course we are already opening up possibilities there that are also susceptible to abuse' (Interviewee 13). For example, duly authorized officials could misuse these tools for private purposes. Furthermore, there is also a risk that digital surveillance will be used for various less serious offences and that the scope will not be limited to the fight against terrorism.

In addition, the data and privacy protection rights of the persons concerned should not be ignored.

> Would probably be a proven way. Probably doesn't always quite coincide with data protection and privacy, but if you're purely looking at efficiency and effectiveness, that's probably an element of what would probably be useful to establish more information. (Interviewee 7)

It is obvious that digital surveillance could come into conflict with various data protection standards. Therefore, clear and unambiguous legal rules are needed. For an assessment of the legal basis, please refer to the following section.

4.4.4 Administrative and judicial assistance

In the following section, the legal aspects of administrative and legal assistance in connection with the international fight against terrorism financing will be discussed. Before doing so, however, some practical aspects will be highlighted from the perspective of investigators in order to develop a better understanding of the need for legislative measures and adjustments of the existing system.

The existing system of administrative assistance is considered outdated due to the following reasons. Nowadays, money often moves faster than administrative assistance. However, in order to be able to combat terrorism financing, immediate action is required in many cases. It would also be necessary to link data and target the use of large volumes of data. Forwarding information to selected states would be helpful in this context. This could be made possible by promoting co-operation between financial intelligence units.

Probably the greatest challenge for investigators to overcome is jurisdictional – their jurisdiction ends at their respective national borders yet perpetrators can move to other jurisdictions within seconds: 'And then before you've ever obtained "assistance" or "detention" anywhere, I mean, there's the money again across all the state lines' (Interviewee 5). So the money is often quicker than the administrative assistance. In practice, this can be problematic because it allows offenders to evade coercive measures and transfer their assets to another country.

Ultimately, co-operation between different countries is still based on an outdated system:

> We have it, I mean, generally in the co-operation between states, I'll say, on the judicial area, so administrative assistance and mutual legal assistance, there we have a nineteenth-century concept, yeah; partly, you still have to send it through the embassies, translate it, authenticate it. (Interviewee 13)

This outdated system slows down investigations. This particularly affects countries that have less advanced legal systems.

A clever offender knows that administrative and judicial assistance procedures in certain countries either take a very long time or are even futile: 'They're probably always half a year behind [administrative assistance], aren't they?' (Interviewee 5). Even less skilled offenders gain this knowledge by simply looking at the police's guide to administrative and legal assistance, which is kindly made available on the Internet. The transfer of funds abroad thus usually remains possible without encountering any problems.

In order to put a stop to terrorism financing, the ability to react immediately is necessary: 'Very difficult at the moment, and then of course again, a world that's even more fast-moving than anything else, and then you have to be able to act immediately and stuff' (Interviewee 5). However, in many cases, the ability to act immediately requires sufficient access to information that helps to substantiate a suspicion. Finally, investigators cannot be allowed to arbitrarily stop transactions. However, clever terrorist financiers structure their transactions in such a way that access to sufficient information is made considerably more difficult. This is particularly successful when several jurisdictions are involved, which rarely or never provide information.

Ultimately, it would be helpful to collect and manage data centrally: 'And I think that's the big challenge but also opportunity, how do we impose data on each other?' (Interviewee 13). The challenge here is to link the data centrally and enable investigators to access the essential information quickly. For example, data could be exchanged between Switzerland and Germany and accessed by investigators in both countries.

One possible approach to this could be enhanced co-operation between financial intelligence units, which would ensure cross-border access to data in real time. There are already initial developments being made in this direction: 'We also have parallel opportunities today also for informal co-operation, I'll say between FIUs, that's one of the examples, also between police agencies that don't have to rely on this judicial requirement now' (Interviewee 13). However, informal co-operation should not be based on the personal relations between employees of financial intelligence units but on a legal basis that regulates and promotes such co-operation.

Among other things, there is the question of whether data may be shared with all other countries or only with selected countries: 'But the fact is that we also have to co-operate with states that do not have the same requirements, and that is a big problem. So do we throw all the principles of the rule of law overboard?' (Interviewee 13). For example, a ban on the use of certain types of evidence is certainly possible and sensible in Switzerland; however, will this prohibition also be consistently observed in other less progressive countries? Nonetheless, the issue of forwarding data to other countries is primarily a problem of data protection law, which is why this question is not dealt with further in this research.

4.4.5 Professional secrets

In the worst-case scenario, perpetrators can use professional secrets as a means of covering up their actions; thus compliance standards on notarizations should be aligned with those of financial service providers. Information should be able to be used to combat terrorism, and the transparency of individuals is considered ideal.

The sharing of professional secrets is dangerous and leads to a considerable potential for abuse to take place. For example, investigations in the area of combating terrorism financing could be misused to gain knowledge about alleged tax evaders. This is obvious, as banks are generally extremely willing to co-operate in the area of terrorism financing and frequently refer to banking secrecy in the area of tax evasion. This behaviour is plausible insofar as the offence of terrorism financing not only protects a higher legal interest than that of tax offences but is also associated with greater reputational risks for financial service providers. While it is not desirable to be reprimanded in the press for aiding and abetting tax evasion, the idea of being accused by the press of not helping to prevent a terrorist attack in which people died due to a bank's lack of co-operation and unwillingness to provide information is likely to be simply unbearable for most bankers. Consequently, financial service providers are extremely willing to co-operate with the authorities in the fight against terrorism financing. The preliminary study even emphasized that the willingness of financial service providers to co-operate was simply exemplary and went beyond expectations.

To ensure that this willingness to co-operate on the part of financial service providers does not one day decline, it is important to guarantee that the information provided is used exclusively for the purposes of combating terrorism financing:

> So, under the heading of terrorism financing, I have what I need today, I get all the information I need. Of course, then I have to use it that way, I'm not allowed to use it for third-party purposes. (Interviewee 13)

Ultimately, this is also in the best interest of customers. Few bank customers are likely to complain that their personal data has been shared with authorities for the purposes of combating terrorism financing. If customers do complain about this, it gives cause to consider why the customer might object. However, should information be shared for a wide variety of purposes, such as combating money laundering and tax evasion, it becomes difficult for customers to see where the boundaries of bank secrecy lie. Each disclosure ultimately increases the risk that the data could fall into the wrong hands.

It is therefore important to relax the rules regarding banking secrecy only selectively. In particular, banks must be able to transfer data to the authorities immediately upon suspicion. In the case of the authorities, on the other hand, they must not misuse these data for other purposes.

However, not only banks are subject to professional secrecy. Lawyers and notaries must also keep the facts entrusted to them confidential. Provided that they do not work as financial service providers on the side, lawyers and notaries are also not subject to the Swiss Money Laundering Act. At the same time, these persons do not as a rule maintain extensive compliance departments, as is expected of banks, for example. However, the (public) deeds signed by lawyers and notaries generally inspire a heightened level of trust. This results in a certain vacuum in the area of control.

Skilled perpetrators use holders of professional secrecy, such as lawyers and notaries, to obtain documents with increased credibility, which smooths the compliance process for financial service providers. The experts complain that lawyers and notaries do not always check transactions closely enough: 'So I think the problem is, there are certain black sheep within the professions who also, for example, take advantage of attorney–client privilege et cetera to cover up certain things' (Interviewee 7). It is therefore important to oblige holders of professional secrecy to take certain compliance measures as well to prevent abuses.

It is also necessary to ensure that lawyers and notaries report suspicious practices to the authorities:

> In principle, this must also be adapted at other levels. Be it with lawyers, be it with notaries, be it, as I said, with authorities. So everywhere where I have the possibility, let's say, to get documentation or something similar, in principle the same standards must prevail. (Interviewee 8)

This possibility currently exists specifically for lawyers and notaries who are active as financial service providers. However, such reports should also be mandatory in all cases that do not concern financial services.

For investigators, the ideal is transparency: 'All right, for the purposes of investigating and combating terrorism or other crime, the ideal situation is if we had completely transparent and glass human beings' (Interviewee 6). Of course, data protection challenges arise in the process – under which circumstances must professional secrecy be maintained and when should a report be made to the authorities? One must also ask whether such a relaxation of professional secrecy rules would actually be in the best interests of the population as a whole.

The author is in favour of selective reporting to selected authorities in the event that terrorism financing is strongly suspected. However, the knowledge gained from this should be used exclusively to combat terrorism financing. This study, however, deals primarily with selected measures of criminal procedure. Therefore, in order to focus on the main issues, it does not go into further detail on the challenges associated with maintaining professional secrecy.

4.5 Pre-study vs main study

A comparison of the results of the preliminary study with those of the main study shows that there are both differences and similarities. In principle, many of the results of the preliminary study were confirmed by the main study's expert interviews. For example, both studies concluded that regular bank transfers – but also parallel banking systems such as hawala banking, cryptocurrencies and physical transfers, among others – could play a role in wealth transfer. Money transfer systems, on the other hand, were only mentioned in passing in the context of online fraud in the preliminary study and were not explicitly linked to terrorism financing. In summary, in the area of money transfers, the findings of the preliminary study could be confirmed by and deepened in the main study.

In the legal sphere, the interviewees in the preliminary study referred primarily to real estate and stock exchange transactions. This largely coincides with the literature analysis.[635] The expert interviews in the main study also referred to trading and construction activities, state support and loans from banks and private individuals. In principle, therefore, in the area of legal sources of income, the main study confirmed and deepened the findings of the preliminary study.

The situation is different with regard to the illegal sources of income used by terrorist financiers. Here, some of the methods mentioned by the interviewees in the preliminary study were not confirmed in the main study. For example, no information on pimping or organ trafficking was provided by the interviewees in the main study. This could be because these topics may only play a marginal role or may already be known to the perpetrators but have not yet attracted the attention of investigators and compliance officers.

Overall, the results of the preliminary study were largely confirmed by the main study. Thus, both the perspectives of the perpetrators and their accomplices as well as those of investigators could be taken into account in the context of the explanations provided in this chapter.

4.6 Overall assessment

The foregoing has highlighted that terrorist financiers are often one step ahead of investigators and compliance experts because the criminal act is often difficult to anticipate as it has yet to occur. While money launderers usually want to deposit already incriminated assets in banks, terrorist financiers often have legal and officially declared sources of income. This means that at the time of the first transaction, the terrorist offence has often not yet been committed.

Unlike money launderers, terrorist financiers have an almost unlimited number of possible sources of income. Some of these sources of revenue were presented as examples at the beginning of this chapter. While offering examples

635 Dalyan, 2008: p. 140.

of likely scenarios, it was by no means an exhaustive overview, as ultimately any form of legal or illegal source of income can be used for the purposes of terrorism financing. Money launderers, on the other hand, derive their assets exclusively from crime; otherwise, they would not even meet the criteria for the offence as described in Art. 305bis CH-StGB, which makes explicit reference to assets derived from crime.

Finally, the argument that the fight against terrorism financing is useless and obsolete anyway, since terrorists can cause significant damage even by carrying out small and inexpensive attacks, should also be addressed. It is true that in many cases even small sums are sufficient in order to plan and carry out a terrorist attack. However, this only covers part of the problem. Terrorist financiers not only support the planning and execution of major attacks but also the training and education of extremists in specially created structures abroad. They also support large terrorist organizations, such as the IS, which take over large areas and create safe havens for terrorists. It cannot therefore be in the best interests of Western countries to stop prosecuting terrorist financiers.

The discussion in this chapter has emphasized how difficult it is to identify terrorist financiers in a timely manner. The author therefore wishes to emphasize that financial service providers are already making a decisive contribution to combating terrorism financing and cannot be held responsible for any weaknesses in the system.

The only suggestion the author has for financial service providers is to take a more holistic view of the compliance process. Currently, compliance officers often focus on formal aspects of the process and neglect the big picture. This is often because internal training focuses on laws and processes but rarely offers information on the behaviour of intelligent offenders. It would make perfect sense to sensitize compliance officers, who are supposed to recognize suspicious behaviour, to how clever terrorist financiers might act. Only those who understand the behaviour of perpetrators can ultimately combat it. However, the primary responsibility for combating terrorism financing cannot be transferred to private parties – it remains with the competent authorities and legislators.

A further delegation of responsibility to private parties would hardly be reasonable, and not only because of the costs involved. It is simply too difficult for banks to recognize what perpetrators intend to do because financial service providers generally do not have recourse to sovereign powers and coercive measures; rather, they rely on the information provided by their clients. If the client succeeds in deceiving the bank in a clever way, the bank's compliance measures are undermined. Therefore, an extension of the compliance measures of financial service providers would not be sufficient to combat intelligent perpetrators. Even if financial service providers were to review every single transaction in detail, which would not be economically viable under any circumstances, these analyses would still be based on the information provided by their customers. It is obvious that the compliance process would still be vulnerable to misperceptions. It is therefore imperative that financial service providers do not bear sole responsibility for combating terrorism financing but are able to co-operate with the authorities.

A question therefore arises as to what the Swiss legislature and competent authorities can do to combat terrorism more effectively. To this end, this study will take a closer look at the options available to law enforcement authorities from a criminal procedure perspective. Consequently, the following chapter discusses selected instruments used by the authorities to combat terrorism financing.

5. Criminal procedural implications of the empirical study

Situated within the framework of the empirical study, the experts who were interviewed highlighted the relevance of five areas to engage in a more effective fight against terrorism financing. In particular, improvements would be required in the following areas:

1. Exchange of information between public authorities and private parties
2. Undercover investigators
3. Digital surveillance
4. Administrative and judicial assistance
5. Trade secrets

The focus of this chapter in particular is on digital surveillance and an extension of the powers of undercover investigators. A comparative legal overview of these coercive measures is provided. In addition, selected weaknesses in criminal procedure are presented and proposed solutions are developed.

Meanwhile, the exchange of information between authorities and private individuals, administrative and judicial assistance and the difficulties associated with professional secrecy are discussed only in passing. Reviewing in its entirety an established system of administrative and mutual assistance cannot be achieved in a single work, and it would also be of limited practical use to analyse only administrative and judicial assistance in the German-speaking world. Ultimately, this is a global challenge. The exchange of information between authorities and private individuals undoubtedly needs to be improved; however, this is not primarily a problem of criminal procedural law but rather an organizational challenge. This process optimization should thus be considered in more detail in a study focusing on business management. Finally, although professional secrets are certainly taken into account in criminal procedural law, ultimately, adjustments would have to be anchored primarily in criminal law. Above all, the abuse of professional secrets would have to be sanctioned more strongly. However, this chapter is primarily concerned with the implications of criminal procedural law.

By contrast, undercover investigations and digital surveillance is core issues of criminal procedure law. These two instruments complement each other perfectly. As soon as the limits of undercover investigations have been reached, digital surveillance can come into play and offer valuable additional insight. For example, in many cases, undercover investigators must first infiltrate and become established in terrorist organizations. Digital surveillance, on the other hand, can be done immediately. However, digital surveillance is not yet permitted in Switzerland. This means that, in addition to the practical necessity of digital surveillance, which results from the explanations of the procedures used by terrorist financiers, suitable legal foundations must also be discussed.

At the same time, undercover investigations complement the use of digital surveillance. It cannot be assumed that perpetrators store all relevant information regarding their crimes on their computers. Undercover investigators can build on the findings of digital surveillance and gather additional information in person.

However, the standards that must be met to engage undercover agents are very high. In addition, undercover agents are often too limited in what they are permitted to do while undercover. Whereas undercover agents in the USA are allowed to commit crimes to maintain their cover, undercover investigators in the German-speaking countries examined here are at most allowed to make test purchases, which makes them relatively easy to uncover.

Undercover investigators and digital surveillance could also help overcome the problem of proving that perpetrators acted intentionally. Anyone who has repeatedly searched the Internet for methods of terrorism financing or referred to methods of transferring assets to the IS in discussions with undercover investigators in chat rooms or on message boards will hardly be able to successfully plead ignorance at a later date after they have successfully transferred funds to a terrorist organization. Since conditional intent is not sufficient under Art. 260^{quinquies} (2) CH-StGB, such evidence would be beneficial.[636]

At the same time, digital surveillance and undercover investigations could also help to prevent the exculpation problem enshrined in Art. 260, paras 3 and 4 CH-StGB. The findings of the undercover investigation and the digital surveillance would provide information about the motives of the perpetrator.

The aim of this chapter is neither to offer a commentary nor summarize the text of the law in full. Rather, this chapter presents the existing legal situation in summary form in order to provide the basis for proposals for legislative measures. Thus, this chapter does not claim to be exhaustive and is deliberately limited to those aspects that are essential for understanding the criminal procedure law implications of the empirical investigation. Therefore, the legal framework will first be explained and then concrete proposals for legislative measures that could enable a more effective fight against terrorism financing will be developed.

636 Stratenwerth & Wohlers, 2013: p. 499.

5.1 Digital surveillance

The surveillance of telecommunications is permissible in most countries in certain circumstances. Digital surveillance (i.e. the systematic, covert searching of hard drives without the knowledge of the person concerned), on the other hand, are considered a far more serious intervention.[637] However, this is necessary to combat terrorism financing and is practised by the National Security Agency (NSA) Terrorist Surveillance Program, among others.[638] In addition to the technical challenges it poses, it also raises numerous legal questions.[639] In particular, are the findings admissible in criminal proceedings?[640]

In the absence of a legal basis for digital surveillance, their findings are inadmissible in many countries.[641] Among other reasons for limiting their admissibility are their breaches of the privacy of the persons concerned and their breaches of data protection rights in general.[642] After all, the state gains access to the digital identity of the persons concerned within the framework of such measures.[643] A question therefore arises as to whether this is a permissible investigative act or amounts to state-sponsored hacking.[644] Consequently, constitutional considerations must be taken into account.[645] This also applies with regard to the confidentiality and integrity of information technology systems and the privacy of the persons concerned.[646]

In particular, digital surveillance is intended to be used to uncover perpetrators who are familiar with the traditional means available to the authorities for monitoring electronic communications. These individuals are unlikely to exchange information with like-minded people via Internet telephony. Rather, they are more likely to succeed in transferring assets for the purpose of terrorism financing without communicating in a monitorable form at all. However, it is

---

637 Rux, 2007: p. 285; Kemper, 2007: p. 105.

638 Wong, 2006: p. 517 f.; Kerr, 2008: p. 225.

639 Pohl, 2007: p. 684 f.

640 Jahn & Kudlich, 2007: p. 57.

641 Hornung, 2007: p. 575.

642 Böckenförde, 2008: p. 925; Bizer, 2007: p. 340; Pfitzmann, 2008: p. 443.

643 Brunst, 2011: p. 618.

644 Hofmann, 2005: p. 121.

645 Schantz, 2007: p. 310 f.; Hömig, 2009: p. 207; Baum & Schantz, 2008: p. 137; Yoo, 2006: p. 565 f.; Balkin & Levinson, 2006: p. 489 f.; Balkin, 2008: p. 1 f.; Maclin, 2007: p. 1259 f.; Thistle, 2008: p. 1197 f.

646 Petri, 2008: p. 443; Denkowski, 2008: p. 5 f.; Posner, 2008: p. 245 f.; Hoffmann-Riem, 2008: p. 1009 f.; Hornung, 2008: p. 299.

well established that terrorists often store suspicious information, such as bomb-making instructions, on their computers.[647]

Terrorist financiers who use cryptocurrencies to transfer assets but refrain from communicating with other people about their activities are difficult to convict by means of telephone surveillance. A clever terrorist financier also uses constantly changing public WLAN networks to access the darknet using a Tor browser. In these cases, it is nearly impossible to catch the target without engaging in digital surveillance.

Hawala bankers who work with couriers and conduct their business in person are also likely to be difficult to convict through conventional telephone surveillance. However, it can be assumed that such hawala bankers have a bookkeeping system in place to keep track of their transactions. While it is possible that individual hawala bankers do not maintain electronic records, it is also reasonable to assume that many hawala bankers do.

A perhaps less obvious, but not to be neglected, benefit of digital surveillance is how they can be used in connection with the personal transfer of assets. This is especially true when it comes to lone wolves who do not discuss their plans with third parties. These perpetrators also generally have to plan and prepare their transfer routes. Nowadays, this is done via the Internet. It can therefore be assumed that such perpetrators may save travel plans on their devices that could be discovered by means of an online search.

Even perpetrators who transfer their assets via the banking system can be exposed through digital surveillance. As a rule, transactions via the banking system must be plausibly justified. In many cases, this is done by the terrorist financier drawing up documents and submitting them to the bank. Digital surveillance could be used to detect such documents.

Transactions that are processed via money transfer service providers can also be detected more quickly by means of digital surveillance. For example, digital surveillance can also be used to view browser histories. This can provide clues to transactions made online via money transfer service providers or provide clues as to which branches the perpetrator has personally visited or will visit in the future.

In summary, then, digital surveillance is suitable for combating the methods of asset transfer for the purposes of terrorism financing outlined in the empirical study. However, they are also vulnerable to abuse. Therefore, a careful balancing of the protection of different legal interests is necessary.

---

647 Ziercke, 2008: p. 62.

In the following, the permissibility of digital surveillance in Switzerland, Liechtenstein, Austria and Germany is discussed in the form of country reports. This analysis serves as the basis for the subsequent recommendation for legislative measures in Switzerland. In particular, all of the hurdles in the countries mentioned will be considered in order to develop a recommendation that is as substantial as possible. Failed attempts to enable digital surveillance will also be included.

5.1.1 Switzerland

5.1.1.1 Switzerland – initial situation

In principle, it should be noted that secret surveillance measures represent a serious and profound intrusion into the privacy of the persons concerned. Since secrecy and privacy are fundamental freedoms in Switzerland, a legal basis is required to invade them. This is particularly important in order not to undermine the principles of the rule of law in Switzerland.[648] For this reason, the abovementioned civil liberties are partially protected by criminal law, specifically by Arts 179bis–179^{quater} CH-StGB.[649] Among other things, the interception and recording of non-public conversations are regulated.[650]

In the case of the physical seizure of devices, stored messages may also be edited. In these cases, no surveillance has taken place within the meaning of Art. 269 CH-StPO and no retroactive data collection has occurred within the meaning of Art. 273 CH-StPO. Legal protection is preserved in that the persons concerned can demand that the records be sealed. If the prosecution wishes to search the electronic records, it must submit a request to unseal them to the competent compulsory measures court. Less clear, however, is the regulation concerning the active interception of emails and text messages. Active interception is always necessary if no physical devices have been seized. In these cases, prior judicial authorization is mandatory.[651] However, digital surveillance go far beyond the interception of messages; thus, prior authorization is undoubtedly required.

The more private a space is, the more serious the intrusion into the private or intimate sphere of the persons concerned.[652] Digital surveillance represent an

648 Jaggi, 2001: p. 1 f.; Eugster & Katzenstein, 2014: Art. 280 CH-stopp point 1.

649 Von Ins & Wyder, 2018; Art. 179^{quater} CH-StGB point 2.

650 Hansjakob, 2014: p. 1635.

651 Forster, 2015: p. 624.

652 Eugster & Katzenstein, 2014; Art. 280 CH-StPO point 29.

extremely serious intrusion, especially in view of the fact that the persons concerned often store their most intimate secrets on their computers – secrets that they would not even share with their closest confidants. Accordingly, the barriers for engaging in digital surveillance must be high.

It is true that the Swiss legislature does not make any explicit differentiation with regard to the observation and recording of events in private premises. However, there is consensus that not all private premises enjoy the same protection. Visual surveillance in private bedrooms and bathrooms is not justified in many cases, taking into account the proportionality and subsidiarity of the measures. Surveillance of a study, on the other hand, is more justifiable. In practice, a question often arises as to which areas are worthy of protection. For example, the area directly in front of the door to a house is also considered protected by Art. 179^{quater} CH-StGB.[653] While it is possible to differentiate between different areas in the case of conventional surveillance measures, it is difficult to make such a distinction in the case of digital surveillance.[654] Anything that can be observed by third parties without putting in a special effort is generally considered public.[655]

If an investigator finds footage on a device during an online search, it must ultimately be sifted through to determine whether it contains extraordinarily intimate recordings. A search based on the file name or the folder in which the recordings were stored would ultimately be too superficial and undoubtedly susceptible to manipulation. At this point, it would be sufficient for offenders to save all suspicious content as 'Private Erotic Recordings' on their device to protect themselves from digital surveillance. This cannot be in the spirit of the legislator.

The use of technical surveillance devices in criminal proceedings usually serves to obtain evidence and thus solve crimes, and a distinction must be made between the use of surveillance devices to prevent crime, which is regulated in the corresponding and applicable police laws.[656] In addition, the question arises as to whether the perpetrator's own devices may be used as surveillance devices.[657] In the past, primarily sound and image recording devices and tracking devices, but also mobile phones, were used as interception devices.[658] These were used for acoustic and optical surveillance as well as for location identification.[659]

---

653 BGE 118 IV, E. 4.
654 Eugster & Katzenstein, 2014: Art. 280 CH-StPO point 34.
655 Riklin, 2014: S. 476.
656 Eugster & Katzenstein, 2014: Art. 280 CH-StPO point StPO
657 Riklin, 2014: p. 475.
658 BGE 133 IV 249, E. 3.3.
659 Hansjakob, 2014: p. 1635.

Surveillance of online telephony (e.g. WhatsApp, Telegram or Viber) has undoubtedly become permissible in Switzerland as a result of the introduction of Art. 269ter CH-StPO, which came into force on 1 January 2018.

Use of special computer programmes for the interception of telecommunications

1. The public prosecutor may order the insertion of special computer programs into a data processing system in order to intercept and extract the content of communications and the marginal data of telecommunications traffic in unencrypted form if:
   a. the conditions laid down in Article 269 (1) and (3) are fulfilled;
   b. it concerns the prosecution of an offence referred to in Article 286 (2);
   c. the previous measures for the interception of telecommunications in accordance with Article 269 have been unsuccessful or the interception would be futile or disproportionately difficult with these measures.

This article ensures that offenders cannot evade telephone surveillance by using encryption technologies. This results in particular from Art. 269ter (1) lit. c. CH-StPO. The terminology used in this context is based on legislation in the postal and telecommunications sector.[660] However, the interception of Internet telephony was also previously permissible.

Finally, Internet telephony is undoubtedly telecommunications traffic within the meaning of Art. 269 (1) CH-StPO.[661] This can be monitored if there are concrete and serious indications that a crime will be committed and the other requirements are met.[662] In particular, the person to be monitored must be a possible perpetrator of a crime.[663]

Since Internet telephony is covered by the secrecy of telecommunications in Art. 43 of the Telecommunications Act (TCA), and Art. 269 CH-StPO provides a sufficient legal basis for lifting it, Internet telephony could also be monitored in the past.[664] The extension of the catalogue has also meant that telephone surveillance is unlikely to be restricted in practice.[665] In principle, a distinction can be made between the conventional surveillance of content, the surveillance of content via direct connection, mere marginal data collection and systematic dragnet

660 Sidler, 2002: p. 116 f.
661 Jean-Richard-dit-Bressel, 2014: Art. 269 CH-StPO point 16.
662 Riklin, 2014: p. 462.
663 Biedermann, 2002: p. 83.
664 Hansjakob, 2011: p. 4.
665 Hansjakob, 2008: p. 109 f.

searches.[666] Half of the measures concentrate on content-based surveillance and half on marginal data collection.[667]

However, problems regularly arose in the process of using this type of surveillance. Internet telephony uses encryption, which is why it cannot be easily intercepted. For technical reasons, it is often necessary to install special software, so-called GovWare, in order to be able to monitor telephone calls.[668] This means that the measures required for the successful monitoring of Internet telephony go far beyond those of conventional telephone monitoring. The latter does not effect a change to the device of the person concerned. The data is merely forwarded by the provider to the authorities. The authorities do not manipulate the device of the person concerned in any way.[669] However, a question arises as to whether this procedure is still covered by Art. 280 CH-StPO.[670]

When monitoring Internet telephony, the authorities usually have to manipulate the device of the person concerned. This requires an intrusion into another person's data processing system within the scope of Art. 143bis CH-StGB.[671] This means that the authorities go well beyond the intrusion justified by Art. 269 CH-StPO, which would otherwise fall under Art. 179bis CH-StGB, namely the violation of telecommunications secrecy.[672] The offence of Art. 179bis CH-StGB is already fulfilled by anyone who puts a listening device into operation in order to use it to listen to another person's non-public conversation.[673]

At this point, one could consider Art. 280, lit. a CH-StPO, which regulates the use of technical surveillance devices for the purposes of intercepting or recording the non-publicly spoken word, as the legal basis for the use of GovWare.[674] This would be obvious for several reasons. First, the legislature has already acknowledged the close relationship between the interception of telecommunications and the use of technical surveillance devices in that the rules governing the interception of telecommunications in Arts 269–279 CH-StPO apply to Arts 280–281 CH-StPO unless specific provisions are applicable.[675] Consequently, urgent

666 Riklin, 2014: p. 458.
667 Hansjakob, 2005: p. 54 f.
668 Jaggi, 2015: p. 276.
669 Hansjakob, 2011: p. 4.
670 Eggimann, 2013: p. 115.
671 Weissenberger, 2018; Art. 143bis CH-StGB Erz. 3.
672 Hansjakob, 2011: p. 4; Von Ins & Wyder, 2018: Art. 179bis CH-StGB point 10.
673 BGE 133 IV 249, E. 3.4–3.6.
674 Riklin, 2014: p. 475 f.
675 Eugster & Katzenstein, 2014; Art. 280 CH-StPO point 4.

suspicion of a crime is presupposed and there are exigent circumstances.[676] In addition, Arts 280 and 281 CH-StPO are regarded as among the first formal and substantive federal legal foundations for state interference in private and confidential spheres.[677] They regulate both acoustic and visual spying.[678]

However, Art. 280 CH-StPO does not list the devices that can be used for surveillance measures.[679] It merely refers to the possible purposes of surveillance.[680] It should also be noted here that Art. 280, lit. a CH-StPO concerns law enforcement authorities' use of devices and not the manipulation of the devices owned by the person being monitored.[681] In Switzerland, a legal basis for the use of GovWare has been created through the Federal Act of 18 March 2016 on the surveillance of Post and Telecommunications Traffic (SPTA).

Nevertheless, it is worth taking a look at the requirements of Art. 281 CH-StPO. In particular, surveillance measures may only be ordered against the accused.[682] In addition, the premises of third parties may only be monitored if there are indications that the accused person is present in them.[683] Furthermore, the use of technical surveillance measures against persons who are deprived of their liberty or who could invoke professional secrecy is generally excluded. It is thus emphasized that the scope of application of technical surveillance measures is defined more strictly than that of the surveillance of postal and telecommunications traffic. With regard to digital surveillance, this means that the strict requirements of Art. 281 CH-StPO should be adopted.[684] Consequently, in addition to the exigent circumstances, the existence of the other prerequisites of Art. 269, paras 1 and 2 CH-StPO are also required.[685] Furthermore, authorization by the compulsory measures court and (with exceptions) subsequent information of the persons concerned are required.[686]

It should be expressly noted that it was not until Art. 269ter CH-StPO that a sufficient legal basis was created for the use of spyware disguised as email.

---

676 Riklin, 2014: p. 477.
677 Eugster & Katzenstein, 2014; Art. 280 CH-StPO point 3.
678 Riklin, 2014: p. 476.
679 Eugster & Katzenstein, 2014; Art. 280 CH-StPO point 22.
680 Hansjakob, 2014: p. 1635.
681 Riklin, 2014: p. 475 f.
682 Hansjakob, 2014: p. 1640.
683 Schmid & Jositsch, 2017: Art. 281 CH-StPO point 2.
684 Eugster & Katzenstein, 2014: Art. 281 CH-StPO point 1.
685 Schmid & Jositsch, 2017: Art. 281 CH-StPO point 4.
686 Riklin, 2014: p. 477.

These spyware programmes provide the investigating authorities with access to numerous pieces of information that go far beyond verbal communication. Such an intrusion into the confidential sphere of the person concerned requires a separate legal basis and cannot be subsumed under Art. 280 CH-StPO.[687]

Consequently, as part of the preparations for the preliminary draft amendment to the SPTA, Article 270[bis] CH-StPO was drafted, which would have read as follows and would have provided a sufficient legal basis for the interception of data[688]:

1. if, in the case of interception of telecommunications, the measures taken to date have been unsuccessful or if other interception measures would be futile or would make interception disproportionately difficult, the public prosecutor may, even without the knowledge of the person being intercepted, order the introduction of computer programmes into a data system in order to intercept and read the data. The public prosecutor shall specify in the surveillance order the type of data it wishes to access.
2. the order shall be subject to the approval of the compulsory measures court.[689]

Demand for a new SPTA came more from the law enforcement authorities than from parliament.[690] One of the issues addressed in the referendum of July 2016 was the extent to which privacy may be restricted for the purposes of fighting crime.[691] However, Art. 270[bis] CH-StPO was not enforced as part of the amendment to the SPTA. It is true that the surveillance of Internet telephony per se was also previously permissible under Art. 269 CH-StPO. However, the installation of software on the equipment owned by the person concerned, which was necessary for technical reasons, was not previously justified by a sufficient legal basis. It can therefore be stated that the monitoring of Internet telephony only receives a sufficient legal basis through the new Art. 269[ter] CH-StPO.[692]

However, digital surveillance go beyond the classic surveillance of telecommunications. Data on a computer can be searched via the Internet without the knowledge of the person concerned. This means that data, which may not even be transmitted, can be viewed by investigators.

---

687 Eugster & Katzenstein, 2014: Art. 280 CH-StPO point 16.

688 Eggimann, 2013: p. 115.

689 Federal Office of Justice, 2011: p. 56.

690 Hansjakob, 2016: p. 429.

691 Hasler, 2016: p. 183.

692 Hansjakob, 2011: p. 5.

According to Art. 246 CH-StPO, data carrier searches are in principle permitted in Switzerland.[693] However, Art. 247 CH-StPO presupposes the knowledge of the person concerned.[694] Article 248 CH-StPO also presupposes the knowledge of the person concerned, as they must be able to request the sealing of the data.[695] This is problematic for several reasons. On the one hand, the data subject may not notice that their data have been searched for a long period of time. At the same time, however, investigators are intruding into the highly personal sphere of the person concerned. This means that a sufficient legal basis is required for such a serious intrusion. The new Art. 269ter CH-StPO does not constitute a sufficient legal basis for searching data carriers via the Internet.

In the draft for the Federal Act on Measures to Safeguard Internal Security (BWIS), there were efforts made to create an explicit legal basis for digital surveillance. There, Article 18m stated:

Secret search of a data processing system

> If specific and current facts or events give rise to the suspicion that a suspected dangerous person is using a data processing system that is available to him or her and is specially secured against access, the Federal Office may search the system. The search may be carried out without the knowledge of the suspected dangerous person.[696]

This proposal also failed. Article 18m is not found in the version of the BWIS that entered into force on 16 July 2012. This means that there is currently no explicit legal basis for digital surveillance in Switzerland. However, such a legal basis is necessary. Finally, digital surveillance is a serious infringement of people's fundamental rights, the breaching of which requires a legal basis in accordance with Art. 36 (1) of the Swiss Federal Constitution (FC).

5.1.1.2 Switzerland – suggestions for legislative measures

5.1.1.2.1 Constitutional aspects

Digital surveillance seriously encroach on the fundamental rights of the persons being targeted and thus require legal justification. Therefore, constitutional considerations are first taken into account in the following. Subsequently, various criminal procedural norms are described to make suggestions. Finally, a concrete proposal for a legal basis for digital surveillance is developed.

---

693 Hansjakob, 2014: p. 1397 f.

694 Riklin, 2014: p. 428.

695 Hansjakob, 2011: p. 5.

696 Federal Council, 2007: p. 11.

First of all, the protection against arbitrariness and the preservation of good faith enshrined in Art. 9 BV should be taken into account, as every person has the right to be treated fairly and in good faith by state bodies.[697] Digital surveillance without a legal basis could lead to arbitrary decisions by the investigating officers. The conditions under which such digital surveillance is permissible must be clearly regulated.

Furthermore, privacy protections must be maintained. According to Art. 13 BV, everyone is entitled to respect for their private and family life and for their communications.[698] However, the protection of privacy may be restricted on the basis of Art. 36 BV. For example, accident insurance companies are permitted to observe policyholders.[699]

Digital surveillance represent a particularly serious intrusion into private and family life. One might think, for example, of private photos on a hard drive. In certain circumstances, the content is so private that the person concerned would not even want to share it with their closest confidants. In other words, the content would not have come into the hands of the investigators throughout the course of standard telecommunications surveillance. However, because a successful online search requires investigators to be able to sift through all the contents of a suspect's hard drive to distinguish relevant files from less relevant ones, investigators would very likely gain knowledge of the contents of these private photos. This raises the question of under which circumstances such a serious intrusion into someone's privacy could be justified.

In addition, digital surveillance without a legal basis could also be in conflict with Art. 26 BV, which guarantees the integrity of personal property, since such searches usually require the installation of spyware on the suspect's device.[700] This means that the suspect's device is tampered with. Such manipulations undoubtedly have a value-reducing effect, because it can be assumed that if the owner decided to sell the device, buyers would be inclined to pay a lower price if they were made aware of the presence of spy software. In the context of digital surveillance, the state thus interferes with the substance of a device or data processing system that is usually owned by a private individual.

Furthermore, the presumption of innocence enshrined in Art. 32, § 1 BV must not be disregarded.[701] This indeed poses a challenge with regard to digital

---

697 Art. 9 BV.

698 Art. 13 BV.

699 BGE 135 I 169, E. 4.4.

700 Art. 26 BV.

701 Art. 32 BV.

surveillance. Provided there is sufficient evidence, an online search is not necessary in many cases as the data carriers can be seized, sealed and subsequently searched as part of a physical search warrant.

Digital surveillance is particularly useful when there is not yet sufficient evidence. However, it is precisely in these cases that the presumption of innocence applies. Only in cases in which sufficient evidence is available, but the investigation is continued for tactical reasons without the knowledge of the suspect, is the online search compatible with Art. 32 (1) BV.

As already mentioned, breaches of a person's fundamental rights under Art. 36 (1) BV require a sound legal justification. Digital surveillance would constitute a serious interference with these rights, which would have to be provided for by law. Such interventions would also have to be proportionate and justified by a public interest or the protection of fundamental rights.[702] This would undoubtedly be the case with digital surveillance for the purposes of combating terrorism financing. The fight against terrorism financing is a public interest. Moreover, it serves, at least indirectly, in the protection of life and limb.

5.1.1.2.2 The usability of knowledge

As mentioned above, in the context of legislative measures to enable digital surveillance, taking a sideways glance at Arts 280–281 CH-StPO is useful. According to Art. 281 CH-StPO, the use of technical surveillance devices is in principle to be restricted to the accused.[703] In the context of surveillance using technical devices, the question regularly arises in practice of how to deal with objects used by the accused.[704] Consider, for example, a third party's vehicle that is shared with the suspect.[705] This problem also exists in the context of digital surveillance. Here, it is worth remembering that the same computer might be used by several family members. If third parties are unintentionally recorded, the information about them cannot be used.[706]

It should also be noted that data processing systems are generally considered a non-public space. The user stores data there without running the risk of it being perceived by third parties. What is to be regarded as 'non-public depends

---

702 Art. 36 BV.

703 Riklin, 2014: p. 477.

704 Eugster & Katzenstein, 2014: Art. 281 CH-StPO, point 3; Schmid & Jositsch, 2017: Art. 281 CH-StPO point 2.

705 Hansjakob, 2014: p. 1641.

706 Riklin, 2014: p. 477.

on the legal interest protected by the penal provision in question as well as on why publicity is presupposed therein as a feature justifying or excluding punishment'.[707] While the Swiss Federal Supreme Court's differentiation is aimed more at the legal interests protected under Art. 179bis CH-StGB, it also provides valuable insights for digital surveillance. In contrast to online forums, where the user must assume that their communications will be perceived by third parties, private data processing systems, which in practice are usually protected by passwords and firewalls, are a non-public space.

In many cases, it is likely to make sense to carry out the online search anyway. However, the non-usability of information vis-à-vis third parties must be taken into account. Thus, the usability of information should only be permissible if an online search would also have been permissible in this case; consider for example, the regulation under Art. 278 CH-StPO.

Furthermore, this raises questions regarding how to proceed if a suspect uses a third party's computer. Here, too, it is helpful to look at the provision of Art. 281 (2) CH-StGB, according to which the surveillance of the premises and vehicles of third parties may be authorized by way of exception if it can be assumed on the basis of certain facts that they are also used by the accused.[708] However, in this case, it cannot only be assumed that there is an abstract possibility of use – it must be possible to ground the assumption in facts indicating that the accused person uses the premises or vehicles.[709] This must be taken into account when granting the warrant.[710]

An analogous regulation is also conceivable for digital surveillance. In particular, it should be proven in the context of digital surveillance that the accused person has used the device to be searched at least once. Nevertheless, presupposing that the device is regularly used by the accused person should be avoided. Indeed, a clever offender could evade digital surveillance by frequently changing devices.

From a practical point of view, a question also arises as to how investigators can determine who owns a computer. After all, the measure is only directed against the accused person and not against third parties.[711] In the case of SIM cards, the customer's data registered at the time of sale are usually used. In the

707 BGE 130 IV 111.
708 Schmid & Jositsch, 2017; Art. 281, § 2 CH-StGB.
709 Eugster & Katzenstein, 2014: Art. 281 CH-StPO point 5.
710 Hansjakob, 2014: p. 1641.
711 Riklin, 2014: p. 477.

case of vehicles, it is obvious to use the vehicle's registration as an indicator of ownership. In the case of computers, it is difficult to determine the user or owner prior to carrying out an online search.[712] Documenting the names of buyers is not customary in computer sales. There is also no obligation to register a computer in one's name afterwards. This is where the new Art. 269ter CH-StPO can provide a remedy. By intercepting and extracting information, it usually becomes apparent who is using the computer. Should this be the accused, an online search could be ordered. A two-stage procedure, in which Art. 269ter CH-StPO is applied first, would make sense.

According to Art. 281 (3) lit. a CH-StPO, technical surveillance measures against persons who are deprived of their liberty are inadmissible because this would be incompatible with the fundamental right to personal freedom.[713] This would also have to be taken into account when introducing a legal basis for digital surveillance. However, the problem only arises to a limited extent here, as prison inmates generally do not have free access to the Internet.

In addition, Art. 281 (3) lit. b CH-StPO excludes the use of technical surveillance measures against certain professional groups.[714] The surveillance of persons holding confidential information is only permissible by way of exception if they themselves are being monitored as suspects.[715] This represents a significant tightening compared to Arts 270 and 271 CH-StPO, as the surveillance of postal and telecommunications traffic of these persons is perfectly permissible.[716] In order to prevent the data processing systems held as professional secrets from being used to protect criminals from digital surveillance, one might be tempted to refrain from upholding such an exception. However, one must bear in mind that this could significantly affect the relationship of trust between lawyers and their clients, as it would hardly be possible to differentiate between the files of the holder of professional secrecy and those of their clients prior to engaging in the online search.

Should one nevertheless argue in favour of engaging in digital surveillance of professional secrecy holders' data processing systems, one should at least consider excluding incidental findings against persons other than the accused from being used. The Federal Supreme Court defines incidental findings as those that

712 Eugster & Katzenstein, 2014: Art. 281 CH-StPO point 6.
713 Riklin, 2014: p. 478; Eugster & Katzenstein, 2014: Art. 281 CH-StPO point 10.
714 Riklin, 2014: p. 478.
715 Hansjakob, 2014: p. 1642.
716 Eugster & Katzenstein, 2014: Art. 281 CH-StPO point 14 f.

'originate from suspicion-driven investigative actions but have nothing to do with this suspicion'.[717]

Article 278 CH-StPO provides valuable suggestions for the use of incidental findings in digital surveillance. In principle, a distinction must be made between incidental findings relating to the accused person and those relating to other persons.[718] Article 278 CH-StPO provides in paragraph 1 that findings concerning other offences not listed in the warrant may be used against accused persons if the surveillance could also be ordered to prosecute those offences.[719] This provision could also be adopted for digital surveillance.

It should be emphasized here that incidental findings should only be admissible if an order for an online search would have been permissible for the accidentally discovered offence.[720] This would ensure that investigating officers could not misuse digital surveillance to solve less serious crimes. Otherwise, it might be possible to feign the prerequisites for an online search. Thus, in all cases, surveillance must be ordered by the public prosecutor and approved by the compulsory measures court. This should also apply to indications of criminal offences.[721] Files on non-usable incidental findings must be retained to ensure that it is possible to verify whether non-usable findings were included in the investigation.[722] Moreover, what is decisive is not what was actually known to the public prosecutor's office, but only what was actually listed in the warrant.[723]

According to Art. 278 (2) CH-StPO, knowledge of offences committed by persons who were not listed as suspects in the surveillance order may also be used during the investigation, provided that the order for a surveillance measure would also have been permissible for these offences.[724] Here it would be obvious to make an exception for digital surveillance. It should be recalled that it must be possible for holders of professional secrecy to store data on their computers without having to fear that investigators will gain access to this information through spyware. For example, lawyers store information about their clients on their computers in the context of preparing a criminal defence.

717 BGE 132 IV 70, E. 6.4.
718 Riklin, 2014: p. 477.
719 Art. 278 (1) CH-StPO.
720 Jean-Richard-dit-Bressel, 2014; Art. 278 (1) CH-StGB.
721 Riklin, 2014: p. 473; Jean-Richard-dit-Bressel, 2014: Art. 278 CH-StGB point 13.
722 Hansjakob, 2014: p. 1620.
723 Jean-Richard-dit-Bressel, 2014: Art. 278 CH-StGB point 14.
724 Art. 278 (2) CH-StPO.

In the case of digital surveillance, findings that arise from the incidental use of a device but concern a person other than the accused should also be regarded as incidental findings.[725] However, these are not considered incidental findings under the existing measures, similar to background conversations.[726] This deviation from the existing privacy rule can be justified by the particularly severe intrusion of digital surveillance.

The provision of Art. 278 (3) CH-StPO on the authorization of incidental findings by the compulsory measures court would also make sense for incidental findings obtained from digital surveillance. This applies in particular to the immediate initiation of the authorization procedure. However, it must be taken into account in this context that finds made by chance are not always immediately detected. Thus, a broad interpretation of the immediate authorization requirement must be assumed. Nonetheless, a period of twenty-four hours after ordering measures for further clarification of the chance find should not be exceeded in any case. The same procedure as the one set out in Art. 276 (1) CH-StPO is applicable here.[727]

In order to prevent serious offences from not being prosecuted due to a failure to obtain timely authorization from the compulsory measures court, the application of Art. 278 CH-StPO for digital surveillance should only be a validity provision within the scope of Art. 141 (2) CH-StPO, which would ensure that it could be used to investigate serious crimes.[728] Otherwise, there would be an absolute ban on its exploitation.[729]

In addition, it should also be possible to reapply for authorization in the case of chance finds from digital surveillance if the circumstances have changed because additional findings are often obtained in the course of complex proceedings by making further clarifications.[730] Restriction to a single authorization could in practice lead to investigators waiting for further clarifications before implementing the first and only authorization procedure, thereby significantly delaying the authorization.

It is also important that the prohibition on the exploitation of incidental findings extends to administrative proceedings. Finally, evidence that does not relate to catalogue offences may not be used. This particularly applies if

725 Riklin, 2014: p. 473.

726 Jean-Richard-dit-Bressel, 2014: Art. 278 CH-StGB point 17.

727 Jean-Richard-dit-Bressel, 2014: Art. 278 CH-StGB point 2; Riklin, 2014: p. 474.

728 Jean-Richard-dit-Bressel, 2014: Art. 278 CH-StGB point 30.

729 Riklin, 2014: p. 474.

730 Jean-Richard-dit-Bressel, 2014: Art. 278 CH-StGB point 32.

subsequent evidence would not have been obtained without the chance find. In such cases, subsequent evidence would also have to remain inadmissible.[731]

Furthermore, professional secrets must remain protected in accordance with Art. 271 CH-StPO.[732] One might think here, for example, of an online search that was authorized on suspicion of terrorism financing and but led to a discovery of tax offences. If the authorization of incidental findings were to be affirmed in these cases, social acceptance of digital surveillance would be significantly jeopardized due to the associated potential for abuse. Again, suspicions of terrorism financing should not be used as an excuse in order to obtain new evidence for tax matters through digital surveillance.

The potential inadmissibility of legitimately collected incidental findings should also be considered.[733] In these cases, there is an absolute ban on exploitation. This also applies to remote effects ("fruit-of-the-poisonous-tree" doctrine).[734]

Subdividing evidence into primary, secondary and tertiary layers should also be avoided to protect the usability of incidental findings from digital surveillance. This makes a distinction between primary evidence, which originates directly from the surveillance measure, secondary evidence, which results from the investigation of the primary evidence and tertiary evidence, which could be obtained based on the secondary evidence. Primary evidence is generally considered unusable and tertiary evidence is considered to be usable.[735] However, this approach suggests that secondary evidence could be usable. This was ruled out above, as digital surveillance is a particularly serious form of intrusion into the privacy and confidentiality of the person targeted and the measure should in any case be prevented from being abused.

It goes without saying that the prohibition on exploiting the results of unauthorized surveillance, as laid down in Art. 277 CH-StPO, should also apply to digital surveillance.[736] In particular, an absolute ban on the exploitation of findings from digital surveillance for which an application for authorization was not approved or was not approved in good time is required. In such cases, the findings must be destroyed immediately.[737] This is particularly important in view

731 Riklin, 2014: p. 474; Jean-Richard-dit-Bressel, 2014; Art. 278 CH-StGB point 36.
732 Riklin, 2014: p. 474.
733 Jean-Richard-dit-Bressel, 2014: Art. 278 CH-StGB point 37.
734 Riklin, 2014: p. 474.
735 Jean-Richard-dit-Bressel, 2014: Art. 278 CH-StGB point 40.
736 Art. 277 CH-StPO.
737 Jean-Richard-dit-Bressel, 2014: Art. 277 CH-StGB point 3.

of the findings associated with digital surveillance and the perceptions of the investigators as well as the public. Should the impression be created that formal errors concerning digital surveillance can be 'cured', this could lead to a loss of confidence in these measures.

In addition, the remote effect of the prohibition of exploitation established in Art. 277 CH-StPO should also apply to digital surveillance. In these cases, an absolute ban on exploitation applies.[738] This means that the findings obtained in the course of an unauthorized online search may not be used for further investigations or for evidentiary purposes.[739] No balancing of interests takes place.[740] The question of the extent to which such a ban on the use of evidence could be used to exonerate the accused does not arise in the case of digital surveillance, if only because unauthorized findings must be destroyed immediately.[741] Thus, any discussion as to whether there was an urgent suspicion of a crime at the relevant time is irrelevant.[742]

In principle, a balancing of interests takes place between the public interest in establishing the truth and the interest of the accused that the evidence not be used.[743] It must be borne in mind that digital surveillance ultimately penetrate the 'mental space' of the person concerned, especially if they have private records, such as a diary or intimate recordings, stored on their device.[744] Furthermore, in addition to the private interest in non-usability, there is also a public interest in not encouraging investigators to obtain evidence unlawfully.[745]

Although, according to the established case law of the Federal Supreme Court, the admissibility of illegally obtained evidence is not ruled out in every case from a constitutional perspective, it is ruled out at least in principle.[746] In the past, the inadmissibility of illegally obtained evidence was affirmed if the evidence itself was inadmissible.[747] However, the evidence is not admissible if legal interests that take precedence over the enforcement of criminal law were violated in order to obtain it.[748]

---

738 Riklin, 2014: p. 472.
739 Jean-Richard-dit-Bressel, 2014; Art. 277 CH-StGB point 4.
740 Riklin, 2014: p. 472.
741 Jean-Richard-dit-Bressel, 2014: Art. 277 CH-StGB point 5.
742 Godenzi, 2012: p. 1246.
743 BGE 130 I 126, E. 3.2.
744 BGE 109 Ia 273, E. 7.
745 BGE 131 I 272 4.1.2.
746 BGE 130 I 126, E. 3.2.
747 BGE 96 I 437, E. 3b.
748 BGE 131 I 272, E. 4.1.2.

Furthermore, a question arises as to what extent Art. 276 CH-StPO could apply to digital surveillance. According to this, the findings obtained from authorized surveillance, which do not appear necessary for criminal proceedings, would have to be kept separately from the case files and destroyed immediately after the end of the proceedings.[749] Among other things, this norm aims to protect third parties and professional secrets.[750]

This obligation to segregate evidence should be interpreted narrowly in the context of digital surveillance with regard to the severity of the intrusion into the private and confidential sphere of the persons concerned. However, we should still speak of segregation and not of destruction. Finally, it cannot be in the spirit of the legislator that information which at first glance appears to be unsuspicious – but which could perhaps be relevant – is destroyed before the investigation is completed.

Furthermore, another question arises regarding under which circumstances the requirements for an online search might be met. Here, it is not possible to simply fall back on Art. 269 CH-StPO, as an online search represents a significantly more serious intrusion than the conventional surveillance of postal and telecommunications traffic. Nevertheless, Art. 269 CH-StPO can offer some valuable suggestions. In particular, Art. 269 (1) lit. b and c CH-StPO can be adopted. Accordingly, the seriousness of the offence must justify the measure.

In addition, previous investigative actions must have been unsuccessful, futile or disproportionately difficult.[751] It would also make sense to draw up a list of predicate offences. However, this catalogue would have to be much shorter than that of Art. 269 CH-StPO. The author proposes that digital surveillance only be permitted for the purpose of combating terrorism financing within the meaning of Art. 260^{quinquies} CH-StPO.

Restricting digital surveillance to a single offence may at first seem too massive and even radical a restriction, but it is a pragmatic proposal. It is hardly conceivable that a law enabling digital surveillance for a broad catalogue of possible cases of application could pass through the legislative process in Switzerland and enter into force. This can be observed in the fact that the much less far-reaching Art. 270bis CH-StPO has already failed.

However, a law limited to combating the financing of terrorism could meet with significantly less resistance, as terrorism and its financing enjoy a very low

749 Art. 276 CH-StPO.

750 Jean-Richard-dit-Bressel, 2014: Art. 276 CH-StGB point 7.

751 Art. 269 (1) CH-StPO.

level of acceptance among the population, and only a few people are likely to be affected by such digital surveillance. While this also applies in principle to other crimes, terrorism financing has a special status due to its potential danger to life and limb.

It goes without saying that the online search, insofar as it is a continuing measure, is terminated immediately if the requirements are no longer met or its authorization or extension is not granted. Thus, an analogous application of Art. 275 CH-StPO is obvious.[752] Provided that the measure is not terminated, an absolute ban on exploitation within the meaning of Art. 277 CH-StPO should apply to the findings obtained after the expiry of the time limit. It therefore makes sense to order termination not immediately but on a specific date and at a specific time.[753]

However, it should be emphasized that there should be no obligation to stop the measure if the online search provides evidence of an ongoing criminal offence.[754] Should an online search reveal that an offender is funding terrorism, it may be essential to continue monitoring these activities.

5.1.1.2.3 Requirements for digital surveillance

For the authorization of digital surveillance and their procedure, Arts 272–274 CH-StPO could be applied mutatis mutandis. According to Art. 272 (1) CH-CPC, authorization from the compulsory measures court would be necessary for digital surveillance. In the case of frequently changing computers, a general licence could exceptionally be granted on the basis of Art. 272 (2) CH-StPO.[755]

This authorization procedure is intended in particular to compensate for the fact that the persons concerned cannot be granted a legal hearing prior to the interception.[756] This regulation also appears to make sense for digital surveillance. After all, it cannot be at the discretion of the investigating officer whether an online search is carried out or not. An authorization procedure is mandatory.

Pursuant to Art. 274 (1) CH-StPO, the public prosecutor shall submit the order and the reasons for it to the compulsory measures court within twenty-four hours of the order for surveillance. According to Art. 274 (2) CH-StPO, the compulsory measures court must decide within five days.[757] In the case of

---

752 Art. 275 (1) CH-StPO.

753 Jean-Richard-dit-Bressel, 2014: Art. 275 CH-StGB point 3; Hansjakob, 2014: p. 1603.

754 Jean-Richard-dit-Bressel, 2014; Art. 275 CH-StGB point 4.

755 Art. 272 CH-StPO.

756 Jean-Richard-dit-Bressel, 2014; Art. 272 CH-StGB point 4.

757 Art. 274 CH-StPO.

digital surveillance, one might be tempted to demand prior authorization due to the seriousness of the intrusion into the privacy and confidentiality of the persons concerned. However, from a practical point of view, this would not be very effective.

Thereafter, the orders as well as their reasons must be formulated clearly. Subsequently, the compulsory measures court must have the opportunity to decide conscientiously on the documents submitted and to formulate a brief but well-reasoned decision. Even if the deadline for the compulsory measures court were to be reduced from five days to forty-eight hours, it must be assumed that digital surveillance could be significantly delayed as a result. Alternatively, rash decisions might have to be taken. Neither of these options seems to be in the best interests of the legislature.

At the same time, however, it must be borne in mind that terrorist financiers can cause considerable damage with their transactions. Among other things, they finance terrorist attacks that pose a threat to public safety. There is therefore a massive time pressure in play. After all, an act might have already been financed but not yet carried out.

Furthermore, due to the international nature of the transactions of terrorist financiers, there is often both a risk of flight and a risk of collusion. Expeditious investigations are therefore of fundamental importance. Therefore, it seems obvious to adopt the existing regulation for digital surveillance as well.

In addition, a notification within the scope of Art. 279 CH-StPO must be made.[758] Pursuant to Art. 279 (1) CH-StPO, the public prosecutor's office must inform the persons under surveillance of the reason for and the nature and duration of the surveillance at the end of the preliminary proceedings, but pursuant to Art. 279 (2) CH-StPO, this notification may be postponed or even omitted with the consent of the compulsory measures court if either would benefit public or private interests.[759]

The purpose of the notification obligation is primarily to ensure that state intrusions into the private sphere are not permanently kept secret and to grant the persons concerned a legal hearing.[760] This is particularly important in the case of digital surveillance, as this is an extremely serious intrusion into the privacy and secrecy of the persons concerned. The idea of the state carrying out

758 Riklin, 2014: p. 475.

759 Art. 279 CH-StPO.

760 Jean-Richard-dit-Bressel, 2014; Art. 279 CH-StGB point 5.

digital surveillance over a long period of time without informing those affected is unlikely to be acceptable to a large proportion of the population.

It is thus important to defuse the problem of secrecy. At the same time, however, it may make sense for investigative tactical reasons to postpone or even omit the notification. A time-limited postponement is conceivable in order not to jeopardize other investigations.[761] Omission is even possible if the communication could put a person's life in danger or endanger public safety.[762] In the case of digital surveillance in the context of investigations into terrorist financiers, the threat to public safety in particular is likely to justify an omission.

With regard to professional secrecy, Art. 271 CH-StPO could also be applied mutatis mutandis to digital surveillance. In particular, an online search of a person subject to maintaining professional secrecy may only be ordered if they are the suspect. Nonetheless, the prosecuting authorities may not obtain knowledge of professional secrets through an online search.[763]

5.1.1.2.4 Art. 298e CH-StPO – a potential solution?

Finally, the question arises as to how such an article should be formulated and at what point in the CH-StPO it should be systematically added. The author argues for its classification under the secret surveillance measures, namely at the end of the eighth chapter of the fifth title of the CH-StPO This would express that digital surveillance could be authorized as a last resort after the exhaustion (or futility) of all other measures. Accordingly, establishing this within the scope of an Art. 298e CH-StPO would be conceivable.

For the wording, one could refer to the drafts of Art. 18m BWIS and Art. 270bis CH-StPO, as well as the existing norms Arts. 269–281 CH-StPO, and supplement the same:

Art. 298e

Secret search of a data processing system

1. If concrete and current facts or incidents give rise to the suspicion that a suspected offender is using a data processing system available to him or her, this system may be searched by the public prosecutor's office if:
   a. there is a strong suspicion that an offence referred to in paragraph 2 has been committed;
   b. the seriousness of the offence justifies the surveillance; and

761 Hansjakob, 2014: p. 1628.

762 Jean-Richard-dit-Bressel, 2014: Art. 279 CH-StGB point 8.

763 Art. 271 CH-StPO.

   c. the investigative measures taken to date have been unsuccessful or the investigations would otherwise be futile or disproportionately difficult.

The search may be conducted without the knowledge of the alleged offender.

2. A search of a data processing system may be ordered for the purpose of prosecuting the offences listed in the following Articles:
   a. 260quinquies StGB
3. The order requires the approval of the compulsory measures court.
4. Accidental findings shall only be admissible if they relate to an offence referred to in subsection 2.
5. In all other respects, the use of searches of a data processing system shall be governed by Articles 280–281.[764]

In drafting Art. 298e CH-StPO, the aspects discussed in this subchapter were taken into account. In particular, the basis for an enumeration of further offences was deliberately resorted to in Art. 298e (2) CH-StPO In the present work, the author has presented the necessity of using digital surveillance for the purposes of combating terrorism financing. At the same time, however, it cannot be ruled out that digital surveillance could also be suitable for the prosecution of other offences.

By means of the legal basis presented here, digital surveillance could be authorized for selected offences. This could make the fight against terrorism financing significantly more effective, especially with regard to the methods outlined in the discussion of the empirical study.

The considerable potential for abuse that digital surveillance offer should be remembered. On the one hand, digital surveillance could be used by the investigating authorities themselves for purposes other than those intended. On the other hand, the technical tools needed for digital surveillance could fall into the wrong hands. However, this applies to almost every technical tool used by investigators. After all, listening devices and tracking devices could also be misused by unauthorized third parties. Nevertheless, appropriate precautions should be taken. The unauthorized misuse of digital surveillance, whether by investigating authorities or by third parties, could cause a stir and lead to resentment and mistrust among the population.

There is also the question of the low political appetite for the possible introduction of an Art. 298e CH-StPO because of the failed attempts in the past to create a legal basis for digital surveillance. Consequently, it would be important

764 Federal Office of Justice, 2011: p. 56; Federal Council, 2007: p. 11; Art. 269 ff. CH-StPO.

to emphasize in the legislative process that digital surveillance would only affect a very small segment of the population. It is important to stress that this measure does not give investigating authorities the power to search any computer. It must also be emphasized that the requirements that must be met to qualify for an online search are very high and that such measures serve to protect the population against terrorist attacks.

5.1.2 Liechtenstein

Ordering the interception of electronic communications is governed by § 103 of the Code of Criminal Procedure of the Principality of Liechtenstein (FL-StPO). It states the following:

> (1) An order for the interception of electronic communications, including the recording of their content, shall be permissible only if it is to be expected that it may assist in the investigation of a criminal offence committed intentionally and punishable by more than one year's imprisonment and if
> 1. the owner of the communication equipment is himself strongly suspected of having committed the offence, or
> 2. there are grounds for believing that a person urgently suspected of the offence is staying with the owner of the installation or will contact him using the installation, unless the owner is one of the persons specified in § 107(1) no. 2, or
> 3. the owner of the facility expressly consents to the monitoring.[765]

However, § 103 FL-StPO does not constitute a sufficient legal basis for digital surveillance. It only regulates the interception and recording of electronic communications. Moreover, § 103 FL-StPO explicitly refers to the 'interception of electronic communications including the recording of their content', which in no way covers the searching of data carriers. A question thus arises here as to how to proceed if an offender does not communicate through but merely stores data on their device.[766]

In Liechtenstein, searches of people and property are regulated in § 91a ff. FL-StPO but do not constitute a sufficient legal basis for digital surveillance. In particular, § 93 (1) FL-StPO provides for a prior interrogation of the person concerned. According to § 93 (2) FL-StPO, this interrogation can be waived if there is an imminent threat or if a particularly notorious person is involved.[767] However, digital surveillance is basically secret and exclude any prior interrogation and

765 § 103 FL-StPO.
766 Stotter, 2012: p. 365 f.
767 Stotter, 2012: p. 273 f.

announcement of the search. Otherwise, the authorities could seize and search the corresponding data carrier in the context of being authorized to search a residence. Engaging in a search via the Internet would be superfluous with the knowledge of the person concerned.

If one were to take the position that an online search based on § 93 (2) FL-StPO would be possible in principle even without informing the person concerned in advance, one would at least have to limit this to cases in which there is imminent danger or the person concerned is particularly notorious.

A further obstacle to digital surveillance arises from § 95 (3) FL-StPO. According to this, the person concerned has the right to be present during the search and to call in a witness. This may also only be dispensed with in cases of imminent danger.[768] According to § 95 (3) FL-StPO, the person concerned must also be provided with a copy of the protocol.[769] This also seems to be incompatible with the secrecy of an online search, as digital surveillance could possibly be carried out repeatedly and over a longer period of time.

Furthermore, it must be taken into account that the sealing of papers that have been seized and are to be searched is also provided for in Liechtenstein. According to § 98 (2) FL-StPO, the person concerned must be given the opportunity to be present during the unsealing. This undoubtedly follows from the text of the law:

> 2) Papers which have been taken into judicial custody and which cannot be recorded immediately shall be placed in an envelope to be sealed with the court seal. The person concerned who may be present during the search shall also be permitted to affix a seal. If an unsealing is carried out, the person concerned shall be requested to attend the same.[770]

This assumes that the individual has knowledge of the search of the papers and the unsealing.[771] However, an online search would be secret and would take place without the knowledge of the person concerned. This does not seem to be in line with § 98 (2) FL-StPO.

Due to the lack of a legal basis and the relatively low number of cases in the Principality of Liechtenstein, there is no direct case law on the admissibility of digital surveillance. However, the Constitutional Court has indirectly dealt with digital surveillance in StGH 2014/051. In an appeal against the decision of the

768 § 95 (3) FL-StPO.
769 Stotter, 2012: p. 276 f.
770 § 98 (2) FL-StPO.
771 Stotter, 2012: p. 351 f.

Supreme Court of 11 March 2014, 14RS.2009.150–185, in which the violation of constitutional rights and rights guaranteed by the ECHR was alleged, the question was, inter alia, whether a request for judicial assistance from Germany, which was based on evidence obtained in the course of an unlawful online search, could be acted upon.

In StGH 2014/051, the issue was, inter alia, that German officials had inadmissibly taken screenshots of the computer of the person concerned every thirty seconds in the course of a surveillance operation by means of spyware and that the mutual assistance proceedings could thus be based on conduct that was punishable by a court in Liechtenstein. This could be contrary to Liechtenstein public policy. The State Court dismissed the complaint because, among other things, the complainant had not succeeded in demonstrating that the requesting authority had obtained the essential information about this spyware, and the complaint was therefore dismissed.[772]

In addition, it must be considered that the online search could constitute an encroachment on secrecy and privacy within the meaning of Art. 32 (1) of the Liechtenstein Constitution (LV).[773] Article 31 (1) LV guarantees the freedom of the person, the right to privacy and the secrecy of correspondence and writings. It goes without saying that this also covers data carriers.

According to Art. 31 (2) LV, a statutory basis is required for the search of a house or person and the letters or writings (or seizure) of the same. Interventions are only permissible if they meet the criteria of the established case law of the State Court. In addition to the existence of a legal basis, the interference must be in the public interest and must not be disproportionate or violate the core content of the fundamental right.[774]

Furthermore, digital surveillance could also violate Art. 34 (1) LV which guarantees the inviolability of private property. Digital surveillance require the installation of spy software. This installation is connected with a considerable interference in the data processing system owned by the person concerned. It can be assumed that spy software changes the substance of the property of the person concerned and ultimately has a diminishing effect on its value. This would also require a legal basis to justify.

In Liechtenstein, no legal basis for digital surveillance is currently planned. Moreover, there are no reports on the use of digital surveillance in Liechtenstein.

---

772 StGH 2014/051, rec. 2.3.

773 StGH 2008/37+88, rec. 5.4; StGH 2007/51, rec. 3.1.

774 StGH 2010/117, provision 31; StGH 2000/65.

It can therefore be assumed that digital surveillance do not (may not) currently take place in Liechtenstein.

The Principality of Liechtenstein can therefore offer no indications for the further development of criminal procedure law to enable digital surveillance in Switzerland since Liechtenstein has neither an appropriate legal basis nor any relevant case law on the subject of digital surveillance.

In principle, the introduction of a new article on digital surveillance would also be conceivable in Liechtenstein. This could be based on the proposed Article 298e for the Swiss Code of Criminal Procedure and anchored in the Liechtenstein Code of Criminal Procedure as § 103a.

Problematic in this context is the fact that the Liechtenstein Code of Criminal Procedure does not contain any regulations on incidental findings. According to § 104 (2) FL-StPO, the only requirement is that the suspect, who is different from the holder of a communications device, must be granted the right to be heard by being given the opportunity to inspect the records resulting from the surveillance if these could lead to criminal proceedings against them.[775] However, this obstacle could be taken into account in a new § 103a FL-StPO and thus overcome.

In summary, it can therefore be stated that digital surveillance is currently not possible in Liechtenstein. However, a suitable legal basis could be created to enable digital surveillance in the future. Article 298e, which was developed for the Swiss Code of Criminal Procedure in the course of this work, could serve as a starting point and be adopted with minor adjustments.

5.1.3 Austria

In Austria, the Code of Criminal Procedure (AT-StPO) has been amended in the following way.

§ 136a.

Monitoring of messages transmitted by means of a computer system

(1) The interception of messages transmitted by means of a computer system shall be permitted under the conditions of section 136(1) no. 3 and (4) if the interference with the computer system is necessary to enable the interception and recording of messages in unencrypted form.

(2) Insofar as this is unavoidable in order to carry out the investigative measure, it shall be permissible to enter a specific dwelling or other premises protected by domestic

775 Jean-Richard-dit-Bressel, 2014: Art. 278 CH-StGB point 43.

law, to search containers and to overcome specific security measures in order to access the computer system.

3. Moreover, interception of communications transmitted by means of a computer system shall be permitted only if it can be ensured that the interception programme
   1. records only data transmitted and received by the computer system and data allowing conclusions to be drawn as to the names or other means of identification of the owners or controllers of the computer systems involved in the transmission of the messages,
   2. is inoperable after the end of the investigative measure or can be removed without permanent damage or impairment of the computer system and the data stored in it, and
   3. does not cause damage or permanent impairment to third party computer systems that are not subject to monitoring.[776]

Ultimately, this draft failed to cover what would ultimately be necessary for an online search and provided exclusively for the monitoring of messages but not for the searching of the device.

In addition, a question arises as to whether § 136a (3) no. 1 AT-StPO would be technically implementable. The (unnoticed) interception of information would require a certain depth of intrusion into a data processing system. While it would certainly be desirable to intercept only the information specified in § 136a (3) no. 1 AT-StPO in the process, this is likely to be extraordinarily difficult from a technical point of view.

Furthermore, it is also necessary to examine whether digital surveillance would be permissible in Austria from a constitutional law perspective. Austrian constitutional law is confusing, since in addition to the Federal Constitutional Law (B-VG), numerous other laws and state treaties also enjoy constitutional status. In the present work, reference is made primarily to the Basic State Law (StGG) in addition to the B-VG.

The inviolability of property is enshrined in Art. 5 StGG. This is particularly problematic with regard to the substance-changing interventions of the investigating authorities on the devices of the persons concerned, which are associated with digital surveillance.

Furthermore, Art. 10 StGG states that the secrecy of correspondence may not be violated.[777] However, this must be put into perspective. Pursuant to § 135 (1) AT-StPO, the seizure of letters is permissible if doing so is necessary to clarify an intentional criminal offence punishable by more than one year's

776 Parliamentary Directorate, 2016: p. 2.
777 Art. 10 StGG.

imprisonment and the person concerned is already in custody or has been put on the wanted list.

Furthermore, Art. 10a StGG emphasizes that the secrecy of telecommunications may not be violated. However, the interception of communications is permissible on the basis of § 135 (3) no. 3 AT-StPO if this appears necessary for the investigation of a criminal offence punishable by imprisonment of more than one year.[778] Such surveillance is also permissible for the clarification or prevention of criminal offences committed by criminal or terrorist organizations.[779] This is particularly the case if the investigation would otherwise be considerably more difficult without it.[780]

Section 136 of the Austrian Code of Criminal Procedure also sets out the requirements for further optical and acoustic surveillance measures.[781] According to § 136 (1) no. 3 AT-StPO, the optical and acoustic surveillance of persons is permissible for the purpose of investigating crimes punishable by a custodial sentence of more than ten years or for the purpose of investigating or preventing crimes committed by a criminal organization or a terrorist group, provided that the surveillance is directed against the accused or against persons who have contact with the accused.[782] The principle of proportionality must always be taken into account.[783]

The originally intended systematic classification of the draft of § 136a AT-StPO would thus make sense. However, since digital surveillance clearly go beyond the monitoring of messages transmitted by way of a computer system, it would make sense to create a § 136b. Here, too, the draft of Art. 298e CH-StPO developed for the Swiss Code of Criminal Procedure could serve as a point of reference.

In principle, § 136b AT-StPO could be subject to the same rules as § 135 and § 136 AT-StPO. It should be emphasized that digital surveillance in Austria could in principle also be used to prevent crimes committed by a terrorist organization. In contrast to Switzerland, preventive investigations in Austria are also regulated in criminal procedure law. This means that the scope of application of a possible § 136b AT-StPO would be significantly more extensive than in Switzerland.

778 Fabrizy, 2011: p. 336 f.

779 § 135 AT-StPO.

780 Reindl-Krauskopf, 2011: § 135 AT-StPO point 41.

781 Bachner-Foregger, 2018: p. 185 f.

782 § 136 AT-StPO.

783 Fabrizy, 2011: p. 342.

5.1.4 Germany

Germany regulates digital surveillance very comprehensively, and other countries could draw inspiration from the German legislation. Consequently, a more detailed presentation of the legal situation in Germany is given here.

5.1.4.1 Delimitations and definitions

In Germany, differentiating between different forms of digital surveillance is necessary. In particular, a distinction must be made between those carried out for the purposes of law enforcement and those carried out as preventive measures. In Germany, digital surveillance is only possible in strict circumstances and are considered a measure that is only applied in a subsidiary manner.[784]

It goes without saying that the interception of telecommunications is in principle subsidiary. Consequently, it is only possible to do if the investigation of the facts or determining the whereabouts of the accused person would be downright hopeless or at least made substantially more difficult by any other means. This particularly applies to digital surveillance.[785] Consequently, the prerequisites for digital surveillance is closely aligned with those for eavesdropping.[786]

Digital surveillance is the surreptitious spying on computers and other information technology systems and only permitted under very strict conditions. However, the most serious criminal offences, which for example endanger the existence of the state, could under certain circumstances justify such a measure.[787] Digital surveillance is primarily about accessing private computer data. This access is made possible either by hacking or by sending a so-called 'Trojan'. Such Trojans transmit the data found on the computer to the outside world. The advantage of using an online search is that this can be done without the knowledge of the person concerned.[788]

In Germany, digital surveillance is now regulated under § 100b DE-StPO and § 49 BKA Law. With regard to the Federal Intelligence Service Act (IntelSA), it must be emphasized that any intelligence gathered through means that have been explicitly excluded by the law is inadmissible. These include measures for which special legal authorization is required but are listed neither in the Federal Act for the Protection of the Constitution nor in the IntelSA, such as digital

784 Kugelmann, 2014: § 20k BKA Law point 7.
785 Kühne, 2015: point 521.1.
786 Singelnstein & Derin, 2017: p. 2647.
787 Kramer, 2014: p. 214.
788 Kühne, 2015: point 527.4.

surveillance. The focus of the present work is on questions of criminal procedure law. Nevertheless, the BKA Law is also dealt with in summary form.

5.1.4.2 BKA Law

In particular, the Act on the Federal Criminal Police Office and Co-operation between the Federation and the Federal States in Criminal Police Matters (Federal Criminal Police Office Act – BKA Law) serves as the basis for preventive measures in Germany. In addition, the police laws of the individual federal states are applicable. However, these are not dealt with in detail here. According to § 4a BKA Law, the Federal Criminal Police Office may take charge of the prevention of threats of international terrorism if a transnational threat exists or if the competence of a land authority is not apparent or if the land authority requests assistance.

5.1.4.2.1 § 20k BKA Law

Section 20k of the Federal Criminal Police Act, the most controversial provision of the entire Federal Criminal Police Act, regulated covert intervention in information technology systems up until 24 May 2018, when it was replaced by a less rigorous version. This provision was subject to the competence norm of Art. 73 (1), no. 9a of the German Basic Law (GG) and could thus only be used to defend against threats of international terrorism.[789] Section 20k BKA Law stated:

> The Federal Criminal Police Office may, without the knowledge of the person concerned, intervene by technical means in information technology systems used by the person concerned and collect data from them if certain facts justify the assumption that there is a danger to
> 1. life, limb or liberty of any person, or
> 2. such public goods, the threat to which affects the foundations or the existence of the state or the foundations of the existence of the people.
>
> A measure in accordance with sentence 1 is also permissible if it cannot yet be established with sufficient probability that damage will occur in the near future if the measure is not carried out, provided that certain facts indicate a threat to one of the legal interests referred to in sentence 1 posed by certain persons in an individual case. The measure may only be carried out if it is necessary for the performance of the task in accordance with section 4a and if this would otherwise be futile or substantially impeded.

789 Kugelmann, 2014: § 20k BKA Law point 2.

(2) It shall be technically ensured that
1. only changes are made to the information technology system that are indispensable for data collection, and
2. the changes made are automatically reversed as far as technically possible when the measure is terminated.

The means used shall be protected against unauthorised use in accordance with the state of the art. Copied data shall be protected against modification, unauthorised deletion and unauthorised disclosure in accordance with the state of the art.

(3) Each time the technical means is used, the following shall be recorded
1. the name of the technical means and the date of its use,
2. the information identifying the information technology system and the non-temporary changes made to it,
3. the information enabling the data collected to be identified, and
4. The organizational unit that carries out the measure.

The log data may only be used to enable the data subject or an authorised public body to check whether the measure in accordance with paragraph 1 was carried out lawfully. They must be retained until the end of the calendar year following storage and then deleted automatically unless they are still required for the purpose specified in sentence 2.

(4) The measure may only be directed against a person who is responsible in accordance with section 17 or section 18 of the Federal Police Act. The measure may also be carried out if other persons are unavoidably affected.
(5) The measure referred to in paragraph 1 may only be ordered by the court on application by the President of the Federal Criminal Police Office or his representative.
(6) The order shall be issued in writing. It shall specify
1. the person against whom the measure is directed, as far as possible with name and address,
2. a description, as precise as possible, of the information technology system which is to be accessed for data collection,
3. the nature, scope and duration of the measure, specifying the end date, and
4. the main reasons.

The order shall be limited to a maximum of three months. An extension of no more than three further months in each case is permissible insofar as the prerequisites for the order continue to apply in the light of the knowledge gained. If the prerequisites for the order no longer apply, the measures taken on the basis of the order shall be terminated immediately.

(7) If there are factual indications for the assumption that the measure would only provide information from the core area of private life, the measure shall be inadmissible. If possible, technical measures shall be taken to ensure that data relating to the core area of private life are not collected. Data collected shall be reviewed without delay under the direction of the court issuing the order in accordance with

> paragraph 5 by the Data Protection Officer of the Federal Criminal Police Office and two other staff members of the Federal Criminal Police Office, one of whom is qualified to hold judicial office, for content relevant to the core area. The data protection commissioner is not bound by instructions when performing this task and may therefore not be disadvantaged (Section 4f (3) of the Federal Data Protection Act). Data concerning the core area of private life may not be used and must be deleted immediately. The facts of the collection of the data and the deletion must be documented. The documentation may be used exclusively for the purposes of data protection control. It shall be deleted when it is no longer required for these purposes, but at the latest at the end of the calendar year following the year of documentation.[790]

Thus, digital surveillance were possible in Germany for preventive purposes under strict conditions.[791]

Pursuant to Art. 20k § 2 BKA Law the technical changes to the data processing system concerned were to be kept to a minimum and reversed insofar as technically possible once the measure had ended. In addition, it had to be ensured that the technical means used, namely the software, and the findings obtained from the online search were secured against unauthorized access.[792]

Furthermore, such digital surveillance were to be recorded. The order for the measure was to be issued in writing by the President of the Federal Criminal Police Office, his representative or a court. Moreover, it could only be directed against a person who was responsible under § 17 or § 18 of the Federal Police Act (i.e. a person who posed a threat). However, it had to be borne in mind that in most cases this person's communication partners were also affected.[793] Therefore, the measure could also be carried out if it was unavoidable that other people would be affected.[794]

However, § 20k (7) BKA Law had a significant weakness. In particular, technical measures had to be taken to ensure that data concerning the core area of private life were not collected.[795] This was particularly important in view of Art. 1 (1) GG, which protects the core area of private life as part of ensuring human dignity.[796] This means that a clever perpetrator only had to disguise all critical files on their computer in such a way that they had to be considered as falling

790 § 20k (1) BKA Law.
791 Kugelmann, 2014; § 20k BKA Law point 2.
792 § 20k (2) BKA Law.
793 Kugelmann, 2014; § 20k BKA Law point 15.
794 § 20k (3–6) BKA Law.
795 § 20k (7) BKA Law.
796 Kugelmann, 2014; § 20k BKA Law point 17.

within the scope of private life by filing instructions for terrorism financing in folder entitled 'private diary', for example, or placing incriminating photos in a folder called 'private nudes'. Accordingly, these files were not allowed to be viewed.

Thus, it can be stated that a legal basis for preventive digital surveillance already existed in Germany. However, the practical usefulness of this legal basis had to be put into perspective due to § 20k (7) BKA Law. In order to be able to effectively combat terrorism financing, § 20k (7) BKA Law would have had to be amended. Thus, all data would have to be collected and subsequently sifted through by employees of the Federal Criminal Police Office who are qualified to hold judicial office. Materials considered to fall under the core area of private life would have had to be deleted in this context. However, an amendment to Art. 1 (1) GG would have been necessary to enable an adaptation of § 20k (7) BKA Law, but such an adjustment was not in the offing.

5.1.4.2.2. § 49 BKA Law

Covert interventions in information technology systems are permitted in the new Federal Criminal Police Act on the basis of § 49. In order to ensure effective national security, it must be possible to access information technology systems – particularly in the context of international terrorism and the increasing use of cryptographic procedures by terrorists. This also applies if the said information technology systems are not used for telecommunications with third parties.[797] Section 49 BKA Law is to be regarded as a lex specialis to § 45 BKA Law.[798] Section 49 BKA Law reads as follows:

> (1) The Federal Criminal Police Office may, without the knowledge of the person concerned, intervene by technical means in information technology systems used by the person concerned and collect data from them if certain facts justify the assumption that there is a danger to
> 1. life, limb or liberty of any person, or
> 2. such public goods, the threat of which affects the foundations or existence of the Federation or of a country, or the foundations of the existence of the people.

797 Schenke, 2019; § 49 BKA Law (point 1).
798 Schenke, 2019; § 49 BKA Law (point 3).

A measure pursuant to sentence 1 is also permissible if
1. certain facts justify the assumption that within a foreseeable period of time damage to the legal interests referred to in sentence 1 will occur in a manner which is at least specific in its nature, or
2. the individual conduct of a person gives rise to the concrete probability that he or she will, within a foreseeable period of time, cause damage to the legal interests referred to in sentence 1.

The measure may only be carried out if it is necessary for the performance of the task in accordance with § 5 and if this would otherwise be futile or substantially impeded.

(2) It shall be technically ensured that
   1. only changes are made to the information technology system that are indispensable for data collection, and
   2. the changes made are automatically reversed as far as technically possible when the measure is terminated.

The means used shall be protected against unauthorised use in accordance with the state of the art. Copied data shall be protected against modification, unauthorised deletion and unauthorised disclosure in accordance with the state of the art.

(3) For each use of the technical means, the following shall be recorded
   1. the designation of the technical means and the time of its use,
   2. the data identifying the information technology system and the changes made to it that are not merely temporary.
   3. The information enabling the identification of the collected data, and
   4. The organizational unit carrying out the measure

The log data may only be used to enable the data subject or an authorised public body to check whether the measure in accordance with subsection 1 was carried out lawfully. They must be retained until the end of the calendar year following storage and then deleted automatically unless they are still required for the purpose specified in sentence 2.

(4) The measure may only be directed against a person who is responsible in accordance with § 17 or § 18 of the Federal Police Act. The measure may also be carried out if other persons are unavoidably affected.

(5) The measure referred to in subsection (1) may only be ordered by the court on application by the President of the Federal Criminal Police Office or his or her representative.

(6) The application shall state:
   1. the person against whom the measure is directed, as far as possible with name and address,
   2. a description, as precise as possible, of the information technology system which is to be accessed for data collection,
   3. the nature, extent and duration of the measure,
   4. the facts of the case and
   5. a rationale.

(6) The order shall be made in writing. It shall specify:
1. the person against whom the measure is directed, as far as possible with name and address,
2. a description, as precise as possible, of the information technology system which is to be accessed for data collection,
3. the nature, scope and duration of the measure, specifying the end date, and
4. the main reasons.

The order shall be limited to a maximum of three months. An extension of no more than three further months in each case is permissible insofar as the prerequisites for the order continue to exist, taking into account the knowledge gained. If the prerequisites for the order no longer exist, the measures taken on the basis of the order shall be terminated immediately.

(7) If there are factual indications for the assumption that the measure would only provide information from the core area of private life, the measure shall be inadmissible. As far as possible, technical measures shall be taken to ensure that data relating to the core area of private life are not collected. Information obtained by means of measures in accordance with paragraph 1 shall be submitted to the ordering court without delay. The court shall decide without delay on the usability or deletion. Data relating to the core area of private life may not be utilised and shall be deleted without delay. The facts of the collection of the data and the deletion shall be documented. The documentation may only be used for the purposes of data protection control. It shall be deleted six months after notification under section 74 or six months after the court has given its consent to the final waiver of notification. If the data protection control pursuant to § 69 (1) has not yet been completed, the documentation shall be retained until its completion.

(8) In the event of imminent danger, the President of the Federal Criminal Police Office or his or her representative may, in consultation with the Data Protection Officer of the Federal Criminal Police Office, decide on the utilisation of the findings. In sifting through the data collected, he or she may avail himself or herself of the technical assistance of two further staff members of the Federal Criminal Police Office, one of whom must be qualified to hold judicial office. The staff of the Federal Criminal Police Office shall be bound to secrecy with regard to the information of which they become aware and which may not be used. The judicial decision pursuant to subsection 7 shall be made up without delay.[799]

For a covert intervention into information technology systems to take place within the scope of § 49 BKA Law, a threat must have been made to an overriding legal interest of superior importance. This danger must be derived from

799 § 49 BKA Law.

certain facts.[800] In addition, certain facts must point to the danger.[801] Similar to the DE-StPO, subsidiarity is also required in § 49 BKA Law.[802] Furthermore, the principle of proportionality must always be upheld. The depth of the intervention is thus to be limited to what is necessary. In particular, as few changes as possible are to be made to the targeted information technology systems. These should be reversed after the surveillance has ended.[803]

Certain authorities (i.e. the president of the Federal Criminal Police Office and their representative) are authorized to apply for covert interventions into information technology systems.[804] There is also a reservation made for judges. This requirement may not be waived even in the case of imminent danger.[805] The surveillance measure is limited to a period of three months and can be extended by a maximum of three months, whereby a proportionality test must be carried out in each individual case.[806] In addition to the name of the person concerned, the application for the intervention must also state the use of the information technology system concerned as well as the type, scope and duration of the covert intervention and the main reasons for it.[807]

It is important that data with highly personal content enjoy special protection. Consequently, these should not be collected in the context of covert interventions into information technology systems.[808] The measure would also be inadmissible if it had to be assumed that knowledge would be obtained exclusively from the so-called core area of private life. In this case, the term 'positive core area prognosis' is used.[809]

According to the opinion of the Federal Constitutional Court (BVerfG), possibilities for information technology safeguards must be made to ensure that no data regarding the core area of private life are collected.[810] However, this is difficult.[811] Theoretically, it may seem possible, for example, to avoid collecting

800 Schenke, 2019; § 49 BKA Law, point 6.
801 Schenke, 2019: § 49 BKA Law point 8.
802 Schenke, 2019: § 49 BKA Law point 10.
803 Schenke, 2019: § 49 BKA Law point 17; Schenke, 2019; § 49 BKA Law point 18.
804 Schenke, 2019: § 49 BKA Law point 26.
805 Schenke, 2019: § 49 BKA Law point 27.
806 Schenke, 2019: § 49 BKA Law point 32; BVerfG 141, 220 point 216.
807 Schenke, 2019: § 49 BKA Law point 31.
808 Schenke, 2019: § 49 BKA Law point 33.
809 Schenke, 2019: § 49 BKA Law point 34.
810 BVerfG 109, 279.
811 Schenke, 2019; § 49 BKA Law point 35.

certain data by means of employing search criteria. For example, one could suggest that a folder with the file name 'private holiday photos' should not be collected. On the perpetrator side, however, this could lead to circumventions by filing plans for criminal offences in folders with names that suggest they pertain to the core area of private life because data relevant to the core area must not be exploited and must be deleted immediately.[812]

5.1.4.3 *Criminal procedural aspects*

In its decision of 24 January 2012, the German Federal Constitutional Court stated that independent specialist legal bases determine the circumstances under which communications may be accessed. For digital surveillance, reference is made in this regard to §§ 100a and 100b DE-StPO.[813]

5.1.4.3.1 *Delimitations and definitions*

In Germany, there was no sufficient legal basis for digital surveillance in the Code of Criminal Procedure until 24 August 2017. This was based, among other things, on the fact that § 102 DE-StPO could not be considered a general search authorization. Section 100a DE-StPO did not constitute a legal basis for digital surveillance since no monitoring of communications between a suspect and a third party was at stake.[814] Digital surveillance cannot be defined as searches within the meaning of §§ 102 ff. DE-StPO because these require a physical substrate.[815] Nonetheless, telecommunications surveillance was and is possible in Germany.[816] This is regulated in § 100a DE-StPO, the first paragraph of which reads as follows:

> (1) Telecommunications may be intercepted and recorded even without the knowledge of the persons concerned if
> 1. certain facts give rise to the suspicion that someone has committed a serious criminal offence referred to in paragraph 2 as a perpetrator or participant, has attempted to commit such an offence in cases where the attempt is punishable, or has prepared such an offence by committing a criminal offence,
> 2. the offence is also serious in the individual case and

812 Schenke, 2019: § 49 BKA Law point 37.

813 Graulich, 2019: § 10 BKAG point 17.

814 Graf, 2018: § 100b DE-StPO point 1.

815 Kramer, 2014: p. 230.

816 Bruns, 2019: § 100a DE-StPO point 1 f.; Günther, 2016: § 100a DE-StPO point 1 f.; Pfeiffer, 2005: § 100a DE-StPO point 2.

3. the investigation of the facts or the determination of the whereabouts of the accused would otherwise be substantially impeded or futile.[817]

However, similar to Switzerland, telecommunications surveillance in the sense of § 100a DE-StPO only covers the surveillance of telecommunications and not the secret search of data carriers.[818]

It could be argued that § 100h (1) no. 2 DE-StPO, which provides for the use of technical means intended for surveillance purposes, is applicable; however, a closer examination thereof shows this to be untrue. After all, digital surveillance is not surveillance, but rather searches, and § 100h (1) no. 2 DE-StPO only concerns surveillance.[819] It must be remembered that encroachments on fundamental rights are only possible under Art. 19, I., GG and may only take place based on concrete and express legal bases. An interpretative derivation from other laws, on the other hand, is not possible. It must be emphasized that § 100h (1) no. 2 DE-StPO does provide for the use of technical means of surveillance which are neither covered by § 100c DE-StPO nor by § 100h (1) no. 1 DE-StPO.[820] However, this definition does not apply to digital surveillance. There is no sufficient legal basis for digital surveillance offered in the Code of Criminal Procedure.[821]

The purpose of an online search is not primarily the constant surveillance of the person concerned but to enable a surreptitious search of their files. In this context, investigators not only collect information about the current actions of the person concerned but may also gain knowledge of their most intimate secrets as a result of seeing what they have stored on their hard drive. In the digital age, data processing systems often serve as memory aids. These reminders of the data subject become visible to investigators in the context of digital surveillance.

Nevertheless, the Code of Criminal Procedure offers valuable suggestions for the design of digital surveillance. This is especially true with regard to the preservation of the core area of the constitutionally guaranteed right to a private life. For example, § 100c (5) DE-StPO requires that wiretapping and recording measures are interrupted immediately once there are indications that there might be an encroachment on the core area of private life.[822] It is important to bear in mind

817 §100a (1) DE-StPO.

818 Graf, 2017: § 100a DE-StPO point 1 f.

819 Hegmann, 2017: § 100h DE-StPO point 1 f.; Bruns, 2019: § 100h DE-StPO point 1; Günther, 2016: § 100h DE-StPO point 1; Pfeiffer, 2005: § 100h DE-StPO point 1.

820 Kühne, 2015: point 531.

821 Kühne, 2015: point 528.1.

822 BVerfGE 109, 279.

that recordings that have already been made must be deleted immediately and would in any case be unusable. If the surveillance measures are to be continued because there is a possibility that further conversations could lie outside the core area of the constitutionally guaranteed right to a private life, for example, then a decision from a court with the authority to issue an order must be obtained in case of doubt – the public prosecutor's office cannot make this decision.[823]

Large-scale eavesdropping can only be ordered by the State Protection Chamber of the District Court.[824] Furthermore, such surveillance measures must also be limited in duration. As a rule, the order may be issued for a maximum of one month, as per § 100d (1) DE-StPO. Extensions for the same length of time can be requested up to five times. Subsequently, a decision by the Higher Regional Court is required.[825]

Surveillance is also permitted against persons who are suspected of being in contact with suspected criminals. This is particularly useful with regard to determining the whereabouts of a suspected perpetrator.[826]

Measures of secret communications monitoring may be subject to a review of their lawfulness and the manner in which they are implemented. As a rule, this can be applied for within two weeks of notification of the measure.[827] Furthermore, subsequent legal protection must of course also be guaranteed in the case of digital surveillance. Here too, the court that ordered the measure should be responsible.[828]

With the entry into force of Art. 3 of the Act on More Effective and Practicable Criminal Procedure, an appropriate legal basis for digital surveillance – namely the new Art. 100b DE-StPO – was created on 24 August 2017. Article 100b DE-StPO regulates under which conditions the information technology systems used by defendants or their associates can be infiltrated as follows[829]:

§ 100b DE-StPO

Online search

(1) Even without the knowledge of the data subject, technical means may be used to intervene in an information technology system used by the data subject and data may be collected therefrom (online search) if

---

823 Kühne, 2015: point 530.1.
824 Kühne, 2015: point 532.
825 Kühne, 2015: point 530.1.
826 § 163 f, I, 3 DE-StPO; Kühne, 2015: point 533.3.
827 Kühne, 2015: § 557.2.
828 Kühne, 2015: § 557.3.
829 Eschelbach, 2020: § 100b DE-StPO point 1.

1. certain facts give rise to the suspicion that a person has committed, or attempted to commit in cases where the attempt is punishable, a particularly serious criminal offence referred to in paragraph 2 as a perpetrator or participant,
2. the offence is also particularly serious in the individual case, and
3. the investigation of the facts or the determination of the whereabouts of the accused would otherwise be substantially impeded or futile.

(2) Particularly serious offences within the meaning of subsection (1) no. 1 are:

1. from the penal code:
   a) Offences of high treason and endangering the democratic constitutional state as well as treason and endangering external security pursuant to §§ 81, 82, 89a, 89c (1) to (4), §§ 94, 95 (3) and 96 (1), in each case also in conjunction with § 97b, as well as §§ 97a, 98 (1) sentence 2, 99 (2) and §§ 100, 100a (4),
   b) Formation of criminal organisations under § 129 (1) in conjunction with subsection (5), third sentence, and formation of terrorist organisations under section 129a (1), (2), (4), (5), first sentence, first alternative, in each case also in conjunction with section 129b (1),
   c) Counterfeiting of currency and tokens under §§ 146 and 151, in each case also in conjunction with § 152, and under §§ 152a (3) and 152b (1) to (4),
   d) Offences against sexual self-determination in the cases of § 176a (2) no. 2 or (3) and, under the conditions specified in § 177 (6) sentence 2 no. 2 of § 177,
   e) Distribution, acquisition and possession of child pornographic writings in the cases of § 184b (2),
   f) Murder and manslaughter under §§ 211, 212,
   g) Offences against personal liberty in the cases of §§ 234, 234a (1), (2), 239a, 239b and trafficking in human beings under section 232 (3), forced prostitution and forced labour under § 232a (3), (4) or (5) second half-sentence, § 232b (3) or (4) in conjunction with § 232a (4) or (5) second half-sentence and exploitation taking advantage of a deprivation of liberty under section 233a (3) or (4) second half-sentence,
   h) Gang theft under § 244 (1) no. 2 and aggravated gang theft under section 244a,
   i) Aggravated robbery and robbery resulting in death under § 250 (1) or (2), § 251,
   j) Predatory extortion under § 255 and a particularly serious case of extortion under § 253 under the conditions specified in the second sentence of § 253 (4),
   k) Commercial receiving of stolen goods, gang trafficking and commercial gang trafficking in accordance with §§ 260, 260a,
   l) Particularly serious case of money laundering, concealment of unlawfully obtained assets pursuant to § 261 under the conditions specified in § 261 (4), second sentence; if punishability is based on the fact that impunity is excluded pursuant to § 261 (9), second sentence, in accordance with section

261 (9), third sentence, but only if the object derives from one of the particularly serious offences specified in nos 1 to 7,
   m) A particularly serious case of corruption and bribery under § 335 (1) subject to the conditions set out in § 335 (2) nos 1 to 3,
2. from the Asylum Act:
   a) Inducement to make an abusive application for asylum under § 84 (3),
   b) Incitement to submit an improper application for asylum on a commercial or gang basis under § 84a (1),
3. from the Residence Act:
   a) Smuggling of aliens under § 96 (2),
   b) Smuggling with fatal consequences or commercial and gang-related smuggling under § 97,
4. from the Narcotics Act:
   a) A particularly serious case of an offence under § 29 (1), first sentence, no. 1, 5, 6, 10, 11 or 13, (3) subject to the condition specified in § 29 (3), second sentence, no. 1,
   b) An offence under §§ 29a, 30 (1) no. 1, 2, 4, § 30a,
5. from the War Weapons Control Act:
   a) An offence under § 19 (2) or § 20 (1), in each case also in conjunction with § 21,
   b) Particularly serious case of an offence under § 22a (1) in conjunction with subsection (2),
6. from the International Criminal Code:
   a) Genocide under § 6,
   b) Crimes against humanity under § 7,
   c) War crimes under §§ 8 to 12,
   d) Crime of aggression under § 13,
7. from the Weapons Act:
   a) A particularly serious case of an offence under § 51 (1) in conjunction with subsection (2),
   b) Particularly serious case of an offence under § 52 (1) no. 1 in conjunction with subsection (5).

(3) The measure may only be directed against the accused. Interference with information technology systems of other persons is only permissible if it can be assumed on the basis of certain facts that
1. the defendant identified in the order under § 100e (3) uses information technology systems of the other person; and
2. the execution of the intrusion into the defendant's information technology systems will not, on its own, lead to the investigation of the facts or to the identification of the whereabouts of a co-defendant.
   1. The measure may also be carried out if other persons are unavoidably affected.

(4) § 100a (5) and (6) shall apply mutatis mutandis with the exception of subsection (5), first sentence, no. 1.[830]

With § 100b DE-StPO an explicit legal regulation for digital surveillance was created. Even before that, digital surveillance were already used in practice. However, this was a legal grey area. The procedure for digital surveillance is now regulated in § 100e DE-StPO.[831]

Digital surveillance is usually carried out without the knowledge of the person concerned. Primarily, information relevant to the investigation, which is stored on the device being searched, is read out.[832] Consequently, the entire data stock is subject to review or monitoring. Data of the person concerned can be collected to a large extent.[833] The fundamental rights to the integrity and confidentiality of information technology systems are thus particularly affected,[834] along with the right to informational self-determination.[835]

Surveillance is carried out secretly and may extend over a longer period of time. It may also cover the usage behaviour of the person concerned. The measure is therefore most comparable to the acoustic surveillance of a person's home. Consequently, the prerequisites for this intervention are based on those for the eavesdropping within the scope of § 100c DE-StPO. According to the opinion represented here, however, digital surveillance is significantly more intrusive than major eavesdropping which can only collect current information.[836] By contrast, an online search can also make information from the past accessible to the investigating authorities. Moreover, microphones or cameras could also be activated in the context of digital surveillance.[837]

The advantage of digital surveillance is, among other things, that a comprehensive picture of the target individual's personality can be created. However, at the same time, they also run the risk of leading to total surveillance.[838]

---

830 § 100b DE-StPO.
831 Eschelbach, 2020: § 100b DE-StPO point 7.
832 Eschelbach, 2020: § 100b DE-StPO point 1.
833 Eschelbach, 2020: § 100b DE-StPO point 2.
834 Beukelmann, 2017: p. 440.
835 Eschelbach, 2020: § 100b DE-StPO point 3.
836 Eschelbach, 2020: § 100b, § 3 DE-StPO.
837 Eschelbach, 2020: § 100b, § 4 DE-StPO.
838 Eschelbach, 2020: § 100b, § 5 DE-StPO.

5.1.4.3.2 Conditions for digital surveillance

The prerequisites for ordering digital surveillance is largely the same as those for telecommunications surveillance, such as certain facts that justify suspecting a person of being guilty of a particularly serious crime.[839] Basically, concrete suspicion of a catalogue offence is required (§ 100b (1) no. 1, (2) DE-StPO).[840] It does not matter whether the offence was carried out or merely attempted; however, merely engaging in the preliminary stages in order to make the attempt is insufficient cause. Committing an offence by omission, on the other hand, is sufficient cause.[841] Thus, perpetration is not required; rather, the suspicion of participation in or an attempted commission of a crime is sufficient.[842]

No increased degree of probability is required. Rather, the existence of concrete facts that indicate that a catalogue offence could exist is sufficient to initiate an online search. This seems questionable in view of the seriousness of the encroachment of an online search on a person's fundamental rights.[843] In principle, simple suspicion is sufficient, but there must be circumstances that indicate to a considerable extent that a serious crime within the meaning of § 100b (2) DE-StPO has been committed. Thus, a certain degree of concretization is required. Nevertheless, the deciding judge or public prosecutor exercises considerable discretion in determining what facts are substantial.[844] The catalogue is exhaustive,[845] but the catalogue of predicate offences in § 100b (2) DE-StPO is limited to particularly serious offences. In particular, a minimum sentence of one year and a maximum sentence of ten years must be assumed.[846]

In addition, the offence suspected in the individual case must be particularly serious.[847] Thus, a maximum degree of severity is required to initiate an online search.[848] Both the wrongdoing and the guilt should be particularly severe. The special gravity of the case must be considered in the sense of weighing all known circumstances.[849] The overall assessment should take into account the

---

839 Krey & Heinrich, 2019: p. 243; Graf, 2018: § 100b DE-StPO point 12.
840 Graf, 2018: § 100b DE-StPO point 12.
841 Eschelbach, 2020: § 100b DE-StPO point 8.
842 Graf, 2018: § 100b DE-StPO point 13.
843 Eschelbach, 2020; § 100b, § 9 DE-StPO.
844 Graf, 2018: § 100b DE-StPO point 12.
845 Eschelbach, 2020: § 100b DE-StPO point 10.
846 Graf, 2018; § 100b DE-StPO point 18.
847 Graf, 2018; § 100b DE-StPO point 14.
848 Eschelbach, 2020: § 100b DE-StPO point 12.
849 BVerfGE 107, 322.

importance of the legal interest violated, the seriousness of the violation in the individual case and the presumed culpability of the accused. The impact of the offence on the victim must also be taken into account.[850]

Furthermore, the proportionality of the measure must always be examined.[851] The investigation of the facts or the establishment of the whereabouts of the person must be made considerably more difficult or even hopeless without it (§ 100b (1), no. 3 DE-StPO). This illustrates the subsidiarity of the measure.[852] The principle of subsidiarity must therefore be observed.[853]

5.1.4.3.3 Persons concerned

The measure should in principle be directed against the accused.[854] However, digital surveillance can affect both the accused and the owner of an information technology system used by the accused. Thus, other people are inevitably affected as well. Accused persons are to be defined according to the established concept.[855]

With regard to the owners of an information technology system used by the accused person, concrete indications are required that clearly suggest such use. Simply having access to the device is not sufficient. Rather, concrete indications are required.[856] Furthermore, there are inevitably affected persons whose data are on the devices that are the subject of the online search.[857]

However, if the accused uses a third party's information technology systems or the monitoring of the accused's own systems will not likely lead to the discovery of evidence or the determination of the accused's whereabouts, then the monitoring of other persons by means of an online search is also permissible to achieve this end.[858]

5.1.4.3.4 Implementation

In the context of digital surveillance, information technology systems are searched. This is done secretly so that the persons concerned are not forewarned.[859]

---

850 Eschelbach, 2020: § 100b DE-StPO point 13; Graf, 2018: § 100b DE-StPO point 15.
851 Graf, 2018: § 100b DE-StPO point 20.
852 Eschelbach, 2020: § 100b DE-StPO point 15.
853 Graf, 2018; § 100b DE-StPO point 16; BVerfGE 109, 342.
854 Graf, 2018; § 100b DE-StPO point 21; Krey & Heinrich, 2019: p. 243.
855 Eschelbach, 2020: § 100b DE StPO point 17.
856 Eschelbach, 2020: § 100b DE-StPO point 18.
857 Graf, 2018: § 100b DE-StPO point 22.
858 Graf, 2018: § 100b DE-StPO point 22.
859 Graf, 2018: § 100b DE-StPO point 9.

Digital surveillance also usually require manipulation of the devices of the persons concerned, such as circumventing passwords, firewalls and other forms of security.[860]

Overcoming the firewall can be achieved in various ways. On the one hand, gaps in the existing operating system can be used. On the other hand, it is possible to install special software on the device. However, the principle of proportionality should always be observed. This means that the technical intervention into the devices of the persons concerned must be limited to the necessary minimum.[861]

In particular, only changes that are absolutely essential for data collection purposes should be made. The changes made should also be reversed – insofar as technically feasible – once the measure has ended. Ideally, the devices should thus be restored to their original state; otherwise, claims for damages could be made by the persons concerned.[862] In particular, there would be a risk that the changes made by the implementing authority to the devices of the persons concerned could lead to security vulnerabilities, and these could also be exploited by third parties for their own purposes.[863]

Furthermore, a question arises as to how to deal with the possible alteration of data as well as how to avoid creating any damage as a result of the online search.[864] In this respect, the legislator largely refers to § 100a (5), sentence 1, no. 1 DE-StPO and thus the principles of conventional telecommunications surveillance.[865]

The protection of the suspect's core area thus only plays a significant role at the level of exploitation.[866] With regard to the protection of the core area, it should be noted that the online search measure is inadmissible under § 100d (1) DE-StPO if knowledge is obtained exclusively from the suspect's core area of private life.[867]

With regard to the technical requirements for the software, the legislator allows the investigating authorities and the court to exercise discretion.[868] As a rule, remote access via a data line is possible.[869] This leads to several challenges.

---

860 Graf, 2018: § 100b DE-StPO point 25.
861 Graf, 2018: § 100b DE-StPO point 27.
862 Graf, 2018: § 100b DE-StPO point 28.
863 Graf, 2018: § 100b DE-StPO point 29.
864 Eschelbach, 2020: § 100b DE-StPO point 22.
865 Eschelbach, 2020: § 100b DE-StPO point 22.
866 Eschelbach, 2020: § 100b DE-StPO point 23.
867 Krey & Heinrich, 2019: p. 244.
868 Eschelbach, 2020: § 100b DE-StPO point 24.
869 Graf, 2018: § 100b DE-StPO point 10.

On the one hand, it may pose a potential threat to the security of IT systems.[870] On the other hand, it is also conceivable that suspects will be able to evade surveillance by using so-called Tor browsers or comparable programmes or by accessing the surveillance via the darknet.[871]

In creating a legal basis for the online search, the legislator has refrained from specifying particular types of equipment. Instead, the term 'information technology systems' is used in general. This makes sense since the ability to engage in digital surveillance was created to be largely independent of technological developments and future trends and capabilities.[872]

Finally, it should be emphasized that the malware must be removed once the measure has been terminated.[873] Third parties should also be prevented from having access to the monitoring software. This means that, as a rule, the software used should be proprietary to the state.[874]

Another question arises as to how investigating authorities can infiltrate the computer systems of those affected. On the one hand, this can happen via a so-called Trojan. On the other hand, investigating officers could also directly access the information technology system of the person concerned. Consequently, § 100b DE-StPO also contains authorization to enter the home of the person concerned using a warrant.[875] In this respect, however, constitutional concerns must be raised with regard to Art. 1 (1) GG and Art. 13 (1) GG. Finally, it cannot be assumed that the owner of the home willingly waives their fundamental rights.[876]

Furthermore, all steps taken must be adequately documented. At a minimum, the documentation must include all preceding steps, the time of deployment of the online search as well as the technical means used and the data collected.[877] With regard to the technical means used, their functional scope and the monitoring software used must at least be documented.[878] Changes to the operating system must also be documented.[879]

---

870 Eschelbach, 2020: § 100b DE-StPO point 25.
871 Eschelbach, 2020: § 100b DE-StPO point 25.
872 Graf, 2018: § 100b DE-StPO point 7.
873 Eschelbach, 2020: § 100b DE-StPO point 26.
874 Eschelbach, 2020: § 100b DE-StPO point 26.
875 Eschelbach, 2020: § 100b DE-StPO point 27.
876 Eschelbach, 2020: § 100b DE-StPO point 27.
877 Graf, 2018: § 100b DE-StPO point 31.
878 Graf, 2018: § 100b DE-StPO point 33.
879 Graf, 2018: § 100b DE-StPO point 34.

5.1.4.3.5 Prohibitions on the use of evidence

Prohibitions of use and restrictions are based on the general principles.[880] It is important to note that only fundamental deficiencies can lead to the findings obtained through the online search being unusable. This would be the case, for example, if there was no order from the competent criminal division of the regional court.[881] On the other hand, simple formal errors, such as violations of the written form requirement, do not lead to inadmissibility.[882]

In addition to formal defects, factual defects of the order for an online search are of course also conceivable. In the absence of a catalogue offence, it must generally be assumed that the evidence is unusable.[883] A prohibition of use with regard to a deficiency in the degree of suspicion only comes into question if the investigating judge has significantly exceeded the discretionary powers of their position.[884] In practice, this should only play a limited role. As a rule, errors of reason do not lead to the inadmissibility of the findings obtained through the online search.[885] However, a violation of the principle of subsidiarity can lead to inadmissibility.[886] Furthermore, there is a ban on the use of evidence for all findings relating to the core area of private life.[887]

If there are no statutory prohibitions on the collection and use of data, the basic prerequisite for non-usability is that the person concerned objects in good time.[888] Article 6 (1), sentence 1 ECHR must always be taken into account in the assessment.[889]

In principle, messages received on the computer during the period of surveillance (emails, chats, etc.) are usable.[890] However, findings that are only indirectly obtained in the context of the online search are often unusable in practice. Consider, for example, a microphone that collects audio information. Although access to this information is available during the online search, it is not necessarily stored on the device. Even if the requirements of §§ 100c and d DE-StPO

880 Graf, 2018: § 100b DE-StPO point 44.
881 Graf, 2018: § 100b DE-StPO point 45.
882 Graf, 2018: § 100b DE-StPO point 46.
883 Graf, 2018: § 100b DE-StPO point 47.
884 Graf, 2018: § 100b DE-StPO point 48.
885 Graf, 2018: § 100b DE-StPO point 49.
886 Graf, 2018: § 100b DE-StPO point 50.
887 BVerfGE StV 2012, 256.
888 Graf, 2018; § 100b DE-StPO point 52; BVerfGE NJW 2012, 907, 911.
889 Graf, 2018; § 100b DE-StPO point 53.
890 Graf, 2018: § 100b DE-StPO point 54.

were met, in practice, there would be an obstacle to its use in the fact that a measure under § 100c DE-StPO was not ordered to obtain it.[891]

With regard to incidental findings, it should be noted that these may only be used for the clarification of further catalogue offences within the scope of § 477 (2) DE-StPO.[892] However, this restriction does not apply to findings in the same criminal proceedings.[893]

5.1.4.3.6 Constitutional aspects

Among other things, digital surveillance encroach on the scope of protection of the integrity and confidentiality of information technology systems.[894] These are considered part of the right to informational self-determination stated in Art. 2 (1) GG in conjunction with Art. 1 (1) GG.[895] Consequently, a balance must be struck between the aforementioned constitutionally guaranteed fundamental rights and the necessity of digital surveillance for criminal prosecution purposes.

The so-called IT fundamental right is part of the general right of personality and protects against encroachments which are not prohibited on the basis of Art. 10 GG or Art. 13 GG. In particular, confidentiality of the processed or stored data is to be guaranteed.[896] This means that the concept of an information technology system must first be defined in terms of the IT fundamental right. This presupposes a certain complexity of the system. In particular, it must be possible in the context of the online search to gain insight into essential parts of the life of the data subject. Furthermore, it is assumed that the person concerned uses the information technology system as their own and that confidential data will therefore be found on it.[897]

From a constitutional point of view, stricter requirements should be placed on digital surveillance intended for repressive purposes than on those intended to protect the public.[898] In principle, it can be stated that the tapping and recording of telephone conversations as well as the surveillance of other forms of communication constitute a serious encroachment on people's fundamental rights – namely Arts 1, I., 2, I., 10 and 13 GG. The privacy of the individual is

891 Graf, 2018: § 100b, point 55 DE-StPO.
892 Graf, 2018: § 100b, point 56 DE-StPO.
893 Graf, 2018: § 100b, point 57 DE-StPO.
894 Schenke, 2019: § 49 BKA Law point 4.
895 Graf, 2018: § 100b DE-StPO point 1.
896 Gercke, 2019: § 100b DE-StPO point 2.
897 Gercke, 2019: § 100b DE-StPO point 3.
898 Eschelbach, 2020: § 100b DE-StPO point 6.

significantly affected. At the same time, it is obvious that communicating via modern media – especially the Internet – is an ideal means of preparing to carry out terrorism offences, for example. Also, surveillance of telecommunications often yields excellent investigative results. It would therefore hardly be justifiable to completely dispense with the surveillance of telecommunications.[899]

In this context, it is worth recalling Art. 1 (1) GG, which describes the dignity of man as inviolable and therefore worthy of protection.[900] This is ultimately the key norm of the German Basic Law.[901] Thus, the question arises as to whether an online search is compatible with Art. 1 (1) GG. In particular, the general right of personality pursuant to Art. 2, § 1 in conjunction with Art. 1 (1) GG includes the fundamental right to guarantee the confidentiality and integrity of information technology systems.[902]

According to Art. 10 (1) GG, the secrecy of telecommunications is inviolable. Pursuant to Art. 10 (2) GG, restrictions of the secrecy of telecommunications require a special legal basis.[903] If

> the restriction serves to protect the free democratic basic order or the existence or security of the Federation or of a country, the law may stipulate that it shall not be communicated to the person concerned and that review by organs and auxiliary organs appointed by the representation of the people shall take the place of legal recourse.[904]

This is mainly relevant in the area of combating terrorism financing since terrorism is undoubtedly a threat to the free democratic basic order. However, Art. 10 (1) GG is only relevant insofar as it concerns state measures through which ongoing communications are monitored.[905]

In extreme cases, one could even describe a serious threat to the existence or security of the German Federation such as the IS, which regards itself not as an association but as a 'state' and has repeatedly announced attacks on Germany. It is true that Art. 10 GG primarily concerns the secrecy of telecommunications and is therefore not yet sufficient as a basis for digital surveillance; however, Art. 10 GG also represents a first step in what will eventually become more far-reaching measures.

---

899 Kühne, 2015: § 520.
900 Art. 1 (1) GG.
901 Hillgruber, 2016: Art. 1 GG point 1 f.
902 1 BvR 370/07 point 166.
903 Baldus, 2016: Art. 10 GG point 7 f.
904 Art. 10 (2) GG.
905 1 BvR 370/07 point 184.

Perhaps more revealing is Art. 13 (1) GG, in which the inviolability of the home is declared. In addition, Art. 13 (2) GG states that searches may only be ordered by a judge or, in case of imminent danger, by other organs provided for by law. However, Art. 13 (3–5) GG is instructive for digital surveillance, and Art. 13, § 3 GG in particular regulates the prosecution of particularly serious crimes by stating that technical aids for the acoustic surveillance of homes in which a suspect is presumed to be can be used provided that any clarification of the facts would otherwise be disproportionately difficult or even impossible to achieve without them. In addition, Art. 13, paras 4–5 GG regulate the conditions for such a measure. It is obvious that technical surveillance may only take place within strictly defined limits.[906]

In particular, according to Art. 13 (4) GG, the court that orders a measure within the meaning of Art. 13 (3) GG must be composed of three judges. Only in cases of imminent danger can the order be made in accordance with Art. 13 (5) GG. In addition, Art. 14 GG may not be disregarded, which applies to property guarantees. In the context of an online search, the search would undoubtedly interfere with the property of the person concerned, especially in the context of the analysis undertaken by the spy software installed on the suspect's device.

On 27 February 2008, the Federal Constitutional Court ruled that digital surveillance is only permissible if there are actual indications of a concrete threat to legal interests of paramount importance. In this context, threats to life, limb, freedom of the person and public goods that affect the existence of the state and the existence of the people therein are considered to be of paramount importance.[907]

However, the ruling of the Federal Constitutional Court of 27 February 2008 also emphasized that digital surveillance is out of the question if there is no existential threat. At the same time, it was emphasized that the state must restrict itself to other investigative powers.[908] In this context, the fundamental right to guarantee the confidentiality and integrity of information technology systems was specifically emphasized.[909]

Such interference is particularly severe in the context of long-term surveillance.[910] Consequently, such serious encroachments on people's fundamental

906 Art. 13 (3) GG; Fink, 2016: Art. 13 GG point 6 f.

907 1 BvR 370/07 point 247.

908 1 BvR 370/07 point 248.

909 Polenz, 2018: point 29 f.

910 Gercke, 2019: point 100b DE-StPO point 5.

rights are only justified if there are indications of a concrete danger to an overwhelmingly important legal interest.[911] In this context, whether the very far-reaching catalogue of offences in § 100b DE-StPO can be justified under constitutional law can be questioned.[912] As stipulated by the Federal Constitutional Court, only offences with a maximum sentence of more than five years are covered by the catalogue of offences.[913]

5.1.4.4 Conclusion

The ability of digital surveillance to avert danger is based on § 49 BKA Law. With regard to the material scope of application of § 100b DE-StPO, it can be stated that law enforcement authorities are permitted to access the information technology systems of the persons concerned and to collect data from them. This is undoubtedly also permissible over a longer period of time. On the other hand, it should not be permissible to activate video or audio functions on the devices of the persons concerned. On the one hand, § 100b DE-StPO is unlikely to be regarded as a sufficient legal basis for this. On the other hand, this raises a question as to whether activating the video or audio function might not constitute an inadmissible spying attack on the home of the person concerned and thus a violation of Art. 13 (3) of the German Constitution.[914]

Section 100b DE-StPO could serve as a model for legislative measures in other countries. In particular, Switzerland, Austria and Liechtenstein could draw inspiration from German legislation and benefit from the experience gained in Germany.

5.2 Undercover investigation

Undercover investigations can make a significant contribution to the fight against terrorism financing.[915] They allow investigators to gain knowledge that would most likely have remained hidden by other means, especially when the police cannot hope to receive intelligence from citizens and thus have to assume fictitious identities themselves in order to penetrate a certain criminal milieu.[916] Both police officers and other investigators are used as operators in this process.[917]

---

911 Gercke, 2019: § 100b DE-StPO point 6.
912 Gercke, 2019: § 100b DE-StPO point 7.
913 BVerfGE 109, 348.
914 Gercke, 2019: § 100b DE-StPO point 11.
915 Webster et al., 2006: p. 225 f.
916 Miller, 1987: p. 34.
917 Marx, 1987: p. 172.

Undercover investigation already represents an essential element of investigative work. Since the 1970s, legal foundations for undercover investigations have been created worldwide.[918]

However, the reach of undercover investigators is often limited. Unlike 'real' criminals, undercover investigators must abide by a wide set of rules. This can be problematic in that it makes undercover agents relatively easy to expose, especially if they are forbidden from committing any crimes while undercover. In some countries, undercover investigators are permitted to make test purchases in order to prove their economic capacity. However, other offences are not allowed. A clever perpetrator can therefore unmask an undercover agent by inciting them to commit a crime – if the undercover officer should look for excuses or outright refuse to commit the crime, the offender might become suspicious.

Consequently, it could be argued that in certain circumstances, an extension of the powers of undercover agents could be useful. For example, it would be a pity if promising investigations against terrorist financiers were scuppered because the perpetrators managed to unmask the undercover agent. Especially in the context of combating terrorism financing, it is important to build trust and survive 'tests of allegiance. Can it ever be permissible to break the law in order to fight crime?[919] While it is possible for undercover agents to commit crimes in the USA, this is prohibited in the European countries examined here, apart from exceptional cases regulated by law.[920]

In Europe, it is difficult to recruit undercover investigators and to infiltrate certain structures, which makes it all the more important not to jeopardize the work of these investigators and to optimize their cover, particularly because of the high personal risks the assume.

At the same time, does it make sense to grant undercover investigators the privilege of committing crimes in the name of the state? After all, this would open up avenues for considerable potential abuse.[921] Undercover investigators could commit criminal offences and claim that these acts were absolutely necessary in order not to jeopardize their cover. In the worst-case scenario, undercover investigators could use their work with the police as a cover for engaging in criminal activity. This ultimately creates significant risks.[922] Thus, strict rules are

918 Marx, 1980: p. 399 f.; Marx, 1982: p. 165 f.
919 Spalek & O'Rawe, 2014: p. 150 f.; Joh, 2009: p. 155 f.
920 Ross, 2007: p. 493; Ross, 2008: p. 239 f.; Roberts, 2000: p. 263 f.
921 Wachtel, 1992: p. 137 f.
922 Brodeur, 1992: p. 105 f.

necessary.[923] Finally, it can be assumed that undercover officers could also be corrupt.[924] Thus, it is often discussed whether undercover investigations are merely creative police work or actually pose a threat to fundamental rights.[925]

In this section, the legal situation regarding Undercover investigations is first considered. In contrast to the comments made on digital surveillance, however, a completely new regulation will not be proposed. Rather, this section explores a question regarding the selective expansion of the powers of undercover investigators. Thus, only the provisions that are essential for understanding this will be discussed in detail. However, in order to create a basis for the discussion, the legal foundations for undercover investigations in Switzerland will be considered as a whole. Subsequently, concrete proposals for legislative measures will be elaborated and explained.

5.2.1 Switzerland

5.2.1.1 Switzerland – initial situation

In Switzerland, a distinction is made between undercover investigations and undercover searches. Undercover investigators establish contact with persons in the criminal milieu through deceptive conduct and build up a relationship of trust in order to solve particularly serious offences.[926] The requirements for an undercover investigation are set out in Art. 285a ff. CH-StPO.

Undercover investigation is ultimately a coercive measure that requires a legal basis. It represents a considerable encroachment on the privacy and personal freedom of the person concerned. Undercover investigations are governed by Arts 285a–298 CH-StPO and are very rare in Switzerland, although precise statistics are not available.[927] In addition, the limits set by Art. 140 CH-StPO must always be observed, according to which deception must always be regarded as an inadmissible method of gathering evidence.[928]

Undercover investigations can be distinguished from undercover searches, which have been regulated since 1 May 2013 by Art. 298a–d CH-StPO.[929] In the context of undercover investigations, police officers carry out shorter

923 Hamilton & Smykla, 1994: p. 135 f.; Dix, 1974: p. 203 f.

924 Girodo, 1991: p. 361.

925 Marx, 1977: p. 34 f.; Hirsch, 2000: p. 1282; Lundy, 1968: p. 634.

926 Hansjakob, 2014: p. 1682.

927 Knodel, 2014: Art. 285a CH-StPO point 1; Hansjakob, 2014: p. 1683.

928 Leuzinger, 2014: p. 168.

929 Knodel, 2014: Art. 285a CH-StPO point 3.

missions without revealing their true identities or intentions. There are various criteria for distinguishing undercover investigations from undercover manhunts.[930]

What differentiates the undercover investigation from the undercover manhunt is in part the need for a cover story.[931] Having a solid cover story helps the undercover investigator to deceive the target persons about their true intentions.[932] This false identity can be secured with documents and should make it easier to contact the target person. Among other things, the establishment of a relationship of trust is in the foreground.[933] Thus, supporting the cover story through the use of documents also serves to set undercover investigations apart.[934]

The establishment of this relationship of trust is usually time-consuming and in many cases entails a lengthy undercover investigation.[935] This can also serve as a delimitation criterion. Undercover searches are usually shorter assignments, whereas undercover investigations often require a long-term approach.

The distinction is also based on the person holding the role of the undercover investigator. While only members of the police are eligible to be undercover manhunters, persons temporarily employed for police tasks can also act as undercover investigators.[936]

Undercover investigation is defined in Art. 285a CH-StPO as follows:

> Undercover investigation occurs when members of the police or persons temporarily employed for police duties, using a false identity (legend) secured by documents, establish contacts with persons through deceptive conduct with the aim of establishing a relationship of trust and penetrating a criminal environment in order to solve particularly serious crimes.[937]

In addition to the fact that both police officers and persons who are only temporarily assigned police tasks can be used as undercover investigators, the definition of Undercover investigation emphasizes that the undercover investigator is equipped with a cover story.

930 Hansjakob, 2014: p. 1680.
931 Knodel, 2014: Art. 285a CH-StPO point 5.
932 Hansjakob, 2014: p. 1682.
933 Riklin, 2014: p. 486.
934 Hansjakob, 2014: p. 1682.
935 Knodel, 2014: Art. 285a CH-StPO point 11.
936 Knodel, 2014: Art. 285a CH-StPO point 6.
937 Art. 285a CH-StPO.

However, the establishment of a relationship of trust in particular presents a challenge for undercover investigators. In this context, it is often necessary to talk about criminal offences. The undercover investigator may even have to participate in crimes to keep up appearances.[938] The undercover investigation is thus almost inevitably associated with a certain intensity of deception.

In contrast to the target persons of undercover manhunts (anyone who carries out criminal transactions), the target persons of undercover investigations tend to share their delinquent behaviour only with those who have overcome certain access barriers.[939] This is plausibly understandable insofar as an undercover search would be sufficient in the case of easily accessible persons and thus an undercover investigation could be dispensed with.

Skilled targets test all new people in their environment by asking them to commit crimes. Since undercover officers are not allowed to commit crimes, it is possible for perpetrators to test the trustworthiness of their new contacts. For example, skilled offenders might ask new people to commit minor crimes for them. Those who consistently refuse in such cases are not necessarily undercover agents. Nevertheless, offenders might view this as an indication of a lack of trustworthiness. Before this aspect can be discussed in more detail, the legal basis for undercover investigations must first be outlined.

The requirements for an undercover investigation are based on the wording of Art. 269 CH-StPO. In particular, according to Art. 269, paras 1–3 CH-StPO, suspicion of a serious criminal offence is required to initiate an undercover investigation. The offences in question are listed exhaustively in the catalogue of offences.[940] Financing terrorism within the meaning of Art. 260^{quinquies} CH-StGB is a catalogue offence.

Launching an undercover investigation requires a catalogue offence, which imposes relatively high requirements that must be met.[941] However, according to Art. 286 CH-StPO only simple suspicion is required. This means that although the target person must be a suspect, the threshold to be met is lower than it is under Art. 269 CH-StPO. In addition, an undercover investigation is also conceivable without suspecting a specific person.[942]

938 Hansjakob, 2014: p. 1683.
939 Knodel, 2014: Art. 285a CH-StPO point 12.
940 Riklin, 2014: p. 487.
941 Hansjakob, 2014: p. 1687.
942 Riklin, 2014: p. 488.

Only requiring sufficient suspicion and not urgent suspicion is based on the fact that the undercover investigation is to be regarded as a coercive measure under criminal procedure law. Pursuant to Art. 197 (1) lit. b CH-StPO, such a measure always requires sufficient suspicion. Otherwise, the order would be disproportionate and therefore inadmissible.[943] However, according to Art. 286 CH-StPO no urgent suspicion is required.[944]

This is particularly noteworthy because undercover investigations represent a more serious interference than the interception of postal and telecommunications traffic, for which an urgent suspicion of an offence is required. However, this is at least partially compensated for by the fact that the catalogue of offences for Undercover investigations is less comprehensive than that for the interception of postal and telecommunications traffic.[945]

Also, for practical reasons, it must not be forgotten that the undercover investigator may come into contact with persons against whom there is no suspicion.[946] This is almost unavoidable in the context of creating the relationship of trust. Thus, the privacy and secrecy of these persons is also affected.

Furthermore, due to the seriousness of the intervention of the undercover investigation, establishing sufficient suspicion of a crime must not be taken lightly. In this context, it must be noted in particular that undercover investigations may not be used exclusively for prevention. However, this argument must also be put into the correct perspective – undercover investigations ultimately always have preventive effects. After all, it is hardly conceivable that an undercover investigator would allow an offender to commit a serious crime simply to justify arresting them afterward.[947]

This is particularly relevant to the fight against terrorism financing. The Undercover investigation ultimately fulfils a dual function here. On the one hand, it helps to gather evidence against terrorist financiers; on the other hand, its presence in the criminal environment can ensure that investigating authorities learn at an early stage about attacks to be financed and can prevent them from happening. This is ultimately a positive side effect of undercover work.

Nonetheless, preventive contact with the target person must be avoided from the point of view of the rule of law because Art. 1 CH-StPO covers the

943 Knodel, 2014: Art. 486 point 14.
944 Hansjakob, 2014: p. 1687.
945 Knodel, 2014: Art. 286 point 15.
946 Hansjakob, 2014: p. 1688.
947 Knodel, 2014: Art. 286 point 16.

prosecution and assessment of criminal offences but does not justify the use of coercive measures to avert danger.[948] Therefore, cantonal police laws are applicable in these cases.[949]

According to Art. 286 (1) lit. b CH-StPO, a certain degree of seriousness of the offence is also required. This means that it must be a catalogue offence that can be judged to be serious in that specific case. This is particularly true with regard to proportionality. Thus, it is not sufficient that only a catalogue offence exists. Ultimately, the violation of the legal interest and the intensity of the offender's intent are decisive.[950]

Art. 286 (1) lit. c CH-StPO also addresses proportionality and subsidiarity. This means that the previous investigations must have been fruitless or futile or disproportionately difficult.[951] Otherwise, the ordering of an undercover investigation is not permissible.[952] This means that before initiating an undercover investigation, whether the same goal could have been achieved using less extreme means must be considered.[953] This is the case, for example, if surveillance measures do not lead to the desired result because the target persons are behaving very cautiously.[954]

In the case of terrorism financing, proportionality should generally be considered. After all, the aim is to prevent the financing of terrorist activities that pose a threat to life and limb. In most cases, the protection of numerous lives is likely to outweigh the accused's right to privacy and confidentiality.

Subsidiarity should also not be a problem in most cases of combating terrorism financing. The empirical study showed how skilfully perpetrators are able to proceed. It is hardly realistic to assume that these individuals will allow themselves to be caught by something as banal as telephone monitoring.

Article 287 CH-StPO sets out the requirements for the persons deployed in undercover investigations. In particular, the deployment of persons who do not have police training requires the approval of the compulsory measures court in accordance with Art. 289, (4) lit. c CH-StPO[955] In any case, therefore, an employment relationship is required.[956] Alternatively, one could consider simple

948 Hansjakob, 2014: p. 1687.
949 Knodel, 2014: Art. 286 point 17a.
950 Knodel, 2014; Art. 286 point 19 f.
951 Hansjakob, 2014: p. 1688.
952 Riklin, 2014: p. 488.
953 Knodel, 2014; Art. 286 point 22.
954 Hansjakob, 2014: p. 1688.
955 Riklin, 2014: p. 488.
956 Knodel, 2014: Art. 287 point 1.

assignments within the scope of an undercover investigation.[957] However, due to the fact that the employment can be terminated at any point in time, there would be an increased possibility of the person changing sides.

This employment relationship offers an advantage in that the undercover investigator is bound to the police on the one hand and receives a fixed salary on the other.[958] This means that undercover investigators are economically independent and therefore more difficult for criminals to influence. Therefore, only members of a police force can be considered as leaders of an undercover investigation.[959]

According to Art. 288 CH-StPO, undercover investigators are provided with a cover story. In particular, Art. 288, paras 1 and 2 CH-StPO set out the requirements for the falsification of documents and assurances to support this cover story.[960] In many cases, documentation is created first.[961]

It should also be stressed that in order for the undercover investigator to be granted anonymity, there must be concrete indications of a threat to mental or physical integrity, since it must be ensured that anonymity is necessary and does not result from a refusal on the part of the police corps to review the investigative work.[962]

The legislature has refrained from listing offences which are admissible so that no tests of allegiance outside this catalogue of offences can be demanded of undercover investigators. Therefore, criminal proceedings must be conducted if an undercover agent commits a criminal offence.[963]

Particularly relevant for the purposes of this paper, however, is Art. 288, § 3 CH-StPO, which regulates the question of the identity under which undercover investigators must answer for any criminal offences.[964] The undercover investigator is in principle prohibited from committing or participating in criminal offences – even minor ones – although the undercover investigator is supposed to behave in a manner that conforms to the criminal milieu and act the part.[965]

---

957 Hansjakob, 2014: p. 1691.
958 Knodel, 2014: Art. 288 point 2.
959 Hansjakob, 2014: p. 1692.
960 Art. 288 CH-StPO.
961 Hansjakob, 2014: p. 1695.
962 Knodel, 2014: Art. 288 point 5 f.
963 Hansjakob, 2014: p. 1696.
964 Riklin, 2014: p. 489.
965 Hansjakob, 2014: p. 1696.

If the limits of Art. 293 CH-StPO are exceeded, the compulsory measures court decides under which identity the undercover investigator must answer. In addition, Art. 317bis CH-StGB states that the undercover investigator is not liable under Arts 251, 252, 255 and 317 CH-StGB.[966]

This question, which at first glance seems banal, has far-reaching consequences. One thinks here, for example, of the setting of the daily rate for monetary fines or the entry of the offence into the investigator's criminal record.[967] However, the risks associated with disclosing the identity of the undercover investigator in criminal proceedings should not be underestimated – doing so ultimately risks putting an undercover investigator who has acted criminally in order to uncover a criminal offence in serious danger.

Therefore, in practice, it is not possible for undercover investigators to act criminally without having to fear serious consequences. However, it must be taken into account that these proceedings can usually be concluded with a penalty order. Therefore, the principle of publicity does not in fact play a major role.[968]

The authorization procedure for Undercover investigations is governed by Art. 289 CH-StPO and is comparable to that for the interception of postal and telecommunications traffic, which is governed by Art. 274 CH-StPO. The Undercover investigation is carried out by the public prosecutor's office and authorized by the compulsory measures court. The authorization must be applied for within twenty-four hours.

However, the twenty-four-hour time limit is merely a regulatory requirement.[969] The compulsory measures court decides within five days. The appellate authority serves as a court of appeal.[970] The approval is of central importance for the usability of the evidence. In the event of non-approval, the evidence cannot be used.[971]

The order shall address, among other things, the duration of the deployment, the investigators to be deployed and the assurance of anonymity.[972] Furthermore, in addition to a summary of the facts of the case, the statement of reasons must also contain an explanation of the reasonable suspicion leading to the order as

966 Knodel, 2014; Art. 288, § 24 f.; Art. 317bis CH-StGB.
967 Knodel, 2014; Art. 288 point 26 f.
968 Hansjakob, 2014: p. 1697.
969 Knodel, 2014; Art. 289 CH-StPO point 3.
970 Riklin, 2014: p. 490 f.
971 BGE 134 IV 266, E. 5.3.
972 Hansjakob, 2014: p. 1700.

well as the purpose of the measures and the need for anonymity.[973] The order shall be made in writing.[974]

From a practical point of view, Art. 290 CH-StPO is of great importance. This regulates the instructions given to the undercover investigator and the lead person on the case by the public prosecutor's office prior to the assignment. These instructions, which make sense from the point of view of the rule of law, relate to the legal situations of undercover investigations.[975] Direct contact between these persons is required. The instructions for the situation at hand, on the other hand, are given by the person in charge and vary from case to case.[976] These must be delivered before the start of the operation.[977] In any case, the instruction should be issued in writing by the public prosecutor's office and signed by the lead person and the undercover investigator.[978]

The role of the lead person is regulated by Art. 291 CH-StPO. Their position is important because they issue instructions to the undercover investigator throughout the operation and they are their only contact person. They instruct the undercover investigator, direct and supervise the operation, carry out risk analyses and documents any findings in the files.[979]

The role of the lead person is also important because no direct contact with the public prosecutor's office is provided for – all instructions are channelled through the lead person for the duration of the assignment.[980] Only the lead person is authorized to issue instructions to the undercover investigator. Consequently, the lead person must be competent and familiar with the undercover investigator's field of operation.[981]

Consequently, leaders are expected to have certain skills and attributes. Leaders should have internationally standardized training to facilitate cross-border operations.[982] Therefore, leaders are usually police officers who have been specially trained for this task.[983] They must have both the necessary technical

973 Riklin, 2014: p. 491.
974 Knodel, 2014; Art. 289 CH-StPO point 4.
975 Hansjakob, 2008: p. 113.
976 Riklin, 2014: p. 492.
977 Hansjakob, 2014: p. 1708.
978 Knodel, 2014; Art. 290 CH-StPO point 3.
979 Hansjakob, 2014: p. 1712.
980 Riklin, 2014: p. 492.
981 Knodel, 2014; Art. 291 CH-StPO point 1.
982 Hansjakob, 2014: p. 1711.
983 Knodel, 2014; Art. 291 CH-StPO point 2.

competence and a strong sense of integrity. They must also be able to assess risks and objectives.[984]

In addition, it makes sense to appoint only one leader at a time in order to avoid communication problems. Furthermore, competencies must be clearly delineated.[985] Otherwise, misunderstandings could arise with potentially serious consequences. For example, providing information on competences and powers in individual cases is the responsibility of the leader.[986]

The tasks of the lead investigator are extremely varied. On the one hand, the leader provides the undercover investigator with instructions about the specific assignment and their powers; on the other hand, the leader also supervises the undercover investigator during the assignment. Furthermore, the leader documents the findings of the undercover investigator and forwards them to the public prosecutor's office.[987]

Should the powers of undercover investigators be extended, the communication channel of the persons involved is of great importance. In this context, Art. 292 CH-StPO, which provides that undercover investigators report continuously and completely to the leading person, must also be observed.[988] Undercover investigators must perform their duties loyally. They are bound by instructions vis-à-vis the person in charge.[989]

The focus of this paper is on Art. 293 CH-StPO, which regulates the extent of the interference permissible through undercover investigations. Since this article is of fundamental importance for the following explanations, it is presented verbatim:

1. Undercover investigators must not arouse a general readiness to commit a crime and must not direct the readiness to commit a crime towards more serious criminal offences. They must confine themselves to concretising an existing intention to commit a crime.
2. Their activity may only be of secondary importance for the decision to commit a specific criminal offence.
3. If necessary, they may make trial purchases to initiate the main business or document their economic performance.

984 Hansjakob, 2014: p. 1712.
985 Knodel, 2014; Art. 291 CH-StPO point 3.
986 Hansjakob, 2014: p. 1712.
987 Knodel, 2014; Art. 291 CH-StPO point 6 f.; Hansjakob, 2014: p. 1713.
988 Art. 292 CH-StPO.
989 Knodel, 2014; Art. 292 CH-StPO point 1 f.

4. If an undercover investigator exceeds the level of permissible influence, this shall be duly taken into account in the assessment of the penalty for the person influenced, or a penalty shall be waived.[990]

In particular, undercover officers are to report their observations. However, they are prohibited from committing offences themselves or inciting offences. There is therefore a prohibition on provocation.[991] Acts that can be considered test purchases or which serve to document the undercover investigator's economic performance are permitted under Art. 293, paras 3 and 4 CH-StPO.[992] The prohibition of other criminal acts is of fundamental importance to ensure compliance with the principles of the rule of law.[993]

It makes sense that undercover investigators are not allowed to demonstrate a general readiness to commit a crime or to direct this readiness to the execution of serious crimes.[994] Undercover investigators must limit themselves to the concretization of already existing intentions to commit a crime. In particular, an undercover investigator may not act as an agent provocateur and provoke the offender to commit a crime. This would ultimately be disproportionate and constitute entrapment.[995] Only the concretization of an intention to commit a crime is permitted.[996]

However, undercover officers must be allowed to behave in a manner appropriate to the role they are playing.[997] Several issues arise from the fact that undercover agents are not allowed to commit crimes. On the one hand, skilled perpetrators may be able to identify undercover investigators by the conduct prescribed for them by law. On the other hand, there is also the question of the usability of the evidence obtained thanks to the crime and the criminal liability of the undercover investigator. In this context, any grounds for justification must always be taken into account.[998]

A daring justification would be a justifiable state of emergency in the sense of Art. 17 CH-StGB. This reads as follows:

990 Art. 293 CH-StPO.
991 Knodel, 2014; Art. 293 CH-StPO point 1.
992 Riklin, 2014: p. 493.
993 Knodel, 2014; Art. 293 CH-StPO point 1.
994 Hansjakob, 2014: p. 1720.
995 Knodel, 2014; Art. 293, § 2 f. CH-StPO.
996 Hansjakob, 2014: p. 1722.
997 Knodel, 2014: Art. 293 CH-StPO point 5.
998 Riklin, 2014: p. 494; Knodel, 2014; Art. 293 CH-StPO point 15.

> A person who commits an act punishable by law in order to save his own or another person's legal interest from an imminent danger which cannot be averted in any other way acts lawfully if he thereby safeguards higher interests.[999]

In principle, therefore, committing minor offences in order to prevent terrorist attacks could be considered permissible. In practice, however, the question of immediacy is likely to arise. In many cases, engaging in criminal offences is necessary in order for an undercover investigator to penetrate a criminal milieu. As soon as the undercover agent is established in the milieu, they may succeed in preventing criminal acts. However, this is problematic for several reasons.

On the one hand, at the time of committing the minor offence, in many cases there is only an abstract threat of danger. This means that the undercover investigator cannot even know at the time of committing minor offences which offences they are aiming to specifically prevent.

On the other hand, preventive investigation (i.e. the use of undercover agents to prevent criminal offences) is inadmissible. Such discoveries can at most be regarded as a by-product of other investigations. Justifying criminal offences on the basis of Art. 17 CH-StGB is therefore unlikely to achieve much.

Article 294 CH-StPO offers greater legal certainty. For undercover investigations, in the context of the prosecution of offences against the Narcotics Act, there is already an exemption from criminal liability in Art. 294 CH-stop. Articles 19–22 of the Narcotics Act of 3 October 1951 do not apply to undercover investigators in these cases, provided that the undercover investigation has been authorized.[1000]

The prerequisite for this, in addition to approval to undertake an undercover investigation for the prosecution of narcotics crime, is above all that the undercover investigator complies with the instructions of the public prosecutor's office and the lead person. In the case of offences committed contrary to instruction, the justification of Art. 294 CH-StPO ceases to apply. In addition, undercover investigators can only invoke Art. 294 CH-StPO if they are acting within the scope of their assignment.[1001]

Finally, Art. 294 is not intended to give undercover investigators impunity to conduct narcotics transactions on their own. If undercover investigators were allowed to trade in narcotics on a blanket basis, lucrative sideline activities could

---

999 Art. 17 CH-StGB.

1000 Riklin, 2014: p. 494.

1001 Knodel, 2014; Art. 294, § 3 f.; Hansjakob, 2014: p. 1726.

develop. However, the regulation concerning narcotics offences is of little help in combating terrorism financing.

A similar provision can also be found in Art. 295 CH-StPO. Specifically, it provides that the Swiss National Bank may make large sums of show money available to undercover investigators at the request of the public prosecutor's office.[1002] In the event of loss, the canton or the confederation is liable.[1003] Consequently, it is important that appropriate protective measures are taken to prevent the loss of the money.

However, Art. 295 CH-CPC is unlikely to have been applied to date in the area of combating terrorism financing. It is reasonable to assume that Art. 295 CH-CPC is currently primarily applied in the area of narcotics offences and at most in connection with money laundering. In certain circumstances, however, this article would also be helpful in the area of combating terrorism financing. However, particular caution must be exercised in this regard. The loss of the money could ultimately contribute to the financing of terrorist attacks.

Articles 296–298 CH-StPO will only be dealt with in summary form here, as they are of limited relevance to the subsequent argumentation on the extension of the powers of undercover investigators. Art. 296 CH-StPO regulates the handling of incidental findings, and these may only be used if an undercover investigation could be ordered to investigate the discovered offence.[1004] Similar rules apply here as in Art. 278 CH-StPO.[1005]

Article 297 CH-StPO regulates the termination of the assignment. This must be done once the requirements of the assignment are no longer being met, authorization or the extension thereof has not been granted or the undercover investigator or their leader disregards instructions or fails to carry out their duties. In this case, too, the regulation on postal and telecommunications traffic, which can be found in Art. 275 CH-StPO, applies in practice.[1006]

According to Art. 298 CH-StPO, the accused person must be informed of the Undercover investigation when the proceedings are concluded at the latest. However, the compulsory measures court may authorize the postponement or

1002 Riklin, 2014: p. 495.
1003 Knodel, 2014; Art. 295 point 8 f.
1004 Art. 296 CH-StPO.
1005 Riklin, 2014: p. 495.
1006 Art. 297 CH-StPO; Riklin, 2014: p. 496.

omission of this notification.[1007] Here too, the procedure outlined in Art. 279 CH-StPO applies in practice.[1008]

For the purposes of demarcation, the undercover search will also be discussed. Undercover investigation is defined in Art. 298a CH-StPO:

1. undercover manhunts occur when members of the police attempt to solve crimes and misdemeanours within the framework of short operations in such a way that their true identity and function are not recognisable and, in particular, conclude fictitious transactions or feign the intention to conclude such transactions.
2. undercover investigators shall not be provided with a legend [cover story] within the meaning of Article 285a. Their true identity and function shall be disclosed in the case files and during interrogations.[1009]

While the author is in favour of extending undercover investigators' powers, he considers their existing powers sufficient. This is especially true with regard to the fact that an undercover investigation can be ordered if there is a need for more extensive powers. An extension of the powers of the undercover investigators is therefore not necessary. For this reason, we will refrain from going into more detail on the provisions on undercover investigations.

5.2.1.2 Switzerland – suggestions for legislative measures

5.2.1.2.1 Extended powers – a necessity?

For reasons of the rule of law, undercover investigators are not permitted to commit criminal offences. The only exceptions to this prohibition enshrined in Art. 293 CH-StPO are the cases regulated in Arts. 293–295 CH-StPO For example, test purchases are permitted. However, an undercover investigator deployed to combat terrorism financing would not be allowed to commit simple theft or fraud.

Now the question arises whether it is at all necessary for undercover investigators to commit offences other than those already provided for. Finally, one could argue that a skilled undercover investigator is able to behave in accordance with the law even in a criminal milieu. In addition, an enumeration of permissible offences could lead to criminals introducing so-called tests of allegiance outside the permissible exceptions, thus failing to solve the problem and merely shifting it elsewhere.

1007 Art. 298 CH-StPO.
1008 Riklin, 2014: p. 497.
1009 Art. 298a CH-StPO.

Several aspects have to be taken into account when answering these questions. On the one hand, one has to consider that the use of undercover agents can only be successful if perpetrators do not succeed in unmasking their new contacts. On the other hand, one must also consider that it is already difficult to recruit undercover agents.

Undercover investigations only make sense if it is not possible for the targets to expose the investigators. However, a clever perpetrator might become suspicious if someone claims to be willing to commit serious crimes (e.g. to finance terrorism) but shies away from committing minor ones.

It is true that the undercover investigator can argue that they are deliberately acting inconspicuously and are not willing to take any risks that could endanger their larger criminal endeavours. However, it is reasonable to assume that other offenders will be unimpressed by such an argument. Nonetheless, this argument is logical and believable in a narcotics context. After all, it makes sense to behave as inconspicuously as possible in order to avoid being targeted by investigators.

The empirical research revealed that it can be assumed that many terrorist financiers are both educated and intelligent. These perpetrators are likely to be aware that undercover agents are attempting to infiltrate organizations in order to combat terrorism financing. Thus, it can be assumed that intelligent and educated perpetrators will implement checks in order to expose undercover agents.

People who are interated in the criminal milieu but who shy away from committing crimes are rather unusual. This odd behaviour could attract the attention of the target persons. Although not every person in the criminal milieu who does not commit minor crimes is automatically suspected of being an undercover agent, such behaviour could be interpreted as an indication of this by some – especially intelligent and well-trained perpetrators.

An undercover investigator may find it necessary for investigative, tactical or self-protection reasons (in the context of a chastity test) to commit minor offences. Those who wish to avoid facing criminal proceedings for engaging in criminal conduct during the course of an assignment might prefer other areas of activity within or outside of the police corps and simply refrain from acting as an undercover investigator altogether.

Finally, from the point of view of the undercover investigator, it makes little sense to expose him or herself to these risks. This may explain why it is already difficult to recruit undercover investigators, especially since they do not receive exorbitantly high remuneration in exchange for the great risks they take. Moreover, even intrinsically motivated investigators might refrain from acting as undercover investigators because of the associated criminal law risks.

5.2.1.2.2 *The authorization procedure*

However, undercover investigators cannot be given a free pass to commit crimes. This would create the significant potential for abuse. Many undercover investigations, especially in the narcotics milieu, are likely to continue to progress without the investigators needing to commit crimes. In these cases, it would make little sense to allow undercover officers to act in an overtly criminal manner.

Prior authorization of criminal offences by leaders also appears impracticable. Undercover officers may be spontaneously asked to commit criminal offences by target persons, but waiting for leader authorization first would not be realistic in such situations.

The author is expressly against a catalogue of prohibited offences because criminals could get a hold of it and use it as a litmus test. Moreover, it would be difficult to ensure proportionality if certain offences were permitted across the board. Instead, it would make more sense to list the permissible offences in the written order of the undercover investigation. These orders are not seen by perpetrators and could give the undercover investigator legal certainty. In these orders, exceptions could be approved in advance that are tailored to the individual case and thus proportionate in each case.

5.2.1.2.3 *Adaptation of Art. 289 CH-StPO – a possible solution?*

Consequently, it would make sense to amend Art. 289 CH-StPO. This could now read as follows:

1. The use of an undercover investigator shall be subject to authorisation by the compulsory measures court.
2. The public prosecutor shall submit the following documents to the compulsory measures court within 24 hours of the order for the undercover investigation:
   a. the arrangement;
   b. the statement of reasons and the procedural documents essential for the approval.
3. The compulsory measures court shall take a decision with brief reasons within 5 days of the order to carry out the Undercover investigation. It may grant authorisation on a provisional basis or subject to conditions, or may request that the files be supplemented or that further investigations be carried out.

4. The authorisation explicitly states:
   a. whether it is permissible to make or alter deeds for the purpose of constructing or maintaining a legend;
   b. whether it is permissible to guarantee anonymity;
   c. whether it is permissible to use persons who have no police training;
   d. under which articles undercover investigators are not liable to prosecution, provided they act within the framework of the authorised undercover investigation and respect the interests of third parties and the principles of proportionality and subsidiarity [emphasis added].
5. The authorisation shall be granted for a maximum period of 12 months. It may be extended once or several times for 6 months at a time. If an extension is necessary, the public prosecutor's office shall submit a reasoned application for an extension before the expiry of the authorised period.
6. If permission is not granted or if permission has not been obtained, the public prosecutor's office shall terminate the operation immediately. All records shall be destroyed immediately. Information obtained through the undercover investigation may not be used.[1010]

The new Art. 289 (4) lit. d CH-StPO would prevent target persons from gaining prior knowledge of the offences permitted to the undercover investigator. This means that tests of allegiance based on a catalogue of offences could be prevented. This represents a significant advantage. In addition, however, the undercover investigator would also be given legal certainty.

In addition, the acts permitted under Art. 289 (4) lit. d CH-StPO could be tailored to the specific individual case. In many cases, no authorization of offences should be necessary. In other cases, offences tailored to the individual facts could be authorized. In this way, undercover investigators could succeed in establishing themselves inconspicuously in the perpetrators' environment without arousing suspicion because even if they had their suspicions, the perpetrators would not know which offences had been authorized.

For example, it might make sense to allow an undercover agent deployed to combat terrorism financing to commit minor thefts. In the course of the empirical study, it was noted that terrorist financiers have a variety of different sources of income. If there is a suspicion that a particular gang is stealing sneakers or cars to generate funds for terrorism financing, undercover officers could be targeted. However, allowing undercover agents to commit narcotics offences

1010 Art. 289 CH-StPO.

with impunity would be of little help in achieving this end. Ultimately, it would be necessary to authorize undercover agents to commit the offence of theft with impunity.

At this point, a question arises as to whether the state can be allowed to harm third parties. This would undoubtedly be the case in the case of theft. Finally, the state would violate the guarantee of property guaranteed in Art. 26 Federal Constitution (BV). According to Art. 26 (1) BV, property is guaranteed. However, according to Art. 26 (2) BV, property restrictions and expropriations are fully compensated for.

In this way, financial losses caused by undercover agents could be fully compensated for at the end of the assignment. This would preserve the core content of Art. 26 BV. Compensation before the end of the assignment would have to be rejected for reasons of investigative integrity.

It goes without saying that acts that harm the interests of third parties, such as homicide (within the meaning of Art. 111 ff. CH-StGB) or rape (within the meaning of Art. 190 CH-StGB) must be excluded. However, a catalogue of offences that can be authorized would in turn lead to tests of allegiance outside this catalogue of offences.

It therefore makes more sense to take a blanket approach to the interests of third parties. It may well be compatible with the interests of third parties that assets are stolen by an undercover agent, provided that compensation is paid in full.

In addition, the principles of proportionality and subsidiarity must be taken into account. It may well be proportionate to steal a car in order to enter terrorist financiers' circle of trust, especially if no other suitable means are available and the owner of the car is fully compensated.

On the other hand, it would undoubtedly be disproportionate to rape a woman as part of an initiation ceremony in order to gather evidence against drug traffickers – especially in view of the fact that rape cannot be compensated for. A gratification would be conceivable, but full compensation is ultimately only possible for property crimes.

Subsidiarity must not be neglected in this context. It is important to the author to emphasize that it goes without saying that undercover investigations involving authorized offences are not intended to cover the whole country. According to Art. 286 (1) lit. c CH-StPO, undercover investigations should only be used if the previous investigations have been fruitless or would have been futile or disproportionately difficult.[1011] Otherwise, the order for an undercover investigation is

1011 Hansjakob, 2014: p. 1688.

not permissible.[1012] Consequently, before the use of an undercover investigation, it must be first be determined whether the same goal could be achieved by milder means.[1013] In addition, it must be noted that the authorization of offences under Undercover investigation should also only take place if the previous Undercover investigations have remained fruitless or would be futile or would be made disproportionately difficult without them. In other words, one can speak of a double subsidiarity and proportionality check.

The political acceptance of such a draft for a new Art. 289 (4) lit. d CH-StPO is difficult to assess ex ante. However, it can be assumed that there will certainly be critical voices. In particular, opponents could point out that it would be the end of the rule of law if undercover investigators were allowed to commit crimes. However, this argument cannot be upheld.

Nevertheless, it must be borne in mind that the principles of proportionality and subsidiarity must be observed when authorizing criminal offences. This means that only crimes that contribute to the protection of higher interests can be authorized (e.g. theft could be authorized if it would help prevent a terrorist attack).

In this context, one should also think of the provisions of Art. 15 ff. CH-StGB, as well as the state of emergency. Ultimately, the population has accepted that police officers shoot perpetrators when there is an acute danger to the lives of third parties. Should it be possible to infiltrate terrorist networks and, in the best case, prevent attacks through minor thefts by undercover officers, a high level of acceptance among the population can be expected, especially if full compensation was offered for pecuniary losses.

However, it must be borne in mind that such a legislative procedure could be debated. Opponents of Art. 289 (4) lit. d CH-StPO, as presented here, could argue that it would legalize criminal acts by the state. Such a legislative project's chances of success are therefore uncertain.

5.2.2 Liechtenstein

In Liechtenstein, no differentiation is made between undercover investigations and undercover manhunts. Undercover investigations are permitted on the basis of § 104b FL-StPO. Pursuant to § 104b (1) FL-StPO, the national police are entitled to deploy police officers or other persons who do not disclose their official position or mandate in the course of an operation and thus conduct undercover

1012 Riklin, 2014: p. 488.
1013 Knodel, 2014; Art. 286 CH-StPO point 22.

investigations. The deployment is permissible if it can thereby further the investigation of a criminal offence.[1014] This is remarkable insofar as the threshold for undercover investigations is thus set low in Liechtenstein. According to the text of the law, no particular seriousness of the crime is required. However, this generosity is relativized in § 104b (2) FL-StPO.[1015]

Pursuant to § 104b (2) FL-StPO, investigations conducted systematically over a long period of time are only permissible if they serve to expose a criminal offence that was committed intentionally and would be punishable by more than one year's imprisonment or to prevent a criminal offence from being planned by a criminal or terrorist organization if the investigation would otherwise be significantly impeded. Thus, according to FL-StPO, preventive investigations to prevent a criminal offence are also permissible. The powers of the FL-CPC thus go beyond those of the CH-StPO. In addition, based on Art. 104b (2) FL-CPC, it is possible to forge documents and use them in legal transactions in order to plausibly secure the identity of the undercover investigator.[1016]

Under Art. 104b (3) FL-StPO, undercover investigations are ordered at the request of the public prosecutor's office. The undercover investigation is ordered by the investigating judge. Pursuant to Art. 104b (3) FL-StPO, the undercover investigation ends when its purpose has been achieved or, in all probability, can no longer be achieved.[1017]

In addition, § 104b (5) FL-StPO regulates the notification of parties or other participants in the proceedings.[1018] This takes place after the investigation has been completed. However, it may be postponed if the purpose of the investigation in this or in another proceeding would otherwise be compromised.[1019]

Furthermore, in Liechtenstein, sham transactions can be carried out on the basis of § 104c FL-StPO. Pursuant to § 104c (1) FL-StPO, the office of the public prosecutor may apply to the regional court for an order authorizing the national police to conduct sham transactions in order to either solve a crime or enable the seizure of assets or objects originating from a crime or threatened with forfeiture or confiscation, if this would otherwise be substantially impeded. In the cases listed, it is also permitted to facilitate fictitious transactions by third parties.[1020]

1014 § 104b (1) FL-StPO.
1015 Stotter, 2012: p. 378 f.
1016 § 104b (2) FL-StPO.
1017 § 104b (3) and (4) FL-StPO.
1018 Stotter, 2012: p. 378 f.
1019 § 104b (5) FL-StPO.
1020 Stotter, 2012: p. 382 f.; § 104c (1) FL-StPO.

Fictitious transactions are also admissible in Liechtenstein.[1021] Sham transactions are defined in § 104c (2) FL-StPO:

> 2) For the purposes of this Act, a sham transaction is the attempted or apparent commission of an offence in so far as it consists in the acquisition, taking possession of, importation, exportation or transit of any article or property which has been alienated, derived from or dedicated to the commission of a crime, or the possession of which is absolutely prohibited.[1022]

Pursuant to § 104c (3) FL-StPO, the execution of sham transactions must be requested by the public prosecutor's office and ordered by the investigating judge. The examining magistrate also instructs the national police to carry out the sham transaction.[1023]

However, the duty of disclosure must always be taken into account in the case of fictitious transactions.[1024] Pursuant to § 104c (4) FL-StPO, the execution of a fictitious transaction must be disclosed to the parties concerned as soon as the purpose of the investigation and other proceedings are no longer jeopardized by such disclosure.[1025]

There are more extensive possibilities for undercover investigators to commit criminal offences in Liechtenstein than in Switzerland. However, these possibilities are also too narrow for the purposes of combating terrorism financing. It is true that under the existing regulation, using a car that has already been stolen would be permissible. The theft of sneakers worth CHF 30, on the other hand, would be prohibited. Thus, an intelligent perpetrator should be able to read the Code of Criminal Procedure and put undercover agents to the test accordingly.

Therefore, an adaptation of criminal procedure law to expand the powers of undercover investigators would also make sense in Liechtenstein. In particular, the draft for the new Art. 289 (4), lit. d FL-StPO, which was developed in the context of the present study, could be used as a guideline. In this context, an adaptation of § 104c FL-StPO would be conceivable.

Specifically, § 104c (3) FL-StPO could be supplemented. The investigating judge could mention in the order which offences the undercover investigator may commit without fear of prosecution. This order would only be known to the investigating judge, the public prosecutor's office and the state police.

1021 Stotter, 2012: p. 382 f.
1022 § 104c (2) FL-StPO.
1023 § 104c (3) FL-StPO.
1024 Stotter, 2012: p. 382 f.
1025 § 104c (4) FL-StPO.

5.2.3 Austria

In Austria, undercover investigations are regulated in § 131 AT-StPO. According to § 131 (1) AT-StPO, undercover investigations are permissible if they serve the purpose of investigating a criminal offence. A distinction has to be made between simple undercover investigations, which can be carried out by the criminal investigation department on its own initiative, and systematic undercover investigations.[1026] Systematic undercover investigations carried out over a long period of time are only permissible if they serve to clarify a criminal offence that was committed intentionally and is punishable by a custodial sentence of more than one year, or to prevent a criminal offence planned by a criminal or terrorist organization, if the investigation would otherwise be significantly impeded.[1027] If a corresponding offence is merely expected, investigations may also be carried out without an order from the public prosecutor's office in accordance with § 54 (3) and (4a) of the Due Diligence Act (SPG).[1028]

The wording of § 131 (1) and (2) AT-StPO is reminiscent of § 104b (1) and (2) FL-StPO and also clearly goes beyond the competences of the Swiss Code of Criminal Procedure, since preventive measures to prevent criminal offences are possible (which in Switzerland are regulated in the police laws).

According to § 131 (2) AT-StPO, it is also possible to produce false documents for the purposes of an undercover investigation and to use them in legal transactions in order to secure the identity of the undercover investigator.[1029] However, this is only the case if the disguise is integral to the investigation.[1030] Here, too, there are similarities with Liechtenstein and Switzerland.

In any case, the undercover investigator is to be led and thus also controlled by the person leading the criminal investigation department.[1031] The undercover investigator is bound by the instructions of the person of trust.[1032] All findings, as well as the circumstances of the assignment, must also be recorded.[1033] Premises protected by the domiciliary right, in particular flats, are to be entered only with the express agreement of the owner, whereby the authorization may not

1026 Fabrizy, 2011: p. 326.
1027 § 131 (1) and (2) AT-StPO.
1028 Zerbes, 2011: § 131, § 7.
1029 § 131(2) AT-StPO.
1030 Zerbes, 2011: § 131(8) AT-StPO.
1031 Fabrizy, 2011: p. 325.
1032 Zerbes, 2011: § 131 AT-StPO point 12.
1033 § 131 (3) AT-StPO.

be brought about by deception.[1034] Thus, the undercover investigator is not permitted to gain entry to a dwelling by feigning false authority.[1035] Covert searches of houses are also prohibited.[1036]

However, fictitious transactions are also admissible in Austria for the purposes of solving crimes. Section 132 AT-StPO provides for sham transactions for the following purposes:

> The execution of a sham transaction is permissible if the investigation of a crime (§ 17 (1) StGB) or the seizure of objects or assets resulting from a crime or threatened with confiscation (§ 19a StGB), forfeiture (§ 20 StGB), extended forfeiture (§ 20b (1) StGB) or confiscation (§ 26 StGB) would otherwise be substantially impeded. Under these conditions, it is also permissible to contribute to the execution of a sham transaction by third parties (§12 third case, StGB).[1037]

This means that undercover investigators are certainly allowed to commit certain criminal offences without having to fear prosecution if the investigation would be significantly impeded by overt methods.[1038] However, this power is limited to the exceptions explicitly listed in the law, which result from § 132 AT-StPO outlined above.[1039] Other offences are prohibited, even if they would be necessary to maintain the facade.[1040]

According to § 133 AT-StPO, an undercover investigation pursuant to § 131 (1) AT-StPO, as well as a sham transaction within the scope of § 132 AT-StPO for the seizure of narcotic drugs or counterfeit money, may be carried out by the criminal investigation department on its own initiative (i.e. without prior authorization by the public prosecutor's office).[1041] Systematic undercover investigations carried out over a longer period of time within the meaning of § 131 (2) AT-StPO, on the other hand, are to be ordered by the public prosecutor's office.[1042]

In principle, it would be possible to take up the proposal for the new Art. 289 (4) lit. d CH-StPO developed in the course of this work and implement an analogous provision for the Austrian Code of Criminal Procedure. The same could be integrated into § 132 AT-StPO by means of a second paragraph. In this case,

---

1034 § 131 (4) AT-StPO.
1035 Fabrizy, 2011: p. 326.
1036 Zerbes, 2011: § 131 AT-StPO point 13.
1037 § 132 AT-StPO.
1038 Zerbes, 2011: § 132 AT-StPO point 1.
1039 Zerbes, 2011: § 131 AT-StPO point 11.
1040 Fabrizy, 2011: p. 325.
1041 Fabrizy, 2011: p. 326.
1042 § 133 AT-StPO.

however, it would have to be ensured that the approval of the actions was granted by a court and not simply by order of the public prosecutor's office.

5.2.4 Germany

Similar to digital surveillance, Germany also has strong legislation in the area of Undercover investigations, which offers valuable suggestions for other countries and thus requires more in-depth treatment.

5.2.4.1 Delimitations, definitions and conditions

Undercover investigation is regulated in Germany in § 110a DE-StPO and is subject to strict requirements due to the potential threat to upholding justice.[1043] The use of undercover investigators is only permissible in the case of criminal offences of considerable importance – necessity alone is not a sufficient justification under the rule of law.[1044] Rather, an explicit legal basis is required. In this context, sufficient indications (i.e. concrete, physically perceptible facts) are required for the existence of a catalogue offence. In addition, the subsidiarity of the use of undercover agents must be taken into account.[1045] A prerequisite for the use of undercover investigators is that the investigation would be considerably more difficult or even futile without them.[1046] However, the significance of the subsidiarity clause is likely to be very limited in practice. Finally, the principle of proportionality must be upheld in any case.[1047]

Section 110a DE-StPO states:

> (1) Undercover officers may be used to investigate criminal offences where there is sufficient factual evidence to suggest that an offence of substantial importance
> 1. in the field of illicit drug trafficking, illicit arms trafficking, counterfeiting of currency or counterfeiting of stamps,
> 2. in the field of state protection (§§ 74a, 120 of the Judicature Act),
> 3. professionally or habitually, or
> 4. organized by a gang member or otherwise
>
> has been committed. Undercover investigators may also be deployed to solve crimes if there is a risk of repetition on the basis of certain facts. The use of undercover agents is only permissible if the investigation would otherwise be futile or considerably more

---

1043 Hegmann, 2017: § 110a DE-StPO point 2.

1044 Kramer, 2014: p. 255; Bernsmann, 1998: p. 220.

1045 Eschelbach, 2020: § 110a DE-StPO point 3; Günther, 2016: § 110a DE-StPO point 7.

1046 Pfeiffer, 2005: § 110a DE-StPO point 1; Bernsmann, 1998: p. 221.

1047 Eschelbach, 2020: § 110a DE-StPO point 18.

difficult. In addition, undercover investigators may be used to solve crimes if the particular importance of the offence requires their use and other measures would be futile.[1048]

The conclusive catalogue listed above was taken verbatim from § 98a (1) DE-StPO.[1049] In contrast to Switzerland, only (domestic) police officers can be used as undercover agents in Germany.[1050] The same are allowed to use false documents if it is necessary for the production or maintenance of the cover story.[1051] Undercover investigators are thus allowed to participate in legal transactions under their cover.[1052] This cover is permanent. Among other things, the name, address, occupation and any family and personal circumstances of the undercover investigator are changed in the cover story in order to protect their true identity.[1053] The undercover investigator's cover story is put together by the police.[1054]

Undercover investigators can act both repressively and preventively. In practice, it is conceivable that an undercover investigator could have been initially active in a preventive police capacity. In the course of their work, they encountered facts that they needed to pursue on the basis of the compulsion to prosecute in the sense of § 152 (2) and § 163 DE-StPO. Consequently, the responsibility was transferred to the public prosecutor's office. If preventive police activities are to continue to be carried out, the relevant operational requirements must continue to be met. Thus, police law remains authoritative in this regard.[1055] Preventive deployment is generally governed by the relevant state police laws.[1056]

The powers of undercover investigators are governed by the Code of Criminal Procedure and the respective police laws. This makes it clear that undercover investigators are also authorized to take preventive police measures within the framework of criminal procedural investigations. At the same time, they are also obliged to prosecute criminal offences of which they have only become aware by chance (§ 163 DE-StPO).[1057]

1048 § 110a (1) DE-StPO.
1049 Günther, 2016: § 110a DE-StPO point 9.
1050 Bruns, 2019: § 110a DE-StPO point 5; BGH StraFo 2007, 331 =NStZ 2007, 713.
1051 § 110a (2) and (3) DE-StPO; Gercke, 2019: § 110a DE-StPO point 6.
1052 Gercke, 2019: § 110a DE-StPO point 17.
1053 Hegmann, 2017: § 110a DE-StPO point 3; BGHSt 41, 64; Gercke, 2019: § 110a DE-StPO point 7.
1054 Gercke, 2019: § 110a DE-StPO point 19.
1055 Hegmann, 2017: § 110a DE-StPO point 10.
1056 Gercke, 2019: § 110a DE-StPO point 9.
1057 Hegmann, 2017: § 110c DE-StPO point 4.

In this research, reference is made primarily to the Code of Criminal Procedure. Undercover investigators must observe the Code of Criminal Procedure in order not to endanger the usability of the results of their work. Even if the limits of police law are somewhat less narrowly defined than those of the Code of Criminal Procedure, the latter is ultimately decisive for determining the usability of the results.[1058]

5.2.4.1.1 Conditions of use

Furthermore, it has to be said that, on the basis of the Code of Criminal Procedure, the use of an undercover investigator is only possible if there is a suspicion of a serious catalogue offence in the sense of § 152, § 2 DE-StPO.[1059] First of all, it must be noted that there must be sufficient factual indications suggesting that a catalogue offence has already been committed.[1060] However, indications that a person is inclined to commit a criminal offence in the future are not sufficient. This suspicion must not be mere conjecture. At the same time, however, it is not necessary to meet a certain level of probability (e.g. an urgent or sufficient suspicion of a crime). Rather, a sufficiently concrete initial suspicion is sufficient.[1061]

Nonetheless, preliminary investigations are not permissible. In practice, however, there is often a combination of criminal procedure law and police law considered which often leads to a softening of the concept of suspicion.[1062] Undercover agents can also be deployed in the run-up to the initial suspicion of danger (based on the state police laws). An exception to the catalogue offences exists in the case of the danger of repetition. It must be emphasized that undercover officers may only be deployed with a dual objective if there is a concrete initial suspicion in combination with a sufficient suspicion of danger within the scope of the state police law.[1063]

It is also necessary that an offence of considerable importance has been committed. These must always be catalogue offences.[1064] At the same time, they must belong at least to the category of medium criminality and thus be capable of significantly disturbing the peace under the law or reducing the public's feelings of and trust in legal certainty.[1065] What is debatable is to what extent the jurisdiction

1058 Gercke, 2019: § 110a DE-StPO point 9.
1059 Gercke, 2019: § 110a DE-StPO point 13; Hegmann, 2017: § 110a DE-StPO point 9.
1060 Bernsmann, 1998: p. 219.
1061 Eschelbach, 2020: § 110a DE-StPO point 13.
1062 Eschelbach, 2020: § 110a DE-StPO point 13.
1063 Gercke, 2019: § 110a DE-StPO point 14; Eschelbach, 2020: § 110a DE-StPO point 13.
1064 Bernsmann, 1998: p. 220.
1065 Eschelbach, 2020: § 110a DE-StPO point 14.

rules according to §§ 74a, 120 GVG apply to state protection offences.[1066] There are no bounds to the subject matter covered in a single criminal proceeding. Operations can therefore take place across proceedings.[1067]

5.2.4.1.2 Covert investigators, informants and police officers not openly investigating

A distinction must also be made between undercover investigators and confidants.[1068] The undercover investigator is defined in § 110a (2) DE-StPO and is considered to be an officer of the police service who investigates under a cover that has been conferred on them and is intended to be permanent.[1069] By contrast, confidants do not usually belong to the police.[1070] However, over a longer period of time, they ultimately support the police in the investigation (or prevention) of crimes.[1071] Even if they partly resort to state resources in doing so, confidants are not subject to the principle of legality.[1072] The use of confidants is often necessary in order to combat serious crimes. Confidants are thus used by authorities in a supportive capacity.[1073] Foreign police officers can also be classified as confidants.[1074] However, there is no explicit special legal basis for their role.[1075]

The question arises as to how to deal with confidants (i.e. informants from within the criminal milieu). In contrast to undercover investigators who are regulated in § 110a ff. DE-StPO, the law does not yet comment on the work of confidants. However, doing so would be imperative. Consider, for example, confidants entering foreign dwellings. Ultimately, this is a serious interference in the rights of third parties. Even if the owner of the dwelling consents to the confidant's entry, the informant's actions are fraudulent since the owner does not know that the person is a police informant. If they were aware, they probably would not have consented to their entry. However, only certain serious

---

1066 Eschelbach, 2020: § 110a DE-StPO point 15.
1067 Eschelbach, 2020: § 110a DE-StPO point 2.
1068 Gercke, 2017: p. 615.
1069 Kühne, 2015: point 534; Hegmann, 2017: § 110a DE-StPO point 1.
1070 Fezer, 1995: p. 971.
1071 Kühne, 2015: point 534.
1072 Gercke, 2019: § 110a DE-StPO point 21.
1073 Eschelbach, 2020: § 110a 11 DE-StPO point 11; Duttge, 1996: p. 564.
1074 BGH NStZ 2007, 713 = StraFo 2007, 331.
1075 Eschelbach, 2000: p. 391.

violations of the law by confidential informants can lead to the inadmissibility of the findings.[1076]

It could also be argued that confidants are already a kind of undercover investigator with extended powers. Confidants often belong to the milieu themselves and sometimes also commit crimes. These crimes are regularly treated with leniency by the police in order not to endanger the position of the undercover agents and thus the gathering of information.[1077] It is interesting that the Ministry of the Interior's budget allocates resources for the remuneration of undercover agents. Nevertheless, there is no legal basis for confidants. Therefore, a question also arises as to whether confidants can also be police officers. In this case, it would be possible to circumvent the restrictions of §§ 110a ff. DE-StPO, which apply to undercover investigators, by allowing police officers to act as confidants instead of undercover investigators. In this case, a prohibition on the use of evidence could possibly come into consideration.[1078]

The use of confidants, which from the point of view of the persons concerned pursues a similar purpose as that of undercover investigators, is often considered a circumvention of § 110a DE-StPO. This is also the case with regard to the risks of self-incrimination and provocation. There is also a risk of falsification of the facts. Among other things, this can constitute a violation of the guarantee of human dignity (Art. 1 (1), 20 (3), 79 (3) GG).[1079]

In addition, undercover investigators are to be distinguished from police officers who are not openly investigating, the German equivalent of Swiss undercover manhunters.[1080] What makes a police officer an undercover investigator is the fact that they permanently participate in legal transactions under a cover story.[1081] Non-publicly investigating police officers appear under false names but without an individual cover story. Police officers investigating suspects on a permanent basis without the use of a cover story are used in Internet investigations, for example, where they can conceal their investigative activities.[1082] The German Federal Supreme Court has subordinated non-publicly investigating police officers to §§ 161 and 163 DE-StPO as an emergency solution.[1083] This enables

1076 Kühne, 2015: point 369; BVerfG NStZ 2000, 489.
1077 Kühne, 2015: point 534.
1078 Kühne, 2015: point 534; BGH NStZ 1995, 514.
1079 Eschelbach, 2020: § 110a DE-StPO point 11.
1080 Kühne, 2015: point 534.1.
1081 Hegmann, 2017: § 110a DE-StPO point 5.
1082 Eschelbach, 2020: § 110a DE-StPO point 9.
1083 BGH NJW 1995, 2237 f.; 1996, 2108.

them to make bogus purchases in the drug scene, for example.[1084] According to the prevailing doctrine, bogus buyers in the drug scene are not undercover investigators because investigators who use a false identity for a single investigative act do not fall under § 110a ff DE-StPO.[1085] In differentiating between officers who do not operate in public and undercover investigators, the decisive factors include how extensive their investigative mandate is, how many persons must be deceived and whether the protection of the investigating officers requires that their identity be kept secret.[1086]

So-called informants are to be distinguished from undercover investigators and confidants.[1087] Informants offer temporary assistance and do not operate under a cover story.[1088] They are not permanently active with the police and only operate in individual cases.[1089]

From an investigative and tactical point of view, the use of undercover investigators is probably preferable to that of confidants. After all, undercover investigators are better trained and, due to their affiliation with the authorities, supposedly more reliable than undercover agents.[1090]

5.2.4.2 Implementation of the operation

Undercover investigators' operations are usually dominated by the police. The public prosecutor's office, on the other hand, usually acts only as an authorizing authority. From the intermediate proceedings onwards, authorization is given by the court. It follows that the control by the judiciary is only limited to some parts of the entire undercover investigation.[1091]

The deployment of undercover investigators must be ordered by the public prosecutor's office or (in the event of imminent danger) by the police.[1092] If an operation is directed against a specific accused person or the undercover investigator is to enter a dwelling which is not generally permitted, a judicial order is

---

1084 Kühne, 2015: point 534.1.
1085 Eschelbach, 2020: § 110a DE-StPO point 10.
1086 Kramer, 2014: p. 255.
1087 Kühne, 2015: point 534; Hegmann, 2017: § 110a DE-StPO point 7.
1088 Bruns, 2019: § 110a DE-StPO point 9.
1089 Kühne, 2015: point 534.
1090 Rogall, 1987: p. 848.
1091 Eschelbach, 2020: § 110a DE-StPO point 2.
1092 Bernsmann, 1998: p. 220.

also necessary. In case of imminent danger, a public prosecutor's order is sufficient (§ 110b (2) DE-StPO).[1093]

Furthermore, it must be considered that undercover investigations pose a potential threat to upholding justice. Finally, undercover investigators take legally relevant actions under their cover stories.[1094]

Similar to Switzerland, the preventive use of undercover officers is regulated in the police laws of the federal and state governments in Germany.[1095] The same restrictions apply to a large extent, which mostly result from constitutional protections. These include, among other things, the protection of the home.[1096] Finally, undercover investigations can lead to total surveillance, to which the protection of the home also falls victim.[1097] This has been discussed above in connection with eavesdropping attacks, which can arise in combination with other covert coercive measures.[1098]

Furthermore, a cover story (i.e. a false identity) must be created for undercover investigators. Reforms were planned to modify the civil status register to support the cover stories of undercover investigators by backing up their aliases; however, these were not implemented by the legislator.[1099]

There is thus only a very low level of protection for cover stories. If there is a threat to life and limb, witnesses are only required to provide information about any previous identities (§ 68 (3) DE-StPO). In the context of a main hearing, however, a witness must state in what capacity he or she obtained the information he or she is recounting (§ 68 (3) DE-StPO). It is problematic in this context that § 110a (3) DE-StPO does provide that documents may be produced, altered and used to maintain or produce cover stories. However, no amendment of public records is provided for. Consequently, cover stories can be found out with relatively little effort.[1100]

A number of challenges arise with regard to cover stories. On the one hand, it must be considered that the undercover agent may have to deceive numerous individuals about their identity. At the same time, their identity may also have to

1093 Kühne, 2015: point 535.
1094 Eschelbach, 2020; § 110a DE-StPO point 4.
1095 Bruns, 2019: § 110a DE-StPO point 2.
1096 Weil, 1992: p. 243 f.; Krüger, 1993: p. 124 f.; Meyer, 1999: p. 49 f.; Baum & Palm, 1994: p. 447.
1097 Seifert, 1992: p. 355 f.
1098 Hassemer, 1992: p. 357 f.
1099 Kühne, 2015: point 535.
1100 Kühne, 2015: point 839.

be kept secret during future criminal proceedings. How these factors will develop is usually impossible to predict at the beginning of the undercover investigator's assignment.[1101] The use of fake documents (even over a longer period of time) alone does not necessarily lead to qualification as an undercover investigator.[1102]

While no fixed period is prescribed for Undercover investigations, they are usually designed to be permanent. However, cover stories do not have to be designed for a specific minimum period of time.[1103] If an operation were not designed to be permanent, it would be grouped under officers acting in a non-public capacity. It is worth mentioning that undercover officers in Germany already have very wide-ranging powers. For example, undercover investigators are allowed to participate in legal transactions as their aliases according to § 110a DE-StPO – they are allowed to found companies or to have themselves entered into the land register (and other registers) under their false name. They are even allowed to appear as plaintiffs or defendants in lawsuits under their alias. These powers, which are reminiscent of intelligence service procedures, are tolerable in the context of Art. 20 (3) GG provided that they appear to be indispensable and sufficiently specific conditions and powers are guaranteed, as well as compliance with the principle of control. In addition, the employer must ensure that the use of undercover agents does not cause damage to third parties.[1104] This means that the employer must pay for any damage caused by the undercover investigator. The employer is also responsible for any liabilities incurred by the undercover investigator once the cover story is lifted.[1105]

5.2.4.2.1 Procedure for the use of undercover agents

The procedure for the use of an undercover investigator is regulated in § 110b DE-StPO:

> (1) The use of an undercover investigator shall only be permitted after the public prosecutor's office has given its consent. If there is imminent danger and the decision of the public prosecutor's office cannot be obtained in time, it shall be obtained without delay; the measure shall be terminated unless the public prosecutor's office consents within three working days. Consent must be given in writing and be limited in time. An extension is permissible as long as the conditions for the deployment continue to exist.

1101 Eschelbach, 2020: § 110a DE-StPO point 5.
1102 Hegmann, 2017: § 110a DE-StPO point 5.
1103 Hegmann, 2017: § 110a DE-StPO point 3.
1104 Eschelbach, 2020: § 110a DE-StPO point 7.
1105 Gercke, 2019: § 110a DE-StPO point 20.

(2) Stakes,
1. directed against a specific defendant, or
2. where the undercover investigator enters a dwelling that is not generally accessible,
require the approval of the court. In the event of imminent danger, the consent of the public prosecutor's office shall suffice. If the decision of the public prosecutor's office cannot be obtained in good time, it must be obtained without delay. The measure shall be terminated unless the court gives its consent within three working days. Subsection (1) sentences 3 and 4 apply mutatis mutandis.

(3) The identity of the undercover investigator may be kept secret even after the assignment has ended. The public prosecutor's office and the court responsible for deciding on consent to the assignment may demand that the identity be disclosed to them. In other respects, in criminal proceedings, the secrecy of the identity is permissible in accordance with § 96, in particular if there is reason to fear that the disclosure would endanger the life, limb or freedom of the undercover investigator or of another person or the possibility of the further use of the undercover investigator.[1106]

The order for an undercover investigation must contain both the substantive and procedural requirements set out in §§ 110a and 110b DE-StPO. In particular, the order must also be substantiated (§ 34 DE-StPO). The lack of prosecutorial or judicial consent can lead to the evidence obtained through a Undercover investigation being unusable. Arbitrary or unjustifiable reasons may also lead to a prohibition of the use of evidence.[1107]

From a practical point of view, it is essential that the initiative for the use of an undercover investigator comes from the police since the public prosecutor's office cannot successfully order the use of an undercover investigator if the police are not willing to make an undercover investigator available.[1108]

Then the police craft the cover story. The public prosecutor's office, however, remains the competent authority and thus oversees the investigative proceedings. In doing so, however, its role is often limited to that of a licensing authority. Due to the element of espionage in undercover investigations, the police often act outside of the classical criminal procedure law.[1109]

In principle, the (written) consent of the public prosecutor's office is always required to initiate an undercover investigation.[1110] Only in cases of imminent

1106 § 110b DE-StPO.
1107 Hegmann, 2017: § 110b DE-StPO point 12.
1108 Eschelbach, 2020: § 110b DE-StPO point 2.
1109 Eschelbach, 2020: § 110b DE-StPO point 2.
1110 Hegmann, 2019: § 110b DE-StPO point 1; BGH NStZ 1996, 48.

danger can the police act alone for the time being. However, the approval of the public prosecutor must be obtained immediately and the approval of the judge within three days (three working days from the day following the order). In this context, it is interesting to note that the mere absence of the prosecutor's approval should not, as a rule, lead to a prohibition of the use of the evidence gathered.[1111]

In addition to the consent of the public prosecutor, that of the court is also required. The investigating judge is responsible for this. However, in view of the high number of staff and the limited availability of information in the area of undercover investigators, the legal protection granted here must be viewed critically. Furthermore, the investigating judge only has to examine the legality, but not the expediency, of the measure. The court's consent is required in any case where the use of an undercover investigator is directed against a specific accused person or against several accused people.[1112]

5.2.4.2.2 Undercover agents and the commission of offences

There is consensus in doctrine and case law that undercover agents may not commit criminal offences. The principle of legality applies to undercover investigators.[1113] This also applies to so-called milieu-related offences.[1114] Thus, undercover investigators are not allowed to commit criminal offences.[1115] The only justifications can be found in the sense of §§ 32, 34, 35 DE-StGB. Undercover investigators' powers correspond to those of normal police officers.[1116] In the past, there have been repeated calls for undercover officers to be able to commit so-called 'milieu-typical crimes'. These have sometimes been justified as strengthening the credibility of the undercover officers concerned. The prevailing doctrine has (rightly) opposed this (in the opinion represented here). In particular, the state must be prevented from disregarding the legal interests of uninvolved third parties who would undoubtedly be the injured parties of these criminal offences.[1117]

1111 Eschelbach, 2020: § 110b DE-StPO point 4.

1112 Eschelbach, 2020: § 110b DE-StPO point 5; Eschelbach, 2020: § 110b DE-StPO point 6; Hegmann, 2017: § 110b DE-StPO point 3.

1113 Eschelbach, 2020: § 110c DE-StPO point 8.

1114 Hegmann, 2017: § 110c DE-StPO point 7.

1115 Eschelbach, 2020: § 110c DE-StPO point 10.

1116 Krey & Heinrich, 2019: p. 249.

1117 Kühne, 2015: point 536.

The powers of undercover investigators are governed by § 110c DE-StPO:

> Undercover investigators may enter a dwelling with the consent of the authorized person using their legend. Consent may not be obtained by feigning a right of entry beyond the use of the legend. In all other respects the powers of the undercover investigator shall be governed by this Act and other statutory provisions.[1118]

This means that the German Code of Criminal Procedure explicitly prohibits undercover agents from committing crimes.[1119] Even milieu-related crimes or so-called tests of allegiance are not permitted. It is an all-encompassing prohibition.[1120] Only the pretence of a crime in the sense of cold case techniques is generally considered permissible.[1121] In exceptional cases, offences may be justified under §§ 32 and 34 DE-StGB or excused under § 35 DE-StGB.[1122] Therefore, in order to create a legal basis in Germany that would allow undercover officers to commit crimes and escape prosecution, one would first have to amend § 110c DE-StPO. However, such plans have failed in the past, due in part to the high value placed on the principle of legality.[1123]

In this context, it must also be taken into account that any extension of the powers of undercover agents to commit criminal offences could not be reasonably limited to supposedly harmless offences. Moreover, such regulations require a legal basis. This means that those operating within the criminal milieu would know what undercover agents would technically be allowed to do and what they could not. If theft were permitted, those in the milieu could demand that suspected undercover officers carry out more serious crimes. The prevailing doctrine here has rightly noted that the spiral would be upward.[1124]

At the same time, a question arises as to whether an exception could be made here in order to combat international terrorism and its financing. The interference with the rights of third parties should be limited in this context, particularly in view of the small number of court proceedings conducted to combat terrorism.

In any case, it is reasonable to assume that the police and the public prosecutor's office are already very reluctant to prosecute possible violations of the law by undercover investigators.[1125] One possible approach to solving this problem is to

---

1118 § 110c DE-StPO.

1119 Hegmann, 2017; § 110c, § 7 DE-StPO.

1120 Bruns, 2019: § 110c DE-StPO point 6; Günther, 2016: § 110c DE-StPO point 39.

1121 Gercke, 2019: § 110c DE-StPO point 8.

1122 Pfeiffer, 2005: § 110c DE-StPO point 2.

1123 Bruns, 2019: § 110c DE-StPO point 6; Günther, 2016: § 110c DE-StPO point 39.

1124 Kühne, 2015: point 536.

1125 Kühne, 2015: point 536.

invoke the fact that, due to the nature of the police's investigative mandate, there is no factual fulfilment at all. For example, police security measures could ensure that acts carried out by an undercover investigator cannot constitute an offence. In addition, the undercover investigator could not be prosecuted for aiding and abetting or inciting a criminal offence due to the lack of intent to complete the offence.[1126]

This approach is elegant and can indeed provide relief in some cases. At the same time, it also easily reaches its limits. Perpetrators from the criminal milieu who want to test a suspected undercover investigator in order to determine whether they are a criminal or a police officer are likely to organize their tests in a correspondingly skilful manner. In conclusion, this raises a question as to whether committing offences under §§ 34 and 35 DE-StGB could be justified.[1127]

According to §§ 110b (2) and 110c DE-StPO, undercover investigators are allowed to enter other people's homes with the consent of the authorized persons.[1128] In particular, undercover investigators have the power to openly enter other people's homes using their alias.[1129] This is not a search in the sense of § 102 ff. DE-StPO but a special regulation in the sense of § 110c DE-StPO. In § 110c DE-StPO, encroachment, Art. 13 (1) GG, was thus specially regulated. It is worth mentioning that this special regulation applies to undercover investigators but not to other types of investigators – neither to openly investigating police officers nor even to confidants. However, this restriction must be put into perspective, since it is assumed that entering a home with the express consent of the owner does not constitute an encroachment on their fundamental rights. Consequently, one can critically question the meaning of § 110c, § 1 DE-StPO.[1130] In this context, there is a question as to how far this can be reconciled with Art. 13 GG. Since the consent of the holder of the domestic right was gained by deception (as it pertains to the identity of the undercover investigator), the consent could therefore be invalid. However, according to the opinion represented here, this deception does not constitute an encroachment on the domestic right, which is why Art. 13 GG is not violated. This is particularly the case in view of the fact that any ineffective consent given by the holder of the domestic right is compensated for by the express statutory provision in § 110c DE-StPO.[1131] At the

1126 Hegmann, 2017: § 110c DE-StPO point 7.
1127 Hegmann, 2017: § 110c DE-StPO point 7.
1128 Hegmann, 2017: § 110c DE-StPO point 1.
1129 Hilger, 1992: p. 525.
1130 Eschelbach, 2020: § 110c DE-StPO point 1.
1131 Kühne, 2015: point 535.

same time, it must be borne in mind that § 110c, § 1 DE-StPO also restricts the actions of undercover investigators. For example, secret searches of apartments are excluded.[1132] Finally, it must be borne in mind that §§ 110a ff. DE-StPO create a constitutive exception to the prohibition of deception.[1133]

However, it is debatable whether police officers who are not openly investigating may enter other people's homes by means of deceiving them about their true identity. This problem could be solved if the material prerequisites for deployment within the meaning of § 110a (1) DE-StPO and judicial approval within the meaning of § 110b (2) sentence 1, no. 2 DE-StPO were met. Finally, the use of an undercover investigator would also be possible in such a case.[1134]

If the deployment of an undercover investigator is specifically directed against a certain person, or if the undercover investigator intends to enter a dwelling that is not generally accessible, the consent of a judge is required.[1135] In principle, the same principles must be applied as in the case of a search order pursuant to § 105 DE-StPO.[1136] The decisive factor is not whether the undercover investigator actually enters the apartment. Rather, a reasonably expected need to enter is to be considered.[1137] Undercover investigators may not engage in any deceptive act beyond their cover story in order to gain access to a dwelling.[1138]

It should be noted that undercover officers have no further powers apart from entering a home using their cover story. In particular, their powers are based on criminal procedure law and the subsidiary applicable police law. According to the legislative conception, undercover investigators are also allowed to take preventive police action. In its judgment 26.04.2017 – 2 StR 247/16, the BGH ruled in favour of a parallel applicability of police and criminal procedure law.[1139]

However, it is interesting to note that undercover investigators can conduct so-called initiative investigations. This means, among other things, that they are not obliged to be instructed according to §§ 136, § 1, 55, § 2, 163a, § 4 and 5 DE-StPO.[1140] However, this must be viewed critically. On the one hand, this can be seen as a violation of § 110c, § 3 DE-StPO. At the same time, such an initiative

---

1132 Eschelbach, 2020; § 110c DE-StPO point 2.
1133 Lagodny, 1996: 372.
1134 Hegmann, 2017: § 110c DE-StPO point 3.
1135 Gercke, 2019: § 110b DE-StPO. point 4.
1136 BGHSt 42, 104.
1137 Gercke, 2019: § 110b DE-StPO point 5.
1138 Gercke, 2019: § 110c DE-StPO point 2.
1139 Eschelbach, 2020: § 110c DE-StPO point 7.
1140 Hegmann, 2017: § 110c DE-StPO point 5.

investigation or questioning without instruction also seems difficult to reconcile with the constitutional principle 'nemo tenetur se ipsum accusare'. The self-incrimination provocation associated with this can also constitute a violation of Art. 1.1 GG. Self-incriminating statements made by the accused might then also only be admissible if they were made without the intervention of the undercover investigator.[1141]

Provided that the requirements for the undercover investigation were fulfilled (i.e. an offence of considerable importance and subsidiarity), self-incriminating statements made by an accused to undercover investigators are in principle also admissible. Exceptions are made, however, if an accused has already invoked their right to refuse to testify and is pressured by the undercover investigator to testify due to a feigned relationship of trust. This would not be compatible with the nemo tenetur principle. Statements which have come about due to coercive actions are also not usable.[1142]

5.2.4.2.3 The undercover investigator as a decoy?

Finally, this raises a question regarding how to deal with behaviour that provokes offences. Within narrow limits, this is considered to be permissible in principle. Even if these limits are exceeded, however, it generally only leads to a mitigation of the sentence. This essentially concerns offences that would not have been committed without the influence of the state.[1143]

In practice, undercover investigators are often used as so-called agent provocateurs. Provocations are only permitted within very narrow limits. For example, it is possible to approach third parties as to whether they would be willing to procure narcotics.[1144] This is often justified by the fact that it is extraordinarily expensive to maintain an undercover investigator and that there is therefore a certain pressure on them to perform. This has been considered admissible in case law but has been taken into account during sentencing. The literature, on the other hand, has been critical of this, since the state actually induces its citizens to commit crimes with such a procedure. The admissibility of a provocation can be reviewed in the context of a procedural complaint in the appeal.[1145]

1141 Eschelbach, 2020: § 110c DE-StPO point 9; Hegmann, 2017: § 110c DE-StPO point 6.
1142 Hegmann, 2017: § 110c DE-StPO point 6.
1143 Eschelbach, 2020: § 110c DE-StPO point 11.
1144 Hegmann, 2017: § 110c DE-StPO, point 9.
1145 Kühne, 2015: point 537; BGH NStZ 2015, 541.

The European Court of Human Rights (ECHR) saw in investigation results uncovered via entrapment a violation of Art. 6, I., 1 ECHR (fair trial principle). In a decision against Portugal (Teixeira), the ECHR declared the corresponding investigation results to be unusable. The First Criminal Senate of the Federal Court of Justice, on the other hand, affirmed the usability in principle in its decision of 18 November 1999. According to this, the role of the state's decoy is only to be taken into account in the legal consequence.[1146] However, this must be viewed critically. In particular, this conduct may constitute an encroachment on the general right of personality (Art. 2.1 in conjunction with Art. 1.1 GG). In the case of coercion, however, the core area of the right of personality as well as the guarantee of human dignity within the meaning of Art. 1.1 GG may also be affected. In any case, the provocation of an unsuspected person is inadmissible.[1147]

In doing so, the BGH relied on the statement repeatedly mentioned by the ECHR in another context that the elaboration of the fundamental principles of the ECHR is governed by national law and is not to be pursued by the ECHR. However, this view is not to be followed. Ultimately, the ECHR did not base its assessment on national law but exclusively on the ECHR. If the ECHR's decision had not concerned Portugal but Germany instead, then the German judiciary would have had to follow the opinion of the ECHR.[1148]

In any case, the potential expansion of the powers of undercover agents discussed in this study must not apply to decoys – a constitutional state must not encourage its citizens to commit more serious crimes or commit a crime at all. Secondly, it would also be extremely dangerous to encourage potential criminals to finance terrorism through decoys. Imagine how quickly the situation would get out of control. In that case, the German state would have financed terrorism through a decoy. If the payment could not be stopped afterwards, this could cost lives. The use of decoys cannot be considered from the outset because of the scope of the offences under discussion.

Foreign undercover investigators are of particular importance in the fight against international terrorism and its financing. The use of foreign undercover investigators finds its legal basis in Art. 14 of the Convention on Mutual Assistance in Criminal Matters between the Member States of the EU. This Convention makes it possible for Member States to agree to accept undercover

---

1146 Kühne, 2015: point 537.1.

1147 Eschelbach, 2020; § 110c DE-StPO point 11.

1148 Kühne, 2015: point 537.1.

agents from each other and to allow them to operate within their territory. However, it is important to bear in mind that foreign undercover investigators are not mentioned in the German DE-StPO and are therefore not subject to § 110a–e DE-StPO. They are therefore de facto on an equal footing with private individuals.[1149] As a rule, undercover police officers from other nations are to be treated like confidants insofar as they are not completely subject to the German legal system.[1150] This means that their misconduct is not to be attributed to the state. Exceptions only exist if state organs themselves have caused the misconduct.[1151]

Furthermore, a question is raised regarding how to deal with information that the undercover investigator perceives but which concerns uninvolved third parties. Prohibitions on the use of evidence outside the catalogue offences of §§ 100a and 110a DE-StPO offer only limited legal protection here.[1152]

This aspect seems particularly problematic with regard to an extension of the powers of undercover agents. After all, such an extension of powers should only be considered to combat the financing of terrorism. If, however, the powers of undercover investigators were to be extended, thereby allowing them to commit certain offences in order to make their cover stories plausible, this would possibly also suggest to criminals who wish to commit other offences outside the financing of terrorism that they are indeed criminals in this case.

5.2.4.2.4 Legal protection

If the conditions for the intervention of an undercover investigator were not met, the evidence obtained by the undercover investigator may not be used. In practice, however, this is often only the case if objective arbitrariness is to be assumed.[1153]

Pursuant to § 101 (7) DE-StPO, within two weeks of being notified of an undercover investigation, an application may be made for a review of its lawfulness and for a review of the manner in which it was carried out.[1154]

It is also possible to obtain legal protection retrospectively. Jurisdiction in this regard lies with the court that was entrusted with ordering the measure. An

1149 Kühne, 2015: point 534.1.
1150 Eschelbach, 2020; § 110a, § 12 DE-StPO; Hegmann, 2017; § 110a, § 8 DE-StPO.
1151 Gercke, 2019: § 110a DE-StPO point 23.
1152 Kühne, 2015: point 401.
1153 Eschelbach, 2020: § 110a DE-StPO point 12; Gercke, 2019: § 110a DE-StPO point 24.
1154 Kühne, 2015: point 557.3.

appeal against any court decision may be lodged immediately (§ 101 (7) DE-StPO). However, this is subject to one restriction: if charges have already been brought, the court will decide on the legality and the manner of execution of the coercive measure as part of its final decision. In this case, an immediate appeal is not possible.[1155]

5.2.4.3 *Constitutional aspects*

The right to secrecy and privacy in the sense of Art. 1 (1) and Art. 10 GG, as well as to informational self-determination in the sense of Art. 2 (1) in conjunction with Art. 1 (1) GG is restricted by the control by undercover agents in the sense of § 110a DE-StPO.[1156] However, the preservation of human dignity within the meaning of Art. 1 GG must remain guaranteed under all circumstances.[1157]

Coercive measures that affect fundamental rights to such a high degree may only be ordered if catalogue offences are concerned. With regard to undercover investigations, these are set out in § 110a (1) nos 1 to 4 DE-StPO. The results of these investigations may then also only be used for the prosecution of said catalogue offences. The problem here is that unusable results often lead to new investigative approaches. Findings obtained within the framework of these new investigative approaches can then be used without restriction.[1158]

Of particular importance for the expansion of the powers of undercover investigators is the reservation of suspicion, the catalogue offence and subsidiarity. Undercover investigations imply particularly severe encroachments on fundamental rights. Therefore, high demands must be placed on the restrictive conditions. They are only permissible if the investigation of the facts and/or the determination of the whereabouts of suspects would otherwise be futile or at least substantially more difficult.[1159]

5.2.4.4 *Conclusion*

Undercover investigators are not permitted to commit criminal offences in view of the principle of legality. Therefore, undercover agents are relatively easy to unmask. It is sufficient for offenders to demand that persons commit criminal

---

1155 Kühne, 2015: point 557.3.
1156 Kühne, 2015: point 402.
1157 Gercke, 2017: p. 619.
1158 Kühne, 2015: point 414.
1159 Kühne, 2015: point 413.

offences in order to test whether they are undercover agents posing as criminals. An expansion of the powers of undercover agents with regard to combating terrorism financing would therefore be desirable.

5.3 Overall assessment of the implications for criminal procedure

In the context of this study, the challenges facing law enforcement agencies in terms of criminal procedure were highlighted. In summary, it can be stated that Germany, in contrast to Liechtenstein, Austria and Switzerland, allows digital surveillance. Thus, law enforcement authorities in Germany have a broader repertoire of investigative tools at their disposal than those in Liechtenstein, Austria and Switzerland.

The advantages of this surveillance method are not limited to its efficiency. It can also be assumed that perpetrators who feel unobserved and do not notice that they are being monitored are less careful with their plans. This also increases their risk of detection.

Moreover, digital surveillance help to overcome the problem of proving that the perpetrators acted intentionally. A perpetrator that has regularly searched the Internet for ways to finance terrorism will hardly be able to claim that they accidentally transferred funds to the IS.

At the same time, the powers of undercover agents in Germany, Liechtenstein, Austria and Switzerland are limited to a very similar extent. Namely, undercover agents are not allowed to commit criminal offences in all four countries. This principle is based on the principle of legality.

In Germany, the limited powers of undercover officers can be at least partially compensated for by digital surveillance. In Liechtenstein, Austria and Switzerland, this possibility does not exist. Thus, it could be argued that Germany is better positioned than Liechtenstein, Austria and Switzerland with regard to combating terrorism financing.

In terms of a summary assessment of the comparison of criminal procedure law, it can be stated with regard to the prevention and prosecution possibilities in Germany, Liechtenstein, Austria and Switzerland that the German law enforcement authorities have greater room to manoeuvre due to the possibility of engaging in digital surveillance. Other countries could take their cues from the experiences of the German authorities, and the legal basis for digital surveillance in Germany could be helpful for legislators in other countries.

6. Summary

The present study analysed how skilful terrorist financiers proceed. Based on a literature analysis, the state of research on the topic of terrorism financing was examined and found that although existing research has dealt with measures to combat terrorism financing, relatively little is currently known about the concrete procedures of terrorist financiers despite this being a basic prerequisite for more effectively combating terrorism financing.

In order to close this research gap, an empirical investigation was undertaken. First, informal interviews were conducted with illicit financial service providers and their helpers as part of a preliminary study. Based on this, formal expert interviews were conducted with compliance specialists and investigators, which were evaluated using a qualitative content analysis according to Mayring due to the exploratory approach of the study. In doing so, the sources of income on the one hand and the transfer of assets of terrorist financiers on the other were examined. Moreover, it was also possible to gain insights into the level of training and characteristics of the perpetrators as well as into the criminal procedural hurdles faced by investigators.

The results of the empirical investigation have shown that in many cases, terrorist financiers are likely to be intelligent and well-trained. Moreover, they can draw on a variety of legal and illegal sources of income. The most promising starting point for combating terrorism financing is thus the transfer of assets. However, here too, the range of methods examined extends from conventional bank transfers to hawala banking and physical transfers.

In the discussion of the empirical results, it became clear that it is difficult to convict terrorist financiers who act intelligently and in a calculated manner – especially since potentially helpful instruments are either not made available to investigators or are only available to a significantly limited extent. Therefore, based on the results of the empirical study, proposals for legislative measures to enable a more effective fight against terrorism financing were developed.

In particular, the (re-)introduction of digital surveillance and an extension of the powers of undercover agents in Germany, Austria, Liechtenstein and Switzerland were discussed. Further research could examine other instruments that would also be helpful in combating terrorism financing. For example, work on adapting administrative and judicial assistance would be conceivable. However, since this is a very extensive topic that can hardly be dealt with in the context of a single book, it has not been discussed in detail here.

The present study also faced some limitations. Due to the significant research gap and the lack of literature on the concrete procedures of the perpetrators studied, an exploratory approach was necessary. Therefore, formal and informal expert interviews were conducted and analysed using a qualitative content analysis according to Mayring. This approach has the advantage of opening up access to a new field. However, it is associated with the disadvantage of significant limitations. This effect is based on the one hand on the selection of a few interview partners, which limits the perspective of the study, and on the other hand on the individual perceptions of the interview partners (and also on their personal background). Furthermore, the results are not representative from a quantitative point of view.

In summary, this work has succeeded in identifying and at least partially closing a significant research gap in this field. Furthermore, the insights gained from the empirical study were used to develop suggestions for the further development of criminal procedure law.

7. Appendix

Appendix 1: Memory transcripts of the informal interviews

(Translated from German into English)

Interviewee 1:

Revenue sources:

General statements:

- Legal sources of income
- Illegal sources of income
- Combination

Sales tax fraud:

- Mobile phones
- Computer chips
- Reverse charge procedure
- Branded clothing
- Textiles

Trade in CO_2 emission allowances:

- Loses importance
- Same procedure as carousel fraud but with CO_2 emission certificates
- No physical transport required as there is with mobile phones, computer chips or textiles
- Fast transfer possible
- Companies in different countries

Trade in raw materials:

- Oil refineries
- Oil production
- Oil processing
- Air attacks a problem
- Logistical challenge
- Political pressure

Trafficking in narcotics:

- Important role
- Several possible approaches
- Combinations are often used
- Cultivation of narcotics
- Export to Europe
- Smuggling
- Retail sales

Trafficking in organs:

- People in Europe who need a donor organ
- Help via personal networks
- Search in terrorist-controlled areas

Human trafficking:

- Labour
- Refugees
- Smuggling of refugees from controlled areas to Europe
- Labour exploitation
- Extremely low wages
- Earnings from facilitating their escape and their work
- Possible conflicts of interest with persons remaining in controlled areas (customs duties, levies, etc.)

Pimping:

- In development
- Prostitution contradicts beliefs of terrorist financiers
- Source of income nevertheless desired
- Refugees provide protection for prostitutes
- Part of the prostitutes' income is for protection
- Use of force if protection is not desired

Protection racket:

- Recruitment of refugees
- Business people are offered protection
- Monetary compensation for protection

- Friendly reminders
- Massive intimidation

Extortionist kidnapping:

- Abduction of persons in terrorist-controlled areas
- High ransom demands
- Significant source of income
- Abduction of persons in Europe
- Low ransom demands
- No involvement of law enforcement authorities
- Small source of income

Theft:

- Recruitment of young refugees
- Theft of sneakers in a department store in Berlin
- Disposal of stolen goods on the black market
- Refugees often poorly integrated
- Refugees do not have legal sources of income
- Easy to inspire refugees
- Radicalization of refugees
- If applicable, no profit sharing for refugees
- Alternatively, small profit shares

Online auction scams:

- Several possible approaches
- Auction of non-existent goods
- Transfer of funds via money transfer systems
- Direct bank transfers
- Avoidance of fiduciary systems
- No delivery of the goods
- Hacking the accounts of existing users
- Transmission of false account data in the name of real sellers

Insurance fraud:

- Deliberately causing damage
- Cash payments from insurance
- Damage to vehicles

- Theft of luxury goods
- No excessive damage to avoid attracting attention from insurance companies

Establishment of car rental companies:

- Leasing of vehicles from renowned manufacturers
- Insurance on the vehicles
- Hiring out of vehicles to straw men
- Moving the vehicles abroad
- Subsequent reporting of the theft to the authorities and insurance company

Real estate deals:

- Very popular
- Legal transactions
- Taxation of income
- Use of a sub-amount for terrorism financing
- Funds not incriminated
- Proof of financing of terrorism only possible if use of funds is documented

Stock market transactions:

- Very popular
- Not illegal
- Difficult to prove terrorism financing unless direct transfers to terrorist groups are made

<u>**Wealth transfer:**</u>

General statements:

- Differentiation between legal and illegal sources of revenue
- Differentiation between cash and electronic balances

Transfers to Turkey:

- Least challenging legal assets
- Officially taxed income from real estate and stock exchange transactions
- Spreading of assets for risk diversification as a plausible justification
- Turkey as a destination
- Cash withdrawal in Turkey
- Handover to terrorists near the border with Syria
- Hardly detectable

Hawala transfer:

- Suitable for cash
- Illcgal assets
- cash clearing

Personal transfer:

- Suitable for cash
- Terrorist financiers travel themselves
- Messenger

Electronic currencies:

- Use of Bitcoin
- Method rather rare
- Preference for personal transfer and remittances through banks and hawala

<u>**Interviewee 2:**</u>

<u>**Revenue sources:**</u>

General statements:

- Legal sources of income
- Illegal sources of income
  - Economic crime (important)
  - Organized crime (important)
  - Petty crime

Sales tax fraud:

- Goods that are easy to transport
- Computer chips
- Mobile phones
- Reverse charge procedure
- Increased attention from tax authorities
- Switching to other sectors, e.g. branded clothing
- Textiles well suited for international business

Trade in CO_2 emission allowances:

- Loses importance
- Same procedure as carousel fraud but with CO_2 emission certificates
- No physical transport required as there is with mobile phones, computer chips or textiles
- Fast transfer possible
- Still in use in practice, although declining

Trade in raw materials:

- Capture oil refineries
- Oil production
- Oil processing
- Declining due to air raids
- Export logistically difficult

Trafficking in narcotics:

- Retail sales
- Small quantities

- Large cities
- Use of auxiliaries
- Recruitment of refugees from Arab countries
- If applicable, entire proceeds of sale remain for terrorism financing
- Consideration of religion in recruitment
- Creation of loyalty to compatriots
- Involve people with financial problems
- Involve persons without alternative gainful employment

Trafficking in organs:

- People in Europe who need a donor organ
- Help via personal networks
- Organ harvesting in Turkey or the Balkans
- Use of refugee routes
- Transplantation in the donor country or exportation

Human trafficking:

- Labour
- Refugees
- Earnings from facilitating their escape and their work
- Possible conflicts of interest with persons remaining in controlled areas (customs duties, levies, etc.)

Pimping:

- In development
- Prostitution contradicts beliefs of terrorist financiers
- Source of income nevertheless desired
- Refugees provide protection for prostitutes
- Use of force if protection is not desired

Protection racket:

- Recruitment of refugees
- Business people are offered protection
- Monetary compensation for protection
- Friendly reminders
- Massive intimidation

Extortionist kidnapping:

- Abduction of persons in terrorist-controlled areas
- High ransom demands
- Significant source of income

Theft:

- Recruitment of young refugees
- Theft of sneakers in a department store in Berlin
- Disposal of stolen goods on the black market
- Radicalization of refugees
- If applicable, no profit sharing for refugees
- Alternatively, small profit shares

Online auction scams:

- Several possible approaches
- Auction of non-existent goods
- Transfer of funds via money transfer systems
- Direct bank transfers

Insurance fraud:

- Damage to vehicles
- Theft of luxury goods
- No excessive damage to avoid attracting attention from insurance companies

Establishment of car rental companies:

- Moving the vehicles abroad
- Subsequent reporting of the theft to the authorities and insurance company

Real estate deals:

- Very popular
- Legal transactions
- Taxation of income
- Use of a sub-account for terrorism financing

Stock market transactions:

- Very popular
- Not illegal

<u>Wealth transfer:</u>

General statements:

- Differentiation between legal and illegal sources of revenue
- Differentiation between cash and electronic balances

Transfers to Turkey:

- Least challenging legal assets
- Officially taxed income from real estate and stock exchange transactions
- Spreading of assets for risk diversification as a plausible justification
- Turkey as a destination

Hawala transfer:

- Suitable for cash
- Suitable for incriminated assets
- Settlement of sums of money among Muslims
- Hawala shops around the world
- Little to no identification requirements

Personal transfer:

- Suitable for cash
- Balkan route
- Works in both directions
- Terrorist financiers travel themselves or send messengers

Electronic currencies:

- Obvious if incriminated assets already exist in electronic currencies

Interviewee 3:

Revenue sources:

General statements:

- Legal sources of income
- Illegal sources of income

Sales tax fraud:

- Carousel scam very popular
- Company A in Country of Origin X sells goods/services to Company B in Country Y
- Export within EU exempt from VAT
- Company B in Country Y sells goods to Company C in Country Y
- Sales tax is incurred but not paid immediately
- Company C sells goods to Company A in Country X
- Export sales tax free
- Company C has sales tax refunded
- Reimbursement to Company C before payment by Company B
- Company B disappears before execution

Trade in CO_2 emission allowances:

- Not specified

Trade in raw materials:

- Capture oil refineries
- Oil production
- Oil processing
- Potential buyers under political pressure

Trafficking in narcotics:

- Controlled areas may be suitable for cultivation of narcotics
- Export to Europe
- Smuggling routes

Trafficking in organs:

- Monetary incentives
- Use of force

- Organ harvesting in Turkey or the Balkans
- Use of refugee routes
- Transplantation in the donor country or exportation

Human trafficking:

- Labour
- Refugees
- Smuggling of refugees from controlled areas to Europe
- Possible conflicts of interest with persons remaining in controlled areas (customs duties, levies, etc.)

Pimping:

- Not specified

Protection racket:

- Monetary compensation for protection
- Friendly memories
- Massive intimidation
- Refugees suitable as perpetrators with little to lose
- Refugees accept low profit sharing

Extortionist kidnapping:

- Abduction of persons in terrorist-controlled areas
- High ransom demands
- Significant source of income

Theft:

- Recruitment of young refugees
- Theft of sneakers in a department store in Berlin
- Disposal of stolen goods on the black market
- Radicalization of refugees
- If applicable, no profit sharing for refugees
- Alternatively, small profit shares

Online auction scams:

- Several possible approaches
- Auction of non-existent goods

- Direct bank transfers
- No delivery of the goods
- Hacking the accounts of existing users
- Transmission of false account data in the name of real sellers

Insurance fraud:

- Deliberately causing damage
- Cash payments from insurance
- No excessive damage to avoid attracting attention from insurance companies

Establishment of car rental companies:

- Leasing of vehicles from renowned manufacturers
- Moving the vehicles abroad
- Subsequent reporting of the theft to the authorities and insurance company

Real estate deals:

- Use of a sub-account for terrorism financing
- Funds not incriminated
- Proof of financing of terrorism only possible if use of funds is documented

Stock market transactions:

- Very popular
- Difficult to prove terrorism financing unless direct transfers to terrorist groups are made

Wealth transfer:

General statements:

- Differentiation between legal and illegal sources of revenue

Transfers to Turkey:

- Least challenging legal assets
- Turkey as a destination
- Cash withdrawal in Turkey
- Handover to terrorists near the border with Syria
- Hardly detectable

Hawala transfer:

- Hand over the cash in a hawala shop in Munich
- Pick up possible within a few minutes from a hawala shop in Turkey

Personal transfer:

- Suitable for cash
- Terrorist financiers travel themselves or send messengers

Electronic currencies:

- Obvious if incriminated assets already exist in electronic currencies
- Preference for personal transfer and remittances through banks and hawala

Interviewee 4:

Revenue sources:

General statements:

- Legal sources of income
- Illegal sources of income

Sales tax fraud:

- Carousel scam very popular
- Goods that are easy to transport
- Computer chips
- Mobile phones
- Reverse charge procedure
- Increased attention from tax authorities
- Switching to other sectors, e.g. branded clothing
- Textiles well suited for international business
- Appointing young jihadists as CEOs
- Inconspicuous environment distracts from intention to leave the country
- Persons anonymous
- Protection of the backers
- No profit sharing

Trade in CO_2 emission allowances:

- No physical transport required as there is with mobile phones, computer chips or textiles
- Fast transfer possible
- Companies in different countries
- Limited traceability

Trade in raw materials:

- Potential buyers under political pressure

Trafficking in narcotics:

- Important role
- Several possible approaches
- Combinations are often used
- Controlled areas may be suitable for cultivation of narcotics

- Sales to end consumers in Europe
- Small quantities
- Large cities
- Deployment of refugees

Trafficking in organs:

- People in Europe who need a donor organ
- Help via personal networks
- Targeted search for donors
- Search in terrorist-controlled areas
- Transplantation in the donor country or exportation

Human trafficking:

- Labour
- Refugees
- Smuggling of refugees from controlled areas to Europe

Pimping:

- Refugees provide protection for prostitutes
- Part of the prostitutes' income is for protection
- Use of force if protection is not desired

Protection racket:

- Recruitment of refugees
- Business people are offered protection
- Monetary compensation for protection
- Friendly memories
- Massive intimidation

Extortionist kidnapping:

- Abduction of persons in terrorist-controlled areas
- High ransom demands
- Significant source of income
- Abduction of persons in Europe
- Low ransom demands
- Small source of income

Theft:

- Recruitment of young refugees
- Theft of sneakers in a department store in Berlin
- If applicable, no profit sharing for refugees
- Alternatively, small profit shares

Online auction scams:

- Auction of non-existent goods

Insurance fraud:

- Deliberately causing damage
- Cash payments from insurance

Establishment of car rental companies:

- Leasing of vehicles from renowned manufacturers
- Insurance on the vehicles
- Hiring out of vehicles to straw men
- Moving the vehicles abroad
- Subsequent reporting of the theft to the authorities and insurance company

Real estate deals:

- Very popular
- Legal transactions

Stock market transactions:

- Very popular
- Not illegal

Wealth transfer:

General statements:

- Differentiation between legal and illegal sources of revenue
- Differentiation between cash and electronic balances

Transfers to Turkey:

- Least challenging legal assets
- Turkey as a destination
- Cash withdrawal in Turkey
- Handover to terrorists near the border with Syria

Hawala transfer:

- Suitable for cash
- Suitable for incriminated assets
- Hand over the cash in a hawala shop in Munich
- Pick up possible within a few minutes from a hawala shop in Turkey

Personal transfer:

- Suitable for cash

Electronic currencies:

- Obvious if incriminated assets already exist in electronic currencies
- Preference for personal transfer and remittances through banks and hawala

Interviewee 5:

Revenue sources:

General statements:

- Legal sources of income
- Illegal sources of income
  - Economic crime (important)
  - Organized crime (important)
  - Petty crime

Sales tax fraud:

- Carousel scam very popular
- Goods that are easy to transport
- Reverse charge procedure
- Increased attention from tax authorities
- Switching to other sectors, e.g. branded clothing
- Textiles well suited for international business
- Appointing young jihadists as CEOs
- Inconspicuous environment distracts from intention to leave the country
- Persons not tangible
- Protection of the backers
- No profit sharing

Trade in CO_2 emission allowances:

- Limited traceability
- Well-known problem
- Reverse charge procedure
- Still in use in practice, although declining

Trade in raw materials:

- Capture oil refineries
- Oil production
- Oil processing
- Potential buyers under political pressure

Trafficking in narcotics:

- Important role
- Controlled areas may be suitable for cultivation of narcotics
- Export to Europe
- Smuggling routes
- Retail sales
- Small quantities

Trafficking in organs:

- People in Europe who need a donor organ
- Help via personal networks
- Targeted search for donors
- Search in terrorist-controlled areas
- Monetary incentives

Human trafficking:

- Labour
- Refugees
- Earnings from facilitating their escape and their work
- Possible conflicts of interest with persons remaining in controlled areas (customs duties, levies, etc.)

Pimping:

- Not specified

Protection racket:

- Refugees suitable as perpetrators with little to lose
- Refugees accept low profit sharing
- Favours easily manipulated, poorly integrated refugees to facilitate radicalization

Extortionist kidnapping:

- Abduction of persons in terrorist-controlled areas
- High ransom demands
- Abduction of persons in Europe
- Small source of income

Theft:

- Recruitment of young refugees
- Theft of sneakers in a department store in Berlin
- Disposal of stolen goods on the black market

Online auction scams:

- Several possible approaches
- Auction of non-existent goods
- Transfer of funds via money transfer systems

Insurance fraud:

- Deliberately causing damage
- Cash payments from insurance
- Damage to vehicles

Establishment of car rental companies:

- Leasing of vehicles from renowned manufacturers
- Insurance on the vehicles
- Hiring out of vehicles to straw men
- Moving the vehicles abroad

Real estate deals:

- Very popular
- Legal transactions
- Taxation of income
- Use of a sub-account for terrorism financing

Stock market transactions:

- Very popular
- Not illegal

Wealth transfer:

General statements:

- Differentiation between legal and illegal sources of revenue
- Differentiation between cash and electronic balances

Transfers to Turkey:

- Least challenging legal assets
- Officially taxed income from real estate and stock exchange transactions

Hawala transfer:

- Not specified

Personal transfer:

- Suitable for cash
- Balkan route
- Works in both directions
- Terrorist financiers travel themselves or send messengers

Electronic currencies:

- Obvious if incriminated assets already exist in electronic currencies
- Use of Bitcoin

Interviewee 6:

Revenue sources:

General statements:

- Legal sources of income
- Illegal sources of income
  - Economic crime (important)
  - Organized crime (important)
  - Petty crime

Sales tax fraud:

- Carousel scam very popular
- Appointing young jihadists as CEOs
- Inconspicuous environment distracts from intention to leave the country
- Persons not tangible
- Protection of the backers
- No profit sharing

Trade in CO_2 emission allowances:

- Not specified

Trade in raw materials:

- Capture oil refineries
- Oil production
- Oil processing
- Export logistically difficult

Trafficking in narcotics:

- Important role
- Retail sales
- Small quantities
- Large cities
- Use of auxiliaries
- Recruitment of refugees from Arab countries
- If applicable, entire proceeds of sale remain for terrorism financing
- Consideration of religion in recruitment
- Creation of loyalty to compatriots

- Involve people with financial problems
- Involve persons without alternative gainful employment
- Refugees assured of family support in case of imprisonment

Trafficking in organs:

- People in Europe who need a donor organ
- Help via personal networks
- Transplantation in the donor country or exportation

Human trafficking:

- Labour
- Refugees
- Smuggling of refugees from controlled areas to Europe
- Labour exploitation

Pimping:

- Not specified

Protection racket:

- Recruitment of refugees
- Business people are offered protection
- Monetary compensation for protection
- Friendly memories
- Massive intimidation

Extortionist kidnapping:

- Abduction of persons in terrorist-controlled areas
- High ransom demands

Theft:

- Refugees often poorly integrated
- Refugees do not have legal sources of income
- Easy to inspire refugees

Online auction scams:

- Hacking the accounts of existing users
- Transmission of false account data in the name of real sellers

Insurance fraud:

- No excessive damage to avoid attracting attention from insurance companies

Establishment of car rental companies:

- Leasing of vehicles from renowned manufacturers
- Subsequent reporting of the theft to the authorities and insurance company

Real estate deals:

- Very popular
- Proof of financing of terrorism only possible if use of funds is documented

Stock market transactions:

- Difficult to prove terrorism financing unless direct transfers to terrorist groups are made

Wealth transfer:

General statements:

- Differentiation between legal and illegal sources of revenue
- Differentiation between cash and electronic balances

Transfers to Turkey:

- Turkey as a destination
- Cash withdrawal in Turkey
- Handover to terrorists near the border with Syria
- Hardly detectable

Hawala transfer:

- Not specified

Personal transfer:

- Not specified

Electronic currencies:

- Obvious if incriminated assets already exist in electronic currencies
- Preference for personal transfer

<u>Interviewee 7:</u>

<u>Revenue sources:</u>

General statements:

- Legal sources of income
- Illegal sources of income
  - Economic crime (important)
  - Organized crime (important)
  - Petty crime

Sales tax fraud:

- Carousel scam very popular
- Company A in Country of Origin X sells goods/services to Company B in Country Y
- Export within EU exempt from VAT
- Company B in Country Y sells goods to Company C in Country Y
- Sales tax is incurred but not paid immediately
- Company C sells goods to Company A in Country X
- Export sales tax free
- Company C has sales tax refunded
- Reimbursement to Company C before payment by Company B
- Company B disappears before execution
- Goods that are easy to transport
- Computer chips
- Mobile phones
- Reverse charge procedure
- Increased attention from tax authorities
- Switching to other sectors, e.g. branded clothing
- Textiles well suited for international business
- Appointing young jihadists as CEOs
- Inconspicuous environment distracts from intention to leave the country
- Persons not tangible
- Protection of the backers
- No profit sharing

Trade in CO_2 emission allowances:

- Loses importance
- Same procedure as carousel fraud but with CO_2 emission certificates

- No physical transport required as there is with mobile phones, computer chips or textiles
- Fast transfer possible
- Companies in different countries
- Limited traceability
- Well-known problem
- Reverse charge procedure
- Still in use in practice, although declining

Trade in raw materials:

- Capture oil refineries
- Oil production
- Oil processing
- Declining due to air raids
- Export logistically difficult
- Potential buyers under political pressure

Trafficking in narcotics:

- Important role
- Several possible approaches
- Combinations are often used
- Controlled areas may be suitable for cultivation of narcotics
- Export to Europe
- Smuggling routes
- Use of aircraft, trucks and ships that deliver relief supplies and otherwise return unloaded
- Retail sales
- Small quantities
- Large cities
- Use of auxiliaries
- Recruitment of refugees from Arab countries
- If applicable, entire proceeds of sale remain for terrorism financing
- Consideration of religion in recruitment
- Creation of loyalty to compatriots
- Involve people with financial problems
- Involve persons without alternative gainful employment
- Refugees assured of family support in case of imprisonment

Trafficking in organs:

- People in Europe who need a donor organ
- Help via personal networks
- Targeted search for donors
- Search in terrorist-controlled areas
- Monetary incentives
- Use of force
- Organ harvesting in Turkey or the Balkans
- Use of refugee routes
- Transplantation in the donor country or exportation

Human trafficking:

- Labour
- Refugees
- Smuggling of refugees from controlled areas to Europe
- Labour exploitation
- Extremely low wages
- Earnings from facilitating their escape and their work
- Possible conflicts of interest with persons remaining in controlled areas (customs duties, levies, etc.)

Pimping:

- In development
- Prostitution contradicts beliefs of terrorist financiers
- Source of income nevertheless desired
- Refugees provide protection for prostitutes
- Part of the prostitutes' income is used for protection
- Use of force if protection is not desired

Protection racket:

- Recruitment of refugees
- Business people are offered protection
- Monetary compensation for protection
- Friendly memories
- Massive intimidation
- Refugees suitable as perpetrators with little to lose

- Refugees accept low profit sharing
- Favours easily manipulated, poorly integrated refugees to facilitate radicalization

Extortionist kidnapping:

- Abduction of persons in terrorist-controlled areas
- High ransom demands
- Significant source of income
- Abduction of persons in Europe
- Low ransom demands
- No involvement of law enforcement authorities
- Small source of income

Theft:

- Recruitment of young refugees
- Theft of sneakers in a department store in Berlin
- Disposal of stolen goods on the black market
- Refugees often poorly integrated
- Refugees do not have legal sources of income
- Easy to inspire refugees
- Radicalization of refugees
- If applicable, no profit sharing for refugees
- Alternatively, small profit shares

Online auction scams:

- Several possible approaches
- Auction of non-existent goods
- Transfer of funds via money transfer systems
- Direct bank transfers
- Avoidance of fiduciary systems
- No delivery of the goods
- Hacking the accounts of existing users
- Transmission of false account data in the name of real sellers

Insurance fraud:

- Deliberately causing damage
- Cash payments from insurance

- Damage to vehicles
- Theft of luxury goods
- No excessive damage to avoid attracting attention from insurance companies

Establishment of car rental companies:

- Leasing of vehicles from renowned manufacturers
- Insurance on the vehicles
- Hiring out of vehicles to straw men
- Moving the vehicles abroad
- Subsequent reporting of the theft to the authorities and insurance company

Real estate deals:

- Very popular
- Legal transactions
- Taxation of income
- Use of a sub-account for terrorism financing
- Funds not incriminated
- Proof of financing of terrorism only possible if use of funds is documented

Stock market transactions:

- Very popular
- Not illegal
- Difficult to prove terrorism financing unless direct transfers to terrorist groups are made

Wealth transfer:

General statements:

- Differentiation between legal and illegal sources of revenue
- Differentiation between cash and electronic balances

Transfers to Turkey:

- Least challenging legal assets
- Officially taxed income from real estate and stock exchange transactions
- Spreading of assets for risk diversification as a plausible justification
- Turkey as a destination
- Cash withdrawal in Turkey

- Handover to terrorists near the border with Syria
- Hardly detectable

Hawala transfer:

- Suitable for cash
- Suitable for incriminated assets
- Settlement of sums of money among Muslims
- Hawala shops around the world
- Little to no identification requirements
- Hand over the cash in a hawala shop in Munich
- Pick up possible within a few minutes from a hawala shop in Turkey

Personal transfer:

- Suitable for cash
- Balkan route
- Works in both directions
- Terrorist financiers travel themselves or send messengers

Electronic currencies:

- Obvious if incriminated assets already exist in electronic currencies
- Use of Bitcoin
- Method rather rare
- Preference for personal transfer and remittances through banks and hawala

Interviewee 8:

Revenue sources:

General statements:

- Legal sources of income
- Illegal sources of income
  - Economic crime (important)
  - Organized crime (important)
  - Petty crime

Sales tax fraud:

- Reverse charge procedure
- Increased attention from tax authorities
- Switching to other sectors, e.g. branded clothing
- Textiles well suited for international business

Trade in CO_2 emission allowances:

- Companies in different countries
- Limited traceability
- Reverse charge procedure
- Still in use in practice, although declining

Trade in raw materials:

- Capture oil refineries
- Oil production
- Oil processing
- Potential buyers under political pressure

Trafficking in narcotics:

- Controlled areas may be suitable for cultivation of narcotics
- Export to Europe
- Smuggling routes
- Use of aircraft, trucks and ships that deliver relief supplies and otherwise return unloaded
- Refugees assured of family support in case of imprisonment

Trafficking in organs:

- People in Europe who need a donor organ
- Help via personal networks
- Targeted search for donors
- Organ harvesting in Turkey or thc Balkans
- Use of refugee routes
- Transplantation in the donor country or exportation

Human trafficking:

- Labour
- Refugees
- Smuggling of refugees from controlled areas to Europe

Pimping:

- Refugees provide protection for prostitutes
- Part of the prostitutes' income is for protection
- Use of force if protection is not desired

Protection racket:

- Recruitment of refugees
- Business people are offered protection
- Monetary compensation for protection
- Favours easily manipulated, poorly integrated refugees to facilitate radicalization

Extortionist kidnapping:

- Abduction of persons in terrorist-controlled areas
- High ransom demands

Theft:

- Recruitment of young refugees

Online auction scams:

- Several possible approaches
- Auction of non-existent goods
- Direct bank transfers

Insurance fraud:

- Damage to vehicles
- Theft of luxury goods
- No excessive damage to avoid attracting attention from insurance companies

Establishment of car rental companies:

- Not specified

Real estate deals:

- Very popular
- Legal transactions
- Taxation of income

Stock market transactions:

- Very popular
- Difficult to prove terrorism financing unless direct transfers to terrorist groups are made

Wealth transfer:

General statements:

- Differentiation between legal and illegal sources of revenue
- Differentiation between cash and electronic balances

Transfers to Turkey:

- Least challenging legal assets
- Officially taxed income from real estate and stock exchange transactions

Hawala transfer:

- Suitable for cash
- Suitable for incriminated assets
- Settlement of sums of money among Muslims

Personal transfer:

- Suitable for cash
- Balkan route

Electronic currencies:

- Obvious if incriminated assets already exist in electronic currencies
- Use of Bitcoin

Interviewee 9:

Revenue sources:

General statements:

- Legal sources of income
- Illegal sources of income
  - Economic crime (important)
  - Organized crime (important)
  - Petty crime

Sales tax fraud:

- Export sales tax free
- Company has sales tax refunded
- Increased attention from tax authorities
- Switching to other sectors, e.g. branded clothing
- Textiles well suited for international business

Trade in CO_2 emission allowances:

- Companies in different countries
- Limited traceability
- Well-known problem

Trade in raw materials:

- Capture oil refineries
- Oil production
- Oil processing
- Potential buyers under political pressure

Trafficking in narcotics:

- Important role
- Several possible approaches
- Combinations are often used
- Recruitment of refugees from Arab countries
- If applicable, entire proceeds of sale remain for terrorism financing
- Consideration of religion in recruitment

- Creation of loyalty to compatriots
- Involve people with financial problems
- Involve persons without alternative gainful employment

Trafficking in organs:

- Use of force
- Organ harvesting in Turkey or the Balkans
- Use of refugee routes
- Transplantation in the donor country or exportation

Human trafficking:

- Earnings from facilitating their escape and their work

Pimping:

- Not specified

Protection racket:

- Refugees suitable as perpetrators with little to lose
- Refugees accept low profit sharing
- Favours easily manipulated, poorly integrated refugees to facilitate radicalization

Extortionist kidnapping:

- Abduction of persons in terrorist-controlled areas
- Small source of income

Theft:

- Easy to inspire refugees
- Radicalization of refugees
- If applicable, no profit sharing for refugees
- Alternatively, small profit shares

Online auction scams:

- Several possible approaches
- Auction of non-existent goods

- Hacking the accounts of existing users
- Transmission of false account data in the name of real sellers

Insurance fraud:

- Deliberately causing damage

Establishment of car rental companies:

- Leasing of vehicles from renowned manufacturers
- Moving the vehicles abroad

Real estate deals:

- Popular
- Legal transactions
- Taxation of income
- Use of a sub-account for terrorism financing

Stock market transactions:

- Very popular
- Not illegal

Wealth transfer:

General statements:

- Differentiation between legal and illegal sources of revenue
- Differentiation between cash and electronic balances

Transfers to Turkey:

- Least challenging legal assets
- Officially taxed income from real estate and stock exchange transactions
- Spreading of assets for risk diversification as a plausible justification

Hawala transfer:

- Suitable for cash
- Little to no identification requirements
- Hand over the cash in a hawala shop in Berlin
- Pick up possible within a few minutes from a hawala shop in Syria

Personal transfer:

- Suitable for cash
- Terrorist financiers travel themselves or send messengers

Electronic currencies:

- Obvious if incriminated assets already exist in electronic currencies
- Preference for personal transfer and remittances through banks and hawala

<u>Interviewee 10:</u>

<u>Revenue sources:</u>

General statements:

- Legal sources of income
- Illegal sources of income
  - Economic crime (important)
  - Organized crime (important)
  - Petty crime

Sales tax fraud:

- Carousel scam very popular
- Increased attention from tax authorities
- Appointing young jihadists as CEOs
- Inconspicuous environment distracts from intention to leave the country
- Persons not tangible
- Protection of the backers
- No profit sharing

Trade in CO_2 emission allowances:

- Loses importance
- Same procedure as carousel fraud but with CO_2 emission certificates
- Still in use in practice, although declining

Trade in raw materials:

- Export logistically difficult
- Potential buyers under political pressure

Trafficking in narcotics:

- Retail sales
- Small quantities
- Large cities
- Use of auxiliaries
- Recruitment of refugees from Arab countries
- If applicable, entire proceeds of sale remain for terrorism financing
- Involve persons without alternative gainful employment
- Refugees assured of family support in case of imprisonment

Trafficking in organs:

- People in Europe who need a donor organ
- Help via personal networks
- Targeted search for donors

Human trafficking:

- Labour
- Refugees
- Smuggling of refugees from controlled areas to Europe
- Labour exploitation
- Extremely low wages

Pimping:

- Refugees provide protection for prostitutes
- Part of the prostitutes' income is for protection
- Use of force if protection is not desired

Protection racket:

- Business people are offered protection
- Monetary compensation for protection

Extortionist kidnapping:

- Abduction of persons in terrorist-controlled areas

Theft:

- Recruitment of young refugees

Online auction scams:

- Auction of non-existent goods

Insurance fraud:

- Cash payments from insurance
- Damage to vehicles

Establishment of car rental companies:

- Leasing of vehicles from renowned manufacturers
- Hiring out of vehicles to straw men
- Damage report

Real estate deals:

- Very popular
- Proof of financing of terrorism only possible if use of funds is documented

Stock market transactions:

- Difficult to prove terrorism financing unless direct transfers to terrorist groups are made

Wealth transfer:

General statements:

- Differentiation between legal and illegal sources of revenue
- Differentiation between cash and electronic balances

Transfers to Turkey:

- Least challenging legal assets
- Spreading of assets for risk diversification as a plausible justification

Hawala transfer:

- Suitable for cash
- Worldwide network

Personal transfer:

- Suitable for cash
- Terrorist financiers travel themselves or send messengers

Electronic currencies:

- Obvious if incriminated assets already exist in electronic currencies
- Use of various cryptocurrencies
- Method rather rare
- Preference for personal transfer and remittances through banks and hawala

Interviewee 11:

Revenue sources:

General statements:

- Legal sources of income
- Illegal sources of income
  - Economic crime (important)
  - Organized crime (important)
  - Petty crime

Sales tax fraud:

- Not specified

Trade in CO_2 emission allowances:

- Not specified

Trade in raw materials:

- Oil production
- Oil processing

Trafficking in narcotics:

- Important role
- Controlled areas may be suitable for cultivation of narcotics
- Export to Europe
- Smuggling routes
- Retail sales
- Small quantities
- Large cities
- Use of auxiliaries
- Recruitment of refugees from Arab countries
- If applicable, entire proceeds of sale remain for terrorism financing

Trafficking in organs:

- People in Europe who need a donor organ
- Help via personal networks
- Organ harvesting in Turkey or the Balkans

- Use of refugee routes
- Transplantation in the donor country or exportation

Human trafficking:

- Labour
- Refugees
- Earnings from facilitating their escape and their work
- Possible conflicts of interest with persons remaining in controlled areas (customs duties, levies, etc.)

Pimping:

- Refugees provide protection for prostitutes
- Part of the prostitutes' income is for protection
- Use of force if protection is not desired

Protection racket:

- Monetary compensation for protection
- Friendly reminders
- Massive intimidation
- Favours easily manipulated, poorly integrated refugees to facilitate radicalization

Extortionist kidnapping:

- Abduction of persons in terrorist-controlled areas
- Significant source of income

Theft:

- Recruitment of young refugees
- Easy to inspire refugees

Online auction scams:

- Several possible approaches
- Auction of non-existent goods

Insurance fraud:

- Deliberately causing damage
- Cash payments from insurance

Establishment of car rental companies:

- Leasing of vehicles from renowned manufacturers
- Subsequent reporting of the theft to the authorities and insurance company

Real estate deals:

- Very popular
- Proof of financing of terrorism only possible if use of funds is documented

Stock market transactions:

- Very popular
- Difficult to prove terrorism financing unless direct transfers to terrorist groups are made

Wealth transfer:

General statements:

- Differentiation between legal and illegal sources of revenue
- Differentiation between cash and electronic balances

Transfers to Turkey:

- Least challenging legal assets
- Officially taxed income from real estate and stock exchange transactions
- Hardly detectable

Hawala transfer:

- Suitable for cash
- Hand over the cash in a hawala shop in Leipzig
- Pick up possible within a few minutes from a hawala shop in Afghanistan

Personal transfer:

- Terrorist financiers travel themselves or send messengers

Electronic currencies:

- Use of Bitcoin
- Method rather rare
- Preference for personal transfer and remittances through banks and hawala

<u>Interviewee 12:</u>

<u>Revenue sources:</u>

General statements:

- Legal sources of income
- Illegal sources of income
  - Economic crime (important)
  - Organized crime (important)
  - Petty crime

Sales tax fraud:

- Not specified

Trade in CO_2 emission allowances:

- Not specified

Trade in raw materials:

- Export logistically difficult
- Potential buyers under political pressure

Trafficking in narcotics:

- Important role
- Export to Europe
- Smuggling routes
- Small quantities
- Large cities
- Consideration of religion in recruitment
- Creation of loyalty to compatriots
- Involves people with financial problems
- Involves people without alternative gainful employment

Trafficking in organs:

- People in Europe who need a donor organ
- Use of force
- Organ harvesting in Turkey or the Balkans
- Use of refugee routes
- Transplantation in the donor country or exportation

Human trafficking:

- Labour
- Refugees
- Smuggling of refugees from controlled areas to Europe
- Labour exploitation

Pimping:

- In development
- Part of the prostitutes' income is for protection
- Use of force if protection is not desired

Protection racket:

- Business people are offered protection
- Favours easily manipulated, poorly integrated refugees to facilitate radicalization

Extortionist kidnapping:

- Abduction of persons in terrorist-controlled areas
- Abduction of persons in Europe

Theft:

- Recruitment of young refugees
- Disposal of stolen goods on the black market

Online auction scams:

- Several possible approaches
- Auction of non-existent goods
- Transfer of funds via money transfer systems
- Direct bank transfers
- Avoidance of fiduciary systems
- No delivery of the goods

Insurance fraud:

- Theft of luxury goods
- No excessive damage to avoid attracting attention from insurance companies

Establishment of car rental companies:

- Leasing of vehicles from renowned manufacturers
- Moving the vehicles abroad

Real estate deals:

- Very popular
- Proof of financing of terrorism only possible if use of funds is documented

Stock market transactions:

- Very popular
- Not illegal

Wealth transfer:

General statements:

- Differentiation between legal and illegal sources of revenue
- Differentiation between cash and electronic balances

Transfers to Turkey:

- Cash withdrawal in Turkey
- Handover to terrorists near the border with Syria
- Hardly detectable

Hawala transfer:

- Little to no identification requirements
- Hand over the cash in a hawala shop in Cologne
- Pick up possible within a few minutes from a hawala shop in Iraq

Personal transfer:

- Suitable for cash
- Terrorist financiers travel themselves or send messengers

Electronic currencies:

- Obvious if incriminated assets already exist in electronic currencies
- Preference for personal transfer and remittances through banks and hawala

Interviewee 13:

Revenue sources:

General statements:

- Legal sources of income
- Illegal sources of income
  - Economic crime (important)
  - Organized crime (important)
  - Petty crime

Sales tax fraud:

- Reverse charge procedure
- Increased attention from tax authorities

Trade in CO_2 emission allowances:

- Loses importance
- Same procedure as carousel fraud but with CO_2 emission certificates
- Reverse charge procedure

Trade in raw materials:

- Declining due to air raids

Trafficking in narcotics:

- Not specified

Trafficking in organs:

- Not specified

Human trafficking:

- Smuggling of refugees from controlled areas to Europe
- Labour exploitation

Pimping:

- Not specified

Protection racket:

- Recruitment of refugees
- Business people are offered protection
- Monetary compensation for protection

Extortionist kidnapping:

- Abduction of persons in terrorist-controlled areas
- No involvement of law enforcement authorities

Theft:

- Recruitment of young refugees
- Easy to inspire refugees

Online auction scams:

- Several possible approaches
- Auction of non-existent goods

Insurance fraud:

- Deliberately causing damage
- Cash payments from insurance

Establishment of car rental companies:

- Insurance on the vehicles
- Hiring out of vehicles to straw men
- Moving the vehicles abroad
- Subsequent reporting of the theft to the authorities and insurance company

Real estate deals:

- Very popular
- Proof of financing of terrorism only possible if use of funds is documented

Stock market transactions:

- Very popular
- Difficult to prove terrorism financing unless direct transfers to terrorist groups are made

<u>Wealth transfer:</u>

General statements:

- Differentiation between legal and illegal sources of revenue
- Differentiation between cash and electronic balances

Transfers to Turkey:

- Least challenging legal assets
- Officially taxed income from real estate and stock exchange transactions
- Spreading of assets for risk diversification as a plausible justification

Hawala transfer:

- Hand over the cash in a hawala shop in Dresden
- Pick up possible within a few minutes from a hawala shop in Istanbul

Personal transfer:

- Suitable for cash
- Terrorist financiers travel themselves or send messengers

Electronic currencies:

- Obvious if incriminated assets already exist in electronic currencies
- Preference for personal transfer and remittances through banks and hawala

Interviewee 14:

Revenue sources:

General statements:

- Legal sources of income
- Illegal sources of income
    - Economic crime (important)
    - Organized crime (important)
    - Petty crime

Sales tax fraud:

- Not specified

Trade in CO_2 emission allowances:

- Not specified

Trade in raw materials:

- Capture oil refineries
- Oil production

Trafficking in narcotics:

- Important role
- Controlled areas may be suitable for cultivation of narcotics
- Export to Europe

Trafficking in organs:

- Organ harvesting in Turkey or the Balkans
- Transplantation in the donor country or exportation

Human trafficking:

- Refugees
- Possible conflicts of interest with persons remaining in controlled areas (customs duties, levies, etc.)

Pimping:

- Not specified

Protection racket:

- Business people are offered protection
- Refugees suitable as perpetrators with little to lose

Extortionist kidnapping:

- Abduction of persons in terrorist-controlled areas

Theft:

- Recruitment of young refugees
- Easy to inspire refugees

Online auction scams:

- Several possible approaches
- Transmission of false account data in the name of real sellers

Insurance fraud:

- Deliberately causing damage

Establishment of car rental companies:

- Leasing of vehicles from renowned manufacturers

Real estate deals:

- Very popular

Stock market transactions:

- Very popular
- Not illegal

Wealth transfer:

General statements:

- Differentiation between legal and illegal sources of revenue
- Differentiation between cash and electronic balances

Transfers to Turkey:

- Least challenging legal assets
- Officially taxed income from real estate and stock exchange transactions
- Spreading of assets for risk diversification as a plausible justification

Hawala transfer:

- Suitable for cash
- Suitable for incriminated assets
- Settlement of sums of money among Muslims
- Hawala shops exists around the world
- Little to no identification requirements

Personal transfer:

- Suitable for cash
- Refugee routes
- Works in both directions
- Terrorist financiers travel themselves or send messengers

Electronic currencies:

- Obvious if incriminated assets already exist in electronic currencies
- Use of Bitcoin
- Method rather rare
- Preference for personal transfer and remittances through banks and hawala

Interviewee 15:

Revenue sources:

General statements:

- Legal sources of income
- Illegal sources of income
  - Economic crime (important)
  - Organized crime (important)
  - Petty crime

Sales tax fraud:

- Carousel scam very popular
- Company disappears before execution
- Goods that are easy to transport
- Textiles well suited for international business
- Appointing young jihadists as CEOs
- Inconspicuous environment distracts from intention to leave the country
- Persons not tangible
- Protection of the backers
- No profit sharing

Trade in CO_2 emission allowances:

- Fast transfer possible
- Companies in different countries
- Limited traceability
- Well-known problem
- Reverse charge procedure
- Still in use in practice, although declining

Trade in raw materials:

- Capture oil refineries
- Oil production
- Declining due to air raids

Trafficking in narcotics:

- Recruitment of refugees from Arab countries
- If applicable, entire proceeds of sale remain for terrorism financing

Trafficking in organs:

- People in Europe who need a donor organ
- Help via personal networks
- Organ harvesting in Turkey or the Balkans
- Use of refugee routes
- Transplantation in the donor country or exportation

Human trafficking:

- Labour
- Refugees

Pimping:

- Prostitution contradicts beliefs of terrorist financiers
- Source of income nevertheless desired

Protection racket:

- Recruitment of refugees

Extortionist kidnapping:

- Low ransom demands
- No involvement of law enforcement authorities
- Small source of income

Theft:

- Refugees do not have legal sources of income
- Easy to inspire refugees
- Alternatively, small profit shares

Online auction scams:

- Hacking the accounts of existing users
- Transmission of false account data in the name of real sellers

Insurance fraud:

- Deliberately causing damage
- Cash payments from insurance

- Damage to vehicles
- Theft of luxury goods

Establishment of car rental companies:

- Leasing of vehicles from renowned manufacturers
- Moving the vehicles abroad

Real estate deals:

- Very popular
- Funds not incriminated
- Proof of financing of terrorism only possible if use of funds is documented

Stock market transactions:

- Very popular
- Not illegal
- Difficult to prove terrorism financing unless direct transfers to terrorist groups are made

Wealth transfer:

General statements:

- Differentiation between legal and illegal sources of revenue
- Differentiation between cash and electronic balances

Transfers to Turkey:

- Least challenging legal assets
- Officially taxed income from real estate and stock exchange transactions
- Cash withdrawal in Turkey
- Handover to terrorists near the border with Syria
- Hardly detectable

Hawala transfer:

- Suitable for cash
- Hand over the cash in a hawala shop in Vienna
- Pick up possible within a few minutes from a hawala shop in Syria

Personal transfer:

- Suitable for cash
- Balkan route
- Works in both directions
- Terrorist financiers travel themselves or send messengers

Electronic currencies:

- Obvious if incriminated assets already exist in electronic currencies
- Use of Bitcoin
- Method rather rare
- Preference for personal transfer and remittances through banks and hawala

Appendix 2: Generalizations of the formal interviews

(Original statement not translated)

Interview partners	Original Statement	Generalization
Interviewee 1	Ich denke mal, das EINE/ EIN wichtiger Bereich ist eigentlich der Austausch zwischen UNTERSCHIEDLICHEN Beteiligten. Ähm das sind vor allem die Ermittlungsbehörden, natürlich, die bestimmte KENNTNISSE haben, Kenntnisse, die man uns auch nicht zur Verfügung stellt, oder BEDINGT nur zur Verfügung stellt.	Exchange between investigative authorities and private parties is important
Interviewee 1	Also Kommunikation zwischen den Beteiligten verbessern, glaube ich, das ist ein wichtiges Ziel. Gerade im Vorfeld.	Improve communication between stakeholders
Interviewee 1	Ich meine, das Gute ist ja auch immer, wenn ich/ haben wir vorher auch gefragt/ äh GESAGT, ähm als Geldwäscher würde ich mir genau solche Literatur holen. Mensch, was empfiehlt denn so der Fachmann? (lacht) Ich meine, wie wäscht man am besten Geld? (holt Luft) Da ist SO viel verfügbar mittlerweile im Internet, dass man da ähm (.) ja auch als Krimineller, äh und die sind da oft besser ausgestattet als die Polizei von mir aus mit ihren auch Topleuten, die sie einkaufen/ einkaufen können.	Perpetrators have access to specialist literature

Interview partners	Original Statement	Generalization
Interviewee 1	Ich meine, wir SIND ja alle jetzt, die Finanzdienstleister aber auch die Kreditinstitute, wir sind ja gehalten ähm Analysen durchzuführen, Monitoring durchzuführen in den äh/ in den Finanzströmen, die wir sehen, in den Transaktionen, die wir sehen.	Transactional analysis
Interviewee 1	Äh üblicherweise, so ist es auch bei UNS im Hause, ähm (.) entwickeln wir Typologien, wir haben beispielsweise hier/ DAS, glaube ich, (unv.) auch eines der/ der führenden Institute ähm, die jetzt insbesondere in den USA dann Zusammenarbeit mit den Behörden, aber auch hier in Europa, und hier auch konkret in Deutschland, (holt Luft) äh Typologien entwickelt haben, zum Beispiel äh Foreign Terrorist Fighters, das/ äh um das Verhalten im finanziellen Bereich zu erkennen.	Typologies for the detection of foreign terrorist fighters
Interviewee 1	Ähm wenn Sie dann sich in die Nähe der syrischen Grenze bewegen, dann wissen wir, dass da AUCH viele dieser Personen sich aufhalten, die ein bestimmtes Profil haben und eine bestimmte Art des Verhaltens, was Finanztransfers anbetrifft, und auch, wenn sie dann nach Syrien gehen, (holt Luft) oder wo immer die sich auch hinbewegen, äh da haben Sie bestimmte Charakteristika, ähm (.) die man auch dann über Analysen erkennen kann.	Proximity to Syria increases risk of detection

Interview partners	Original Statement	Generalization
Interviewee 1	Ähm (.) aber DA ist halt auch die/ die, ich sage mal, Herausforderung hier äh eine zielführende und auch risikoorientierte natürlich (holt Luft) äh (.) Klassifizierung vorzunehmen, und auch dann die Finanzströme entsprechend zu analysieren.	Transactional analysis
Interviewee 1	Ähm wenn ich das mal ganz/ ganz ALLGEMEIN formuliere, ähm dann wissen wir, dass es häufig sich um/ um junge MÄNNER handelt, die zwischen 18 und 30 Jahre alt beispielsweise sind, (holt Luft) wir sehen auch eine Zunahme an FRAUEN, die das unterstützen, und auch AKTIV äh werden. Aber da hätten wir schon mal etwas, sozusagen, JA, es sind oft junge Männer, die ähm (..) eine bestimmte Historie auch haben. Äh auch möglicherweise was ihre ähm/ also NICHT-Deutsche, die aber einen deutschen Ausweis haben, aber woanders GEBOREN sind möglicherweise/ ähm (..) die äh sich in einer bestimmten Art und Weise VERHALTEN.	Avoid certain profiles (male, between 18 and 30, etc.)
Interviewee 1	Wenn sie also jetzt in die/ beispielsweise in die/ äh nach Syrien REISEN wollen, dann sehen wir, dass die ein bestimmtes Verhalten haben, WIE sie sich bewegen, wo sie Geld in EMPFANG nehmen oder auch Geld schicken.	Certain behaviours increase risk of detection

Interview partners	Original Statement	Generalization
Interviewee 1	Kleinstbetriebe, die sie nutzen, ähm (.) wir sehen Sympathisanten auch mit bestimmten Charakteristika, die dann ähm (…) äh beispielsweise (lacht auf) auch mal in einer Art (.) Pressearbeit aktiv sind, mit Pressearbeit meine ich jetzt EHER so auch Facebook oder andere Internet/ (holt Luft) soziale Netzwerke, also Internetplattformen, dann nutzen, wo Sie auch mit bestimmten Methoden das erkennen können oder auch recherchieren können.	Facebook search
interviewee 1	Sie sehen auch bestimmte/ bestimmte Netzwerke, wie dann Transaktionen sich zwischen bestimmten ähm/ (..) sagen wir mal, äh vielleicht ein ganz konkretes Kriterium oder ETWAS konkreter, wäre, dass EINE Person (unv.) Netzwerk äh WIEDER hat von vielen anderen Personen aus verschiedenen europäischen Ländern, durchaus auch äh immer wieder kleinere Betriebe zugeschickt. Und sie sind dann wie so eine Art Spinne in einem Netzwerk auch erkennbar.	Networks between certain persons
Interviewee 1	Und Sie überschreiten einen bestimmten Betrag, dann lassen wir die Auszahlung nicht mehr zu, sondern schicken das Geld zurück, und reagieren dann WEITER.	Exceeding certain amounts

Interview partners	Original Statement	Generalization
Interviewee 1	Eine einzelne/ nur EINE Transaktion sticht erst mal gar nicht ins AUGE, 50 Euro, 100 Dollar, was auch immer, (holt Luft) man ist dann auf einmal überrascht, wenn man grosse Netzwerke erkennt, wo wirklich HUNDERTE von Menschen ähm untereinander vernetzt sind und Gelder kreuz und quer schicken, die dann ein Indikator sein können für diese terroristischen Aktivitäten.	Networks between certain persons
Interviewee 1	Und wenn Sie noch WEITER gehen, ich meine, was WIR auch zum Beispiel machen, dass wir wirklich über bestimmte NAMEN analysieren, gucken, ob wir etwas GLAUBEN erkannt zu haben, gehen wir in Facebook. Und da sind wir oft überrascht, was wir da in Facebook sehen können, auch an (holt Luft) ähm ja an Meinungsäusserungen.	Facebook search
Interviewee 1	Gerade bei der Verrechnung von Spitzen können Sie das in bestimmten Banken wahrscheinlich erkennen, wenn/ über bestimmte Methoden.	Clearing via banks risky

Interview partners	Original Statement	Generalization
Interviewee 1	Das ist korrekt. Die sind zwar ähm/ ich meine, wenn man es ganz DRASTISCH sieht, dann ist in Deutschland zumindestens unterliegen sie AUCH dem Geldwäschebekä mpfungsgesetz, und müssten EIGENTLICH auch, wenn sie Verdachtsfälle haben, die MELDEN. (holt Luft) Werden Sie nur nicht sehen. Das macht kein Mensch äh in dieser Branche, weil sie halt nicht ähm (holt Luft) SO überwacht werden wie jetzt die Kreditinstitute durch eine/ durch eine Aufsichtsbehörde. Es gibt halt die Gewerbeaufsichtsämter, aber die gucken da nicht in SOLCHE Bereiche rein.	Lack of supervision
Interviewee 1	Aber Stichwort Hawala, ähm das würden Sie erkennen können, theoretisch nachher über die Verrechnung von Spitzen unter Umständen, aber es ist extrem SCHWIERIG.	Clearing via banks risky
Interviewee 1	Das ist für uns auch eines der KONKRETEN Kriterien, die wir entwickelt haben, wenn sich jemand ganz/ wie sie sich jetzt in VERSCHIEDENEN Ländern bewegen und immer wieder äh Gelder in Empfang nehmen, wenn es auch Kleinstbeträge sind.	Movement profiles

Interview partners	Original Statement	Generalization
Interviewee 1	Die befinden sich sozusagen auf dem Weg nach Syrien, und sie gehen vielleicht nach einem HALBEN Jahr wieder zurück. Also so etwas, also jetzt äh aus welchen Gründen auch IMMER, ähm (holt Luft) äh kommen zurück nach Deutschland. Das sind Verhaltensweisen, die wir sehen. Und da gibt es auch bestimmte Kriterien, die man/ die WIR jetzt entwickelt haben, die finden Sie sicherlich auch woanders, bei anderen Häusern, äh die dann zu einer Auffälligkeit führen, und die dann konkret durch Mitarbeiter bei uns bearbeitet wird, der dann (.) sich diesen Vorfall anschaut und äh recherchiert und dann WEITERE (holt Luft) Möglichkeiten nutzt.	Movement profiles
Interviewee 1	Da gibt es VIELE Methoden, (holt Luft), wie man Dinge erkennen kann durch Echtzeitkriterien, durch nachgelagerte Kriterien.	Real-time criteria and ex post analyses

Interview partners	Original Statement	Generalization
Interviewee 1	Das wäre natürlich für Finanzdienstleister und auch für Banken interessant, wenn man diese Liste bekommen könnte, und könnte dann auch GEZIELTER recherchieren ähm und auch dann im Austausch äh die Informationen natürlich dann den Behörden zur Verfügung stellen. Und das sind natürlich Personen auch, die mögen noch nicht äh den/ im Stadium eines/ eines TERRORISTEN sein, und vielleicht irgendwo im Vorstadium irgendwo im WEITESTEN Sinne damit zusammenhängt, ähm vielleicht auch nicht, vielleicht auch UNSCHULDIG reingeraten sind.	Exchange of information (lists of dangerous persons) between authorities and banks
Interviewee 1	Ähm natürlich haben Sie immer das Problem, auch wenn Sie solche Listen an PRIVATE Institute geben, dass die dann nicht mehr so richtig unter Kontrolle sind und dann vielleicht in Hände geraten, wo sie nicht hin sollen. (holt Luft) Ähm aber das wäre, glaube ich, gerade im Bereich der Kommunikation zwischen Behörde, wie gesagt: den Ermittlern, und der Privatindustrie, jetzt in diesem Fall dann halt Finanzdienstleister oder auch BANKEN.	Lack of control over information exchanged

Interview partners	Original Statement	Generalization
Interviewee 1	Das geschieht teilweise auch/ also wir arbeiten da auch beispielsweise konkret mit den Behörden ZUSAMMEN, also ich jetzt auch als Person zum Beispiel mit dem Bundeskriminalamt oder mit ähm durchaus auch Verfassungsschutz, wo man dann drüber nachdenkt, und äh das auch relativ offenlegt: WIE verhält sich denn einer, ein Sympathisant, der IS unterstützt, oder wie verhält sich auch tatsächlich ein Foreign Terrorist Fighter?	Exchange of information (typologies) between public authorities and financial service providers
Interviewee 1	Aber da gibt es VIELE Methoden, und ähm (holt Luft) WICHTIG ist da immer wieder auch dann, denke ich auch, die/ wirklich der AUSTAUSCH auch mit den Behörden. Ähm (.) nicht nur Polizeibehörden, sondern Aufsichtsbehörden oder (holt Luft) äh Institute, Gruppierungen, die es da gibt, bis hin zu den Kollegen ähm von anderen Instituten.	Exchange between different authorities (police, supervision) and private persons
Interviewee 1	Durch die enge Zusammenarbeit auch mit den Behörden.	Close co-operation
Interviewee 1	Das ist ja üblich. Also das ist nicht nur/ nicht nur im Bereich des Terrorismus, sondern ganz andere ähm kriminelle Aktivitäten, wie Menschenhandel, Menschenschmuggel, oder DROGEN-Handel, dann werden in der REGEL Personen vorgeschoben. Das ist so ein Verhalten, das durchaus BEKANNT ist, und das finden Sie in der Szene genauso.	Use of straw men

Interview partners	Original Statement	Generalization
Interviewee 1	/Wenn// man sich also jetzt in der TÜRKEI, sagen wir mal, in die Türkei GELD schicken/ sich schicken, zu jemandem in die Türkei, und ähm Sie überschreiten bestimmte BETRÄGE, so können wir erst mal vom GRUNDSATZ her überall in der Türkei das Geld abheben, egal, wo Sie sind. Das geht immer so. Es geht von EINEM Land in ein anderes Land, und es ist nicht BEGRENZT auf eine Stadt oder Region.	Send money to Turkey
Interviewee 1	Wenn wir aber sehen, dass der Empfänger in der Türkei das Geld nicht in Istanbul abhebt, sondern, sagen wir mal, in einer der Grenzstädte.	Avoid border towns

Interview partners	Original Statement	Generalization
Interviewee 1	Ja, das sehen wir/ ich meine, das sehen Sie auch, wir haben auch Beispiele hier, wo Sie gerade sagten, ein VATER, äh der sich auch in dieser Alters- äh -gruppe bewegte, der seinem SOHN Geld geschickt hat, der sich in Syrien befand und auch im KAMPF mitgewirkt hat. (holt Luft) Da habe ich gesagt, der Sohn hatte einfach/ wollte sich einfach mal eine COLA kaufen, hatte kein Geld dafür. Und ähm dem fehlten bestimmte westliche Annehmlichkeiten. Und über diesen/ ja, aufgrund DIESER Situation äh, Geld wurde über UNS transferiert, wir haben das der Polizei gemeldet, die Polizei hat uns hinterher noch mal informiert, dass es wirklich so platt war, dass der/ der JUNGE da ähm bestimmte BEDÜRFNISSE hatte äh und in der TAT auch Cola trinken wollte und dafür GELD brauchte.	Transfer funds to family members
Interviewee 1	Da sind wir beim Thema Strohmann. (holt Luft) Ähm (.) das ist völlig üblich, dass sie da ähm/ dass Dritte vorgeschoben werden. Das ist wie in ALLEN kriminellen Bereichen, also beim Drogenhandel auch, beim Geldwaschen dort/.	Marshal

Interview partners	Original Statement	Generalization
Interviewee 1	Aber ähm natürlich wird ein Mitarbeiter auch, wenn da ein offizieller Stempel drauf ist einer/ einer/ ja, einer Behörde, äh dem MEHR Glauben schenken, als wenn das so ein Wischiwaschipapier ist. Und dann wird man auch oft nicht weiter nachfassen.	Use public documents
Interviewee 1	Muss man nur aufpassen, äh ich hatte auch einen Kollegen der Polizei, der hat mal gesagt, was DIE ganz gern machen (unv.) die gingen gelegentlich zu äh bestimmten Auktionen, die sind dann nicht als Polizisten erkennbar, und BEOBACHTEN, (.) ähm wer da so sitzt, und was die so machen	Risks of discovery in the case of trade in cultural goods at auctions
Interviewee 2	Aber es kommt auch immer darauf an, wie das dokumentiert ist. Und äh, was/ was Zahlungszweck ist, und äh, wie gut äh, man diese überweisende und diese empfangende Stelle auch kennt dann, oder.	Payment purpose and documentation influence detection risk
Interviewee 2	Überweisungen, und äh, und irgendein Zahlungsempfänger, und irgendein Grund. Und dann halt irgendwie etwas sagen, was man auch, äh, sagen wir, belegen könnte, oder.	Choose a documentable reason for payment
Interviewee 2	Irgendwelche Aufträge, oder Rechnungen, oder sonstige Finanzierungsdokumente.	Create invoices, orders and financing documents

Interview partners	Original Statement	Generalization
Interviewee 2	Man wird höchstens mal, sagen wir, in der Finanzindustrie damit konfrontiert, wenn die darüber reden, welche (unv.,?) Attacken laufen, und dann halt eben Erpressungsgelder verlangt werden, die dann halt in diesen Fällen zumeist über die Bitcoins bezahlt werden müssen.	Payment of extortion money in Bitcoin
Interviewee 3	Bei Geldwäsche hat man ja meistens irgendwelche verdächtigen Transaktionen, die da äh auffallen und dann letztendlich die Bank dazu bringen, da 'ne Meldung zu machen. Bei der Terrorismusfinanzierung äh läuft das ja ein bissel anders, dass wir/ die Gelder äh kommen teilweise aus legalen Quellen, teilweise kleine Beträge, die dann zusammen auf 'nem grossen Konto zusammengeführt werden. Is also wirklich sehr, sehr schwierig, das zu erkennen.	Legal sources
Interviewee 3	Die Frage, wo ist das Geld hin, muss das Geld jetzt ins Ausland raus oder muss es ins Inland reinkommen. Das sind ja schon mal zwei verschiedene Ansatzpunkte, wo ich sagen muss, wie muss ich das Geld nach Deutschland bekommen, damit ichs hier verwenden kann für zum Beispiel Terroranschläge oder was muss ich umgekehrt machen.	Funds are transferred both domestically and abroad

Interview partners	Original Statement	Generalization
Interviewee 3	Auffälligkeiten festmachen, weil da etwa/ entweder ein grösserer Betrag abgeht oder aber ins Ausland verfügt wird, wo man sich vorstellen könnte, das könnte der Terrorismusfinanzierung dienen.	Transferring large amounts abroad increases the risk of detection
Interviewee 3	Nur, aber wenn der nach Syrien reisen würde, hätten wir schon jede Menge Verdachtsmomente, um den nur zu melden.	Travel to Syria is suspicious
Interviewee 3	Der/ // der zwar vertraulich, aber da is/ da is auch gewarnt/ da wird gewarnt, wie Terrorkämpfer, also die jetzt sich nach Syrien absetzen, um da kämpfen zu wollen bei der IS, ähm wie sie sich vorher verhalten. Da gibt's so Muster, die dann beschrieben sind, wo man als Bank auch merken könnte, hoppala, das könnte jetzt gefährlich werden.	Preparation of the trip to Syria is suspicious
Interviewee 3	Aber ansonsten hmhm ist es äusserst schwierig, das zu erkennen, weils, wie gesagt, oft kleinere Beträge sind, die weder beim Ein- noch beim Ausgang grossartig auffallen.	Smaller amounts do not attract attention
Interviewee 3	Is billiger als Swift und/ und vor allen Dingen is es (.) nicht von irgendeiner Aufsicht zu kontrollieren.	No supervision
Interviewee 3	Das sind meistens Familienangehörige.	Involve family members

Interview partners	Original Statement	Generalization
Interviewee 3	Ähm wenn jetzt, sage ich mal, 'ne Familie aus der Türkei oder hier arbeitet ein/ ein/ ein/ ein türkischer Mitbewohner und/ und weist dann seiner Familie jeden Monat 2.000 Euro nach Hause aus seinen Einkünften her, das is ja nicht verdächtig, das ist auch normal.	Transfers to family members
Interviewee 3	Muss natürlich immer der Empfängername, wenn man den googeln kann und das ist 'ne NGO, die man nachvollziehen kann, dann is das in Ordnung für uns. Wenn es, sage ich mal, an den Roten Halbmond geht, is es für mich auch in Ordnung. Wenn's aber hingegen irgendwo was ist, wo ich/ was ich wirklich nicht nachvollziehen könnte, dann würden wir eher Verdacht (.) // haben. //	Referrals to reputable NGOs
Interviewee 3	In (Mitsch) haben wir sehr viele Touristen aus Katar. Ähm dass einer von denen Geld A mitbringen würde auf der einen Seite oder dass er sich hierher Geld überweisen lässt. Das ist ganz legal.	Disguised as a tourist from Qatar for remittances from abroad
Interviewee 3	Da gibt's Geschäftsleute, die sind millionenschwer. Und wenn der von zu Hause Geld bekommt und dann anschliessend hier äh das Geld auf ein/ auf ein Konto sich überweisen lässt und dann abhebt und dann wieder verteilt, (.) das kann man gar nicht nachvollziehen. (.)	Cash withdrawals and subsequent cash distribution

Interview partners	Original Statement	Generalization
Interviewee 3	Da spielt das keine Rolle, wie er da/ (.) was wer für Geld hat. Das Geld ist ganz legal hergekommen von einer Bank aus Katar und wird dann gar nicht mehr näher geprüft oder Mittelherkunft wird da auch nicht mehr geprüft in dem Augenblick.	Legal source of funds
Interviewee 3	Ich überweise einfach das Geld, wenn ich hier jemand drüben finanzieren will, an eine Bank in Dubai zum Beispiel, die gilt ja nicht so als/ als/ als total gefährdet, und über Dubai werden die Gelder dann wiederum innerarabisch dann verteilt.	Remittances to Dubai and subsequent distribution in the Arab region
Interviewee 3	Spenden, verdeckte Spenden sind dann, die also offiziell als Spenden getätigt werden und dann aber inoffiziell doch dem Terrorkampf dienen sollen. Ähm aber die können genauso gut sich auch kriminell verhalten.	Disguised as donations
Interviewee 4	Wenn sie wie gesagt, ein, ein Mosaik aus einer christlichen Kirche rausreissen, das wäre wohl schlecht zu transportieren, das muss anders gehen, das muss dann über Container gehen oder ü/ über andere Transportmittel. Ich würde denken, wenn man Flüchtlingsrouten nimmt, dann muss man doch relativ kleinformatige Sachen mit sich führen, oder?	Trade in cultural goods

Interview partners	Original Statement	Generalization
Interviewee 4	Ähm ansonsten, das ist jetzt eher der ägyptische Bereich, Papyri sind natürlich auch sehr sehr fragil, äh, Sie finden Sie aber trotzdem auf eBay. Also (lacht) auch so was wird offensichtlich rausgeschmuggelt.	Trade in papyri
Interviewee 4	Ja, wenn Sie die zu Geld machen wollen, müssen Sie die ja eigentlich verkaufen. Und ähm, ja dafür müsste man dann wiederum, ähm, einmal jemanden finden, der das offiziell für Sie tun kann, ja gut, es sei denn, Sie haben da einen privaten, äh, Kunstliebhaber oder eben Antikenliebhaber an der Hand, dem das egal ist, ob die Sachen sozusagen einen ähm, einen gewissen Stammbaum an Papieren haben kann oder nicht.	Trade in art and antiques
Interviewee 4	Wenn das Ganze aber dann schon über den offiziellen Antikenhandel geht, dann muss so ein Gegenstand irgendwann mal eben Papiere kriegen.	Trade in antiques

Interview partners	Original Statement	Generalization
Interviewee 4	Fälschungen muss man auch immer mit relativ viel Aufwand betreiben, ansonsten fliegen die relativ flott auf und äh ich glaube beinahe, zur Terrorismusfinanzierung wäre es einfacher, man man äh äh plündert ein lokales Museum, äh eben, zum Beispiel ähm im ähm vorderen Orient und verhökert die Sachen dann, äh, weil man dann sozusagen, also ich ich, dem Entsprechenden, der das aufkaufen würde, auch gleich versichern kann, dass das Originale sind (lacht), weil weil eben sie sind ja eben aus einem musealen Zusammenhang.	Trade in antiques
Interviewee 4	Und ähm, wenn man dann einen Wissenschaftler dazu bewegen kann, sich dieses Stück anzugucken, eine Expertise auszustellen und äh dann gegebenenfalls das Ganze auch noch zu publizieren, dann erhöht sich der Wert dieses Stückes natürlich.	Illegal transfer of cultural property
Interviewee 4	Die Sachen müssen ausser Landes geschmuggelt werden und dann, ja, werden die verkauft.	Smuggling
Interviewee 4	Also das wäre dann sozusagen der Weg vom Quellenland über einen Freihafen, über ein ein neutrales Drittland bis hin auf den europäischen, oder ähm, ja, amerikanischen, bis hin zum asiatischen Markt.	Smuggling via free port to Europe, America or Asia
Interviewee 5	Ja ich habe, ich habe eben so das Gefühl, dass die legalen Einkünfte doch einen grösseren, also einen rechten Teil ausmachen, oder?	Legal sources

Interview partners	Original Statement	Generalization
Interviewee 5	Die hinkt wahrscheinlich immer ein halbes Jahr hinterher, oder?	Administrative assistance too slow
Interviewee 5	Ist halt immer sehr schwerfällig und träge und, ähm, ich denke, das muss weitgehend über persönliche, schon im Rahmen der Rechtsordnung natürlich, aber schon über persönliche Kontakte läuft das dann.	Administrative assistance too slow
Interviewee 5	Im Moment sehr schwierig und dann natürlich wieder eine Welt, die noch schnelllebiger ist als alles andere und dann muss man sofort handeln können und so.	Immediate action required
Interviewee 5	Das waren dann auffallend viele Personen involviert in diese Geldflüsse, alle mit arabischen Namen.	Numerous people with Arabic names are suspects
Interviewee 5	Das sind dann ja Rechnungen für nicht erbrachte Leistungen sozusagen. Das war ja dann, dass, so fiktive Rechnungen waren es, ja genau.	Bills for services not rendered
Interviewee 5	Ja klar. Und in unserem Fall war das/ ging das auf ein Bankkonto in Dubai.	Remittances to Dubai
Interviewee 5	Ja, man muss wahrscheinlich halt auch Strohmänner finden.	Marshal
Interviewee 5	Tarnen, Scheinunternehmungen gründen. So halt einfach.	Set up dummy companies
Interviewee 5	Plausibilität ist schon ganz wichtig, damit das nicht gleich so ins Auge sticht.	Ensure plausibility

Interview partners	Original Statement	Generalization
Interviewee 5	Ähm, da hat man, ähm, Telefonnummern gehackt. Und zwar, ähm, nicht benutzte Telefonnummern, also wenn man jetzt eine grosse Unternehmung nimmt. Ähm. Die haben ja so eine interne Telefonanlage mit ganz vielen internen Nummern. Und wenn man jetzt weiss, dass auf dieser Nummer, dass da gerade niemand arbeitet an diesem Pool, diese Nummer also nicht vergeben ist intern, und man es dann schafft, auf so eine Nummer sich einzuhacken, dann kann man über diese Nummer Anrufe generieren.	Misuse of telephony systems
Interviewee 5	Ja, also bei uns fängt es ja schon mit der gesetzlichen Grundlage an, dass wir das eigentlich gar nicht dürfen beziehungsweise uns so enge Grenzen gesetzt sind.	Weak legal basis
Interviewee 5	Ist auch sehr aufwendig, sehr kostenintensiv, personalintensiv. Ähm. Langjährige Ermittlungen sind das.	Cost and personnel intensive
Interviewee 5	Aber ich denke, das ist halt, bis man eine Person so aufgebaut hat, dass ihre/ dass ihr gesamtes Umfeld halt stimmt, ihre gesamte Legende, die man ihr geben kann, das ist schon sehr aufwändig.	Elaborate

Interview partners	Original Statement	Generalization
Interviewee 6	Das Ganze ist ursprünglich ausgerichtet gewesen unter der Prämisse, dass Terrorismusfinanzierung eigentlich eine Finanzierung von Terrororganisationen als grosse Organisation oder als grosses Netzwerk und vor allem als einheitliches Netzwerk und somit etwas, das fassbar ist, und im grossen Stil finanziert werden kann, das war, glaube ich, grundsätzlich der Hintergedanke.	Combating terrorism financing targeted at large organizations and networks
Interviewee 6	Wir sehen immer mehr die Lonesome-Wolf-Attacken oder eben völlig un/ also nicht unkoordiniert oder zumindest nicht mehr so zentrale Strukturen, wie das vielleicht ursprünglich bei der Al-Qaida war oder im Moment wieder bei ISIS auftritt.	Trend away from central structures to single perpetrators
Interviewee 6	Und man braucht jetzt nicht grossartige oder grossartige Mengen oder Beträge an Ressourcen. Um eben einen wesentlichen Schaden und einen Schockzustand in einer Gesellschaft hervorzurufen, braucht man eben nicht mehr so viele Ressourcen, mittlerweile. Da reichen niederschwellige Angriffe wie Messerattacken in Zügen oder sonst wie.	Small sums sufficient for terrorism

Interview partners	Original Statement	Generalization
Interviewee 6	Insofern, das wird wohl die grösste Problematik sein, denn es wird wohl kaum aus/ man kann kaum Einzelpersonen, vor allem, die noch nicht am Radar sind, möglicherweise erst zukünftig etwas vorhaben, vom kommerziellen, wirtschaftlichen Leben, so wie es in der Gesellschaft der Fall ist, ausschliessen können.	Single perpetrator difficult to identify
Interviewee 6	Wobei wahrscheinlich eingeschränkt, eingeschränkter wird die Möglichkeit jetzt wirklich schon im regulierten Finanzbereich sein, nämlich insbesondere über normale Bankkonten.	Normal bank accounts inconspicuous
Interviewee 6	Muss man sich eingestehen, gerade bei der Terrorismusfinanzierung muss man sich eingestehen, dass das nicht alles vollends erfassbar ist. Es ist vielleicht noch etwas, was man nicht gerne laut ausspricht, aber wenn man absolut, also wenn man nicht absolute Kontrolle und Überwachung haben möchte, und insbesondere, wenn es so etwas wie eine Cash Economy noch gibt. Da rede ich nicht einmal von Hawala, wo man nicht einmal Cash braucht, um das zu setteln, wird man ein gewisses Restrisiko und solche Situationen, wie Sie sie geschildert haben, so ein Restrisiko, das wird man nicht gänzlich ausschalten können.	100 per cent certainty is not possible

Interview partners	Original Statement	Generalization
Interviewee 6	Ja, ja, aber das ist die grundsätzliche Problematik, weil man hier versucht, einen Regelungsbereich zu erschaffen, der, um zu funktionieren, einen totalen, fast schon totalitären Eingriff in alle Lebensbereiche oder zumindest in alle relevanten kommerziellen Lebensbereiche bedeuten würde.	Interventions in all areas of life are necessary
Interviewee 6	Bei Terrorismusfinanzierung glaube ich einfach, dass es wesentlich schwieriger ist, durch Transaktionsanalysen etwas zu finden, ganz im Gegensatz zu Money Laundering. Hier hat man einfach eine Gleichschaltung der Systematik erreicht, weil man das Ganze unter einem grossen Begriff AML/CTF hat.	Transactional analyses only of limited help
Interviewee 6	Aber auf der einen Seite ist die Mittelherkunft die relevante oder Geldwäsche, und bei der Terrorismusfinanzierung ist es die Mittelverwendung.	Source of funds vs application of funds
Interviewee 6	Und hier habe ich auch ein Frequentierungsproblem, weil das eine liegt in der Vergangenheit, das andere liegt in der Zukunft.	Use of funds lies in the future
Interviewee 6	Also ich glaube, dass das nach wie vor weniger über den Finanzbereich das Ganze läuft, sondern eher über den Warenhandel und Cash, über Cashtransport.	Cash transport more vulnerable than the banking sector
Interviewee 6	Noch dazu können Sie so etwas wie ein Steuersystem aufziehen.	Tax systems as sources of financing for the IS

Interview partners	**Original Statement**	**Generalization**
Interviewee 6	Na gut, für die Zwecke der Ermittlung und Bekämpfung von Terrorismus oder sonstiger Kriminalität, der Idealfall, wenn wir den vollkommen gläsernen und transparenten Menschen hätten.	Transparent human being as an ideal case
Interviewee 6	Also da sind die entsprechenden Systeme sehr wohl schon sehr ausgebaut, und die/ also diese Institute sind natürlich auch sensibilisiert im Hinblick auf diese Regionen.	High sensitivity with regard to specific regions
Interviewee 6	Nun ja, besonders zu hinterfragen, es ist/ das wäre so, wie wenn man fragen würde, alle Fahrzeuge, die in die Himmelsrichtung Türkei unterwegs sind oder vielleicht sogar direkt in die Türkei fahren, müssten einer speziellen Kontrolle unterliegen. Also, die Frage ist, inwiefern ist das überhaupt noch praktikabel? Es sind 99,9 Prozent Überweisungen wahrscheinlich völlig legitim, und in dieser Masse an Finanzströmen wird der eine oder andere Euro sein, der möglicherweise vom Sympathisanten an, weiss ich nicht, Familienangehörige oder sonst irgendjemanden oder Personen, die eben in dem Kampfgebiet tätig sind oder dorthin zumindest immer wieder pendeln, an die überwiesen.	Suspicious transactions get lost in legitimate transactions

Interview partners	Original Statement	Generalization
Interviewee 6	Das liegt dann halt bei der Bank, diejenigen Ausreisser herauszufiltern, wo möglicherweise ein Indiz vorliegt, dass das Ganze doch möglicherweise einen anderen Hintergrund hat.	Transactional analysis
Interviewee 6	Wobei zugegebenermassen, gerade bei der Terrorismusfinanzierung es den Banken irrsinnig schwerfallen wird, Einzelpersonen nur aufgrund einzelner, wahrscheinlich auch Kleinstbeträge und Überweisungen diesbezüglichen Verdacht, dass diese in Verdacht geraten.	Small amounts difficult to detect
Interviewee 6	Grundsätzlich ist es das Leichteste für eine Bank natürlich, wenn man mit Personenlisten arbeitet.	Lists of persons
Interviewee 6	Und der zweite Faktor sind einfach Überweisungen in gewisse Regionen. Kennen wir Beispiele, wo Institute gewisse Regionen, also auch wirklich Filialen oder Banken in bekannten Regionen, zum Beispiel auch in Bosnien, die bekanntermassen extremistische Gruppierungen beherbergen, dass diese explizit auch von den Systemen gepflegt werden.	Suspicious regions

Interview partners	Original Statement	Generalization
Interviewee 6	Dass der Überprüfungsstandard und der Sorgfaltsstandard nicht der ist, der die meisten Länder gerne sehen würden, insbesondere, wenn solche Transaktionen angestossen werden bei Handyshops oder sonstigen Handelstreibenden, die als Agenten auftreten für diese grossen Unternehmen. Das wissen wir auch.	Low standard of verification for mobile phone shops
Interviewee 6	Und da kann ich, vor allem, wenn ich nicht spezifische Namen von Personen habe, wird es sehr schwer sein, hier aufgrund Zahlungsverhaltens im Bagatellbereich oder im niederschwelligen Bereich mir einen Reim nur aus dem Zahlungsverhalten einen Reim darauf zu machen, ob derjenige jetzt irgendwie beabsichtigt, terroristische Aktivitäten zu finanzieren damit. Also der Anknüpfungspunkt ist eigentlich nur, und das ist natürlich auch der Anknüpfungspunkt zu den Intelligence Agencies: die Person, das Verhalten der Person.	Suspicious behaviour
Interviewee 6	Also legitimierte Bankkonten und Überweisungen von Bankinstituten, insbesondere im EWR- und EU-Raum direkt in diese Krisengebiete, sagen wir jetzt Syrien oder Irak oder sonst wo, das wird unauffälligerweise nicht mehr möglich sein.	Direct transfers to crisis areas impossible

Interview partners	Original Statement	Generalization
Interviewee 6	Dazu stellt sich die Frage, ob überhaupt eine relevante Infrastruktur überhaupt noch zur Verfügung steht auf Empfängerseite in Syrien.	No suitable infrastructure in Syria
Interviewee 6	Na ja, rein schon von der, jetzt ohne, dass/ das wird jetzt schwierig/ das ist insofern schon geeignet, weil wiederum, es gibt kein legitimiertes, fixes Konto dahinter, das heisst, es gibt keine ständige Infrastruktur, die auf eine Person zugerechnet werden kann.	No imputability to a specific person
Interviewee 6	Bitcoin und Co., bekanntermassen über das Darknetz, schon eine gewisse Beliebtheit in kriminellen Kreisen. Es würde mich wundern, wenn hier nicht nur normale Rauschgiftdelikte oder sonstige, wesentlich härtere Delikte begangen werden, sondern auch eben so was wie Terrorismusfinanzierung.	Bitcoin popular on the darknet
Interviewee 6	Ich glaube, dass das wahrscheinlich einer der Hauptkanäle ist, das ist meine persönliche Meinung.	Main channel
Interviewee 6	Da wird man überweisungstechnisch vielleicht wirklich noch auf Money Transfers zurückgreifen, wobei auch hier, denke ich, mittlerweile die Infrastruktur einfach auf der Empfängerseite in einem Land wie Syrien wohl kaum vorhanden sein wird.	Infrastructure on the recipient side may be limited

Interview partners	Original Statement	Generalization
Interviewee 6	Anderes wird wahrscheinlich, ganz, ganz banal, wird über den/ normal über den Handel funktionieren, also dass man Finanzierungen jetzt nicht nur mit reinem flüssigem Cashmittel oder sonstigen Finanzmitteln macht, sondern dass man finanziert mit Ressourcen oder mit Financing-in-Kind, also mit sonstigen Unterstützungshandlungen, Spenden, Sachgütern und Sonstiges.	Financing in kind, donations and trade
Interviewee 6	Wir haben natürlich, gerade bei gewissen Regionen in Zentraleuropa, wo vielleicht die Diaspora aus der Türkei traditionell stärker vertreten ist, auch völlig legitime grosse Ströme, Finanzströme, in das jeweilige Land.	Legitimate flows from Central Europe as a cover
Interviewee 6	Also wenn man einen soliden Background hat und vor allem eine solide Transaktionshistorie, wo man auf eine durchschnittliche Überweisungs/ sagen wir mal so, Überweisungsprofil schliessen kann, dann wird man wohl auch einen Grossteil dieser Transaktionen relativ schnell plausibilisieren können.	Build a solid transaction history
Interviewee 6	Dass es auch solche Überweisungen gegeben hat, von unterschiedlichen Personen, jedoch unter dem gleichen Namen, das ist auch sehr wohl bekannt.	Different people under the same name

Interview partners	Original Statement	Generalization
Interviewee 6	Man muss auch sagen, wir kennen das von Erfahrungsberichten, von Leuten, die aus den Krisengebicten aus Syrien gekommen sind und hier Asyl gesucht haben. Die haben oftmals auch nicht mehr die Möglichkeit, sich auf dem geregelten Finanzweg, theoretisch, wenn sie zu Hause ein Vermögen haben oder ein Bankguthaben haben oder sonst irgendwie Guthaben auf Banken oder sonstigen Konten haben, sie können mittlerweile nicht mehr darauf zurückgreifen. Einfach, weil es Sperren gibt, wird seitens der Organisationen, die ein gewisses Gebiet derzeit besetzen oder es ist halt immer noch die syrische Regierung, die sind dann mitunter darauf angewiesen, auf solche Netzwerke wie ein Hawala-Netzwerk zurückzugreifen.	Transfer from crisis area via bank not possible
Interviewee 6	Für einige gibt es auch rein praktikable Gründe, warum die Person, auch wenn sie in Wien ist und theoretisch hier schon ein Konto hat, noch immer auf Hawala zurückgreifen muss, einfach, weil man die Schwierigkeiten im Land B, also in dem Fall in Syrien, hat und nichts anderes machen kann, weil man sonst das Geld nicht über die Grenze bekommt. Das wäre die eine Richtung. Natürlich in die andere Richtung ist das Ganze natürlich auch zugänglicher, keine Frage.	No bank in Syria

Interview partners	Original Statement	Generalization
Interviewee 6	Die Frage ist allerdings, und das ist schon zumindest zu hinterfragen, was kann ich mir dann/ also eincashen werde ich es wohl relativ schwer können, irgendwo in Syrien. Also ich gehe mal davon aus, sehr viele Abnehmer für Bitcoins oder sonstige virtuelle Währungen wird es nicht geben.	Limited tradability of Bitcoin in Syria
Interviewee 6	Das heisst wiederum, ich könnte, wenn ich die Bitcoins als Zahlungsmittel oder als Finanzmittel akzeptieren will, als Terrorist, und damit arbeiten will, kann ich mir dann wiederum im Darknet für Bitcoins möglicherweise Waffen oder sonstiges Material beschaffen.	Using Bitcoin to pay for weapons on the darknet
Interviewee 6	Also hier müsste man zumindest irgendwo das nächste Land heranziehen, wo man so etwas wie eine informelle Bitcoin-Wirtschaft hat, wo einzelne, vielleicht Warenhändler oder sonst irgendjemand Bitcoins akzeptiert oder wo es zumindest die Möglichkeit gibt, Bitcoins auszucashen und wiederum in Cash umzuwandeln.	Search for countries with a Bitcoin exchange
Interviewee 6	Ich glaube auch, der Attentäter von München war im Darknet unterwegs, um sich die Glock zu besorgen.	Using Bitcoin to pay for weapons on the darknet

Interview partners	Original Statement	Generalization
Interviewee 6	Man hat da relativ oft vor Augen so etwas wie in Syrien, wo es eine relativ unbehelligte Grenze zur Türkei gegeben hat, wo man auch weiss, dass sehr viele Personen und Güter diese Grenze überqueren und relativ frei.	Use border between Syria and Turkey
Interviewee 6	Also, das können legitime Einkommensquellen sein, das kann ein Gehalt sein, das kann Arbeitslosenunterstützung, staatliche Unterstützung, das kann alles Mögliche sein.	Salary or state support
Interviewee 6	Ich denke mal, dadurch, dass es immer wieder zu solchen Attacken kommt und man weiss, dass diese Personen im Internet radikalisiert wurden oder durch gewisses Material im Internet, und dennoch nicht auf diese Personen draufgekommen ist, zeigt umso mehr, wie schwierig das einfach ist. Das sind einfach Regelungsbereiche oder das sind einfach Bereiche des Lebens, die einfach den Alltag betreffen, so wie jeder den kennt bei uns. Und das sind dann nur kleine Elemente, die möglicherweise ein Indiz geben können.	Individual elements as circumstantial evidence
Interviewee 6	Ja, das ist wahrscheinlich eine der wesentlichsten oder der intelligentesten Formen der Bekämpfung, weil man hier vielleicht wirklich auf die einzelnen Zellen eingehen kann.	Flexibly adjustable to cells

Interview partners	Original Statement	Generalization
Interviewee 6	Aber wenn man sich in gewissen sozialen Bereichen frei bewegen kann, eben, weil man als solcher aufgenommen wird als einer der Ihren, dann kann das durchaus einen Intelligence-Mehrwert produzieren.	Intelligence added value
Interviewee 7	Ähm (.) ein Grossteil kommt tatsächlich aus/ aus/ aus (.) 'ner Art Steuererhebung.	Tax collection
Interviewee 7	Also das ist schon/ ich sage mal, dieser Anspruch, Islamischer Staat, die sich als Staat sehen, die eine gewisse Infrastruktur haben, also die 'ne gewisse Besteuerung erfordert. Aber das Interessante ist auch, was die sagten. Der/ wirklich der überwiegende Teil der Finanzierung kommt aus/ das ist so 'ne Art Ponzi-Scheme, den die aufgesetzt haben, aus Plünderungen.	Taxation and looting by the IS
Interviewee 7	Dass man also tatsächlich durch/ durch Gebietsgewinne, durch/ durch Landgewinne letztendlich bestehende Infrastruktur, Vermögen konfisziert, plündert und dann über graue Märkte, über Schwarzmärkte in den Handel bringt.	Looting
Interviewee 7	Das können (.) Kulturgüter sein, das können Konsumgüter sein. Also das ist letztendlich 'ne Umverteilung, 'ne Konfiszierung und Umverteilung, quasi 'ne Plünderung von/ von/ von Vermögensgegenständen.	Looting

Interview partners	Original Statement	Generalization
Interviewee 7	Wenn es um den Review von Transaktionen äh geht, letztlich das Mindset aber auch auf GWG, äh auf Geldwäscherei, auf Muster von Geldwäscherei, äh aber Terrorismusfinanzierung einfach in den Köpfen noch nicht existiert.	Focus on money laundering rather than terrorism financing
Interviewee 7	Ja, ich/ ich glaube, die/ die Muster der (.) Terrorismusfinanzierung sind, glaube ich, bei den meisten Leuten gar nicht bekannt. Und/ und deswegen ist es einfach auch schwierig, diese zu finanz/ äh diese zu identifizieren.	Patterns of terrorism financing partly unknown
Interviewee 7	Und bevor Sie dann mal irgendwo 'nen Amtshilfegesuch oder 'ne Arrestierung erwirkt haben, ich meine, da ist das Geld schon wieder äh üb/ über alle Ländergrenzen hinweg.	Money faster than administrative assistance
Interviewee 7	Also es ist/ Also ich glaube, das Problem ist, es gibt innerhalb der Berufsstände hmhm gewisse schwarze Schafe, die sich auch (.) zum Beispiel das Anwaltsgeheimnis, et cetera zu eigen machen, um/ um äh gewisse Sachen zu verschleiern.	Professional secrets as a concealment tool
Interviewee 7	Und // und da haben Sie einfach, ich sage mal, mittels der Ihnen als/ als Bank zur Verfügung stehenden (.) Compliance-Datenbanken null Zugriff, ne.	Limitations of compliance databases

Interview partners	**Original Statement**	**Generalization**
Interviewee 7	Sei es // das Geld geht an 'nen/ 'nen Verein, an/ an/ (.) äh oder an 'ne Privatperson oder an ein Geschäft, wer dahinter steht, woher der kommt, (.) das/ das bleibt für Sie intransparent, ne.	Beneficial owners of the beneficiary are often not known
Interviewee 7	Da haben Sie null Chance hier. Da haben Sie null Chance. Also ich glaube, damit würden Sie so durchkommen hier jetzt.	Low risk of detection
Interviewee 7	Äh es finden insofern alle/ alle Standards, die wir haben im Bereich Geldwäschereibekämpfung, (KYC) findet da nicht statt.	No AML or KYC standards
Interviewee 7	Und ähm (.) Sie haben keinerlei Chance, letztendlich durch, so wie das System angelegt ist, den wirtschaftlich Berechtigten ultimativ finanzieren/ äh zu identifizieren.	No identification of the beneficial owner possible
Interviewee 7	Das heisst, innerhalb dieser ganzen Prozesskette von fünf, sechs, sieben Schritten, (.) da seh' ich nur anderthalb Schritte, (.) ja. Und/ und da die Informationen zu verknüpfen und/ und/ und 'ne Faktenbasis zu schaffen, die es mir erlaubt, das dann rich/ richtig zu beurteilen, das ist faktisch nicht gegeben.	Bank sees only part of the process

Interview partners	Original Statement	Generalization
Interviewee 7	Was/ was meine Kenntnis ist, einfach nur auf die bewährten zurück. Einerseits äh Identifizierung des wirtschaftlichen Berechtigten und/ und dann das Monitoring äh der Transaktionen und das Matching gegen Listen, Sanktionslisten, EU-Listen, äh Geldwäscherei, (unv.) Checklisten, et cetera. Das heisst, (.) ich glaube, (.) es/ es besteht keine grooosse Sensibilität, was eigentlich der Unterschied genau ist zwischen Terrorismusfinanzierung oder Geldwäscherei.	Terrorism financing is mixed up with money laundering
Interviewee 7	Nur weil/ weil die jetzt an der Grenze liegen da zu/ zu den Krisengebieten und es einen gewissen Influx gibt im ganzen Land, heisst ja nicht, dass per se jede Geschäftstätigkeit in der Türkei rechtswidrig ist od/ oder letztendlich Geldwäscherei oder Terrorismusfinanzierungsverdacht automatisch gegeben ist.	Turkey not per se suspicious
Interviewee 7	Und ich meine, das ist natürlich ein perfektes System, was auch angelegt ist natürlich dann auch, äh äh (.) die Beneficial Ownership geheim zu halten, zu verschleiern und/ und kann natürlich dann auch genutzt werden für/ für illegale Transaktionen.	Concealment of the beneficial owner
Interviewee 7	Es müsste eigentlich möglich sein, ohne dass jemals ein Finanzinstitut damit in Berührung kommt.	Without contact points with financial institutions

Interview partners	Original Statement	Generalization
Interviewee 7	Und/ und äh äh wenn Sie da Menschen rüberkriegen, dann kriegen Sie natürlich auch Bar- oder Vermögenswerte da rüber.	Refugee routes suitable for money transfer
Interviewee 7	// innerhalb // der Bank sehe. Und das ist einfach das/ die Krux, dass/ dass/ dass wir äh als Berater oder als Anwälte immer nur diesen Snapshot sehen. Das heisst, Sie haben letztendlich 'ne Kette von/ von Ereignissen, Sie haben irgendwo (.) die Quelle (.) und von der Quelle bis hin zum Empfänger haben Sie verschiedene Prozessschritte.	Banks do not see the whole process
Interviewee 7	Und/ und wir wissen alle, nichts ist so flüchtig auf dieser Welt wie Geld.	Fast transfers
Interviewee 7	Und nichts ist so schnell wie Geld. Also das heisst, ich kann ja mittlerweile innerhalb von Sekunden Geld von A nach B transferieren und (.) unbegrenzte Summen.	Fast transfers
Interviewee 7	Es ist das typische Nutzen von Strohmännern, um eben den Finanzplatz, den Sektor als Medium zu nutzen, um/ um Gelder zu transferieren an (.) terroristische Organisationen, an ein Individuum, die (.) Anschläge geplant haben, et cetera.	Use of straw men
Interviewee 7	Also ich glaube, das ist wirklich das grosse Risiko ähm für Schweizer Finanzinstitute, dass mittels Strohmänner die Herkunft und/ und dann die Zie/ Ziele, die Empfänger verschleiert werden …	Use of straw men
Interviewee 7	Einerseits Strohmänner	Use of straw men

Interview partners	Original Statement	Generalization
Interviewee 7	Was natürlich auf der anderen Seite ein Problem ist, sind zum Beispiel/ das können Stiftungen sein, das/ das können Kulturvereine sein, das können (.) irgendwelche Unterstützergruppen sein, die sich nach aussen hin irgend 'nen Anstrich geben, wie/ wie/ ja, wie gesagt, diese ganzen Kulturvereine, die Sie hier haben, die ganzen NGOs, äh irgendwelchen Non-Governmental Organizations, die sich 'nen Anstrich geben als gemeinnützig, wohltätig. Aber dahinter verbirgt sich letztendlich 'ne/ ich sage mal, eine Organisation, die einer (.) politischen Organisation, einer terroristischen Organisation nahesteht.	Cultural associations and foundations as a cover
Interviewee 7	Das heisst // Sie brauchen ja immer, ich sage mal, irgendwo/ (.) wenn/ wenn Sie/ angenommen Sie sind 'ne terroristische Vereinigung, irgendwo (.) 'nen legalen Arm in die Gesellschaft hinein, in dem Sie, ich sage mal, A rekrutieren, Werbung, Lobbying betreiben.	Create legal structures for advertising and lobbying

Interview partners	Original Statement	Generalization
Interviewee 7	Und was ich mir vorstellen kann, ist natürlich, wenn Sie gerade im/ im Bereich ähm (.) ähm (.) Transaktionen in die Türkei ansprechen, dass Sie natürlich im Rahmen der Flüchtlingsbewegung, dass/ dass wir natürlich viele Leute haben, die aus den Krisengebieten, wo es terroristische Aktivitäten gibt, in/ ich sage mal, in westliche oder in nahe westliche Länder immigriert sind, da jetzt (.) 'ne legale äh äh (.) Identität oder ein legales Leben aufgebaut haben, sind registriert, haben ein Geschäft, et cetera. Und da können natürlich die History/ wo kommen die Leute her, was für Beziehungen haben die, das können Sie nur schwer nachvollziehen, ne.	Using refugees as a cover
Interviewee 7	Wenn Sie/ wenn Sie es/ dann auch noch irgendwie ein Splitting machen und/ und bleiben unter irgendwelchen kritischen Schwellenwerten, (.) da haben Sie als Bank keine äh/ (.)	Distribute assets
Interviewee 7	Und/ und Sie haben natürlich, ich sage mal, aufgrund der sprachlichen Unterschiedlichkeiten und/ und/ und der/ (.) der Ferne trotzdem nicht/ nicht die Chance, das alles irgendwie in/ berechtigte Zweifel zu ziehen. Gerade wenn Sie dieses Beispiel mit der notariellen Beurkundung et cetera bringen dann, ne. (.)	Use notarial certification

Interview partners	Original Statement	Generalization
Interviewee 7	Also wenn es 'ne plausible Geschichte ist, die rund ist und/ und Sie auf der Gegenseite sagen, Sie haben da ein valides Business und es hat vielleicht sogar schon 'ne gewisse History, das ist jetzt nicht gerade erst seit äh/ seit ein, zwei Monaten registriert im Markt, et cetera.	Plausible business with history
Interviewee 7	Ähm der hat vielleicht renommierte Kunden auch irgendwo, äh hat 'ne gute Webpage mit/ mit allen Zipp und Zapp. Also das äh/ das fällt Ihnen da nicht auf. (.)	Renowned customers and website
Interviewee 7	Und // und diese Handelsrouten, das sind einfach Landwege gewesen, weil die Häfen blockiert waren, diese Handelsrouten und/ und das heisst, auch diese Logistik dahinter, die funktioniert heute immer noch.	Use trade routes (land routes)
Interviewee 7	Existiert, sondern das stammt zum Teil wirklich eben noch gerade, diese Route, äh äh aus/ aus dem Oil-for-Food-Programm. Und ich meine, in der/ in der Türkei ein legales Business aufzubauen, ist, glaube ich, nicht sonderlich schwierig.	Establish a legal business in Turkey

Interview partners	Original Statement	Generalization
Interviewee 7	Aber // aber die Leute, die an diesem Part/ oder an diesem System partizipieren und gewinnen, das heisst, die Leute, die diese Wertgegenstände über die Grenzen schaffen, die das Geld wieder rücktransferieren, ähm da/ das besteht seit Jahrzehnten und/ und das kann, wie gesagt, ähm (.) einerseits der/ der Schmuggel oder der Transfer von/ von/ von materiellen Gegenständen sein und dann auf der anderen Seite natürlich auch die Rückführung von/ von Geldern.	Involve experienced smugglers
Interviewee 7	Dass // dass Sie sagen, ähm Sie haben ein/ ein System, dieses (Hawala)-System zum Beispiels, weil's einfach auf/ auf Mittelsmännern und Vertrauen beruht, ne, wo letztendlich am Ende des Tages mal irgendwann ein Clearing stattfindet, aber es ist alles bargeldbasiert, und Sie haben einfach Ihre Mittelsmänner irgendwo sitzen, wo Sie natürlich als/ ja, ich sag mal, als/ als (.) jemand, der ein westliches Bankensystem gewohnt ist, natürlich überhaupt keinen Zugriff haben, weil's einfach ein komplett paralleles Bankensystem ist, ne.	Cash transactions based on trust and middlemen

Interview partners	Original Statement	Generalization
Interviewee 7	Ähm (seufzt leise) das ist 'ne gute Frage. Also ich weiss, dass es das gibt. Ähm (.) ähm ich weiss es eigentlich (.) inoffiziell von/ von, ich sag mal, Hilfsorganisationen, die, ich sag mal, das Problem haben, stellen Sie sich vor, Sie sind 'ne Hilfsorganisation und Sie wollen/ Es gab 'ne Katastrophe irgendwo in 'nem Gebiet, wo es einfach keine westliche Bank gibt, die Dollar annimmt oder so.	Aid agencies as a cover
Interviewee 7	Sie müssen irgendwo nach, ich sage mal, Mittelafrika Geld bringen, um da helfen zu wollen. Da greifen diese Hilfsorganisationen zum Beispiel auf Parallelbankensysteme, auf Cash-Systeme zurück.	Aid agencies as a cover
Interviewee 7	Ich meine, das Ganze geht ja letztendlich über irgendwelche Rechenkapazitäten.	Increase computing power
Interviewee 7	Letztendlich, Sie/ ich meine, Sie können ja Bitcoins erwerben, wenn Sie an anteil/ am System teilnehmen und einfach Rechenkapazität zur Verfügung stellen und können so durch dieses System intern letztendlich, (.) ja, (.) Kaufkraft erwerben …	Provide computing capacity
Interviewee 7	indem Sie Rechenkapazität zur Verfügung stellen.	Provide computing capacity
Interviewee 7	Also das heisst, hier hat man diesen Umweg über das/ den Kauf von Infrastruktur, die Möglichkeit, daran zu partizipieren.	Build infrastructure

Interview partners	Original Statement	Generalization
Interviewee 7	Und ich meine, wir haben natürlich Länder jetzt, wie Frankreich und/ und so, die gewisse Limite aussprechen wollen und trotzdem auch gewisse (KYC-)Regeln über diese Prepaid-Karten ziehen wollen. Also ich glaube, das wär schon wieder zu/ zu offensichtlich, oder?	Avoid prepaid cards
Interviewee 7	Ja, ich/ Und das ist, glaube ich, die/ diese Flüchtlingsrouten oder Schmugglerrouten oder wie auch immer Sie die da nennen wollen, ich meine, da gibt's 'ne bestehende Infrastruktur. Das funktioniert.	Use refugee routes
Interviewee 7	Da gibt's äh äh/ da gibt es Logistiker, Schleuser, was auch immer Sie/ oder wie Sie die nennen wollen.	Involve smugglers
Interviewee 7	Und gerade jetzt, wenn wir über Barwerte reden oder/ oder gerade Prepaid-Karten. Ich meine, das ist ja wahrscheinlich noch leichter dann als irgendwelche Menschen rüberzuschmuggeln, wo Sie äh Papiere brauchen et cetera. Und dann/	Use prepaid cards
Interviewee 7	Ja, so 'ne Prepaid/ Ich meine, Prepaid-Karte, ich meine, das is/ dann haben Sie (.) 'nen Haufen kleiner Kärtchen. Ich meine, wie/ das fällt keinem auf.	Use prepaid cards
Interviewee 7	Das heisst, Sie sehen eigentlich als/ als Finanzintermediär immer nur, A wo kommst Geld rein (durch diesen) Strohmann und B wo gehts Geld wieder raus, eventuell auch wieder ein Strohmann oder unsere türkische Bank, et cetera.	Use of straw men

Interview partners	Original Statement	Generalization
Interviewee 7	Und/ und ich glaube, das ist einfach auch die Krux äh ähm (.) bei der Ermittlung grundsätzlich, dass Sie einfach über das äh äh Nutzen von Strohmännern, von Konstrukten, von Gesellschaften eben 'ne (.) sehr lange Prozesskette haben und um dieses Ganze, dieses Big Picture dann zu etablieren und wenn es über Ländergrenzen hinweg geht, über verschiedene Finanzinstitutionen, verschiedene Banken, et cetera, die Informationen zusammenzubekommen.	Use of straw men and company constructs
Interviewee 7	Und dann wird das Geld transferiert und es ist innerhalb von Sekunden/ Wenn Sie das mal nachträglich investigieren, dann landet das erst auf (.) 'nem Konto 'ner westlichen Bank, aber von da geht's dann nach China und von der chinesischen Bank dann in tausend Himmelsrichtungen. Da haben Sie null Chance, das Geld jemals wieder zu finden. (leise) Also das ist äh (.) illusorisch.	Transfers to Chinese banks and subsequent dispersal
Interviewee 7	Sie können letztendlich auch Bitcoins anders erwerben als jetzt über/ über 'ne Bank oder/ oder über/ äh äh über 'nen Finanzdienstleister.	Purchase Bitcoin anonymously

Interview partners	Original Statement	Generalization
Interviewee 7	Wäre wahrscheinlich ein probates Mittel. Deckt sich wahrscheinlich nicht immer ganz mit der/ (schmunzelnd) mit dem Datenschutz (lacht) und dem Persönlichkeitsschutz. Äh (.) aber wenn Sie rein auf die/ auf die Effizienz und Effektivität abzielen, ist das wahrscheinlich ein Element, was/ was/ was wahrscheinlich probat wäre, weitere Informationen zu etablieren, ja.	Effective and efficient, but questionable under data protection law
Interviewee 7	Das können sein, wie gesagt, dann Drogenhandel oder andere Sachen.	Drug trafficking
Interviewee 7	Was wir gesehen haben, dass der Grossteil der Versicherungsbetrügereien wirklich Fälle von organisierter Kriminalität sind.	Insurance fraud
Interviewee 7	// Also das // ist jetzt wirklich der Grossteil, wo fingiert von/ über fingierte Autofällen/ Un/ Unfällen, über/ über Diebstähle, wo Sie wirklich, ich sag mal, ähm Netzwerke haben von Leuten, die äh bewusst, ich sag mal, Versicherungspolicen zeichnen und/ und Schaden melden, fingieren.	Insurance fraud
Interviewee 7	Und das sind letztendlich immer gewisse/ gewisse Netzwerke, die da agieren. Sind immer dieselben Player. Und/ und (.) also Versicherungsbetrug ist ein Grossteil wirklich ein Problem, organisierte Kriminalität.	Insurance fraud

Interview partners	Original Statement	Generalization
Interviewee 7	Also ich glaube, dass/ dass es ohne klassische Intelligence wahrscheinlich sehr, sehr schwierig ist, also ohne äh/ ohne dass ich das jetzt aus der Erfahrung sagen könnte.	Investigations without classical intelligence are difficult
Interviewee 7	Ich meine, die Behörden sind da angewiesen auf Insiderwissen. Sei es Sie haben 'nen Verdeckten Ermittler, der/ den Sie beauftragt haben unter Einschleusen oder Sie kaufen 'ne Art Whistleblower oder Kronzeugen raus.	Insider knowledge required
Interviewee 7	Hm ich glaube, ohne diese Art von Informationen werden Sie sonst nie da ankommen. Wenn Sie wirklich (.) äh äh mühselig die Prozesskette nachgehen müssen mit/ mit Amtshilfe, da kommen Sie nie ans Ziel.	Without undercover investigators, there is hardly any chance of success
Interviewee 7	Ich glaube, Sie sind angewiesen auf entweder Verdeckte Ermittler oder Whistleblower, Kronzeugen, die aus der Organisation kommen, umfallen und/ und äh (.) die dann aus dem Nähkästchen plaudern.	Insider knowledge required

Interview partners	Original Statement	Generalization
Interviewee 7	Und/ und ich meine, ohne dass ich da jetzt aus der Erfahrung spräche, aber meine Vermutung ist einfach relativ gross, was wir gesehen haben, (.) äh zum Beispiel als das ganze ähm (.) Iran-Oil-for-Food-Programm lief. Das sind ja diese Handelsrouten. Ich meine, das ist ja belegt mittlerweile, dass äh in/ in der Zeit der 90er und 2000er, als dieses Oil-for-Food-Programm lief, dass der Schwarzhandel mit/ mit dem Öl über (.) zum Teil auch die Türkei lief.	Trade in oil via Turkey
Interviewee 7	Ich will nicht ausschliessen, dass es da noch über Firmenkonstrukte jetzt äh äh (.) in den/ in den grösseren Bereich jetzt/ jetzt Umsatzsteuerbetrügereien, et cetera gehen mag. Das/	Sales tax fraud via company constructs
Interviewee 8	Ich meine, man darf sich ja nicht den Illusionen hingeben, dass das – gerade bei Terrorismus – dass das alles nur – in Anführungszeichen – irgendwelche Fanatiker sind, die Hochhäuser in die Luft jagen wollen und dann irgendwelche Menschen mit reinziehen. Die gibt es auch, aber da gibt es wahrscheinlich natürlich auch hochintelligente Menschen im Hintergrund, die mit einer vergleichbaren Ausbildung, ja wirklich die Schwachstellen suchen.	Perpetrators are intelligent and well trained
Interviewee 8	Also das heisst, man hat hier mittlerweile einen, ja, auf der Gegenseite durchaus gleichwertigen Gegner, sage ich mal.	Perpetrators are competent

Interview partners	Original Statement	Generalization
Interviewee 8	Ich weiss nicht, wie Ihre Erfahrung ist, sage ich jetzt mal, von Ihren bisherigen Tätigkeiten heraus, aber man sieht ja schon, dass die immer cleverer werden.	Perpetrators are clever
Interviewee 8	Dritter Punkt, um das vielleicht auch nochmal zu sagen, für mich ist die fortschreitende Technisierung des Ganzen auch ein, ich will nicht sagen, ein Risiko, aber auch ein Fakt, der die Arbeit schwieriger gemacht hat.	Progressive mechanization complicates investigations
Interviewee 8	Ich will mal so ein Beispiel nennen, aber das ist bei mir hier so ein Lieblingsthema, worüber ich stundenlang schwadronieren könnte, dass gewisse Bereiche unfassbar hart reguliert sind und manche Bereiche aber, wo es aus meiner Sicht offensichtlich ist, dass da aus freien Stücken gar nichts passiert.	Certain industries are not regulated
Interviewee 8	Der intelligente Terrorismusfinanzierer macht im Prinzip genau das, was er tun möchte, und erklärt das einfach nur gut.	Intelligent offenders have plausible explanations for their behaviour
Interviewee 8	Ich sage mal so, das sind ja nicht nur noch, sage ich mal, irgendwelche schlimmen Ziegenhirten, die dann irgendwie mit der Kalaschnikow auf irgendwelche Leute feuern. Das sind ja wirklich durchaus gut ausgebildete Menschen dahinter, die sich so einem Ziel verschrieben haben, leider.	Perpetrators are well trained

Interview partners	Original Statement	Generalization
Interviewee 8	Das, was Sie aus der Geldwäsche lernen können, kann man natürlich auch auf das Thema Terrorismusfinanzierung übertragen.	Similarities between money laundering and terrorism financing
Interviewee 8	Es gibt Lücken in Prozessen, sei es in der Verwaltung, sei es bei Gericht, die man, wenn man das genau weiss, gut nutzen kann.	Perpetrators exploit loopholes in the administration
Interviewee 8	Bei der Geldwäsche sind wir ja praktisch schon paranoid und gucken: Wo könnte da irgendwas Grösseres reinkommen? Bei der Terrorismusfinanzierung haben wir schon Gelder, die als sauber deklariert wurden, die auch schon geprüft wurden – also das ist ja praktisch der Unterschied dazu, ein wirklich spannendes Thema, wie ich finde – dass die also erst mal gar nicht den Verdacht (unv. #00:37:32.5#) erregen.	Funds of terrorist financiers are often not incriminated
Interviewee 8	Persönlich glaube ich, dass wir Terrorismusfinanzierung nie einfangen können, weil es immer solche Schlupflöcher gibt.	Terrorism financing cannot be combated
Interviewee 8	Wenn Sie einen guten haben – in Anführungszeichen –, der die Prozesse halt kennt und ausnutzen kann, wird er sie austricksen. Gerade wenn die richtig viel Geld zur Verfügung haben. Die Kleinen, sage ich mal, Unauffälligen, die kriegen Sie, weil die einfach nicht die Ressourcen haben.	Competent offenders do not get caught

Interview partners	Original Statement	Generalization
Interviewee 8	Und das ist ja genau das Spannende daran, dass Sie also praktisch die Kleineren kriegen, aber die Grossen, die richtig schweren Brocken, die kriegen Sie nur ganz schwer zu sehen. Ich glaube, da müssen Sie dann, ja, auf ganz anderer Ebene angreifen.	Only small offenders get caught
Interviewee 8	Das zeigt ja, wenn man sich ein bisschen mit dem Thema auseinandersetzt, findet man einfach Möglichkeiten, die es dem einzelnen Unternehmen fast unmöglich macht, das auch rauszufinden. Weil dieser Gesamtzusammenhang, den kriegen Sie nicht mit.	Skilled offenders do not get caught
Interviewee 8	Da ist mir doch vollkommen egal, ob ich jetzt hinten raus noch eine Strafe bekomme für Terrorismusfinanzierung, wenn ich vorne raus irgendwie, keine Ahnung, ein Bombenattentat oder sowas finanziert habe. Das ist dann das kleinere Übel, wo ich sage: Ja gut, dann kriegst du halt da, wenn es rauskommt, auch noch zwei Jahre. Aber wenn ich da vorher schon, ich sage mal, Mittäter bin, sage ich mal, oder Urheber für ein Bombenattentat oder sowas, wie es in Paris passiert ist (unv. #00:56:27.9#), dann ist es doch vollkommen egal.	Penalties for terrorism financing do not act as a deterrent
Interviewee 8	Ich glaube, auch da ist vielleicht noch eine Schwäche der Terr orismusfinanzierungsbekämp fung, dass die Aufsichts- oder Ermittlungsbehörden eigentlich zu langsam sind.	Investigating authorities are too slow

Interview partners	Original Statement	Generalization
Interviewee 8	Es gibt einfach zu viele Einfallstore, die man im Hinterkopf haben muss, wie das laufen kann, warum das so laufen kann, und ich glaube einfach mittlerweile, dass die Professionalität auf der anderen Seite so gross geworden ist, dass man eben vorsichtig sein muss, zu glauben, man kann das alles noch durch eine singuläre Massnahme abfangen. Also singulär im Sinne von: Ich kann das nicht alles alleine bei den Finanzinstituten liegen lassen, weil die nur einen Teil der Prozesskette sind.	Perpetrators are too competent to be caught by financial service providers
Interviewee 8	Ansonsten, wie gesagt, aber das ist halt eine persönliche Schlussnote, wenn ich das mal sagen darf, viele der Sachen, die wir aktuell machen, werden verkauft unter dem Deckmantel der Geldwäscheprävention und/oder der Terrorismusfinanzierung, dienen aber nach meinem Verständnis eher dem Thema Steuerfahndung.	Combating the financing of terrorism serves tax investigations
Interviewee 8	Im Prinzip muss das auch auf anderen Ebenen auch angepasst sein. Sei es bei Rechtsanwälten, sei es bei Notaren, sei es, wie gesagt, bei Behörden. Also überall dort, wo ich die Möglichkeit habe, sage ich mal, eine Dokumentation oder Ähnliches zu besorgen, müssen im Prinzip die gleichen Standards herrschen.	Standards for notarizations

Interview partners	Original Statement	Generalization
Interviewee 8	Die Wahrscheinlichkeit, dass uns da jemand unterrutscht, der komplett anonym ist und irgendwie durch Zufall reinkommt, das ist eigentlich nicht darstellbar oder ist nicht möglich.	Anonymity almost impossible
Interviewee 8	Wir kennen unseren Kunden wirklich und wir kennen auch den Hintergrund des Kunden.	Backgrounds of customers known
Interviewee 8	Das heisst, da lassen wir gesondert durch den Berater prüfen, was der Hintergrund einer Zahlung ist.	Verification of the background of the payments
Interviewee 8	Das ist das, was ich eingangs meinte. Wie gut kenne ich eigentlich meinen Kunden, ja?	Backgrounds of customers known
Interviewee 8	Die Presse von (unv. #00:20:15.6#), da kommen Sie heute nicht mehr drum herum. Wenn Sie feststellen, da ist irgendjemand dabei, der nicht seriös ist, dann sollten Sie tunlichst anfangen, mal nachzudenken in Ihrer Bank, warum man vielleicht diesen Geschäftspartner nicht mehr in Zukunft haben möchte.	Press analysis
Interviewee 8	Wenn jemand wirklich so präzise vorgeht, wirklich, sage ich mal, von den Unterlagen her eine Nachvollziehbarkeit stattfindet, glaube ich, ehrlich gesagt, dann bekommen Sie den im Zweifel gar nicht.	Traceability of documentation reduces risk of detection
Interviewee 8	So, das heisst, wir haben eine komplette Parallelwährung, die Sie aber wieder umtauschen können in reales Geld.	Parallel currency exchangeable into common currencies
Interviewee 8	So, ist aber null reguliert.	No regulation

Interview partners	Original Statement	Generalization
Interviewee 8	Ja, warum soll ich denn irgendwie, sage ich mal, ganz böse, sage ich mal, eine Überweisung machen, wenn ich einfach über so ein Verschlüsselungssystem, also über künstliche Währung, eigentlich alles darstellen kann, was ich möchte?	Good alternative to classic bank transfers
Interviewee 8	Also nochmal, nicht dass die Banken alle sauber sind, bitte nicht so verstehen, aber ich glaube, die Wahrscheinlichkeit, dass man über die Banken noch was darstellen kann, ist deutlich schwieriger oder unwahrscheinlicher, als wenn Sie in andere Bereiche gehen.	Banks control more than other industries
Interviewee 8	Und es ist unfassbar schwer nach meinem Verständnis, die wenigen Bösen – und ich glaube, es sind wirklich wenige – von der überragenden grossen guten Masse zu unterscheiden.	Perpetrators difficult to distinguish from normal customers
Interviewee 8	Sie merken ja, egal, welches Beispiel wir diskutieren, es gibt einfach unfassbar viele Möglichkeiten, die eben ausserhalb der Banken liegen, und die Banken kriegen eben nur einen Teil dieses Prozesses mit, nicht den Gesamtprozess, und dadurch, ja (...) können die gar nicht alles aufdecken, was da gefordert ist.	Banks do not see the whole process
Interviewee 8	Wenn Sie nur einen Teil des Prozesses sehen, können Sie nicht das Gesamtbild beurteilen. Das ist aktuell die Schwierigkeit in der Bank, das ist meine Überzeugung.	Banks do not see the whole process

Interview partners	Original Statement	Generalization
Interviewee 8	Dass man wirklich weiss, mit welchem Kunden habe ich zu tun, und vor allen Dingen, was sind die Geschäftspartner meines Kunden.	Disclose customers and their business partners
Interviewee 8	Ich meine, weiss ich, warum der dort eigentlich Gelder hat, warum der dahin überweisen will?	Explanations for transactions
Interviewee 8	Kann ich das nachvollziehen?	Ensure traceability
Interviewee 8	Kann ich das plausibilisieren?	Ensure plausibility
Interviewee 8	Onlinebanken. Die wissen im Zweifel gar nicht, was da hinten dran steht, oder die sehen das gar nicht.	Online banks do not know background
Interviewee 8	Sie haben ja auch, sage ich mal, Spezialdienstleister, ich will es jetzt nicht Ethno-Banking nennen, das hört sich so komisch an, aber die sich genau auf gewisse Volksgruppen spezialisiert haben.	Specialized financial service providers for specific regions
Interviewee 8	Das sind türkische Banken, die hier eine Niederlassung aufgemacht haben, die (unv. #00:19:24.3#), die gezielt auf Migranten zielen und sagen: Wir möchten euch als Kunden werben.	Turkish banks with branches in Germany
Interviewee 8	Ja, an deutsche regulierte Vollbanken würden wir immer überweisen.	German regulated full-service banks as partners
Interviewee 8	Also das fängt schon damit an, dass Sie die Sprache im Zweifel nicht sprechen, oder wenn es ganz hart kommt, noch nicht mal die Schrift entziffern können.	Documents in foreign languages

Interview partners	Original Statement	Generalization
Interviewee 8	Oh, ich fang jetzt plötzlich an, an die Türkei zu überweisen oder nach Russland oder, keine Ahnung, irgendwohin, das ist auffällig. Komme ich aber hin und sage: So, ich hab hier ein internationales Unternehmen, ich mach Transport, hab eine schöne Homepage dazu, wo ich auch sehen kann: Ach guck mal, der macht Transporte in den Nahen Osten. Wegen mir sagt er auch, spezialisiert für, keine Ahnung, Krankentransport oder Ähnliches. Dann läuft das wunderbar.	Plausibility check of foreign transfers through international company structure in the transport sector
Interviewee 8	Also so ein Klassiker, sage ich mal, der auch damals durch die Presse gegangen ist, machen Sie ein Bestattungsunternehmen auf. Hört sich im ersten Moment ein bisschen komisch an, aber wenn Sie sagen: Na ja, wir haben halt viele Leute, die in ihrer Heimat beerdigt werden wollen, dann haben Sie auf jeden Fall schon mal jemanden, der Ihnen plausibel erklären kann, warum die regelmässig unten vor Ort im Nahen Osten ist.	Set up a funeral home
Interviewee 8	Und wenn Sie dann noch sagen: Ja, und die zahlen dann eben teilweise auch bar, haben Sie auch einen Grund, warum Sie Geld reinbekommen.	Cash company
Interviewee 8	Und auf einmal haben Sie ein Profil, wo Sie sagen: Ungewöhnlich, aber macht Sinn.	Select a meaningful profile

Interview partners	Original Statement	Generalization
Interviewee 8	Wie gesagt, Sie müssen halt parallel diese (unv.) auch betreiben, schöne Homepage et cetera. Firmeneintrag und so weiter, aber schon sind Sie im Prinzip da erst mal, was die Wahrnehmung angeht, zumindest nachvollziehbar.	Build up companies with a homepage and company entry
Interviewee 8	Ein Intelligenter macht sich diese Vorurteile zu eigen und guckt eigentlich: Wie komme ich zu einem Profil in der Überwachung, was risikoarm ist?	Using biases to create low-risk profiles
Interviewee 8	Und das heisst, ich suche mir erst mal die Lücken. Zum Beispiel, wenn ich jetzt eben sage, ich transferiere Gelder für die Terroristenfinanzierung in die Türkei, um bei Ihrem Beispiel zu bleiben, suche ich mir eben als Vehikel eine deutsche Firma, wahrscheinlich eine GmbH, weil die am günstigsten ist, die regelmässig Geschäftsbeziehungen in die Türkei hat.	Establish a limited liability company with business relations in Turkey
Interviewee 8	Zum Beispiel Reiseveranstalter könnte ich sein.	Establish a tour operator
Interviewee 8	Dann mache ich idealerweise auf der türkischen Seite auch nochmal eine Firma auf, die auch am besten irgendwie so/ Dann kann ich zwischen diesen beiden Sachen ständig was hin- und hertransferieren.	Establish a company in Turkey
Interviewee 8	Und das Perfide daran: Je häufiger Sie das machen, umso unauffälliger wird das, ja?	Frequency increases plausibility

Interview partners	Original Statement	Generalization
Interviewee 8	Weil, wenn Sie da sagen, bei der ersten Transaktion: Oh, guck mal, der hat da was überwiesen. Dann macht man den ersten Scheck und stellt fest, ja, okay, ist in Ordnung. Beim zweiten Mal auch. Aber beim 10. oder 20. Mal sagt man sich: Ach ja, stimmt, die machen schon seit langer Zeit Geschäfte mit denen, das ist in Ordnung.	Frequency increases plausibility
Interviewee 8	Durch die Wiederholung wird es weniger auffällig, als man meinen könnte.	Frequency increases plausibility
Interviewee 8	Reiseveranstalter, klar, und dann liefert man die Ware nicht. Also man sagt zum Beispiel: Ich nehme dem Kontingent ab für 100 Betten im Monat, den ganzen Sommer und dann war ich halt schlecht im Verkauf und hab jetzt leider nicht so viele Betten an den Mann gebracht, aber die 100 Betten muss ich halt trotzdem bezahlen.	Establish tour operators and create fictitious quotas

Interview partners	Original Statement	Generalization
Interviewee 8	Also ich verklage jetzt (unv.) und sage, keine Ahnung, Sie haben meinen Hund erschossen, dadurch ist mir ein emotionaler Schaden entstanden von 100.000 Euro. Dass ich keinen Hund habe, hat damit nichts zu tun. Ich kann jeden Blödsinn vor Gericht behaupten. So, das packe ich in eine Klageschrift, stelle das dem Amtsgericht zu. Das Amtsgericht kriegt das und sieht, na ja, da ist eine Klageschrift, so. Und dann geht das Ihnen zu und Sie müssen erwidern. Das Thema ist, nach der deutschen Prozessordnung, wenn Sie nichts dazu sagen und bei Gericht auch nicht erscheinen trotz Aufforderung, wird dem Kläger Recht gegeben, sofern die Klage nachvollziehbar ist.	Seek judgments by default

Interview partners	Original Statement	Generalization
Interviewee 8	Also Klassiker ist: Autounfall, Auto ist beschädigt, war eine Luxuskarosse, 60.000 Euro, so. Und auf einmal stellen Sie fest: Ja, da hab ich eine Klage. Ich antworte nicht drauf und dann gibt es, wenn Sie im Termin nicht erscheinen, ein Versäumnisurteil. Und dieses Versäumnisurteil ist ein vollwertiges Gerichtsurteil. So, und dann überweisen Sie auf einmal, Sie an mich, die 60.000 oder 100.000 Euro und wenn die Frage ist, warum ist das so gewesen, zeigen Sie ein Urteil eines deutschen Gerichts vor, wo ich sage: Höherer Qualitätsnachweis als eine gerichtliche Anordnung, das zu machen, können Sie ja gar nicht haben.	Seek judgments by default
c	Ja, der macht das, weil er dazu gerichtlich verurteilt wurde. Keiner ist ja freiwillig bereit, sich vom Gericht verurteilen zu lassen, kommt dann natürlich. Und automatisch ist dieses Thema durch.	Seek judgments by default
Interviewee 8	Also Tourismushochburgen, da stellen Sie halt eine Seite vom Hotel online und sagen: Da und da ist das Hotel, und da können Sie hinfliegen. Wie Sie gesagt haben, kaufen ein Bettenkontingent von, keine Ahnung, 5000 Übernachtungen pro Jahr, und am Ende des Tages gibt es kein Hotel, das Geld wird trotzdem überwiesen. Nun sind Sie noch so clever und machen auf Holidaycheck und Clubreisen irgendwie 30 Bewertungen drauf und schon sieht das Ding doch rund aus.	Set up tour operators and advertise fictitious quotas on websites

Interview partners	Original Statement	Generalization
Interviewee 8	Ich gehe also in Deutschland mit meinem Geld zur HSBC, sage: Hier auf mein Konto, den und den Betrag, und jetzt überweist das doch auf mein Konto bei der HSBC in, keine Ahnung, nehmen wir die Türkei oder nehmen wir den Iran oder wo die auch immer vertreten sind.	Choose banks with branches abroad
Interviewee 8	Das heisst also, ich kriege dann über eine Konzernstruktur es hin, dass das Geld transferiert wird. Und vor Ort wird kein Mensch prüfen, ob das unsauber ist, weil das kommt ja aus dem Mutterhaus oder aus irgendeiner Schwestergesellschaft.	Choose banks with branches abroad
Interviewee 8	Ich prüfe bei uns innerhalb der Konzernstruktur ja auch nicht, ob das in Ordnung ist.	Use lower audits within group structures
Interviewee 8	Ich muss mir nur eine gute Geschichte ausdenken.	Ensure plausibility
Interviewee 8	Ich glaube, auf der Gegenseite sind mittlerweile Leute da, die die Strukturen kennen und diese Strukturen ausnutzen können.	Involve experts
Interviewee 8	Eine Bank, die zwar eine türkische Mutter hat, aber hier eine deutsche Registrierung hat, deutsche Beaufsichtigung, dann ist das für mich ein Inländer.	Choose banks with Turkish parent companies

Interview partners	Original Statement	Generalization
Interviewee 8	Aber wenn Sie sagen, ich habe hier, keine Ahnung, 100.000 Euro zur Hand, um eben, keine Ahnung, eine deutsche GmbH aufzumachen, noch einen Partner auf der, keine Ahnung, türkischen Seite, sagen wir mal, mit dabei, um dann ein paar Webseiten zu hosten, um da vielleicht auch irgendwie, sage ich mal, den Eindruck entstehen zu lassen, dass da irgendwas hinten dran ist, also wenn ich das hinkriege und dieses Kapital habe, um mir einen Deckmantel zu bauen, dann finden Sie es nicht mehr raus.	Set up cover in Germany and Turkey with GmbH
Interviewee 8	Geld leihen	Borrow
Interviewee 8	Das ist quasi so eine Art Funding durch Privatleute.	Financing by private individuals
Interviewee 8	Das heisst, Sie sagen: Ich hab hier den und den Kreditbedarf, den und den Preis bin ich bereit zu zahlen, und die Plattform stellt eigentlich nur noch den Kontakt her zwischen den Kreditsuchenden und anderen Leuten, die sagen: Okay, ich gebe Geld dafür.	Platforms put lenders and borrowers in touch with each other
Interviewee 8	Dann sagen die halt: Wir sind hier nur Vermittler, aber gehen nicht selber praktisch ins Risiko.	Platforms as intermediaries without risk

Interview partners	Original Statement	Generalization
Interviewee 8	So, das heisst, Sie haben eine wunderbare Anonymität über das Netz geschaffen. Und gehen Sie davon aus, dass diese Plattform, sonst würden die sich ja nicht tragen, nicht dem Standard, sage ich mal, der Kreditbeschaffung entsprechen, sei es Deutsch, Schweizerisch oder überhaupt irgendeines anderen Landes, die sind weitestgehend noch Wildwest.	Platforms are anonymous
Interviewee 8	Also die Rückzahlung überprüft die Plattform im Zweifel gar nicht.	Repayment is not verified by platforms
Interviewee 9	Oder Sie haben tatsächlich auch illegale Quellen, das heisst, der IS finanziert sich ja auch selber durch Zwangsabgaben.	Compulsory levies
Interviewee 9	Die hat/ überall kommt die Geldwäsche zusammen mit der Terrorismusfinanzierung. Das, das wäre auch ein Ansatz, Sie mal drüber sich auslassen sollten kritisch, ob das nicht eigene Institutionen und eigene Prozesse oder so, wie auch immer, nach sich ziehen sollte.	Money laundering and terrorism financing are mixed up
Interviewee 9	Terrorismus ist immer ein, ein, ein Türöffner, nicht nur für Gesetzesänderungen sondern auch für, für massive Massnahmen.	Terrorism financing as a gateway for tough measures

Interview partners	Original Statement	Generalization
Interviewee 9	Erst mal ist/ hat man ja ein primäres Ziel. (unv.) der IS, der Islamische Staat, will sich finanzieren. Der überlegt sich ja nicht gerade, "was passiert 'n, wenn irgendwo ein Ermittlungsverfahren läuft?"	Preliminary proceedings do not deter offenders
Interviewee 9	Dass da Leute in, in Molenbeek in Brüssel sitzen, die brauchen bloss/ die brauchen im Grunde nur ihre Gewehre, äh, zu finanzieren, um dann irgendwo hinzugehen und Leute zu erschiessen, äh, oder die müssen Waffen halt beschaffen. Das ist ja/ Finanzierung muss ja auch nicht nur Geld sein. Das kann ja auch eben (die?) Tatmittel sein, Waffen beschaffen zum Beispiel nur.	Terrorism financing can also be carried out through the means of crime
Interviewee 9	Sie haben ganz normale Einnahmen. Der, der Bin Laden war Erbe eines grossen Baukonzerns in Saudo A/ Saudi-Arabien und war Millionär und hat damit, (.) ziemlich einfach wahrscheinlich, die Anschläge in 9/11 finanziert, indem er aus legalen Bauunternehmen/ aus den Gewinnen eines Bauunternehmens oder eines Konzerns hat er seinen/ die Leute, die die Anschläge gemacht haben, im nötigen Masse finanziert.	Legal income from construction companies

Interview partners	Original Statement	Generalization
Interviewee 9	Da hat jemand seinem, seinem Bruder 1.000, 2.000 Euro geschickt (.) und der hat hier vor Gericht dann eben das Problem, oder nicht er, sondern die Justiz hatte das Problem, nachzuweisen, dass das IS-Finanzierung war, wenn der gesagt hat, "mein Bruder war krank, ich musste ihm 'ne Arzt/ der musste 'ne Arztrechnung bezahlen. Das ist 'ne reine familiäre Sache, ich musste dem/ der ist in Syrien, ich weiss gar nicht, wa/ vom IS weiss ich nix", sagte er dann, "ich hab' dem 1.000 oder 2.000 Euro geschickt oder Dollar, weil er mir sagte, er braucht das Geld. Der ist krank."	Referrals to sick family members
Interviewee 9	Nicht/ und da/ das andere sind V-Leute. Und Verdeckte Ermittler, Polizei, die haben/ hatten schon früher, so viel kann ich mal verraten, auch Leute mit Migrationshintergrund, Muslime, bei der/ als Beamt/ die dann Deutsche wurden, als Beamte im BKA tätig.	Undercover investigators with a migration background

Interview partners	Original Statement	Generalization
Interviewee 9	Egal. Es ist eine grössere Hürde solche/ selbst die Kollegen sozusagen, Kollegen zu gewinnen, die in dem Bereich – ich hatte kein Glück bis dahin – Verdeckte Ermittler sein wollen. Die haben da so 'n bisschen 'ne gewisse, (.) wie soll ich sagen, 'ne ethnische Loyalität, Pro/ Problem der ethnischen Loyalität sogar gehabt, dass die sagen, "nee, das will ich nicht. Das mag ich nicht." Also, das, das/ die Gewinnung verdeckter Ermittler, das stellen Sie sich nicht zu einfach vor.	Undercover investigators with a migration background are difficult to recruit
Interviewee 9	V-Leute, gut, das geht jetzt eher. (Denkweise?) ist eher, dass man Leute aus der Szene direkt hat, die dann für die Polizei arbeiten. Ist ja auch im, im Rechtsextremismus und im Linksextremismus durchaus ja üblich, mit, mit/ auch mit sehr grossen Problemen.	V-men are easier to recruit
Interviewee 10	Das ist ja bei der Terrorfinanzierung so, dass, ähm, die Herkunft der Vermögenswerte sowohl legal als auch illegal sein kann. Und eigentlich dann die Verwendung, also die Terrorfinanzierung an sich, dann illegal ist. Das macht die Ermittlungen natürlich etwas schwierig. Weil das völlig legal erworbenes Vermögen sein kann. Und die Leute auch nicht notwendigerweise schon irgendwelche Vormerkungen haben im strafrechtlichen Bereich.	Investigations difficult as assets are not incriminated

Interview partners	Original Statement	Generalization
Interviewee 10	Da/ die zweite Schwierigkeit, die mir dazu einfallen würde, ist, dass das ähm, national und auch international einfach einer sehr hohen Koordinierung der Behörden bedarf. Da durchwegs sehr unterschiedliche Behörden mit der Bekämpfung betraut sind.	International co-ordination of co-operation between authorities required
Interviewee 10	Aber ich glaube aber, grundsätzlich alles, was für den Transfer von Vermögenswerten geeignet ist, ist natürlich auch für potentielle Terrorismusfinanzierung geeignet.	Any type of asset transfer is eligible for terrorism financing
Interviewee 10	Wenn es eine ganz normale Banküberweisung ist, kann natürlich alles sein. Und allein der Umstand, dass das jemand in die Türkei transferiert hat, heisst nicht notwendigerweise, dass das Geld mit Terrorfinanzierung zu tun hat	Bank transfers to Turkey
Interviewee 11	Und dann natürlich regional, regional durch die Erhebung von Zwangsabgaben, Zwangszöllen ähm, Schutzgebühren, Strassenzöllen, Sondersteuern und so weiter und so fort. Also hm, (.) zum Beispiel der (..) in Syrien (seufzend) oder im Irak praktizierte IS auch die Enteignung von ähm, Immobilien oder Landwirtschaftsgütern und da müssen die Leute ihr Eigentum quasi mieten, wenn sie es benutzen wollen, nicht? Also das ist Raubrittertum, nicht?	Compulsory levies, compulsory duties, protective charges, road tolls, special taxes, expropriation

Interview partners	Original Statement	Generalization
Interviewee 11	Das Problem ist, dass zum Zweck der Terrorismusfinanzierung ähm, sehr geringe Beträge, äh, wenn überhaupt, über das Frankensystem transferiert werden, oder?	Small sums sufficient for terrorism
Interviewee 11	Wobei eigentlich zu sagen, dass das eher die Ausnahme darstellt äh, (unv.), das sind äh, sehr geringe Beträge, weil ähm, es ist ähm, festzuhalten, dass man heute einen Anschlag ähm, problemlos äh, durchführen kann, für ein paar tausend Franken.	Small sums sufficient for terrorism
Interviewee 11	Wenn überhaupt Transaktionen stattfinden, ähm, über das elektronische Transaktionssystem vom Finanzinstitut ähm, (.) in der Regel nicht festgestellt werden kann, dass hier ein krimineller Zweck verfolgt wird.	Criminal purpose cannot usually be established
Interviewee 11	Zuordnung des Bitcoins oder der Währung zu einem wirtschaftlich Berechtigten ist äh, äusserst schwierig, oder?	Assignment of Bitcoin to the beneficial owner is difficult
Interviewee 11	Ich meine, die Überwachung von (Hawala?-)Transaktionen ist nicht möglich.	No monitoring possible
Interviewee 11	Ja, die müsste man eigentlich, wenn man sagt, das ist ein erhöhtes Risiko, muss man eine Abklärung des äh, wirtschaftlichen Hintergrundes machen und den dokumentieren.	Clarification of the economic background can take place
Interviewee 11	Die Leute sind sehr seriös, weil sie sehr viel riskieren, wenn es nicht klappt.	Serious
Interviewee 11	Und es ist auch kostengünstig, so.	Cost-effective

Interview partners	Original Statement	Generalization
Interviewee 11	Dass Terrorismus auch über den Handel finanziert wird.	Financing through trading activities
Interviewee 11	Man kann zum Beispiel das Geld äh, physisch transportieren. Man kann auch jemanden anrufen äh und ihn veranlassen, dass er jemandem, der sich meldet ähm, einen Kredit zur Verfügung stellt, in Form eines (unv.) Geschäftes, also eines (Bargeschäftes?). Da gibt es verschiedene Methoden, die es unmöglich machen,	Physical transport of cash or credit
Interviewee 11	(Hawala?-)Banker gibt es natürlich in Regionen, die nicht über ein ähm, fortschrittliches Banksystem verfügen, oder anders gesagt, wo der Zugang zu Banken für den Grossteil der Bevölkerung nicht möglich ist.	Involve countries without advanced banking systems
Interviewee 11	Aber ich meine, es geht ja einfach darum, ich meine, (.) wenn, wenn man natürlich Geld in gefährdete Regionen schickt oder Geld aus gefährdeten Regionen bekommt, dann ist das klar, es gibt Hochrisikoländer, das ist sicher Syrien, Irak, Afghanistan und so weiter. Ähm, Libanon, was auch immer, das sind so Risikoländer. Und dort muss man das (unv.) Risiko aufgrund des Domizilstaates oder des Destinationsstaates evaluieren, das ist ganz klar.	Avoid high-risk countries
Interviewee 11	Durch die (unv.), sondern auch über den Verkauf von (Raubkunst?). (.) Ähm, also illegaler Kulturgütertransfer, wobei, das passiert vor allem auf dem Schwarzmarkt.	Illegal transfer of cultural property

Interview partners	Original Statement	Generalization
Interviewee 12	Praktisch haben wir aber bei der/ bei der Terrorismusfinanzierung ähm im Gegensatz zur/ zur/ zur reinen Geldwäsche 'ne/ 'ne Mischfinanzierung. Das heisst, wir haben (.) ähm/ wir haben teilweise legale Quellen über/ über Spenden, et cetera. Und als aber auch das gesamte Spektrum der (.) ähm/ der kriminellen Aktivitäten.	Legal and illegal sources of income
Interviewee 12	Äh da können Sie halt auch schon mit 1.000 Euro richtig viel erreichen.	Small sums sufficient for terrorism
Interviewee 12	Sondern es gibt so viele ähm alternative Möglichkeiten, Gelder über Landesgrenzen hinweg zu bringen. Also in erster Linie die/ die/ die Dienstleister, wie/ wie Western Union, et cetera, die das äh wesentlich schneller können, wesentlich billiger können.	Fast and inexpensive
Interviewee 12	Und auf der anderen Seite aus Sicht der Behörden ähm ist bei/ äh bei/ bei der ganzen Office-Arbeit, bei der Prävention ein/ ein/ unbedingt erforderlich/ ein sehr hohes Mass an Abgeschottenheit erforderlich/ Abgeschottenheit erforderlich. Also das heisst, diese Informationen kann man, darf man aus/ aus rechtsstaatlichen äh Gründen gar nicht weitergeben.	Seclusion

Interview partners	Original Statement	Generalization
Interviewee 12	Äh das/ das ist/ das ist sehr schwer. Ob man zusätzlich bei der/ der nötige Austausch zwisch/ zwischen den Strafverfolgern und äh/ und/ und der Wirtschaft im weitesten Sinne äh teilweise gar nicht erfolgen darf.	Information may not be exchanged
Interviewee 12	Ähm wir vergeben Kredite (.) und da wäre die einzige Möglichkeit, (.) ähm (.) sich das im/ im (Bildungsgeschäft) sich zu besorgen, also mittels/ äh mittels Krediten, die man/ die man bekommt über einen gewissen Zeitraum im Rahmen der Auszahlung ähm und/ und wo dann erst Jahre später so die (Zahlung) einsetzt. (.) Also (.) ähm ist aber/ das/ wir sind ja nicht äh/ nicht alleiniger Anbieter im Markt von solchen/ von solchen, ich sage mal (Bildungsfinanzierungen), ähm aber mit Sicherheit einer der/ der/ der grossen insgesamt.	Scam education loans
Interviewee 13	Aber auch Steuern erhebt.	Tax collection
Interviewee 13	Also hier sind jetzt nicht ganz so viel, aber im Prinzip, was der IS macht, ist, er erhebt tatsächlich Zölle und zwar in dem Gebiet, wo er es kontrolliert, da werden wir mit unseren Massnahmen, Ermittlungen nicht viel ausrichten können, also ich kann nichts machen hier in Liechtenstein, was den IS daran hindern sollte.	Duties

Interview partners	Original Statement	Generalization
Interviewee 13	Zum Beispiel bei Abhebungen von Banken muss jeder eine Steuer abliefern und zwar je nach Religion, Christen ein bisschen mehr, Muslime ein bisschen weniger, gibt es da einen Steuertarif.	Tax collection
Interviewee 13	Das haben wir natürlich relativ deutlich erlebt mit dem Aufkommen des Islamischen Staates und eigentlich relativ schnell gemerkt dann, dass alles, was wir gemeint haben zu wissen über Terrorismusfinanzierung, eigentlich aus dem Wissen post Nine Eleven entstanden ist.	Knowledge of terrorism financing based on 9/11
Interviewee 13	Na, das kommt darauf an, ich glaube, es gibt nicht DIE Terrorismusfinanzierung.	Different types of terrorism financing
Interviewee 13	Wir hatten dann, ich glaube, etwa 2003, 2004/5 herum relativ genaue Kenntnis, wie sich Al-Qaida finanziert hat, und haben daraus dann die entsprechenden Massnahmen abgeleitet.	Measures based in part on knowledge of Al-Qaeda
Interviewee 13	Und vielleicht ein Grund, warum man dieses Phänomen jetzt so lange nicht eindämmen konnte oder immer noch Mühe hat damit, ist, dass diese Organisation völlig anders strukturiert ist und eben auch völlig anders finanziert ist als Al-Qaida.	New structures function differently than Al-Qaeda

Interview partners	Original Statement	Generalization
Interviewee 13	Auf die zu einfache Antwort, also es gibt nicht die Terrorismusfinanzierung, man kann auch nicht sagen, die man macht, sondern es ist jede, wenn man einmal so von den Organisationen, vor allem ist, jede Organisation hat ihre Eigenheiten.	Individual characteristics of the organizations
Interviewee 13	Was jetzt für den Islamischen Staat ganz besonders schwierig macht, ist, dass der Islamische Staat natürlich gelernt hat aus Al-Qaida, also so unverwandt sind die beiden ja nicht, gibt es auch noch persönliche Beziehungen.	IS has learned from Al-Qaeda
Interviewee 13	Und im Unterschied Al-Qaida hatte ja eigentlich nie ein grosses Geldproblem am Anfang, weil sie hatten ja genügend Vermögenswerte aus der bin-Laden-Familie, bin Laden selber war ja vermögend.	Al-Qaeda had assets from the beginning.
Interviewee 13	Da ging es eigentlich mehr darum, das Geld, das man hat, möglichst beisammenzuhalten und niemandem Zugriff darauf zu gewähren.	Preservation of assets was a priority for Al-Qaeda
Interviewee 13	Wo der IS im Gegensatz dazu arm und klein angefangen hat und gewachsen ist.	IS had few assets to begin with
Interviewee 13	Und eigentlich, je grösser die Organisation wurde, desto mehr sich so verhalten hat, wie ein Staat sich verhält.	Organizations behave like states
Interviewee 13	Und darum ist der Begriff Islamischer Staat eben nicht ganz falsch, generieren aber ihre Einkünfte aus dem eigenen Herrschaftsbereich.	Income from own domain

Interview partners	Original Statement	Generalization
Interviewee 13	Al-Qaida war immer extern finanziert, also zum Teil intern bin-Laden-Vermögen und andere, aber im Wesentlichen extern durch Donations, also es war eigentlich eine spendenfinanzierte Organisation.	Al-Qaeda externally funded
Interviewee 13	Darum hat man bei der Bekämpfung eigentlich auch, Hauptansatzpunkt war zum einen Listing von Personen, die Geld haben oder Zugriff zu Geldern haben, und zum anderen das Unterbinden von Spenden.	Person listings for the suppression of donations
Interviewee 13	Beim IS ist es fast umgekehrt, IS bekommt zwar auch Spenden, hängt aber nicht davon ab, sondern der IS generiert Einkommen, indem er Ölquellen auch nutzt.	IS generates its own income
Interviewee 13	Also eine völlig andere Ausgangslage als jetzt bei Al-Qaida.	Different starting position than Al-Qaeda
Interviewee 13	Man muss zuerst einmal gucken, welche Organisation, was man eigentlich anschaut, um die Hintergründe der Finanzierung zu verstehen.	Analysis of the organization as a prerequisite for understanding the financing
Interviewee 13	Und wenn man dann jetzt noch weitergeht über die beiden hinaus und Boko Haram sieht, die auch wieder Eigenheiten haben, die eher an den IS erinnern.	Boko Haram is similar to IS
Interviewee 13	Und erst dann eigentlich daraus abgeleitet die richtigen Massnahmen machen kann.	Derive measures from analysis

Interview partners	Original Statement	Generalization
Interviewee 13	Das Zweite ist, ein ganz anderes Kapitel sind die Terroranschläge durch Einzeltäter, die einfach radikalisiert sind durch die Ideologie, aber nicht bei wirklich einer Organisation sind, also die Lone Wolves, wahrscheinlich Nizza und wahrscheinlich Ansbach und ein paar andere.	Single perpetrator difficult to identify
Interviewee 13	Hier ist es schon so, dass die AUCH darauf achten, unterdessen ist auch Teil der Ausbildung dieser Terroristen oder des Materials, dass sie sich finden und zueignen, möglichst keine Spuren zu hinterlassen.	Terrorists trained to avoid leaving traces
Interviewee 13	Also möglichst versuchen, dass wenn sie irgendwo ihre Waffen besorgen oder ihr Auto mieten, sie selber riskieren das Leben, ihnen ist egal, wenn sie auffliegen, aber möglichst ihr Umfeld nicht auffliegen zu lassen.	Terrorists try not to expose their environment
Interviewee 13	Und da ist man dann ganz anders, da geht es nicht darum, dass die Geld brauchen, um den Anschlag zu begehen, sondern dass die Terrorismusfinanzierung dort eigentlich ein nützliches Instrument ist, weil man über die Finanzierungsströme, also, ich sage einmal, die Auswertung des Bankkontos eines solchen Attentäters ist wahrscheinlich mindestens so aufschlussreich wie die Auswertung seines Handys.	Analysis of the financing flows of the assassins provides information about their environment

Interview partners	**Original Statement**	**Generalization**
Interviewee 13	Und viele dieser Lone Wolves sind ja dann doch Teil auch von informellen Fällen, also man verspricht sich, und das ist auch nachgewiesen nach den Anschlägen in Paris, man kann schon relativ schnell weitere Mitglieder von Zellen oder Anverwandte aufspüren, wenn man weiss, wer wem, wo, wann Geld überwiesen hat.	Analysis of the financing flows of the assassins provides information about their environment
Interviewee 13	Hier hat es eigentlich einen Paradigmenwechsel gegeben, also bei, am Anfang nach Nine Eleven ging es darum, die Finanzquellenorganisationen auszutrocknen, um die Organisation lahmzulegen.	Early drying up of financial flows
Interviewee 13	Das ist eigentlich bei Al-Qaida gar nicht einmal so schlecht gelungen, Al-Qaida spielt heute wirklich keine grosse Rolle mehr. Welcher Teil hier ferngesteuerte Bomben und welcher Teil die Finanzierungsbemühungen hatte, welchen Anteil daran, das ist hypothetisch, aber ich glaube, geschadet hat es auf jeden Fall nicht.	Al-Qaeda was weakened by CFT
Interviewee 13	Beim Islamischen Staat glaubt man auch, dass die Massnahmen Wirkung zeigen, der Islamische Staat hat deutlich weniger Geld zur Verfügung als noch am Anfang.	IS is weakened by CFT

Interview partners	**Original Statement**	**Generalization**
Interviewee 13	Aber die grösste Herausforderung ist wahrscheinlich schon bei diesen Einzeltätern, bei den kleinen Zellen, die ja sehr mobil, sehr unabhängig von der zentralen Organisation arbeiten und dort ist, glaube ich, die Zielsetzung der Massnahmen, nicht mehr die auszutrocknen, weil die gar nicht so viel Geld brauchen, sondern der Charme der Massnahmen liegt darin, erstens das Umfeld zu erkennen, was ich schon gesagt habe, und zweitens aber auch, und jetzt wird es natürlich spannend, mit Zuhilfenahme von diesen Erkenntnissen, die man schon hat, Täter überhaupt, mögliche zukünftige Täter überhaupt erst aufzuspüren.	Single perpetrator difficult to identify
Interviewee 13	Also, wenn man weiss, dass diese Leute typischerweise Autos mieten mit Prepaid-Karten, ja, kann man daraus, zusammen mit ein paar anderen Merkmalen, die typisch ist für diese Täter, schon einspeisen und sagen: "Hier, halt. Kann man das dann nicht erkennen im Moment, wo jemand ein Auto mietet, um den wenigstens zu observieren", ne?	Individual perpetrators identifiable on the basis of certain behaviours
Interviewee 13	Also ich sage nicht, dass jeder, der mit Prepaid-Karte ein Auto mietet, observiert werden muss, aber wenn er zusätzlich noch andere Merkmale hat, ich sage einmal jung, männlich, radikalisiert, dann kann das einen Alarm auslösen.	Recognize suspicious behaviour

Interview partners	Original Statement	Generalization
Interviewee 13	Und ich glaube schon, dass zunehmend die Mittel da, die Kenntnisse aus der Finanzierung helfen, einen Beitrag dazu leisten, solche Leute aufzuspüren.	CFT makes an important contribution
Interviewee 13	Also es geht eigentlich jetzt mehr darum, die Nadel im Heuhaufen erst zu finden, als die Illusion zu haben oder vielleicht die beschränkten Möglichkeiten zu haben eine ganze Organisation hier lahmzulegen mit Terrorismusfi nanzierungsmassnahmen.	Fighting individual perpetrators vs entire organizations
Interviewee 13	Also das ist eigentlich für mich eine wichtige Erkenntnis, in den letzten zwei, drei Jahren sind die Erwartungen eine andere geworden, die Zielsetzung ist anders geworden.	Changed objective
Interviewee 13	Möglichst ohne Spuren zu hinterlassen	Terrorists trained to avoid leaving traces
Interviewee 13	Oder wenn Spuren hinterlassen werden, dann die so normal aussehen zu lassen, dass sie eben nicht entdeckt werden können.	Terrorists make their traces look inconspicuous
Interviewee 13	Was ja schon einmal anders ist als früher, ich glaube, wenn vor fünf Jahren ein Terroranschlag gewesen wäre, hätte man eigentlich gar nicht so gross geguckt, wo die ihr Geld herhaben und wohin das Geld gegangen ist.	Terrorism financing increasingly in focus
Interviewee 13	Weg aus dem formellen Sektor, eine sehr starke Neigung zu modernen Zahlungsmitteln, sehr starke Neigung zum Gebrauch von Technologie, also Mobile Payment Services.	Strong trend towards modern technologies and mobile payment services

Interview partners	Original Statement	Generalization
Interviewee 13	Also jede, ich sage einmal, Innovation auf dem Finanzmarkt vor allem zur Übermittlung von Geldern, vor allem zum Transferieren von Geldern ausserhalb des formalen Bankensektors, die wird aufgenommen.	Innovations for transfer of funds are included
Interviewee 13	Wir sehen zunehmend Hinweise auf die Verwendung von Kryptowährung, auch wenn das jetzt noch nicht sich durchgesetzt hat als Lieblingsmittel der Terroristen, aber wenn es eine Möglichkeit gibt, die wenigen Transaktionen, die sie machen müssen, aber ein paar müssen sie halt schon machen, dann sicher ausserhalb des Bankensektors.	Transactions outside the banking sector
Interviewee 13	Und man darf die nicht immer nur isoliert betrachten, also nicht ein Indikator heisst, es ist ein Terrorist dahinter, sondern ist dann immer eine Kombination von mehreren solchen Indikatoren, die Hinweise darauf geben kann.	Observe combination of several indicators
Interviewee 13	Also, und das sieht schon anders aus als das, was wir noch vor zehn Jahren hatten, wo wir immer typischerweise versucht haben, diesen finanziellen Unterstützer, diesen Scheich halt zu finden, der Al-Qaida unterstützt, da sind wir heute schon breiter aufgestellt.	Broad scope of investigations into terrorism financing

Interview partners	Original Statement	Generalization
Interviewee 13	Was wir machen können, ist dafür sorgen, dass das Geld nicht weiter fliesst, aber der IS, ist halt schon, weil es vor allem über den Schmuggel herausgeht, sind eigentlich die Nachbarländer gefragt.	Focus on countries neighbouring crisis regions
Interviewee 13	Ja, das ist aber, wobei die Täter, also von denen wir hier reden, das sind ja Verrückte, oder? Also irgendwelche 23-jährige Arbeitslose, die sich irgendwo radikalisiert haben, ich weiss nicht, ob die so intelligent sind.	Perpetrators not usually intelligent
Interviewee 13	Das dürfte einfach schwieriger sein und ich sage einmal, lieber dort ansetzen, wo man es sehen kann und das richtigmachen, anstatt zu sehr im Fischteich zu buddeln.	Focus on counter-terrorism activities
Interviewee 13	Ich meine, wenn das einmal auffällt und erfolgreich ist, dann werden Leute natürlich wieder ausweichen und andere Methoden finden.	Further development of methods
Interviewee 13	Zum einen, weil der IS immer noch über erhebliche Geldmittel verfügt, versucht er eher in seinem Herrschaftsgebiet noch mehr Geld zu machen, als das Risiko einzugehen, im Ausland sich zu exponieren zu stark.	Focus of the IS on its own territory of rule

Interview partners	Original Statement	Generalization
Interviewee 13	Also es gibt Lösegeldversicherungen, aber ich denke einmal mehr an diese Konzerne, die halt weltweit tätig sind und die eine generelle Police haben, was immer ihren Mitarbeitern passiert, zahlt die Versicherung oder entschädigt die Gesellschaft für die Kosten, ja. Die Versicherung kann nicht in Anspruch nehmen für sich, dass sie im Notstand ist, ja, kein Mensch zwingt sie diese Police anzubieten, aber die Versicherung hat ja ein grösseres Risiko sich der Terrorismusfinanzierung schuldig zu machen, wenn sie solche Kosten entschädigen würde.	Ransomware insurance as a risk industry
Interviewee 13	Also ein grosses Thema ist natürlich, dass wir ganz vorsichtig sein müssen, schnelle Rückschlüsse zu ziehen.	No hasty conclusions
Interviewee 13	Mit Terrorismus ist heute eine Keule natürlich, die ein Arsenal auslöst von Massnahmen, also da kann man die auch ganz schnell in die Bredouille bringen.	Many measures possible
Interviewee 13	Also hier, was vielleicht so eine der Schwierigkeiten ist, die Erkenntnisse, die man heute gewinnen kann, man hat ja viel mehr Mittel als früher, dass man hier aufpasst, dass man nicht über die Stränge schlägt.	Do not take excessive measures

Interview partners	**Original Statement**	**Generalization**
Interviewee 13	Weil es ist natürlich, Big Data ist natürlich eine Sorge für Datenschützer, ne, hier kommen wir in einen Zielkonflikt herein, wobei ich kann heute hundert Leute fragen, was ihnen wichtiger ist, Terrorismusbekämpfung oder Datenschutz, und ich kriege 99-mal die gleiche Antwort. Der Hundertste war ein Treuhänder.	Counter-terrorism often more important than data protection
Interviewee 13	Aber mir geht es ja nicht so sehr um den Täter, der hat sich ja vielleicht schon in die Luft gejagt, mir geht es vor allem darum, einen möglichen Anschlag zu vermeiden, indem man Gelder sicherstellt.	Preventing attacks by seizing funds
Interviewee 13	Ich glaube, generell haben wir, also wir haben zum einen eine wichtige Rolle der Nachrichtendienste und zum anderen haben wir eine wichtige Rolle der Finanzermittler und die beiden haben sich bis jetzt noch nicht einmal in den gleichen Raum gesetzt, ja?	Communication between intelligence services and Financial Intelligence Units not yet sufficient

Interview partners	Original Statement	Generalization
Interviewee 13	Das andere ist tatsächlich, wie können wir es schaffen, einen Schnitt, den Fuss vor die Tat zu kriegen, ja? Also schon, wenn Sie die Anschläge in Paris ansehen, dann war eigentlich alles da, man wusste, die Täter haben Spuren gelegt, ne? Es waren Daten und Erkenntnisse in Belgien vorhanden, es waren Daten und Erkenntnisse in Frankreich vorhanden. Und obwohl die beiden Staaten die gleiche Sprache sprechen, gut zusammenarbeiten, keine Probleme miteinander haben, alle Kanäle sind offen, es sind EU-Staaten, man hat es nicht gesehen, man hat es erst nachher gesehen, was da abgeht.	Fatal consequences of sluggish communication
Interviewee 13	Und ich glaube, dass das die grosse Herausforderung, aber auch Chance ist, wie können wir Daten miteinander verhängen?	Link data
Interviewee 13	Wie können wir, das berühmte Stichwort, Big Data nutzen, um schneller zu sein, um Anschläge zu verhindern, um Leute aus den Verkehr zu nehmen oder zumindest unter Beobachtung zu setzen, ohne dass wir Gefahr laufen, dass es dann die Falschen trifft?	Targeted use of large data volumes
Interviewee 13	Aber es ist ja schon so, dass wir hier auch mit Staaten zusammenarbeiten müssen, die eben nicht die gleichen Anforderungen haben, und das ist schon ein grosses Problem. Also schmeissen wir alle rechtsstaatlichen Grundsätze über Bord?	Forwarding of information to selected countries

Interview partners	Original Statement	Generalization
Interviewee 13	Wir haben es, ich meine, generell in der Zusammenarbeit zwischen Staaten, ich sage einmal, auf dem justiziellen Bereich, also Amts- und der Rechtshilfe, da haben wir ein Konzept aus dem 19. Jahrhundert, ne, zum Teil muss man es noch über die Botschaften schicken, übersetzen, beglaubigen.	Obsolete system of mutual assistance
Interviewee 13	Und wir haben heute auf der anderen Seite ein Finanzsystem, das ihnen erlaubt innerhalb Sekunden Transaktionen in zig verschiedene Länder umzuleiten.	Fast financial system
Interviewee 13	Und um die gleiche Transaktion nachzuvollziehen, brauchen Sie drei Jahre, ja?	Administrative assistance too slow
Interviewee 13	Wir haben auch parallel dazu heute schon Möglichkeiten auch der informellen Zusammenarbeit, ich sage einmal, zwischen FIU, das ist eines der Beispiele, auch zwischen Polizeibehörden, die jetzt nicht auf diese justizförmliche Anforderung angewiesen sind.	Informal co-operation between FIUs
Interviewee 13	Also ich glaube, wir müssen noch stärker unterscheiden, was ist Intelligence, wo geht es darum, Informationen rasch zugänglich zu machen.	Make information readily available
Interviewee 13	Also unter dem Titel Terrorismusfinanzierung habe ich heute das, was ich brauche, ich bekomme alle Informationen, die ich brauche. Natürlich muss ich sie dann auch so verwenden, ich darf sie ja nicht für Drittzwecke verwenden.	Use information only for counter-terrorism purposes

Interview partners	Original Statement	Generalization
Interviewee 13	Ich frage mich manchmal, ob die Betroffenen selber sich dann nicht noch Fesseln eigentlich anziehen, die es gar nicht mehr geben sollte. Ob vielleicht viele im Privatsektor denken, zum Beispiel: Ja, wir dürfen vielleicht gar nicht zu den Behörden kommen, weil wir Berufsgeheimnisse haben.	Hesitant reactions on the part of the professional secrecy bodies
Interviewee 13	Bei der Organisation, beim IS selber, ich glaube, dort ist die Reihenfolge der Finanzierungsquellen oder die Wichtigkeit immer noch im Vordergrund, also erst einmal das Geld, das der IS selber hat, das ist zwar ein Thema für die, ja, gut, für das Konfliktgebiet, sage ich einmal, im weitesten Sinne.	Existing assets in conflict areas
Interviewee 13	Solange der IS die Gelder nur in seinem Territorium verwenden kann, geht es ja noch, aber, ich glaube, auch die Nachbarländer Irak, Jordanien, Türkei vor allem sind da gefragt.	Transfer via neighbouring countries as a challenge
Interviewee 13	Sehr häufig fliegen halt die nach Istanbul, reisen dann an die Grenze und leeren dann an den Geldautomaten in der letzten türkischen Stadt vor dem Grenzübertritt, plündern die noch einmal ihr Konto, also die kommen dann mit ihren fünf-, sechstausend Euro ins Krisengebiet.	Cash withdrawals in area bordering Syria is suspicious

Interview partners	**Original Statement**	**Generalization**
Interviewee 13	Und das ist etwas, was man erkennen kann, also hier kann natürlich eine türkische Bank durchaus einen wichtigen Beitrag leisten, indem man solche Transaktionen als ungewöhnlich erfasst und auswertet.	Transactional analysis
Interviewee 13	"Moment einmal, du bist einmal in dieser südtürkischen Stadt gewesen, du hast dein Konto geplündert, das ist ein Indikator und dich schauen wir einmal genauer an."	Suspicious transactions as a starting point for further investigations
Interviewee 13	Also ich sage, dass das/ Nur ist es so eben, ist gerade beim Geldautomatengeschäft, die Bank, wo sie den Zug vornehmen, die weiss nicht, ob das Konto geplündert wird oder nicht. Die weiss ja nicht, wie viel auf dem Konto ist, die sieht einfach, da werden tausend Euro bezogen, das kann aber schon auch ein Tourist sein, der ein Teppich kauft, oder?	Difficult to differentiate between terrorism financing and legitimate cash withdrawals
Interviewee 13	Also hier sind schon Banken im, nahe am Kriegsgebiet waren, türkische Banken, die ja auch gut sind, die ja professionell aufgestellt sind, die haben da wahrscheinlich schon eine besondere Verantwortung.	Turkish banks as an alternative to Syria
Interviewee 13	Das war natürlich ein grosses Thema bei Al-Qaida, wusste man auch, weil es dort eben vor allem darum ging, Geld ins Konfliktgebiet zu bringen, und da war Hawala fast die einzige Möglichkeit.	Access to conflict areas

Interview partners	Original Statement	Generalization
Interviewee 13	Ich würde meinen, wenn man so eine Transaktion, wie ich sie skizziert habe, so eine strukturierte, denkt, könnte Hawala zwischen oder nach der Bankreform Cash durchaus eine Rolle spielen.	Combination with bank transfer
Interviewee 13	Also ich glaube, im Bereich Lösegeld könnte ich mir durchaus vorstellen, dass das immer noch eine Rolle spielt.	Suitable for ransom payment
Interviewee 13	Natürlich ist es so, und hier kommt die internationale Zusammenarbeit ins Spiel, wenn natürlich jetzt eine belgische Behörde jemanden sowieso schon beobachtet, sieht, der fliegt nach Istanbul, wenn diese Information dann schnell in die Türkei gehen kann, dort an die Banken gelangen kann und der macht das in Istanbul, dann könnte man das auch entdecken.	Exchange of information (lists of dangerous persons) between authorities and banks
Interviewee 13	Das sind junge Männer, die digital aufgewachsen sind und vertraut sind. Ich meine, bin Laden wusste wahrscheinlich nicht, was E-Banking ist, die wissen, was hier E-Wallets sind, ja?	Digital natives as perpetrators
Interviewee 13	Ich würde einmal vermuten, da würde man wahrscheinlich eher den Weg über die Golfstaaten machen, wo ja, man darf nicht ganz vergessen, der IS hat sich da massgeblich am Anfang auch aus den Golfstaaten finanziert.	Detour via Gulf States

Interview partners	Original Statement	Generalization
Interviewee 13	Also ich bringe eben das Beispiel, dass irgendjemand einen grossen Geldbetrag in Istanbul hat und hat einen arabisch klingenden Namen, aber mit französischer Staatsangehörigkeit. Vielleicht ist es ein braver Familienvater, der einen Teppich kaufen will oder dem die Brieftasche gestohlen wurde und dringend Cash braucht, um sein Hotel zu bezahlen.	Cite carpet purchase or wallet loss in Istanbul as justification
Interviewee 13	Wie gesagt, auch hier natürlich wertvoll, weil schnell und eben nicht an irgendwelche Grenzen, formalen Grenzen haltmachend.	Quickly
Interviewee 13	Also ich sage einmal, wenn eine deutsche Bundesanwaltschaft so etwas macht, dann habe ich kein Problem damit, wenn der russische Inlandsgeheimdienst das macht, dann (lachen) ist wahrscheinlich nicht so toll.	Differentiation by country
Interviewee 13	Weil wir öffnen natürlich da schon Möglichkeiten, die auch missbrauchsanfällig sind.	Vulnerable to abuse
Interviewee 13	Also wahrscheinlich ist das Rezept darin, ja, diese Möglichkeiten müssen genutzt werden, das schulden wir den Leuten, wenn sie Sicherheit haben wollen, oder wir müssen so ehrlich sein und zu den Leuten hingehen und sagen: "Das könnte man tun, das machen wir nicht, damit ist aber die Sicherheit nicht eine hundertprozentige."	Lower security without digital surveillance
Interviewee 13	Wenn Unternehmen, also Ölquellenschmuggel betreibt.	Oil trading

Interview partners	Original Statement	Generalization
Interviewee 13	Ganze Bevölkerungsgruppen von der Lösegeldindustrie betreibt und halt der Versklavung der Jesiden sind darauf gerichtet, damit Lösegeld zu generieren.	Ransomware
Interviewee 13	Antiquitätenhandel zu einem gewissen Bereich und ich sage einmal, ist eigentlich mehr der Schmuggel von Antiquitäten, der besteuert wird, wo Zölle erhoben werden.	Trade in antiques
Interviewee 13	Wir haben den Bereich Schmuggel, wo der IS immer noch viel finanziert, und eben den Bereich Menschenhandel.	Human trafficking
Interviewee 13	Und dann noch beim Schmuggel spezifisch die Antiquitäten.	Trade in antiques
Interviewee 13	Da sind schon gewisse Bedenken dann, dass in diesen Ländern vielleicht nicht die Staaten selber, aber viele Leute natürlich auch davon profitieren vom IS das Öl abzunehmen oder die ausgebeuteten oder geraubten Kunstwerke.	Smuggling
Interviewee 13	Und danach wird es dann ganz schwierig, also Öl ist das einmal vermischt, werden Sie da nicht mehr, der Ölhändler, der dann viel später erst das Öl kauft, da dürfte es zu spät sein anzusetzen.	Oil trading
Interviewee 13	Sicher gibt es eine Entführungsindustrie, also der IS, Boko Haram, auch viele andere entführen gezielt Leute.	Ransomware
Interviewee 13	Der den Ermittlungsbehörden hilft, sich einmal an die Fersen von jemandem zu setzen und allenfalls jemanden hochzugehen.	Facilitates further investigation

Interview partners	**Original Statement**	**Generalization**
Interviewee 13	ist wahrscheinlich eine der wenigen Möglichkeiten, die man hat, überhaupt in diese Felder.	One less option
Interviewee 13	Für den IS selber relativ schwierig, weil diese Organisation ist sehr geschickt aufgebaut, die haben da eigentlich nicht ein Hauptquartier, wo man einen einschleusen kann und dann alles erfährt, eine sehr dezentrale Organisation.	Decentralized organization of the IS as an obstacle
Interviewee 13	Vielversprechend wahrscheinlich dort im europäischen Umfeld, wo sie tatsächlich Schläferzellen haben, aus denen heraus sich ein Anschlag erzielen lässt.	Ideal for sleeper cells in Europe
Interviewee 13	Also ich glaube, die belgische Zelle und so weiter, das sind lohnenswerte Ziele für Verdeckte Ermittler.	Belgian cell as a worthwhile destination
Interviewee 13	Den Lonely Wolf, der da irgendwo zuhause sich Gewaltvideos anschaut und sich irgendwie radikalisiert und dann einen Lastwagen mietet, den werden sie, so viele Verdeckte Ermittler gibt es gar nicht, also, wenn sie da jedem einen oder drei oder fünf hinterherhängen und da haben wir die Ressourcen nicht.	Lone wolf not available

Interview partners	Original Statement	Generalization
Interviewee 13	Ich glaube, man muss die beschränkten Mittel, die man ohnehin schon hat bei den Verdeckten Ermittlern, das ist ja hoch riskant für die Betroffenen auch, muss man dort ansetzen, wo es am meisten Sinn macht, und das ist wahrscheinlich beim Aufspüren und Infiltrieren von erkannten Zellen, die eine hohe Wahrscheinlichkeit haben, dass einer davon dann tatsächlich einen Anschlag vornimmt.	Targeted use necessary
Interviewee 14	Und die/ Eben diese Splittergruppen, diese Attentäter von Paris und Brüssel, wahrscheinlich jetzt auch in Istanbul, das ist nicht aufwendig, ein paar tausend Euro, die die nötig haben, um quasi da ihre Ressourcen zu kaufen, also Miete zu tragen, Lebensmittel zu kaufen. Die Waffen sind auch nicht wahnsinnig teuer. Da ist man mit ein paar tausend Euro dabei	Strikes are not costly
Interviewee 14	eben als terroristische Organisation würde ich schauen: Kann ich mich selber finanzieren? Dann bin ich natürlich viel unabhängiger oder eher Land und Quellen erschliessen, wo ich weiss, da gibt es immer Opfer, die wir da uns aussuchen können.	Terrorist groups are self-financing

Interview partners	Original Statement	Generalization
Interviewee 14	Ja das ist natürlich das absolute Highlight oder/ Was Geldwäsche oder Terrorfinanzierung erreichen möchte, dass das durch Quellen kommt, die legal sind und so geschickt konstruiert werden kann, dass die Quelle legal ist, aber auch der Verwendungszweck dann legal aussieht.	Legal sources
Interviewee 14	Und die Frage ist: Wenn dann diese Geldhändler, dieser (unv.) dann seinerseits quasi Geschäfte macht, bleibt er eventuell bei seiner Hausbank hängen.	Clearing via banks risky
Interviewee 14	Also ich persönlich würde viel eher in die Richtung gehen von diesen neuen Technologien. Da sind die Behörden wirklich noch hinterher.	Authorities are not up to date
Interviewee 14	Aber doch, es gibt immer ein Risiko, dass man da Spuren hinterlässt, ja. Aber das ist beim Bargeld genau das Gleiche. Sie können nicht grosse Bargeldsummen irgendwie unsichtbar in den Markt integrieren. Irgendwo fällt das immer auf.	Risk of leaving traces
Interviewee 14	Die Entwicklung geht so schnell voran und den Behörden fehlt einfach das Geld.	Authorities are not up to date
Interviewee 14	Ja also ich denke zuletzt geht das in bar. Also die brauchen ja das Geld (unv.), um das/ Ja quasi um die (unv.) betreiben zu können, um Einkäufe tätigen zu können.	Cash transport of funds for purchases

Interview partners	Original Statement	Generalization
Interviewee 14	Also eine Bank in der Schweiz kann sagen: (unv.) Türkei ist für mich nicht ein erhöhtes Risiko, weil sie unterstehen einer Bankenaufsicht und gemäss (unv.) gehen sie nicht auf/ Mit erhöhtem Risiko versehen und werden sich da auch nicht die grossen Fragen stellen.	Swiss banks can refuse business relations with Turkey
Interviewee 14	Also sprich zusammengefasst: Ja, es können Überweisungen gemacht werden in die Türkei, wird nicht von Gesetzes wegen als Hochrisiko angesehen werden müssen, ausser die Bank setzt sich selber über gewisse Risikokriterien und sagen: "Türkei ist für mich erhöhtes Risiko."	Turkey is not considered a high-risk country
Interviewee 14	Es ist ein Thema und bleibt ein Thema, weil wenn man mit quasi diesem informellen Bereich benutzt oder/ Dann schaut niemand nach, oder?	No supervision
Interviewee 14	Das ist möglich, aber das ist natürlich schon ein Gebiet, wo keine Aufsicht besteht und der überhaupt nicht transparent ist und das bietet natürlich ganz viele Möglichkeiten auch Vermögenswerte von A nach B zu verschieben.	No supervision
Interviewee 14	Also die Bitcoins, ich finde das ein super spannendes Thema, hochkomplex, absolut nicht transparent,	Lack of transparency
Interviewee 14	Aber man hat keine Ahnung, wer sich hinter einer Bitcoin-Adresse verbirgt. Das ist komplett anonym, verschlüsselt, man hat keine Ahnung, wer dahintersteckt.	Anonymity

Interview partners	Original Statement	Generalization
Interviewee 14	Und ja, weil es eben technisch anspruchsvoll ist (unv.), überhaupt nicht transparent ist, ist es natürlich ein super geeignetes Mittel, um die Vermögenswerte von A nach B zu verschieben, solange die Teilnehmer an das System Bitcoin glauben, funktioniert das auch.	Lack of transparency
Interviewee 14	Aber es ist sehr leicht versteckbar, es ist verschlüsselbar.	Easy to hide
Interviewee 14	Man kann grosse Summen quasi in Bitcoin umwandeln und wenn ich das in bar haben müsste, dann brauche ich grosse Lagerplätze und da ist eben das Verlustrisiko, sei es durch Diebstahl, sei es durch Verlust, sei es durch Raub, sei es durch Brand oder irgendwelche Elementarschäden.	Reduced storage risk
Interviewee 14	Für diese Terroristen, die da in, ja nicht so westlichen Ländern, aber die ausserhalb des Operationsgebietes vom IS arbeiten, also quasi direkt im Zielort arbeiten, ist schon eine Rolle. Die müsse quasi ihren Lebensunterhalt finanzieren und ich glaube nicht, dass die finanzielle Unterstützung des IS erhalten.	Financing living expenses in the West

Interview partners	Original Statement	Generalization
Interviewee 14	Miete müssen sie zahlen, sie müssen Essen kaufen können, sie müssen quasi die Waffenmunition, Sprengstoff kaufen, aber da bewegen wir uns nicht wirklich im Bereich von ein paar 10.000 Euro. 10, 20 pro Person. Das klingt zwar nach viel, für jemanden, der arbeitslos ist, aber das hat man schnell beisammen. Und gerade wenn man noch (unv.) tätig ist oder im Drogenhandel drinnen (unv.) keine Berührungsängste, Diebstahl, Erpressung, ja? Und dann wird das quasi so finanziert.	Financing livelihood in the West through theft, drug trafficking and extortion
Interviewee 14	Ich weiss nicht, wie genau die Behörden dort hingucken. Also es heisst zumindest, dass die internationale Kooperation etwas schwierig ist mit den Behörden in Dubai.	Taking advantage of the lack of co-operation from the authorities in Dubai
Interviewee 14	Also Türkei gilt in dem Sinne/ Es ist nicht auf einer Sanktionsliste der (unv.) und das bedeutet, dass die Aufsicht über den Bankenbereich als gleichwertig empfunden wird.	Turkish banks' supervision considered equivalent
Interviewee 14	Aber dann kann das Geld dort sicher bar abgehoben werden.	Cash withdrawals
Interviewee 14	Wenn man das kombiniert oder das quasi mit Handel vermischt wird oder dass eine Warenlieferung gemacht oder nicht gemacht wird oder eine Rechnung gestellt wird, aber nicht geliefert wird und dann hat man natürlich wieder die Möglichkeit, Vermögenswerte von A nach B zu verschieben.	Combination with trade and use of fictitious invoices

Interview partners	Original Statement	Generalization
Interviewee 14	Was ist der (unv.) Wert eines Produktes oder wie können die bestimmen, ob diese Maschine wirklich so viel 100.000 Euro kostet oder nicht?	Difficult to determine value of machines
Interviewee 14	Oh, es ist ein hoher Betrag und gibt es eine Rechtfertigung für das? Ja, es gibt ein Dokument oder einen Vertrag. Okay, den schauen wir uns an. Um was geht es da? Ah, Dienstleistungen, ja das ist schon etwas, was verdächtig wäre. Dienstleistungen ist ein schwammiger Begriff.	Avoid invoices for services
Interviewee 14	Aber wenn irgendeine Maschine geliefert wird und da steht, die kostet eine halbe Million und der Betrag war eine halbe Million, (unv.) mein Einwand. Das ist dann für die meisten Banken genügend. Die hinterfragen dieses Dokument gar nicht.	Machine bills
Interviewee 14	Die sind schon froh, dass es ein Dokument oder sogar eine Urkunde gibt, die besagt: Diese Maschine ist eine halbe Million Euro wert.	Procure documents
Interviewee 14	Ich sage mal ich bin da wirklich compliant, ich komme freiwillig zu euch. Dann ist auch die Bank froh, wenn sie diese Dokumente hat, ablegen kann, zusammenheften kann und dann sagt: "Wir haben ja eine Dokumentation."	Provide documentation to the bank voluntarily

Interview partners	Original Statement	Generalization
Interviewee 14	Ich weiss nicht, ob ich von vorneherein so kommen würde. Aber wenn die Frage kommt, dann würde ich das gleich liefern und sagen: "Ja, selbstverständlich. Wir verstehen, dass Sie Compliance-Pflichten haben, dass Sie Aufklärungspflichten haben und wir wissen das. Ist nicht das erste Mal, dass wir gefragt werden. Bitte schön, hier sind die Unterlagen."	Provide documentation to the bank upon first request
Interviewee 14	Und dann kommt man wunderbar schön/ Verfasst das Dossier, welches alle sagen wir mal schwierigen Fragen plausibel beantwortet. Würde ich schon so machen, ja. Deswegen (unv.) und sagen: "Ja, wissen wir, die Problematik."	Keep well prepared documents for the bank
Interviewee 14	Von vornherein kommen würde ich jetzt eher nicht, das käme mir komisch vor. Aber wenn dann die Frage kommt, ja, sofort, selbstverständlich, finden wir gut.	Provide documentation to the bank upon first request
Interviewee 14	Stempel sind immer gut, das ist so unglaublich.	Use a stamp
Interviewee 14	Ich würde das so offiziell wie möglich aussehen lassen, super Geschichte.	Create an official documentation

Interview partners	Original Statement	Generalization
Interviewee 14	Aber es gibt sagen wir mal Personengruppen aus bestimmten Regionen und die wollen Geld in die Heimatländer überweisen, und wenn man weiss, man hat eine Community, sage ich mal von Asiaten oder Philippinen oder das können auch Brasilianer sein und man hat einen Zugang zu diesen Gruppen, dann kann man ja mal fragen. "Wo kann ich Geld günstig überweisen?" Und da wird sofort gesagt: "Geh zu dem!" oder "Geh zu dieser Frau!"	Contact by members of certain ethnic groups
Interviewee 14	Also das ist für mich ein Transportkanal für Menschen, aber auch für Güter oder auch für Geld.	Use refugee routes
Interviewee 14	Wenn die Leute dann wieder freiwillig zurückgehen, dann kann es sein, dass sie wieder Gelder mitnehmen, das ist durchaus möglich, aber beim Transport selber meist nicht (unv.) fliesst.	Use refugee routes
Interviewee 14	Man braucht auch ein elektronisches Portemonnaie, ein E-Wallet dazu und nur noch die Adresse oder nur noch die physikalische, elektronische Adresse (unv.)	Create an e-wallet
Interviewee 14	Dann kaufen Sie sich einen billigen Computer, ein billiges Notebook und dann ist man mit ein paar Hundert Franken dabei und das ist ja nichts. Und dann wechselt man das Ding wieder und schmeisst das weg.	Constantly changing, inexpensive notebooks

Interview partners	Original Statement	Generalization
Interviewee 14	Ja, wie gesagt, die öffentlichen Netze, das ist schon so. Wo keine Handynummer notwendig ist, um sich einzuloggen. Es gibt nach wie vor Personen, die ihr Netzwerk nicht schützen und so weiter und so fort.	Use publicly accessible WLAN networks
Interviewee 14	Die müssen am/ Entweder gehen Sie (unv.), wo Sie diese kaufen können und das andere Geld quasi oder Vermögenswerte auf Gegenleistung einzahlen können.	Acquisition of Bitcoin with cash or tangible assets
Interviewee 14	Aber wahrscheinlich muss man schon in Buchgeld umwandeln oder auch in Bargeld umwandeln können oder dann auch einen Gegenpart finden, der bereit ist, quasi Bitcoins gegen einen anderen Wert zu verkaufen.	Find exchange partners
Interviewee 14	Entweder über einen Bitcoins-Change oder man findet direkt Leute.	Find a Bitcoin exchange or exchange partner
Interviewee 14	Immobilie verkauft und ich lege das jetzt in Bitcoin an. Ich hätte es auch in Edelmetall anlegen können, in Aktien anlegen, dann hätte es die Bank noch einigermassen unter Kontrolle, weil das in einem Wertschrift- oder Edelmetalldepot dann eingebucht wird, aber bei den Bitcoins wäre das nicht der Fall.	Investment of assets in Bitcoin
Interviewee 14	Darum muss es über Mittelsleute laufen. Da sind wir wieder bei Nachbarländern, Syrien, Irak oder Türkei, da ist es durchaus möglich, dass so Vermögenswerte gemacht werden.	Middlemen in countries neighbouring crisis areas

Interview partners	Original Statement	Generalization
Interviewee 14	Ja natürlich, natürlich. Es ist keine (unv.) könnte auch ein Tochterunternehmen in der Türkei aufmachen oder ich finanziere die.	Establish and finance a subsidiary in Turkey
Interviewee 14	Die machen Beratungsteams oder was auch immer und muss auch wieder Investitionen tätigen und braucht ihrerseits wieder Beratungen (unv.). Da kann man das Geld wirklich weiter schicken.	Consultancy and investment as justification for capital requirements
Interviewee 14	Andere terroristische Organisationen, die das nicht haben oder die sind ganz klar im Drogenhandel tätig, ganz klar, sie sind in Entführungen und Erpressungen tätig und das sind so die Quellen und das funktioniert nach wie vor noch und die Frage ist: Kann man diesem Herr werden und in Ländern wie Pakistan, denke ich, ist das komplett unmöglich.	Drug trafficking
Interviewee 14	Ja die klassischen Entführungen, wo/ Also egal wo, ob das jetzt der IS ist oder in Pakistan der Fall ist oder in, nach wie vor, in Lateinamerika der Fall ist oder in Afrika der Fall ist, wo halt eine westliche Geisel/ Wirklich, das ist eine Investition.	Kidnappings

Interview partners	Original Statement	Generalization
Interviewee 14	Ich weiss, dass Menschenhandel ein grosses Thema ist in Westafrika. Es gibt dort immer noch Sklaven in verschiedenen Ländern. Die lokalen Stämme profitieren vom Menschenhandel oder die schmuggeln oder schleusen Leute durch diese Ader und zum Teil sind diese Stämme ja auch/ Haben sich angeschlossen oder beim Al-Qaida, Maghreb und wie sie alle heissen, ja, ist schon ein Thema, aber, glaube ich regional beschränkt, denke ich jetzt mal.	Human trafficking
Interviewee 14	Wenn ich natürlich sagen wir mal Selbstfinanzierer bin, das ist natürlich die ideale Situation. Der IS hat ja diese Möglichkeit, indem sie nach wie vor ja noch Zugriff auf Ölquellen hat und das wäre für mich erste Priorität, wenn man dann quasi Zugang hat, zu solchen Quellen.	Oil trading
Interviewee 14	Ich denke mal, wenn man das Öl etwas günstiger auf den Markt wirft als quasi der Weltmarktpreis. Dann gibt es immer Abnehmer, die sagen: "Okay das ist ein Schnäppchen, eine Schnäppchenmöglichkeit oder wir lehnen das ab." Klar muss man da Leute schmieren und ich nehme jetzt mal an, Dokumente fälschen oder verfälschen, aber sobald man ein Produkt mit einem interessanten Preis anbietet, dann gibt es immer Leute (unv.), die bereit sind darauf einzusteigen und sich einen Deut scheren, woher dieses Öl kommt, garantiert.	Oil trading

Interview partners	Original Statement	Generalization
Interviewee 14	Ja, ich könnte mir schon vorstellen, man muss schon über ein Beziehungsnetz verfügen oder in der Branche, aber das ist ja/ (unv.) ist das eine. Das (unv.) muss ja noch transportiert werden.	Trade oil through relationships in the industry
Interviewee 14	Also wenn man jetzt Betrügerei auch als Wirtschaftskriminalität anschaut, dann ja, ist jede Form der Kriminalität, die Geld produziert, um solche Terroristen zu finanzieren, ist ein Thema.	Fraud
Interviewee 14	Und ich weiss, dass mit Produktfälschungen oder einige terroristische (unv.) sich finanziert haben in der Vergangenheit oder mit Kreditkartenbetrügereien.	Counterfeit products
Interviewee 15	Also grundsätzlich äh, grundsätzlich ist die Terrorismusfinanzierung, meines Erachtens, geringere Beträge möglich als bei der klassischen Geldwäsche.	Terrorism financing possible with small amounts
Interviewee 15	Nur, es ist halt schwierig, weil ich kann nicht einkaufen beim Aldi mit Bitcoin oder an der Tankstelle.	Not a common currency in retail
Interviewee 15	Aber man kommt da als Nicht-Teil dieser Community kaum rein.	Difficult access
Interviewee 15	Also Sie müssten schon aus dieser Volksgruppe sein, damit Sie das Urvertrauen von (Hawala?) da bekommen.	Difficult access

Interview partners	Original Statement	Generalization
Interviewee 15	Aber Bitcoins selber, kommt auf dasselbe heraus, Sie brauchen ein Konto, ein Wallet, ich brauche ein Wallet, um zu einem gewissen (Stichtag?) wechseln wir, wechselt dieser Wallet.	Create an e-wallet
Interviewee 15	Da gibt es dann einen Ausgleich, der geschaffen wird. Ähm, aber im Prinzip ist es ähm, eine Sache für Betroffene, ne? Das ist eine Grundidee (unv.) der gibt es und sagt, bitte, ich möchte meiner Mutter einen Kühlschrank zukommen lassen. Gibt es Geld mit Provision oder Abzug und ihr wird der Kühlschrank vor die Tür gestellt, ne?	Clearing (balancing of peaks)

Appendix 3: Document citations

(Quotes not translated)

Category	Generalization	Quote	Interview partners
General statements			
	Exchange between investigative authorities and private parties is important	Ich denke mal, das EINE/ EIN wichtiger Bereich ist eigentlich der Austausch zwischen UNTERSCHIEDLICHEN Beteiligten. Ähm das sind vor allem die Ermittlungsbehörden, natürlich, die bestimmte KENNTNISSE haben, Kenntnisse, die man uns auch nicht zur Verfügung stellt, oder BEDINGT nur zur Verfügung stellt.	Interviewee 1
	Perpetrators have access to specialist literature	Ich meine, das Gute ist ja auch immer, wenn ich/ haben wir vorher auch gefragt/ äh GESAGT, ähm als Geldwäscher würde ich mir genau solche Literatur holen. Mensch, was empfiehlt denn so der Fachmann? (lacht) Ich meine, wie wäscht man am besten Geld? (holt Luft) Da ist SO viel verfügbar mittlerweile im Internet, dass man da ähm (.) ja auch als Krimineller, äh und die sind da oft besser ausgestattet als die Polizei von mir aus mit ihren auch Topleuten, die sie einkaufen/ einkaufen können.	Interviewee 1

Category	Generalization	Quote	Interview partners
	Perpetrators are intelligent and well trained	Ich meine, man darf sich ja nicht den Illusionen hingeben, dass das – gerade bei Terrorismus – dass das alles nur – in Anführungszeichen – irgendwelche Fanatiker sind, die Hochhäuser in die Luft jagen wollen und dann irgendwelche Menschen mit reinziehen. Die gibt es auch, aber da gibt es wahrscheinlich natürlich auch hochintelligente Menschen im Hintergrund, die mit einer vergleichbaren Ausbildung, ja wirklich die Schwachstellen suchen.	Interviewee 8
	Progressive mechanization complicates investigations	Dritter Punkt, um das vielleicht auch nochmal zu sagen, für mich ist die fortschreitende Technisierung des Ganzen auch ein, ich will nicht sagen, ein Risiko, aber auch ein Fakt, der die Arbeit schwieriger gemacht hat.	Interviewee 8
	Certain industries are unregulated	Ich will mal so ein Beispiel nennen, aber das ist bei mir hier so ein Lieblingsthema, worüber ich stundenlang schwadronieren könnte, dass gewisse Bereiche unfassbar hart reguliert sind und manche Bereiche aber, wo es aus meiner Sicht offensichtlich ist, dass da aus freien Stücken gar nichts passiert.	Interviewee 8

Category	Generalization	Quote	Interview partners
	Intelligent offenders have plausible explanations for their behaviour	Der intelligente Terrorismusfinanzierer macht im Prinzip genau das, was er tun möchte, und erklärt das einfach nur gut.	Interviewee 8
	Similarities between money laundering and terrorism financing	Das, was Sie aus der Geldwäsche lernen können, kann man natürlich auch auf das Thema Terrorismusfinanzierung übertragen.	Interviewee 8
	Perpetrators exploit loopholes in the administration	Es gibt Lücken in Prozessen, sei es in der Verwaltung, sei es bei Gericht, die man, wenn man das genau weiss, gut nutzen kann.	Interviewee 8
	Funds of terrorist financiers are often not incriminated	Bei der Geldwäsche sind wir ja praktisch schon paranoid und gucken: Wo könnte da irgendwas Grösseres reinkommen? Bei der Terrorismusfinanzierung haben wir schon Gelder, die als sauber deklariert wurden, die auch schon geprüft wurden – also das ist ja praktisch der Unterschied dazu, ein wirklich spannendes Thema, wie ich finde – dass die also erst mal gar nicht den Verdacht erregen.	Interviewee 8
	Only small offenders get caught	Und das ist ja genau das Spannende daran, dass Sie also praktisch die Kleineren kriegen, aber die Grossen, die richtig schweren Brocken, die kriegen Sie nur ganz schwer zu sehen. Ich glaube, da müssen Sie dann, ja, auf ganz anderer Ebene angreifen.	Interviewee 8

Category	Generalization	Quote	Interview partners
	Penalties for financing terrorism do not act as a deterrent	Da ist mir doch vollkommen egal, ob ich jetzt hinten raus noch eine Strafe bekomme für Terrorismusfinanzierung, wenn ich vorne raus irgendwie, keine Ahnung, ein Bombenattentat oder sowas finanziert habe. Das ist dann das kleinere Übel, wo ich sage: Ja gut, dann kriegst du halt da, wenn es rauskommt, auch noch zwei Jahre. Aber wenn ich da vorher schon, ich sage mal, Mittäter bin, sage ich mal, oder Urheber für ein Bombenattentat oder sowas, wie es in Paris passiert ist, dann ist es doch vollkommen egal.	Interviewee 8
	Investigating authorities are too slow	Ich glaube, auch da ist vielleicht noch eine Schwäche der Terrorism usfinanzierungsbekämp fung, dass die Aufsichts- oder Ermittlungsbehörden eigentlich zu langsam sind.	Interviewee 8
	Combating the financing of terrorism serves the purpose of tax investigation	Ansonsten, wie gesagt, aber das ist halt eine persönliche Schlussnote, wenn ich das mal sagen darf, viele der Sachen, die wir aktuell machen, werden verkauft unter dem Deckmantel der Geldwäscheprävention und/oder der Terrorismusfinanzierung, dienen aber nach meinem Verständnis eher dem Thema Steuerfahndung.	Interviewee 8

Category	**Generalization**	**Quote**	**Interview partners**
	Focus on money laundering and not on terrorism financing	Wenn es um den Review von Transaktionen äh geht, letztlich das Mindset aber auch auf GWG, äh auf Geldwäscherei, auf Muster von Geldwäscherei, äh aber Terrorismusfinanzierung einfach in den Köpfen noch nicht existiert.	Interviewee 7
	Patterns of terrorism financing partly unknown	Ja, ich/ ich glaube, die/ die Muster der (.) Terrorismusfinanzierung sind, glaube ich, bei den meisten Leuten gar nicht bekannt. Und/ und deswegen ist es einfach auch schwierig, diese zu finanz/ äh diese zu identifizieren.	Interviewee 7
	Strikes are not costly	Und die/ Eben diese Splittergruppen, diese Attentäter von Paris und Brüssel, wahrscheinlich jetzt auch in Istanbul, das ist nicht aufwendig, ein paar tausend Euro, die die nötig haben, um quasi da ihre Ressourcen zu kaufen, also Miete zu tragen, Lebensmittel zu kaufen. Die Waffen sind auch nicht wahnsinnig teuer. Da ist man mit ein paar tausend Euro dabei.	Interviewee 14

Category	Generalization	Quote	Interview partners
	Terrorist groups are self-financing	Also eben als terroristische Organisation würde ich schauen: Kann ich mich selber finanzieren? Dann bin ich natürlich viel unabhängiger oder eher Land und Quellen erschliessen, wo ich weiss, da gibt es immer Opfer, die wir da uns aussuchen können.	Interviewee 14
	Money laundering and the financing of terrorism are mixed up.	Die hat/ überall kommt die Geldwäsche zusammen mit der Terrorismusfinanzierung. Das, das wäre auch ein Ansatz, Sie mal drüber sich auslassen sollten kritisch, ob das nicht eigene Institutionen und eigene Prozesse oder so, wie auch immer, nach sich ziehen sollte.	Interviewee 9
	Terrorism financing as a gateway to tougher measures	Terrorismus ist immer ein, ein, ein Türöffner, nicht nur für Gesetzesänderungen sondern auch für, für massive Massnahmen.	Interviewee 9
	Preliminary proceedings do not deter offenders	Erst mal ist/ hat man ja ein primäres Ziel. (unv.) der IS, der Islamische Staat, will sich finanzieren. Der überlegt sich ja nicht gerade, "was passiert 'n, wenn irgendwo ein Ermittlungsverfahren läuft?"	Interviewee 9

Category	Generalization	Quote	Interview partners
	Terrorism financing can also be carried out by means of crime	Dass da Leute in, in Molenbeek in Brüssel sitzen, die brauchen bloss/ die brauchen im Grunde nur ihre Gewehre, äh, zu finanzieren, um dann irgendwo hinzugehen und Leute zu erschiessen, äh, oder die müssen Waffen halt beschaffen. Das ist ja/ Finanzierung muss ja auch nicht nur Geld sein. Das kann ja auch eben (die?) Tatmittel sein, Waffen beschaffen zum Beispiel nur.	Interviewee 9
	International co-ordination of co-operation between authorities required	Da/ die zweite Schwierigkeit, die mir dazu einfallen würde, ist, dass das ähm, national und auch international einfach einer sehr hohen Koordinierung der Behörden bedarf. Da durchwegs sehr unterschiedliche Behörden mit der Bekämpfung betraut sind.	Interviewee 10
	Any type of asset transfer is suitable for terrorism financing.	Aber ich glaube aber, grundsätzlich alles, was für den Transfer von Vermögenswerten geeignet ist, ist natürlich auch für potentielle Terrorismusfinanzierung geeignet.	Interviewee 10

Category	Generalization	Quote	Interview partners
	Legal and illegal sources of income	Praktisch haben wir aber bei der/ bei der Terrorismusfinanzierung ähm im Gegensatz zur/ zur/ zur reinen Geldwäsche 'ne/ 'ne Mischfinanzierung. Das heisst, wir haben (.) ähm/ wir haben teilweise legale Quellen über/ über Spenden, et cetera. Und als aber auch das gesamte Spektrum der (.) ähm/ der kriminellen Aktivitäten.	Interviewee 12
	Funds are transferred both domestically and abroad	Die Frage, wo ist das Geld hin, muss das Geld jetzt ins Ausland raus oder muss es ins Inland reinkommen. Das sind ja schon mal zwei verschiedene Ansatzpunkte, wo ich sagen muss, wie muss ich das Geld nach Deutschland bekommen, damit ich's hier verwenden kann für zum Beispiel Terroranschläge oder was muss ich umgekehrt machen.	Interviewee 3
	Combating the financing of terrorism targeted at large organizations and networks	Das Ganze ist ursprünglich ausgerichtet gewesen unter der Prämisse, dass Terrorismusfinanzierung eigentlich eine Finanzierung von Terrororganisationen als grosse Organisation oder als grosses Netzwerk und vor allem als einheitliches Netzwerk und somit etwas, das fassbar ist, und im grossen Stil finanziert werden kann, das war, glaube ich, grundsätzlich der Hintergedanke.	Interviewee 6

Category	Generalization	Quote	Interview partners
	Trend away from central structures to single perpetrators	Wir sehen immer mehr die Lonesome-Wolf-Attacken oder eben völlig un/ also nicht unkoordiniert oder zumindest nicht mehr so zentrale Strukturen, wie das vielleicht ursprünglich bei der Al-Qaida war oder im Moment wieder bei ISIS auftritt.	Interviewee 6
	Single perpetrator difficult to identify	Insofern, das wird wohl die grösste Problematik sein, denn es wird wohl kaum aus/ man kann kaum Einzelpersonen, vor allem, die noch nicht am Radar sind, möglicherweise erst zukünftig etwas vorhaben, vom kommerziellen, wirtschaftlichen Leben, so wie es in der Gesellschaft der Fall ist, ausschliessen können.	Interviewee 6
	Normal bank accounts inconspicuous	Wobei wahrscheinlich eingeschränkt, eingeschränkter wird die Möglichkeit jetzt wirklich schon im regulierten Finanzbereich sein, nämlich insbesondere über normale Bankkonten.	Interviewee 6

Category	Generalization	Quote	Interview partners
	100 per cent certainty is not possible	Muss man sich eingestehen, gerade bei der Terrorismusfinanzierung muss man sich eingestehen, dass das nicht alles vollends erfassbar ist. Es ist vielleicht noch etwas, was man nicht gerne laut ausspricht, aber wenn man absolut, also wenn man nicht absolute Kontrolle und Überwachung haben möchte, und insbesondere, wenn es so etwas wie eine Cash Economy noch gibt. Da rede ich nicht einmal von Hawala, wo man nicht einmal Cash braucht, um das zu setteln, wird man ein gewisses Restrisiko und solche Situationen, wie Sie sie geschildert haben, so ein Restrisiko, das wird man nicht gänzlich ausschalten können.	Interviewee 6
	Interventions in all areas of life are necessary	Ja, ja, aber das ist die grundsätzliche Problematik, weil man hier versucht, einen Regelungsbereich zu erschaffen, der, um zu funktionieren, einen totalen, fast schon totalitären Eingriff in alle Lebensbereiche oder zumindest in alle relevanten kommerziellen Lebensbereiche bedeuten würde.	Interviewee 6

Category	Generalization	Quote	Interview partners
	Transaction analysis only of limited use	Bei Terrorismusfinanzierung glaube ich einfach, dass es wesentlich schwieriger ist, durch Transaktionsanalysen etwas zu finden, ganz im Gegensatz zu Money Laundering. Hier hat man einfach eine Gleichschaltung der Systematik erreicht, weil man das Ganze unter einem grossen Begriff AML/CFT hat.	Interviewee 6
	Source of funds vs application of funds	Aber auf der einen Seite ist die Mittelherkunft die relevante oder Geldwäsche, und bei der Terrorismusfinanzierung ist es die Mittelverwendung.	Interviewee 6
	Use of funds lies in the future	Und hier habe ich auch ein Frequentierungsproblem, weil das eine liegt in der Vergangenheit, das andere liegt in der Zukunft.	Interviewee 6
	Tax systems as sources of financing for the IS	Noch dazu können Sie so etwas wie ein Steuersystem aufziehen.	Interviewee 6
	Knowledge of terrorism financing based on 9/11	Das haben wir natürlich relativ deutlich erlebt mit dem Aufkommen des Islamischen Staates und eigentlich relativ schnell gemerkt dann, dass alles, was wir gemeint haben zu wissen über Terrorismusfinanzierung, eigentlich aus dem Wissen post Nine Eleven entstanden ist.	Interviewee 13

Category	Generalization	Quote	Interview partners
	Different types of terrorism financing	Na, das kommt darauf an, ich glaube, es gibt nicht DIE Terrorismusfinanzierung.	Interviewee 13
	Measures based in part on knowledge of Al-Qaeda	Wir hatten dann, ich glaube, etwa 2003, 2004/5 herum relativ genaue Kenntnis, wie sich Al-Qaida finanziert hat, und haben daraus dann die entsprechenden Massnahmen abgeleitet.	Interviewee 13
	Preservation of assets was a priority for Al-Qaeda	Da ging es eigentlich mehr darum, das Geld, das man hat, möglichst beisammenzuhalten und niemandem Zugriff darauf zu gewähren.	Interviewee 13
	IS had few assets to begin with	Wo der IS im Gegensatz dazu arm und klein angefangen hat und gewachsen ist.	Interviewee 13
	Organizations behave like states	Und eigentlich, je grösser die Organisation wurde, desto mehr sich so verhalten hat, wie ein Staat sich verhält.	Interviewee 13
	Income from own domain	Und darum ist der Begriff Islamischer Staat eben nicht ganz falsch, generieren aber ihre Einkünfte aus dem eigenen Herrschaftsbereich.	Interviewee 13
	Watchlists for the suppression of donations	Darum hat man bei der Bekämpfung eigentlich auch, Hauptansatzpunkt war zum einen Listing von Personen, die Geld haben oder Zugriff zu Geldern haben, und zum anderen das Unterbinden von Spenden.	Interviewee 13

Category	Generalization	Quote	Interview partners
	IS generates its own income	Beim IS ist es fast umgekehrt, IS bekommt zwar auch Spenden, hängt aber nicht davon ab, sondern der IS generiert Einkommen, indem er Ölquellen auch nutzt	Interviewee 13
	Terrorists trained to avoid leaving traces	Hier ist es schon so, dass die AUCH darauf achten, unterdessen ist auch Teil der Ausbildung dieser Terroristen oder des Materials, dass sie sich finden und zueignen, möglichst keine Spuren zu hinterlassen.	Interviewee 13
	Analysis of the financing flows of the assassins provides information about their environment	Und da ist man dann ganz anders, da geht es nicht darum, dass die Geld brauchen, um den Anschlag zu begehen, sondern dass die Terrorismusfinanzierung dort eigentlich ein nützliches Instrument ist, weil man über die Finanzierungsströme, also, ich sage einmal, die Auswertung des Bankkontos eines solchen Attentäters ist wahrscheinlich mindestens so aufschlussreich wie die Auswertung seines Handys.	Interviewee 13
	Early drying up of financial flows	Hier hat es eigentlich einen Paradigmenwechsel gegeben, also bei, am Anfang nach Nine Eleven ging es darum, die Finanzquellenorganisationen auszutrocknen, um die Organisation lahmzulegen.	Interviewee 13

Category	Generalization	Quote	Interview partners
	IS is weakened by CFT	Beim Islamischen Staat glaubt man auch, dass die Massnahmen Wirkung zeigen, der Islamische Staat hat deutlich weniger Geld zur Verfügung als noch am Anfang.	Interviewee 13
	Individual perpetrators identifiable on the basis of certain behaviours	Also, wenn man weiss, dass diese Leute typischerweise Autos mieten mit Prepaid-Karten, ja, kann man daraus, zusammen mit ein paar anderen Merkmalen, die typisch ist für diese Täter, schon einspeisen und sagen: "Hier, halt. Kann man das dann nicht erkennen im Moment, wo jemand ein Auto mietet, um den wenigstens zu observieren", ne?	Interviewee 13
	Recognize suspicious behaviour	Also ich sage nicht, dass jeder, der mit Prepaid-Karte ein Auto mietet, observiert werden muss, aber wenn er zusätzlich noch andere Merkmale hat, ich sage einmal, jung, männlich, radikalisiert, dann kann das einen Alarm auslösen.	Interviewee 13
	Strong trend towards modern technologies and mobile payment services	Weg aus dem formellen Sektor, eine sehr starke Neigung zu modernen Zahlungsmitteln, sehr starke Neigung zum Gebrauch von Technologie, also Mobile Payment Services.	Interviewee 13

Category	Generalization	Quote	Interview partners
	Innovations for transfer of funds are included	Also jede, ich sage einmal, Innovation auf dem Finanzmarkt vor allem zur Übermittlung von Geldern, vor allem zum Transferieren von Geldern ausserhalb des formalen Bankensektors, die wird aufgenommen.	Interviewee 13
	Observe combination of several indicators	Und man darf die nicht immer nur isoliert betrachten, also nicht ein Indikator heisst, es ist ein Terrorist dahinter, sondern ist dann immer eine Kombination von mehreren solchen Indikatoren, die Hinweise darauf geben kann.	Interviewee 13
	Broad scope of investigations into terrorism financing	Also, und das sieht schon anders aus als das, was wir noch vor zehn Jahren hatten, wo wir immer typischerweise versucht haben, diesen finanziellen Unterstützer, diesen Scheich halt zu finden, der Al-Qaida unterstützt, da sind wir heute schon breiter aufgestellt.	Interviewee 13
	Focus on countries neighbouring crisis regions	Was wir machen können, ist dafür sorgen, dass das Geld nicht weiter fliesst, aber der IS, ist halt schon, weil es vor allem über den Schmuggel herausgeht, ist in eigentlich die Nachbarländer gefragt.	Interviewee 13

Category	Generalization	Quote	Interview partners
	Ransomware insurance as a risk industry	Also es gibt Lösegeldversicherungen, aber ich denke einmal mehr an diese Konzerne, die halt weltweit tätig sind und die eine generelle Police haben, was immer ihren Mitarbeitern passiert, zahlt die Versicherung oder entschädigt die Gesellschaft für die Kosten, ja. Die Versicherung kann nicht in Anspruch nehmen für sich, dass sie im Notstand ist, ja, kein Mensch zwingt sie diese Police anzubieten, aber die Versicherung hat ja ein grösseres Risiko sich der Terrorismusfinanzierung schuldig zu machen, wenn sie solche Kosten entschädigen würde.	Interviewee 13
	No hasty conclusions	Also ein grosses Thema ist natürlich, dass wir ganz vorsichtig sein müssen, schnelle Rückschlüsse zu ziehen.	Interviewee 13
	Preventing attacks by seizing funds	Aber mir geht es ja nicht so sehr um den Täter, der hat sich ja vielleicht schon in die Luft gejagt, mir geht es vor allem darum, einen möglichen Anschlag zu vermeiden, indem man Gelder sicherstellt.	Interviewee 13

Category	Generalization	Quote	Interview partners
	Communication between intelligence services and FIUs not yet sufficient	Ich glaube, generell haben wir, also wir haben zum einen eine wichtige Rolle der Nachrichtendienste und zum anderen haben wir eine wichtige Rolle der Finanzermittler und die beiden haben sich bis jetzt noch nicht einmal in den gleichen Raum gesetzt, ja?	Interviewee 13
Revenue sources – Legal			
	Borrow	Geld leihen	Interviewee 8
	Financing by private individuals	Das ist quasi so eine Art Funding durch Privatleute	Interviewee 8
	Platforms put lenders and borrowers in touch with each other	Das heisst, Sie sagen: Ich hab hier den und den Kreditbedarf, den und den Preis bin ich bereit zu zahlen, und die Plattform stellt eigentlich nur noch den Kontakt her zwischen den Kreditsuchenden und anderen Leuten, die sagen: Okay, ich gebe Geld dafür.	Interviewee 8

Category	Generalization	Quote	Interview partners
	Legal income from construction companies	Sie haben ganz normale Einnahmen. Der, der Bin Laden war Erbe eines grossen Baukonzerns in Saudo A/ Saudi-Arabien und war Millionär und hat damit, (.) ziemlich einfach wahrscheinlich, die Anschläge in 9/11 finanziert, indem er aus legalen Bauunternehmen/ aus den Gewinnen eines Bauunternehmens oder eines Konzerns hat er seinen/ die Leute, die die Anschläge gemacht haben, im nötigen Masse finanziert.	Interviewee 9
	Financing through trading activities	Dass Terrorismus auch über den Handel finanziert wird.	Interviewee 11
	Salary or state support	Also, das können legitime Einkommensquellen sein, das kann ein Gehalt sein, das kann Arbeitslosenunterstützung, staatliche Unterstützung, das kann alles Mögliche sein.	Interviewee 6
Revenue sources – Illegal			
	Taxation and looting by the IS	Also das ist schon/ ich sage mal, dieser Anspruch, Islamischer Staat, die sich als Staat sehen, die eine gewisse Infrastruktur haben, also die 'ne gewisse Besteuerung erfordert. Aber das Interessante ist auch, was die sagten. Der/ wirklich der überwiegende Teil der Finanzierung kommt aus/ das ist so 'ne Art Ponzi-Scheme, den die aufgesetzt haben, aus Plünderungen.	Interviewee 7

Category	Generalization	Quote	Interview partners
	Compulsory levies, compulsory duties, protective charges, road tolls, special taxes, expropriation	Und dann natürlich regional, regional durch die Erhebung von Zwangsabgaben, Zwangszöllen ähm, Schutzgebühren, Strassenzöllen, Sondersteuern und so weiter und so fort. Also hm, (.) zum Beispiel der (..) in Syrien (seufzend) oder im Irak praktizierte IS auch die Enteignung von ähm, Immobilien oder Landwirtschaftsgütern und da müssen die Leute ihr Eigentum quasi mieten, wenn sie es benutzen wollen, nicht? Also das ist Raubrittertum, nicht?	Interviewee 11
	Trade in oil via Turkey	Und/ und ich meine, ohne dass ich da jetzt aus der Erfahrung spräche, aber meine Vermutung ist einfach relativ gross, was wir gesehen haben, (.) äh zum Beispiel als das ganze ähm (.) Iran-Oil-for-Food-Programm lief. Das sind ja diese Handelsrouten. Ich meine, das ist ja belegt mittlerweile, dass äh in/ in der Zeit der 90er und 2000er, als dieses Oil-for-Food-Programm lief, dass der Schwarzhandel mit/ mit dem Öl über (.) zum Teil auch die Türkei lief.	Interviewee 7
	Sales tax fraud via company constructs	Ich will nicht ausschliessen, dass es da noch über Firmenkonstrukte jetzt äh äh (.) in den/ in den grösseren Bereich jetzt/ jetzt Umsatzsteuerbetrügereien, et cetera gehen mag.	Interviewee 7

Category	Generalization	Quote	Interview partners
	Fraud	Also wenn man jetzt Betrügerei auch als Wirtschaftskriminalität anschaut, dann ja, ist jede Form der Kriminalität, die Geld produziert, um solche Terroristen zu finanzieren, ist ein Thema.	Interviewee 14
	Counterfeit products	Und ich weiss, dass mit Produktfälschungen oder einige terroristische (unv.) sich finanziert haben in der Vergangenheit	Interviewee 14
	Scam education loans	Ähm wir vergeben Kredite (.) und da wäre die einzige Möglichkeit, (.) ähm (.) sich das im/ im (Bildungsgeschäft) sich zu besorgen, also mittels/ äh mittels Krediten, die man/ die man bekommt über einen gewissen Zeitraum im Rahmen der Auszahlung ähm und/ und wo dann erst Jahre später so die (Zahlung) einsetzt. (.) Also (.) ähm ist aber/ das/ wir sind ja nicht äh/ nicht alleiniger Anbieter im Markt von solchen/ von solchen, ich sage mal, (Bildungsfinanzierungen), ähm aber mit Sicherheit einer der/ der/ der grossen insgesamt.	Interviewee 12
	Drug trafficking	Das können sein, wie gesagt, dann Drogenhandel oder andere Sachen.	Interviewee 7

Category	Generalization	Quote	Interview partners
	Insurance fraud	// Also das // ist jetzt wirklich der Grossteil, wo fingiert von/ über fingierte Autofällen/ Un/ Unfällen, über/ über Diebstähle, wo Sie wirklich, ich sag mal, ähm Netzwerke haben von Leuten, die äh bewusst, ich sag mal, Versicherungspolicen zeichnen und/ und Schaden melden, fingieren.	Interviewee 7
	Drug trafficking	Andere terroristische Organisationen, die das nicht haben oder die sind ganz klar im Drogenhandel tätig, ganz klar, sie sind in Entführungen und Erpressungen tätig und das sind so die Quellen und das funktioniert nach wie vor noch und die Frage ist: Kann man diesem Herr werden, und in Ländern wie Pakistan, denke ich, ist das komplett unmöglich.	Interviewee 14
	Kidnappings	Ja die klassischen Entführungen, wo/ Also egal wo, ob das jetzt der IS ist oder in Pakistan der Fall ist oder in, nach wie vor, in Lateinamerika der Fall ist oder in Afrika der Fall ist, wo halt eine westliche Geisel/ Wirklich, das ist eine Investition.	Interviewee 14

Category	**Generalization**	**Quote**	**Interview partners**
	Human trafficking	Ich weiss, dass Menschenhandel ein grosses Thema ist in Westafrika. Es gibt dort immer noch Sklaven in verschiedenen Ländern. Die lokalen Stämme profitieren vom Menschenhandel oder die schmuggeln oder schleusen Leute durch diese Ader und zum Teil sind diese Stämme ja auch/ Haben sich angeschlossen oder beim Al-Qaida, Maghreb und wie sie alle heissen, ja, ist schon ein Thema, aber, glaube ich regional beschränkt, denke ich jetzt mal.	Interviewee 14
	Trade in cultural goods	Wenn sie wie gesagt, ein, ein Musee/ ein ein Mosaik aus einer christlichen Kirche rausreissen, das wäre wohl schlecht zu transportieren, das muss anders gehen, das muss dann über Container gehen oder ü/ über andere Transportmittel. Ich würde denken, wenn man Flüchtlingsrouten nimmt, dann muss man doch relativ kleinformatige Sachen mit sich führen, oder?	Interviewee 4

Category	Generalization	Quote	Interview partners
	Misuse of telephony systems	Ähm, da hat man, ähm, Telefonnummern gehackt. Und zwar, ähm, nicht benutzte Telefonnummern, also wenn man jetzt eine grosse Unternehmung nimmt. Ähm. Die haben ja so eine interne Telefonanlage mit ganz vielen internen Nummern. Und wenn man jetzt weiss, dass auf dieser Nummer, dass da gerade niemand arbeitet an diesem Pool, diese Nummer also nicht vergeben ist intern, und man es dann schafft, auf so eine Nummer sich einzuhacken, dann kann man über diese Nummer Anrufe generieren.	Interviewee 5
	Financing livelihood in the West through theft, drug trafficking, extortion	Miete müssen sie zahlen, sie müssen Essen kaufen können, sie müssen quasi die Waffenmunition, Sprengstoff kaufen, aber da bewegen wir uns nicht wirklich im Bereich von ein paar 10.000 Euro. 10, 20 pro Person. Das klingt zwar nach viel, für jemanden, der arbeitslos ist, aber das hat man schnell beisammen. Und gerade wenn man noch (unv.) tätig ist oder im Drogenhandel drinnen (unv.) keine Berührungsängste, Diebstahl, Erpressung, ja? Und dann wird das quasi so finanziert.	Interviewee 14

Category	Generalization	Quote	Interview partners
<u>Transfer possibilities</u>			
Banking system			
Banking system – General suitability			
	Banks control more than other industries	Also nochmal, nicht dass die Banken alle sauber sind, bitte nicht so verstehen, aber ich glaube, die Wahrscheinlichkeit, dass man über die Banken noch was darstellen kann, ist deutlich schwieriger oder unwahrscheinlicher, als wenn Sie in andere Bereiche gehen.	Interviewee 8
	Perpetrators difficult to distinguish from normal customers	Und es ist unfassbar schwer nach meinem Verständnis, die wenigen Bösen – und ich glaube, es sind wirklich wenige – von der überragenden grossen guten Masse zu unterscheiden.	Interviewee 8
	Banks do not see the whole process	Sie merken ja, egal, welches Beispiel wir diskutieren, es gibt einfach unfassbar viele Möglichkeiten, die eben ausserhalb der Banken liegen, und die Banken kriegen eben nur einen Teil dieses Prozesses mit, nicht den Gesamtprozess, und dadurch, ja (…) können die gar nicht alles aufdecken, was da gefordert ist.	Interviewee 8

Category	Generalization	Quote	Interview partners
	Terrorism financing is mixed up with money laundering	Was/ was meine Kenntnis ist, einfach nur auf die bewährten zurück. Einerseits äh Identifizierung des wirtschaftlichen Berechtigten und/ und dann das Monitoring äh der Transaktionen und das Matching gegen Listen, Sanktionslisten, EU-Listen, äh Geldwäscherei, (unv.) Checklisten, et cetera. Das heisst, (.) ich glaube, (.) es/ es besteht keine grooosse Sensibilität, was eigentlich der Unterschied genau ist zwischen Terrorismusfinanzierung oder Geldwäscherei.	Interviewee 7
	Turkey not per se suspicious	Nur weil/ weil die jetzt an der Grenze liegen da zu/ zu den Krisengebieten und es einen gewissen Influx gibt im ganzen Land, heisst ja nicht, dass per se jede Geschäftstätigkeit in der Türkei rechtswidrig ist od/ oder letztendlich Geldwäscherei oder Terrori smusfinanzierungsverdacht automatisch gegeben ist.	Interviewee 7
	Banks do not see the whole process	// innerhalb // der Bank sehe. Und das ist einfach das/ die Krux, dass/ dass/ dass wir äh als Berater oder als Anwälte immer nur diesen Snapshot sehen. Das heisst, Sie haben letztendlich 'ne Kette von/ von Ereignissen, Sie haben irgendwo (.) die Quelle (.) und von der Quelle bis hin zum Empfänger haben Sie verschiedene Prozessschritte.	Interviewee 7

Category	Generalization	Quote	Interview partners
	Fast transfers	Und nichts ist so schnell wie Geld. Also das heisst, ich kann ja mittlerweile innerhalb von Sekunden Geld von A nach B transferieren und (.) unbegrenzte Summen.	Interviewee 7
	Smaller amounts do not attract attention	Aber ansonsten hmhm ist es äusserst schwierig, das zu erkennen, weils, wie gesagt, oft kleinere Beträge sind, die weder beim Ein- noch beim Ausgang grossartig auffallen.	Interviewee 3
	No suitable infrastructure in Syria	Dazu stellt sich die Frage, ob überhaupt eine relevante Infrastruktur überhaupt noch zur Verfügung steht auf Empfängerseite in Syrien.	Interviewee 6
	Turkish banks as an alternative to Syria	Also hier sind schon Banken im, nahe am Kriegsgebiet waren, türkische Banken, die ja auch gut sind, die ja professionell aufgestellt sind, die haben da wahrscheinlich schon eine besondere Verantwortung.	Interviewee 13
Banking system – Concrete approach			
	Use of straw men	Das ist ja üblich. Also das ist nicht nur/ nicht nur im Bereich des Terrorismus, sondern ganz andere ähm kriminelle Aktivitäten, wie Menschenhandel, Menschenschmuggel, oder DROGEN-Handel, dann werden in der REGEL Personen vorgeschoben. Das ist so ein Verhalten, das durchaus BEKANNT ist, und das finden Sie in der Szene genauso.	Interviewee 1

Category	Generalization	Quote	Interview partners
	Disclose customers and their business partners	Dass man wirklich weiss, mit welchem Kunden habe ich zu tun, und vor allen Dingen, was sind die Geschäftspartner meines Kunden.	Interviewee 8
	Explanations for transactions	Ich meine, weiss ich, warum der dort eigentlich Gelder hat, warum der dahin überweisen will?	Interviewee 8
	Ensure traceability	Kann ich das nachvollziehen?	Interviewee 8
	Ensure plausibility	Kann ich das plausibilisieren?	Interviewee 8
	Online banks do not know background	Onlinebanken. Die wissen im Zweifel gar nicht, was da hinten dran steht, oder die sehen das gar nicht.	Interviewee 8
	Specialized financial service providers for specific regions	Sie haben ja auch, sage ich mal, Spezialdienstleister, ich will es jetzt nicht Ethno-Banking nennen, das hört sich so komisch an, aber die sich genau auf gewisse Volksgruppen spezialisiert haben.	Interviewee 8
	Turkish banks with branches in Germany	Das sind türkische Banken, die hier eine Niederlassung aufgemacht haben, die (unv. #00:19:24.3#), die gezielt auf Migranten zielen und sagen: Wir möchten euch als Kunden werben.	Interviewee 8
	Documents in foreign languages	Also das fängt schon damit an, dass Sie die Sprache im Zweifel nicht sprechen, oder wenn es ganz hart kommt, noch nicht mal die Schrift entziffern können.	Interviewee 8

Category	Generalization	Quote	Interview partners
	Plausibility check of foreign transfers through international company structure in the transport sector	Oh, ich fang jetzt plötzlich an, an die Türkei zu überweisen oder nach Russland oder, keine Ahnung, irgendwohin, das ist auffällig. Komme ich aber hin und sage: So, ich hab hier ein internationales Unternehmen, ich mach Transport, hab eine schöne Homepage dazu, wo ich auch sehen kann: Ach guck mal, der macht Transporte in den Nahen Osten. Wegen mir sagt er auch, spezialisiert für, keine Ahnung, Krankentransport oder Ähnliches. Dann läuft das wunderbar.	Interviewee 8
	Founding a funeral home	Also so ein Klassiker, sage ich mal, der auch damals durch die Presse gegangen ist, machen Sie ein Bestattungsunternehmen auf. Hört sich im ersten Moment ein bisschen komisch an, aber wenn Sie sagen: Na ja, wir haben halt viele Leute, die in ihrer Heimat beerdigt werden wollen, dann haben Sie auf jeden Fall schon mal jemanden, der Ihnen plausibel erklären kann, warum die regelmässig unten vor Ort im Nahen Osten ist.	Interviewee 8
	Cash company	Und wenn Sie dann noch sagen: Ja, und die zahlen dann eben teilweise auch bar, haben Sie auch einen Grund, warum Sie Geld reinbekommen.	Interviewee 8

Category	Generalization	Quote	Interview partners
	Build up companies with a homepage and company entry	Wie gesagt, Sie müssen halt parallel diese (unv. #00:25:13.9#) auch betreiben, schöne Homepage etc. Firmeneintrag und so weiter, aber schon sind Sie im Prinzip da erst mal, was die Wahrnehmung angeht, zumindest nachvollziehbar.	Interviewee 8
	Using biases to create low-risk profiles	Ein Intelligenter macht sich diese Vorurteile zu eigen und guckt eigentlich: Wie komme ich zu einem Profil in der Überwachung, was risikoarm ist?	Interviewee 8
	Establish a limited liability company with business relations in Turkey	Und das heisst, ich suche mir erst mal die Lücken. Zum Beispiel, wenn ich jetzt eben sage, ich transferiere Gelder für die Terroristenfinanzierung in die Türkei, um bei Ihrem Beispiel zu bleiben, suche ich mir eben als Vehikel eine deutsche Firma, wahrscheinlich eine GmbH, weil die am günstigsten ist, die regelmässig Geschäftsbeziehungen in die Türkei hat.	Interviewee 8
	Establish a tour operator	Zum Beispiel Reiseveranstalter könnte ich sein.	Interviewee 8
	Establish a company in Turkey	Dann mache ich idealerweise auf der türkischen Seite auch nochmal eine Firma auf, die auch am besten irgendwie so/ Dann kann ich zwischen diesen beiden Sachen ständig was hin- und hertransferieren.	Interviewee 8

Category	Generalization	Quote	Interview partners
	Frequency increases plausibility	Und das Perfide daran: Je häufiger Sie das machen, umso unauffälliger wird das, ja?	Interviewee 8
	Frequency increases plausibility	Weil, wenn Sie da sagen, bei der ersten Transaktion: Oh, guck mal, der hat da was überwiesen. Dann macht man den ersten Scheck und stellt fest, ja, okay, ist in Ordnung. Beim zweiten Mal auch. Aber beim 10. oder 20. Mal sagt man sich: Ach ja, stimmt, die machen schon seit langer Zeit Geschäfte mit denen, das ist in Ordnung.	Interviewee 8
	Frequency increases plausibility	Durch die Wiederholung wird es weniger auffällig, als man meinen könnte.	Interviewee 8
	Establish tour operators and create fictitious quotas	Reiseveranstalter, klar, und dann liefert man die Ware nicht. Also man sagt zum Beispiel: Ich nehme dem Kontingent ab für 100 Betten im Monat, den ganzen Sommer und dann war ich halt schlecht im Verkauf und hab jetzt leider nicht so viele Betten an den Mann gebracht, aber die 100 Betten muss ich halt trotzdem bezahlen.	Interviewee 8

Category	Generalization	Quote	Interview partners
	Seek judgments by default	Also ich verklage jetzt (unv. #00:30:19.5#) und sage, keine Ahnung, Sie haben meinen Hund erschossen, dadurch ist mir ein emotionaler Schaden entstanden von 100.000 Euro. Dass ich keinen Hund habe, hat damit nichts zu tun. Ich kann jeden Blödsinn vor Gericht behaupten. So, das packe ich in eine Klageschrift, stelle das dem Amtsgericht zu. Das Amtsgericht kriegt das und sieht, na ja, da ist eine Klageschrift, so. Und dann geht das Ihnen zu und Sie müssen erwidern. Das Thema ist, nach der deutschen Prozessordnung, wenn Sie nichts dazu sagen und bei Gericht auch nicht erscheinen trotz Aufforderung, wird dem Kläger Recht gegeben, sofern die Klage nachvollziehbar ist.	Interviewee 8
	Choose banks with branches abroad	Ich gehe also in Deutschland mit meinem Geld zur HSBC, sage: Hier auf mein Konto, den und den Betrag, und jetzt überweist das doch auf mein Konto bei der HSBC in, keine Ahnung, nehmen wir die Türkei oder nehmen wir den Iran oder wo die auch immer vertreten sind.	Interviewee 8
	Use lower audits within group structures	Ich prüfe bei uns innerhalb der Konzernstruktur ja auch nicht, ob das in Ordnung ist.	Interviewee 8
	Involve experts	Ich glaube, auf der Gegenseite sind mittlerweile Leute da, die die Strukturen kennen und diese Strukturen ausnutzen können.	Interviewee 8

Category	Generalization	Quote	Interview partners
	Cultural associations and foundations as a cover	Was natürlich auf der anderen Seite ein Problem ist, sind zum Beispiel/ das können Stiftungen sein, das/ das können Kulturvereine sein, das können (.) irgendwelche Unterstützergruppen sein, die sich nach aussen hin irgend 'nen Anstrich geben, wie/ wie/ ja, wie gesagt, diese ganzen Kulturvereine, die Sie hier haben, die ganzen NGOs, äh irgendwelchen Non-Governmental Organizations, die sich 'nen Anstrich geben als gemeinnützig, wohltätig. Aber dahinter verbirgt sich letztendlich 'ne/ ich sage mal, eine Organisation, die einer (.) politischen Organisation, einer terroristischen Organisation nahesteht.	Interviewee 7
	Create legal structures for advertising and lobbying	Das heisst // Sie brauchen ja immer, ich sage mal, irgendwo/ (.) wenn/ wenn Sie/ angenommen Sie sind 'ne terroristische Vereinigung, irgendwo (.) 'nen legalen Arm in die Gesellschaft hinein, in dem Sie, ich sage mal, A rekrutieren, Werbung, Lobbying betreiben.	Interviewee 7

Category	Generalization	Quote	Interview partners
	Using refugees as a cover	Und was ich mir vorstellen kann, ist natürlich, wenn Sie gerade im/ im Bereich ähm (.) ähm (.) Transaktionen in die Türkei ansprechen, dass Sie natürlich im Rahmen der Flüchtlingsbewegung, dass/ dass wir natürlich viele Leute haben, die aus den Krisengebieten, wo es terroristische Aktivitäten gibt, in/ ich sage mal, in westliche oder in nahe westliche Länder immigriert sind, da jetzt (.) 'ne legale äh äh (.) Identität oder ein legales Leben aufgebaut haben, sind registriert, haben ein Geschäft, et cetera. Und da können natürlich die History/ wo kommen die Leute her, was für Beziehungen haben die, das können Sie nur schwer nachvollziehen, ne.	Interviewee 7
	Distribute assets	Wenn Sie/ wenn Sie es/ dann auch noch irgendwie ein Splitting machen und/ und bleiben unter irgendwelchen kritischen Schwellenwerten, (.) da haben Sie als Bank keine äh/ (.).	Interviewee 7
	Use notarial certification	Und/ und Sie haben natürlich, ich sage mal, aufgrund der sprachlichen Unterschiedlichkeiten und/ und/ und der/ (.) der Ferne trotzdem nicht/ nicht die Chance, das alles irgendwie in/ berechtigte Zweifel zu ziehen. Gerade wenn Sie dieses Beispiel mit der notariellen Beurkundung, et cetera bringen dann, ne. (.)	Interviewee 7

Category	Generalization	Quote	Interview partners
	Avoid prepaid cards	Und ich meine, wir haben natürlich Länder jetzt, wie Frankreich und/ und so, die gewisse Limite aussprechen wollen und trotzdem auch gewisse (KYC-) Regeln über diese Prepaid-Karten ziehen wollen. Also ich glaube, das wär schon wieder zu/ zu offensichtlich, oder?	Interviewee 7
	Transfers to Chinese banks and subsequent dispersal	Und dann wird das Geld transferiert und es ist innerhalb von Sekunden/ Wenn Sie das mal nachträglich investigieren, dann landet das erst auf (.) 'nem Konto 'ner westlichen Bank, aber von da gehts dann nach China und von der chinesischen Bank dann in tausend Himmelsrichtungen. Da haben Sie null Chance, das Geld jemals wieder zu finden. (leise) Also das ist äh (.) illusorisch.	Interviewee 7
	Taking advantage of the lack of co-operation from the authorities in Dubai	Ich weiss nicht, wie genau die Behörden dort hingucken. Also es heisst zumindest, dass die internationale Kooperation etwas schwierig ist mit den Behörden in Dubai.	Interviewee 14
	Cash withdrawals	Aber dann kann das Geld dort sicher bar abgehoben werden.	Interviewee 14

Category	Generalization	Quote	Interview partners
	Provide documentation to the bank upon first request	Ich weiss nicht, ob ich von vorneherein so kommen würde. Aber wenn die Frage kommt, dann würde ich das gleich liefern und sagen: "Ja, selbstverständlich. Wir verstehen, dass Sie Compliance-Pflichten haben, dass Sie Aufklärungspflichten haben und wir wissen das. Ist nicht das erste Mal, dass wir gefragt werden. Bitte schön, hier sind die Unterlagen."	Interviewee 14
	Keep well-prepared documents for the bank	Und dann kommt man wunderbar schön/ Verfasst das Dossier, welches alle sagen wir mal schwierigen Fragen plausibel beantwortet. Würde ich schon so machen, ja. Deswegen (unv.) und sagen: "Ja, wissen wir, die Problematik."	Interviewee 14
	Provide documentation to the bank upon first request	Von vornherein kommen würde ich jetzt eher nicht, das käme mir komisch vor. Aber wenn dann die Frage kommt, ja, sofort, selbstverständlich, finden wir gut.	Interviewee 14
	Use a stamp	Stamps are always good, it's so amazing.	Interviewee 14
	Consultancy and investment as justification for capital requirements	Die machen Beratungsteams oder was auch immer und muss auch wieder Investitionen tätigen und braucht ihrerseits wieder Beratungen (unv.). Da kann man das Geld wirklich weiter schicken.	Interviewee 14

Category	Generalization	Quote	Interview partners
	Referrals to sick family members	Da hat jemand seinem, seinem Bruder 1.000, 2.000 Euro geschickt (.) und der hat hier vor Gericht dann eben das Problem, oder nicht er, sondern die Justiz hatte das Problem, nachzuweisen, dass das IS-Finanzierung war, wenn der gesagt hat, "mein Bruder war krank, ich musste ihm 'ne Arzt/ der musste 'ne Arztrechnung bezahlen. Das ist 'ne reine familiäre Sache, ich musste dem/ der ist in Syrien, ich weiss gar nicht, wa/ vom IS weiss ich nix", sagte er dann, "ich hab' dem 1.000 oder 2.000 Euro geschickt oder Dollar, weil er mir sagte, er braucht das Geld. Der ist krank."	Interviewee 9
	Create invoices, orders and financing documents	Irgendwelche Aufträge, oder Rechnungen, oder sonstige Finanzierungsdokumente.	Interviewee 2
	Referrals to reputable NGOs	Muss natürlich immer der Empfängername, wenn man den googeln kann und das ist 'ne NGO, die man nachvollziehen kann, dann is das in Ordnung für uns. Wenn es, sage ich mal, an den Roten Halbmond geht, is es für mich auch in Ordnung. Wenn's aber hingegen irgendwo was ist, wo ich/ was ich wirklich nicht nachvollziehen könnte, dann würden wir eher Verdacht (.) // haben. //	Interviewee 3

Category	Generalization	Quote	Interview partners
	Disguised as a tourist from Qatar for remittances from abroad	In (Mitsch) haben wir sehr viele Touristen aus Katar. Ähm dass einer von denen Geld A mitbringen würde auf der einen Seite oder dass er sich hierher Geld überweisen lässt. Das ist ganz legal.	Interviewee 3
	Cash withdrawals and subsequent cash distribution	Da gibt's Geschäftsleute, die sind millionenschwer. Und wenn der von zu Hause Geld bekommt und dann anschliessend hier äh das Geld auf ein/ auf ein Konto sich überweisen lässt und dann abhebt und dann wieder verteilt, (.) das kann man gar nicht nachvollziehen (.).	Interviewee 3
	Legal source of funds	Da spielt das keine Rolle, wie er da/ (.) was wer für Geld hat. Das Geld ist ganz legal hergekommen von einer Bank aus Katar und wird dann gar nicht mehr näher geprüft oder Mittelherkunft wird da auch nicht mehr geprüft in dem Augenblick.	Interviewee 3
	Disguised as donations	Spenden, Verdeckte Spenden sind dann, die also offiziell als Spenden getätigt werden und dann aber inoffiziell doch dem Terrorkampf dienen sollen. Ähm aber die können genauso gut sich auch kriminell verhalten.	Interviewee 3

Category	Generalization	Quote	Interview partners
	Avoid high-risk countries	Aber ich meine, es geht ja einfach darum, ich meine, (.) wenn, wenn man natürlich Geld in gefährdete Regionen schickt oder Geld aus gefährdeten Regionen bekommt, dann ist das klar, es gibt Hochrisikoländer, das ist sicher Syrien, Irak, Afghanistan und so weiter. Ähm, Libanon, was auch immer, das sind so Risikoländer. Und dort muss man das (unv.) Risiko aufgrund des Domizilstaates oder des Destinationsstaates evaluieren, das ist ganz klar.	Interviewee 11
	Legitimate flows from Central Europe as a cover	Wir haben natürlich, gerade bei gewissen Regionen in Zentraleuropa, wo vielleicht die Diaspora aus der Türkei traditionell stärker vertreten ist, auch völlig legitime grosse Ströme, Finanzströme, in das jeweilige Land.	Interviewee 6
	Cite the purchase of a carpet or the loss of a wallet in Istanbul as justification	Also ich bringe eben das Beispiel, dass irgendjemand einen grossen Geldbetrag in Istanbul hat und hat einen arabisch klingenden Namen, aber mit französischer Staatsangehörigkeit. Vielleicht ist es ein braver Familienvater, der einen Teppich kaufen will, oder dem die Brieftasche gestohlen wurde und dringend Cash braucht, um sein Hotel zu bezahlen.	Interviewee 13

Category	Generalization	Quote	Interview partners
Banking system – detection risk			
	Transaction analyses	Ich meine, wir SIND ja alle jetzt, die Finanzdienstleister aber auch die Kreditinstitute, wir sind ja gehalten ähm Analysen durchzuführen, Monitoring durchzuführen in den äh/ in den Finanzströmen, die wir sehen, in den Transaktionen, die wir sehen.	Interviewee 1
	Typologies for the detection of foreign terrorist fighters	Äh üblicherweise, so ist es auch bei UNS im Hause, ähm […] entwickeln wir Typologien, wir haben beispielsweise hier/ DAS, glaube ich, [unintelligible] auch eines der/ der führenden Institute ähm, die jetzt insbesondere in den USA dann Zusammenarbeit mit den Behörden, aber auch hier in Europa, und hier auch konkret in Deutschland, (holt Luft) äh Typologien entwickelt haben, zum Beispiel äh Foreign Terrorist Fighters, das/ äh um das Verhalten im finanziellen Bereich	Interviewee 1
	Anonymity almost impossible	Die Wahrscheinlichkeit, dass uns da jemand unterrutscht, der komplett anonym ist und irgendwie durch Zufall reinkommt, das ist eigentlich nicht darstellbar oder ist nicht möglich.	Interviewee 8

Category	Generalization	Quote	Interview partners
	Backgrounds of customers known	Wir kennen unseren Kunden wirklich und wir kennen auch den Hintergrund des Kunden.	Interviewee 8
	Verification of the background of the payments	Das heisst, da lassen wir gesondert durch den Berater prüfen, was der Hintergrund einer Zahlung ist.	Interviewee 8
	Press analysis	Die Presse von (unv.) da kommen Sie heute nicht mehr drum herum. Wenn Sie feststellen, da ist irgendjemand dabei, der nicht seriös ist, dann sollten Sie tunlichst anfangen, mal nachzudenken in Ihrer Bank, warum man vielleicht diesen Geschäftspartner nicht mehr in Zukunft haben möchte.	Interviewee 8
	Traceability of documentation reduces risk of detection	Wenn jemand wirklich so präzise vorgeht, wirklich, sage ich mal, von den Unterlagen her eine Nachvollziehbarkeit stattfindet, glaube ich, ehrlich gesagt, dann bekommen Sie den im Zweifel gar nicht.	Interviewee 8
	Limitations of compliance databases	Und // und da haben Sie einfach, ich sage mal, mittels der Ihnen als/ als Bank zur Verfügung stehenden […] Compliance-Datenbanken null Zugriff, ne.	Interviewee 7
	Beneficial owners of the beneficiary are often unknown	Sei es // das Geld geht an 'nen/ 'nen Verein, an/ an/ […] äh oder an 'ne Privatperson oder an ein Geschäft, wer dahinter steht, woher der kommt, […] das/ das bleibt für Sie intransparent, ne.	Interviewee 7

Category	Generalization	Quote	Interview partners
	Transferring large amounts abroad increases the risk of detection	Auffälligkeiten festmachen, weil da etwa/ entweder ein grösserer Betrag abgeht oder aber ins Ausland verfügt wird, wo man sich vorstellen könnte, das könnte der Terrorismusfinanzierung dienen.	Interviewee 3
	Criminal purpose cannot usually be established	Wenn überhaupt Transaktionen stattfinden, ähm, über das elektronische Transaktionssystem vom Finanzinstitut ähm, […] in der Regel nicht festgestellt werden kann, dass hier ein krimineller Zweck verfolgt wird.	Interviewee 11
	Numerous people with Arabic names are suspects	Da waren dann auffallend viele Personen involviert in diese Geldflüsse, alle mit arabischen Namen.	Interviewee 5
	High sensitivity with regard to specific regions	Also da sind die entsprechenden Systeme sehr wohl schon sehr ausgebaut, und die/ also diese Institute sind natürlich auch sensibilisiert im Hinblick auf diese Regionen.	Interviewee 6

Category	Generalization	Quote	Interview partners
	Suspicious transactions get lost in legitimate transactions	Nun ja, besonders zu hinterfragen, es ist/ das wäre so, wie wenn man fragen würde, alle Fahrzeuge, die in die Himmelsrichtung Türkei unterwegs sind oder vielleicht sogar direkt in die Türkei fahren, müssten einer speziellen Kontrolle unterliegen. Also, die Frage ist, inwiefern ist das überhaupt noch praktikabel? Es sind 99,9 Prozent Überweisungen wahrscheinlich völlig legitim, und in dieser Masse an Finanzströmen wird der eine oder andere Euro sein, der möglicherweise vom Sympathisanten an, weiss ich nicht, Familienangehörige oder sonst irgendjemanden oder Personen, die eben in dem Kampfgebiet tätig sind oder dorthin zumindest immer wieder pendeln, an die überwiesen.	Interviewee 6
	Cash withdrawal in area bordering Syria is suspicious	Sehr häufig fliegen halt die nach Istanbul, reisen dann an die Grenze und leeren dann an den Geldautomaten in der letzten türkischen Stadt vor dem Grenzübertritt, plündern die noch einmal ihr Konto, also die kommen dann mit ihren fünf-, sechstausend Euro ins Krisengebiet.	Interviewee 13

Category	Generalization	Quote	Interview partners
	Differentiation between terrorism financing and legitimate cash withdrawals difficult	Also ich sage, dass das/ Nur ist es so eben, ist gerade beim Geldautomatengeschäft, die Bank, wo sie den Zug vornehmen, die weiss nicht, ob das Konto geplündert wird oder nicht. Die weiss ja nicht, wie viel auf dem Konto ist, die sieht einfach, da werden tausend Euro bezogen, das kann aber schon auch ein Tourist sein, der ein Teppich kauft, oder?	Interviewee 13
Parallel banking systems			
Parallel banking systems – general suitability			
	Concealment of the beneficial owner	Und ich meine, das ist natürlich ein perfektes System, was auch angelegt ist natürlich dann auch, äh äh (.) die Beneficial Ownership geheim zu halten, zu verschleiern und/ und kann natürlich dann auch genutzt werden für/ für illegale Transaktionen.	Interviewee 7
	No supervision	Das ist möglich, aber das ist natürlich schon ein Gebiet, wo keine Aufsicht besteht und der überhaupt nicht transparent ist und das bietet natürlich ganz viele Möglichkeiten auch Vermögenswerte von A nach B zu verschieben.	Interviewee 14

Category	Generalization	Quote	Interview partners
	Difficult access	Also Sie müssten schon aus dieser Volksgruppe sein, damit Sie das Urvertrauen von (Hawala?) da bekommen.	Interviewee 15
	No supervision	Is billiger als Swift und/ und vor allen Dingen is es […] nicht von irgendeiner Aufsicht zu kontrollieren.	Interviewee 3
	Serious	Die Leute sind sehr seriös, weil sie sehr viel riskieren, wenn es nicht klappt.	Interviewee 11
	Cost-effective	Und es ist auch kostengünstig, so.	Interviewee 11
	Access to conflict areas	Das war natürlich ein grosses Thema bei Al-Qaida, wusste man auch, weil es dort eben vor allem darum ging, Geld ins Konfliktgebiet zu bringen, und da war Hawala fast die einzige Möglichkeit.	Interviewee 13
	Combination with bank transfer	Ich würde meinen, wenn man so eine Transaktion, wie ich sie skizziert habe, so eine strukturierte, denkt, könnte Hawala zwischen oder nach der Bankreform Cash durchaus eine Rolle spielen.	Interviewee 13
	Suitable for ransom payment	Also ich glaube, im Bereich Lösegeld könnte ich mir durchaus vorstellen, dass das immer noch eine Rolle spielt.	Interviewee 13

Category	Generalization	Quote	Interview partners
Parallel banking systems – concrete approach			
	Cash transactions based on trust and middlemen	Dass // dass Sie sagen, ähm Sie haben ein/ ein System, dieses (Hawala-)System zum Beispiels, weils einfach auf/ auf Mittelsmännern und Vertrauen beruht, ne, wo letztendlich am Ende des Tages mal irgendwann ein Clearing stattfindet, aber es ist alles bargeldbasiert, und Sie haben einfach Ihre Mittelsmänner irgendwo sitzen, wo Sie natürlich als/ ja, ich sag mal, als/ als [...] jemand, der ein westliches Bankensystem gewohnt ist, natürlich überhaupt keinen Zugriff haben, weils einfach ein komplett paralleles Bankensystem ist, ne.	Interviewee 7
	Aid agencies as a cover	Ähm (seufzt leise) das ist 'ne gute Frage. Also ich weiss, dass es das gibt. Ähm [...] ähm ich weiss es eigentlich [...] inoffiziell von/ von, ich sag mal, Hilfsorganisationen, die, ich sag mal, das Problem haben, stellen Sie sich vor, Sie sind 'ne Hilfsorganisation und Sie wollen/ Es gab 'ne Katastrophe irgendwo in 'nem Gebiet, wo es einfach keine westliche Bank gibt, die Dollar annimmt oder so.	Interviewee 7

Category	Generalization	Quote	Interview partners
	Combination of trade and use of fictitious invoices	Wenn man das kombiniert oder das quasi mit Handel vermischt wird oder dass eine Warenlieferung gemacht oder nicht gemacht wird oder eine Rechnung gestellt wird, aber nicht geliefert wird und dann hat man natürlich wieder die Möglichkeit, Vermögenswerte von A nach B zu verschieben	Interviewee 14
	Difficult to determine value of machines	Was ist der Wert eines Produktes oder wie können die bestimmen, ob diese Maschine wirklich so viel 100.000 Euro kostet oder nicht?	Interviewee 14
	Avoid invoices for services	Oh, es ist ein hoher Betrag und gibt es eine Rechtfertigung für das? Ja, es gibt ein Dokument oder einen Vertrag. Okay, den schauen wir uns an. Um was geht es da? Ah, Dienstleistungen, ja das ist schon etwas, was verdächtig wäre. Dienstleistungen ist ein schwammiger Begriff.	Interviewee 14
	Procure documents	Die sind schon froh, dass es ein Dokument oder sogar eine Urkunde gibt, die besagt: Diese Maschine ist eine halbe Million Euro wert.	Interviewee 14

Category	Generalization	Quote	Interview partners
	Contact with members of certain ethnic groups	Aber es gibt sagen wir mal Personengruppen aus bestimmten Regionen und die wollen Geld in die Heimatländer überweisen und wenn man weiss, man hat eine Community, sage ich mal von Asiaten oder Philippinen oder das können auch Brasilianer sein und man hat einen Zugang zu diesen Gruppen, dann kann man ja mal fragen. "Wo kann ich Geld günstig überweisen?" Und da wird sofort gesagt: "Geh zu dem!" oder "Geh zu dieser Frau!"	Interviewee 14
	Clearing (balancing of peaks)	Da gibt es dann einen Ausgleich, der geschaffen wird. Ähm, aber im Prinzip ist es ähm, eine Sache für Betroffene, ne? Das ist eine Grundidee [unintelligible] der gibt es und sagt, bitte, ich möchte meiner Mutter einen Kühlschrank zukommen lassen. Gibt es Geld mit Provision oder Abzug und ihr wird der Kühlschrank vor die Tür gestellt, ne?	Interviewee 15
	Physical transport of cash or credit	Man kann zum Beispiel das Geld äh, physisch transportieren. Man kann auch jemanden anrufen äh und ihn veranlassen, dass er jemandem, der sich meldet ähm, einen Kredit zur Verfügung stellt, in Form eines [unintelligible] Geschäftes, also eines (Bargeschäftes?). Da gibt es verschiedene Methoden, die es unmöglich machen,	Interviewee 11

Category	Generalization	Quote	Interview partners
	Involve countries without advanced banking systems	(Hawala?) Banker gibt es natürlich in Regionen, die nicht über ein ähm, fortschrittliches Banksystem verfügen oder anders gesagt, wo der Zugang zu Banken für den Grossteil der Bevölkerung nicht möglich ist.	Interviewee 11
	Financing in kind, donations and trade	Anderes wird wahrscheinlich, ganz, ganz banal, wird über den/ normal über den Handel funktionieren, also dass man Finanzierungen jetzt nicht nur mit reinem flüssigem Cashmittel oder sonstigen Finanzmitteln macht, sondern dass man finanziert mit Ressourcen oder mit Financing-in-Kind, also mit sonstigen Unterstützungshandlungen, Spenden, Sachgütern und Sonstiges.	Interviewee 6

Category	Generalization	Quote	Interview partners
	Transfers from crisis areas via banks not possible	Man muss auch sagen, wir kennen das von Erfahrungsberichten, von Leuten, die aus den Krisengebieten aus Syrien gekommen sind und hier Asyl gesucht haben. Die haben oftmals auch nicht mehr die Möglichkeit, sich auf dem geregelten Finanzweg, theoretisch, wenn sie zu Hause ein Vermögen haben oder ein Bankguthaben haben oder sonst irgendwie Guthaben auf Banken oder sonstigen Konten haben, sie können mittlerweile nicht mehr darauf zurückgreifen. Einfach, weil es Sperren gibt, wird seitens der Organisationen, die ein gewisses Gebiet derzeit besetzen, oder es ist halt immer noch die syrische Regierung, die sind dann mitunter darauf angewiesen, auf solche Netzwerke wie ein Hawala-Netzwerk zurückzugreifen.	Interviewee 6

Category	Generalization	Quote	Interview partners
	No bank in Syria	Für einige gibt es auch rein praktikable Gründe, warum die Person, auch wenn sie in Wien ist und theoretisch hier schon ein Konto hat, noch immer auf Hawala zurückgreifen muss, einfach, weil man die Schwierigkeiten im Land B, also in dem Fall in Syrien, hat und nichts anderes machen kann, weil man sonst das Geld nicht über die Grenze bekommt. Das wäre die eine Richtung. Natürlich in die andere Richtung ist das Ganze natürlich auch zugänglicher, keine Frage.	Interviewee 6
Parallel banking systems – detection risk			
	Clearing via banks risky	Gerade bei der Verrechnung von Spitzen können Sie das in bestimmten Banken wahrscheinlich erkennen, wenn/ über bestimmte Methoden.	Interviewee 1

Category	Generalization	Quote	Interview partners
	Lack of supervision	Das ist korrekt. Die sind zwar ähm/ ich meine, wenn man es ganz DRASTISCH sieht, dann ist in Deutschland zumindestens unterliegen sie AUCH dem Geldwäschebekä mpfungsgesetz, und müssten EIGENTLICH auch, wenn sie Verdachtsfälle haben, die MELDEN. (holt Luft) Werden Sie nur nicht sehen. Das macht kein Mensch äh in dieser Branche, weil sie halt nicht ähm (holt Luft) SO überwacht werden wie jetzt die Kreditinstitute durch eine/ durch eine Aufsichtsbehörde. Es gibt halt die Gewerbeaufsichtsämter, aber die gucken da nicht in SOLCHE Bereiche rein.	Interviewee 1
	No AML or KYC standards	Äh es finden insofern alle/ alle Standards, die wir haben im Bereich Geldwäschereibekämpfung, KYC findet da nicht statt.	Interviewee 7
	No identification of the beneficial owner possible	Und ähm […] Sie haben keinerlei Chance, letztendlich durch, so wie das System angelegt ist, den wirtschaftlich Berechtigten ultimativ finanzieren/ äh zu identifizieren.	Interviewee 7
	No monitoring possible	Ich meine, die Überwachung von (Hawala?) Transaktionen ist nicht möglich.	Interviewee 11

Category	Generalization	Quote	Interview partners
Cryptocurrencies			
Cryptocurrencies – general suitability			
	Parallel currency exchangeable into common currencies	So, das heisst, wir haben eine komplette Parallelwährung, die Sie aber wieder umtauschen können in reales Geld.	Interviewee 8
	No regulation	So, ist aber null reguliert.	Interviewee 8
	Good alternative to classic bank transfers	Ja, warum soll ich denn irgendwie, sage ich mal, ganz böse, sage ich mal, eine Überweisung machen, wenn ich einfach über so ein Verschlüsselungssystem, also über künstliche Währung, eigentlich alles darstellen kann, was ich möchte?	Interviewee 8
	Without contact points with financial institutions	Es müsste eigentlich möglich sein, ohne dass jemals ein Finanzinstitut damit in Berührung kommt.	Interviewee 7
	Anonymity	Aber man hat keine Ahnung, wer sich hinter einer Bitcoin-Adresse verbirgt. Das ist komplett anonym, verschlüsselt, man hat keine Ahnung, wer dahintersteckt.	Interviewee 14
	Lack of transparency	Und ja, weil es eben technisch anspruchsvoll ist [unintelligible], überhaupt nicht transparent ist, ist es natürlich ein super geeignetes Mittel, um die Vermögenswerte von A nach B zu verschieben, solange die Teilnehmer an das System Bitcoin glauben, funktioniert das auch.	Interviewee 14

Category	Generalization	Quote	Interview partners
	Easy to hide	Aber es ist sehr leicht versteckbar, es ist verschlüsselbar.	Interviewee 14
	Reduced storage risk	Man kann grosse Summen quasi in Bitcoins umwandeln und wenn ich das in bar haben müsste, dann brauche ich grosse Lagerplätze und da ist eben das Verlustrisiko, sei es durch Diebstahl, sei es durch Verlust, sei es durch Raub, sei es durch Brand oder irgendwelche Elementarschäden.	Interviewee 14
	Not a common currency in retail	Nur, es ist halt schwierig, weil ich kann nicht einkaufen beim Aldi mit Bitcoin oder an der Tankstelle.	Interviewee 15
	Bitcoins popular in the darknet	Bitcoin und Co., bekanntermassen über das Darknetz, schon eine gewisse Beliebtheit in kriminellen Kreisen. Es würde mich wundern, wenn hier nicht nur normale Rauschgiftdelikte oder sonstige, wesentlich härtere Delikte begangen werden, sondern auch eben so was wie Terrorismusfinanzierung.	Interviewee 6
Cryptocurrencies – concrete approach			
	Increase computing power	Ich meine, das Ganze geht ja letztendlich über irgendwelche Rechenkapazitäten.	Interviewee 7

Category	Generalization	Quote	Interview partners
	Provide computing capacity	Letztendlich, Sie/ ich meine, Sie können ja Bitcoins erwerben, wenn Sie an anteil/ am System teilnehmen und einfach Rechenkapazität zur Verfügung stellen und können so durch dieses System intern letztendlich, […] ja, […] Kaufkraft erwerben …	Interviewee 7
	Create an e-wallet	Man braucht auch ein elektronisches Portemonnaie, ein E-Wallet dazu und nur noch die Adresse oder nur noch die physikalische, elektronische Adresse (unv.)	Interviewee 14
	Constantly changing, inexpensive notebooks	Dann kaufen Sie sich einen billigen Computer, ein billiges Notebook und dann ist man mit ein paar Hundert Franken dabei und das ist ja nichts. Und dann wechselt man das Ding wieder und schmeisst das weg.	Interviewee 14
	Use publicly accessible WLAN networks	Ja, wie gesagt, die öffentlichen Netze, das ist schon so. Wo keine Handynummer notwendig ist, um sich einzuloggen. Es gibt nach wie vor Personen, die ihr Netzwerk nicht schützen und so weiter und so fort.	Interviewee 14
	Acquiring Bitcoins with cash or non-cash assets	wo Sie diese kaufen können und das andere Geld quasi oder Vermögenswerte auf Gegenleistung einzahlen können.	Interviewee 14
	Find Bitcoin exchange or exchange partner	Entweder über einen Bitcoins-Change oder man findet direkt Leute.	Interviewee 14

Category	Generalization	Quote	Interview partners
	Investment of assets in Bitcoins	Immobilie verkauft und ich lege das jetzt in Bitcoin an. Ich hätte es auch in Edelmetall anlegen können, in Aktien anlegen, dann hätte es die Bank noch einigermassen unter Kontrolle, weil das in einem Wertschrift- oder Edelmetalldepot dann eingebucht wird, aber bei den Bitcoins wäre das nicht der Fall.	Interviewee 14
	Payment of extortion money in Bitcoins	Man wird höchstens mal, sagen wir, in der Finanzindustrie damit konfrontiert, wenn die darüber reden, welche Attacken laufen, und dann halt eben Erpressungsgelder verlangt werden, die dann halt in diesen Fällen zumeist über die Bitcoins bezahlt werden müssen.	Interviewee 2
	Limited tradability of Bitcoins in Syria	Die Frage ist allerdings, und das ist schon zumindest zu hinterfragen, was kann ich mir dann/ also eincashen werde ich es wohl relativ schwer können, irgendwo in Syrien. Also ich gehe mal davon aus, sehr viele Abnehmer für Bitcoins oder sonstige virtuelle Währungen wird es nicht geben.	Interviewee 6

Category	Generalization	Quote	Interview partners
	Using Bitcoin to pay for weapons on the darknet	Das heisst wiederum, ich könnte, wenn ich die Bitcoins als Zahlungsmittel oder als Finanzmittel akzeptieren will, als Terrorist, und damit arbeiten will, kann ich mir dann wiederum im Darknet für Bitcoins möglicherweise Waffen oder sonstiges Material beschaffen.	Interviewee 6
	Look for countries with Bitcoin exchange	Also hier müsste man zumindest irgendwo das nächste Land heranziehen, wo man so etwas wie eine informelle Bitcoin-Wirtschaft hat, wo einzelne, vielleicht Warenhändler oder sonst irgendjemand Bitcoins akzeptiert oder wo es zumindest die Möglichkeit gibt, Bitcoins auszucashen und wiederum in Cash umzuwandeln.	Interviewee 6
Cryptocurrencies-risk of detection			
	Authorities are not up to date	Also ich persönlich würde viel eher in die Richtung gehen von diesen neuen Technologien. Da sind die Behörden wirklich noch hinterher.	Interviewee 14
	Risk of leaving traces	Aber doch, es gibt immer ein Risiko, dass man da Spuren hinterlässt, ja. Aber das ist beim Bargeld genau das Gleiche. Sie können nicht grosse Bargeldsummen irgendwie unsichtbar in den Markt integrieren. Irgendwo fällt das immer auf.	Interviewee 14

Category	Generalization	Quote	Interview partners
	Assignment of Bitcoin to the beneficial owner is difficult	Zuordnung des Bitcoins oder der Währung zu einem wirtschaftlich Berechtigten ist äh, äusserst schwierig, oder?	Interviewee 11
Money transfer systems			
Money Transfer Systems – general suitability			
	Fast and inexpensive	Sondern es gibt so viele ähm alternative Möglichkeiten, Gelder über Landesgrenzen hinweg zu bringen. Also in erster Linie die/ die/ die Dienstleister, wie/ wie Western Union, et cetera, die das äh wesentlich schneller können, wesentlich billiger können.	Interviewee 12
	Cannot be traced back to a specific person	Na ja, rein schon von der, jetzt ohne, dass/ das wird jetzt schwierig/ das ist insofern schon geeignet, weil wiederum, es gibt kein legitimiertes, fixes Konto dahinter, das heisst, es gibt keine ständige Infrastruktur, die auf eine Person zugerechnet werden kann.	Interviewee 6
	Infrastructure on the recipient side may be limited	Da wird man überweisungstechnisch vielleicht wirklich noch auf Money Transfers zurückgreifen, wobei auch hier, denke ich, mittlerweile die Infrastruktur einfach auf der Empfängerseite in einem Land wie Syrien wohl kaum vorhanden sein wird.	Interviewee 6

Category	Generalization	Quote	Interview partners
Money transfer systems – concrete approach			
	Send money to Turkey	/Wenn// man sich also jetzt in der TÜRKEI, sagen wir mal, in die Türkei GELD schicken/ sich schicken, zu jemandem in die Türkei, und ähm Sie überschreiten bestimmte BETRÄGE, so können wir erst mal vom GRUNDSATZ her überall in der Türkei das Geld abheben, egal, wo Sie sind. Das geht immer so. Es geht von EINEM Land in ein anderes Land, und es ist nicht BEGRENZT auf eine Stadt oder Region.	Interviewee 1
	Avoid border towns	Wenn wir aber sehen, dass der Empfänger in der Türkei das Geld nicht in Istanbul abhebt, sondern, sagen wir mal, in einer der Grenzstädte.	Interviewee 1

Category	Generalization	Quote	Interview partners
	Transfer funds to family members	Ja, das sehen wir/ ich meine, das sehen Sie auch, wir haben auch Beispiele hier, wo Sie gerade sagten, ein VATER, äh der sich auch in dieser Alters- äh gruppe bewegte, der seinem SOHN Geld geschickt hat, der sich in Syrien befand und auch im KAMPF mitgewirkt hat. (holt Luft) Da habe ich gesagt, der Sohn hatte einfach/ wollte sich einfach mal eine COLA kaufen, hatte kein Geld dafür. Und ähm dem fehlten bestimmte westliche Annehmlichkeiten. Und über diesen/ ja, aufgrund DIESER Situation äh, Geld wurde über UNS transferiert, wir haben das der Polizei gemeldet, die Polizei hat uns hinterher noch mal informiert, dass es wirklich so platt war, dass der/ der JUNGE da ähm bestimmte BEDÜRFNISSE hatte äh und in der TAT auch Cola trinken wollte und dafür GELD brauchte.	Interviewee 1
	Use straw men	Da sind wir beim Thema Strohmann. (holt Luft) Ähm […] das ist völlig üblich, dass sie da ähm/ dass da Dritte vorgeschoben werden. Das ist wie in ALLEN kriminellen Bereichen, also beim Drogenhandel auch, beim Geldwaschen dort/.	Interviewee 1

Category	Generalization	Quote	Interview partners
	Use public documents	Aber ähm natürlich wird ein Mitarbeiter auch, wenn da ein offizieller Stempel drauf ist einer/ einer/ ja, einer Behörde, äh dem MEHR Glauben schenken, als wenn das so ein Wischiwaschipapier ist. Und dann wird man auch oft nicht weiter nachfassen.	Interviewee 1
	Different people under the same name	Dass es auch solche Überweisungen gegeben hat, von unterschiedlichen Personen, jedoch unter dem gleichen Namen, das ist auch sehr wohl bekannt.	Interviewee 6
	Digital natives as perpetrators	Das sind junge Männer, die digital aufgewachsen sind und vertraut sind. Ich meine, bin Laden wusste wahrscheinlich nicht, was E-Banking ist, die wissen, was hier E-Wallets sind, ja?	Interviewee 13
Money transfer systems – risk of detection			
	Proximity to Syrian border increases detection risk	Ähm wenn Sie dann sich in die Nähe der syrischen Grenze bewegen, dann wissen wir, dass da AUCH viele dieser Personen sich aufhalten, die ein bestimmtes Profil haben und eine bestimmte Art des Verhaltens, was Finanztransfers anbetrifft, und auch, wenn sie dann nach Syrien gehen, (holt Luft) oder wo immer die sich auch hinbewegen, äh da haben Sie bestimmte Charakteristika, ähm (.) die man auch dann über Analysen erkennen kann.	Interviewee 1

Category	Generalization	Quote	Interview partners
	Avoid certain profiles (male, between 18 and 30 etc.)	Ähm wenn ich das mal ganz/ ganz ALLGEMEIN formuliere, ähm dann wissen wir, dass es häufig sich um/ um junge MÄNNER handelt, die zwischen 18 und 30 Jahre alt beispielsweise sind, (holt Luft) wir sehen auch eine Zunahme an FRAUEN, die das unterstützen, und auch AKTIV äh werden. Aber da hätten wir schon mal etwas, sozusagen, JA, es sind oft junge Männer, die ähm (..) eine bestimmte Historie auch haben. Äh auch möglicherweise was ihre ähm/ also NICHT-Deutsche, die aber einen deutschen Ausweis haben, aber woanders GEBOREN sind möglicherweise/ ähm (..) die äh sich in einer bestimmten Art und Weise VERHALTEN.	Interviewee 1
	Certain behaviours increase risk of detection	Wenn sie also jetzt in die/ beispielsweise in die/ äh nach Syrien REISEN wollen, dann sehen wir, dass die ein bestimmtes Verhalten haben, WIE sie sich bewegen, wo sie Geld in EMPFANG nehmen oder auch Geld schicken.	Interviewee 1

Category	Generalization	Quote	Interview partners
	Facebook search	Kleinstbetriebe, die sie nutzen, ähm […] wir sehen Sympathisanten auch mit bestimmten Charakteristika, die dann ähm (…) äh beispielsweise (lacht auf) auch mal in einer Art […] Pressearbeit aktiv sind, mit Pressearbeit meine ich jetzt EHER so auch Facebook oder andere Internet/ (holt Luft) soziale Netzwerke, also Internetplattformen, dann nutzen, wo Sie auch mit bestimmten Methoden das erkennen können oder auch recherchieren können.	Interviewee 1
	Networks between certain persons	Sie sehen auch bestimmte/ bestimmte Netzwerke, wie dann Transaktionen sich zwischen bestimmten ähm/ (..) sagen wir mal, äh vielleicht ein ganz konkretes Kriterium oder ETWAS konkreter, wäre, dass EINE Person [unintelligible] Netzwerk äh WIEDER hat von vielen anderen Personen aus verschiedenen europäischen Ländern, durchaus auch äh immer wieder kleinere Betriebe zugeschickt. Und sie sind dann wie so eine Art Spinne in einem Netzwerk auch erkennbar.	Interviewee 1
	Exceeding certain amounts	Und Sie überschreiten einen bestimmten Betrag, dann lassen wir die Auszahlung nicht mehr zu, sondern schicken das Geld zurück, und reagieren dann WEITER.	Interviewee 1

Category	Generalization	Quote	Interview partners
	Movement profiles	Die befinden sich sozusagen auf dem Weg nach Syrien, und sie gehen vielleicht nach einem HALBEN Jahr wieder zurück. Also so etwas, also jetzt äh aus welchen Gründen auch IMMER, ähm (holt Luft) äh kommen zurück nach Deutschland. Das sind Verhaltensweisen, die wir sehen. Und da gibt es auch bestimmte Kriterien, die man/ die WIR jetzt entwickelt haben, die finden Sie sicherlich auch woanders, bei anderen Häusern, äh die dann zu einer Auffälligkeit führen, und die dann konkret durch Mitarbeiter bei uns bearbeitet wird, der dann […] sich diesen Vorfall anschaut und äh recherchiert und dann WEITERE (holt Luft) Möglichkeiten nutzt.	Interviewee 1
	Real-time criteria and ex-post-analyses	Da gibt es VIELE Methoden, (holt Luft) wie man Dinge erkennen kann durch Echtzeitkriterien, durch nachgelagerte Kriterien	Interviewee 1
	Low standard of verification in mobile phone shops	Dass der Überprüfungsstandard und der Sorgfaltsstandard nicht der ist, der die meisten Länder gerne sehen würden, insbesondere, wenn solche Transaktionen angestossen werden bei Handyshops oder sonstigen Handelstreibenden, die als Agenten auftreten für diese grossen Unternehmen. Das wissen wir auch.	Interviewee 6

Category	Generalization	Quote	Interview partners
Personal transfer			
Personal transfer – general suitability			
	Refugee routes suitable for money transfers	Und/ und äh äh wenn Sie da Menschen rüberkriegen, dann kriegen Sie natürlich auch Bar- oder Vermögenswerte da rüber.	Interviewee 7
	Cash transport of funds for purchases	Ja also ich denke zuletzt geht das in bar. Also die brauchen ja das Geld [unintelligible], um das/ Ja quasi um die [unintelligible] betreiben zu können, um Einkäufe tätigen zu können	Interviewee 14
	Main channel	Ich glaube, dass das wahrscheinlich einer der Hauptkanäle ist, das ist meine persönliche Meinung	Interviewee 6
Personal transfer – concrete approach			
	Use trade routes (land routes)	Und // und diese Handelsrouten, das sind einfach Landwege gewesen, weil die Häfen blockiert waren, diese Handelsrouten und/ und das heisst, auch diese Logistik dahinter, die funktioniert heute immer noch.	Interviewee 7

Category	Generalization	Quote	Interview partners
	Involve experienced smugglers	Aber // aber die Leute, die an diesem Part/ oder an diesem System partizipieren und gewinnen, das heisst, die Leute, die diese Wertgegenstände über die Grenzen schaffen, die das Geld wieder rücktransferieren, ähm da/ das besteht seit Jahrzehnten und/ und das kann, wie gesagt, ähm […] einerseits der/ der Schmuggel oder der Transfer von/ von/ von materiellen Gegenständen sein und dann auf der anderen Seite natürlich auch die Rückführung von/ von Geldern.	Interviewee 7
	Use refugee routes	Ja, ich/ Und das ist, glaube ich, die/ diese Flüchtlingsrouten oder Schmugglerrouten oder wie auch immer Sie die da nennen wollen, ich meine, da gibt's 'ne bestehende Infrastruktur. Das funktioniert.	Interviewee 7
	Involve smugglers	Da gibt's äh äh/ da gibt es Logistiker, Schleuser, was auch immer Sie/ oder wie Sie die nennen wollen.	Interviewee 7

Category	Generalization	Quote	Interview partners
	Use prepaid cards	Und gerade jetzt, wenn wir über Barwerte reden oder/ oder gerade Prepaid-Karten. Ich meine, das ist ja wahrscheinlich noch leichter dann als irgendwelche Menschen rüberzuschmuggeln, wo Sie äh Papiere brauchen et cetera. Und dann/	Interviewee 7
	Use border between Syria and Turkey	Man hat da relativ oft vor Augen so etwas wie in Syrien, wo es eine relativ unbehelligte Grenze zur Türkei gegeben hat, wo man auch weiss, dass sehr viele Personen und Güter diese Grenze überqueren und relativ frei.	Interviewee 6
Personal transfer – risk of detection			
	Travel to Syria is suspicious	Nur, aber wenn der nach Syrien reisen würde, hätten wir schon jede Menge Verdachtsmomente, um den nur zu melden.	Interviewee 3
	Preparation of the trip to Syria is suspicious	Der/ // der zwar vertraulich, aber da is/ da is auch gewarnt/ da wird gewarnt, wie Terrorkämpfer, also die jetzt sich nach Syrien absetzen, um da kämpfen zu wollen bei der IS, ähm wie sie sich vorher verhalten. Da gibt's so Muster, die dann beschrieben sind, wo man als Bank auch merken könnte, hoppala, das könnte jetzt gefährlich werden.	Interviewee 3

Category	Generalization	Quote	Interview partners
Counter-terrorism instruments			
Exchange of information between private individuals and authorities			
	Exchange of information (lists of dangerous persons) between authorities and banks	Das wäre natürlich für Finanzdienstleister und auch für Banken interessant, wenn man diese Liste bekommen könnte, und könnte dann auch GEZIELTER recherchieren ähm und auch dann im Austausch äh die Informationen natürlich dann den Behörden zur Verfügung stellen. Und das sind natürlich Personen auch, die mögen noch nicht äh den/ im Stadium eines/ eines TERRORISTEN sein, und vielleicht irgendwo im Vorstadium irgendwo im WEITESTEN Sinne damit zusammenhängt, ähm vielleicht auch nicht, vielleicht auch UNSCHULDIG reingeraten sind.	Interviewee 1

Category	Generalization	Quote	Interview partners
	Lack of control over information exchanged	Ähm natürlich haben Sie immer das Problem, auch wenn Sie solche Listen an PRIVATE Institute geben, dass die dann nicht mehr so richtig unter Kontrolle sind und dann vielleicht in Hände geraten, wo sie nicht hinsollen. (holt Luft) Ähm aber das wäre, glaube ich, gerade im Bereich der Kommunikation zwischen Behörde, wie gesagt: den Ermittlern, und der Privatindustrie, jetzt in diesem Fall dann halt Finanzdienstleister oder auch BANKEN.	Interviewee 1
	Exchange of information (typologies) between authorities and financial service providers	Das geschieht teilweise auch/ also wir arbeiten da auch beispielsweise konkret mit den Behörden ZUSAMMEN, also ich jetzt auch als Person zum Beispiel mit dem Bundeskriminalamt oder mit ähm durchaus auch Verfassungsschutz, wo man dann drüber nachdenkt, und äh das auch relativ offenlegt: WIE verhält sich denn einer, ein Sympathisant, der IS unterstützt, oder wie verhält sich auch tatsächlich ein Foreign Terrorist Fighter?	Interviewee 1

Category	Generalization	Quote	Interview partners
	Seclusion	Und auf der anderen Seite aus Sicht der Behörden ähm ist bei/ äh bei/ bei der ganzen Office-Arbeit, bei der Prävention ein/ ein/ unbedingt erforderlich/ ein sehr hohes Mass an Abgeschottetheit erforderlich/ Abgeschottetheit erforderlich. Also das heisst, diese Informationen kann man, darf man aus/ aus rechtsstaatlichen äh Gründen gar nicht weitergeben.	Interviewee 12
	Exchange of information must not take place	Äh das/ das ist/ das ist sehr schwer. Ob man zusätzlich bei der/ der nötige Austausch zwisch/ zwischen den Strafverfolgern und äh/ und/ und der Wirtschaft im weitesten Sinne äh teilweise gar nicht erfolgen darf.	Interviewee 12
Undercover investigators			
	Investigations without classical intelligence are difficult	Also ich glaube, dass/ dass es ohne klassische Intelligence wahrscheinlich sehr, sehr schwierig ist, also ohne äh/ ohne dass ich das jetzt aus der Erfahrung sagen könnte.	Interviewee 7
	Insider knowledge required	Ich meine, die Behörden sind da angewiesen auf Insiderwissen. Sei es Sie haben 'nen Verdeckten Ermittler, der/ den Sie beauftragt haben unter Einschleusen oder Sie kaufen 'ne Art Whistleblower oder Kronzeugen raus.	Interviewee 7

Category	Generalization	Quote	Interview partners
	Without undercover investigators, there is hardly any chance of success	Hm, ich glaube, ohne diese Art von Informationen werden Sie sonst nie da ankommen. Wenn Sie wirklich […] äh äh mühselig die Prozesskette nachgehen müssen mit/ mit Amtshilfe, da kommen Sie nie ans Ziel.	Interviewee 7
	Undercover investigators with a migration background	Nicht/ und da/ das andere sind V-Leute. Und Verdeckte Ermittler, Polizei, die haben/ hatten schon früher, so viel kann ich mal verraten, auch Leute mit Migrationshintergrund, Muslime, bei der/ als Beamt/ die dann Deutsche wurden, als Beamte im BKA tätig.	Interviewee 9
	Undercover investigators with a migration background difficult to recruit	Egal. Es ist eine grössere Hürde solche/ selbst die Kollegen sozusagen, Kollegen zu gewinnen, die in dem Bereich – ich hatte kein Glück bis dahin – Verdeckte Ermittler sein wollen. Die haben da so 'n bisschen 'ne gewisse, […] wie soll ich sagen, 'ne ethnische Loyalität, Pro/ Problem der ethnischen Loyalität sogar gehabt, dass die sagen, "nee, das will ich nicht. Das mag ich nicht." Also, das, das/ die Gewinnung Verdeckter Ermittler, das stellen Sie sich nicht zu einfach vor.	Interviewee 9

Category	Generalization	Quote	Interview partners
	Confidants are easier to recruit	V-Leute, gut, das geht jetzt eher. (Denkweise?) ist eher, dass man Leute aus der Szene direkt hat, die dann für die Polizei arbeiten. Ist ja auch im, im Rechtsextremismus und im Linksextremismus durchaus ja üblich, mit, mit/ auch mit sehr grossen Problemen.	Interviewee 9
	Weak legal basis	Ja, also bei uns fängt es ja schon mit der gesetzlichen Grundlage an, dass wir das eigentlich gar nicht dürfen beziehungsweise uns so enge Grenzen gesetzt sind.	Interviewee 5
	Cost and personnel intensive	Ist auch sehr aufwendig, sehr kostenintensiv, personalintensiv. Ähm. Langjährige Ermittlungen sind das.	Interviewee 5
	Flexibly adjustable to cells	Ja, das ist wahrscheinlich eine der wesentlichsten oder der intelligentesten Formen der Bekämpfung, weil man hier vielleicht wirklich auf die einzelnen Zellen eingehen kann.	Interviewee 6
	Decentralized organization of the IS as an obstacle	Für den IS selber relativ schwierig, weil diese Organisation ist sehr geschickt aufgebaut, die haben da eigentlich nicht ein Hauptquartier, wo man einen einschleusen kann und dann alles erfährt, eine sehr dezentrale Organisation.	Interviewee 13

Category	Generalization	Quote	Interview partners
	Ideal for sleeper cells in Europe	Vielversprechend wahrscheinlich dort im europäischen Umfeld, wo sie tatsächlich Schläferzellen haben, aus denen heraus sich ein Anschlag erzielen lässt.	Interviewee 13
	Belgian cell as a worthwhile destination	Also ich glaube, die belgische Zelle und so weiter, das sind lohnenswerte Ziele für Verdeckte Ermittler.	Interviewee 13
	Lone wolf difficult to reach	Den Lonely Wolf, der da irgendwo zuhause sich Gewaltvideos anschaut und sich irgendwie radikalisiert und dann einen Lastwagen mietet, den werden sie, so viele Verdeckte Ermittler gibt es gar nicht, also, wenn sie da jedem einen oder drei oder fünf hinterherhängen und da haben wir die Ressourcen nicht.	Interviewee 13
	Targeted use necessary	Ich glaube, man muss die beschränkten Mittel, die man ohnehin schon hat bei den Verdeckten Ermittlern, das ist ja hoch riskant für die Betroffenen auch, muss man dort ansetzen, wo es am meisten Sinn macht, und das ist wahrscheinlich beim Aufspüren und Infiltrieren von erkannten Zellen, die eine hohe Wahrscheinlichkeit haben, dass einer davon dann tatsächlich einen Anschlag vornimmt.	Interviewee 13

Category	Generalization	Quote	Interview partners
Digital surveillance			
	Effective and efficient, but questionable under data protection law	Wäre wahrscheinlich ein probates Mittel. Deckt sich wahrscheinlich nicht immer ganz mit der/ (schmunzelnd) mit dem Datenschutz (lacht) und dem Persönlichkeitsschutz. Äh […] aber wenn Sie rein auf die/ auf die Effizienz und Effektivität abzielen, ist das wahrscheinlich ein Element, was/ was/ was wahrscheinlich probat wäre, weitere Informationen zu etablieren, ja.	Interviewee 7
	Individual elements as circumstantial evidence	Ich denke mal, dadurch, dass es immer wieder zu solchen Attacken kommt und man weiss, dass diese Personen im Internet radikalisiert wurden oder durch gewisses Material im Internet, und dennoch nicht auf diese Personen draufgekommen ist, zeigt umso mehr, wie schwierig das einfach ist. Das sind einfach Regelungsbereiche oder das sind einfach Bereiche des Lebens, die einfach den Alltag betreffen, so wie jeder den kennt bei uns. Und das sind dann nur kleine Elemente, die möglicherweise ein Indiz geben können.	Interviewee 6

Category	Generalization	Quote	Interview partners
	Quick	Wie gesagt, auch hier natürlich wertvoll, weil schnell und eben nicht an irgendwelche Grenzen, formalen Grenzen haltmachend.	Interviewee 13
	Differentiation according to countries	Also ich sage einmal, wenn eine deutsche Bundesanwaltschaft so etwas macht, dann habe ich kein Problem damit, wenn der russische Inlandsgeheimdienst das macht, dann (lachen) ist wahrscheinlich nicht so toll.	Interviewee 13
	susceptible to abuse	Weil wir öffnen natürlich da schon Möglichkeiten, die auch missbrauchsanfällig sind.	Interviewee 13
	Lower security without digital surveillance	Also wahrscheinlich ist das Rezept darin, ja, diese Möglichkeiten müssen genutzt werden, das schulden wir den Leuten, wenn sie Sicherheit haben wollen, oder wir müssen so ehrlich sein und zu den Leuten hingehen und sagen: "Das könnte man tun, das machen wir nicht, damit ist aber die Sicherheit nicht eine hundertprozentige."	Interviewee 13
Administrative and judicial assistance			
	Money faster than administrative assistance	Und bevor Sie dann mal irgendwo 'nen Amtshilfegesuch oder 'ne Arrestierung erwirkt haben, ich meine, da ist das Geld schon wieder äh üb/ über alle Ländergrenzen hinweg.	Interviewee 7

Category	Generalization	Quote	Interview partners
	Administrative assistance too slow	Die hinkt wahrscheinlich immer ein halbes Jahr hinterher, oder?	Interviewee 5
	Immediate action required	Im Moment sehr schwierig und dann natürlich wieder eine Welt, die noch schnelllebiger ist als alles andere und dann muss man sofort handeln können und so.	Interviewee 5
	Link data	Und ich glaube, dass das die grosse Herausforderung, aber auch Chance ist, wie können wir Daten miteinander verhängen?	Interviewee 13
	Targeted use of large data volumes	Wie können wir, das berühmte Stichwort Big Data nutzen, um schneller zu sein, um Anschläge zu verhindern, um Leute aus dem Verkehr zu nehmen oder zumindest unter Beobachtung zu setzen, ohne dass wir Gefahr laufen, dass es dann die Falschen trifft?	Interviewee 13
	Forwarding of information to selected countries	Aber es ist ja schon so, dass wir hier auch mit Staaten zusammenarbeiten müssen, die eben nicht die gleichen Anforderungen haben, und das ist schon ein grosses Problem. Also schmeissen wir alle rechtsstaatlichen Grundsätze über Bord?	Interviewee 13

Category	Generalization	Quote	Interview partners
	Obsolete system of mutual assistance	Wir haben es, ich meine, generell in der Zusammenarbeit zwischen Staaten, ich sage einmal, auf dem justiziellen Bereich, also Amts- und der Rechtshilfe, da haben wir ein Konzept aus dem 19. Jahrhundert, ne, zum Teil muss man es noch über die Botschaften schicken, übersetzen, beglaubigen.	Interviewee 13
	Informal cooperation between FIUs	In parallel, we already have possibilities for informal co-operation, I would say between FIUs, that is one of the examples, also between police authorities, which are not dependent on this formal judicial requirement.	Interviewee 13
Trade secrets			
	Standards for certifications	Im Prinzip muss das auch auf anderen Ebenen auch angepasst sein. Sei es bei Rechtsanwälten, sei es bei Notaren, sei es, wie gesagt, bei Behörden. Also überall dort, wo ich die Möglichkeit habe, sage ich mal, eine Dokumentation oder Ähnliches zu besorgen, müssen im Prinzip die gleichen Standards herrschen.	Interviewee 8
	Professional secrets as a concealment tool	Also es ist/ Also ich glaube, das Problem ist, es gibt innerhalb der Berufsstände hmhm gewisse schwarze Schafe, die sich auch […] zum Beispiel das Anwaltsgeheimnis, et cetera zu eigen machen, um/ um äh gewisse Sachen zu verschleiern.	Interviewee 7

Category	Generalization	Quote	Interview partners
	Transparent/ trans-parent human being as an ideal case	Na gut, für die Zwecke der Ermittlung und Bekämpfung von Terrorismus oder sonstiger Kriminalität der Idealfall, wenn wir den vollkommen gläsernen und transparenten Menschen hätten.	Interviewee 6
	Use information only for counter-terrorism purposes	Also unter dem Titel Terrorismusfinanzierung habe ich heute das, was ich brauche, ich bekomme alle Informationen, die ich brauche. Natürlich muss ich sie dann auch so verwenden, ich darf sie ja nicht für Drittzwecke verwenden.	Interviewee 13

Appendix 4: Interview Guide

(Translated from German into English [for original version see below])

1. Which difficulties do you see in combating the financing of terrorism? How do intelligent perpetrators finance terrorism? How would you finance terrorism?
2. Which sources of income do terrorists have?

   You have not yet mentioned white-collar crime. To what extent is white-collar crime suit;able for financing terrorism?
   - Sales tax fraud
   - CO2 emissions
   - Commodity trading (especially oil)

   You have not yet mentioned organised crime. To what extent is organised crime suitable for financing terrorism?
   - Drug trafficking
   - organ trafficking
   - Trafficking in human beings
   - Pimping
   - Protection rackets
   - kidnapping

   You have not yet mentioned petty crime. To what extent is petty crime suitable for financing terrorism?
   - Theft
   - eBay fraud
   - Insurance fraud
   - Car rentals (sales to Eastern Europe)

   You have not yet mentioned legal sources of income. To what extent are legal sources of income suitable for financing terrorism?
   - Real estate
   - Stock market transactions

   How do terrorists transfer their assets?

   To what extent are banks, for example in Turkey, suitable for transferring terrorists' assets?

   To what extent is offsetting among Muslims, for example through hawala, suitable for transferring terrorists' assets?

To what extent is personal transfer, for example in the context of leaving the country, for example to Syria, suitable for transferring terrorist assets?

To what extent are cryptocurrencies, such as Bitcoin, suitable for transferring terrorist assets? 4.

4. Which difficulties arise in investigations to combat terrorist financing?
   - Which difficulties arise with regard to undercover agents?
   - Which difficulties arise with regard to online searches?
   - Which difficulties arise with regard to administrative and legal assistance?
   - Which difficulties arise with regard to professional secrecy?

(Original, German version)

1. Welche Schwierigkeiten ergeben sich aus Ihrer Sicht bei der Bekämpfung der Terrorismusfinanzierung? Wie finanzieren intelligente Täter Terrorismus? Wie würden Sie Terrorismus finanzieren?

2. Welche Einnahmequellen haben Terroristen?

   Sie haben die Wirtschaftskriminalität noch nicht erwähnt. Inwiefern eignet sich die Wirtschaftskriminalität, um Terrorismus zu finanzieren?
   - Umsatzsteuerbetrug
   - CO_2-Emissionen
   - Rohstoffhandel (insbesondere Öl)

   Sie haben die organisierte Kriminalität noch nicht erwähnt. Inwiefern eignet sich die organisierte Kriminalität, um Terrorismus zu finanzieren?
   - Drogenhandel
   - Organhandel
   - Menschenhandel
   - Zuhälterei
   - Schutzgelderpressung
   - Entführungen

Sie haben die Kleinkriminalität noch nicht erwähnt. Inwiefern eignet sich Kleinkriminalität, um Terrorismus zu finanzieren?
- Diebstahl
- eBay-Betrug
- Versicherungsbetrug
- Autovermietungen (Verkauf nach Osteuropa)

Sie haben legale Einnahmequellen noch nicht erwähnt. Inwiefern eignen sich legaleEinnahmequellen, um Terrorismus zu finanzieren?
- Immobilien
- Börsengeschäfte

3. Wie transferieren Terroristen ihre Vermögenswerte?

Inwiefern eignen sich Banken, beispielsweise in der Türkei, um Vermögenswerte von Terroristen zu transferieren?

Inwiefern eignet sich die Verrechnung unter Muslimen, beispielsweise durch Hawala, um Vermögenswerte von Terroristen zu transferieren?

Inwiefern eignet sich die der persönliche Transfer, zum Beispiel im Rahmen einer Ausreise, zum Beispiel nach Syrien, um Vermögenswerte von Terroristen zu transferieren?

Inwiefern eignen sich Kryptowährungen, wie beispielsweise Bitcoin, um Vermögenswerte von Terroristen zu transferieren?

4. Welche Schwierigkeiten ergeben sich bei den Ermittlungen zur Bekämpfung der Terrorismusfinanzierung?

- Welche Schwierigkeiten ergeben sich im Hinblick auf Verdeckte Ermittler?
- Welche Schwierigkeiten ergeben sich im Hinblick auf Onlinedurchsuchungen?
- Welche Schwierigkeiten ergeben sich im Hinblick auf die Amts- und Rechtshilfe?
- Welche Schwierigkeiten ergeben sich im Hinblick auf Berufsgeheimnisse?

Appendix 5: Preliminary Publications

Excerpts from the present work have already been published or accepted for publication. In consultation with Prof. Dr. Dr. h.c. Hans-Heiner Kühne, an overview of the preliminary publications has not been included.

www.ingramcontent.com/pod-product-compliance
Ingram Content Group UK Ltd.
Pitfield, Milton Keynes, MK11 3LW, UK
UKHW020258051026
15470UKWH00021B/1322

9 783631 864326